Windows NT 4:
The Complete Reference

Griffith Kadnier

Osborne **McGraw-Hill**

Berkeley New York St. Louis San Francisco
Auckland Bogotá Hamburg London Madrid
Mexico City Milan Montreal New Delhi Panama City
Paris São Paulo Singapore Sydney
Tokyo Toronto

Osborne **McGraw-Hill**
2600 Tenth Street
Berkeley, California 94710
U.S.A.

For information on translations or book distributors outside the U.S.A., or to arrange
bulk purchase discounts for sales promotions, premiums, or fundraisers, please
contact Osborne/McGraw-Hill at the above address.

Windows NT 4: The Complete Reference

234567890 DOC 9987

ISBN 0-07-882181-9

Publisher
Brandon A. Nordin

Editor-in-Chief
Scott Rogers

Acquisitions Editor
Joanne Cuthbertson

Project Editor
Emily Rader

Associate Project Editor
Cynthia Douglas

Editorial Assistant
Gordon Hurd

Technical Editor
Steve Apiki

Copy Editors
Judith Brown
Alex Miloradovich
Dennis Weaver

Proofreaders
Karen Mead
Rhonda Holmes

Indexer
David Heiret

Computer Designer
Lance Ravella

Illustrator
Leslee Bassin

For my mother,
Genevieve, who will always be with me.

And to my father,
Arthur, who always supported my decisions.

And not least, to my dear wife Jeanne Marie.
Without her my life would be empty.

I love you all.

Contents

PART I

Getting Started

IIIII **1 Exploring a New Technology** 3

PART II

Learning the Basics

PART III

Connecting with Windows NT

PART IV

Inside Windows NT

PART V

For Programmers and Power Users

Acknowledgments

I would like to thank all of the many people who helped bring this book to print. Writing as a columnist did not fully prepare me for the amount of time and work needed to publish a book like this. Thanks go to all of my editors, art personnel, and staff at Osborne/McGraw-Hill. I especially want to thank my wife, Jeanne Marie. She not only had to put up with all of the various minicrises that go along with writing a multipart book, but she also pitched in like a trooper, with fantastic help along the way, and never complained (a little maybe) of my continual absence. I'd like to give my two cats, Samson and Claudius, a big hug, since I've also not seen enough of them lately. I know I'll find them somewhere around one of the computers.

Introduction

Since 1991, I have been involved with Windows NT, first as a developer and consultant at Microsoft Corporation, and then using the operating system and developing kernel and user mode drivers and custom applications for it. Even though I have programmed for the other Windows platforms since their inception, I am continually amazed at the resilience and applicability of NT as an evolving operating system.

When you think of an operating system in terms of what it is actually doing for you, the many processes involved in making a character or graphic appear on the screen, or the thousands of steps that are taken in saving a file, it's easy to be truly astonished. These complexities are not things one should have to contemplate every day, but with so much of our daily lives being augmented by the computer, they are worth considering, even if just for a moment.

With each successive release, NT has become more usable. It is rapidly gaining momentum as the operating system of choice for industries as diverse as film and recording studios, nationwide retail stores, and the Department of Defense. You can see this in the offerings of the thousands of software houses that used to offer only Windows 3.1 and Windows 95 products. (It's always a good idea to check out the software support base for an operating system before you buy and install. Many fine operating systems have become relics overnight because, for various reasons, developers and software companies did not agree to produce products for them.)

Despite the fact that Microsoft has always had vocal opposition from people who complain about technical aspects of the Windows family of operating systems or who worry that the company will take over the world and quash diversity, Windows 95 and NT become more successful every month. Any successful, large corporation, especially one that sets standards, will face similar hostility, as its products become ubiquitous. But despite these complaints, the Windows platforms, along with their parent, MS-DOS, are almost single-handedly responsible for the proliferation of desktop computers during the last 10 years.

It should be obvious that open design, high-volume products will always win over the largest audience, whose primary fear is obsolescence. The cards are always going to be stacked against companies that try to play it too close to the belt. IBM and Microsoft started an openness policy back in the 1980s that is still unprecedented in the computer hardware and software world. They have regularly published full specifications and programming information for both hardware and software offerings. This has not hurt them, as it would seem to do at first. Instead of keeping a proprietary, closed system, like Apple Computer's Macintosh (which, of course, is a fine product), they published specifications and operating system internals and then provided BIOS and OS licensing policies that ended up driving a unit market of over 150 million. Such policies might not allow as much profit per sale, but oh boy, what a potential customer base!

It is on the needs of this customer base that NT is built. The choice is becoming clear for users of desktop computers made within the last few years: if your 16MB Pentium computer can run Windows 95, it can run NT, and with the critical software and driver support now being provided for NT, the question of which operating system to use is really becoming moot.

About This Book

As you read this book, you will find the answers to many of the questions you have about NT. Hopefully, you'll learn a little about the history of NT and how it came to be the premiere operating system it is today. It is a privilege to be able to put as much information as possible into printed form, for your enjoyment and reference, and if I have glossed over your favorite subject, it is only because limited space has dictated the extent to which some aspects of NT could be covered. I have tried to keep most of the dry, super-technical discussions to a minimum, since this book is intended to reach beyond the programmer and systems analyst audiences.

How This Book is Organized

Part 1 introduces you to NT—its history, architecture, installation, and setup. This part of the book also takes you through your first NT session, along with pointers on how to tailor your system to your liking. Also covered are the basics of networking and how to pick the right mix of network tools and protocols for your particular needs. Since networking and internetworking are so critical to a modern NT installation, this book pays special attention to these issues throughout.

Part 2 introduces you to the NT desktop, where you will interact with the operating system. It covers all of the salient points about usage of the desktop for navigation, application execution, and customization. Part 2 then goes on to cover the command prompt (console) operation so familiar to MS-DOS and Unix users, file system navigation, two very important applications whose use can help to diagnose proper operation, and the tuning of your system. Then I turn to a favorite subject of mine—Multimedia. You'll learn how NT is being used by television and film companies to create special effects and animation, and discover the many other visual, aural, and sensory uses for NT's multimedia components.

Part 3 covers networking issues such as how to set up and administer TCP/IP, a critical task if you plan to link your network with a Unix system or if you want to provide connections to that shimmering oasis, the Internet. I also cover TCP/IP configuration using some special services available to you, to make this task easier. Lastly, in this section, you will be introduced to NT's Remote Access Service (RAS) and to Dial-Up Networking, services that connect you to the outside world.

As you continue into Part 4, you will be presented with overviews of NT's internal components and explanations of how they work. This information is introductory matter but is as meaningful to administrators and informed users as it is to programmers who need a general outline when contemplating NT programming. We will talk about RPC, DDE, the security subsystem, the Registry, and several BackOffice issues.

Part 5 continues deeper into NT's internal processes, with coverage of NT's major operating system components—the Kernel, user subsystems, device drivers, OLE, printing, and support for an important, if esoteric, subject: real-time programming. These subjects are not for the faint of heart, but technical coverage has been paired down to the essentials, leaving the reader with points that may be researched in depth at a later time.

Finally, Part 6 covers the Internet and intranets. Using NT as a tool for Internet connection, or to support an in-house Web-based information tool, are two of the most popular applications of this operating system. With NT Server, you can install a fully functional, world-class Internet site that includes World Wide Web and FTP services, or set up internal network-based information services that allow you to provide tools such as online newsletters, policy communications, and email.

The book closes with an extended appendix, aimed at diagnosis and repair of a poorly performing or inoperable NT installation. Special attention is paid to proper hardware setup, and many tips are provided to help you improve performance or find and repair problems that may crop up during installation and tuning. All of the diagnostic methods presented presuppose that you have upgraded your NT system with the latest Service Pack, which Microsoft makes available for bug fixes and additions from time to time.

I sincerely hope that you find this work to be informative and enjoyable. Thank you for purchasing this book, and great luck using NT!

Griff Kadnier
Edmonds, Washington
May, 1997

PART ONE

Getting Started

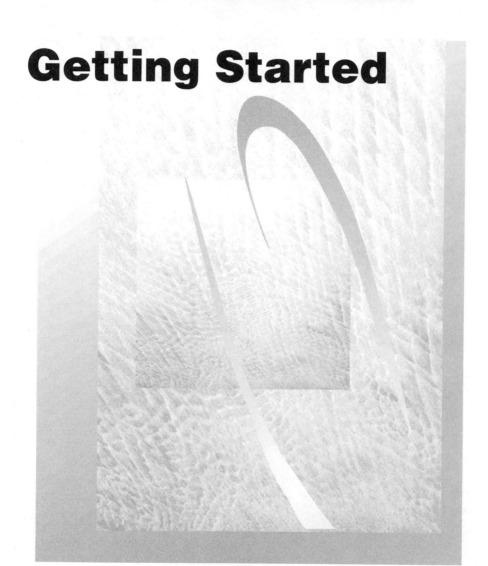

Chapter One

Exploring a
New Technology

In this chapter, we will explore the history and design decisions that went into the making of NT. We'll also discuss, as an overview, the features and models that form the architecture of NT 4. To give you a grounding for the chapters to come, we'll examine some of the differences between NT 4 and its competitors and antecedents. We'll also look at an overview of the client/server model, which is important for understanding how and why NT works as it does.

The Windows NT Advantage

In July of 1993, the computing world was presented with the first release of a totally new and revolutionary operating system: Microsoft Windows NT. Performance and features that previously had been accessible only on $20,000 workstations became instantly available to anyone with a high-end personal computer. It was as if suddenly you could buy and drive a Ferrari for the price of a Yugo! All of the promises that computer hardware manufacturers had made for 32-bit PCs could finally be realized. Up to that moment, most users of 32-bit PCs (for example, those containing Intel 386, 486, or Pentium processor chips) could only find 16-bit operating systems and software to run, severely crippling their computing power.

REMINDER: *To get the most from this book, you should possess a basic knowledge of how an operating system works. A rudimentary understanding of networking is also assumed, as NT is used primarily on a local area network (LAN) or wide area network (WAN) environment.*

Windows NT is now Microsoft Corporation's premier operating system. It has become a workhorse and a standard for corporations, scientific establishments, and consumers. With newer releases, NT has become the operating system of choice in many computing environments. Designed around a powerful and well thought-out 32-bit software architecture, the primary features that allow NT to use the full power of today's processors are

- **Scalability:** The ability to run on a single PC chip with a single user up to a multiuser, multiprocessor networked installation.
- **The Windows GUI:** The familiar graphical user interface it presents to the world.

Now, with the advent of version 4—with its new features, improvements in speed, and the Windows 95 look and feel—Windows NT has become the most important, powerful, and usable operating system on the market.

A Cooperative Computing Model

Windows NT 4.0 operations are based on a client/server computing model. This is a model in which the computing workload (for an application or for the operating system routines) is shared between the server—or the service-providing piece of software—and the client, end-user application, or software process. It is a cooperative relationship that divides the workload evenly between machines or processes on a single machine.

NOTE: This ability to parcel out processing in a coordinated way increases performance by using otherwise idle system resources, and it enhances shared usage of resources as a whole, reducing redundant system routines, application code, and memory overhead.

Two Distinct Versions

By extending and refining the NT client/server model, Microsoft has created two distinct and complimentary versions of the NT operating system:

- Windows NT Workstation
- Windows NT Server

To the casual observer, they are very alike, but as we shall see in later chapters, each version has a unique role to fill in a total computing environment. For now, just keep in mind that these two versions work together. They share many features in common but also have their own unique capabilities.

A Wide Range of Solutions

Microsoft has invested upwards of 2,000 worker years (4 years x 400 employees for NT 3.1, plus another 2 years x 150–200 employees for current releases) in making Windows NT the most robust, inclusive, and capable operating system for both the client (workstation) and server markets. No other operating system of NT's size, capability, and scope can be found today as an out-of-the-box solution to so many different computing needs.

NOTE: To get an idea how wide the coverage and capabilities of NT are, some of the first major customers employing NT included the international banking community at one end of the spectrum and NASA at the other.

A Modular and Extensible System

We are going to examine NT as a sum of its parts, because that is precisely how it was constructed. Unlike other "one-size-fits-all" operating systems, NT is constructed as a modular and extensible operating system. Modularity, a la Unix, can have its drawbacks when it comes to integration and system administration, but NT distinguishes itself as follows:

- **Tight integration:** Its built-in coupling of various subsystem functions that operate smoothly and efficiently together.

- **Component granularity:** Its ability to load and keep in memory only those bits of code needed immediately. This increases speed and allows efficient use of physical memory space.

NT is extensible like Unix; that is, many add-on modules and opportunities for expansion exist. NT is also cohesive like VMS, because it is a complete and integrated environment in which you know and feel that you can handle any given maintenance or computing task. Yet NT is familiar and easy to use like MS-DOS, Windows 3.1, or Windows 95.

Mini-Glossary

GRAPHICAL USER INTERFACE (GUI)   The graphical "picture" presented to the user to interact with the computer. Contrasts with the older style character-based interfaces used in computers where all input and output is presented to the user as "typewriter style" characters.

OPERATING SYSTEM (OS)   The underlying software that allows a computer to accomplish other tasks. The OS handles interaction with the GUI, the disk storage, the printer, the network, and so on.

UNIX   An older, but still widely used workstation OS. Many extensions, very well known.

VMS   The widely used operating system native to Digital Equipment Corporation computers.

MS-DOS   Microsoft Disk Operating System. The character-based operating system that was a precursor to Microsoft Windows and Windows NT.

OBJECT-ORIENTED TECHNOLOGY   A scheme in which the attributes of individual functions or files are abstracted so they can be treated in similar ways at a higher level in the operating system or application.

A New User Interface

With the release of Windows NT 4, a new pseudo-object-oriented user interface—using folders, cabinets, and shortcuts to represent files and collections of files or program actions—becomes the standard, first introduced, in part, as the GUI for Windows 95. In this chapter and throughout this book, we will be looking at what this new interface has to offer and contrasting it against the older Windows 3.1/Windows for Workgroups style.

REMINDER: *This book is primarily concerned with the new Windows NT 4 operating system and when and how you can best use it. However, if you're familiar with the older 3.1 interface, it's still available to you as a customized choice in the form of the Program Manager, the File Manager, and so on.*

A Broader Spectrum of Support

Windows NT 4 now has support for workstation-like graphics with OpenGL—a high-end graphics language used in the workstation market. NT 4 also incorporates a wide range of hardware support, which is crucial for choosing a platform on which to base your NT installation. These are just a few of the evolutionary changes that make this version of NT so easy to use and profitable to utilize. We'll be covering each of these changes in detail in subsequent chapters.

The History of NT

With each successive release since its initial release in July of 1993, Windows NT has significantly matured, becoming more robust and useful. Even back in 1993, however, pioneer users could not believe how solid the NT 3.1 release was as a first offering. Up to 100,000 beta sites were involved, and few major errors were ever reported by that group.

Maximizing Code Stability

An interesting note is that within the development group, code stability was always maximally enforced. Throughout its development cycle, NT's developers were constantly made aware of the need not to regress, or break the checked-in build.

NOTE: *Checked-in code is the code base sitting on or being migrated to the master build machines. A developer checks in his or her code after thorough testing and review by peers and merges the changes with the master build files—those files used to actually make the released version of the product.*

Although it was never observed, a story floated around that a developer who broke the build would be made to wear a set of antler horns for an entire day! The developers were strictly controlled by program management as to what they could add, fix, or change, and when they could do so. Nightly builds of NT resulted in a life cycle per release of usually no more than two or three days. There were 807 builds of the official NT source code before the official first release.

Adding to its stability was the fact that from late 1991 on, most team members were at least in part, self-hosted; that is, they had to develop NT on NT. Up until then, Microsoft OS/2, Assembler, and Windows 16-bit platforms, along with some customized utilities, were used as tools to edit and compile the original modules and assemble the original pieces of code. This led to an initial release that was stable not only in its user configuration, but from a software design engineer's standpoint as well.

The application program interface (API), the kernel routines, and the low-level hardware access software were thoroughly tested by the engineers writing the operating system. Digital Equipment Corporation, NCR, Olivetti (MIPS), and many others worked closely with Microsoft, even locating on-site expert personnel to help customize the various versions of NT to be offered.

Architectural Integrity

The main architect, and arguably the father of the NT operating system, is David Cutler. Dave worked as a chief architect on the DEC VMS operating system before coming to Microsoft in 1988, and many of the principles that Dave designed into NT came as a result of his experience with and desire to improve on and scale VMS.

NOTE: VMS is a large, mission-critical operating system. It has many admirable features for a mainframe computer, but does not scale down readily.

Design elements were also taken from a project started in 1985 at Carnegie Mellon University called MACH. The Micro-kernel ArChitecture operating system is a relative of NT in some particularly unique ways:

- **Micro-kernel architecture:** This limits the functions supported by the micro-kernel and enables multiple, user-level servers. This is a central feature of NT. The core of the NT operating system is a very small collection of software routines that provide the basis upon which all other parts of the operating system are built. This kind of design enables an operating system to be chameleonlike; the operating system can easily be ported, or rewritten, to run on a different hardware platform. Also, because the core routines are written to enable multiple upper-level support systems, scenarios like running a Windows 32-bit program *alongside* a Unix-style or MS-DOS–style program, become possible.

- **Interprocess communication (IPC) functionality:** At the kernel level, this feature is used as a building block for the rest of the system. IPC is the ability of one *process* or program to communicate with another while both are running alongside each other. Many operating systems do not allow this kind of interaction at the kernel level. Therefore, in other operating systems, communication between programs must be accomplished at a more abstract level, if at all, taking more system resources and introducing inefficiencies.

- **Different and multiprocessor support:** NT supports closely and loosely coupled multiprocessors and a variety of different commercially available workstations. Many operating systems support only one hardware platform and run on only one processor.

- **Application and programming interfaces:** NT, like MACH, provides for more than one API set. Win32, POSIX, OS/2, and Win16/MS-DOS are all supported in NT. Most operating systems support only one basic API set.

Developmental Continuity

With the advent of NT 3.5, 3.51, and now 4, each successive release builds on the previous one—never changing gears enough to cut off users of the prior release. This continuity is important and reassuring. Microsoft's long-term plan is to meld Windows NT and Windows 95 into one support platform. The strategy is simple. Microsoft has had to offer several versions of its Windows platform operating system up until now. With the release of Windows 95, Microsoft has essentially abandoned 16-bit platforms and no longer offers Windows for Workgroups, a 16-bit OS, and is directing Windows 95 at the home user. NT may someday become a home platform, since entrepreneurs are already embracing it for the at-home work environment. This will drive future user-friendly refinements.

 NOTE: *The next release of Windows 95 is aimed at eventual development of an always-on, appliance-type computer for the home. The Intel Corporation is now developing low-power processors for this home appliance platform. For the business and workstation market, Microsoft has already publicly stated that its goal is to move everyone toward NT in the next few years.*

The Win32 Interface

If a potential user needs to know one thing about NT or any other Microsoft operating system in the future, it can be summed up in one word: Win32. Win32 is the 32-bit compatible application program interface—the exposed operating system routines that developers and administrators can call and employ when writing software for the NT platform. For instance, if a program needs to communicate with the user, store a file on disk, print to a printer, or use the network, it will use the routines exposed by the Win32 API to do so.

REMINDER: *We'll be looking at how Win32 affects what you do in NT, and how you do it, in the chapters coming up.*

The Win32 API has become the de facto standard for all development in NT, Windows 95, and beyond. Based on the 16-bit Windows 3.1 and Windows for Workgroups APIs, the extension to 32 bits added many new and more appropriate functions and capabilities to the programming interface upon which all Windows development is made.

Mini-Glossary

WIN32   The Windows 32-bit application program interface (API).

MULTITASKING   The ability of an OS to support more than one simultaneously running application, preemptively or nonpreemptively.

MULTITHREADING   The ability to have nonlinear program execution or blocked execution within a program while execution continues elsewhere within the application.

POSIX, OS/2   Two NT-supported subsystems that allow their respective native programs to be executed.

REMOTE PROCEDURE CALL (RPC)   An OS method of sharing process execution between servers or server processes on NT.

The Complete OS in a Box

For many reasons, NT 4 gives the user abilities that can be had only in part in other current operating systems. Multithreading, multitasking, support for legacy-style applications from the Windows 3.1/DOS world, security, remote access, and NT's many other inherent features come in the box, ready to be used immediately.

A Multithreaded System

Multithreaded means that a program or application may have more than one "thread" of execution. A *thread* is simply part of a program that is allowed to run asynchronously, to completion, while the main program code continues on about its other work. Most older programs and operating systems allow only one thread of execution, effectively negating the idea of threading.

The linear model of execution in a classic computer dictates that a program executes its routines from start to finish in a linear fashion. Multithreading is a little like walking and chewing gum at the same time (and maybe even taking two steps forward and one back too!). It allows a program to *apparently* accomplish more than one task at a time with multiple threads of duplicated logic acting on different data sets, or for a thread of the program to wait on a task that requires, for instance, some external stimulus, while the main portion of the program continues with other tasks.

NOTE: *Threads are transparent to the user; only programmers need to know how to manipulate threads. The user only needs to know that threaded support in an OS such as NT makes an application more powerful and smoother in its operation. We'll look more into threading in Chapter 19.*

Preemptive Multitasking

Multitasking is a related ability of more advanced operating systems like NT. There are two different types of multitasking: nonpreemptive and preemptive.

REMINDER: *An operating system that allows multitasking enables a user to have more than one program running at the same time. If you want to run a tax program and have a calculator program running in the background, you need multitasking.*

The Nonpreemptive World

In an OS that only supports nonpreemptive multitasking, any single application that hogs the computer's processing power can slow the entire computer down. The programs themselves have to be carefully written to yield to other programs running at the same time. Sometimes, a crashed program—a program that has become stuck in a nonresponsive state or that has caused a fault—can take down the entire computer system in a nonpreemptive multitasking OS. This is generally undesirable. It would be horrible if your teeth were nonpreemptively multitasked! If one tooth was injured or broken, you wouldn't be able to chew with any of the others. Not exactly fail safe.

Putting the OS in Control

In a preemptively multitasked system like Windows NT, the OS itself has full control over which program gets to run at any specific time. The OS deals out time slots to all running processes and switches away from each process at given intervals to allow all other processes a shot at running.

Insider Info

Protected virtual memory ensures that multiple applications can run simultaneously without interfering with one another or with the operating system. Virtual memory schemes allow computers to have much more linear address space than what they physically have installed in RAM. Virtual memory has been implemented on many operating systems, using paged-disk files to swap chunks of a process context back and forth transparently.

NT happens to have an extremely efficient mechanism for doing this. It also has the ability to provide memory to each process as if it were the only program being executed, protecting the program and its address space from any other program running concurrently. In older OSs, this protection mechanism was not available, and a badly behaved or invasive program could overwrite another's address space or compromise security by, say, reading another program's memory or files to obtain passwords or supposedly secure information.

Support for DOS, Windows, and Win32

NT contains support for programs written for MS-DOS, 16-bit Windows, and the Microsoft Win32 API. This assures backward compatibility with thousands of existing programs, while offering Win32 as a more powerful and easy-to-use API on which to base current software. Character-based "console" applications can be hosted—a useful alternative to fully graphical programs. Additionally, POSIX-compliant and character-based OS/2 version 1.xx applications can run on NT. POSIX is a compliant subset of the Unix operating system.

NOTE: Many thousands of existing programs are POSIX compliant and can be run with little or no change on an NT system. OS/2 version 1.xx programs run on Microsoft and IBM's older OS/2 platforms, and NT has support for most of these older version OS/2 applications.

Other Special Features

Included are dial-up connectivity and remote access, integrated networking, a very robust security model, installable file systems, a full set of administration tools, inter-server communication via RPC (Remote Procedure Calls), which we will discuss at length in Chapter 15, and more. Windows NT supports thousands of x86-based uniprocessor systems, many multiprocessor systems, MIPS, PowerPC, and DEC Alpha systems. In addition, Windows NT has extensive peripheral support for video adapters, network adapters, SCSI adapters, communications, multimedia, tape devices, and printers.

The Client/Server Model In-Depth

Windows NT was designed as Microsoft's flagship operating system offering. It was the first Microsoft operating system to employ a model of computing that shares the processing and execution of an application or piece of code internally *and across* networks in order to gain in performance and flexibility. Of significant importance is NT's internal client/server model, in which the internal processes responsible for running the operating system divide the work efficiently—a concept that may, at first, be confusing because of its apparent double meaning.

NOTE: *This is the client/server model on a "silicon" scale, which we'll look at in Chapter 20. Here, we'll discuss the "macro" model encompassing client/server technology on a larger scale.*

The Front and Back Ends

In the most generic sense, client/server architecture splits an application into a front-end *client* component that runs on the workstation, and a back-end *server* component that runs on the server (see Figure 1-1). On the front end, the client portion of the application typically consists of a user interface that can launch the application, provide input, manipulate data, and display results. On the back end, the server waits for requests from clients. When it receives a request, the server processes it and provides the results of the requested service back to the client.

NOTE: *Server processes manage shared resources and perform processor-intensive operations, such as record sorting in a database, or protocol translation in a communications server.*

Performance and Security

An example of an application that uses NT security is a client/server database, such as a SQL (Structured Query Language) server, that extracts only the specific data requested, so traffic and overhead are reduced and the network maintains high performance. Additionally, security and data integrity are maintained centrally on the server because client workstations are given controlled, sometimes encrypted, access to the central database or data set housed physically on the server.

NOTE: *Microsoft SQL Server is a high-performance, client/server relational database management system (RDBMS) designed to support high-volume transaction processing like online order entry, as well as decision and support applications like sales analysis, on PC-based local area networks (LANs).*

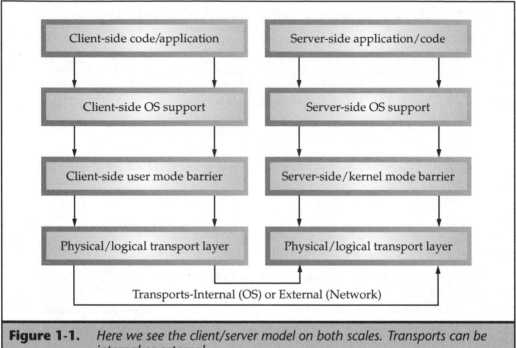

Figure 1-1. *Here we see the client/server model on both scales. Transports can be internal or external*

Networking Power

As personal computer networks have developed more capabilities, organizations have begun to transfer important data processing functions from mainframe and minicomputers to LANs. With the client/server model, a corporation can provide its workstation users with access to centrally controlled services such as databases, communication gateways, and electronic mail systems. In this environment, the role of the network server is critical, and the reliability and security of the LAN assumes even greater importance.

Client/server is an efficient computing model because it handles processing where it makes the most sense, split between more powerful servers and desktop machines. The client/server front end is traditionally either a prepackaged or customized application that is able to present and manipulate data in a graphical, easy-to-use, understandable fashion. The client is networked to the back-end server application that is responsible for storing, retrieving, and protecting data.

Systems Integration and Economy

Client/server computing provides the framework for integrating heterogeneous systems and applications. Users gain access to up-to-date data when they need it, without compromising security, and they can use familiar tools, such as spreadsheets and database systems, to access it. This architecture is also less expensive to deploy than traditional mainframes and minicomputers. It involves reduced hardware costs and lower software maintenance costs, while providing for leverage with existing systems.

NOTE: *For instance, older PCs can add processing power when added to a network. Sharing expensive servers and peripheral devices (e.g., printers) across a large base of clients leverages costs. Collections of PCs (using RPC) can also do the work of minicomputers and mainframes.*

Scalability and Access Control

Client/server systems are easily scalable. A system can add new processors, servers, and clients as needs increase. Back-end services such as databases can be shared by several front-end applications (for example, spreadsheets and custom ordering tools). Network administrators can centrally manage servers and desktops in a client/server computing environment. Administrators can change desktop and server configurations, maintain security, update user permissions, or troubleshoot problems from any workstation on the network.

Data movement is minimized and security is maximized. The server controls the data and processes requests, then transfers only requested and authorized data to the desktop client machine. This reduces network traffic and allows the network to support more users—a factor that's especially important with the new remote and wireless technologies that connect users with limited bandwidth network channels.

The Two Flavors of NT

Windows NT comes in two versions that differ significantly in respect to networking. These versions are called Windows NT Workstation and Windows NT Server. The standard NT Workstation supports peer-to-peer networking connections. NT Server includes tools for server networking, remote access administration, and server administration. Microsoft optimized both Windows NT Workstation and Windows NT Server to serve their individual intended purposes.

TIP: *Windows NT Workstation is an excellent client OS for users who need the power, scalability, fault tolerance, or security it offers. Windows NT Server is a powerful server environment for users who need the power of its application server, file and print services, or remote access capabilities.*

Windows NT Server can be user-configured for optimized file and print server performance or application server performance, allowing you to tune it for maximum throughput depending on the type of server usage. Windows NT Workstation does not have this feature. Windows NT Workstation performs about the same as Windows NT Server up to approximately ten different, simultaneous inbound user connections. This enables Windows NT Workstation to function well in a small-peer environment.

TIP: *Windows NT Server is the correct choice if you want to deploy a server in a larger environment or want to scale your network in the future.*

In total, these optimizations have an impact on the performance of Windows NT Workstation when used as a server. Peer networking is supported for basic connectivity between users on a network. Although NT Workstation allows you to make unlimited outbound connections to server resources and technically supports more than the historic maximum of ten simultaneous inbound connections, this obviously would not be sufficient for setting up an Internet web site or to service many remote connections from a field sales force. NT Server would be needed for these purposes.

TIP: *While Windows NT Server can certainly provide excellent file and print services, it can also be used extensively as an application server platform for database and other services. The Windows NT Server file and print capabilities can be selectively implemented.*

Windows NT Server

Windows NT Server enables implementation of client/server applications such as database, messaging servers, or communications gateways on many different types of networks. Windows NT Server also provides built-in, secure file, and print sharing services for a range of operating systems, including MS-DOS, Windows 3.1, Windows 95, Unix, OS/2, and the Macintosh. To access and share information on local and remote networks, Windows NT supports network transports such as NetBEUI and a routable TCP/IP transport. NT Server also supports IBM protocols such as DLC for access to IBM OS/400 systems along with the SNA Server, which allows Windows systems to connect to IBM SNA mainframes and minicomputers.

Insider Info

NT Server builds on the NT operating system, adding centralized management, centralized security, advanced fault tolerance, and connectivity to remote clients. NT Server is a complete file and print server, and it is the central platform for building the server portion of client/server applications.

MIS managers can use NT Server to centrally manage security, user accounts, and configuration information across multiple domains. This results in the ability of users to access resources across the network with a single logon, subject to the appropriate authorization.

Special Capabilities

Windows NT Server includes the following special capabilities:

- **Dynamic Host Configuration Protocol (DHCP) server service:** Both Windows NT Workstation and Server support DHCP, which is a standard for the automatic configuration of IP (Internet Protocol) hosts. DHCP was designed to reduce the complexity of IP network administration.

- **Windows Internet naming service (WINS):** WINS provides a distributed database for registering and querying dynamic computer name-to-IP address mappings in a routed network environment. If you are administering a routed network, WINS is your best choice for name resolution, because it is designed to solve the problems that occur with name resolution in complex Windows internetworks.

- **Data protection features (disk striping, RAID 5, disk mirroring):** RAID stands for redundant array of independent disks. Fault-tolerant disk systems are categorized in RAID levels, each level offering various mixes of performance, reliability, and cost. Each level uses a different algorithm to implement fault tolerance.

- **Remote Access Server (RAS):** This service can handle 255 concurrent incoming calls. (Windows NT Workstation is limited in this respect, at least by license.) Remote Access Service is designed to provide transparent network access for PCs running NT or Windows 95/Windows for Workgroups operating systems. RAS is discussed in Chapter 13.

- **Gateway Services for NetWare (GSNW):** GSNW allows users to connect to what appear to be NT Server resources, but which, in reality, are resources that exist on a NetWare server connected with the Windows NT network. This capability allows Windows NT Server to act as a nondedicated gateway to NetWare file systems.

- **Services for Macintosh:** This allows Macintosh clients to access file and print resources on the Windows NT Server, and allows Microsoft network and Macintosh clients to access AppleTalk-based printers.

- **Account lockout security:** The account lockout feature enables you to make NT Server more secure from intruders who try to log on by guessing the passwords of existing user accounts.

- **Network Client Administrator:** A utility used to install MS-DOS client software from the Windows NT Server CD.

- **Administrative tools:** These include Server Manager, User Manager, and User Manager for Domains.

The BackOffice Suite

Because Windows NT Server is optimized as a server platform, it is required to run the following Microsoft BackOffice Suite products:

- **Systems Management Server (SMS):** This is an administrative manager suite that adds remote administration, configuration, and inventory capabilities to an NT network.

- **SNA server:** This provides a complete pathway to utilize an NT server as an IBM AS400 or other IBM-style gateway.

- **SQL server:** This implements the server side software for the ever popular SQL database language and system.

- **Exchange Server:** Just now coming online, this feature offers complete mail and messaging services.

- **The Internet Information Server (IIS):** This provides Internet protocol and World Wide Web hosting capabilities for NT 4.

- **Distributed File System (DFS) Server:** This allows data (files) distributed across multiple servers to appear as if it belongs to a single file directory or tree. With a single DFS directory tree, users and administrators can cohesively access information regardless of physical location.

- **Index Server:** This server works with NT Server and IIS to provide access to all of the documents stored on an intranet or Internet site. It allows full-text searches and retrieval of all types of information from any Web.

Mini-Glossary

NetBEUI The NetBIOS extended user interface (NetBEUI) protocol.

TCP/IP (TRANSMISSION CONTROL PROTOCOL/INTERNET PROTOCOL) A networking protocol that provides communication across interconnected networks.

DLC (DATA LINK CONTROL PROTOCOL) Allows NT computers to operate in IBM SNA environments and to connect to mainframes and minicomputers.

SNA (SIMPLE NETWORK ARCHITECTURE) SERVER Links desktop personal computers to IBM mainframe and midrange computers.

Windows NT Workstation

While many will require the extra horsepower of NT Server, the standard version of NT, called NT Workstation (sometimes abbreviated as NT WkSta), comes ready to run as a stand-alone product supporting peer-to-peer networking. This product acts as a "client" in our macro client/server relationship. Included with the delivery are local administration tools and a full set of utilities.

 NOTE: *NT WkSta is capable of running any NT-compatible application with the exception of server-specific software integrated into NT Server. NT WkSta is not optimized for server applications. That is part of the NT Server product.*

Comparisons and Contrasts

Both versions of NT offer common functionality and complementary functions to perform as a single unit. Each version differs and is optimized only within its role based upon a server/workstation scenario. Each version implements different roles in integrated networking for basic file and print sharing and easy access to LAN or WAN resources. For instance, a single-user version of NT Remote Access Service (RAS) allows users to access their system and the network remotely. A complete, multiuser version is included with the Windows NT Server.

 NOTE: *Built-in workgroup features—including electronic mail and group scheduling—enhance workgroup productivity. Graphical administration tools—including Performance Monitor and Event Viewer—make it easy to optimize Windows NT platforms from anywhere on the network.*

Windows NT Server has no innate limit on the number of users who can be connected, respective of client licensing. Windows NT Workstation, on the other hand, imposes a licensed maximum of ten inbound simultaneous connections (incoming connections from external clients) with an unlimited number of outbound connections (outgoing connections to an external server or other workstation). This limitation used to be enforced by the software, but it has been removed for compatibility reasons. You still must have NT Server to legally use more than ten concurrent incoming connections. The base Server product doesn't include these client licenses. These are purchased separately.

Vive La Différence!

Although NT Workstation and NT Server use the same basic kernel, NT Server has been optimized as an application's file and print server, and NT Workstation has been optimized as a network client. Its file handling and printing capabilities are suited best to handling local requests, on the same machine or local network.

NOTE: *Both systems are built around the same basic kernel (GUI, Win32 API, Shell) and both have high-level security features. NT Workstation is meant to connect peer-to-peer workgroups, typically within a single area or site on a departmental or office level.*

With NT Server you get greater fault tolerance and wider network capabilities and connectivity features. NT Server can perform remote access administration. You can perform administrative duties from a remote station instead of having to perform them at the server's station. With NT Server comes additional support for AppleTalk, enabling Apple Macintosh users to coexist on an NT network.

Both NT and NT Server allow connection of hardware systems running NetWare, Banyan VINES, and Microsoft LAN Manager networks, as well as Windows for Workgroups and Windows 95. Administrators also have sophisticated control over file and directory accessibility and user-rights on a network running NT, even with Windows for Workgroups clients.

NOTE: *A host of activities such as read/write privileges, programmer privileges, forcing obligatory password changes or uniqueness, backing up files, forcing a system shutdown, and changing the system time can be individually assigned on a user-by-user basis. Administrators also can opt to build an audit trail using an automatic event logger—recording who logs on and off the system, which files and directories were accessed, and other details.*

To the user, the sharing of network resources in NT is an extension of the model used in Windows for Workgroups and Windows 95. To share a directory, simply highlight the directory's file folder in Explorer and set its sharing properties from the properties sheet, available with a right mouse click on the File/Properties menu item. To share a printer, open the printers folder, choose a printer, and set its sharing properties sheet from the Printers/Properties menu item.

Insider Info

Important distinctions exist between the NT/Windows 95 and Windows for Workgroups sharing models. When you share a resource such as a directory or a printer in Windows for Workgroups, security is set at the share level; that is, you have the option of declaring some properties about the share, such as whether the directory is read-only or read/write. Specific network users who will have access to the resource aren't declared. You can declare a password, but this restricts access only to people who don't know the password.

With NT (and Windows 95), shares can be restricted to use by individual users or to preset groups of users. When a user tries to access a resource, the resource server (that is, the workstation containing the shared resource) checks the identity of the potential client and either grants or refuses access to the resource based on the user's identity (username and password).

The advantage over what can be obtained on a standard Windows for Workgroups or Windows 95 peer-to-peer network is that your NT server can be protected by C2 level password protection, assignable user privileges, and fault-tolerant hard disk functions. Not only can Windows for Workgroups and Windows 95 workstations access FAT partitions on the server, they can also indirectly take advantage of the advanced features of the NTFS file system such as long filenames (not the case for Windows for Workgroups), security, and media fault-detection and repair.

Windows NT Versus Other OSs

My OS is better than your OS, because. . . You'll hear these zealous statements in every corner of the computing world. From editors to databases, everyone has a favorite, and everyone has an opinion. Let's take a look at where NT figures into this global discussion and where NT surpasses its competition.

Although some NT users will be making the move from Unix or OS/2, most newcomers to NT will be migrating upward from the DOS/Windows/Windows 95 platforms. Let's look at how NT compares to DOS/Windows/Windows 95 setups and briefly discuss the advantages and disadvantages of NT over its predecessors (see Figure 1-2).

DOS Compatibility

Despite the enormous popularity of Windows 3.1 and Word for Windows, these GUIs are really only shells placed over DOS. It has been estimated that more than 150 million copies of DOS are in existence and that more than 25,000 applications are available for it. As a result, no MIS professional or computer user would want to discount the importance of DOS compatibility when making an operating system choice.

DOS was not designed to be a multitasking operating system or to have a GUI tacked on top of it. In other words, Windows 3.1 and Windows for Workgroups are add-ons. As any Windows user knows, crashes and incompatibilities often show up in Windows as a result of this arrangement. When one Windows program (or DOS program running under Windows) crashes, it might very well bring the whole system and any other running applications to its knees. This is particularly a problem with Windows 3.0. Windows 3.11, and Windows for Workgroups are more forgiving, but still, limitations in the architecture of DOS prevent building a crashproof shell.

What of Windows 95?

Windows 95 has addressed much of this problem. However, with the Win16 lock still in place, an errant 16-bit executable can still crash, or cause a lockup of Windows 95. This is an important point to keep in mind when deciding on which OS to employ in which role.

	Windows 3.1/ Windows for Workgroups	Windows 95	Windows NT 4
Win16 support	★	★	★
Win32 support		★	★
Threading		★	★
Multitasking	★	★	★
Preemptivity		★	★
Win32S	★	★	★
Named pipes/mail slots		★	★
RPC		★	★
Logging			★
Object security			★
Advanced GDI			★
OLE	★	★	★
COM		★	★
Networking	★	★	★
Server			★
Unicode			★

Figure 1-2. *The Windows family sits for a feature comparison portrait*

A certain level of "crashability" can usually be tolerated in a client machine running only user application software. However, one could argue that stability is paramount where files and data are being stored or routed, and this is where NT has the advantage. If an application client crashes or locks, one station is retrievably involved. On the other hand, if a company's files are corrupted in total, stored on a less stable repository machine, a much more serious failure path is involved.

Windows NT and the DOS Console

How does NT's DOS Console work, and how does NT do DOS without the limitations of DOS? First, when NT boots, real MS-DOS does not. You can install NT so that you have a "dual boot," or even a "triple boot" system for booting DOS or Windows 95, but never do you load anything other than NT's boot loader when booting NT.

 NOTE: *NT does have a core operating system for keyboard and screen I/O, managing loadable device drivers, and handling disk I/O requests—similar to what DOS does in Windows 3.x and Windows for Workgroups. Layered on that, NT contains modules called "subsystems" that emulate the DOS environment. (There are also modules for POSIX, OS/2, 16-bit Windows, and 32-bit Windows environments.) The DOS subsystem provides all the system services that DOS normally does. However, these functions are integrated seamlessly into NT. They are not layered below it.*

The "DOS box" or Console is not a DOS session per se, as it is in Windows 3.1/Windows for Workgroups. In the latter, Windows actually spawns a session of DOS, running COMMAND.COM. In NT, the system architects decided to offer DOS's functionality while avoiding the limitations of DOS. They utilize the benefits of NT CPU scheduling, system security, and crash protection. This is achieved through DOS emulation via a 32-bit application called CMD.EXE, which is a superset of MS-DOS that not only provides MS-DOS compatibility but also lets you run Windows, OS/2, and POSIX applications from the command line.

Flexible, Configurable DOS

The DOS session that is created when you run a DOS application from the command window (CMD.EXE) is quite flexible in that it is configurable. Just as DOS that boots on a PC can be configured from AUTOEXEC.BAT and CONFIG.SYS, the DOS session that gets created within NT can be configured with loadable device drivers. The NT DOS emulator supports all the usual DOS commands, and NT-specific extensions.

When you launch a DOS program under NT, a VDM (virtual DOS machine) is created that tricks the DOS program into thinking it's running on its own PC. You can think of a VDM as a mini-PC within your PC. It has its own version of all of the resources available on the computer and thinks that it is running as an entire machine in and of itself. NT sets up one VDM for each DOS application you run.

 NOTE: *Each VDM has all the hooks needed to handle both 16-bit and 32-bit DOS calls in compliance with DOS 6. A full 16MB of standard DOS, segmented application, and data memory space is supplied to the VDM. In addition, support for most popular memory managers is included.*

I/O Intercepts and System Security

In order for NT to ensure data security and system stability, its DOS emulator intercepts all I/O processes, routing data to their destinations. This is handled by I/O interceptors, which in turn hand data to the NT executive for dispatching. Any traditionally designed DOS programs that perform their I/O using standard DOS system calls will run under NT as expected. Those that write directly to hardware for which device drivers prevent direct access—for example, the hard-disk drives—will be intercepted by NT, leading to an error message and/or termination of the program. Typical programs that do this are disk caching and communications applications. Overall, this approach provides a high level of system security.

> **NOTE:** *If your DOS application requires a loadable device driver to operate, you might have trouble running it in NT because the driver won't be loaded. If NT allowed loading of device drivers, it would have to compromise security features in the NT Executive because many device drivers attempt to access hardware directly. With time, modified versions of DOS applications are becoming available for NT.*

Dealing with 16-Bit Windows

As with DOS applications, 16-bit Windows programs run in an emulation VDM created on the fly by NT. You launch a 16-bit Windows application in NT just as you do from Windows 3.x. That is, one can double-click on icons in Explorer, in the NT Program Manager, from the Start menu, or they may be launched from the Run command on the Start menu. You can also type the program's .EXE filename at the DOS prompt (called the command prompt in NT's console) or enter the program's name in the Task List box.

From information in the header of the file, NT then recognizes the 16-bit Windows program and launches a VDM, just as when you run a DOS program. The VDM includes DOS and an emulation of Windows called Windows on Windows (WOW). As with DOS emulation, the Windows emulation intercepts all of the standard system calls. When a program makes a call to a standard Windows 3.x API, WOW intercepts the call and routes it to the appropriate target. Some APIs are mapped to internal code integrated into the WOW subsystem. The Windows NT 32-bit Graphics Device Interface (GDI) manages the display of the application on-screen for such things as image and text display. As with DOS applications, only well-behaved Windows applications are likely to run successfully under NT.

OS/2 and Windows NT

Windows NT and IBM's OS/2 have similar beginnings. Both were conceived at Microsoft. IBM and Microsoft were joint developers of OS/2 when a falling-out between the two companies developed. Subsequently, the companies went their own ways and developed their 32-bit operating systems independently. Due to their common ancestry and similar design philosophies, OS/2 and NT have many similar features.

In general, NT is much more robust than OS/2. It has more advanced capabilities and offers better device support. You can easily crash OS/2 by locking the message queue, inappropriately altering GDI memory, or installing a bad MS-DOS device driver. NT guards against these situations with protected memory space. No process may inadvertently access any memory space that does not belong to it. Also, DOS device drivers are not used in NT, and they are the source of many memory-related troubles in the MS-DOS and OS/2 world.

How OS/2 Works

OS/2 is a multithreaded, preemptive multitasking operating system with a graphical user interface similar to Windows. It runs only on Intel-based processors. It can run 16- and 32-bit OS/2 applications, as well as 16-bit Windows and 16-bit DOS applications.

NOTE: Although IBM has vaguely planned such support for the future, OS/2 does not support the Win32 API. OS/2 doesn't run Win32 or NT 32-bit applications or programs written exclusively for Windows for Workgroups.

OS/2's multitasking works differently than NT's in the way it queues I/O requests from applications. OS/2's design can result in I/O bottlenecks that can slow system responsiveness as perceived by the user, whereas NT isn't likely to suffer in this way.

The graphical interface in OS/2 is called the Workplace Shell or the Presentation Manager. Unlike Program Manager and File Manager, however, it's more object-oriented. Similar to the new NT 4 shell, OS/2 applications actually can modify the Workplace Shell, creating new operating system objects that can take advantage of OS/2's built-in functionality. These features then can be used by the application.

REMINDER: Both NT and OS/2 support large amounts of memory. For example, the addressable memory area for both is 4GB. However, NT gives each application up to 2GB, and OS/2 limits applications to 512MB.

OS/2 doesn't use TrueType fonts, except when running Windows applications. Otherwise, it uses Adobe's ATM. Although ATM is available for Windows 3.1 and Windows for Workgroups/Windows 95, most Windows users prefer TrueType because it's built into Windows, and TrueType fonts are readily available.

OS/2 HPFS Versus NTFS

OS/2 supports an advanced file system similar to NT's called HPFS or High Performance File System. It supports filenames up to 254 characters long, as well as "extended attributes" above and beyond the normal DOS (FAT) attribute settings (date, time, system, hidden, archive, and read/write).

REMINDER: Extended attributes allow programs to store notes about a file, such as key phrases, the editing history of the file, the author of the file, and so on, as part of the directory entry.

NT offers similar but superior features in NTFS due to its support for access control security that enables an administrator to assign individual and group permission rights to every file and directory. NT's fault-tolerant and error-recovery features also exceed those of OS/2.

OS/2 and Networking

Connectivity is OS/2's strong point. Due to its IBM background, SNA (Systems Network Architecture) is well supported. This is an important feature in the many settings that historically have been connected to IBM mainframes. In addition, many other popular protocols such as TCP/IP, APPC, NetBIOS, and LU 6.2 are supported. This allows OS/2 machines to connect as workstations (clients) on most popular LANs.

NOTE: *One particularly strong point is that an OS/2 machine can perform as a Novell NetWare server, although NT—with the addition of add-on modules—can also support Novell file and print services.*

OS/2 and DOS

At the time of NT's initial release, OS/2 was more successful at running DOS and Windows 3.x applications without error. This was partly because OS/2 had been around longer and bugs had been resolved, but mostly because NT's security prevents programs not in strict compliance with API rules from violating protected subsystems. It's a trade-off between compatibility and robustness at this point, with robustness taking the upper hand. This situation is changing rapidly.

The Unix Universe

Unix is no longer the "black magic" operating system usable only by engineers and computer scientists. Its popularity among nonacademics is on the rise as a graphical, high-performance operating system. In fact, much of Windows NT has its origins in a variant of Unix called MACH, developed at Carnegie-Mellon University.

NOTE: *In the last several years, standardization of Unix among its many vendors (most notably OSF) has resulted in its gaining an even stronger foothold in the marketplace. Major players in the Unix market are SCO, IBM, DEC, and Sun Soft, with their products SCO Unix, AIX, ULTRIX, and Solaris, respectively.*

What They Have in Common

NT and Unix have much in common. The multiprocessing, multitasking, and networking capabilities of NT's I/O Manager, Object Manager, and Process Manager—and parts of the NT Kernel, which are discussed in depth in Chapter 19—owe much to Unix's own architecture, as well as to VMS design concepts. In addition, Unix and NT have another important commonality. It's called RPC (Remote

Procedure Call) support. This feature allows NT to offload computing tasks to another networked CPU (that is, a workstation). Such a chore typically is a subtask or thread of a currently executing program or procedure.

NOTE: Windows NT Server provides RPC support services that let programs written to take advantage of them do so. Use of RPC can result in very efficient execution of complex programs, in effect turning a network into a huge multiprocessor computer that can be dynamically assigned to any number of tasks that network users are running.

DEVICE DRIVERS   A major similarity between NT and Unix is in how they interact with devices attached to the computer. In order to design an operating system that's as flexible as possible, Unix and NT both connect to the world through device drivers that appear as files. When either Unix or NT wants to send data to or fetch data from a screen, keyboard, I/O port, memory, or disk file, the same internal approach is used—they simply route the process to a device that appears to the operating system as a file. Regardless of the physical nature of the device (such as a keyboard, a memory location, or a COM port), all of these objects are treated in the same manner.

MEMORY ACCESS   Another major similarity is the way NT and Unix use memory. Both can access a large, "flat" memory space of many megabytes. NT and the newest 32-bit Unix implementations don't have to deal with any of the problems inherent in a 16-bit PC application's need for a segmented addressing scheme.

NT typically offers a memory space of 4GB per application. This is virtual memory, of course. Actually, only 2GB of that space is available for the application, the rest is for NT's internal use. Many Unix systems offer about this same amount.

NOTE: Both systems prevent applications from stepping on each other's toes, because memory blocks allotted to one process or application can be protected from access by another process.

The Great GUI Debate

Through the years, a number of graphical interfaces for Unix have appeared. Due to the open design philosophy of Unix, however, these interfaces have had very little standardization. One of the key advantages of NT over Unix is the Windows GUI, an interface that through popularity has more or less become the standard. In the Unix world, contending GUIs such as X Window, OPEN LOOK, and Motif present problems for users and applications developers alike. Users can be confused when jumping between systems with different GUIs, and developers have to decide which GUI or GUIs they'll tune their application for.

Where Unix Shines

Unix has some advanced features (such as distributed file services and parallel processing) that NT does not. A huge cadre of Unix experts worldwide has been developing utilities, applications, and extensions for many years. Microsoft is only in the initial stages of developing support for NT. However, Unix is problematical; it's not fully standardized and it also requires significant software maintenance.

How NT Captures the Prize

The popularity of DOS and Windows applications in nonspecific applications such as spreadsheets, databases, and word processors will ensure NT's success and that of other Windows derivatives like Windows 95. This makes NT the better choice for most power-user business needs—whether on the network or on the stand-alone desktop. Though NT is much like Unix in terms of features, it's elegant and more efficient.

What's Next

With so many features, Windows NT presents a prodigious amount of power to the user. With the release of Windows 95 and competing operating systems such as OpenMach, Unix, and OS/2, it is even more important to understand the subtle as well as major differences between these products in your quest for the ideal OS.

TIP: *The chapters in this book will introduce you gently, and then more furiously to the roller coaster of concepts and implementations available in the Windows NT operating system. Stay with us; it's going to be a fun ride!*

We are going to be covering quite a bit of ground in the next chapters. We'll take a look at the insides of NT, networking, some internal systems that affect the way you work as a user, and then we'll look at various configurations and configurable parameters. Finally, we'll put the pedal to the metal and jump into NT's abilities and facilities for power users and even developers.

Chapter Two

Analyzing NT's Architecture

This chapter provides a thorough grounding in the ideas and architecture that define Windows NT. If you are contemplating the use or administration of an NT installation, this information will give you an insider's advantage when the time comes to make configuration and installation choices. This chapter will also introduce you to the idea of a subsystem—the largest element that the NT operating system can be broken into.

NOTE: While it's easy to install NT out of the box, it's hard to configure this operating system optimally. The nitty-gritty in later chapters will help you to fully utilize and understand how to administer NT, even develop an NT application. Many decisions about what hardware to buy, network to employ, or application suite to use will be justified by what you learn in this chapter and throughout this book.

The Kernel and Its Subsystems

Windows NT is more than the sum of its parts, but its parts are what define the system's capabilities. The *kernel,* the core routines that NT is built around, is designed to be extensible by the addition of various subsystems that are layered on top. Let's suppose that NT's kernel, comprising all low-level noninteractive routines, forms a permeable logic barrier called Kernel mode. Then, also, let's call all of the OS software above that barrier—the parts of the software that can directly converse with and be used by an application—User mode. This is how NT's architects talk about the NT OS components.

Mini-Glossary

KERNEL MODE   NT's lowest level of operation. All physical device control and low-level OS control is accomplished in this mode.

USER MODE   Where all subsystems and application code run. User mode is distinguished from Kernel mode in several ways: No User mode program may directly access a physical device or process, and security protections are in full force in User mode, which is not true for Kernel mode. We'll see what else Kernel mode can mean and do in Chapter 19.

SUBSYSTEMS   Those parts of NT that implement whole blocks of functionality: i.e. Win32, OS/2, POSIX, and the Security subsystem.

The Kernel Mode/User Mode Barrier

This Kernel mode/User mode barrier is the central pivot around which OS interaction in NT is designed. NT is a study in abstraction. In order to keep a user's programs from crashing the entire system, compromising security, or taking direct control of a physical device (which might crash the system, present a security threat, or at the very least, cause the system to run poorly), NT groups all of the low-level functions that control physical devices and processes into the kernel. Therefore, a word processor or file manager program, which would run in the logical space we are calling User mode, cannot directly control the disk drives or display adapter. The User mode program must package its requests to use physical devices, and then call upon a Kernel mode OS routine to handle those requests.

The tasks performed by the two modes break down as follows:

- **Kernel mode:** These routines handle physical access to devices such as the system motherboard electronics and CPU, disk drives and tape drives, keyboard and display adapter. Kernel mode OS software is also responsible for handling the lowest levels of access to memory space, multitasking, threading, and scheduling. All of the logical and physical device routines are further broken down into units that can be replaced or extended to support new and different devices and device schemes. These smaller replaceable units are usually referred to as *device drivers*.

- **User mode:** This is the part of NT that does not (and cannot) directly control a physical device or basic underlying process like multitasking. Any and all applications and all of NT's subsystems run in User mode. User mode programs and subsystems package their requests to use system resources and then call through to Kernel mode routines.

Insider Info

It's important that we understand the Kernel mode/User mode distinction in order to understand the role that subsystems play in NT. Subsystems are implemented as User mode OS components. They present different application support platforms to the user: Win32, OS/2, Win16, and so on. If you try to run a Windows 3.1 program, for instance, you will be using the Win16 subsystem, sometimes called Windows on Windows (WOW).

By knowing what is available to you and how these subsystems interact, you will be able to make the choices that result in a smooth and useful deployment of NT. After you understand these concepts, you will see why you want to make the choice to implement some programs and stay away from trying to use others.

What is unique to NT is the central importance that extensible subsystems play. They are the building blocks with which NT's architects assembled the OS. The major application-level subsystem is Win32.

The Win32 Subsystem

The Win32 subsystem comprises of several modules, which when grouped together, provide a coherent 32-bit application interface (see Figure 2-1). Win32 is consistent (within the capabilities of the platform) across the entire Microsoft Windows family of operating systems. It presents homogenous functions and procedures across supported OS's (NT, W95, Win3.1 (Win32s)) and allows applications to run successfully on all Windows installations—while still taking advantage of the unique features and capabilities of any given platform.

 NOTE: *Differences in the implementation of Win32, say between NT and Windows 95, depend on the capabilities of the underlying platform. For example, C2-type security functions (those aimed at fulfilling Department of Defense security guidelines) are available only in NT's version of Win32.*

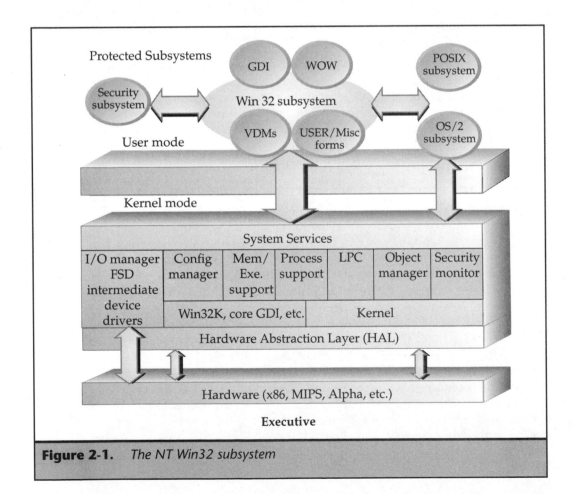

Figure 2-1.   *The NT Win32 subsystem*

The Application Program Interface (API)

The Microsoft Win32 Application Program Interface (API) provides a wide range of functions that allow 32-bit applications access to the unique features and capabilities of the Microsoft Windows operating system. The Win32 API consists of the following functional categories:

- The Graphics Device Interface (GDI)
- System Services and Information
- Multimedia
- Window Creation and Management
- Remote Procedure Calls (RPCs)
- Win32 Extensions

Mini-Glossary

GRAPHICS DEVICE INTERFACE (GDI)   The part of Win32 and the kernel that implements display and drawing functions.

REMOTE PROCEDURE CALL (RPC)   A mechanism to spread processing over more than one machine. A way to execute certain parts of a program's code on a remote machine.

SHELL   The part of NT that appears on the screen behind an application (e.g., the main window, control panel, etc., and all of the associated code behind these elements).

DYNAMIC LINKABLE LIBRARY (DLL)   A type of file that contains reusable code and data—sharable among applications or operating system code.

HYPERTEXT MARKUP LANGUAGE (HTML)   The programming language used to create Web pages on the Internet.

The Graphics Device Interface (GDI)

Windows NT 4 extends the GDI (Graphics Device Interface) of Windows 3.x, Windows 95, and prior versions of NT not only by extending high-level graphics functionality, which we will discuss in Chapter 10, but, as a departure from NT 3.x, by moving some of its functionality down into the NT Executive (in Win32K.sys), in Kernel mode for speed. This is one of the exceptions NT 4 makes to its internal client/server mechanism. The GDI is the portion of the Windows OS that allows the application to present information to the user in graphics mode. Almost all of the graphical interaction that a user has with output on screen and out to a printer or other display device, is controlled by the GDI. The GDI works in concert with other portions of the OS to present information to the user in the form of bitmap pictures, like the dots that make up a newspaper picture.

NOTE: *Until now, workstation graphics on platforms such as Silicon Graphics or Sun have far surpassed what was available on the Windows 3.1, 16-bit platform, Windows 95 (with its limited OpenGL add-ons), or in the first versions of NT. Designers and graphic artists had to use very expensive, niche-market software and hardware to do professional-quality work. NT now allows most of this high-end graphics functionality to be hosted on a more cost-effective platform.*

The Win32 GDI provides many functions that applications can use to generate graphical output for displays, printers, and other devices. Using GDI functions, a program can draw text, lines, complex curves, polygons, and bitmapped images. The color and style of any element may be controlled by the choice of drawing objects—pens, brushes, and fonts—that are available in stock form, or created on the fly. Complex graphics primitives such as paths, and support for OpenGL, a high-end graphics language, are also available. To the user, this means that high-powered graphics programs (for example, the broadcast-quality SoftImage tools that advertising agencies use to create 3-D flying and rotating images) can now be used with NT. Functionality like this used to cost $50,000 and up, with host computers costing $20,000 to $100,000, or more, on top of that.

Win32 applications can direct output to a physical device—such as a display, plotter, or printer—or to a logical device—such as an in-memory bitmap or graphics metafile. Logical devices give Win32 applications the means to store output in a form that is easy to send to a physical device or to manipulate internally for programmatic purposes. Once an application has valid output in the form of a memory image, or graphics metafile, it can manipulate and/or output that image quickly and repeatedly, sending the output to any number of physical devices in a standardized form.

System Services and Information

System services are a subset of Win32 that gives applications access to the resources of the computer and the lowest-level features of the underlying operating system, such as memory, console I/O, file system drivers, threads, and processes. An application uses system service functions to manage and monitor the resources that the application needs to complete its work.

NOTE: *An application might use memory management functions to allocate and free memory. It might also use memory management to thread and process management and synchronization functions to start and coordinate the operation of multiple applications—or multiple threads of execution within a single application.*

System service and information functions also provide access to files, directories, and input and output devices. Win32 file I/O functions give applications access to files and directories on disks and other storage devices on the local computer and on computers in a network. The Win32 network functions create and manage connections to shared resources, such as remote directories and printers on computers in the network. Communications functions read from and write to communications ports as well as controlling the operating modes of these ports. For NT networks, the security functions give applications access to secure data as well as protecting data from intentional or unintentional access or damage.

Insider Info

System service functions provide methods for applications to share resources with other applications. For example, an application can make useful procedures available to all applications by placing these procedures in dynamic link libraries (DLLs). Applications access these procedures by using DLL functions to load the libraries and to retrieve the addresses of the procedures. A Win32 application can share global data (such as bitmaps, icons, fonts, and strings) by adding these resources to the file for an application or DLL. Applications retrieve the data by using the Win32 resource functions to locate the resources and load them into memory.

System service functions provide access to information about the system and other applications. For example, system information functions let applications determine specific characteristics about the computer, such as whether a mouse or joystick is present and what dimensions the visible elements of the screen have. Registry and initialization functions allow the storage of application-specific information in globally visible system files, so new instances of the application or even other applications can retrieve and use this information.

There are services that also let applications share information with applications running on the same computer or on other computers in a network. Applications can copy information between processes by using the mailslots and pipe functions to carry out interprocess communication (IPC), as discussed in Chapters 1 and 15.

Multimedia

NT is becoming a premier platform for high-end graphics animation and sound processing in the motion picture, television, advertising, music, and even scientific workstation markets. Those beautiful NASA re-creations of spacecraft flybys and the newest Terminator-type movie effects all rely on support for multimedia functions in the OS. NT's multimedia layer gives applications access to high-quality audio, music, and video. Multimedia functions enhance and expand the capabilities of graphics and presentation applications, giving users the ability to combine these forms of communication with more traditional forms of computer output.

Using multimedia functions, applications can create documents and presentations that incorporate music, sound effects, and video clips as well as text and graphics (see Figure 2-2). The multimedia functions also provide services for file I/O, media control, joystick, and event timers used in synchronization of audio and video playback and recording. Applications use audio functions to play and record audio data using waveform, musical instrument digital interface (MIDI), and auxiliary audio formats.

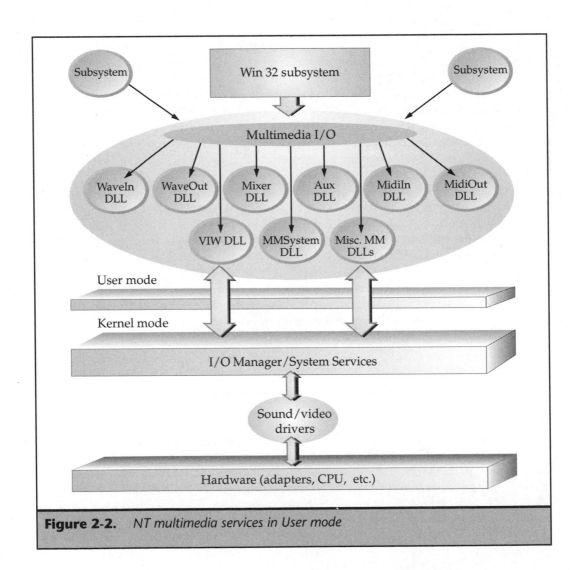

Figure 2-2. *NT multimedia services in User mode*

NOTE: *When playing audio, an application can mix sounds by routing selected audio to specified devices. To ensure efficient storage of audio data, the audio functions provide access to audio compressors and decompressors through the Audio Compression Manager.*

Insider Info

Applications use video functions to capture video clips, compress the clips, and control their playback. An application captures video clips by using simple messages to access video and wave audio acquisition hardware, such as a videotape machine, and to stream selected video clips to disk. To store video data efficiently, an application can use the video compressors and decompressors provided by the Installable Compression Manager. That way, only a fraction of the space required by a multimedia file is actually physically used. Applications can play back video clips either on the computer screen or on other media devices by indirectly using the Media Control Interface (MCI), a simple abstracted control interface used extensively by such programs as MacroMedia Director and Adobe Premier.

Applications use file I/O functions to store and retrieve the different types of multimedia data. An application can use unbuffered and buffered I/O with multimedia files, access and navigate Resource Interchange File Format (RIFF) files, and integrate custom I/O functions for multimedia data types. Intrinsic support is provided for the audio/video interleaved (AVI) file format, which allows the recording, storage, and playback of digital video clips consisting of both video and audio data. An AVI file is a RIFF file that has an extensible file architecture.

MCI provides a common set of high-level commands through which applications control media devices, such as animation devices, audio CDs, digital video devices, MIDI sequencers, video overlay devices, video discs, VISCA videotape recorders (VCR), and waveform (digital sound) devices (.WAV, .AU, and similar formats). To communicate with a device, an application sends messages or command strings through MCI. Think of MCI as a batch language for multimedia devices. The corresponding device handler interprets the message or string and executes the appropriate command at the device.

Applications use joystick functions to support up to two or more joystick devices. An application can retrieve information about a joystick, calibrate the sensitivity, and receive messages related to movement and button activity. Multimedia timer functions provide high-resolution timing for single or periodic events, such as keeping track of playback position on an audio file.

Window Creation and Management

Window management gives Win32 applications the means to create and manage a user interface. Almost all Win32 applications are associated with at least one main (possibly invisible) window. Applications generate output for a window using the Graphics Device Interface (GDI) functions. Because all windows share the display screen, applications do not usually receive access to the entire screen. The Win32 subsystem and its display interface drivers manage output so that it is generally fit within a window, and logically tied to any user interaction. Applications output graphics to a window in response to a request from an application or a system notification.

REMINDER: Graphics in the Win32 driven GUI can be text, line drawings, or bitmaps.

RECEIVING INPUT   Applications receive mouse, keyboard, and possibly port input in the form of Win32 messages. The system translates mouse movement, button clicks, keystrokes, and characters received from, say, a modem into input messages and places these messages into a queue for the application. A Win32 application uses menus and popup, or temporary, windows to present a list of commands to the user. For user input, keyboard accelerators are application-defined combinations of keystrokes and keyboard shortcuts that the system translates into messages. Accelerators typically correspond to commands in a menu and generate the same messages.

TIP: NT comes in many international versions that remap the keyboard and display to fit a particular language. This may be crucial to your use of NT if, for example, you require input and output in Cyrillic, Hebrew, or Arabic.

DIALOG BOXES AND POPUPS   Applications often respond to user input by prompting the user for additional information with dialog boxes or popups. A dialog box, or *dialog,* is a temporary window that displays information or requests input (see Figure 2-3).

REMINDER: A dialog box typically includes controls, which are small, single-purpose windows that display buttons and boxes for the user to make choices or enter information. There are often controls for entering text, scrolling text, selecting items from a list of items, and more.

Dialog boxes manage and process the user's input, making this information available to the application so that it can complete the requested command. A popup is sort of like a *thought cloud*—a small window that provides contextual information to the user, usually self-dismissing.

CLIPBOARD FUNCTIONS   Window management functions provide many other features which relate to windows. For example, Clipboard functions provide the means to copy and paste information within the same window, between windows in

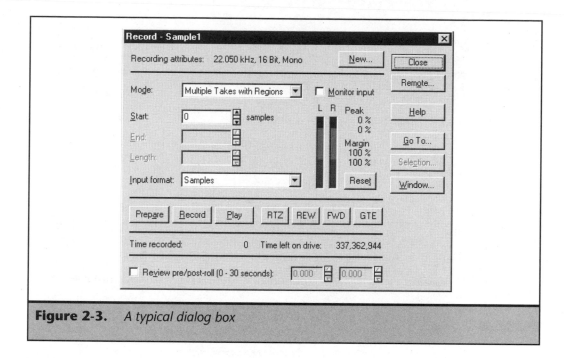

Figure 2-3. *A typical dialog box*

the same application, and between windows in different applications. Applications also use the Clipboard functions to carry out dynamic data exchange (DDE). DDE operations let applications exchange information without requiring specific direction from the user.

Remote Procedure Calls (RPCs)

Remote procedure calls (RPCs) give applications the means to carry out distributed computing, letting Win32 applications tap the resources and computational power of other computers, all of which are linked through a network. Using RPC, the creation of distributed applications becomes possible, each consisting of a client that presents information to the user and one or more servers that store, retrieve, and manipulate data or handle other computing tasks for the client. Shared databases, remote file servers, and remote printer servers are examples of RPC-type distributed applications. Chapter 15 takes a closer look at RPCs.

INVOKING STUB PROCEDURES   A distributed application running as a process in one address space makes procedure calls that execute in an address space on another computer. Within the application, such calls appear to be standard local procedure calls, but these calls invoke stub procedures that interact with the RPC mechanism to carry out the necessary steps to execute the call on a remote machine. RPC manages the network communications needed to support such functionality, even details such as network protocols (see Figure 2-4).

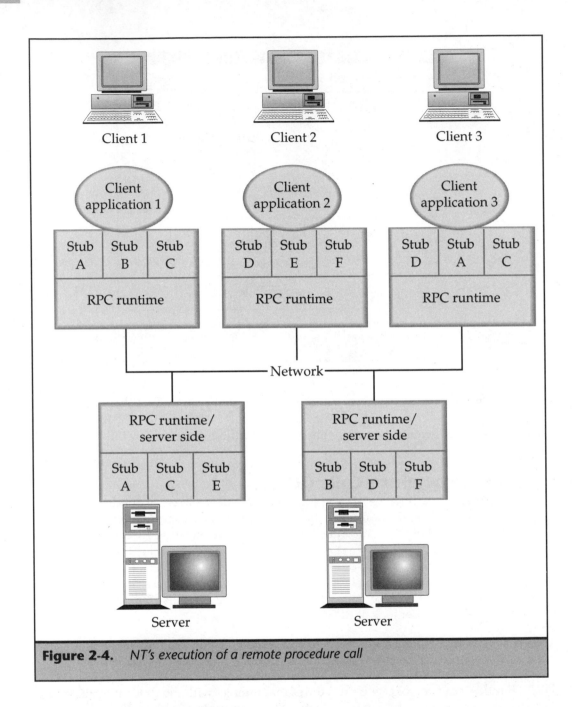

Figure 2-4. *NT's execution of a remote procedure call*

IN NETWORKED ENVIRONMENTS In a networked environment, applications may be divided into separate processes that run on different computers. The benefit of

RPC, and the real reason for using it, is that RPC allows potentially complex functions to execute on remote (and potentially very powerful) computers. The sharing of the computational burden can significantly speed up some applications, particularly database queries. A distributed database might be set up using RPC to share lookup capability over more than one machine on the network. This would allow the database to act upon multiple sets of data almost simultaneously.

NOTE: *The remote procedure call facility provided in Windows NT is compatible with the Open Software Foundation's (OSF) Distributed Computing Environment (DCE) specification. Windows NT workstations can use RPC to interoperate with any other workstations that support this standard.*

Win32 Extensions

Win32 extensions provide services and capabilities beyond the basic services of Win32. These extensions expand on services already provided or provide unique services that are used by only a subset of Win32 applications, which, therefore, do not need to be available most of the time as base functions. Win32 extensions consist of the following:

- **Common controls and common dialog boxes:** The extensions needed to implement common user interface elements such as file open dialogs.

- **Data decompression and file installation:** Extensions that allow automatic installation of sets of files.

- **Dynamic Data Exchange (DDE) and network DDE management:** The ability to exchange information in the background or by using the clipboard as an intermediary across two or more applications.

- **Shell extension:** Association extensions to customize the user interface.

COMMON CONTROLS AND DIALOG BOXES   These extensions simplify the creation and management of controls and dialog boxes. The common controls provide predefined windows that applications can use in dialog boxes to give the user a wider array of ways to view and input information. The common dialog boxes provide predefined dialog boxes that applications can use to prompt the user for information needed to complete common commands, such as the Open, Save, and Print commands in the File menu or printer setup routines.

DATA COMPRESSION AND FILE INSTALLATION   The data decompression and file installation libraries provide useful functions for applications that install files. The Lempel-Ziv (an efficient compression algorithm named after the mathematicians who formulated it) data decompression DLL (dynamic link library) provides functions that applications use to expand files that have been compressed using the Microsoft file compression utility (COMPRESS.EXE). The file installation DLL provides functions that make it easier for applications to analyze currently installed files and install new files properly.

DDE AND NETWORK DDE   The Dynamic Data Exchange (DDE) management and network DDE DLLs simplify the process of exchanging data with other applications. Dynamic data exchange gives an application the means to exchange data without requiring user interaction. The network DDE library provides functions that applications use to connect to DDE servers on other computers in the network. These functions provide DDE code that an application needs to access the network and ensure security across network connections.

SHELL EXTENSIONS   The Windows NT shell is extensible. NT Applications can extend the shell in a number of ways. A shell extension enhances the shell by providing additional means of manipulating file objects, by simplifying the task of browsing through the file system and networks, or by giving the user easier access to tools that manipulate objects in the file system.

TIP: If you like, you can create a shell extension that adds menu items to the context menu of specific types of files, or you can create a shell extension that allows you to assign an icon to specific types of files. An example of this can be found in Netscape's Commerce Server. It creates a new association for HTML files and assigns the big N icon to them.

Networks Support Infrastructure

Microsoft provides four basic transport drivers (i.e., protocols) with Windows NT:

- TCP/IP (Transmission Control Protocol/Internet Protocol)
- NWLink (IPX/SPX)
- NetBEUI (NetBIOS Extended User Interface) or NBF (NetBEUI Frame)
- DLC (Data Link Control)

Insider Info

Windows NT installs TCP/IP and NWLink by default, primarily because IPX is the most common protocol in PC networks, and it has relatively simple configuration requirements. However, administrators can modify installation scripts (the SETUP.INF files) to install other protocols by default. Administrators should install the minimum protocols necessary, because multiple protocols usually result in higher memory requirements, more complex client configuration and network administration, and higher support and software license costs.

Because of the Internet and its technical abilities as an interface to Unix and non-PC networks, the TCP/IP protocol is becoming the de facto standard. You should seriously think of installing TCP/IP as a primary first choice. The more popular protocols have a larger base of experienced support and design engineers, and studies of router-based LAN backbones with at least 250 nodes in Fortune 500 companies conclude that TCP/IP is used on 95 percent of all such networks, while SPX/IPX is used on 87 percent.

NetBEUI usage is limited primarily to Microsoft and IBM PC network environments. SPX/IPX has been the most popular protocol in PC network environments, and if you must support an infrastructure that includes legacy machines networked with this protocol (most notably NetWare systems), support is built in.

TCP/IP

Windows NT includes an implementation of TCP/IP. Since TCP/IP is available for many diverse operating systems—such as Unix, VMS, NetWare, and OS/2—Windows NT can use TCP/IP to communicate with these different operating systems. TCP/IP also provides compatibility with the global Internet.

NOTE: *Microsoft completely redesigned the TCP/IP transport driver in Windows NT 4, providing many enhancements over the streams-based TCP/IP transport driver in Windows NT 3.1.*

NWLink (IPX)

Novell NetWare currently has the largest market share among PC-based network operating systems. NetWare's native Network Layer protocol is IPX, a Novell proprietary descendant of the Xerox XNS protocol. Microsoft implements the lower-level NetWare protocols in the NWLink transport driver, which includes IPX, SPX, RIPX, and NBIPX.

NetBIOS (The Network Basic Input/Output System)

The NetBIOS standard, which was originally developed for IBM in 1983, defines two entities:

- **A Session Layer interface:** This is a standard API for user applications to submit network I/O and control directives to underlying network protocol software. NetBIOS commands are submitted via Network Control Blocks (NCBs).

- **NetBIOS Frames Protocol (NBFP):** This is a session management/data transport protocol. It functions at the Session and Transport layers to perform the network I/O to accommodate the NetBIOS interface command set.

NBF (NetBEUI)

IBM first introduced the NetBEUI protocol specification in 1985. It is optimized for departmental LANs or LAN segments. The Windows NT NBF (NetBIOS Frame) transport driver implements the IBM NetBEUI specification, and is compatible with the NetBEUI shipped with past Microsoft networking products.

Insider Info

NT networking drivers and software generally adhere to two different standards, using the OSI networking model (discussed in Chapter 5) as a framework: the Network Driver Interface Specification (NDIS) and the Transport Driver Interface (TDI). These two specifications allow NT to support almost any kind of networking hardware, driver, or transport protocol, without requiring changes to the surrounding software layers. This makes NT much easier to configure and more flexible in its support of various network configurations. When contemplating a third-party protocol or driver, try to make sure it is NDIS- or TDI-compliant. By doing so, you will likely guarantee smooth installation and operation.

NOTE: NetBEUI support may be important in NT LANs that plan to be backward compatible with older Microsoft and IBM networks. Its use is limited almost exclusively to Microsoft LAN Manager, Windows NT, Windows for Workgroups, LAN Manager for Unix, and IBM PCLAN and LAN server environments.

Data Link Control (DLC)

Unlike the other protocols in Windows NT, the DLC (Data Link Control) protocol is not designed to be a primary protocol for use between PCs. DLC only provides applications with direct access to the data link layer, and thus is not used by the Windows NT network redirector or controller. Because the redirector cannot use DLC, this protocol is not used for normal session communication between Windows NT computers.

NOTE: SNA Server for NT Server uses DLC as its primary transport for communicating with IBM mini and mainframe devices.

NOTE: All of NT's network protocols are self-tuning, but can be helped to perform at peak efficiency by following the basic performance-enhancing guidelines found in Appendix A. You can also refer to the NT Resource Kit for specific parameter entries that you may make or customize for each protocol. These parameters are contained in NT's Registry, and you can use NT's registy editors, covered in Chapter 17, to enter new values or to customize entries that already exist.

Security Models

If this were a perfect world, we wouldn't need to worry about protecting our data from being exposed to and accessed by anyone. Because almost all data requires some level of protection (and some data and code must be protected from almost all access), NT offers security in varied levels and on most operations and services provided.

Who Needs It?

Let's clarify why you might need security. You may not have to bother with security at all, unless you have (or are writing) a server application. This is an application that several users can access and that provides data structures restricted to only a subset of those users. For stand-alone computers (that is, machines that are not tied into a network), you can have a service that starts up as Windows NT boots and keeps running even as multiple users log on and off the same machine. This service could provide information that is visible only to a few users. For example, if you wish to compile usage patterns or logon data, you might want to restrict access to that data to the machine's administrator(s).

System-Level Restrictions

A number of privileges are restricted on the system level. For example, the system registry is protected so that only users with special privileges are allowed to add device drivers to the system, or—for security reasons—a malicious user won't misuse a device driver's ability to monitor user input to spy on other users' work.

Security can also help stabilize your system. Consider a poorly written device driver installed by an unauthorized user. Such a driver could crash the machine while another user is working. By restricting the ability to register new device drivers to trusted users, we can shield a Windows NT machine from this kind of misuse.

Server Application Security

A large number of stand-alone server applications that also function over a network will benefit from some kind of hook into the security system. For example, a database server might handle several users at the same time—some of whom may not be allowed to see portions of the data in a given database. Let's say that everybody in your company needs to query your inventory database. Administration will need to access all the information on all items (prices, markup, etc.), whereas others in the company should only be able to see inventory numbers and quantity or ordering information. If you restrict the database fields that contain sensitive information to administrative personnel, you can, in effect, allow everyone in the organization to use the same database without compromising security and privacy.

Domain Group Access

Each Windows NT domain (or domain group) keeps a database of users that the domain knows about. A user who wishes to work on a computer within a Windows NT domain must identify himself or herself using a username and password. As soon as the security system verifies the password against the user database, the user (and every process he or she starts) is associated with an access token, an internal data structure that identifies the user.

Right and Privilege Verification

Windows NT uses two mechanisms that cause failed accesses:

- Verification against rights
- Verification against privileges

A *right* pertains to an action on an object, such as the right to suspend a thread or the right to read from a file. Rights are always associated with a certain object and a known user. For example, the right to read from a file must be associated with a file (to which this right is applied) and with a user who does or doesn't have that right. Likewise, the right to suspend a thread is useless unless it is associated with a specific thread and a user.

A *privilege* is a predefined right that pertains to operations on the system. For example, there are privileges to debug applications, to back up and restore storage devices, and to load drivers. Privileges are centered around users, not objects. Furthermore, whereas rights require the specification of an action (for example, to read a file or to suspend a thread), privileges do not (that is, the user either does or does not hold them). The action that goes with the privilege is implied in the privilege itself.

Application Support

All applications that run on NT depend upon one or more underlying support mechanisms. Applications that must migrate from a Windows 3.1, Windows for Workgroups, or DOS environment will find almost complete support in NT 4. Let's take a look at the part of NT that assures you of being able to run these "foreign" applications, and why you don't necessarily need to upgrade all of your existing applications to Win32 now.

Mini-Glossary

WINDOWS ON WINDOWS (WOW)   The code in NT that allows a Win 3.1 (Win16) application to run.

VIRTUAL DOS MACHINE (VDM)   An NT internal construct that sets up what amounts to a complete DOS PC (logically) within the memory space of the NT machine. This VDM is separate from Win32 applications and runs as if it were a complete PC in itself.

Windows on Windows (WOW)

WOW is the "glue" that binds 16-bit Windows-based (and some MS-DOS-based) applications to the Windows NT operating system. Windows NT unifies a number of diverse operating systems onto a single, integrated desktop. The subsystem architecture of Windows NT makes this integration possible. Operating systems are mimicked by an environment constructed on top of the low-level Windows NT kernel (see Figure 2-5).

Virtual DOS Machines

MS-DOS and 16-bit Windows emulation are not supplied by environment subsystems per se. Instead, a Win32-based application called a virtual DOS machine (VDM) provides a complete MS-DOS machine environment. MS-DOS and 16-bit Windows-based applications are run within VDMs, which run as clients of the Win32 subsystem (and also call native services from time to time).

> *NOTE: Each MS-DOS application runs within its own VDM process. Windows 3.1 is considered one MS-DOS application, so all Windows 3.1-based applications normally share one VDM, but this is selectable when starting the application.*

The Role of Win32

Because the Win32 subsystem and the new kernel routines handle all video output, the other environment subsystems and VDMs must direct the output of their applications to the Win32 subsystem or directly to the kernel for display. The VDM running 16-bit Windows-based applications translates their output calls into Win32 calls and sends them via messages to the Win32 subsystem, or a call is made directly into the kernel.

The OS/2 and POSIX subsystems, as well as any VDMs running MS-DOS-based applications, also direct their applications' character-mode output to the Win32 subsystem or kernel routines. This output is displayed in character-mode windows called consoles. An environment subsystem can also have many client applications running. Each subsystem keeps track of its clients and maintains any global information the client applications share.

> *NOTE: Though several subsystems and VDMs may be running, Win32 is the only environment that makes itself visible. To the user, it appears that Windows runs all the applications.*

Win16 Applications

As of Windows NT 4, Win16 applications in separate VDMs are supported. The interface is this:

- If running the item in Explorer or from the desktop, check Run in Separate Memory Space in the Program Item Properties dialog box.

- If you are starting from the command prompt, the Start command supports a /SEPARATE option.

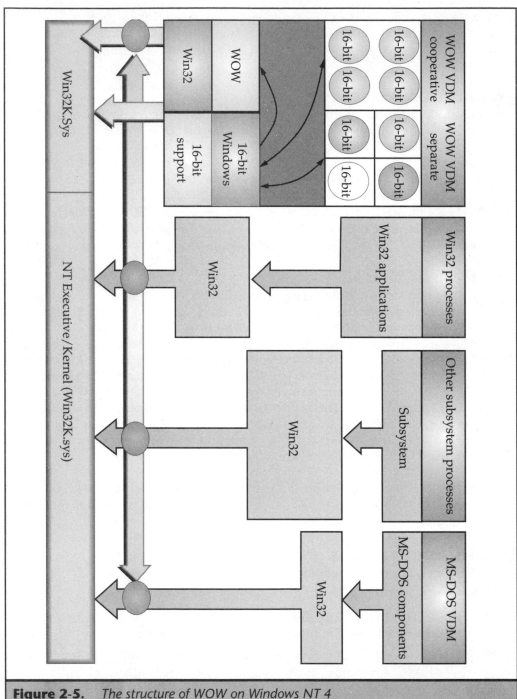

Figure 2-5.   *The structure of WOW on Windows NT 4*

> **TIP:**   *Because of their support in NT 4, a large number of 16-bit Win 3.1-style applications can be used directly, obviating the need to purchase 32-bit updates immediately. This can be quite a cost factor when, let's say, a system administrator plans to upgrade to NT on 200 workstations but cannot afford the extra cost of upgrading 200 copies of a Win 3.1-style word processor or spreadsheet. MS-DOS utilities such as file finders and editors can also be used on NT, avoiding the need to purchase all new software suites.*

Non-Windows Applications

Migration paths don't always follow the DOS/Win16 to NT route. Many users of both OS/2 and Unix systems are now looking to migrate to NT 4. NT offers many standardized interface improvements and capabilities versus the hodgepodge of Unix. OS/2's penchant for crashing, and its inability to fully support Win32-compliant applications also boost the move to NT.

OS/2 Support

The OS/2 subsystem enables automatic support for OS/2 version 1.x character-based applications. All that is required is to type the name of the application, and it will be run in a console window. The OS/2 subsystem is only loaded into memory when it is needed, so the fact that this support exists does not mean you will pay a penalty if you don't use it.

Support for the High Performance File System (HPFS) has been removed in NT 4, so you'll have to reformat your HPFS drives, and you won't be able to use an HPFS-specific utility or application. The support left in NT 4 for OS/2 is only there so that applications that have been used in prior versions of NT can be migrated without shock. Otherwise, NT plans no further development or further support for OS/2.

POSIX Support

POSIX (Portable Operating System Interface) began as an effort by the IEEE (Institute of Electrical and Electronics Engineering) community to promote the portability of applications across Unix environments by developing a clear, consistent, and unambiguous set of standards. POSIX is not limited to the Unix environment, however. It can also be implemented on non-Unix operating systems, as was done with the IEEE Standard (POSIX.1) Implementation on Virtual Memory System (VMS), Multiprogramming Executive (MPE), and the Conversion Technology Operating System (CTOS). POSIX actually consists of a set of standards that range from POSIX.1 to POSIX.12.

The POSIX subsystem (see Figure 2-6) is implemented in Windows NT as a protected server. POSIX applications communicate with the POSIX subsystem through a facility in the NT Executive known as a local procedure call (LPC).

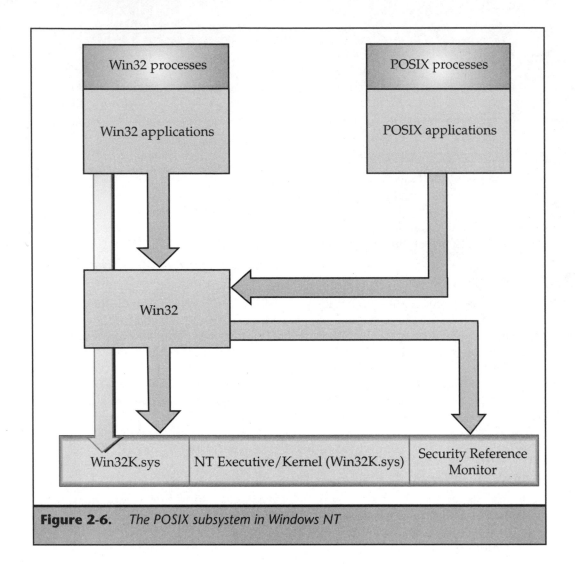

Figure 2-6. *The POSIX subsystem in Windows NT*

NOTE: *The POSIX subsystem, as well as each POSIX application, runs in its own protected address space that protects it from any other application that might be running on Windows NT. POSIX applications are preemptively multitasked with respect to each other and to other applications running in the system.*

STARTING THE POSIX SUBSYSTEM POSIX applications can be started from a Windows NT console-window command prompt, File Manager, Program Manager, or by invocation from within another POSIX application. The following files, found in the System32 directory, are required to support the POSIX subsystem and run POSIX applications:

- PSXSS.EXE (the POSIX subsystem server)
- PSXDLL.DLL (the POSIX dynamic link library)
- POSIX.EXE (the POSIX console session manager)

POSIX FILE SYSTEM SUPPORT   POSIX requires a certain amount of functionality from the file system, such as the ability for a file to have more than one name (or hard links), and case-sensitive file naming. The MS-DOS-style FAT (File Allocation Table) file system does not support these features, which is another reason why a new file system was required for Windows NT. NTFS (NT File System) supports both hard links and case-sensitive naming.

NOTE: If you want to run in a POSIX-conforming environment, you need at least one NTFS disk partition on your computer.

You can run POSIX applications from any Windows NT file system. If the application does not need to access the file system, it will run with no problems. However, if the application does require access to the file system, there is no way to guarantee that it will behave correctly on a non-NTFS disk partition.

NOTE: By default, when you install Windows NT for the first time, the user's right to bypass traverse checking is granted to everyone. This right allows a user to change directories through a directory tree even if the user has no permission for those directories.

POSIX AND NT PRINTING SUPPORT   The POSIX subsystem itself does not directly support printing, but Windows NT supports redirection and piping between subsystems. If your POSIX application writes to stdout (that's what Unix hackers call the console or terminal—the screen!), and you have connected or redirected either your serial or parallel ports to a printer, you can redirect the output of a POSIX application to that printer.

NOTE: The POSIX.1 specification does not have a requirement for access to remote file systems, but as with any of the other subsystems, the POSIX subsystem and POSIX applications have transparent access to any Win32 remotely connected file system.

COMMUNICATING WITH OTHER SUBSYSTEMS   Windows NT supports a common command processor that can run commands from any of the subsystems. In addition, Windows NT supports piped input and output between commands of different subsystems. Figure 2-7 illustrates how a POSIX application interacts with other components of the Windows NT operating system.

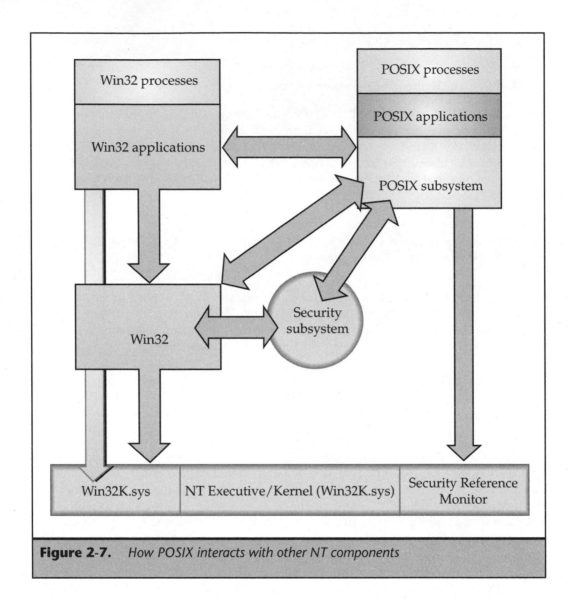

Figure 2-7. *How POSIX interacts with other NT components*

USING A SINGLE COMMAND SHELL   A certain amount of functionality can be gained by using a single command shell of Windows NT. From an administration and programming point of view, although not elegant, it is possible to put a Win32 graphical front-end on a POSIX application by using the redirection of stdin and stdout (our two Unix geek acronyms for the keyboard, and the screen, respectively).

NOTE: *POSIX applications have no direct access to any of the facilities and features of the Win32 subsystem, such as memory mapped files, networking, graphics, or dynamic data exchange.*

What's Next

In this chapter, we have taken the first steps into the internals of NT. The journey is far from over, but you should now be a bit more comfortable with the extent and scope of the specific information to come. You have learned why NT is the leader in portable operating systems today, and why, no matter what platform you're coming from, NT will fit your future needs. We will take an in-depth look at some of NT's internals in the chapters to come—why and how they affect your hardware, applications, and support choices.

But for now, let's jump in with both feet and go through an NT installation. Chapter 3 covers NT 4 installation, from breaking the seal on the package to the first time you log in. There is a lot more to installing NT than merely shoving a CD-ROM or scads of disks into the computer. We'll cover some little-known but important aspects of installation, and show you how to cut an hour off of your first install!

Chapter Three

Setting Up Your System

In this chapter, we are going to go from the unopened box to a running system. We'll examine some of the basic choices that you will have to make before you even insert the first disk. As more than just an aside, we'll take a peek at what makes an optimal system—hardware-wise. Even an optimally installed NT OS will not perform to your expectations if the hardware it's running on isn't set up right.

TIP: As you read through this chapter, some tips and information will appear in Insider Info boxes outside the regular flow of the text. These contain lessons learned the hard way and knowledge not generally available. These tidbits are put down in black and white for you to take heed of and use. They are signposts to guide you.

With the insights you are going to gain from this chapter, you can prevent many hours and even days of troubleshooting after an initial installation of NT 4. You will also be able to make the initial configuration choices that will enable you to optimize your system and add functionality to NT later on, without backing up and having to start over.

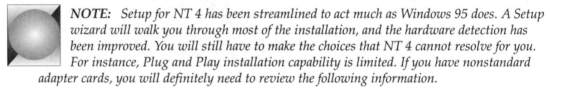

NOTE: Setup for NT 4 has been streamlined to act much as Windows 95 does. A Setup wizard will walk you through most of the installation, and the hardware detection has been improved. You will still have to make the choices that NT 4 cannot resolve for you. For instance, Plug and Play installation capability is limited. If you have nonstandard adapter cards, you will definitely need to review the following information.

Choosing the Right Hardware

With so many choices and preferences in hardware, we are not going to get into which manufacturer is better or which display card runs faster. That argument is between your salesman and your wallet. From the most basic of standpoints, almost all of the Intel Pentium and high-end 486-class computers sold are capable of running NT 4 just fine. The same can be said for the DEC Alpha, PowerPC, and MIPS platforms available. So why would we want to even think about hardware, if it's just this simple? The answer is that it is much more complicated. Now, brace yourselves, because we are going to talk bits and bytes, a necessary evil.

CAUTION: Microsoft has dropped NT support for Intel 386-type computers. They are underpowered and not sold anymore, so don't plan an installation—even for low-powered workstations—around 386-class computers.

Over and above your choice of "box," there are a few factors that, when taken into account, will help you make the right decisions about hardware. We will stick with the Intel x86 (486, Pentium, and Pentium Pro) architecture for the purposes of this discussion, because probably 90 percent of all NT installations are made on x86 platforms. Many of the same factors, however, apply equally to the other platforms for

NT. We will go through these one at a time, building up our ideal NT computer as we go. (See Table 3-1 for a basic road map of NT hardware requirements.)

Mini-Glossary

DOMAIN   A logical (abstract) group, controlled by a server, to be joined by individual computers needing access to the resources and security it provides. A domain is a grouping of computers and users that eases administration of the computers and user accounts. NT Server is required to create a domain. The NT Servers on your network will all share a common user account and security database, thus enabling each user to have a single account which is recognized on all servers in the domain. Security policies such as how long passwords remain valid are also held in common by all servers in a domain. NT workstations can also be members of a domain; the benefit they derive is the ability to recognize user accounts that are created on the servers in the domain, but security policies on a workstation are always independent of the domain security policies.

INDUSTRY STANDARD ARCHITECTURE (ISA)   An 8-bit, and later a 16-bit, *expansion bus* that provides a buffered interface from *devices* on *expansion cards* to the PC internal bus. The most common expansion bus found on PC-compatible *motherboards*.

EISA   A 32-bit PC *expansion bus* designed as a superset of the Industry Standard Architecture (ISA) bus. This bus was designed to expand the speed and data width of the PC expansion bus, while still supporting older ISA cards.

I/O ADDRESSING   Input/output port addresses. The microprocessor's way of communicating information in 8-,16-, or 32-bit chunks to and from the outside world (peripherals). I/O ports on an IBM PC-compatible computer range from 0000h to FFFFh (in base 16).

INTERRUPT REQUEST (IRQ) SETTINGS   A method by which a *device* can request to be serviced by the device's software driver. The *motherboard* uses a programmable interrupt controller (PIC) to monitor the priority of the requests from all devices. When a request occurs, the microprocessor suspends the current operation and gives control to the device driver associated with the interrupt number issued. Many devices only support raising requests of specific numbers. Settable IRQ numbers for IBM PC-type machines range from IRQ 0 through 15.

PERIPHERAL COMPONENT INTERCONNECT (PCI)   A high-performance 32-bit or 64-bit bus designed to be used with devices that have high bandwidth requirements, such as the display subsystem.

Role/Component	Client/Workstation	Server/Domain Server
Motherboard	ISA, PCI slots available	EISA(ISA), PCI slots available
CPU	486-Dx4-75/Dx4-100, Pentium 90, 120, 133, 166, 200 (high speeds are required for CAD)	Pentium 90, 120, 133, 166, 200, Pentium Pro, Multiprocessor configurations
Power supply	200/220 watt standard supply	230 to 275 watt HD supply
Available card slots	2 to 3 slots; 2 ISA, 1 PCI	3 to 5 slots, 3 EISA(ISA), 2 PCI
Available drive bays	1 extra for hard disk drive	2 to 4 extra for hard disk, tape backup drives
Memory (RAM)	20MB to 64MB	32MB to 128MB
Hard disk capacity	1.2GB to 4.1GB	2.1GB to >9GB

Table 3-1. *Basic NT Computer Hardware Choices*

Motherboard and Power Supply

Depending on how your NT hardware is going to be used—workstation or server, CAD or database—there are a few basic qualities that the actual computer case and motherboard/power supply should have. First, you must take into account what kind of NT installation you will be aiming for. How much space is inside the case and on the motherboard for such things as extra hard disk drives or additional adapter cards?

TIP: You will need at least one empty slot for a network card. Almost all NT systems are networked. It's a good idea to always have at least one motherboard slot available. There are many consumer-based computers coming into the market now that have a total of just three motherboard adapter slots! Stay away from them.

We also want to make sure that the rating on the power supply is sufficient. If the system that you are building or buying requires many adapter cards or multiple internal disk drives, the power supply ratings become critical. As you can see from Table 3-1, typical ratings are from 200 to 275 watts.

NOTE: You will also have to decide what your own requirements are for memory and hard disk space, although there are some lower limits which you should pay heed to. These subjects are covered in detail in the next two sections of this chapter.

Random Access Memory (RAM)

Now that we know pretty much what our box is going to look like, let's flesh it out so we can make up a plan of attack for our NT 4 installation. First of all, let's talk memory. RAM is more than important in NT. The architects have tried to tune NT's working set (the operating system code actually resident in RAM at any one time) so NT will run on a computer with as little RAM as possible.

 CAUTION: *There have been various informational releases by Microsoft indicating that the architects' goal was 8MB of RAM. This somewhat misleading figure would include enough spare RAM to run applications, utilities, and the like. Also keep in mind that this figure is for NT Workstation, not NT Server. The final figures for minimal RAM in an NT installation turn out to be about 12MB for Workstation.*

It Takes Much More

Well, it just can't be done right with even 12MB of RAM. The minimum amount for NT Workstation, to achieve a functional machine, is 16MB of RAM, and on NT Server, the number is 24MB. The virtual memory scheme in NT (the design that allows big chunks of code and data not being used at the moment to be written temporarily to disk and then read back just before it's needed) will not function properly without at least 16MB of RAM.

The Vicious Virtual Memory Cycle

What happens is that as the computer reads OS code, data, and application code into memory, a vicious circle starts in low memory installations (<16MB). As the system fills up available RAM, the virtual memory system *pages* (or moves onto disk) large chunks of what it deems the least important code or data in order to make room for what it deems to be the most important. As this happens (on a machine with minimal RAM), the operating system becomes almost locked in a cycle of paging data out and immediately reading it back into memory, constantly trying to satisfy its idea of where equilibrium will be reached. This is most notable where large application programs are used, or multiple-network protocols and connections put a strain on resources.

TIP: *Although NT Workstation runs fairly well with 16MB of RAM and NT Server with 24MB, a performance increase of up to 25 percent (and a drastic reduction in memory paging to disk) can be gained by installing at least 20~24MB and 32MB, for NT Workstation and NT Server, respectively.*

Hard Disk Space

A full NT installation without applications or development tools can run upwards of 100MB, so you have to think about hard disk space. NT's paging file, the one used for the virtual memory swapping we just discussed, can easily grow to between 30 and 70MB, so there can be up to 200MB used before you even install one application! As hard disk drive prices drop, it doesn't make sense to install any less than a 1.2GB hard disk as your primary drive. If you have many applications, or you are going to work with large databases, CAD, or multimedia files, plan on at least a second 1.2GB hard disk drive or possibly a 2.1GB drive. If you are planning an NT Server installation, a total of at least 4GB of hard disk is a better number to work with.

REMINDER: We are planning out the ideal workstation or server, so remember, these are guidelines. A 486Dx2-66 with 16MB of memory and a 500MB disk drive can be used as an NT server, although in a severely limited capacity.

Tape Backup Systems

If you are planning to use your NT system as a server, work with large graphics files, have data storage requirements that involve the temporary storage of information that you don't necessarily want to keep on disk forever, or have critical data that must be redundant, you will need a tape backup drive. Tape backup for NT couldn't be easier. Tape drives in several formats are directly supported. Drives are available in 250MB to greater than 8GB capacities. DAT (Digital Audio Tape) drives are a good choice, offering 2GB and greater capacity at very high speed and low cost.

NOTE: The Backup Manager, which is included as an NT administrative tool in both Server and Workstation versions, completely automates a tape backup session. See the following chapter for a detailed discussion on working with NT Backup.

CD-ROM Drives

Although it is not critical that you have a CD-ROM drive installed on each computer in your local network, it is mandatory that you have at least one CD-ROM drive available and visible in your local network. NT 4 no longer ships on floppy disks. Anyway, who would choose to swap 60 or so disks in and out of a floppy drive when CD-ROM drives cost so little!

Getting Ready to Install

When you've resolved the necessary hardware issues covered in the first part of this chapter, it's important to gather certain information and make some decisions before you start NT Setup and install the program. Here's what you need to know and do:

- **Adapter cards:** Whatever type of computer you have, it is important to know what brands of adapter cards you have installed and how they are set up before attempting an installation of NT 4.

■ **I/O addressing:** Find out the settings that a card needs to function in the I/O address space of your computer.

■ **Interrupt request settings (IRQs):** The levels (numbered 0 through 15) that your card is set to respond to, should be known; although in some cases, NT will automatically detect these for you.

■ **Printer model and port:** If you have a printer connected directly to your computer, you'll need to know the printer model and port used by the printer, usually LPT1 or LPT2.

■ **Computer name:** You should have planned out the computer name for your NT workstation or NT server. In the case of a server, you need to know whether it will be a domain controller or a server and the name of the NT domain for which your computer will be a primary or backup domain controller. (This issue is covered in detail later in this chapter.) If your computer will not play the role of domain controller, you'll need to know the name of the domain or workgroup that this computer will join.

■ **Emergency repair disk:** You will need a high-density floppy disk of the correct size for disk drive A. There is no need to preformat this disk. Label it "NT 4 Emergency Repair disk" and set it aside until NT Setup prompts you to insert it. (We will cover this subject fully later in this chapter.)

■ **Keeping an older version:** If you want to keep an old installation of NT 3.1 or 3.5x on the same computer where you are installing NT 4, you can install NT 4 in the same domain and use the same computer name as long as this computer is not a server and the primary domain controller.

> *CAUTION: This version of NT is slightly more sensitive to hardware that is, or has been, misconfigured. In tests, an NT 3.51 machine, running fine for over a year, was upgraded to NT 4 with a great deal of difficulty. It turns out that IRQs were overlapped on some of the adapter cards (this shows up mostly on network, disk, and multimedia adapters), and this kept NT 4 from successfully completing the setup process, where 3.51 didn't seem to mind. Lesson: know your hardware and its settings before you start the install!*

Using NT Setup

How you start NT Setup (the Windows NT 4 installation program) depends on the source media you are using to install NT—from a CD-ROM drive (for all types of supported CD-ROM drives) or from a shared network directory. There is also the variable of how you start the setup process. If you are installing from Windows 95, and you insert the setup CD in your local CD-ROM drive, it will "auto-run," causing an introduction screen to be displayed automatically, offering to run NT Setup. If you are installing from MS-DOS, you will be using a program on the setup CD called

WINNT.EXE. If an older version of NT is already installed on your computer, you can also run a program called WINNT32.EXE to upgrade the operating system or perform a new install.

 CAUTION: *You cannot install NT on a drive configured with any disk compression products. If you use Drivespace, Doublespace, Stacker, or any other utility of the sort, uninstall it first or pick another drive to install to. If the compressed disk is the primary boot disk, you must uninstall the compression product.*

Installing from a CD-ROM Drive on a Non-Windows 95 Machine

To start NT Setup from a CD-ROM drive on a machine that does not have Windows 95 installed, follow these steps:

1. Reboot your computer, making certain to first insert the NT Boot Disk in the appropriate boot drive, or from MS-DOS, with the NT 4.0 CD in your CD-ROM drive, change to the \I386 directory and type **winnt.exe**.

2. If you rebooted with the NT Boot Disk in drive A, then when Setup asks for Setup Disk #2 and then Setup Disk #3, insert the disk in the appropriate boot drive. Otherwise, Setup will prompt you to insert blank formatted floppy disks to create boot disks, for archival and repair purposes.

3. If Setup asks for the NT 4.0 CD, insert it in the CD-ROM drive.

4. Follow the instructions on the screen to complete the setup process.

5. Have a fourth blank formatted high-density floppy ready for the step in the setup process where you are asked to create an emergency repair disk.

Installing from a CD-ROM Drive on a Windows 95 Machine

To start NT Setup from a CD-ROM drive on a machine that already has Windows 95 installed, follow these steps:

1. Insert the NT 4.0 CD in the CD-ROM drive.

2. The auto-run feature of Windows 95 will automatically display the NT 4.0 CD-ROM introduction screen, shown in Figure 3-1. Choose to set up NT.

3. Setup will prompt you to insert blank formatted floppy disks to create boot disks.

4. Setup will then copy some initial files to your C drive and ask you to reboot the computer, with the boot disk that you created in step 3 inserted in drive A.

5. Follow the instructions given in the previous section, from step 2; then follow the further steps on the screen to complete the setup process.

6. Have a fourth blank formatted high-density floppy ready for the step in the setup process where you are asked to create an emergency repair disk.

Installing from a Network Drive

To install NT Workstation or NT Server from a network drive, you or your network administrator must first copy the NT 4 master files to a shared network directory as described later in this chapter. Perform the following procedure from the computer where you want to install NT. This method uses either a program called WINNT.EXE or a similar 32-bit version for upgrade on an older NT installation, called WINNT32.EXE, to prepare your computer for running NT Setup. (WINNT(32).EXE can be used to upgrade your existing NT 3.x workstation or server or to install NT 4 for the first time.)

 NOTE: *You can also use this method to install NT on computers with SCSI hard disks or CD-ROM devices that are supported under MS-DOS, as in the previous examples given for installing from CD-ROM.*

1. Have ready four blank formatted high-density floppy disks of the correct size for your computer's boot drive. Label the first three disks "Setup Boot Disk,"

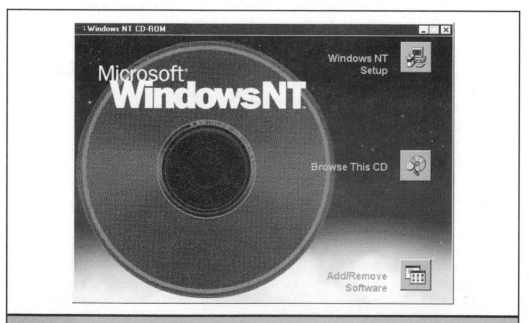

Figure 3-1.   *The NT CD-ROM introduction screen*

"Setup Disk #2," and "Setup Disk #3," and the fourth disk "Emergency Repair Disk."

2. Connect to the directory that contains the NT master files:

   ■ **On MS-DOS clients, you will be using WINNT.EXE:** Use your MS-DOS network to connect to the shared network directory that contains the NT master files.

   ■ **On Windows 3.x, Windows for Workgroups, or Windows 95 clients, you will be using WINNT.EXE:** Use Explorer or File Manager to connect to the network directory that contains the master files for the new version of NT 4.

   ■ **On Windows NT clients, you will be using WINNT32.EXE:** Use Explorer or File Manager to connect to the network directory that contains the master files for the new version of NT 4.

   ■ **You may also use the WINNT.EXE program from a local CD-ROM device:** Insert the NT 4.0 CD in the CD-ROM drive, and then, while running MS-DOS or Windows/Windows 95, change to the \I386 directory on the CD-ROM drive. (For example, if the CD-ROM is drive E, change to the E:\I386 directory.) Then, at the MS-DOS command prompt or through the Run command, type **winnt** and press ENTER.

3. You will be asked to confirm the NT 4 source directory (as shown in the following illustration). Type the path for the directory where the master files are stored (the same directory you switched to in step 2).

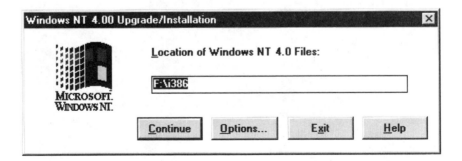

4. When prompted, insert the blank formatted high-density floppy disk labeled Setup Disk #3 in drive A. After some files are copied to Setup Disk #3, you will be prompted to insert the high-density floppy disk labeled Setup Disk #2 and then the Setup Boot Disk in drive A. Setup will advise you of its progress with messages like the one shown here. This process creates the three startup disks

required for setup. After the necessary files are transferred, a message asks you to press ENTER to restart the computer.

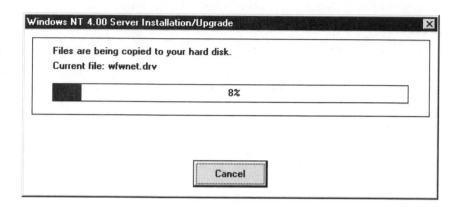

5. Follow the instructions on the screen to complete the setup process.

TIP: *Make sure you keep the setup and emergency repair disks that WINNT.EXE or WINNT32.EXE creates during installation. If you have problems with your installation, you may need those disks to repair your operating system.*

Choosing Setup Options

Early in the setup process you must choose options that allow you to control how NT 4 gets installed. This is a two-part process. First, basic options will be shown to you. These include

- **Detection of special disk controllers:** NT 4.0 Setup can detect SCSI adapters, CD-ROM drives, and special disk controllers for use with NT. You should let NT 4.0 Setup detect these devices and install appropriate drivers, including those for which you have a device support disk from a manufacturer for mass storage devices. You should only skip this automatic detection when you know that detection causes Setup to fail.

- **The install disk partition and directory:** This is where the NT 4 files will be installed.

- **Video, mouse, and keyboard layout:** If you have an NT-compatible driver from the hardware manufacturer for a video adapter card, mouse, or keyboard, follow the instructions on the screen for installing them from your manufacturer's disk.

Once you have finished the basic setup, the NT 4.0 Setup wizard will start, and you will be given the opportunity to configure further options. The Custom setup steps are designed for power users who want more control over how NT 4 is installed on their computers. Within this part of Setup, you can override default values or accept recommended settings for the following:

- **Components and applications:** You can choose the specific NT 4 components you want to install and the existing applications you want to run with NT.

- **Virtual memory:** You can select specific settings for this feature.

- **Printer:** Here's where you can choose the local printer connections for your computer.

- **Network configuration:** You can choose any additional network adapters or other network components you want to install and configure during NT 4.0 Setup.

Setting Up for Mass Storage

NT 4.0 Setup automatically checks for mass storage devices, including SCSI adapter cards, proprietary interfaces for CD-ROM drives, and special disk controllers (such as arrays) in your computer. In Setup, you can choose to bypass this detection. However, it is strongly recommended that you let Setup perform detection for mass storage devices unless you already know that detection causes Setup to fail.

CAUTION: If you skip this special detection for mass storage devices and your computer uses a special controller or SCSI adapter for your hard disk, NT 4.0 Setup will not be able to configure your hard disk to use NT.

During detection, Setup looks for mass storage devices and presents you with a list of all the devices it finds. If you accept the list of devices that Setup detects, Setup installs and configures those mass storage devices. You can also choose to specify additional mass storage devices—for example, if you have a disk with special device drivers from a hardware manufacturer.

TIP: You can choose to install additional SCSI adapters after setup is complete by running the Add New Hardware icon in the Settings/Control Panel, accessed from the Start button.

The Licensing Agreement

You will now come to a screen that shows Microsoft's licensing agreement for NT. Read it and page down to the bottom, where you will be given the chance to agree, and go on. If you do not agree, you may quit Setup here. Otherwise, press F8 to continue the process.

Choosing the Installed Hardware and Software Components

You will now be presented with a screen that shows you what NT discovered about the basic hardware/software setup of your computer. If you have no changes to make, press ENTER; otherwise, you may change the selected components by using the arrow keys to highlight a selection, followed by the ENTER key to see choices. Use this setup feature if you *must* change a selection at this time.

Insider Info

NT 4.0 Setup allows you to choose a basic video display mode for running Setup. At the end of Setup, you have the opportunity to configure and test the actual video display mode to be used with NT.

To change the video resolution or colors after setup is complete, choose the NT 4.0 Display icon in the Settings/Control Panel, accessed from the Start button. To change the keyboard or mouse configuration after setup is complete, choose Keyboard and Mouse icons in the Settings/Control Panel, accessed from the Start button.

Making Directory Decisions

After you choose to accept the detected hardware configuration, you must make some basic decisions to prepare your computer for NT 4. First, you must make decisions about the disk partition where you want to install NT 4, the file system to be used on the NT 4 disk partition, and the directory where the system files will be stored; whether to install NT 4 on the same partition (and if this is an NT upgrade, in the same directory with a previous version of Windows NT, if present).

Specifying Disk Partitions

A disk partition is a logical way to assign part or all of a physical hard disk to a logical drive. A partition can be any size from 1MB to the entire hard disk. The partition where you plan to store NT 4 files must be on a nonremovable hard disk and must have enough unused disk space to hold all the files (about 100MB).

Formatting the Partition

The system partition is the partition that has the hardware-specific files needed to load NT 4. On an Intel-based computer, the operating system boots from the active system partition on the first internal hard disk. This means that NT 4 looks for certain files in the root directory of the C drive (Disk 0) when you start your computer. This partition must be formatted with either the NTFS or FAT file system for NT 4 to start, and it cannot be a compressed partition. It must be formatted with the FAT file system if you want to run both NT 4 and MS-DOS, Windows 3.x, Window for Workgroups, or Windows 95.

On RISC-Based Computers

RISC-based computers can have several system partitions that are configurable by the manufacturer's configuration program, and each system partition must be formatted for the FAT file system. If you want to use NTFS, you need to create at least one FAT system partition of at least 2MB plus a second partition large enough to contain all the files you want to protect with NTFS. Specific steps to set up RISC-based disk systems vary, so you should consult your hardware documentation.

 CAUTION: If your hard disk contains stripe sets, volume sets, or mirrors, these elements appear on the Setup screen as "NT 4.0 Fault Tolerance." Be careful not to delete any of these elements. Also, do not delete partitions that contain data you want to keep.

Mini-Glossary

DISK PARTITION   A portion of a physical disk that functions as though it were a physically separate unit. A partition is usually referred to as either a primary or an extended partition.

PRIMARY PARTITION   A portion of a physical disk that can be marked as active for use by an operating system. Active means that the POST (power-on self-test) routine can locate a boot sector on the partition. There can be up to four primary partitions (or up to three if there is already an extended partition) per physical disk. A primary partition cannot be subpartitioned.

EXTENDED PARTITION   This is created from free space on a hard disk and can be subpartitioned into one or more logical drives. The free space in an extended partition can also be used to create volume sets or other kinds of volumes for fault-tolerance purposes. Only one of the four partitions allowed per physical disk can be an extended partition, and no primary partition needs to be present to create an extended partition.

LOGICAL DRIVE   An abstract representation of a whole or part of a whole physical disk or RAM-based storage media. Logical drive A is the first floppy drive. Logical drive C is the first partition of the first physical hard disk or RAM-based storage installed.

MIRROR SETS   In disk mirroring, partitions on two drives store identical information so that one is the mirror of the other. All data written to the partition on the primary disk is also written to the mirror, or secondary, partition. If one disk fails, the system can use the data from the other disk. Only NT Server can create and break mirror sets.

NT FILE SYSTEM (NTFS)   NTFS supports object-oriented *applications* by treating *files* as *objects* with user-defined and system-defined *attributes*. It provides all the capabilities of the FAT and HPFS file systems without many of their limitations.

SMALL COMPUTER SYSTEM INTERFACE (SCSI)   An I/O bus designed as a method of connecting several classes of peripherals to a host system without requiring modifications to generic hardware and software.

STRIPE SETS   NT Server disk striping (RAID Level 0) creates a disk file system called a stripe set by dividing data into blocks and spreading them in a fixed order across all disks in an array. By adding data to all partitions in the set at the same rate, disk striping offers the best performance of all NT disk management strategies.

REDUCED INSTRUCTION SET COMPUTING (RISC)   In RISC architectures, the design goal is to execute one or two instructions in every clock cycle. The price for this speed is a simpler instruction set, and hence a compiler needs to generate about 20 percent more instructions to do a given job.

SYSTEM PARTITION   A portion of a physical disk that can be accessed by the POST (power-on self-test) routine to locate a boot sector and system boot files. Always a primary partition.

VOLUME SETS   Volume sets effectively use memory under NT Server by combining free disk space on from 1 to 32 physical disks into a single volume with a single drive letter.

With Older NT Versions

When you install NT 4, Setup checks to see whether a previous version of Windows NT is installed on your computer. If a version of Windows NT is already on your computer, you can install NT 4 in the same directory. This allows NT 4 to configure the working environment based on the existing NT environment and to support all the features of existing Windows-based applications.

 NOTE: *When NT 4 is installed, configuration settings are added automatically, so you can still start your computer using the previous operating system. If you choose to install NT 4 in your Windows directory, Setup skips the following steps for selecting a partition, file system, or directory.*

Using Only NT 4

If you will use only the NT 4 operating system, make a single partition and format it with either FAT or NTFS, as described in the upcoming section, "Selecting a File System." On an existing system that contains files you want to keep, maintain all existing partitions. You can place the NT 4 files on any partition with sufficient free space.

With Other Operating Systems

If you want to use another operating system such as MS-DOS, Windows 95, or an older version of NT in addition to NT 4, you must first have installed that OS. Otherwise, later installation of the other operating system might overwrite the NT 4 system files, making it impossible to start NT 4 without using the emergency repair process, which is referred to later in this chapter.

Make sure the system partition (the C drive) is formatted with the appropriate file system. For example, if you already have Windows 95 installed and want to keep it, preserve the C partition and keep the file system as FAT. You can place the NT 4 files on any uncompressed partition with sufficient free space.

 NOTE: *You cannot install NT 4 on a compressed drive created with a compression utility. Also, NT 4 considers space created on a FAT partition using the UNDELETE feature in MS-DOS version 6.2 as used space.*

To use NTFS and have access to another operating system, you must have at least two disk partitions. Format the C drive with FAT, so that NT 4 and your other operating system can use it. Format the second partition with NTFS. You can place the NT 4 files on any uncompressed partition with sufficient free space. If you are installing NT 4 on a computer currently configured to start either OS/2 or MS-DOS/Windows 95 using the boot command, NT 4.0 Setup sets up your system so that you can run NT 4 or whichever operating system (MS-DOS/Windows 95 or OS/2) you last started before running NT 4.0 Setup.

CAUTION: HPFS (High Performance File System) is no longer supported by NT. If you are running OS/2 and have an HPFS partition, you must copy your files to a FAT partition and then reformat your HPFS partition during installation.

Selecting a File System

NT 4 can use the following two file systems:

- NT 4 File System (NTFS)
- File Allocation Table (FAT)

You can set up NT 4 on a partition with an existing file system, or you can choose to use a new file system. You can format a partition for NTFS or FAT during setup. For an unformatted partition, you can choose to format it with either the NTFS or FAT file system.

Here are some rules of thumb:

- Choose the FAT option if you want to access files on that partition when running NT, MS-DOS, Windows 95, or OS/2 on your computer.

- Choose the NTFS option if you want to take advantage of the features in NTFS, and do not need to run another operating system. (Windows 95 has limited support for NTFS partition visibility.)

- For an existing partition, you'll probably want to choose the default option, which is to keep the current file systems intact, preserving all existing files on that partition.

Converting FAT to NTFS

You can choose to convert an existing FAT partition to NTFS so you can use NT 4 security. This preserves existing files, but only NT 4 has access to files on that partition after conversion. You can choose to reformat an existing partition to the NTFS or FAT file system, which erases all existing files on that partition. If you choose to reformat the partition as NTFS, only NT 4 will have access to files created on that partition.

NOTE: After running Setup, you can always change file systems on any partitions. However, to preserve data, you cannot convert an NTFS partition to any other file system without backing up all the files, reformatting the partition (which erases all files), and then restoring the files from the backup. You must also back up data before repartitioning a hard disk.

Insider Info

NTFS supports complete NT 4 security, so you can specify who is allowed various kinds of access to a file or directory. NTFS also keeps a log of activities to restore the disk in the event of a power failure or other hardware problems. NTFS supports file and directory names of up to 255 characters and supports extended file attributes. It also automatically generates correct MS-DOS filenames so that files can be shared with MS-DOS users. This allows a program designed to run under other operating systems, such as MS-DOS, access to NTFS files when it runs under NT.

The disadvantages include the fact that NTFS is only recognized by NT. When the computer is running another operating system, that operating system cannot access files on an NTFS partition on the same computer.

The File Allocation Table (FAT) file system allows access to files when your computer is running another operating system, such as MS-DOS, Windows 95, or OS/2. The FAT system is the most widely used file system for PCs. FAT supports long filenames under NT, but files are not protected by the security features of NT. FAT cannot support extremely large files and is not as fault tolerant as NTFS. For example, FAT has no automatic disk restore features.

If you choose to convert the file system on an existing partition to NTFS, the conversion does not take place until all of Setup is complete and you first start your computer with NT 4. So if you quit Setup before it is completed, the file system on that partition is not converted.

Selecting a Directory

After you specify the partition and select a file system for NT, Setup suggests a directory where it will install the NT 4 files. You can accept the directory name that Setup picks or type the directory name you prefer. If you did not choose to upgrade an existing installation of NT and Setup detects a version of NT in the directory where you chose to place the new NT 4 files, it asks if you want to choose another directory. If you do so, Setup will automatically configure your computer so that you can run both versions of NT. If you install NT 4 as a new installation and into a directory that contains a previous installation of NT or NT Server, Setup overwrites the earlier version without preserving any custom settings or user accounts.

 CAUTION: If you want to replace an existing version of NT and keep your system settings and security accounts, be sure to choose the Setup option for upgrading the operating system.

Configuring NT 4

After Setup tests your disk drives and copies some initial files, rebooting again in the process, you will see the NT 4 logo for the first time, and all subsequent information will appear in NT 4 "wizard" dialog boxes such as the one shown in Figure 3-2. You can use standard Windows user interface keyboard and mouse techniques for all actions during this part of setup. You can also press the F1 key for context-sensitive help. You will be asked about:

- **Gathering information on your computer:** The Setup wizard will inspect your computer and gather information on the setup options that you wish to use.

- **Installing networking:** The wizard will walk you through the installation of your network components.

- **Finishing Setup:** All "household" duties will be performed, and finalized settings will be made for NT Setup.

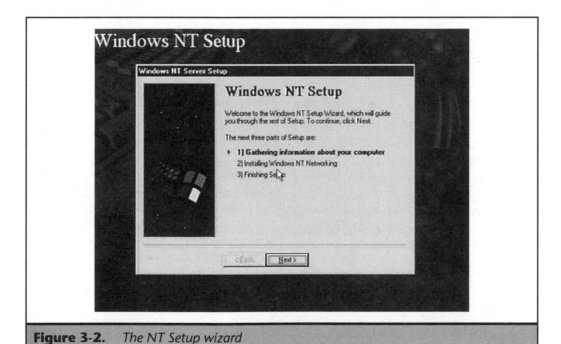

Figure 3-2.   *The NT Setup wizard*

During the early part of Setup, you will be asked to pick what kind of actions you want Setup to perform. These choices are expressed as Typical, Portable, Compact, and Custom. These options specify how many of NT's optional components you want installed on your computer. For instance, for a limited size hard disk, on a notebook computer, you would choose Portable. All of the options except Custom make automatic choices for you. Picking Custom allows you to fine-tune your installation, but requires you to know more and make choices that otherwise would be automatically set up.

With either the automatic or Custom setup options, you must next supply the following information:

- **A name:** You must supply a name and possibly a company name that NT 4 will use to identify you for various operations and administrative purposes. You must type a response and verify your response for Setup to continue.

- **A CD-key for product identification and authentication:** This number can be found on the jewel case cover of your NT 4 CD. You must type a response for Setup to continue.

- **A computer name:** NT uses this name to identify this computer on the network. Use any name you like, as long as you use legal naming conventions. The name must be 15 characters or less and must be different from any other computer name, domain name, or workgroup name on the network. You can make up your computer name, or if you are on a company network, you may need to ask your network administrator if a specific name has been assigned for your computer. If you are going to run automated logon scripts, do not use spaces in the computer names of the domain controllers in the network.

- **The administrator account password:** The built-in administrator account must now be assigned a password. Enter the password twice to confirm it.

- **Domain controller role:** For NT Server setup, you will need to indicate whether this computer will have a role as a domain controller in NT 4 domain security. A domain controller authenticates domain logons and maintains the security policy and master user database for a domain. (You will specify whether this is a primary domain controller or backup domain controller later in Setup.)

CAUTION: *If you are installing NT Server, be sure to decide on the security role for this NT 4 computer before beginning setup. You cannot change a server to a domain controller (or vice versa) without reinstalling NT 4.*

- **Floating point workaround:** On certain steppings of the Pentium CPU, a floating point error may occur in rare instances. If NT Setup indicates that your Pentium has this problem, you may wish to use NT's workaround scheme, which is to turn off the numeric processor portion of the CPU and emulate its action in software.

- **Emergency disk creation:** Remember that fourth disk you formatted at the start of setup? Well, here's where you get to tell NT to create an emergency recovery disk with it. Although you can create this disk later, using a utility called RDISK.EXE, you should always choose to do this during setup. You won't actually create this disk until the last part of setup.

Mini-Glossary

DOMAIN CONTROLLER   There is no single database that is shared by all servers in a domain; there is a single computer called the domain controller that "owns" the master copy of the user account and security database. This master copy is then replicated (copied) to all other servers in the domain. When the domain controller is unavailable, no changes can be made to the domain's user account security database. If necessary, any server may be promoted to be the domain controller at any time.

INTERNET PACKET EXCHANGE/SEQUENCED PACKET EXCHANGE (IPX/SPX)   Popular in NetWare networks. Provides support for the Novell implementation of the NetBIOS protocol. The IPX/SPX-compatible protocol can be used by Client for NetWare Networks to communicate with NetWare servers or computers running File and Printer Sharing for NetWare Networks. This protocol can also be used by Client for Microsoft Networks to communicate with computers running Windows for Workgroups, Windows 95, or NT that are running the same protocol. NetWare's native Network Layer protocol is IPX, a Novell proprietary descendant of the Xerox XNS protocol.

NETBIOS EXTENDED USER INTERFACE (NETBEUI)   IBM introduced this protocol specification in the mid 1980s. It is optimized for departmental LANs or LAN segments. The Windows NT NetBEUI Frame (NBF) transport driver implements the IBM NetBEUI specification.

NWLINK   NWLink is an implementation of the IPX/SPX protocols popular in NetWare networks. In addition, it provides support for the Novell implementation of the NetBIOS protocol.

REMOTE ACCESS SERVICE (RAS)   Designed to provide transparent network access for PCs running a Windows operating system. Users run RAS, or the Dial-Up Networking option (discussed in Chapter 13), on a remote PC and initiate a connection to the RAS server via a modem, X.25, or ISDN card. The RAS server, running on an NT server-based PC connected to the corporate network, then provides network access to the remote PC.

TRANSMISSION CONTROL PROTOCOL/INTERNET PROTOCOL (TCP/IP)
NT includes an implementation of TCP/IP. In general usage, the term TCP/IP refers to a suite of protocols. Since TCP/IP is available for many diverse operating systems such as Unix, MVS, VM, VMS, NetWare, and OS/2, NT can use TCP/IP to communicate with these different operating systems. TCP/IP also provides compatibility with the Internet.

■ **Optional setup tasks:** For Custom setup, a dialog box like the one shown in Figure 3-3 asks you to select optional setup tasks to be performed, including installing optional components such as accessories and games, multimedia applications, and accessibility options. You also specify messaging components to be installed here. Choose the Details button to see which components are selected in each displayed category.

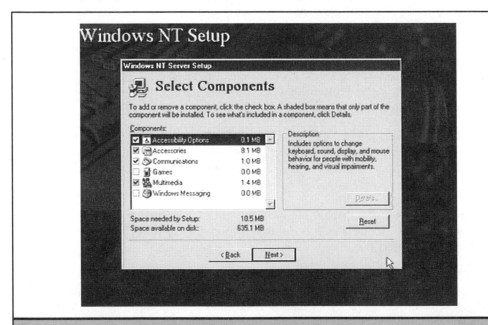

Figure 3-3.   *Optional component setup in the wizard*

Network Adapter Card Setup

The automatic options for setup check for a network adapter card in your computer and install the first one recognized (see Figure 3-4). Some types of network cards may not be recognized automatically. If Setup cannot identify your adapter card (and therefore thinks you don't have one), it asks if you want to install Remote Access Service (RAS)—for users connecting to a network through a modem. If you do not choose this option, Setup will display a dialog box that asks you to select the name of the card you want to install.

NOTE: If you are installing NT Server and your computer will be a domain controller, you must install the network. If, however, your computer will not be a domain controller, or you are installing NT Workstation and you do not want to install network software, choose Cancel in the dialog box, and continue with the rest of the setup tasks.

Detecting the Card

Custom setup first asks whether the computer should be networked, and if it is wired to a network, or if you want to install Remote Access Service (RAS)—for users connecting to a network through a modem. After you have made your choice, and assuming a wired network, Setup will search for the network card in your computer. If you cancel

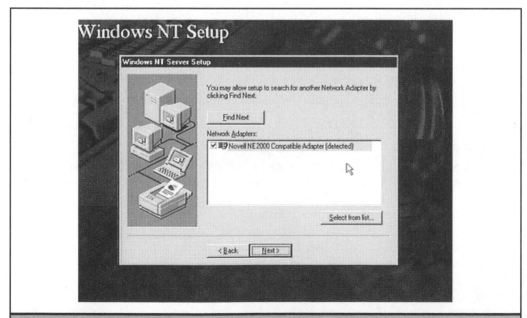

Figure 3-4. *The Network Adapter Detection wizard*

detection, Setup will ask you to select an adapter card make and model from its list. If you choose detection, Setup looks for a network adapter card. It stops at the first one it identifies and asks you to select one of three options:

■ You can accept the identified network card, in which case Setup installs the supporting network software for you.

■ You can choose Search again, which causes Setup to search for another network adapter card.

■ You can choose Select from List, which causes Setup to stop detection and display the Network Adapter Setup listbox.

NOTE: If Custom setup cannot identify an adapter card to install or if you do not choose any of the detected cards, Setup informs you that there are no more network cards and asks you to choose Detect to try again. If, instead, you choose Continue, you have the option of installing Remote Access Service (RAS) or manually selecting an adapter card. Also, the detection process may lock up your computer. If it does, you will have to reboot and choose the network adapter from the list, rather than detecting it.

Installing and Configuring the Network Card

If you accept the card that Setup detects, Setup installs and configures it, and then displays a dialog box with the adapter card settings. If Setup cannot completely validate adapter card settings or if potential hardware conflicts exist, Setup warns you and allows you to change the settings. After Setup installs a network adapter card, it may display the Adapter Card Setup dialog box, so you can select the correct interrupt request (IRQ) number, I/O base port address, memory buffer address, and other settings. For many adapter cards, the settings are configured automatically, so you don't have to identify settings.

Insider Info

If you are upgrading from NT 3.1 or 3.5, the Adapter Card Setup dialog box will not appear, because your old configuration settings are still correct. However, if you previously installed the TCP/IP protocol for your network configuration, Setup will request new TCP/IP information.

During Setup, the Network Settings dialog box appears after you configure the first network card so you can install additional network cards and driver software. If you choose to install additional network components, you might be asked to insert additional disks with support software for your card.

If Setup cannot start the network after network adapter card settings are determined, you will have a chance to go back and select different network configuration settings, or you can choose to skip network setup and set the configuration after NT 4.0 Setup is finished.

Selecting Network Protocols

During this phase of setup, NT 4 will ask you to select one or more network protocols to install (see Figure 3-5). Following are the primary network protocols you can choose:

■ **TCP/IP:** A suite of networking protocols that provide communication across interconnected networks, such as the Internet. TCP/IP is rapidly becoming the protocol of choice for many installations. Select this option if your computer is on an interconnected network with many different types of hardware and operating systems, or if you want to communicate with machines running operating systems such as Unix, especially those on a WAN. This is NT's default protocol.

■ **NWLink IPX/SPX Compatible Transport:** For many sites, this is the standard network protocol. It supports routing, and it can support NetWare client/server applications, where applications communicate with IPX/SPX. Choose this option if your computer is connected to or communicates with a NetWare network, or will be used in a trusted domain. Be sure to enable the NWLink NetBIOS support option for running this protocol over Microsoft networks, where you will be communicating with Windows for Workgroups or Windows 95 clients. Otherwise these clients will not be automatically visible to your NT workstations and servers when sharing directories or resources.

■ **NetBEUI:** This protocol is usually used in small department-sized local area networks of up to approximately 200 clients. Choose this option if other clients on your network use NetBEUI as a transport protocol. (NetBEUI is installed automatically if you install RAS and do not configure a network adapter card, although this is controllable—see Chapter 13.)

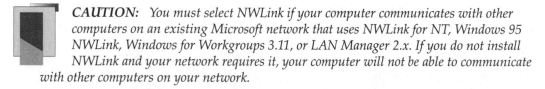

CAUTION: You must select NWLink if your computer communicates with other computers on an existing Microsoft network that uses NWLink for NT, Windows 95 NWLink, Windows for Workgroups 3.11, or LAN Manager 2.x. If you do not install NWLink and your network requires it, your computer will not be able to communicate with other computers on your network.

If you are unsure which network protocol to choose, select a default of NWLink IPX/SPX with NWLink NetBIOS—or ask your network administrator. After setup is completed, you can use the Network option in the Start/Settings/Control Panel to add or remove any available transports you may require for your system.

Workgroup and Domain Membership

At this point, in a Workstation setup, NT will ask you to make the computer a member of an existing domain, or workgroup. In order to register a new computer installation with the domain controller, you can also specify the automatic creation of a machine account, a domain-related security record on the domain controller.

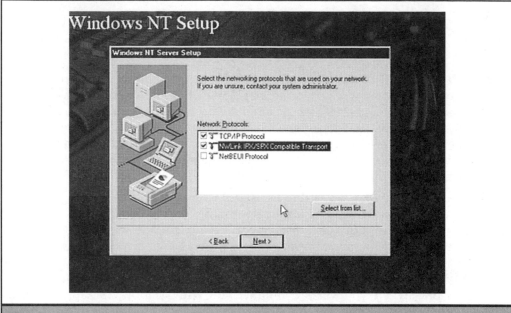

Figure 3-5. *Choosing network protocols*

If you will not be joining a domain at this time, choose to join a workgroup. If you don't know what to do, or have not set up any workgroups or domains yet, just allow the defaults to be registered, and go on.

Domain Controller/Server Setup

After you enter your choices for the network configuration settings in an NT Server installation, Setup will display a dialog box so that you can identify the domain for the computer you are using. Do you want it to serve as a backup domain controller, or do you want to create a new domain where the computer will be the primary domain controller?

CAUTION: Creating a domain has important security consequences that you should understand before proceeding. Before you create a domain, be sure to read Chapter 16.

As a Primary Controller

If you are setting up a primary domain controller, and want to create a new domain, remember to enter your chosen domain name in the setup dialog that allows you to name a new domain.

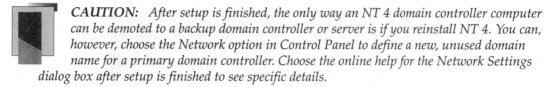 *CAUTION:* *After setup is finished, the only way an NT 4 domain controller computer can be demoted to a backup domain controller or server is if you reinstall NT 4. You can, however, choose the Network option in Control Panel to define a new, unused domain name for a primary domain controller. Choose the online help for the Network Settings dialog box after setup is finished to see specific details.*

As a Backup Controller

If a computer account already exists for your computer and you want your computer to join a domain as a backup domain controller, select the Backup Domain Controller option. In the appropriate box, when displayed, type the known domain name. (Remember, domain names cannot contain spaces.) When you're finished, choose the OK button.

 NOTE: *If a computer account does not exist, you must enter the name and password of an administrator account to be used to authorize the creation of a new account. For example, in the appropriate box, type a name and password for the domain administrator account, and then choose the OK button.*

As a Server

You may wish simply to specify that this computer should act as a normal server within a known domain. If you want to join a domain as a normal server, select the Server option. In the appropriate box, when displayed, type the known domain name. (Remember, domain names cannot contain spaces.) When you're finished, choose the OK button.

 NOTE: *As with a backup domain controller, if a computer account does not exist, you must enter the name and password of an administrator account to be used to authorize the creation of a new account.*

Installing Internet Information Server

During setup, you will have the option to install Internet Information Server (IIS)—the integrated Internet/intranet server that supplies WWW, FTP, and GOPHER services. If you intend to use this server as a supplier of Internet or intranet content, check this box during setup. For more information on IIS, see Chapter 25.

Time and Video Display Choices

NT 4.0 Setup will now ask you to specify the local time zone and make choices about time settings, using a graphical display and dropdown listbox. After you set the time and choose the Close button, the Display utility appears so that you can configure your Making video choices video display (see Figure 3-6). Set your display preferences,

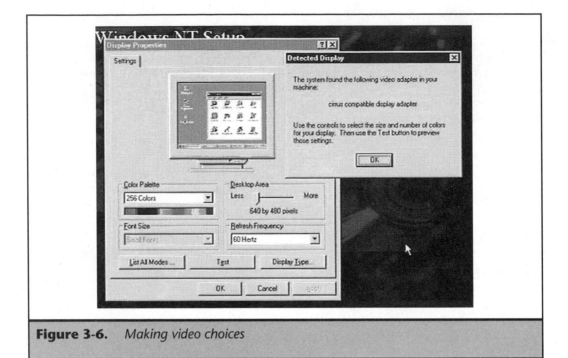

Figure 3-6. *Making video choices*

and press the Test button to try them out. If you want to make changes to your video configuration after running Setup, use the Display option in Control Panel.

Completing the Setup Process

After you follow the instructions to create the emergency repair disk (if you choose to do so), Setup completes the final installation steps. If you have done an NT Server installation and your computer is going to act as a backup domain controller, Setup copies security account information from the primary domain controller. This activity takes several minutes, depending on the size of the security database. If you choose Cancel in the message that announces database replication (copying), the system will instead replicate the database as soon as you reboot your computer.

When setup is finished and a message asks you to restart your computer, remove any disks from the floppy disk drives and choose the Reboot button. When the boot loader menu appears, let it time out, or press ENTER. As NT boots, the logon message appears, as shown next.

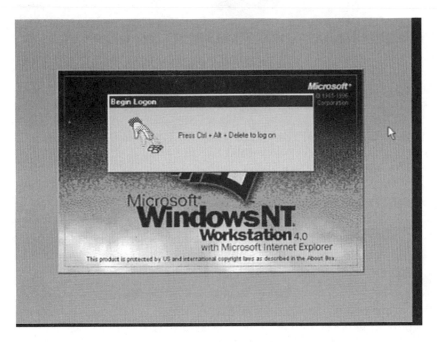

As indicated, press CTRL+ALT+DEL to log on. In the Welcome dialog box, type and confirm your password and then select the OK button.

Insider Info

For an Intel-based computer, the following files are copied to the root directory on the C drive: BOOT.INI, BOOTSECT.DOS (if another operating system is on your computer), NTLDR, and NTDETECT.COM. Also, if you have a SCSI disk that is not visible from MS-DOS (that is, not seen by the computer's BIOS), the NTBOOTDD.SYS file is copied.

These files should *never* be deleted because NT 4 will not start without them. For a RISC-based computer, HAL.DLL and OSLOADER.EXE are copied to the \OS\WINNT directory on your system partition. These files also should *never* be deleted. These files are all read-only, hidden, system files. If any of these files are missing on your system, you can use the emergency repair disk to restore them.

Setting Up Server Master Files

This section is written for the power user or administrator responsible for installing NT 4 on multiple computers. We'll assume that you have already installed NT 4 on a single computer and are familiar with NT 4 commands and procedures.

You can install NT 4 on multiple computers by first copying the NT 4 master source files to a shared directory on a network computer, as described in the following section. You then use WINNT.EXE or WINNT32.EXE to install or upgrade NT 4 on each computer, as described earlier in this chapter.

NOTE: *You can also use this method to install NT 4 on Intel-based computers with SCSI or CD-ROM devices that are supported under MS-DOS but are not supported by NT 4. On RISC-based computers, you can use WINNT32.EXE to upgrade or reinstall the operating system when NT 4 is already installed.*

Copying the Master Source Files

When you copy the NT 4 master files, you can set up the shared directory using any type of network, such as Microsoft LAN Manager 2.1 or Novell NetWare. The directory containing the NT 4 files must be accessible from MS-DOS to all users who will be using WINNT.EXE or WINNT32.EXE.

NOTE: *Before you can copy the master NT 4 files onto a network directory, the network must be operational. You must have read/write permission to the network directory where you want to copy the NT 4 files, and other users must have read access to that directory.*

To copy the master NT 4 files onto a network computer:

- Share the \I386, \MIPS, \PPC or \ALPHA directories of the NT 4 compact disc in the CD-ROM drive connected to a network computer, depending on the type of computer you have.

- Or, connect to the drive where you want to install the NT 4 master files and create the shared directory on the drive that will contain the NT 4 master files.

- Then, open a DOS session, and XCOPY the NT 4 files to the shared directory you created using this syntax: *xcopy /s cdrom:\platform share_directory*. For example:

```
xcopy /s f:\i386 \\winnt40.src\x86
```

Users or administrators can now connect to this shared directory to follow the setup procedures for installing NT 4 from the network, as described earlier in this chapter.

What's Next

In this chapter, we've learned how to choose the right hardware and set up NT 4 from scratch. Just knowing some of the pitfalls will save you hours of setup time and months of tuning and twiddling to get your system right.

In the next chapter, we'll look at starting your system for the first time. You'll have a chance to get to know the user interface in NT 4 and find out how to set up and use the many applications that ship with the program. You'll also find out how to set up your desktop and create a personal environment that allows you to work more efficiently.

Chapter Four

Interacting with the Program

In this chapter, we'll take a look at how to start Windows NT, glance at some of the built-in applications, and learn to use several of the administrative tools. When you have finished these pages, you'll know how to configure NT 4's new UI (user interface), set up preferences, work with hard disks and files, and administer some of the more sophisticated tools that are made available to you.

NOTE: NT 4's most visible improvement is the addition of the Windows 95-style user interface (UI). This new user shell, or front end, is a marked improvement over the Windows 3.1-style UI that NT used previously. The controls and menus are more accessible, easier to read, and make sense almost immediately, even to a novice user. We'll be examining the Windows NT 4 UI in greater detail in Part 2 of this book.

Starting NT 4

Upon boot, or startup, NT 4 makes itself ready to accept commands from authorized personnel. Because NT is a password-protected, secure system, you must provide it with an identity before you can begin to use the system. This is the process of logging on to NT. When you log on, you are telling the operating system who you are. With that knowledge, and using the database of known and authorized users, NT customizes itself with your individual settings, adjusts privilege levels, and registers you as an active user.

Before you can enter your username and password, you must first boot the computer and choose to start NT from the multiboot menu that will be presented to you at initial computer power-on. This is a character-oriented menu that allows you to choose which installed operating system, or variant, you would like to start.

First, turn on your computer, and use the up/down arrow keys to highlight NT Workstation, Server, or a safe-mode variant (see Figure 4-1 and Appendix A). You may then press ENTER. You may also allow the startup timer to expire, which will then automatically start the highlighted operating system.

After the initial boot sequence, which might take a minute or two, you will be presented with the logon invitation dialog, as shown in the following illustration. Press CTRL+ALT+DEL to log on.

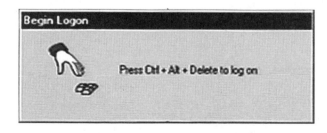

```
OS Loader V4.00

Please select the operating system to start:


    Windows NT Workstation Version 4.00
    Windows NT Server Version 4.00
    Windows NT Server Version 4.00 [VGA mode]
    Windows NT Workstation Version 4.00 [VGA mode]
    Microsoft Windows

Use ↑ and ↓ to move the highlight to your choice.
Press Enter to choose.
```

Figure 4-1.   *The multiboot startup screen*

NOTE: The CTRL+ALT+DEL sequence, also called the Secure Attention Sequence (SAS), is part of the front-end security shield that NT provides for your safety and privacy. Always start NT by using this sequence or its equivalent (such as a smartcard being inserted into a reader). Don't assume that you can securely log on to the system if you see any other dialog already displayed on the screen. Start over, by issuing the CTRL+ALT+DEL sequence, and then proceed to enter your username, password, and domain information in the Logon Information dialog, discussed next.

The Logon Information Dialog

The Logon Information dialog, shown in Figure 4-2, provides three fields in which you enter information that uniquely identifies you as a valid user of the system and directs NT to attempt domain logon. First enter the username that identifies you on the system. This may be one that you chose during setup, or it may have been issued to you by your system administrator. Subsequently, each time you log on to this machine, NT will fill in this field, presenting the username of the last logged-on user on this computer.

Now enter your password. This may be any combination of letters and numbers, up to 14 characters in length, and may initially have been assigned to you, or set up by

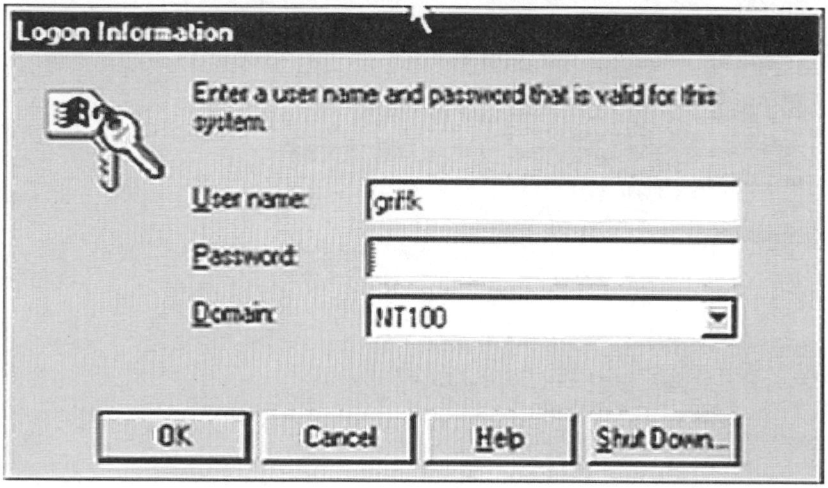

Logon Information

Enter a user name and password that is valid for this system.

User name: grifk

Password:

Domain: NT100

| OK | Cancel | Help | Shut Down... |

Figure 4-2. *The Logon Information dialog*

you as in Chapter 3. You may be required to change this password the first time you log on to the system (see the material on the User Manager in Chapter 16 to learn how you can control usernames and password parameters).

The last part of the logon involves choosing the domain that you will log on to. If you are logging on to your local machine only, choose its name in the drop-down Domain list. (Note that a local computer's name is also a local domain.) A local domain account is stored locally on the computer, while a server domain account is stored on the NT domain controller that you choose in this field. If you are logging on to a wider domain, you will have been given a domain user account (and machine account) on that domain already. Alternatively, you will have to set up your membership using NT Server's User Manager for Domains (see Chapter 16) and the Control Panel/Network applet, discussed in Chapter 6. If you have already set up the domain membership, select the name of the NT Server domain. Finally, choose the OK button.

NOTE: *You can only log on to a domain from a computer that has a machine account on that domain and therefore belongs to the domain.*

Once you have completed the logon procedure, you can begin to run applications, use file and printing resources, and share your files with other users on the network.

Logging On from a Dial-up or Remote Access Service Client

To log on to remote domains across an unwired dial-up connection, you can use the Dial-Up Networking facilities anytime during your active session. You can also specify a logon to that domain from the Logon Information dialog.

For automatic logon to a remote domain, you must have previously installed Dial-Up Networking, which will result in the display of the Logon using the Dial-Up Networking checkbox within the Logon Information dialog. By selecting this checkbox, you are directing NT to attempt a logon to a Remote Access Server (RAS—see Chapter 13) and domain whose access is controlled by that RAS-enabled computer. You must, of course, have already been granted access to the RAS and must have a valid domain username and password.

TIP: *To improve response time over a dial-up connection, turn off domain browsing. Otherwise, NT will attempt to browse the domain whenever you open Explorer or a File/Open dialog, connect to a network drive, or attempt to find printers or other resources. The combined network traffic over a modem (dial-up) connection can severely affect the responsiveness of your computer.*

The NT Security Dialog: Logging Off or Quitting NT

You may, at any time during an active session, choose to invoke the NT Security dialog, shown in Figure 4-3. This dialog allows you to log off the workstation. It also allows you to shut down the computer, to lock the workstation with your password, to change your password easily, and to work with the Task Manager.

To invoke the Security dialog, press CTRL+ALT+DEL. You may now choose among several buttons:

- **Lock Workstation:** Choosing this button results in the workstation being locked and inaccessible to anyone but yourself. You must unlock the station by issuing the CTRL+ALT+DEL sequence and reentering your password.

- **Logoff:** Choose this button to log the current user off NT and to return to the initial logon invitation dialog, where the CTRL+ALT+DEL sequence must be entered to log another user on.

- **Shut Down:** Use this button to completely shut down the system. You will be given the choice of shutting down the computer, ready for power-off, or restarting the computer as if it was booting up after power-on. Either of these options logs the current user off the system before executing.

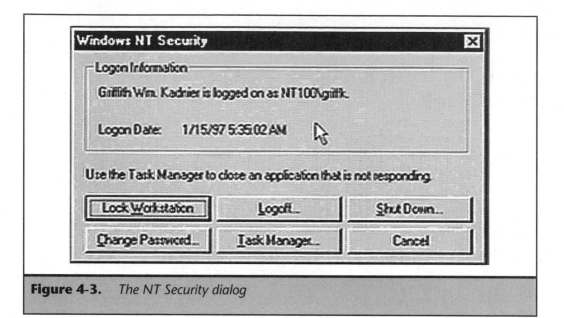

Figure 4-3. *The NT Security dialog*

 CAUTION: *Never shut down a computer actively running NT 4 by using the computer's power or reset switch. This may result in disk corruption or loss of data. Always use the Security dialog's Shut Down button so NT can gracefully close all processes and flush its data to disk before the computer halts or restarts.*

■ **Change Password:** Use this button to display the Change Password dialog, shown in the following illustration. You will be asked to enter your old password and then a new one, with confirmation. If the password is a domain password, the domain controller will be contacted in order to accomplish the task.

- **Task Manager:** Use this button to display the NT Task Manager, where you may pick from among three dialogs to manipulate applications and processes or display quick performance statistics on the local workstation. The Task Manager is discussed next.

- **Cancel:** Choose this button to cancel the Security dialog and return to the NT desktop.

The NT Task Manager

The Task Manager application displays three dialogs allowing you to control and monitor applications and processes that are running on your NT system. The dialogs, described in the following sections, allow you to work with different aspects of executing applications and tasks.

Applications

All of the user-level applications (tasks) currently running on the local workstation are listed in the Applications dialog. The status of each application is listed alongside the name (see Figure 4-4). If an application becomes unresponsive, you can use this dialog to check its status or end the program.

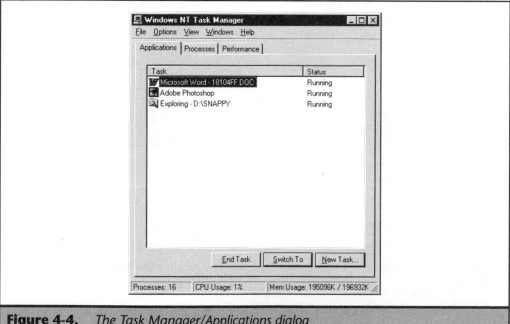

Figure 4-4.   *The Task Manager/Applications dialog*

Use the View menu in the Task Manager to control how the various data is presented by choosing options for display that contextually change with the active dialog. You can manipulate the task list in several ways by choosing the buttons at the bottom of the dialog:

- **End Task:** Highlight a task in the list and choose this button to immediately end that task. If the task is in an unresponsive state, an override dialog may also appear, asking if you want to wait to see if the task becomes responsive again, or to unequivocally end it.

- **Switch To:** Switches NT to the highlighted task immediately. Similar to the ALT+TAB switching mechanism on the desktop, with greater target control.

- **New Task:** Choosing this button results in the display of the Create New Task dialog, similar to the Start/Run dialog (see Chapter 6). It allows you to start a new task directly.

Processes

The Processes dialog lists all of the processes, typically system and helper tasks, that are currently executing on the local computer. Again, you can control what information is displayed from the Task Manager's View menu. In the case of the Processes dialog (Figure 4-5), you can choose to show data and statistics for each process by choosing the Select Columns menu choice, covering the following topics:

- **Image Name:** Always present. The name of the image on disk.
- **PID (Process Identifier):** Optional. The process ID that NT uses to identify this process.
- **CPU Usage:** Optional. The percentage of CPU resource allocated to this process.
- **CPU Time:** Optional. The actual CPU time that this process has used.
- **Memory Usage:** Optional. Memory usage for this process.
- **Memory Usage Delta:** Optional. Instantaneous change in memory usage.
- **Page Faults:** Optional. The number of page faults for this process (page faults result in a paging or memory selector reassignment).
- **Page Faults Delta:** Instantaneous change in page faults for this process.
- **Virtual Memory Size:** Size of virtual memory committed to this process.
- **Paged Pool:** Optional. The memory available to general processes and programs.
- **Non-paged Pool:** Optional. The memory available to the kernel.
- **Base Priority:** The base scheduling priority assigned to this process.
- **Handle Count:** Number of open handles that this process is using.
- **Thread Count:** Number of threads created by this process.

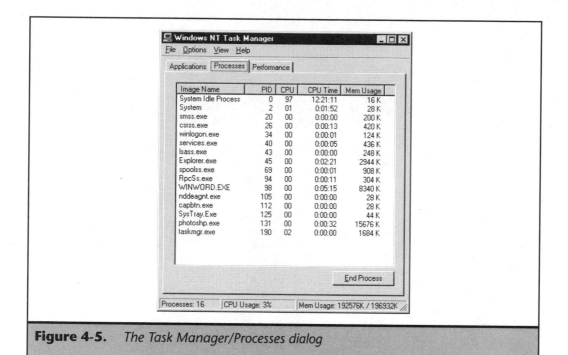

Figure 4-5. *The Task Manager/Processes dialog*

Additionally, you may use the End Process button after highlighting a process in the list to immediately end that process. If you choose this button, you will be warned that ending a process in this way can have deleterious side effects. Always know what you are doing here, since process manipulation can lock up NT and cause data loss.

Performance

The Task Manager/Performance dialog (Figure 4-6) lets you explore how NT and your PC are being loaded by the various tasks and processes that are currently executing. You receive information on instantaneous loading on the CPU, with a historical graph, as well as moment to moment memory usage with trend information. Kernel memory statistics, file cache and physical memory use, and commit memory for system and application are also provided.

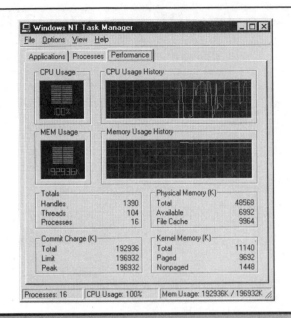

Figure 4-6. *The Task Manager/Performance dialog*

Mini-Glossary

GROUP   An account that contains other accounts, which are called members. Groups provide an easy way to grant common capabilities to several users, because all rights and permissions assigned to a group are provided to its members.

NT SERVER DOMAIN   Besides providing the same network-browsing capabilities as a workgroup, an NT Server domain is a collection of computers that can recognize the same user accounts. Membership in a domain is assigned by the domain administrator in an NT Server network.

USER ACCOUNT   A user account consists of all the information that NT 4 uses to allow someone to use a computer—including the username, a description, a password, and the groups to which that user belongs.

WORKGROUP   A collection of computers that appear under the same workgroup name on the network. This grouping makes it easy to find directories or printers shared by people you work with.

Joining Workgroups and Domains

When logging on to a networked NT machine, you will become a member of either a workgroup—a collection of local peer machines—or you will become an NT domain member. Domain members have security and resource rights given to them and administered by a remote NT Server that performs the function of a domain controller.

An NT domain controller holds the security database for domain members that can join and receive special access to the resources that the domain controller governs. An NT Server can be set up to act as a domain controller, a backup domain controller, or a stand-alone server for file and print sharing. You may have joined a workgroup or domain already, when you originally set up NT. In that case, use the following instructions as a guide on how to change membership or computer name.

Before you can join a workgroup or an NT Server's domain, you must log on to the computer as a member of the Administrators group. Next, open the Start/Settings/Control Panel/Network applet, where you will be presented with the Identification dialog. The computer name and domain or workgroup membership name will be displayed.

Choose the Change button. This will bring up the Identification Change dialog. You can do several things now:

- **Change the computer name:** You can enter a new name by which this computer will subsequently be known.

- **Enter the name of a workgroup or domain that you wish to join:** Use the Member of field to enter the name of an existing workgroup or domain. If your computer is not a member of an NT domain, you must set up your user accounts on the local machine, using User Manager. If you are joining a domain, the user accounts must be registered on the domain controller, using User Manager for Domains. Both types of accounts can coexist, since the local user accounts are only used when logging on to the local machine's domain (the local machine). To create user accounts (and groups), follow the procedures in the section covering the User Manager in Chapter 16.

- **Create a computer account in the domain:** When joining a domain, you must also set up an account for the local computer. You can do this with the domain controller's Server Manager application, which you can reach through Computer | Add to Domain, or you can accomplish the same task by checking this box and entering the name of a domain user and the user's password. That domain user must have been granted sufficient privileges to be able to add workstations to the domain.

Security and Backup Administration

Data loss and compromise are the most serious security and operational breaches that you are likely to encounter. Use the list of suggestions on the next page when contemplating plans for security and backup procedures in your NT installation.

■ Create user accounts with User Manager that give only specific rights to regular users. Never give administrative rights to regular users of the system.

■ Use the NTFS file system for greater data integrity and security features.

■ Enforce password control and require users to change passwords frequently.

■ Use the NT Backup application (covered later in the chapter) to keep offline copies of all your important data and system files.

■ Turn on security auditing and logging, and then plan to review the security logs on a weekly basis (see the discussion of the Event Viewer in Chapter 7).

Mini-Glossary

FILE ALLOCATION TABLE (FAT)   The file system used by the MS-DOS/ Windows 95 operating systems. FAT does not provide security. FAT is required for the system partition if you also use MS-DOS or Windows 3.1/95 on your computer.

NT FILE SYSTEM (NTFS)   An advanced file system that supports file recovery, extremely large storage media, and long filenames. NTFS is required if you want maximum data security for your installation, and is recommended if NT is the only operating system on your computer.

Floppy and Hard Disk Administration Tools

Before a hard disk can be used to store files for application or operating system use, it must be prepared by partitioning and formatting it with a layout and structure that the OS can recognize and use (see Chapter 14). Partitioning is used to prepare a hard disk's logical layout. This lets you, for instance, make two logical disks (C and D) out of a single physical disk drive. By partitioning a disk, you also tell the system how large you want it to be, and with what minimal storage units (allocation unit) it should be formatted. A hard disk that will be used by NT must be formatted with either the NTFS or FAT file systems. A floppy disk to be used with NT must be formatted with the FAT file system.

Formatting with the FAT file system gives you flexibility in working with operating systems and lets you use some of the many tools that work with the FAT file system, but you also inherit all of FAT's vulnerabilities and shortcomings. On the other hand, if you format a hard disk with NTFS, NT will log all file transactions, scan for and fix bad sectors automatically, and make backup copies of configuration information. Using NTFS, NT is capable of ensuring file integrity and recovery.

With NT's tools, you can manage both floppy and hard disks. For floppy disks, the Format command line utility will help you prepare a disk for use. For hard disks, NT provides more than one way to administer them. Primarily, you will use the Disk Administrator application (discussed next), which you run from the Start / Programs / Administrative Tools (Common) menu. This application allows you to partition, format, and label volumes using either NTFS or FAT. You can also work with volume sets, extended volumes, stripe sets, and mirror sets. You must be logged on as a member of the Administrators group to work with Disk Administrator. Some of these operations require that you format the disks with the NTFS file system.

Alternatively, you can start a command line session and issue the *fdisk, format,* and *label* commands from a DOS box (command prompt).

Using the Disk Administrator

Open Disk Administrator (see Figure 4-7) by selecting Start | Programs | Administrative Tools (Common), or by entering **windisk.exe** from a command prompt. You must be logged on as a member of the Administrators group to do so. The main Disk Administrator window will display a graphical representation of all

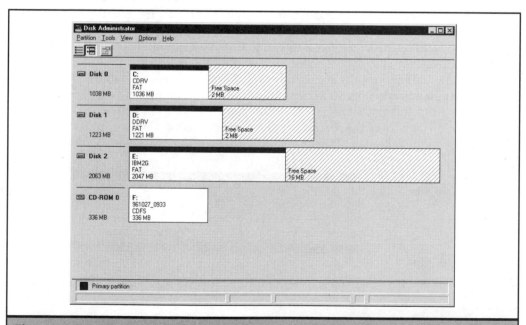

Figure 4-7.   *The Disk Administrator window*

the physical disks and their partitions that are presently connected to your computer. A status line at the bottom of the window shows information on selected partitions.

Mini-Glossary

FREE SPACE An unused and unformatted portion of a hard disk that can be partitioned or subpartitioned. Free space within an extended partition is available for the creation of logical drives. Free space that is not within an extended partition is available for the creation of a partition, with a maximum of four partitions allowed.

VOLUME A partition or collection of partitions that has been formatted for use by a file system. An NT 4 volume can be assigned a drive letter and used to organize directories and files.

Working with Partitions

As mentioned earlier, before you can use a hard disk with NT, it must be partitioned and formatted. Disk Administrator lets you manage partition creation and deletion directly. You can create up to four partitions per physical disk drive. Other operating systems may not recognize all of the partitions that you create, so use care in laying out the disk partition structure if you intend to use other operating systems with your hard disk drives.

In addition to the four primary partitions that you can create per drive, one of them may be an extended partition, with the capability of being assigned any number of logical drives. The number of logical drives you may have per extended partition is only limited by the size of the partition and the system constraints when using volume and stripe sets. The following illustration shows examples of disk partitioning:

▦ Disk 1 1916 MB	D: DDRV FAT 1914 MB			F: Unknown 2 MB		

| ▦ Disk 2

642 MB | M:

NTFS
150 MB | N:
FAT-A
FAT
75 ME | O:
ntfs-B
NTFS
75 ME | I:
FAT-B
FAT
100 MB | J:
ntfs-c
NTFS
100 MB | L:
ntfs-d
NTFS
142 MB |

The Boot Partition

The boot partition is the partition that contains NT operating system files that NT uses to execute. This includes the %SystemRoot% directory. These files can be in the same location as the boot/startup files in the system partition (see the next section), but the boot partition cannot be part of a stripe or volume set.

The System Partition

The system partition is the partition, always on disk 0, and always formatted in either NTFS or FAT, that contains startup and NT boot-operating system files. This partition holds the NTLDR, NTDETECT.COM, BOOT.INI, and other startup files. Disk Administrator must mark this partition as active. This tells the boot loader that the partition should be used for startup. There can be only one active partition.

Drive Letters and Assignments

Hard disks take up drive letters from C through Z. Drives A and B are reserved for floppy disk drives. NT allows you to create more than 24 drives (volumes), but only 24 volumes can have drive letters. Usually, NT can manage the placement of physical disks and their partitions within a hardware installation. NT will assign drive letters as needed. Until Disk Administrator is used on an NT machine, drive assignments are treated as in MS-DOS. First, each primary partition on each hard disk gets assigned a letter starting with C. The system partition (active) is usually assigned as C. Then, NT assigns each logical drive on each physical disk the next available drive letter. Assignment then continues with the secondary partitions on each physical disk.

You can control this assignment with static drive letters that never get reassigned. In this way, a specific drive, containing applications that are path specific, will not change letters, which might affect the application-drive mapping. When new hard disks are added to an existing installation, their assignments do not affect statically assigned drive letters.

Insider Info

On an x86 PC, the operating system must boot from the active system partition on the first physical hard disk (Disk 0). This is always the Master drive in a two-drive (E)IDE system. On SCSI systems, this is drive select 0.

If you have both SCSI and (E)IDE systems installed, and unless you have special hardware and driver setups, disk 0 will always reside on the Master (E)IDE drive.

Creating Primary Partitions

When you create a primary partition, NT will only use a contiguous disk space that can hold the partition. If a partition is created from a free space that is bordered by other partitions, it cannot exceed the size of that free space.

To create a partition, select an area of free space on the target disk and choose Partition | Create. The Create Primary Partition dialog (see Figure 4-8) will display

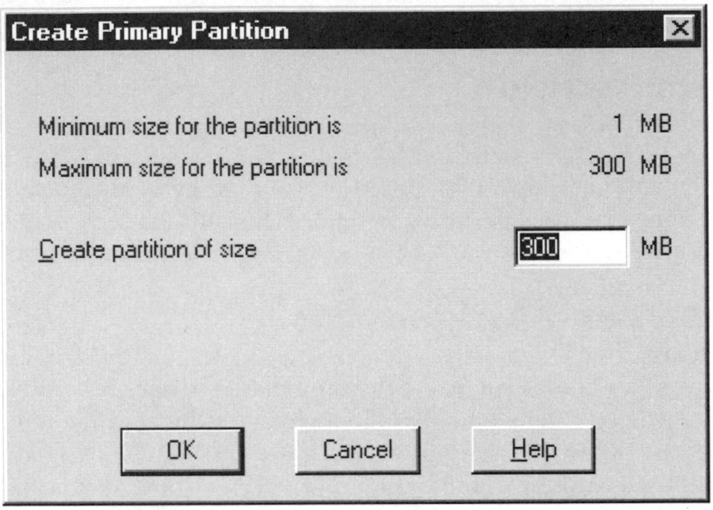

```
┌─────────────────────────────────────────────────────────┐
│ Create Primary Partition                             [X] │
│                                                           │
│                                                           │
│   Minimum size for the partition is           1  MB      │
│   Maximum size for the partition is         300  MB      │
│                                                           │
│                                                           │
│   Create partition of size            [300]   MB         │
│                                                           │
│                                                           │
│                                                           │
│                                                           │
│      ┌─────────┐    ┌─────────┐    ┌─────────┐          │
│      │   OK    │    │ Cancel  │    │  Help   │          │
│      └─────────┘    └─────────┘    └─────────┘          │
└─────────────────────────────────────────────────────────┘
```

Figure 4-8.   *The Create Primary Partition dialog*

minimum and maximum sizes for the primary partition, and will suggest a size. Enter the size, or accept the suggested size, and then choose the OK button.

Creating Extended Partitions

If you have budgeted disk space, and have not created more than three primary partitions on the target disk, you may also create an extended partition. You can use an extended partition to create multiple logical drives or to create volume or stripe sets for use in fault-tolerant and recovery schemes. *Fault-tolerance* is a feature of NT, using NTFS, which makes use of schemes that are partially immune to read or write faults due to disk surface or hardware failure (see Chapter 14 for more information).

   To create an extended partition, select an area of free space on the target disk and choose Partition | Create Extended. The Create Extended Partition dialog (see Figure 4-9) will display minimum and maximum sizes for the extended partition, and will suggest a size. Enter the size, or accept the suggested size, and then choose the OK button.

Creating Logical Drives on Extended Partitions

Select an area of free space in an extended partition and choose Partition | Create. The Disk Administrator will display what the minimum and maximum sizes for the logical drive can be. The Create Logical Drive dialog will display minimum and maximum sizes for the extended partition, and will suggest a size. Enter the size, or accept the suggested size, and then choose the OK button.

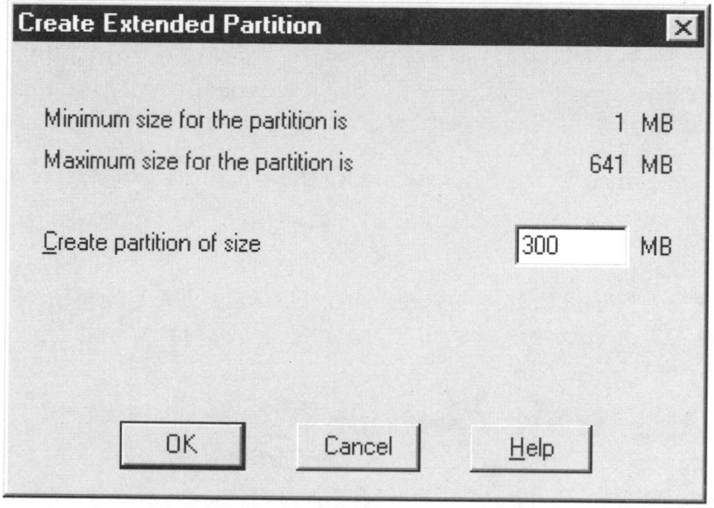

Figure 4-9. *The Create Extended Partition dialog*

Formatting and Labeling Partitions

After you create a primary or extended partition, you must write the configuration changes to disk, format, and optionally label each primary partition or extended partition set so that these partitions can be used with NT.

First, write the partition changes that you have made back to disk using the Partition I Commit Changes Now command. Next, choose the Tools I Format command. The Format dialog will be displayed. You must now specify parameters controlling how you want the disk to be formatted and labeled:

- **Capacity:** Unused for hard disks.

- **File System:** Select the file system you want to format this drive with—FAT or NTFS.

- **Allocation Unit Size:** The size, in bytes, of the unit used when making allocations of space on the drive. The lower this number is, the less space is wasted. The higher this number is, the faster the access, especially for large files. The default is a trade-off between these two extremes and should usually be correct.

- **Volume Label:** Optionally enter a label for this drive. This helps identify the drive while in use.

■ **Format Options:** NT can scan for bad sectors in the partition during the formatting process. If you do not want to do this, choose Quick Format. You cannot use Quick Format on mirror or stripe sets with parity. If the Enable Compression checkbox is used, the drive will be formatted so that NT uses compression when reading and writing files on this drive.

After you have filled in these fields, choose the OK button to start formatting the disk drive.

CAUTION: A final warning message will be displayed before formatting begins. If you choose Yes at this point, the disk will be formatted and all previous data will be lost.

Marking the Active Partition

Select the primary system partition. Choose the Partition I Mark Active command. You will be advised that the partition has been marked active and will be used as such when you restart your computer. Be sure to commit these changes before you quit Disk Administrator.

The Tools/Properties Dialog

Select and highlight a formatted volume. Choose the Tools I Properties command. This will result in the display of the properties dialog for the drive that you have selected. You can now perform several actions.

In the General dialog, where statistics for the volume are listed, enter the label you wish to give the drive. To commit the label change, choose OK. In the Tools dialog, you may choose to perform an error check on this volume (which will usually be deferred until the next time NT boots). You can also choose to perform a backup of the volume. Finally, if you have a third-party disk defragmenter installed, you can invoke it from here (see Figure 4-10). For a discussion of disk performance, see Appendix A.

Assigning Drive Letters

Select a partition or logical drive. Now choose the Tools I Assign Drive Letter command. This will result in the display of the Assign Drive Letter dialog. Choose to assign a drive letter and pick one from the list, or choose not to assign a drive letter. In cases where you have more than 24 volumes, you might want to assign and remove drive letters on the fly. This command and dialog will allow you to accomplish these tasks without rebooting the machine. When you have finished, choose the OK button to commit any changes.

Deleting Partitions and Logical Drives

Select the partition or logical drive, and then choose the Partition I Delete command. You will receive a message warning you that all data in the partition or logical drive

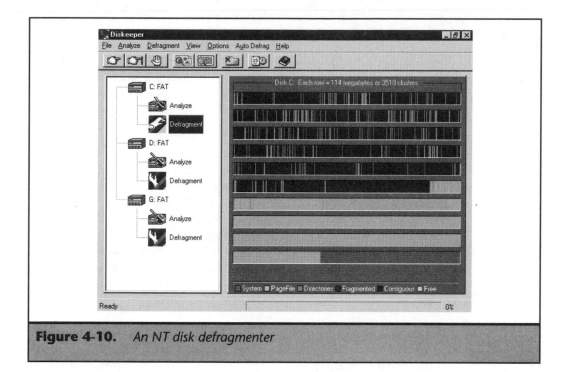

Figure 4-10. *An NT disk defragmenter*

will be lost. If you choose Yes in this Confirm message box, the partition or logical drive will be deleted, and its space will be freed.

NT will not let you delete a system or boot volume. Also, you cannot delete individual partitions that are part of a set without deleting the entire set.

CAUTION: Back up files on partitions, volumes, and logical drives you wish to delete. Once you have done so, NT cannot recover data on a deleted entity.

Saving and Restoring Disk Configurations

You can save and restore disk configuration information in the same way that you save and restore emergency backup configuration parameters. Using Disk Administrator's Save, Restore, and Search commands on the Partition/Configuration menu, you can act on configuration information covering drive letters, volume sets, stripe sets with and without parity, and mirror sets. The Search variant lets you look for previously saved configuration information files on drives in your computer.

Use the Save command each time you make a change to your disk's configuration. A message will appear telling you what is to be saved, and that it will be saved to floppy disk. Insert a floppy disk into drive A and choose the OK button.

Use the Restore command to restore disk configuration information from a previously saved floppy disk. A message will appear telling you that the restore operation will overwrite your current disk configuration information. Any changes made during the current session will also be lost. Insert the floppy disk containing a saved configuration and choose the OK button. Disk Administrator will restore the information and shut down your computer in preparation for restart.

Volume and Stripe Sets

Volume sets are only available in the NT operating system. They implement a scheme for efficient use of free space areas on a disk or disks. Volume sets allow you to combine many different-sized areas of free space, on up to 32 physical disks, into one logical volume set that is seen by applications as a single partition.

If you create volume sets on MS-DOS partitions, those partitions will no longer be usable by MS-DOS or Windows 95 since only NT knows how to deal with them.

Stripe sets are created similarly to volume sets, but each member partition of the stripe set *must* be on a different disk. All of the partitions will be made approximately the same size.

TIP: *Volume sets may increase throughput by spreading the I/O load on large database files, for instance, across more than one drive. They also provide a way to free up drive letters that would otherwise be taken up by the much smaller constituent spaces that they are made up of.*

Creating Volume and Stripe Sets

You choose free space areas to create a volume set in the same way as you use the Windows selection mechanism for other purposes: Hold down CTRL and then select the first free space area, continuing to press CTRL while selecting all of the other areas. Next, choose Partition | Create Volume Set. The Create Volume Set dialog (Figure 4-11) will be displayed, showing the minimum and maximum sizes for the volume set, along with the recommended size. Enter the size you want and choose the OK button. If you choose less than the total available space, NT will spread the entered space value across all disks to create more or less equal partitions. The volume set will be assigned a single drive letter.

To create a stripe set, follow the same selection criteria as with volumes, but make sure that each free area to be used is on a different disk. Then choose the Partition | Create Stripe Set command. The Create Stripe Set dialog will be displayed, showing the minimum and maximum sizes for the stripe set, along with the recommended size. Enter the size you want and choose the OK button. Equally sized unformatted partitions, divided and normalized across each physical disk, will be created. The stripe set will then be assigned a single drive letter.

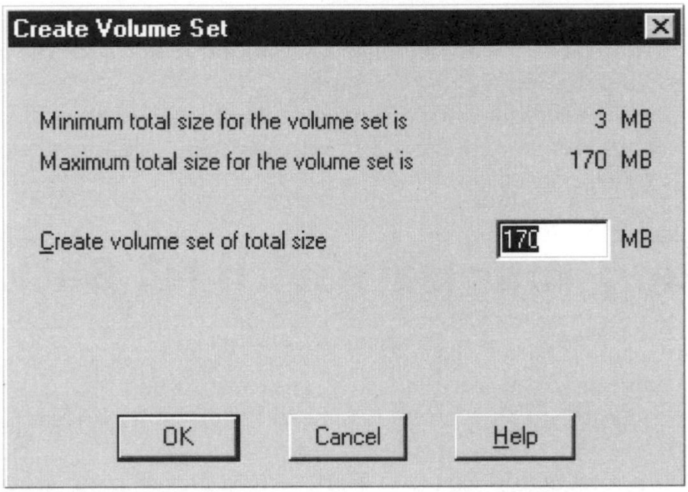

Create Volume Set   ☒

Minimum total size for the volume set is   3 MB

Maximum total size for the volume set is   170 MB

Create volume set of total size   [170]   MB

[OK]   [Cancel]   [Help]

Figure 4-11.   *The Create Volume Set dialog*

Deleting Volume and Stripe Sets

Select the volume or stripe set. Now, choose the Partition | Delete command. All data on the volume or stripe set will be lost, so back it up before you choose this command. In the Confirm dialog, choose the Yes button.

Extending Volume Sets

You can extend NTFS volumes (that are not part of stripe or mirror sets) and volume sets by adding free space. Select the existing volume or volume set and the free space you wish to extend the volume or volume set with. Now choose the Partition | Extend Volume Set command. The Extend Volume Set dialog will be displayed, showing the minimum and maximum sizes for the volume set, along with the recommended size. Enter the size you want and choose the OK button.

Disk Administrator will shut down and restart the system when you commit your changes and quit, extending and formatting the new volume or volume set area without affecting the data already contained in the volume or volume set.

Committing Changes and Exiting Disk Administrator

Upon exit, and if you have made any changes to your disk structures, Disk Administrator will display a reminder about committing changes and ask if you want to save your work. Unless you answer Yes to this question, or you have explicitly chosen the Partition I Commit Changes Now command, none of your work will be saved permanently. If you answer Yes, Disk Administrator will save the changes and display a confirmation dialog with an OK button.

Some actions that you request may require a reboot, and when this is the case, such as when a volume set is extended, Disk Administrator will initiate a complete computer restart upon exit.

Protecting Your Data with NT Backup

NT Backup helps you to protect against data loss from computer crashes, hardware and drive failures, and erasures of any kind. Backup allows you to work with a supported tape drive as if you were choosing files to be copied with Explorer (see Chapter 6). You can back up and restore files to and from either FAT or NTFS file systems, and sets of files can be viewed from a tape's catalog.

NT Backup supports SCSI 4 mm DAT, floppy controller or parallel-style QIC-80/3010/3020 and Travan drives, IDE-QIC-157, and SCSI minicartridge drives, as well as custom drives from many manufacturers. Multiple connected devices are supported, but only one may be active at any time.

This section reviews the steps needed to perform a full backup and restore cycle. Using Backup's graphical user interface, we will survey the commands for total and selective backups and restores. Backup may also be used across the network, to back up a remote resource on any connected computer on which you have sufficient permissions.

With Backup, you can use any supported tape backup drive and some special commands, such as Erase, Format, and Retension, which we will describe later. You can back up and restore both local and remote files on NTFS and FAT volumes with or without data compression and verification passes, making normal, copy, incremental, differential, and daily backups.

Backup also allows you to select files for backup or restore by volume, directory, and filename. You can view and save log information on tape operations, and you can use one tape for multiple backups, or use many tapes for large backups that span more than one tape.

Finally, you can select files to be restored from a tape catalog and redirect a tape restore's destination drive and directory.

Starting Backup

Choose Start I Programs I Administrative Tools (Common), or enter **ntbackup.exe** at a command prompt, to start Backup (see Figure 4-12). The main Drives window will be displayed along with a Tapes window. A status bar appears at the bottom of the main window, providing backup operation status.

NT checks for a tape drive that has been installed and then initializes it when you start Backup. The tape drive should be powered up before you start Backup.

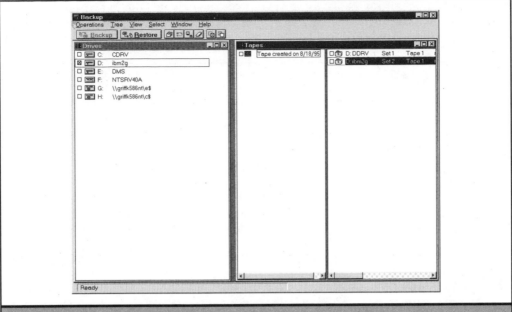

Figure 4-12.   *The NT Backup main window*

Tape Hardware and Drivers

When you open Backup for the first time, or have recently installed a new backup device, an error message will be displayed, telling you that no tape drive is installed or has been detected, or that the drive was detected, but the driver is not loaded. At this time, you must install a device driver for your tape backup drive and reboot your computer to activate the driver.

In order to detect your tape drive and install a driver for it, open the Tape Devices applet in Start/Settings/Control Panel. Choose the Devices tab, and then choose the Detect button. NT will attempt to detect your tape drive and install drivers for it. You may be asked to supply the directory path where a driver file may be found. If NT cannot detect your drive automatically, or you choose to add a device driver for it manually, open the Drivers tab and choose the Add button. A list of supported manufacturers and devices will be displayed. Choose a driver from this list, or if you have a custom device driver, choose the Have Disk button. The latter method will ask you for the drive and path to the custom driver files.

Choose a model from the list, or load your custom driver. After NT installs the driver and you have dismissed the dialog, you will have to restart your computer to enable the tape device driver.

Insider Info

You must have two kinds of permission to back up files. First, you must have file access permissions on the drive that you are trying to back up. An alternative would be to log on as a member of the Administrators or Backup Operators group. Members of the Backup Operators group have special permission to bypass normal security and file permissions so that they can use backup devices without being granted full administrative rights. However, because they have these file access permissions, they hold a powerful card. These operators also have restore privileges, so they can overwrite files that would normally be protected. Never grant untrusted individuals Backup Operators rights!

The Backup Menus

The Operations menu is where most of the action takes place. In this menu are commands for starting a backup, restoring a volume or volumes from a backup tape, cataloging a tape, and various commands that control tape utilities. The Hardware Setup command lets you select a tape drive target or source, if more than one device is installed.

The Tree, View, and Window menus provide commands for manipulating Backup's windows in the same way as Explorer manipulates its views. The Select menu mirrors the action of clicking on a highlighted selection box.

Choosing Files to Back Up or Restore

Using the Drives window for backup, which lists connected resources in the same hierarchical way as Explorer (see Chapter 6), or the Tapes window for restore, you can select whole drives (drives on tape for restore), individual subdirectories, or individual files. You may select entities in one of two ways: Either point at an entity's checkbox and click once to check and again to uncheck, or highlight an entity and use the Select | Check or Uncheck commands. You can also use the check/uncheck toolbar icons. Figure 4-13 shows a sample window with files marked for backup.

Operations Commands

After you have selected files, directories, or drives to back up or restore, you will use the Operations menu commands to perform the task that you choose. This menu allows you to perform all backup and restoration duties, as well as tape maintenance.

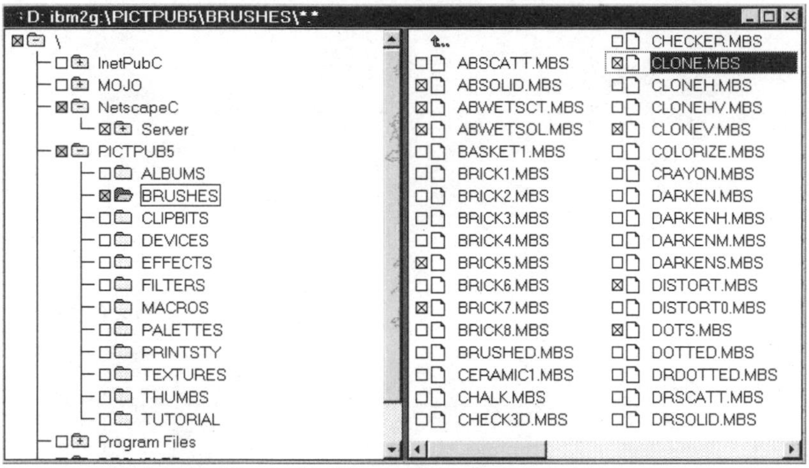

Figure 4-13. *Selecting files in the Backup window*

Operations|Backup

To perform a backup, choose Operations | Backup. This will result in the display of the Backup Information dialog (see Figure 4-14). The information at the top of the dialog tells you what tape is loaded, when this tape was originally created, and by whom. Then comes the Tape Name field where you can type in a name up to 32 characters long.

The next section in the upper portion of the dialog lets you specify options for this backup: verification, access restriction, and hardware compression. To the right of these options, the Operation section lets you choose whether to append the backup to any that already exist on this tape, or to overwrite any existing backup, starting anew. Also, you can back up the local Registry if this checkbox is active and selected. The Backup Local Registry checkbox is only active if the local drive, on which the Registry database is stored, is selected.

There are two remaining sections at the bottom of the dialog. Backup Set Information first denotes the drive name you are backing up from. Then, two fields are provided: the Description field for your comments (up to 32 characters long), which may be any string you choose to enter; and the Backup Type list that lets you make a choice of backup method—Normal (full), Copy, Differential, Incremental, or Daily.

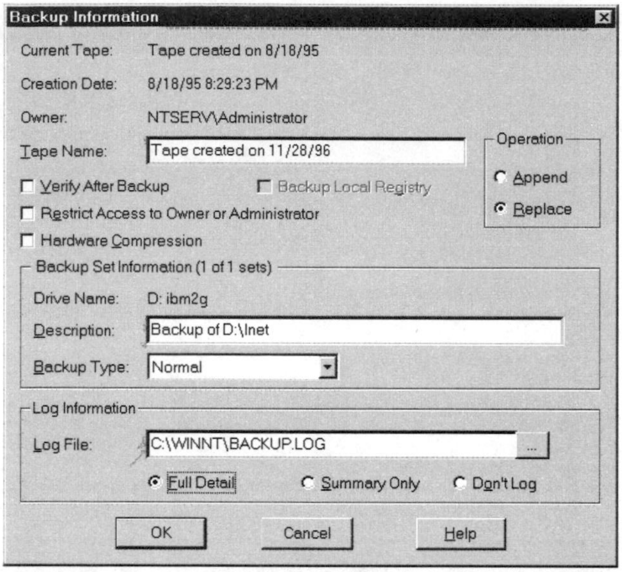

Figure 4-14. *The Backup Information dialog*

Finally, the Log Information section allows you to enter the path and name of the log you wish Backup to write its status log to, and underneath this field, selection buttons for the level of detail you wish to include in the log.

BACKUP SETS   In the Backup Set Information portion of the Backup Information dialog, the text also shows how many backup sets have been selected (in parentheses). A *backup set* is a collection of related files, existing on a single drive, to be backed up in a single backup operation.

If more than one drive is selected, or files that are on more than one drive are selected, Backup will define a set for files existing on each drive that your file set spans. A scroll bar will appear, which is used for locating which backup set is selected so that you can enter a different description and select different backup types for each set displayed.

VIEWING BACKUP STATUS   Once you have started the backup, the Backup Status dialog will be displayed (see Figure 4-15). The top of the dialog shows totals for the number of directories, files, and bytes backed up, as well as elapsed time, corrupted files, and skipped files.

The second status area shows a hierarchical, graphical view of the current drive/set being backed up. The third area is the log/status Summary area, where a

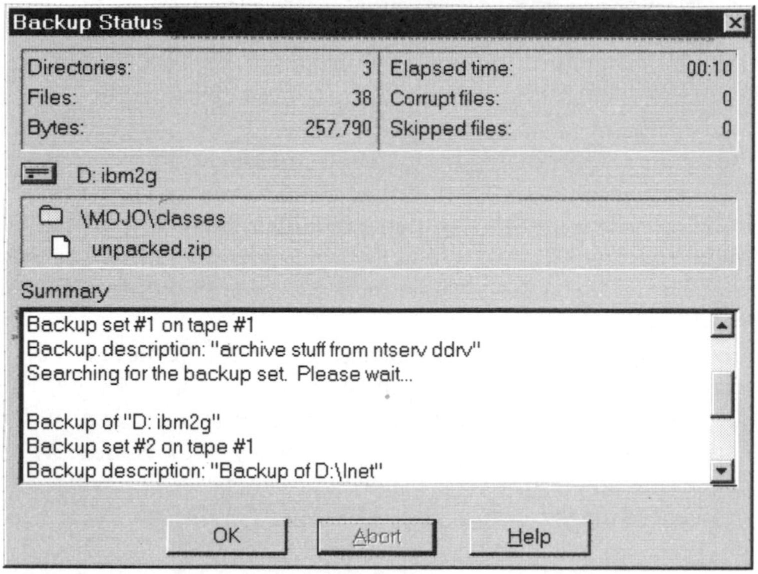

Backup Status   ☒

Directories:	3	Elapsed time:	00:10
Files:	38	Corrupt files:	0
Bytes:	257,790	Skipped files:	0

▤   D: ibm2g

☐   \MOJO\classes
☐   unpacked.zip

Summary

```
Backup set #1 on tape #1
Backup description: "archive stuff from ntserv ddrv"
Searching for the backup set. Please wait...

Backup of "D: ibm2g"
Backup set #2 on tape #1
Backup description: "Backup of D:\Inet"
```

[OK]   [Abort]   [Help]

Figure 4-15.   *The Backup Status dialog*

summary of what is written to the log is displayed. The Backup Status dialog also contains an Abort button, with which you can stop the backup at any time.

> **NOTE:**   *If many drives (sets) or set-files are backed up, to the point at which the tape becomes full before the backup is done, Backup will display the Insert New Tape dialog. You will then be prompted to insert another tape. This will repeat until the backup has completed, or until you abort the backup. A series of backup tapes created in this way is called a* family set.

Operations | Restore

In order to be fully functional, a backup program must have some way of reloading backed up files, or a way of moving these files to another disk. Backup provides both kinds of functionality. Using the Operations | Restore command, you will have full control over and access to single backup sets and files for restoration to their original disk and directories, or to an alternate of your choice.

First, using the Tapes window in the same manner as the Drives window, make your selections from the hierarchical display. When you first open the tape to be restored, Backup will catalog it for you, reading restoration information from the tape's directory. Family sets have the directory information on the last tape in the set.

After you have chosen Operations | Restore, the Restore Information dialog will be displayed (see Figure 4-16). You should have already picked which drives or files will be restored in the Tapes window. Information about the current tape is displayed in the top portion of the dialog window next to Tape Name, Backup Set, Creation Date, and Owner.

The Restore section of this dialog has two entry fields: Restore to Drive is a dropdown list that gives you a choice of drives on which to restore these files. The Alternate Path field lets you enter a pathname to which the restore will take place, with this pathname as a root directory. As an alternative, you may choose the ... button, which will bring up a browse dialog where you may choose the path you want to restore to.

Two checkboxes also appear in the Restore section: First, Restore Local Registry allows you to restore the Registry from a previously saved copy on tape. This overwrites the Registry database files, so you must be very careful. Second, the Restore File Permissions checkbox, when active, allows you to restore any permissions that existed on the files when they were backed up. Otherwise, the restored files receive the permissions information of the restore's target directory.

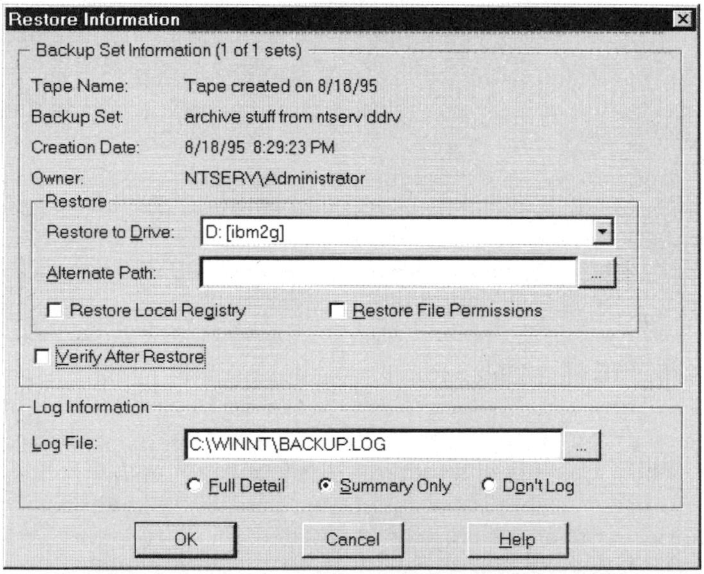

Figure 4-16. *The Restore Information dialog*

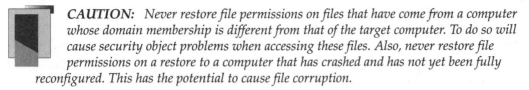 **CAUTION:** *Never restore file permissions on files that have come from a computer whose domain membership is different from that of the target computer. To do so will cause security object problems when accessing these files. Also, never restore file permissions on a restore to a computer that has crashed and has not yet been fully reconfigured. This has the potential to cause file corruption.*

Finally, the Log Information section allows you to enter the path and name of the log you wish Backup to write its status log to and, underneath this field, selection buttons for the level of detail you wish to include in the log.

VIEWING RESTORE STATUS Once you have started the restore, the Restore Status dialog will be displayed (see Figure 4-17). The top of this dialog shows totals for the number of directories, files, and bytes backed up, as well as elapsed time, corrupted files, and skipped files.

The second status area shows a hierarchical, graphical view of the current drive/set being backed up. The third area is the log/status Summary area, where a summary of what is written to the log is displayed. The Backup Status dialog also contains an Abort button, with which you can stop the backup at any time.

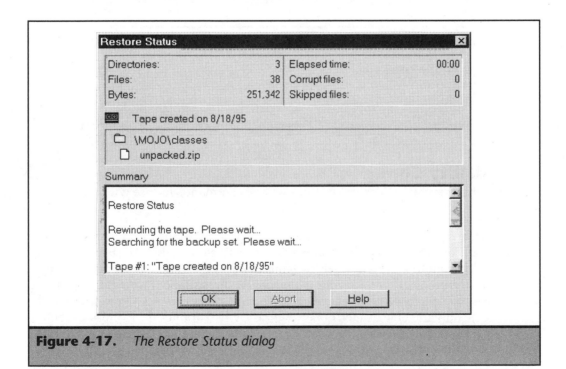

Figure 4-17. *The Restore Status dialog*

Operations|Catalog

Whenever an unknown tape is inserted in the drive, or you wish to restore from a tape, the preliminary information that is displayed in the Tapes window shows only the first backup set. Whether you just want to know what's on the entire tape, or you want to restore files and directories from other known sets, you can catalog the tape in one of two ways.

First, you can double-click on the first set icon in the Tapes window. As an alternative, you can issue the Operations | Catalog command. This will read the tape's directory and display a fully expandable list of all backup sets contained on the tape. You can also click the Catalog button on the toolbar.

Any of these actions will result in the display of the Catalog Status dialog, shown in the following illustration. This dialog shows you status for the tape cataloging action and provides an Abort button to stop the cataloging process. Upon completion, the catalog list will be shown in the Tapes window. The catalog display will contain question marks where individual catalogs have not been loaded. Double-click on any set icon displayed in the Tapes window in order to display its hierarchical tree. If needed, a catalogue operation will be performed automatically.

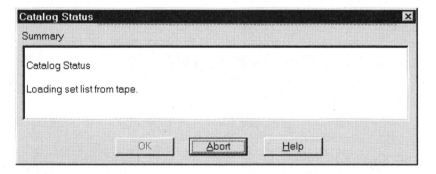

Tape Utility Commands

The Operations menu in Backup furnishes several commands for use with your tape backup device:

- **Erase Tape:** When issued, this command will result in the erasure of the entire tape. Backup will display an Erase Tape warning dialog to confirm that you really want to erase a tape. The original name and creation date of the tape in the drive is displayed for your reference. The Erase Tape warning dialog also lets you specify erasure type on capable drives. You can pick Quick Erase to erase only the tape header, or Secure Erase, when applicable, to erase the entire tape. This may take several hours to complete, depending on the tape technology in use.

- **Retension Tape:** When issued and applicable, this command fast forwards and then rewinds the tape, under tension, to eliminate slack.

TIP: *Four mm DAT and 8 mm tapes do not require retensioning, secure erasure, or formatting, so those commands are disabled.*

■ **Eject:** This command ejects the tape in a tape drive that is capable of doing so.

■ **Format Tape:** When issued, this command formats QIC (Quarter Inch Cartridge) or other types of minicartridge tape, because they act like a floppy disk and must therefore be formatted.

Insider Info

Swapping and using backup tapes between two or more models or brands of tape drives can look like a hardware error condition, and NT might issue an error pertaining to the tape drive. This can be caused by proprietary or mismatched tape compression schemes. To erase a tape that is exhibiting such errors, use the Backup application, invoked from a command line, and augmented with the */nopoll* switch. Do *not* use the */nopoll* switch for any operation other than erasure!

Operations|Exit

To exit Backup, choose Operations | Exit. Be sure to eject the tape cartridge before exiting. You can eject the tape under software control or manually, depending on the technology and model of the tape drive.

What's Next

In this chapter, we have covered the basic operations for starting NT and shutting it down properly, for using local and domain-style logon procedures and the Task Manager. We also looked at how NT manages your files and disks, how the Disk Administrator works, and how to use the NT Backup program.

In the next chapter, we'll take a closer look at networking. We'll explore the flexibility of NT's open architecture and the OSI reference model. We'll also discuss how to choose the right adapter cards and protocols so you can set up NT 4 to do the networking job you want it to.

Chapter Five

Getting Ready to Network

Whcn you start to plan and install the ideally connected NT 4 machine, you must set out to choose the types of network adapter cards, drivers, and protocols to use; and since NT has an open architecture, you have a lot of flexibility in this decision. Choice brings the promise of excellence in anything we do, but to make a choice such as this, we need to know all we can about what alternatives NT offers.

NT supports both the Network Driver Interface Specification (NDIS) and Transport Driver Interface (TDI) standards. These standards are designed to make NT's networking layers as configurable and efficient as possible. At a higher level, the support for WinSock 1.1/2.0 is probably the most important aspect of network programming support in NT. Many applications and programming platforms support this specification and have products that depend on its presence in a target operating system. NT also supports a variant of the Unix STREAMS protocol, which makes porting to NT much more straightforward.

The extensible nature of NT's networking layer, coupled with a published way in which to take advantage of these standards, allows NT to communicate with many third-party networking products. This means you have a variety of network adapter cards, protocols, applications, and network topologies to choose from.

Understanding Networking Basics

Before exploring the specific drivers and protocols supported by NT, you should understand the OSI reference model, which is the underpinning of most modern networking concepts, including those embodied by NT. On the physical side, you will also want to know the basics about the purpose of network interface cards, their drivers, and transport protocols.

Any overview of NT networking must include a look at the actual installation procedures that support your choice of driver and protocol, which will be covered here and in Chapters 6 (the Control Panel applets introduction), 11, and 12. If you already understand the topics we'll be covering in the next few sections, you can skip ahead to the material on choosing a network adapter card later in this chapter.

The OSI Reference Model

In 1978 the International Standards Organization (ISO), in conjunction with interested industry leaders, developed a new framework for computer networking. This source design was called the Open Systems Interconnect (OSI) reference model. The reason for this model's inception was to standardize the many different networking schemes that were starting to proliferate. To this end, ISO set out to suggest standards for the flow of data in a network, from the basic physical connections of the network, all the way up to the applications used by computer operators.

The aim of the OSI model, then, is to provide a common framework for network design that allows new and existing applications to cooperatively carry out distributed processing tasks (across a network connection), irrespective of the type of computer on which they are running. The OSI model divides network functionality into seven distinct layers. Each of these layers can be thought of as a separate software process or task, but they cooperate with each other on a given machine. The organization allows each layer to communicate locally only with its surrounding layers, but between hosts, or network connections, each layer can communicate with its corresponding remote layer through the lower layers on each side of the connection.

The OSI model provides only a guideline for implementation and a method by which designers may qualify their design decisions. An actual implementation need not use physically separate processes to implement each layer. In fact, an OSI-compliant protocol may include functions that span several levels of responsibility, blurring the distinction between these theoretical layers. OSI's seven layers, shown in Figure 5-1, are defined as follows:

- **Application layer 7 (programs):** Applications that use network services reside in this layer. The bidirectional transmission of messages to and from these programs is the ultimate goal of all lower-level protocols. Application layer clients include Telnet, FTP, and any other network-enabled program.

- **Presentation layer 6 (data interpretation):** This layer formats data for display or printing and translation. Data translation and encryption is also performed in this layer. Presentation layer protocols include HTTP.

- **Session layer 5 (control of sessions between hosts):** This layer establishes connections or "conversations" between hosts over the network. Session layer protocols include TCP, Named Pipes, and NetBIOS.

- **Transport layer 4 (transmission control):** This layer provides flow control and data ordering services. Transport layer protocols include TCP, UDP, NetBIOS/NetBEUI, and SPX.

- **Network layer 3 (flow control and routing):** This layer provides services for transmitting datagrams over the network to a remote host, assigning of addresses, and data packet routing. The transmissions are "connectionless"; datagrams sent in this way can be sent or received out of order and their transmission is not guaranteed. Network layer protocols include IP and IPX, a Novell protocol.

- **Data Link layer 2 (maintenance and release of data):** This layer, also known as the Media Access Control (MAC) layer, is responsible for making and breaking logical links, assembly of bits from the physical layer into frames, detection of physical errors, and notification of such errors. Data Link implementations include the following protocols: IEEE 802.2 (LLC), IEEE 802.3, IEEE 802.5 (token-ring), and PPP LCP (Point-to-Point Protocol for serial communication).

- **Physical layer 1 (physical media definition):** This layer defines the physical media used to communicate through the network. This can be coaxial cable, FDDI (fiber), RS-232, or even RF. This layer defines physical implementation specifics such as the type of cable, frequency, terminations, and so on. Physical layer implementations include Ethernet 10Base2, 10BaseT, and 100BaseT; also, token-ring, Arcnet, FDDI, and, for example, wireless (e.g., Spread Spectrum FM).

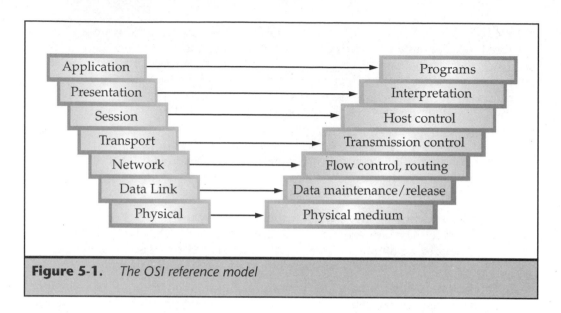

Figure 5-1. *The OSI reference model*

When OSI-compliant computers converse across a network, levels of OSI reference layer software existing on each host assume they are communicating with the same layer on the other host. For example, the Presentation layers on both hosts communicate through the transparent services of all of the lower levels on each host without knowing that they are not directly connected to each other (see Figure 5-2). This is true at any level of the model; the software designer, without affecting any other layer, can replace whole blocks of functionality.

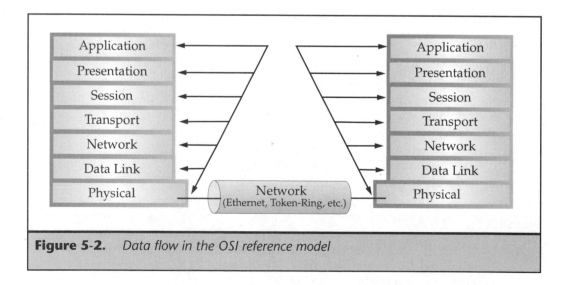

Figure 5-2. *Data flow in the OSI reference model*

Mini-Glossary

NETWORK ADAPTER CARD Sometimes called a network interface card or NIC, the network adapter card is a hardware adapter that allows your computer to function on a network.

ADAPTER CARD (NIC) DRIVER A software program layer that controls an adapter card at the physical level. This driver is responsible for actually controlling the NIC's integrated circuits, I/O channel, and so forth. More properly called a *network interface card device driver*.

PROTOCOL DRIVER A software program that translates the data sent on the network so that it can be understood both by the sending and receiving computers.

BINDING The process of associating a protocol driver with a NIC and establishing a communication channel between the two. NT performs protocol binding every time you add or change protocols in the Control Panel/Network applet.

NETWORK DRIVER INTERFACE SPECIFICATION (NDIS) In 1989 Microsoft and 3Com jointly developed a standard defining an interface for communication between the OSI model Data Link (MAC) layer and the transport protocol drivers handled by the Network and Transport layers. NDIS defines the software interface used by network transport protocols to communicate with a NIC. NDIS provides the ability for multiple transport protocols to share a single physical NIC.

NT STREAMS An operating system-level support system and environment for network transport protocols that facilitates the porting of existing STREAMS-based stacks from other environments to NT. It is a full tool set for the development of communication services.

TRANSPORT DRIVER INTERFACE (TDI) The Transport Driver Interface implements a low-level network application program interface (API) that all NT transport drivers expose to higher level software.

Network Cards, Drivers, and Protocols

A network adapter card is an electronic circuit that provides one or more electrically and mechanically compatible I/O ports following some standard, such as Ethernet 10BaseT (twisted-pair Ethernet), to which network cable can be physically connected. The adapter card (what we shall call a NIC—network interface card—from now on), under direction of a software driver, electronically transmits data coming from the computer onto the network, and also receives data from the cable, making it available to the computer (Figure 5-3).

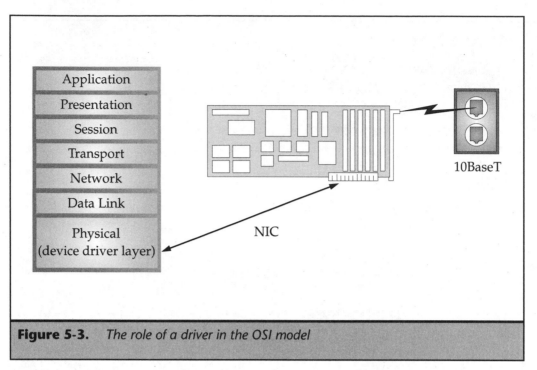

Figure 5-3. *The role of a driver in the OSI model*

All networked computers, by definition, have a NIC, whether built into the motherboard electronics, or as a separate plug-in card. This also means that all networked, NIC-equipped computers must have several installed layers of supervisory software to enable the NIC to function.

The lowest level of software for NIC support is driver, or device driver, software. A NIC device driver is customized to the exact make and model of NIC that you install. It is responsible for managing the lowest levels of network interface, including the actual memory, I/O ports, and registers on the NIC itself. Following the levels up from the device driver layer, NIC supervisory software includes at least one protocol driver, which implements the transport protocol—that part of the NIC's software that provides an interface between the low-level drivers and upper-level network processes and applications. Protocol drivers wrap and unwrap data to make it understandable when transmitted to a remote host and when received from a remote host. Low-level NIC driver software can be implemented in discrete driver layers or as a single entity, called a *monolithic driver*.

Multiple Protocol Support

As long as a NIC/driver combination adheres, even loosely, to the OSI model, and each computer that needs to converse with another is using a compatible protocol and physical network interface, they will be able to communicate across the network. Computers using modern operating systems, such as NT, can be configured to use more than one network protocol at a time. A computer so equipped can have, for instance, simultaneous NetBIOS/NWLink and TCP/IP conversations with other computers running those protocols. A computer running more than one protocol stack, or driver set, then, can have multiple connections to other computers that are running only one of the protocol stacks in use. If you build up a server, for instance, you might want it to support all of the popular protocols, so that it can receive connections from any kind of workstation configuration on your network.

The permutations are endless, limited only by the inherent abilities of each protocol and each computer. Usually, a computer is set up to favor one protocol over another and to use it as its default when making new connections. When you install multiple protocols on a computer, you choose the order in which the computer will use them. The default protocol is also called the primary protocol.

NT 4 ships with and supports compliant NDIS drivers and protocol stacks, which let you use more than one protocol and driver This also means that you can use more than one physical NIC (this kind of installation is called *multihomed*).

Insider Info

NDIS, the basis for plug-in functionality in network protocol-NIC/driver support, provides built-in functionality that enables any workstation to use any combination of any compliant protocol driver or drivers in concert with any compliant NIC device driver and physical hardware. All protocol and NIC drivers shipped with NT 4 conform to NDIS, so there is built-in support for multiple protocols tied into one NIC, and multiple NICs (multihoming) existing in one computer installation. Older style monolithic drivers are not able to share installation with each other, meaning that only one protocol can be supported at a time with them. This makes NDIS support very attractive in disparate installations.

Because NDIS separates protocols from the NIC driver, NT can support many different brands and designs of NICs with no change to the upper-level protocol driver. This makes support for differing installations much simpler; you need only install the correct lower-level NIC driver for each card that a protocol will support.

Further Adaptability: What Is the TDI?

NT uses a special interface to communicate directly between the OSI Session and Transport layers, as they are implemented within the operating system. This special interface is called the Transport Driver Interface (TDI). TDI provides a back door into the NT network communication mechanism for the use of such NT components as the server and redirector processes, whose responsibilities range over the entire network implementation. Such NT components use the TDI to communicate directly with the installed transport protocols.

A Cousin to NDIS

As NDIS standardizes NIC physical-to-transport protocol communication, TDI does the same for transport protocol-to-high-level networking components. The common interface mechanism implemented by TDI lets NT components like the redirector communicate directly with any installed protocol transport. Using TDI, these upper-level network components do not need to know specifics about the protocol transport they are talking to. Thus, like NDIS, TDI is an abstraction mechanism.

Any TDI-compliant transport protocol can work with any TDI-compliant upper-level component. TDI allows NT to have greater functionality by offering the possibility of network Transport and Session layer replacement, if, for instance, new functionality is made available in a third-party product. Nonstandard or custom protocols, NDIS support for a custom hardware device (like a multiport serial board), and new network redirectors and servers can be made as plug-ins using the TDI.

NetBIOS Support

NetBIOS support in NT 4 is critical for those processes that need this functionality. NT fully supports NetBIOS and is therefore fully compliant with NetBIOS applications and services. NT's NetBIOS components are optionally removable if not needed, but support and performance overhead is not an issue.

The Session layer NetBIOS components work alongside the TDI for situations that require compatibility at this level. You must enable NetBIOS by installing the NetBIOS interface in the Control Panel/Network applet (see Figure 5-4). NetBIOS will only be used in specific situations where software requests it.

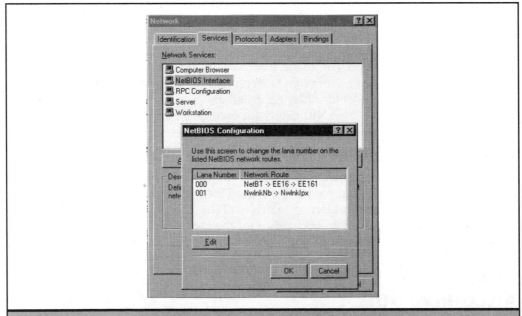

Figure 5-4. *The NetBIOS interface, installed as a network service*

Mini-Glossary

BUS WIDTH　The bus width of a network card is the number of bits used to connect the card to the computer bus, usually 8, 16, 32, or 64 bits. This determines how much data can be transferred across the card's interface with the bus at any one time.

ETHERNET　In the late 1960s, the University of Hawaii developed a wide area network called ALOHA. The basis for future designs came from their use of a scheme called Carrier-Sense Multiple Access with Collision Detection (CSMA/CD). Using the Carrier Sense method, a network card waits online for quiescent periods during which it will send data. This scheme also allows the physical cable to simultaneously support multiple NICs, with detection and correction of data collision, when two or more NICs are active at once.

　　This network design was the foundation for Xerox Ethernet. Xerox's involvement with Ethernet resulted in their first product offerings in 1975. In cooperation with Intel and DEC, Xerox then released specifications for 10Mbps Ethernet, which subsequently became the IEEE 802.3 specification.

TOKEN-RING　Physically, a local area network that is an implementation of the IEEE 802.5 standard; a physical manifestation of the token-ring access method. Token-ring refers mostly to the access method employed, not a ring shape.

ISA/EISA　Industry Standard Architecture (ISA) is an 8-bit or 16-bit PC expansion bus that provides a buffered interface from devices on expansion cards to the internal bus. This is the most common expansion bus found on PC-compatible motherboards. EISA is a 32-bit PC expansion bus designed as a superset of the ISA bus, which expands the speed and data width while still supporting older ISA cards. EISA has been largely supplanted by the PCI specification.

PERIPHERAL COMPONENT INTERCONNECT (PCI)　A high-performance 32-bit and sometimes (internally) 64-bit bus, 132Mbps adapter standard designed to be used with devices that have high bandwidth requirements, such as the display subsystem. Since 1985, the industry has released improved PC buses that have met with limited acceptance. The IBM Micro Channel (MCA) bus features a 32-bit bus width, with up to 40Mbps throughput; the EISA bus also has a 32-bit bus width with 33Mbps maximum throughput; and the VESA Local Bus has a 32-bit bus with up to 200Mbps throughput.

　　As a result of newer processors and increasing throughput and ease of installation demands, Intel designed an open bus specification that was aimed at, but not exclusive to, the 64-bit Pentium processor. PCI is plug-and-play capable, so no switch or jumper settings are normally required. Also, PCI supports concurrency, so more than one operation can take place at once. PCI's features have made it the most popular PC adapter standard today, after ISA.

LOCAL AREA NETWORK (LAN)   Two or more computers and / or network devices, such as network printers, which are physically connected and can share local resources. LAN usually refers to a network segment that exists physically and logically within a discrete geographical area, such as a single building. A LAN might have a gateway connection to another LAN, or to a WAN, but that further connection is not generally considered to be part of the LAN. PCs that need to share storage and printer resources are connected locally, with cabling and NICs, to implement a LAN. To fit the definition, the logical grouping, along with reasonable proximity, is of primary importance. The connection technology is actually immaterial and could possibly include wireless or serial line technology.

WIDE AREA NETWORK (WAN)   A network that provides data communication capability in areas larger than those serviced by a LAN, and with computers that do not necessarily belong to the local grouping, logically or physically. A WAN can be implemented with regular telephone lines, dedicated leased lines, interconnected subnetworks within an organization, or geographically, through the use of relay stations such as satellite links or a distributed network such as the Internet.

The Hardware Choice—Selecting a NIC

When you go to the computer store to purchase a NIC, or a salesperson calls on you, you will be presented with hundreds of brands and models. First, you can choose from among the various connection technologies that your planned or in-place network supports—Ethernet, token-ring, and so on. Also make sure to match the cabling technology you want to use, such as thinnet or 10/100BaseT twisted pair).

Ethernet is undoubtedly the most popular connection technology in use today. The most widely used Ethernet topologies are

- **10Base2 (thinnet):** A bussed Ethernet connection technology that uses coaxial cable (usually RG50/8) that can carry a signal up to approximately 600 feet without the need for a signal repeater. 10Mbps throughput.

- **10Base5 (thicknet):** A bussed Ethernet connection technology that uses coaxial cable (usually RG-8/11, about double the diameter of RG50/8-thinnet) that can carry a signal up to approximately 1,640 feet without the need for a signal repeater. 10Mbps throughput.

- **10BaseT (twisted pair):** A point-to-point Ethernet connection technology using an unshielded twisted-pair (UTP) cable that can carry a signal up to about 325 feet. This is, then, the maximum distance between any workstation and the hub that the workstation is connected to. 10Mbps throughput.

- **100BaseT (twisted pair):** A point-to-point Ethernet connection technology using an unshielded twisted-pair (UTP) cable that can carry a signal up to about 325 feet. As with 10BaseT, this is the maximum distance between any workstation and the hub that the workstation is connected to. 100Mbps throughput.

> **TIP:** *If you're installing thinnet or thicknet (coaxial) Ethernet, a few words about the cabling may be in order here. Coaxial-based Ethernet is very sensitive to improper cabling and termination. The bus must go from machine to machine, without branching. You must not have any three-way connections (i.e., three cables connected in a T or star shape) on the network. The cable must also be terminated on both ends with a 50ohm resistor termination device, and if you are connecting thicknet, you must attach the network to your NIC using an Ethernet transceiver. This unit either plugs into the 15-pin AUI (Attachment Unit Interface) port on your NIC, or may be connected by some sort of shielded cable. If you fail to properly set up a thinnet or thicknet installation, NT will, at best, fail to start the network. In extreme cases, NT may lock up or crash when these guidelines are not followed.*

Match the NIC with a Driver

Many commercially sold NICs do not ship with drivers for NT. Or they ship with drivers for older versions of NT, which may or may not work with NT 4. This is principally due to the strong sales numbers of, and thus the need of smaller companies to concentrate development on, Windows 95.

This situation is rapidly changing. With the powerful upswing in sales of the NT OS and shipping of OEM NT systems, more and more manufacturers are now offering NIC support for NT in their primary driver set. This is especially true in the server and corporate markets. Leading NIC makers such as 3Com, Xircom, Intel, and DEC now offer full NT NDIS-compliant driver support.

Added to this is the fact that NT ships with native support for over 100 of the most popular NICs, or variations that are supported indirectly. Many network cards are installable as the generic NE2000 type, so native support in NT is probably more on the order of hundreds of different cards.

Always make sure to check that a driver is available before you purchase your NICs. First, check for native NT drivers. Also check with the NIC manufacturer, as they very often have driver sets that exploit special features and performance options not obtainable in the generic versions.

Network Performance Issues

Physical performance on the network and in NICs depends mostly on the following three elements:

- The type of communications standard (Arcnet, Ethernet, etc.) and routing
- Computer interface bus width, such as ISA (16/32-bit) or PCI
- Onboard memory and controller to perform concurrent operations, relieving the burden on the main CPU(s)

Network Topology

Throughput, and therefore total performance, is just as dependent on the basic network topology and connection as it is on the computers and NICs that are employed within the network. If you install Ethernet 10BaseT, for instance, you are never going to be able to approach the network speeds that are required to ship uncompressed real-time video around the network.

Also of importance is how your network gets routed. If you are on a subnetwork where heavy traffic is routed across a gateway, you are likely to experience a performance bottleneck at that point (for more information on performance issues, see Appendix A).

Bus Width

You should always try to match the data path width of your NIC with that of the computer bus it will be used with. The best performance comes with a close match between the computer and NIC bus width, since this combination results in the most efficient movement of data across the adapter-to-bus boundary. The data path width will most likely be 16, 32, or possibly 64 bits wide.

Smart NICs

Adapters with built-in processors and memory can perform much better than "dumb" adapters. Smart NICs can employ their internal processing and memory power in maximizing throughput at the physical boundary by operating in full-duplex mode (both sending and receiving data at one time), and by buffering network data packets bound for, and coming from, the network.

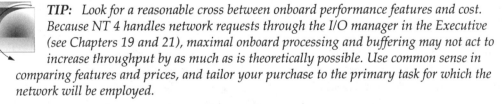

TIP: *Look for a reasonable cross between onboard performance features and cost. Because NT 4 handles network requests through the I/O manager in the Executive (see Chapters 19 and 21), maximal onboard processing and buffering may not act to increase throughput by as much as is theoretically possible. Use common sense in comparing features and prices, and tailor your purchase to the primary task for which the network will be employed.*

Installing the Network Driver

With NT, when you set up a network card in a computer, installation of the appropriate driver is almost always very simple. Using either the Setup program or the Network applet in the Control Panel, choose the name of the NIC from the list. The new network card driver will be automatically bound to all NDIS-compliant protocols currently running on the computer, and if any protocols are added later, they will also automatically be bound to the NIC's driver.

Choosing a Protocol

Microsoft provides eight networking protocols, out of the box, for use with NT:

- TCP/IP
- NWLink (IPX/SPX)
- NWLink NetBIOS (installed with other protocols—ancillary)
- NetBEUI
- Data Link Control
- Point to Point Tunneling
- Streams Environment
- AppleTalk

You must choose how to use one or more of these protocols on your network. The selections you make will depend on which protocols you need to support for compatibility with existing networks that you must link up with.

If you are building a LAN from scratch, and there are no preexisting conditions that must be met, all the better. The following sections discuss the uses, advantages, and disadvantages of each protocol listed.

What TCP/IP Offers

TCP/IP (Transmission Control Protocol/Internet Protocol), discussed in Chapters 11 and 25, was developed originally from networking protocol concepts that eventually became a Defense Advanced Research Projects Agency (DARPA) research project on interconnected networks. The principal advantages of TCP/IP are that it is in use by many millions of computers worldwide, and it was designed to be a routable protocol—able to cross gateways and network boundaries easily, able to operate on, and link together, a wide variety of computer architectures.

TCP/IP is actually a suite of protocols, each having its place in a scheme that provides a complete service set. It is the protocol that provides compatibility for a wide range of hardware and operating systems with the Internet, the worldwide collection of networks and gateways that has become so popular. TCP/IP is the default protocol for NT installations.

 NOTE: *Connection to the Internet is becoming increasingly important for businesses and individuals alike. From email to World Wide Web browsing, the Internet is now a must if you intend to do business or keep in touch with the extended world community. TCP/IP is the only network protocol that will enable you to connect your NT workstations and servers with this global network.*

SNMP Network Management for TCP/IP

Installing and using TCP/IP is no bed of roses. Because it allows so much latitude and functionality, it has been designed to be very configurable. There are strategies that you can use to minimize the impact of TCP/IP installation and operation overhead, and we'll look at them in depth in Chapters 11 and 12.

One important utility, allowing administrators to monitor and control TCP/IP remote hosts and gateways, is the Simple Network Management Protocol (SNMP). This utility is used widely to manage TCP/IP-connected computers, whether they are running NT, Unix, or another operating system. There are two parts to NT-SNMP: a service that runs on client machines that are to be administered (the SNMP agent), and an application that you use from an NT server, the SNMP management tool. SNMP management tools are also available from many third-party sources.

 NOTE: If you wish to set up the TCP/IP performance counters in Performance Monitor, as described in Chapter 7, you will also need to install the SNMP agent service on all target machines on your network.

Insider Info

SNMP was designed in the 1980s as an answer to common network management problems. SNMP allows for management of remote hosts by an administrator, using one of the available SNMP manager applications and an SNMP agent running on the target host or gateway. The mechanisms that SNMP employs are outwardly simple. SNMP exchanges network information by using special messages (known as *protocol data units* or PDUs). A PDU is a data object that contains variables with both titles and values. A set of objects that an SNMP-managed service or protocol uses is referred to as its management information base (MIB). SNMP employs these objects to monitor and manage a network. Special objects, called *traps*, are used to monitor network events such as computer reboots or shutdowns.

A strong advantage of SNMP is that it is widely used. This means that there is a great deal of support for this service. Major vendors of internetwork software and hardware such as bridges and routers design their products to support SNMP.

With TCP/IP and the SNMP service, a remote NT host can report its status to the SNMP manager application, or the SNMP manager can request this information from the remote host.

Pros and Cons of TCP/IP

When considering TCP/IP for your NT network, use the following list of advantages and disadvantages to help make your decision:

Advantages of TCP/IP	Disadvantages of TCP/IP
Allows interconnection with many different operating systems and computers. Supports LANs and WANs.	Not as fast as NWLink or NetBEUI for nonrouted LANs.
Provides automatic Internet connectivity.	Requires a great deal of setup and administrative overhead to maintain.
Provides routing support.	Requires independent name resolution schemes such as DNS (see Chapter 11).
Supports Windows Sockets 1.1/2.0.	No drawbacks.
Supports SNMP management.	Requires agent service on all managed machines; minor network overhead.
NetBIOS over TCP/IP support; allows, for instance, connection to Unix servers running Samba or other utilities.	Requires exacting setup overhead and management.
Allows connection-oriented (TCP) *and* connectionless (UDP) data broadcasts.	Data delivered by UDP can be lost or disregarded.

Mini-Glossary

MANAGEMENT INFORMATION BASE (MIB)   The SNMP and TCP/IP services use sets of objects known as management information bases (MIBs). A MIB is a collection of objects, defining the form and meaning of management messages, which variables a host must maintain, and the representation of these variables in management-system messages. Each managed service has its own set of objects, embodied in a MIB.

SIMPLE NETWORK MANAGEMENT PROTOCOL (SNMP)   A standard network management protocol used widely in NT, Unix, and other operating systems. It allows the transmission and reception of information and commands between a supervisory application and a managed resource. Using the SNMP agent service and TCP/IP, any NT computer can report status and events to an SNMP control application.

TRAP   An SNMP alert sent by a remote host running an SNMP agent. A trap reports an important system event, such as shutdown or possibly a security violation.

IPX/SPX The proprietary transport protocols used by Novell NetWare and generalized for use in NT as the NWLink protocol. The Sequential Packet exchange is Novell's implementation of SPP (Sequenced Packet Protocol). The Internetwork Packet exchange is a Novell NetWare protocol similar to IP (Internet Protocol).

DATA LINK CONTROL (DLC) A transport protocol defined by IBM. DLC is the IBM Systems Network Architecture layer responsible for transmission of data between two nodes over a physical link. It is mainly used to communicate with IBM mainframes and minicomputers, typically model 3270 controllers or AS/400 machines. In addition, NT can use DLC to communicate with network printers.

What NWLink IPX/SPX Offers

NWLink IPX/SPX is the NDIS-compliant NT version of the IPX/SPX protocol. IPX/SPX is used on Novell NetWare networks and is a principal protocol for use on Microsoft networking installations. NWLink is TDI compliant and has support for NetBIOS and Windows Sockets.

If you want to support easy integration of NetBIOS name resolution for Microsoft networking, using, for instance, Windows 95 clients, install NWLink along with the NetBIOS interface. Along with compatibility for NetWare, the NWLink IPX/SPX protocol can be your primary NT protocol for small, routable LANs.

NOTE: NT also provides further Novell NetWare services in the form of Client Services for NetWare (for workstations) and the Gateway Service for NetWare (for servers).

Use the following list to examine the pros and cons of installing NWLink IPX/SPX:

Advantages of NWLink IPX/SPX	**Disadvantages of NWLink IPX/SPX**
Supports Novell NetWare connectivity.	Used with NetBIOS name resolution broadcasts; slight overhead on NT networks.
Routable	Not as fast as NetBEUI for small LANs.
Seamlessly supports Microsoft networking for easy client integration.	Will not route over most ISP backbones.

What NetBEUI Offers

NetBEUI was developed in 1985 by IBM in response to a need for a small, fast network protocol in installations of less than about 200 computers. This meant that most insular

LANs could benefit from the adoption of NetBEUI. Many LANs still use this protocol as a primary connection mechanism today.

IBM optimized NetBEUI's design for very high performance, when used in these small LAN installations. NetBEUI is the fastest, yet least capable protocol shipped with NT today. However, it has its uses. For instance, if you are setting up a small LAN with the need to stream video across local computers, NetBEUI might be a good choice.

Use the following list of pros and cons to decide on an installation of NT-NetBEUI:

Advantages of NetBEUI	**Disadvantages of NetBEUI**
Optimized for small, local networks.	Will not route.
Little control packet overhead; best speed of all popular protocols for LAN use.	Is not suited for subnetwork or LAN-WAN use. Performance falls off rapidly as the number of users increases beyond theoretical limits.
Good error recovery.	In certain cases, can easily cause broadcast storms.
Small OS support overhead.	Limited connection potential.

Insider Info

NT's version of NetBEUI does not exhibit the limitations found in some older versions of the protocol. It is NDIS/TDI compliant and does not have a limitation on sessions/NIC, as did older versions. Also, NT-NetBEUI is capable of changing its performance characteristics on the fly.

NT-NetBEUI is actually a NetBIOS Frame (NBF) protocol. This is in contrast to older versions of the protocol which, because they were not NDIS and TDI compliant, were implemented as monolithic drivers. NT-NetBEUI (NBF) is a complete emulation of IBM NetBEUI and is totally compatible with all existing NetBEUI-compliant applications and services. However, since NetBEUI cannot be routed, you should plan to install NT-NetBEUI along with another routable protocol if you plan to use your network with a gateway or router, providing access to a wider area network.

What the Data Link Control Protocol Offers

DLC, the Data Link Control protocol, is designed to be a secondary connection protocol. It is primarily for use in an NT system that needs to access IBM mainframes or minicomputers, or needs to use the resources of a printer that attaches directly to the network cable instead of to a serial or parallel port on a print server. The DLC protocol functions with a direct relationship to the OSI model's Data Link layer, instead of using the Network and Transport layers as other NT protocols do.

To use Data Link Control, add the DLC protocol in addition to whatever protocols are in primary use on NT computers that need to communicate with IBM equipment or networked printers. The DLC protocol need only be installed on those computers that will actually use its services.

TIP: *If you are using DLC in support of a networked printer, you need only install DLC on the computer that will act as the print server.*

What the Point-to-Point Tunneling Protocol Offers

The Microsoft Point-to-Point Tunneling (PPTP) Protocol provides you with a mechanism for using a public data network, such as the Internet, to implement a private and secure virtual network between NT installations or compatible operating systems using PPTP. With the PPTP protocol, data encryption is standard, so privacy is assured, even though the primary connection mechanism is a public network. PPTP also encapsulates other protocols via TCP/IP. This technology can be used on a Remote Access Server connection to ensure privacy, even when dialups go through a public WAN and standard applications are being used.

Use the following list of pros and cons to decide on an installation of NT-PPTP:

Advantages of PPTP	Disadvantages of PPTP
Allows private virtual networks using public data channels.	Requires special TCP/IP setup.
Can encapsulate other protocols for use across a PPTP connection.	Using PPTP, general adapter (NIC) use with other protocols is disabled.
Provides strong encryption across public channels.	Must have PPTP-enabled connection on both sides of conversation.

What the STREAMS Environment Offers

The NT STREAMS environment installs the support and tools that you will need to port Unix-style STREAMS-based protocols and drivers to the NT platform. NT STREAMS also provides a runtime support environment for STREAMS network protocols and terminal drivers.

Support is possible for STREAMS-based protocols, such as TCP/IP and XTP, as well as X.25, AppleTalk, and specialized protocols from various vendors. See the NT

SDK and DDK for complete information on porting and programming to the NT STREAMS environment.

What the AppleTalk Protocol Offers

The NT AppleTalk protocol provides support for Apple Computer's network architecture and network protocols. If you intend to run Services for Macintosh on an NT server, or if you need to support a network that has Macintosh clients, functioning partially as an AppleTalk network, you will need to install this protocol.

Additionally, if you have Macintosh clients who will be sending documents to printers attached to an NT print server, or you want to enable NT clients to send documents to printers on an AppleTalk network, you must install the AppleTalk protocol.

LANA Numbers

Whenever NT 4 installs the IPX/SPX or NWLink with NetBIOS protocol, each binding of the protocol to a NIC will be assigned a LANA (local area network adapter) number. The LANA number for each binding is assigned automatically by NT and is used to identify a specific adapter on the LAN. Some NetBIOS applications require the proper use of LANA numbers, and NT allows you to override its default LANA number assignments.

Only change these LANA numbers if your NetBIOS application requires a specific number. To set LANA numbers, use the Control Panel/Network applet. (See Chapter 6 for more information on the Network applet in the Control Panel.)

Installing NICs, Protocols, and Services

Installation of NICs and networking protocols takes place in the Start/Settings/ Control Panel/Network applet. This applet is where you will both set up and maintain your network adapters, protocols, and services (see Figure 5-5). Although every different kind of setup has its own variations, you will always use the general procedures and guidelines set out in the sections that follow.

Installing a NIC

Open the Network applet, which will present a dialog with five tabs. Select the Adapters tab to see the Adapters dialog (see Figure 5-6).

Now choose the Add button, which will result in the display of the Select Network Adapter dialog (see Figure 5-7). Here, choose from among the list of supported NICs, and then choose OK. As an alternative, you can load a custom NIC driver from disk by choosing the Have Disk button and following the prompts.

The system will ask you to insert the NT distribution files into your CD-ROM, or as an alternative, you may then specify a network or hard disk location where NT can

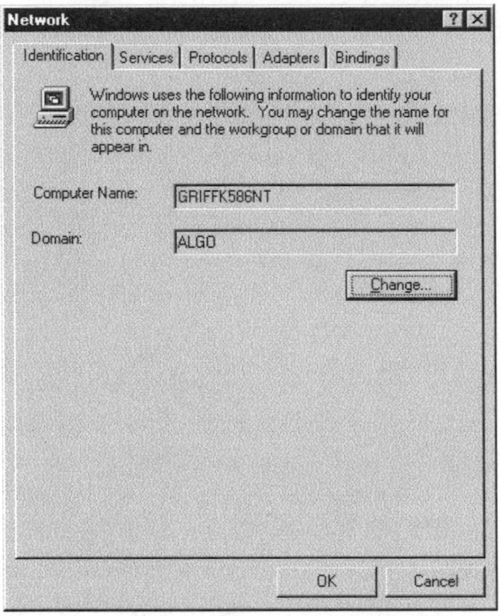

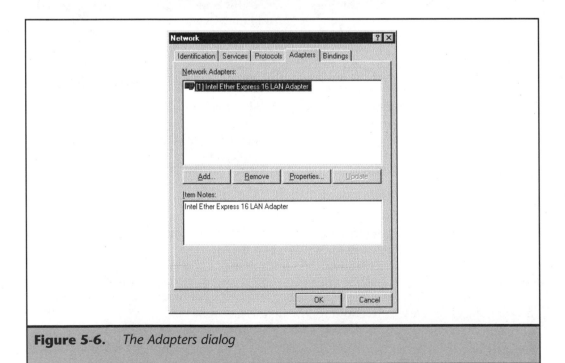

Figure 5-5. *The Control Panel/Network applet*

Figure 5-6. *The Adapters dialog*

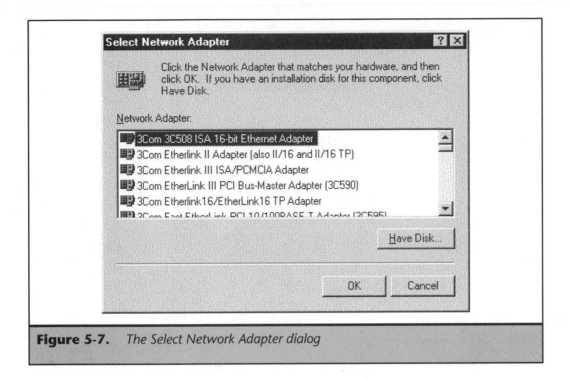

Figure 5-7. *The Select Network Adapter dialog*

find the support files that it will need to complete installation. After NT has copied
files and installed the NIC, close the Network applet dialogs and reboot. NT will
perform a bindings analysis before shutdown. Set any parameters or settings as
needed in the specific adapter dialog, selected by double-clicking the adapter's listing
in the Adapters dialog's Network Adapters list. You can also use this dialog to remove
an adapter from use.

Installing a Protocol

Open the Network applet and select the Protocols tab, which will result in a
presentation of the Protocols dialog (see Figure 5-8).

Now choose the Add button, which will result in the display of the Select Network
Protocol dialog (see Figure 5-9). Here, choose from among the list of supported
protocols, and then choose OK. As an alternative, you can load a custom protocol from
disk by choosing the Have Disk button and following the prompts.

The system will ask you to insert the NT distribution files into your CD-ROM, or
as an alternative, you may then specify a network or hard disk location where NT can
find the support files that it will need to complete installation. After NT has copied
files and installed the protocols, close the Network applet dialogs and reboot. NT will
perform a bindings analysis before shutdown. Set any parameters or settings as
needed in the specific protocol dialog, selected by double-clicking the protocol's listing

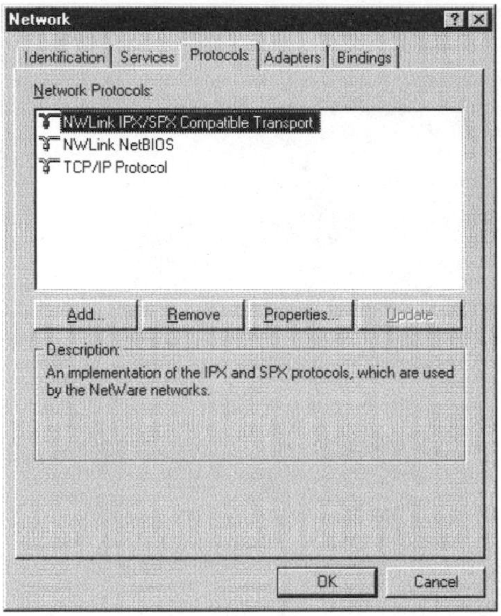

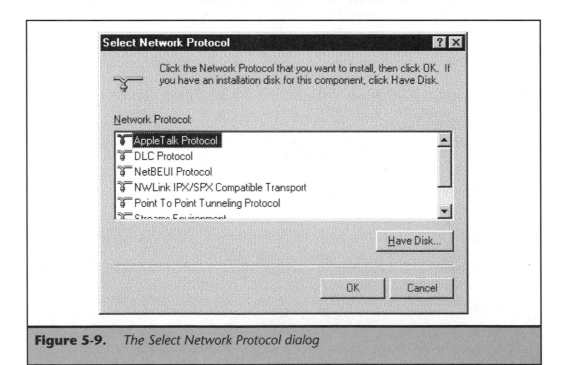

Figure 5-8. *The Protocols dialog*

Figure 5-9. *The Select Network Protocol dialog*

in the Protocols dialog's Network Protocols list. You can also use this dialog to remove a protocol from use.

Installing a Service

Open the Network applet and select the Services tab, which will result in a presentation of the Services dialog (see Figure 5-10).

Now choose the Add button, which will result in the display of the Select Network Service dialog (see Figure 5-11). Here, choose from among the list of supported services, and then choose OK. As an alternative, you can load a custom service from disk by choosing the Have Disk button and following the prompts.

The system will ask you to insert the NT distribution files into your CD-ROM, or as an alternative, you may then specify a network or hard disk location where NT can find the support files that it will need to complete installation. After NT has copied files and installed the service, close the Network applet dialogs and reboot. NT will perform a bindings analysis before shutdown. Set any parameters or settings, if any, as needed in the specific service dialog, selected by double-clicking the service's listing in the Services dialog's Network Services list. You can also use this dialog to remove a service.

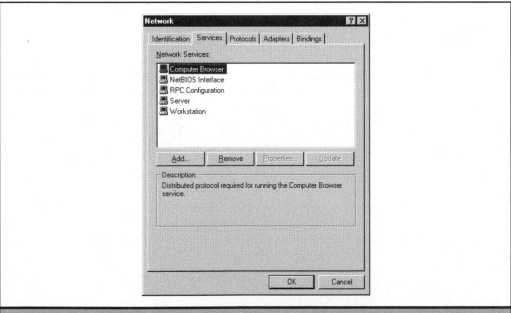

Figure 5-10. *The Services dialog*

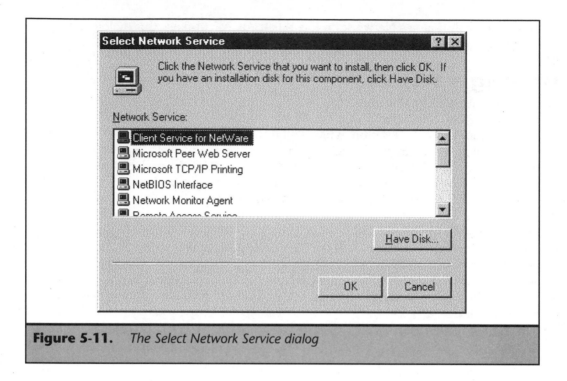

Figure 5-11. *The Select Network Service dialog*

What's Next

As we've seen in this chapter, NT offers many choices in installation, configuration, and administration. Don't be daunted by all this detail. It will all come together as we go through subsequent chapters—especially those in Part Three of this book. Stay with it, and soon you'll be up and running—the right way!

Now that we've gotten off to a good start with an overview of NT's architecture, setup procedures, interface, and networking issues, let's go on to Part Two of this book. This is where we'll be taking a closer look at the basics—the tools and utilities that help you get the most out of NT 4 on a day-to-day basis.

PART TWO

Learning the Basics

Chapter Six

The Desktop

All of the action in NT happens on or begins with the desktop. As a metaphor, the NT desktop is very much like the physical one that you would find in a typical office. Graphically, the NT desktop presents an overall view into the application and data files that are available from and stored on your computer and network resources. This chapter examines the individual elements of the desktop and looks at how you can manipulate and customize your desktop—setting functional preferences and machine parameters—by working with the various Control Panel applets.

The Graphical User Interface

The desktop, shown in Figure 6-1, presents a graphical user interface (GUI) that allows you to manipulate the various functions that your computer is capable of performing, such as running applications, manipulating files and data, connecting to a network, and so on. Traditionally, all of these functions have been available from a teletype-like command-line interface (and still are to some degree, both in NT's console interface—see Chapter 8—and in other modern operating systems).

NOTE: *NT can be partially manipulated from the command line in a console session, but as functionality and features increase and are improved, the GUI desktop interface becomes necessary and even more desirable. The console session user faces the daunting challenge of starting and running applications, setting parameters, and repeatedly typing long command lines; exactly the kind of situation that is so simplified by graphical user interfaces.*

Figure 6-1.   *The NT 4 desktop*

The entire desktop is designed to present information and let you work with data and files in a coherent, easy-to-manipulate environment. One of the principal design philosophies behind GUI desktops is the abstraction of data. Users do not need to know the exact command-line invocation for an application, and can easily identify a data set or subdirectory by its pictorial representation rather than some arcane alphanumeric name. GUIs are actually rooted in the early Xerox PARC technologies and have been tested and used to present a more natural user environment to users of Windows, Macintosh, Unix, and various other operating systems for the past 10 to 15 years.

Working with Icons

NT presents information in a hierarchical form, and the desktop represents data and executable application files—stored on disk or intrinsically available—by displaying little graphical pictures called icons. These icons represent a "black-box" view of the links and parameters needed to execute an application or retrieve data information from a target file. Desktop icons have the ability to instance and store these parameters so that they can represent not only the data or application that they point to but also the methods of invocation or association needed to work with the target file. We'll discuss all of this in depth later in this chapter.

Rather than type **start c:\myapps\cad\bin\ver50\new\patched\drawapp.exe/ T/nologo** at a console prompt, a user simply aims the mouse or trackball pointer at an abstract icon, clicks a button, and launches the application. This iconic representation carries with it all of the command-line invocation, parameters, and settings needed to start and run the target application. All of the parameters are, however, hidden and obscured, by design.

The Folder Metaphor

Another kind of desktop icon—specially reserved for use by NT—is a representation called a folder. The folder icon is a metaphor for the folders stored in an office file cabinet. Folders represent collections of files that are usually, but not necessarily, stored on disk in the traditional directory and subdirectory structure. When you click on a folder icon, the system doesn't run an application or retrieve data for manipulation. Rather, the folder opens to display iconic representatives of the files and applications that are logically grouped within that folder (see Figure 6-2). Folders can also contain other folders, and so on. Thus, the hierarchical nature of data storage in the FAT (File Allocation Table) or NTFS (New Technology File System) file systems is actually extended and enhanced by the use of folders.

The Start Menu

You activate the Start menu to do the following:

■ Start applications

- Make system settings
- Search for files and folders
- Work with system help
- Shut down or log off the computer

Insider Info

Because some of the desktop elements refer to and act on folders and files, there is not always a one-to-one relationship between desktop icons, target applications, or data files. The hierarchical nature of folder elements mimics the underlying disk volume structure only peripherally.

Folders can reflect the contents of a particular disk volume directory and can contain iconic shortcuts to applications or data in totally different logical and physical locations. This makes folders an extended, top-level representation of the directory/subdirectory hierarchical storage paradigm, as they depict more of an object-oriented, black-box view of reality than traditional storage structures, linking local and remote (network-connected) resources into a unified *use*, rather than *location*, view.

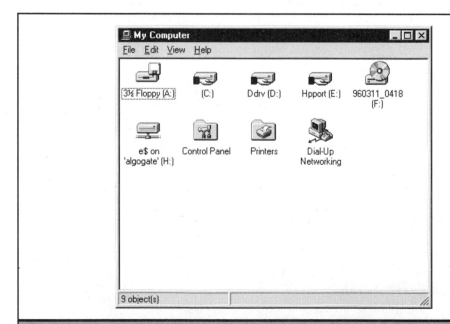

Figure 6-2. *Icons representing folders, applications, and data*

The Start menu (shown here) appears when you select the Start button and causes the desktop to display a series of (sometimes) cascading menus to appear just above the button. The main menu choices are examined in the following sections.

The Programs Option

When you select Programs from the Start menu, a list of menu items appears on a subordinate, cascading menu. The Programs menu, shown in Figure 6-3, displays application icons and several subsequent cascading menus, which represent folders of

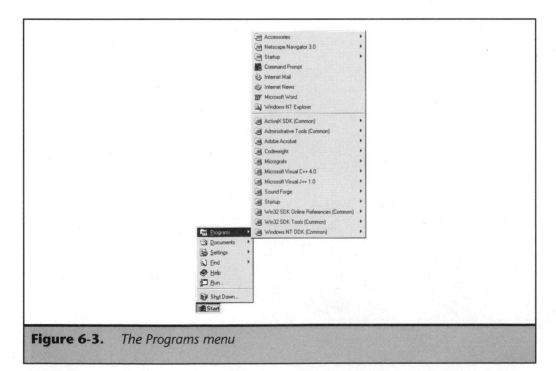

Figure 6-3. *The Programs menu*

executable programs and other registered programs and documents on your computer. The menus represent the available files using descriptive text, icons, and an arrow in the right margin of the menu item, directing the user to open the next submenu. To select a menu item, slide the mouse over each successively subordinate menu until you find the item you want to activate and execute. Click on that item and the application will run or the document will load into its viewer/editor.

The Documents Option

If you have recently worked with any documents—such as text files, word processing documents, spreadsheet files, or similar registered document types—their names appear in the Documents menu, as shown in Figure 6-4. This list of most recently used (MRU) documents provides you with a shortcut for reopening these files for further editing or manipulation. Instead of having to start the application again and then manually loading your document back into the program, you can simply choose the document from the Documents menu. NT automatically starts the application, loads the document immediately, and returns control to you, ready for editing, viewing, or other work.

The Settings Option

The Settings menu item will lead you to three further choices: Control Panel, Printers, and Taskbar. The dialog boxes and windows that each of these choices then show have setting choices or applets for changing systemwide settings and behavior and options

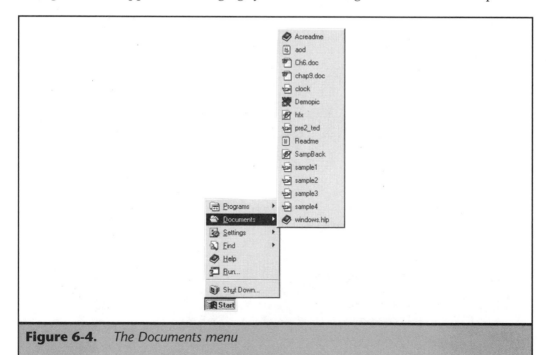

Figure 6-4.   *The Documents menu*

for installing both hardware and software. Because there are so many functions controlled by the Settings menu, the following sections explain them in depth.

The Control Panel

Select the Control Panel option on the Settings menu to see a window like the one shown in Figure 6-5. The many icons all relate to system configuration and control. These icons represent mini-applications, or *applets*, that allow you to set parameters, load software, configure software and hardware, and control the operation of various system and application services and preferences.

 NOTE: *The content of the Control Panel window is variable. In other words, if a certain service or application is installed on your computer, it may add its own applet to the Control Panel. If you don't have a multimedia device, for example, you may not see an applet that would be used to control that device unless you add the hardware and install its supporting software.*

The following sections go through the basic Control Panel applets one by one and cover their major functionality and interfaces. Almost all Control Panel applets provide specific help—pertaining to a specific device and manufacturer—so use the contextual help in Control Panel when dealing with aftermarket devices or third-party software drivers. They all have device-specific variations on the general descriptions offered here. There are slight differences in the applet mix in NT Workstation as opposed to NT Server.

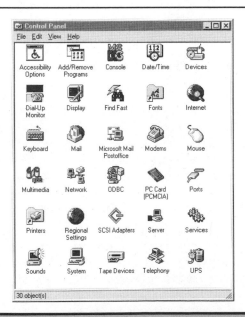

Figure 6-5. *The Control Panel*

ACCESSIBILITY OPTIONS   This applet controls options that are built into NT, but usually turned off, to make the operating system behave in a way that is more accessible to persons with disabilities. The tabbed dialog box includes options for the following:

- **Keyboard:** This dialog box contains three sections. StickyKeys, FilterKeys, and ToggleKeys all control how interaction with the keyboard can be customized to allow the keyboard to behave in different ways. StickyKeys allows the CTRL, ALT, DEL key combination to be pressed one at a time instead of simultaneously. FilterKeys allows you to adjust the sensitivity of the keyboard and its repetition rate so that keys can be pressed momentarily without registering and repetition rates can be slowed down. ToggleKeys allows the system to generate tones when the NUM LOCK, CAPS LOCK, and SCROLL LOCK keys are pressed.

- **Sound:** This dialog box contains two sections: SoundSentry and ShowSounds. SoundSentry allows NT to generate visual warnings when a system sound is generated. ShowSounds signals your applications, if capable, that they should use visual cues and captions instead of only sounds when signaling an action or error.

- **Mouse:** Using MouseKeys, you can direct the system to allow input that mimics mouse movement by using the numeric keypad on your keyboard. You can also control the actual pointer speed and toggle for the MouseKeys feature with this dialog box.

- **General:** This dialog box has three sections. The first two pertain to how NT resets the accessibility features and how it notifies you of their state. The third section, SerialKey, lets you attach an augmentative communication device for alternative input to a serial port.

ADD/REMOVE PROGRAMS   This dialog box has two tabbed sections: Install/ Uninstall and Windows NT Setup.

- **Install/Uninstall:** This dialog box has two sections. The first section really only consists of an Install button, prompting you to insert the software contained on CD or disk. Once you have done so, and then selected Install, the individual software setup's script or wizard will install and register the software. The second section is a list that shows all of the applications and controls registered as installed in your NT configuration. If you wish to add options to or remove one of these items, select it and press the Add/Remove button.

- **Windows NT Setup:** This dialog box allows you to add or remove basic NT operating system components. If, for instance, you need to add accessibility options to your NT installation, check the Accessibility Options box and choose OK or Apply. The reverse is also possible. To remove a basic NT OS option, uncheck the box beside the option you wish to remove and choose the OK or Apply button.

CONSOLE   This applet has many options and settings that affect the overall behavior of any console window that you open. To learn about specific settings and options, see Chapter 8.

DATE/TIME   This feature has the following options:

- **Date & Time:** This dialog box allows you to visually set the date and manipulate a clock to set the system time.
- **Time Zone:** Use this dialog box to set your time zone information. You do this by using the dropdown menu above the world map, telling NT what time zone you are in. Also, make sure you check the "Automatically adjust clock for daylight savings changes" if needed.

DEVICES   This applet lists all of the available device drivers in your system and their current state (enabled, disabled, started, etc.). It lets you control which device drivers are to be enabled, and at what point in the boot process they are to be started. You must have administrator permissions to work with the Devices applet.

- **Start:** This button will start (if possible) a stopped device when pressed.
- **Stop:** This button will stop a device when pressed.

CAUTION: Be careful using this feature. If you stop a device that is needed by NT, you can cause the computer to lock up or crash.

- **Startup:** When this button is chosen, a dialog box lets you set the startup type for the chosen device. The startup type controls when, in the boot process, a device is started.

NOTE: This is important since some devices need to be started first before others can start. Also, some devices need to start after others have initialized—for synchronization purposes.

The startup types include

Boot	Starts the device right after the computer boots into NT
System	Starts the device right after initial boot as the system starts
Automatic	Starts the device after the boot and system start

Manual	Lets you start the device programmatically or through the Devices applet
Disabled	Does not allow the start of the device by a user at all

- **HW Profiles:** This lets you configure a set of devices dependent on a hardware profile. You use hardware profiles to configure NT to use different sets of hardware, depending on these profiles for configuration. An example of using this feature would be when NT is installed on your portable computer. If you have a docking station at your office, with extra hardware capability, you would want at least two hardware profiles: one for on the road with minimal hardware, and one for the office with docking station and add-on hardware.

DIAL UP MONITOR   This property dialog box is used to display status and set options for dial-up modem-type networking. This is now effectively NT's client-side implementation of RAS, which has been changed and improved in NT 4. (See Chapter 13 to learn more about RAS, the Remote Access Service, and dial-up networking in general.) Dial-up Networking in NT 4 also lets you connect to non-RAS hosts using a plethora of options and protocols, which we will examine in Chapter 13.

- **Status:** This property dialog box displays various statistics about the device connection that you choose in the dropdown listbox at the top of the dialog box. It's only active after a connection is made.

- **Summary:** Use this dialog box to discover which remote dial-up devices are connected to which remote networks, and with which users. Remote connections to networks can be multilinked, using multiple devices. The Summary dialog box enumerates all active and inactive connections and devices installed on your computer.

- **Preferences:** Use this property dialog box to tell Dial-Up Networking how to display its status to you when active. You can play a sound based on dial-up events, include the status indicators in the taskbar, and control which indicators are displayed.

DISPLAY   This applet allows you to control almost all aspects of how your display hardware is configured. It also allows you to set wallpaper, screen savers, window coloring schemes, and Plus! features—such as icons for standard desktop elements, window display control, and screen font anti-aliasing to make the screen fonts appear smoother.

- **Background:** This contains two options for the desktop background, Pattern and Wallpaper. Pattern allows you to choose from several editable backgrounds, and Wallpaper allows you to choose from a set of bitmap images. Use Pattern if you want to paint the background with a uniform design, or Wallpaper if you want to display a bitmap. If you choose a wallpaper, you have two options: Center and Tile. Center displays the bitmap image in the middle of the desktop, and Tile enlarges the bitmap to cover the entire desktop surface.

- **Screen Saver:** This allows you to choose a screen saver to be activated after a controllable period of inactivity. Many optional screen savers are available from third parties, and NT ships with 12 different types.

- **Appearance:** You can pick the color scheme to use as a default for window elements such as the title bar and menu area colors. Control over separate elements is possible, and you can set custom colors for each supported element.

- **Plus!:** This dialog box allows you to select options that include the setting of icons for desktop elements such as the Recycle Bin. Also selectable are visual settings that include using large icons on the desktop, showing windows as they are dragged, anti-aliasing of screen fonts, multicolored icons, and tiling the desktop wallpaper.

- **Settings:** This most useful property dialog box lets you set up your display hardware—using customizable color depth and font size—and control the resolution and refresh rate for your display hardware and monitor. When you change resolutions, NT walks you through a test of the changes, letting you back out of them—if, for instance, the chosen resolution is not fully supported by your display monitor, which would render the display unreadable.

FONTS   This applet opens a window that displays, as icons, all of the installed and registered fonts that your NT system knows about. The window displays icons with their font names. When you select one of these icons, a secondary window opens to show you the complete graphical rendering of that font set. Use this applet to check on installed fonts and their capabilities.

INTERNET   This applet allows you to control aspects of operation in Microsoft Internet Explorer (IE). This is the same applet that is activated with the View I Options menu choice in Internet Explorer itself.

- **General:** Use this property dialog box to control the display of multimedia elements in Web pages. Turn off multimedia to speed up the display on a slow connection. Also controllable are the colors used to display windows in Internet Explorer and the colors used for following hyperlinks. You can also use this dialog box to select the toolbar elements displayed in the IE application.

- **Connection:** If you connect to the Internet through a proxy server (see Chapters 18 and 25), you can enter the proxy port addresses for each service in this dialog box.

- **Navigation:** You can use this dialog box to customize your startup page, aiming IE at any valid HTML document. Also use this dialog box to control the history list of visited sites kept by IE in its data cache.

- **Programs:** Use this dialog box to tell IE what mail and news applications to use when retrieving that data. Also use this dialog box to set preferences for viewers of certain file types, such as .BMP bitmaps, so IE can use those viewers when displaying Internet content. This dialog box also allows you to set IE as your default browser application.

- **Security:** Use this dialog box to control three different security-related aspects of the IE browser. First, use the section entitled "Content advisor" to set Ratings filters so that material labeled with higher ratings cannot be downloaded by children. Also, use the section on certificates to obtain or use signed digital certification. This option is used to positively identify you when transacting business on the Internet. Last, you can use this dialog box to control what kinds of "active" content, such as ActiveX controls (see Chapter 26), can be downloaded and run by IE.

- **Advanced:** Use this property dialog box to control settings and options relating to how IE warns you about receiving and sending data that may be a security threat, how temporary files are used and stored, and how certain elements of Web pages are displayed.

KEYBOARD This applet allows you to set options for how the keyboard responds, which character set it's mapped to, and what kind of keyboard is attached.

- **Speed:** Use this dialog box to set the amount of time it takes before a held-down key begins to repeat (move the Repeat delay slider) and to adjust the speed at which the characters repeat (move the Repeat rate slider). Also use it to control the on-screen cursor blink rate.

- **Input Locales:** Use this dialog box to select a mapping scheme for the keyboard. In scenarios where a foreign keyboard mapping must be used, this is the property dialog box that allows you to set that mapping relationship.

- **General:** Use this drop-down list to select the kind of keyboard that you have attached to your computer. In some cases, you may have more than one kind of keyboard. This dialog box is used in case you have to make that choice.

MAIL AND MICROSOFT MAIL POST OFFICES Use these applets to control how Microsoft Exchange/Mail preferences are administered on the local computer. It controls user preference settings and administers users' mailboxes, passwords, and so on. The main functions of these applets have to do with setting up mailboxes for different users who might have access to a workstation. Maintenance functions and options are beyond the scope of this chapter, and you should refer to the Exchange or Microsoft Mail documentation for complete operation instructions.

MODEMS Use this applet to install and administer modems for use with Dial-Up Networking (see Chapter 13), the Hyperterminal application, and applications such as voice mail that use telephony features. When installing or adding a modem, this applet will start an installation wizard that can automatically detect your modem, or allow you to choose one from a list of known modems. The wizard will also assign a COM port for use with this modem.

■ **Modem configurations:** After a modem is installed, you can use the Modem Administration dialog box to edit your choice, to delete it, or to set properties for it. The General tab of the Properties dialog box allows you to enter the maximum connect speed and speaker volume for the modem. The Connection tab can be used to set the hardware connection preferences for the COM port in use. Such options as data bits, parity, and stop bits are controllable from here. Also controllable are call preferences such as waiting for a dial tone and canceling the call after trying to connect for a number of seconds.

■ **Advanced modem settings:** The Advanced button opens another dialog box that lets you set advanced options to control flow and error control, as well as data compression. Any extra setting that may need to be used with a particular modem can be entered here, and if you want a log of modem activity for troubleshooting, check the "Record a log file" option box.

Insider Info

In many cases, new or unregistered modem types cannot be directly configured through the standard modem setup wizard. If you find yourself in this spot, you can use the Advanced property dialog box on the Modem Properties dialog box to overcome many problems.

For example, say you have a Motorola BitSurfR Pro ISDN modem that you wish to configure NT 4 to use. If there is no entry in the NT modem database for the BitSurfR Pro (and so the wizard will not detect it), first mark the "Don't detect my modem; I will choose it from a list" check box in the Add Modem wizard. Second, pick the closest manufacturer and modem on the list. In this case, a Motorola BitSurfR. Because these two models are sufficiently different to cause problems in exact setup, and if you have to use V120 or Multilink PPP protocols to connect to a host, you would normally be out of luck. However, using the Modem Properties/Connection tab in the Advanced property dialog box after an installation session, you can enter the proper initialization string into the Extra settings edit field, something like

    AT&F&C1&D2\Q3%A2=95@B0=2%A4=1

This gets sent out to the modem after any NT-initiated modem setup, so your hardware is then set up correctly, no matter how the internal NT script sent its initialization parameters.

MOUSE   You use this option as follows:

- **Buttons:** Use this dialog box to configure the primary action button on your mouse. If you are right-handed, the default would be the left mouse button. Also, use this dialog box to configure and test the double-click speed for activating applications.

- **Pointers:** This dialog box allows you to choose pointer schemes and individual pointers for each type of mouse pointer and hourglass that can be displayed.

- **Motion:** Use this dialog box to set the acceleration or pointer speed. This is also used for setting the Snap to Default option, which positions the mouse cursor on the default action button when a dialog box is displayed.

- **General:** If you change mouse hardware, you should use this dialog box to change drivers and specifications for the installed hardware.

MULTIMEDIA   The multimedia Control Panel settings work in the following ways:

- **Audio:** This dialog box is used to select volume settings and preferred playback and recording devices for multimedia files. For recording, the default quality (digitization frequency) is also selectable.

- **Video:** This dialog box is used to control how video is displayed on playback—in a window or full screen. The default is to play back video in a window.

- **MIDI:** This dialog box allows you to select options for mapping the MIDI output to a physical device. Usually, this device has one of two outputs: an internal router that plays MIDI over the multimedia adapter's speaker output, or an MPU-401-compatible MIDI output port that routes MIDI to a cable output for use with an external keyboard or synthesizer. The second option on this dialog box, "Custom configuration," allows you to map each MIDI output channel to either the internal or external outputs individually, or to selectively disable channels altogether.

- **CD Music:** This property dialog box allows you to assign or change a drive letter, associated with the CD-ROM drive, and to set the electronic volume level for the CD-ROM drive's headphone jack output, if available.

- **Devices:** The Devices dialog box is the most useful and complicated property dialog box for working with multimedia devices. Since this section is so variable and is different for most installations, it is covered here only in the most generic sense. The properties listed here cover all facets of the multimedia devices installed on your computer. Every driver interface, whether for software support or as a hardware driver, is enumerated in this dialog box. When you expand a category, you will see the installed device listed, if any. You can then double-click on the item or use the Properties button to call up the dialog box for setting the parameters of a particular device or driver. When the dialog box is displayed, it may or may not have a Settings button enabled. If it does, you can move further into this device's configuration dialog box by choosing that Settings button. If the device has hardware settings, you will find them here. Some devices and drivers have software configuration controls embedded in the dialog box, and some devices are self-configuring. A typical dialog box for setting sound card parameters is shown in Figure 6-6.

NETWORK   This applet covers all facets of setup, administration, and operation for all network interfaces and services. Whether you are configuring TCP/IP for a network interface card (NIC) or you are installing the Remote Access Service (RAS) manager for Dial-Up Networking, the various dialog boxes contained in this applet are used.

■   **Identification:** Selecting the tab that brings up this property dialog box will result in the display of the current computer name—the name you have given to identify this computer on the network—and the workgroup or domain membership. If your computer is registered as a member of an NT domain, the domain name is displayed here. If you have set up this computer to belong only to a local workgroup, the workgroup name appears. When you join a domain, a valid NT machine account must exist on the domain controller for your workstation. If it already exists, it must be reset or deleted so your workstation can rejoin that domain with its current profiles, which are used to form a valid domain machine account. In the dialog box that is shown when you choose the Change button on the Identification dialog box, you can enter a workgroup or domain name. You can also add your machine to the domain by creating a new account on the domain controller and supplying a valid account name and password (valid in terms of an account on the domain controller), which has sufficient permission to add your machine's account.

■   **Services:** This property dialog box is variable in its content, depending on the network services installed on your computer. The dialog box lists all of the services that are configured for use, and depending on what service you choose within the list, may display—by choosing the Properties button—a configuration or information dialog box for settings and parameters. As an example, look at the dialog box shown in Figure 6-7, which is displayed when Remote Access Service (RAS) is selected.

■   **Protocols:** This dialog box displays the currently installed network protocols. The setup dialog boxes for entering or changing parameters for each of the installed protocols are available by selecting a protocol from the list and then choosing the Properties button. As an example, the dialog box for TCP/IP settings is shown in Figure 6-8. The TCP/IP example then displays further property dialog boxes that allow you to set TCP/IP parameters for your installation. (See Chapters 11 and 12 for further information on TCP/IP.)

■ **Adapters:** This property dialog box displays any and all network interface cards (NICs) that you have installed. By choosing Properties, further dialog boxes may appear, giving you the chance to set hardware parameters—such as IRQs and I/O addresses—for each of the NICs that you have installed. Some NICs may be totally self-configuring, so you cannot set them in the Properties portion of this dialog box.

■ **Bindings:** This property dialog box lists connections between network protocols, services, and NICs. You can control the order in which your computer looks for connections and information on the network by adjusting the hierarchy displayed in this dialog box. Only users and administrators should change the order of these items. As an example of using this dialog box, one might want the RAS to have first shot at trying for information when the network is polled, if this installation was running on a portable computer.

ODBC   This applet lets you configure data sources and set options for the ODBC drivers used in your installation. A data source is a set of resources used to work with data. It may be as simple as a collection of database files, or it may be as complete as the specification of a database server application, its server files, and the network connections that must be made for access to the server. These data sources are set on a per-user basis. If you wish to set a global resource, do so by choosing the System DSN

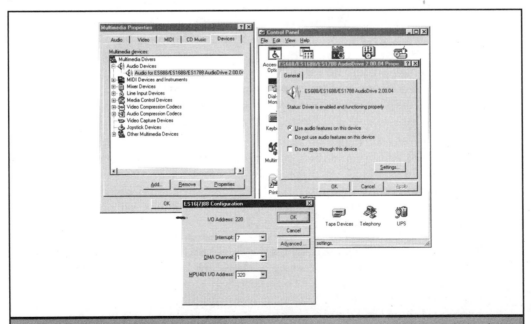

Figure 6-6.   *Configuring a sound card in the Multimedia applet's Devices dialog box*

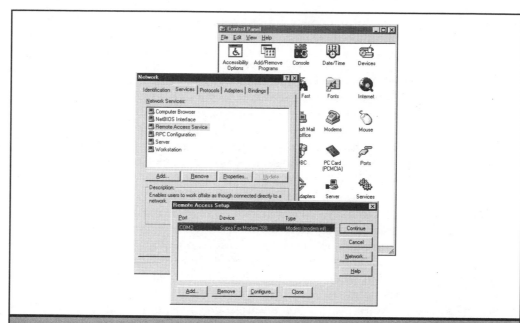

Figure 6-7. *The Network applet's Services dialog box and properties box for Remote Access Service*

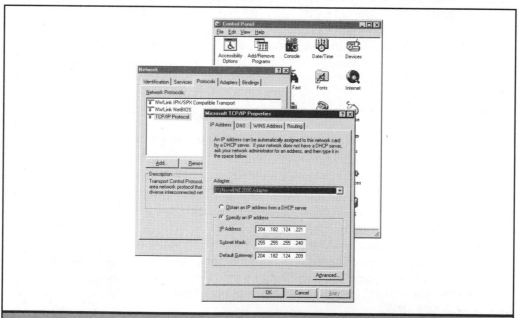

Figure 6-8. *The Protocols dialog box and settings box for TCP/IP*

button and entering the information for the data source there. Also included in this applet is a browsing tool, shown when you choose the Drivers button, that allows you to see which ODBC drivers are installed, along with their version levels.

PC CARD (PCMCIA)   This applet allows you to control setup and system settings pertaining to the use of PCMCIA-type hardware. Typically, a PCMCIA card has user-specific settings along with some global settings, such as I/O addresses, that need to be controlled. Use this applet to make changes to a card's settings or to configure a new card for use. Typically, this applet is not present in most installations. Only when a PCMCIA controller is recognized during setup, as in a notebook computer, do you have access to this Control Panel applet.

NOTE: The support for PCMCIA card slots in NT 4 is just starting to mature. It is only possible to use certain PCMCIA controllers, and many of the newer notebook computers are not supported yet. If you have PCMCIA equipment that must be supported, be sure to check with your manufacturer before planning your NT 4 deployment, since it is always six months to a year before drivers and support for the newest features and chipsets come online. Additionally, third parties are now working on, or have released, NT 4 versions of their PCMCIA card manager programs, so you may want to check with your supplier for information on this type of support solution (bypassing NT's built-in support altogether).

PORTS   This applet allows you to control systemwide settings for the serial or COM ports installed in your computer. The ports list in this applet's dialog box shows the available COM ports and allows you to set communications parameters for these ports. Parameters include Baud Rate, Data Bits, Parity type, number of Stop Bits, and Flow Control. Flow Control can be Xon/Xoff, Hardware, and None. Use Hardware for most modems and direct serial connections, Xon/Xoff for most printers, and None for special purposes only.

NOTE: If you have a mouse connected to a COM port, you should not adjust settings for that port, and it may not even appear as a resource in the ports list.

PRINTERS   This applet is actually mirrored in two other sites within the NT desktop. You can also find it in the main Settings menu at the same level as the Control Panel menu choice and as an item in the My Computer window opened from the My Computer icon. The Printers window and its contents, opened from this applet icon, display installed and network-connected printers for your computer. Also available is the Add Printer icon, which opens the Add Printer wizard for installing new printers. For complete instructions on administering printers or using the Add Printer wizard, see Chapter 24.

REGIONAL SETTINGS   The uses for this applet are as follows:

- **Regional Settings:** You can control the way dates, currency, and numbers are displayed by choosing Regional Settings in the dropdown listbox within this property dialog box. You can set your choice as the default locale by checking the Default box.

- **Number:** Use this property dialog box to set individual facets of the display method for quantities represented by numbers. Measurement systems, numbers displayed to the right of a decimal point, and the display of leading zeros are just a few of the settings available here.

- **Currency:** Use this property dialog box to set individual facets of the display method for quantities represented in monetary units. Display and digit-grouping symbols are just a few of the settings available here.

- **Time:** Use this property dialog box to set individual facets of the display method for quantities representing time—24 hour, forms of AM and PM, and the like.

- **Date:** Use this property dialog box to set individual facets of the display method for quantities representing dates. Calendar systems and long or short date styles can be set here.

- **Input Locales:** This lists and allows you to add locales—with display and keyboard mappings—to be loaded each time you start your computer. It's also used to set the key sequences for switching between these loaded locales.

SCSI ADAPTERS   The SCSI adapter features function as follows:

- **Devices:** This lists the installed adapters and enumerates the physical devices attached to each. Choose the Properties button to show individual adapter and device settings and information. For an adapter, the properties shown include CardInfo, Driver, and Resources (physical settings). For an attached device, such as a hard disk drive, the properties shown include General (device manufacturer information) and Settings (the parameters pertaining to the device's relationship with the adapter).

- **Drivers:** This lists installed drivers and their running state, and lets you add or delete drivers.

SERVER   This applet and its associated dialog boxes work in the following ways:

- **Usage Summary:** This portion of the Server dialog box displays a summary of connections and resources being used on the computer.

- **Users:** When this button is pressed, a dialog box is shown that lets you view a list of all the users connected to your computer over the network. If you select a user, you can view a list of all open resources for that user. The Users dialog box also allows you to disconnect one or all users connected to the computer.

■ **Shares:** When this button is pressed, a dialog box is shown that lets you view a list of the computer's shared resources. You can also select a single resource and get a list of all the connected users. This dialog box also lets you disconnect one or all users from the computer.

■ **In Use:** When this button is pressed, a dialog box is shown that lets you view a list of open shared resources and enables you to close one or all resources.

■ **Replication:** When this button is pressed, a dialog box is shown that lets you administer directory replication. For a workstation, you can only import directories and files from other computers. Servers can specify the path to user logon scripts, export copies of directories and files for storage on other computers, or import directories and files from other computers.

■ **Alerts:** When this button is pressed, a dialog box is shown that lets you view and administer a list of users and computers that are notified of an administrative alert generated by the local computer. Types of alerts include security and permissions, printer problems, and power loss or shutdown.

SERVICES This applet, shown in Figure 6-9, lets you list the services available to you in NT. It also lets you configure those services. The configuration involves enabling, disabling, starting, and stopping the boot sequence, as well as controlling the point in

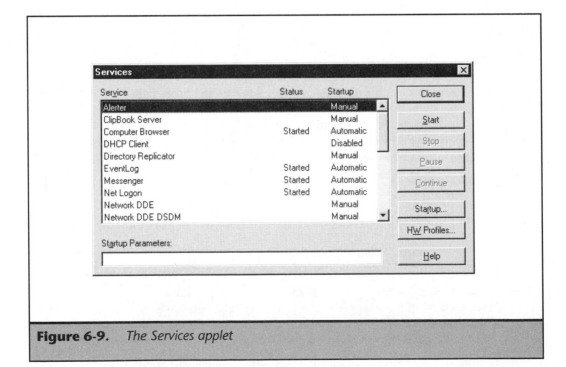

Figure 6-9. *The Services applet*

the boot sequence at which a service starts up. You can also assign services to hardware profiles to control which profile attempts to use a service.

The default services that ship with NT and their explanations are listed here. In addition to these default services, other services appear in the list depending on what network protocols and such have been installed.

- **Alerter:** This service sends notifications of administrative alerts originating on the local computer to selected users and computers. It works in conjunction with the Messenger service.

- **ClipBook Server:** This service enables functionality in the ClipBook Viewer, allowing ClipBook pages to be accessed remotely.

- **Computer Browser:** This service maintains a periodically refreshed list of computers, providing the list to applications and services that request it.

- **Directory Replicator:** This service replicates directories and files between computers.

- **Event Log:** This service supports event logging for system, security, and applications categories.

- **Messenger:** This service supports the Alerter service, and direct administration, as a message transceiver.

- **Net Logon:** In NT Workstation, this service provides pass-through authentication of domain account logons. In NT Server, this service carries out authentication of domain account logons and synchronizes the domain's security database between the primary domain controller and other NT servers (which may act as backup domain controllers).

- **Network DDE:** This service handles the protocol layer and security for dynamic data exchange (DDE) over the network.

- **Network DDE DSDM (DDE Share Database Manager):** This service handles shared DDE conversations for the Network DDE service (NDDE).

- **NT LM Security Support Provider:** This service handles security for programs using remote procedure calls (RPCs) other than through named pipes.

- **Remote Procedure Call (RPC) Locator:** This service provides RPC name services by managing the RPC name service database to distributed applications.

- **Remote Procedure Call (RPC) Service:** This service implements the RPC subsystem for NT.

- **Schedule:** This service manages execution scheduling for commands and applications that are set up to run at a specified time and date.

- **Server:** This service implements sharing for files, printers, and named pipes. It also provides ancillary RPC support.

- **Spooler:** This service implements the print spooler, providing spooling services to the printer subsystem.

- **UPS:** This service supports the use of an uninterruptible power supply. The service can be set to provide alerts and controlled shutdown and reboot of the computer system.

- **Workstation:** This service implements local network connectivity and client-side communications functions.

SOUNDS Use this applet to assign sounds to program events. The applet's dialog box is divided into three sections: Events, Sound, and Schemes. This is analogous to the sounds design in Windows 95, in which individual sounds can be applied to certain events, and whole "schemes" of sounds, assigned to the popular events in NT, can be assigned and saved as a set.

To set a sound for an event, select the event you want to assign a sound to in the Events list. Next, in the Sound list, select the sound you want NT to generate when the event is generated. You can browse for a sound to assign, and with the Preview portion of this dialog box, you can play a sound before assigning it to an event. Repeat this process for all events that you wish to assign sounds to. You can use your own sounds in the form of .WAV files if you want to. Lastly, you can save a set of your event-to-sound settings by selecting Save As in the Schemes portion of the dialog box, providing a name, and selecting the OK button. Your scheme appears in the Schemes list and is applied whenever you log on.

SYSTEM The System Properties dialog box has tabs that allow you to change systemwide settings for such things as environment variables, performance and paging file usage, and startup or shutdown options. The General tab of the System Properties dialog box is shown in Figure 6-10. The categories are as follows:

- **General:** This dialog box is for information purposes only. It provides the NT version, registration information, and your computer's vital statistics.

- **Performance:** This dialog box allows you to control the priority boost for foreground applications and the virtual memory, or paging file, settings for your computer. Use the application priority boost slider to control how much of a priority boost, and hence what tasking balance, the foreground application gets. This makes applications that have focus respond slightly faster than applications doing work in the background. For a file server, you might want to decrease foreground boost slightly. Selecting the Virtual Memory/Change button displays a dialog box with current paging file assignments. You can set these according to the recommendations or to a value that you have calculated to be optimal. Also, you can control the upper limit on how large you want the registry to grow.

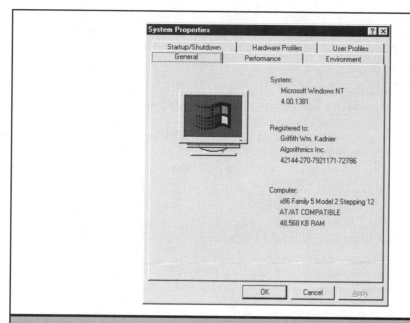

Figure 6-10. *The System Properties dialog box, General tab*

TIP: *NT installs a conservatively-sized, single-paging file on the system drive. It is a good rule of thumb to allow for a paging file to exist on each primary physical hard disk. By doing this, you can increase paging efficiency and decrease swapping time. For instance, if you have two physical hard disk drives, assign a swap file to both C: and D:—the first partitions on each physical disk—and make each of their size limits at least as large as the default that was installed by NT. (See Appendix A for more information on this technique.)*

■ **Environment:** This dialog box displays the environment variables that are currently set for both the system as a whole (those that don't change on a per-user basis) and the variables that are only in effect for the currently logged-on user. Environment variables are used by applications and services, and there may be times when you need to edit, delete, or add them. To do so, select the variable you want to work with in either list, and its name and value appear in the edit fields at the bottom of the dialog box. You can edit the values and select Set to save, or you can select Delete to erase that variable from the list.

■ **Startup/Shutdown:** Whether you have another operating system installed or not, you boot into NT using the Multi-boot menu. This menu displays at least two choices: NT Workstation (Server) 4, and NT Workstation (Server) 4 (VGA mode). You might also have selections for other operating systems. These selections are available in the Startup dropdown listbox. Select the choice you wish to have as default and also enter a value to wait before using this choice. Under Recovery Options, you can select an action to take when NT enters the Stop mode—where a critical error has been encountered and the system must be shut down. You can choose to log an event, send an alert to other computers, write debugging information to a file, or just automatically reboot.

- **Hardware Profiles:** When multiple configurations of your hardware exist—such as with a portable computer that may have an extended docking station with extra hardware—you can configure NT to boot with different hardware profiles, depending on what is attached. Use this dialog box to edit hardware profiles and also to control booting-time waits for profile selection.

- **User Profiles:** User profiles contain all of the settings relating to your user logon personality and all of the settings for your customized desktop (which icons are displayed, colors, etc.). You can choose to have a single user profile that "roams" the network and is used at each workstation you log on to, or you can have multiple local-user profiles. Use this dialog box to control how you want to use your user profiles, and whether you want a single-roaming or multiple-individual profile.

TAPE DEVICES   This applet allows you to use NT's backup facility to back up a local or network-connected resource. Use this dialog box to list and configure, or search for, installed tape devices.

- **Devices:** This dialog box shows the currently configured tape devices available on your machine. Use the Detect button to search for a device and install it.

- **Drivers:** This dialog box lists installed drivers for tape devices on your machine. If you wish to add a driver, select the Add button here and follow the prompts. This dialog box can also be used to remove and uninstall a driver.

TELEPHONY   NT uses telephony devices to interface with and use standard driver interface routines for modems and related devices. In order to use Dial-Up Networking or the Phone Dialer application, you must tell NT a few basic things about how it should set parameters for its telephony drivers.

- **My Locations:** Use this dialog box to set basic parameters that tell NT where you are and how you dial out from your location. Included are area code, physical location, dialing prefixes, calling card parameters, call waiting disablement, and whether you need tone or pulse dialing. Telephony drivers and applications use this information to control how they interface with the physical telephone network.

- **Telephony Drivers:** This dialog box lists the installed drivers that relate to telephony functions, giving you a chance to add drivers that you may receive from software suppliers or to remove old or unused drivers. Selecting a driver in the list may also enable the Properties button, and selecting this results in the display of the specific properties dialog box for that component.

UPS It is always preferable to have an uninterruptible power supply (UPS) attached to your NT installation. A UPS is much more than a backup power source for smooth shutdown of a system when primary power has failed. It can smooth spikes and filter the power, and in certain security or quality of service installations, it may be necessary because of regulations or parametric requisites. Most UPSs have a serial-line interface, which allows them to control and be controlled by an NT COM port. The UPS applet helps you set up the UPS service—a control application for UPS operation.

- **UPS Configuration:** This dialog box, shown in Figure 6-11, lets you configure parameters for the UPS interface and what signals it works with. The UPS Configuration portion of this dialog box allows you to set parameters for UPS operation, the COM port to use, and—depending on which parameters you check or uncheck—you may be asked to enter information in the sections entitled UPS Characteristics and UPS Service. See the NT help file and your UPS manufacturer's recommendations for specific information.

- **Execute Command File:** This option allows you to run a command file or application before the system is shut down due to a power failure. The command must execute within 30 seconds to close all network connections and return.

- **UPS Configuration:** Depending on how you have chosen options in the UPS Configuration section, you may be asked to specify battery life and recharge time here. Enter the battery life per charge and the recharge time per minute of runtime.

- **UPS Service:** Depending on how you have chosen options in the UPS Configuration section, you may be asked to specify the time between an initial power failure and alert message and the delay time between successive alerts.

Printers

The Settings menu's Printers choice is relatively straightforward compared to the variety of the Control Panel. This menu choice results in the display of a window that contains icons representing the printers you have installed or the printers available to you over a network connection. Also available is the Add Printer icon, which opens the Add Printer wizard for installing new printers.

NOTE: *For complete instructions on administering printers or using the Add Printer wizard, see Chapter 24.*

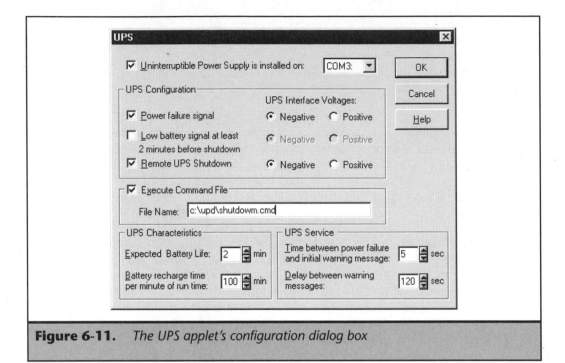

Figure 6-11. *The UPS applet's configuration dialog box*

Taskbar

Choosing Taskbar in the Settings menu results in the display of the Taskbar Properties dialog box (see Figure 6-12). This dialog box allows you to work with settings that pertain to the way the taskbar and its icons display.

NOTE: See "Using the Taskbar," a little later in the chapter for more information about the taskbar.

TASKBAR CONTROLS   You can control whether the taskbar is always shown on top of a window and whether it automatically hides or recedes to the bottom of the screen when not needed. You can also control the size of the icons shown in the taskbar and whether the system clock is shown.

THE START MENU PROGRAMS TAB   Another tab on the dialog box, Start Menu Programs, allows you to customize your Start menu and clear the Documents MRU list. To add or remove an item, select the appropriate button. The Advanced button displays a complete enumeration of the Start menu and allows you to navigate it so that you can see and edit menu items displayed in their proper hierarchy. The Advanced option uses Explorer, discussed in Chapter 9.

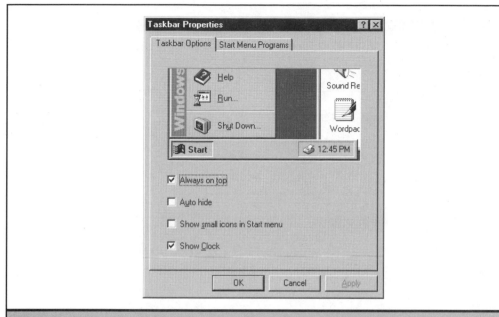

Figure 6-12. *The Taskbar Properties dialog box*

The Find Option

The third option on the Start menu is Find. By choosing this option, followed by a subordinate command, you can search for specific files or folders or for a specific computer attached to your network using its computer name.

The Files or Folders Item

When you select the Find All Files item from the Find menu, the Find dialog box appears. It lets you search for files or folders on your local computer or on a shared computer connected on the network. The three tabs on the dialog box use different search criteria to control the search.

NAME & LOCATION   From this tab, you can enter the name of a file that you are searching for. The name may include wildcards if you don't know the full name, as shown in Figure 6-13. For instance, typing **mydoc*.*** would find all files starting with *mydoc* and ending with any legal filename characters and any extension name. From this tab, you also control where you want to search for these files. Enter the name of the disk volume or drive letter you wish to perform the search on. You can also search on connected network resources. Use the dropdown listbox or Browse button to find a network resource or subdirectory. You can also search subdirectories by checking the "Include subfolders" option in the dialog box.

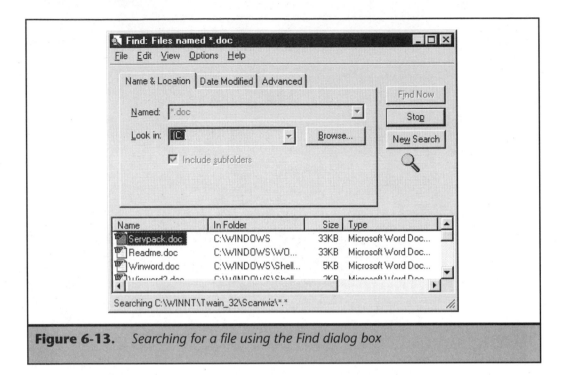

Figure 6-13.   *Searching for a file using the Find dialog box*

DATE MODIFIED   From this tab, you can control search criteria relating to date and time. You can enter a range of time in which the files were created, or you can specify that you wish to search for files that were created during a previous period of days or months. The default time criteria is *all files*.

ADVANCED   From this tab, shown in Figure 6-14, you can enter criteria pertaining to the type of file you wish to search for. Enter an extension type such as **.exe** or **.doc**. You can also search for files that contain a word or phrase by entering the data into the "Containing text" field. Finally, you can limit your search to files within a specific size range by entering the size criteria in the "Size is" fields.

The Find Dialog Box Menus

Across the top of the Find dialog box, the menu items that pertain to searches include the File and Options menus, where you can save the results of a search, open folders that you have found through a search, and control the case sensitivity of a textual search.

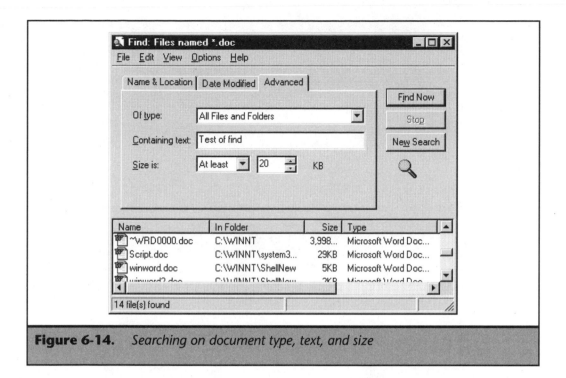

Figure 6-14. *Searching on document type, text, and size*

The Help Option

NT 4's help system allows you to look through the main table of contents, search for a keyword, or find a subject by looking for words that might be contained in a particular subject's help text. You choose how you wish to use system help by selecting a tab on the Help Topics dialog box to denote the help method you wish to employ.

The first time you use a help file, NT creates an index of keywords with which it performs searching and matching, as shown in Figure 6-15. Help asks if you want to maximize search capabilities, minimize disk usage, and so on. You should always choose to maximize search capabilities—unless you are short on free disk space—since this creates a larger cross-reference file.

The Run Option

Just like the old-style command-line interfaces, the Run dialog box, accessed from the Start menu, allows you to enter a command line directly, without having to be in a console window.

You can type in the path and name of an application or batch file—along with any options, switches, or parameters—as if you were issuing this command from the console prompt. You can start a DOS, Win16, Win32, OS/2, or POSIX application in this way. The dropdown listbox in the Run dialog box contains a list of the most recently used Run commands, which you can reselect.

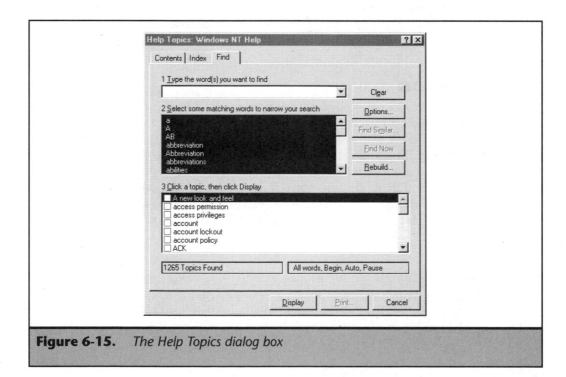

Figure 6-15. *The Help Topics dialog box*

The Shut Down Option

The last item on the Start menu switches NT to a secure desktop and displays the Shut Down Windows dialog box, which contains several choices.

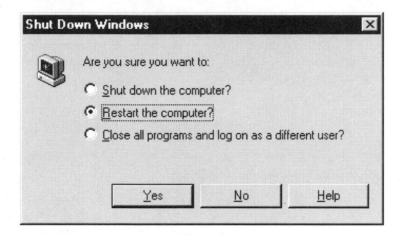

 NOTE: *The secure desktop and logon/logoff features are part of the NT security subsystem and may vary slightly on your particular installation if the replaceable parts of the subsystem have been modified—for example, smartcard readers.*

The Shut Down Windows dialog box lets you do the following:

- Shut down the computer
- Restart the computer
- Close all programs and log on as a different user

Choose the action you wish to take by selecting one of the radio buttons. You can also cancel the operation by choosing No or Cancel, which returns you to the desktop.

Using the Taskbar

The taskbar has three elements: the Start button, the bar itself, and an area to the extreme right that shows system applet icons and the system clock if selected. The Start button has already been discussed, so the following sections briefly cover the other elements of the taskbar.

 NOTE: *See the earlier section "Taskbar" for information about display options.*

Working with Applications

When you start an application, its icon appears in the taskbar. If the application has focus (is the foreground task), the icon appears as a button that has been depressed. If applications are in the background—or they are completely minimized, so they do not show their windows on screen—they also appear on the taskbar. When you select an application, NT switches to that application, restoring the window to the desktop and giving it keyboard and mouse focus. You can also toggle between running applications by repeatedly pressing ALT+TAB. As the taskbar fills with running applications, each icon becomes smaller, lining up side by side.

Other Taskbar Elements

The third element in the taskbar is the area to the extreme right where system applets show their state or run as iconized entities. The system clock runs in this area, and the volume control for multimedia adapters runs here, too. If these elements have settings, you can click on their icons, and a settings window opens.

The Desktop User Area

The area of the screen where applications are displayed and where you interact with them is the desktop user area. Any application that displays a window or dialog box displays it in this area. As screen real estate is usually limited, most applications have at least two states: iconic, which means they appear only on the taskbar, and active, which means they appear on the general desktop with or without focus. You can create a shortcut icon anytime and move it to the Desktop directory so that it shows up in this way.

 TIP: To create a shortcut icon on the desktop, press the right mouse button, which brings up the shortcut menu for the desktop. Now select New, then Shortcut, and follow the Create Shortcut dialog to enter the command line (what application you want to attach to the shortcut), and to select a name for the shortcut icon. Once you have completed the dialog, the shortcut will immediately appear on your desktop.

Shortcut Menus

Almost all of the elements available from the desktop have shortcut menus containing options that can be accessed by clicking the right mouse button. These shortcut menus vary in content, depending on what kind of element they are associated with. Most often, these menus allow you to set the item's properties, links, and appearance. They might also have options to cut, copy, paste, or perform item-specific duties. An example of a shortcut menu is shown here:

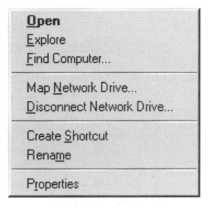

Desktop Item Properties

All items (icons, windows, etc.) showing on the desktop have properties that can be accessed quickly from the quick menus if, in context—such as relating to an application icon—a Properties action choice is available. The dialog box that is displayed by selecting this action allows you to inspect and edit the properties relating to the item. You can generally control the related file's attributes and set the parameters that link the item to its application. These parameters usually include the target file's location, the starting directory, a shortcut key for invocation, and the type of window in which to start the application. Figure 6-16 shows a typical properties dialog box for a desktop item.

System Elements

Some icons are automatically displayed on the desktop. These icons are for the system elements contained in NT's desktop directory. Items that appear on the desktop can be accessed without opening the Start menu. These system elements are discussed in the following sections.

My Computer

When selected, the My Computer icon brings up a window with icons representing the available local and connected network resources. These include logical disk drives and network shares, as well as shortcuts to the Control Panel, the Printers window, and Dial-Up Networking.

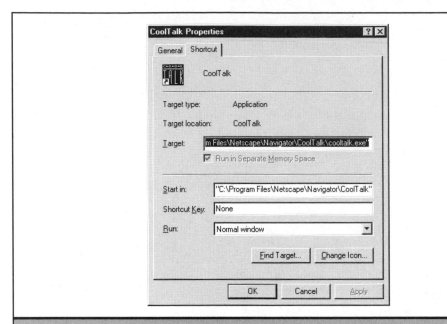

Figure 6-16. *Many desktop items can be accessed through dialogs like this CoolTalk Properties dialog box*

Network Neighborhood

From the Network Neighborhood icon, you are presented with a window that allows you to move quickly through, and copy, delete, select, or run, any connected network resource you have permission to access and manipulate. Resources include network-connected shares (disk drives or subdirectories) and networked printers.

Inbox

The Inbox icon, when selected, opens your Exchange Inbox. The Inbox is where you receive messages and faxes when using Microsoft Exchange messaging to send and receive mail.

Internet Explorer

Microsoft Internet Explorer, a World Wide Web (WWW) browser (see Chapters 25 and 26), is included with NT 4. If you have an intranet or Internet connection, choose this icon to start the Internet Explorer browser, where you can access WWW and FTP resources on sites that you connect to.

Recycle Bin

The Recycle Bin is a fail-safe mechanism that NT 4 (and Windows 95) uses when you choose to delete files from your system. No files are actually deleted until you "empty" the Recycle Bin, giving you the chance to back out of a delete transaction.

My Briefcase

You can use My Briefcase to keep multiple copies of files (contained on different machines, such as between a desktop computer and a laptop you use when traveling) in sync with each other. The Briefcase does all of the work involved in reconciling differences between sets of files and updating the older set automatically when instructed to.

The My Briefcase application is used by creating symbolic links to your shared desktop (local) files by dragging these files into the Briefcase on a remote machine, such as a laptop. (You would do this while connected.) Once these files have been updated on a remote resource such as a laptop, you would choose the "Update All..." option in the Briefcase menu, causing all desktop files to be updated automatically from the laptop or remote machine. You can also use this feature to keep multiple workstations in a small LAN updated from a single source.

For more information on this feature, follow the "Welcome to the Windows Briefcase" help when you first start this application.

What's Next

Next, we'll take a little detour to look at two of the built-in NT applications that are going to become your friends as you assemble and configure your NT system. These are not trivial utilities. They are equally as relevant to an administrator with 500 workstations to configure as they are to a single user.

The Event Viewer and Performance Monitor open the door to understanding what is going on inside your NT system. If you have just installed NT and are having configuration problems, you'll love these applications. On the other hand, a seasoned NT user always has these tools on hand to light the way. The understanding you gain by using these two applications is applicable even when a user is just curious, so let's get busy and see what's under NT's hood right now.

Chapter Seven

The Event Viewer and Performance Monitor

It's all well and good to have the power of NT 4 at your fingertips, but you can't effectively organize your installation or use of NT without knowing what is happening inside the operating system while it runs. If you need to know why a service has not started or what to do about tuning a certain parameter for a network or system component, NT provides you with two tools that will soon become your friends in both the Workstation and Server models of the program: The Event Viewer and the Performance Monitor.

As you read through this chapter, you'll quickly find out how to work with both tools and learn how to manipulate and collate the information they return.

Working with the Event Viewer

When you first start NT 4, you might get an event error dialog box. This is a normal occurrence in a system that is not properly or wholly configured. To find out what error the system is trying to inform you of, you'll need to know how to use NT's Event Viewer—a tool that monitors various kinds of events in your system that are recorded in logs.

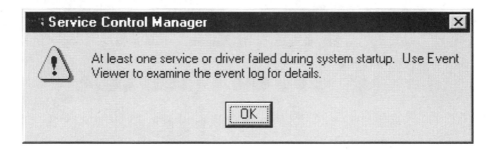

Insider Info

In the NT operating system, an event is defined as a notification from the operating system signaling the occurrence of an error, warning, notice, or result in a system or application module. Events are not necessarily errors or failures, but for some critical error events—such as a memory protection error, a full disk drive, server connection error, hardware failure, or a backup power supply problem—NT may notify you by logging an event and by displaying a message on your screen.

NT may choose not to interrupt your work if the event does not require immediate attention. In this case, the event will be silently added to the event log file, where you can view it later. NT automatically starts the event log service each time you boot NT, and the level of detail for event logging is configurable.

You use Event Viewer to view and manage event logs and to diagnose problems and inefficiencies on your system. You can also save event logs to view later or to generate reports about your NT installation. The detailed information that follows runs you through the basics:

- Viewing event logs
- Sorting, filtering, and searching events
- Setting options for event logging
- Specific events and their meaning
- Saving, exporting, and using event logs

How It Works

NT records system events in three different log files, depending upon what category the specific event falls under:

- **The system log:** Used to record events that pertain to system components. As an example, an event notifying you of a device driver failure or a network error would be recorded in the system log.

- **The security log:** Used to record security related events. Any change to the security system, dependent upon your Audit settings (see Chapter 16) will be logged to this file. For example, the system might log failed logon attempts, indicating a possible break-in, or access violations on NT objects. Almost any security related event can result in a notification entry in the security log.

- **The application log:** This file is used to log events that are generated by applications. When an application executes, it may produce messages and notifications that result in immediate or delayed messages and errors. These notifications may result in abnormal program termination (as in the case of an application that needs to write data to a file, where the disk drive is full) or messages that warn of some impending situation. For example, an application may warn that it's data files need to be compressed or upgraded. These application generated messages will be logged in the application log file.

 TIP: *To control the security events you want audited, choose the Audit Policy dialog from the Policies menu in User Manager as outlined in Chapter 16. To control file and directory permissions and access, choose the Properties/Sharing/Permissions dialog from Explorer, as outlined in Chapter 9.*

Starting and Quitting the Program

You start and quit Event Viewer in the same way as any application, from the Start/Administrative Tools menu, from an explicit shortcut icon on the desktop, or through access in the My Computer folder. To quit Event Viewer, from the Log menu, choose Exit.

The Event Viewer Window

Once you have selected the type of log you wish to display in Event Viewer, you will
be able to view events (sorted by age) and filter the events to view (based upon age
ranges, type of information, user info, and Event ID). You will be able to set threshold
values for the size of each log and how long these logs should be recorded before
being overwritten. This can be important because log files can grow very large over a
short period if maximum information levels are being logged.

You can search for events too, based on any detail related to the event. You can
save event logs in their native format (as .EVT files) or in text format (both raw and
comma delimited). The Event Viewer will display events from the log of your choice,
listing them line by line, showing information about each event—by date, time,
source, category, Event ID, user, and computer name (see Figure 7-1). The events
will include an informational icon in the first column indicating the seriousness
of the event.

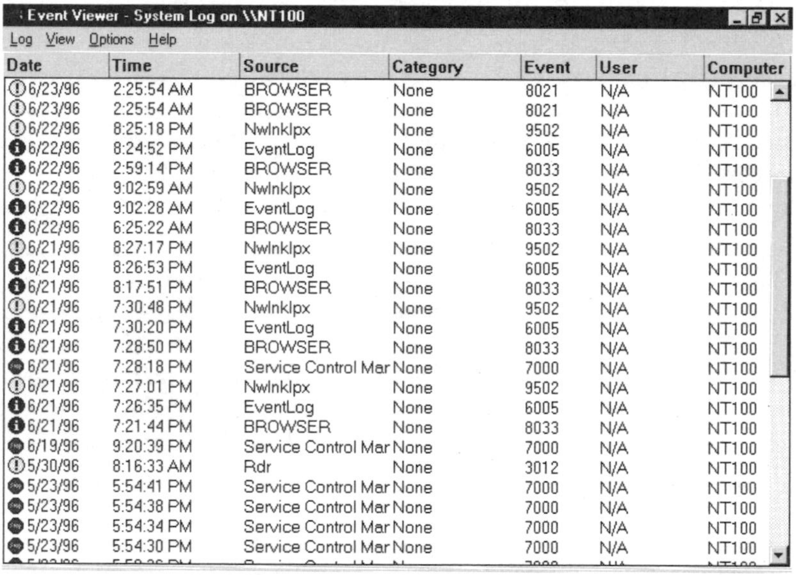

Date	Time	Source	Category	Event	User	Computer
6/23/96	2:25:54 AM	BROWSER	None	8021	N/A	NT100
6/23/96	2:25:54 AM	BROWSER	None	8021	N/A	NT100
6/22/96	8:25:18 PM	Nwlnklpx	None	9502	N/A	NT100
6/22/96	8:24:52 PM	EventLog	None	6005	N/A	NT100
6/22/96	2:59:14 PM	BROWSER	None	8033	N/A	NT100
6/22/96	9:02:59 AM	Nwlnklpx	None	9502	N/A	NT100
6/22/96	9:02:28 AM	EventLog	None	6005	N/A	NT100
6/22/96	6:25:22 AM	BROWSER	None	8033	N/A	NT100
6/21/96	8:27:17 PM	Nwlnklpx	None	9502	N/A	NT100
6/21/96	8:26:53 PM	EventLog	None	6005	N/A	NT100
6/21/96	8:17:51 PM	BROWSER	None	8033	N/A	NT100
6/21/96	7:30:48 PM	Nwlnklpx	None	9502	N/A	NT100
6/21/96	7:30:20 PM	EventLog	None	6005	N/A	NT100
6/21/96	7:28:50 PM	BROWSER	None	8033	N/A	NT100
6/21/96	7:28:18 PM	Service Control Mar	None	7000	N/A	NT100
6/21/96	7:27:01 PM	Nwlnklpx	None	9502	N/A	NT100
6/21/96	7:26:35 PM	EventLog	None	6005	N/A	NT100
6/21/96	7:21:44 PM	BROWSER	None	8033	N/A	NT100
6/19/96	9:20:39 PM	Service Control Mar	None	7000	N/A	NT100
5/30/96	8:16:33 AM	Rdr	None	3012	N/A	NT100
5/23/96	5:54:41 PM	Service Control Mar	None	7000	N/A	NT100
5/23/96	5:54:38 PM	Service Control Mar	None	7000	N/A	NT100
5/23/96	5:54:34 PM	Service Control Mar	None	7000	N/A	NT100
5/23/96	5:54:30 PM	Service Control Mar	None	7000	N/A	NT100

Figure 7-1. *The Event Viewer window*

Mini-Glossary

The Event Viewer window columns use the following terms designed to explain what it's registered events are, and where they originate from:

SOURCE   Source refers to the software module that initiated or logged the event, which can be either an application name (such as PowerPoint), a DLL being used by the system or an application (such as OLE2.DLL), or a base component of the system (such as a device or system driver). For example, NwLnkIpx would indicate an event pertaining to the NWLink (IPX/SPX) network driver. Service Control Manager events refer to any service or device that couldn't start because of, say, an I/O port or parameter error.

CATEGORY   Category pertains to the subtype of event with respect to the Source event. Most events will be marked for all categories, and, although all logs have this option, categories are generally used only for the Security log entries. If a source contains categories, you can choose the events you wish to see in View/Filter Events.

EVENT ID   Event ID's refer to a specific number given to an event by the module that logged that event. These numbers are generally useful only to support personnel.

USER   This is the user that was logged on to the computer at the time the event was logged. An N/A entry indicates that it was not user specific or could not determine the user.

COMPUTER   Because Event Viewer can determine the computer where an error occurred and lets you inspect another computer's event logs, this column indicates the computer name for the computer where the event originated from.

Interpreting the Icons

There are icons on the left side of the Event Viewer screen that describe NT's classification of the event, such as:

■ **Information:** This denotes a successful return or result from the execution of an application function or system service. Not all modules will log this event, but it is available for software to use, informing the user of an event for tracking purposes.

- **Error:** This icon denotes critical problems. An error event informs you of unrecoverable errors such as hardware failures or system services problems (e.g. the failure of the serial port driver to load at startup).

- **Warning:** This denotes logged events that are significant but not critical (e.g. may need your attention in the near future or rectification for administrative purposes). A warning event might be logged by the Rdr (Network Redirector) service if your application needs to access a share on a remote computer but the connection has been broken.

- **Success Audit:** This will inform you of successful operation when an audited security object is accessed. An attempt to connect to a shared resource, such as a remote directory, can result in this event being logged.

- **Failure Audit:** This informs you of unsuccessful or denied operations on audited security objects. An attempt to access a shared resource for which no security access is allowed—such as an administrative share, where no user privileges exist—can result in an audit failure being logged.

Security and the Event Log

Even users logged on as "Guest", the lowest default security privilege, can view the System and Application logs. However, the user must be given specific Administrator rights (see Chapter 16) in User Manager to be granted viewing and administration privileges for the Security log. Also, the clearing of logs and the right to change log attributes are granted only to users with administrative access.

When viewing a remote computer's event logs, you must have sufficient privilege on the remote system. If you are trying to view or administer a remote computer's logs, and both you and that computer are part of a domain, make sure that the domain controller, from whom you gain access rights, is properly setup to grant you those remote domain-wide rights.

Viewing Individual Event Logs

Event Viewer allows you to choose the type of log (System, Security, or Application), and which computer that log resides on, for subsequent viewing and administration. When you start Event Viewer, the System log for your local computer will be displayed. You can change computers, choosing to inspect another computers logs, or you can change the type of log you wish to view from the Log menu.

TIP: In order to display more information, or make the information more readable in the Event Viewer window, you can change display fonts and their size. You can change the font that you want to use in the Event Viewer windows by choosing the Options/Font dialog.

Choosing Another Computer

To view another computer's event log, choose Computer from the log menu as shown in Figure 7-2. The dialog will access the network for you, and display the available computers which you can select. Domains and workgroups will be listed, if available, and once you have selected the local or remote computer, the System log for that computer will be displayed. You may also type the name into this dialog. If the computer you select is remote, and the communications link is slow, such as a RAS connection, you may want to check the Low Speed Connection box in this dialog. When this box is selected, NT will try to optimize network access when resolving computer names. This may result in a partial list for a large domain.

 TIP: *If you typically access Event Viewer over a modem—say from a RAS connection or from another type of slow connection—you may want to set the default for connection to Low Speed Connection in the Options menu.*

Viewing the Logs

When started, Event Viewer shows the System log by default. To select another log, select System, Security, or Application from the Log menu (see Figure 7-3). Each time

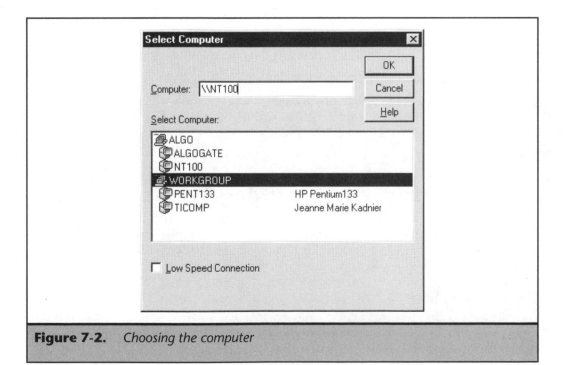

Figure 7-2. *Choosing the computer*

Event Viewer - System Log on \\NT100			
Log View Options Help			
✓ System	Source	Category	Event
Se<u>c</u>urity	NwlnkIpx	None	9502
Application	EventLog	None	6005
<u>O</u>pen...	BROWSER	None	8033
Sa<u>v</u>e As...	NwlnkIpx	None	9502
	EventLog	None	6005
C<u>l</u>ear All Events	BROWSER	None	8033
Log Se<u>t</u>tings...	NwlnkIpx	None	9502
	EventLog	None	6005
Select Computer...	BROWSER	None	8033
	BROWSER	None	8021
E<u>x</u>it Alt+F4	BROWSER	None	8021
ⓘ 6/25/96 11:38:26 AM	BROWSER	None	8021
ⓘ 6/24/96 5:37:58 AM	NwlnkIpx	None	9502
❶ 6/24/96 5:37:29 AM	EventLog	None	6005
❶ 6/24/96 5:31:26 AM	BROWSER	None	8033
ⓘ 6/23/96 2:25:54 AM	BROWSER	None	8021

Figure 7-3. *Choosing the log*

that you choose a log, that log is refreshed, reflecting the most recent changes. The log will not be refreshed again until it is closed and reopened or refreshed manually. If you wish to refresh the log manually, choose Refresh from the View menu.

REMINDER: *Remember, to view and administer the security log, you must be logged on as a member of the Administrators group or be given equal security access.*

Sorting, Filtering, and Searching Events

By default, the log that you have chosen is displayed in its entirety and sorted by age. Once you have selected this log, you may then proceed to apply several sort and filter criteria to narrow your view. You can also filter and search for events based on the event description text or type, time, user, or computer.

Event Sorting

As stated above, by default, the displayed events appear sorted with the latest at the head of the list. You can reorder listed events by age by choosing Newest First or Oldest First from Event Viewer's View menu.

NOTE: *The time-sort order that you setup will become the default for all subsequent sessions if you check Save Settings On Exit from the Options menu before you quit Event Viewer. The next time you start Event Viewer, the sort order and any other options that you have set will be in effect.*

Event Filtering

You may apply filters to your view of a specific event log. Filters allow you to narrow your view of the event log by including only those events that meet your filter criteria. By default, all events are displayed. If you want to filter certain events, choose the Filter Events dialog from the View menu. As with sorting, your filter choices will be applied to subsequent Viewer sessions if you check Save Settings On Exit from the Options menu before you quit Event Viewer.

 NOTE: *Filtering does not permanently affect the event log. All events are always logged, irrespective of any filters you might apply while in Event Viewer. The filters you set deal only with the display of events from a log while in the Viewer.*

To set a filter on logged events, choose Filter Events from the View menu. You will be presented with the Filter dialog box, which lets you specify the kind of filtering you wish to apply to your log view (see Figure 7-4).

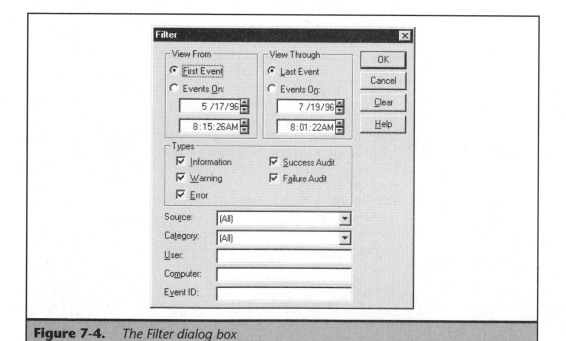

Figure 7-4. *The Filter dialog box*

The following list shows the options available in the Filter dialog box:

Choose	To Apply a Filter Pertaining to:
View From	There are two choices: **First Event:** Denotes viewing from the very first event, by date and time, in the log **Events On:** Denotes viewing from a date and time that you specify. Events before this date and time will not be displayed.
View Through	There are two choices: **Last Event:** denotes viewing through to the very last event recorded, by date and time, in the log **Events On**: Denotes viewing through a date and time that you specify. Events after this date and time will not be displayed.
Types	There are five general types: **Information:** Events that denote a successful return or result from the execution of an application function or system service. Not all modules will log this event, but it is available for software to use, informing the user of an event for tracking purposes. **Warning:** Events that denote logged events that are significant but not critical (e.g. may need your attention in the near future or rectification for administrative purposes). A warning event might be logged by the Rdr (Network Redirector) service if your application needs to access a share on a remote computer, but the connection has been broken. **Error:** Events that denote critical problems. An error event informs you of unrecoverable errors such as hardware failures or system services problems. **Success Audit:** Events that inform you of successful operation when an audited security object is accessed. An attempt to connect to a shared resource, such as a remote directory, can result in this event being logged. **Failure Audit:** This informs you of unsuccessful or denied operations on audited security objects. An attempt to access a shared resource, for which no security access is allowed (such as an administrative share, where no user privileges exist) can result in an audit failure being logged.
Source	The source of an event that you wish to display logged event items for. This could be an application, a device driver, or a system service or component.

Choose	To Apply a Filter Pertaining to:
Category	The category of event with respect to the source event. Most notably, this will be a security item such as Object Access or Account Management.
User	A case insensitive user name to match on.
Computer	A case insensitive computer name to match on.
Event ID	The actual event ID number. This ID is unique within the scope of the event itself.

NOTE: Using the Clear button will result in resetting the filter parameters to the default. To turn off filtering altogether, select All Events from the View Menu. All Events and Filter Events are mutually exclusive and reflect their states by the placement of a check by their menu entries in the View menu.

Event Searching

When you have large log files, or know exactly what you are looking for, you may want to use Event Viewer's search capabilities. You invoke a search by using the Find dialog from the View menu. You can search for events that match the same kind of input criteria that allow you to filter events: Types, Source, Category, Event ID, Computer, User, and one additional parameter, Description.

In order to perform a search, invoke the Find dialog (see Figure 7-5) and select any or all of the Types of events you want to find, noting that they are not mutually exclusive. Next, if you wish, enter parameters for Source, Category, Event ID, Computer, and User as you did when specifying a filter, explained earlier in this chapter. If you want to find events with certain text contained in their descriptions (see the following section), enter that text in the Description edit box, typing as much of the description as you wish to match. The Find function will search for incomplete sentences and single words within the event description bodies. Use the Direction buttons to specify which direction to search the list of events, relative to your present position in the Viewer window. To perform the actual search, press the Find Next button.

NOTE: You can step through found entries by repeating the Find Next button or by pressing F3. The clear button will reset the default search criteria.

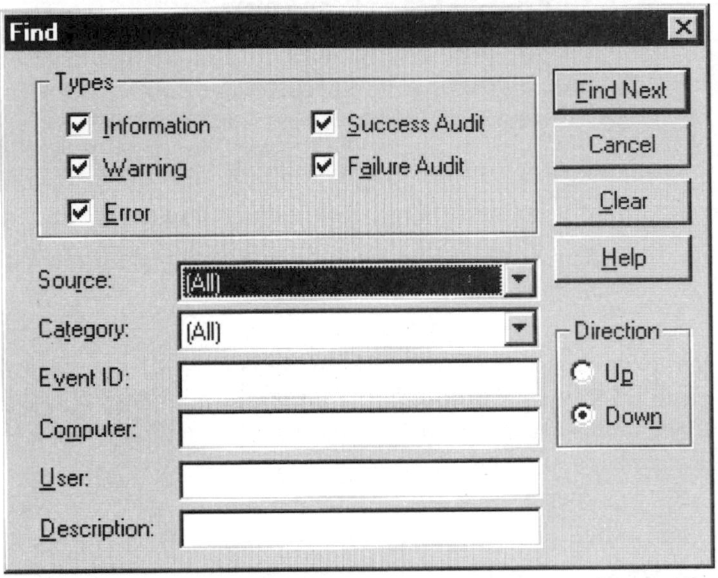

Figure 7-5.   The Find dialog box

Looking at Detailed Information

Some events may have a detailed explanation attached to them (e.g. covering the reason an event was logged). The event Detail dialog box, invoked by the Detail command from the View menu, displays any textual description and associated hexadecimal data generated for a selected event (see Figure 7-6). An event may have verbose description and data, or there may be little, or none. You use this information to gain insight into what is happening inside your system. Product support engineers can also use this data to diagnose problems and workarounds with applications or system components.

You can also bring up the details about an event by double-clicking on the event you want to view details about. To continue with details for the next or previous events, use the Next or Previous buttons in the Details dialog.

NOTE: If you export a log to text or comma-delimited text format, the hexadecimal event data will be lost; only the event description will be saved. If you need to preserve the hexadecimal data, use the .EVT file format to save your logs.

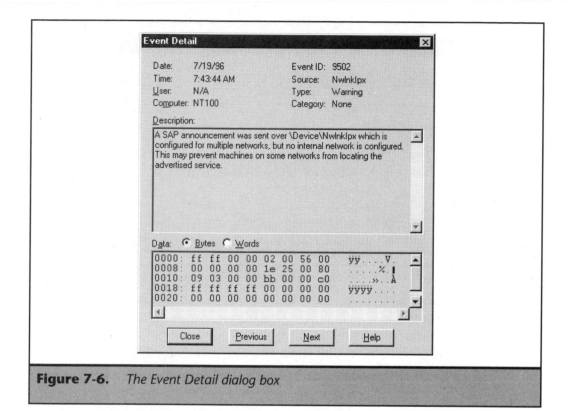

Figure 7-6. *The Event Detail dialog box*

Setting Log Options

When global parameters for logging events need to be set, you will use the Log Settings command from the Log menu. This will bring up the Event Log Settings dialog (see Figure 7-7), which allows you to set the not-to-exceed maximum size for each type of log. This dialog also allows you to set criteria for overwriting each type of log, if they become full.

TIP: To enforce logging of all security related events and to ensure security logs do not get overwritten, you can set audit policies in the User Manager (see Chapter 16) that force the system to halt when the security log is full.

To review, as above, select the log that you wish to set parameters for in the Change Settings for area. You may also use the Maximum Log Size area to control how large any log will be allowed to become. The default is 512 kilobytes, and you may change this up or down in 64K increments.

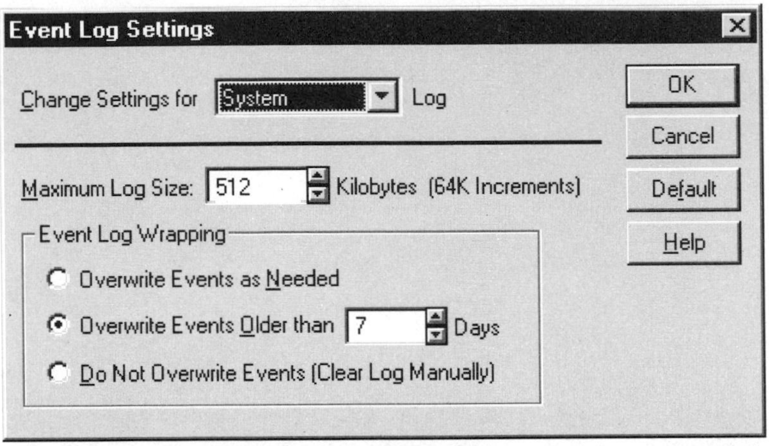

Figure 7-7. *The Event Log Settings dialog box*

Select an Event Log Wrapping parameter to control how NT will manage the selected log over time. The options include:

■ **Overwrite Events as Needed:** This directs NT to write new events to the selected log even after the log is full. Any new event will be written in place of the oldest event in the specified log.

■ **Overwrite Events Older than:** This is the default. NT will keep events for a certain number of days before overwriting them. Useful for automatic maintenance of periodic logging.

■ **Do Not Overwrite Events (Clear Log Manually):** Directs NT to never automatically clear this log. This is used for catching critical events and needs manual intervention when logs are full. It's also used in critical situations where all events should be saved.

Clearing an Event Log

When you specify that events cannot be overwritten for a specific log (e.g. the Do Not Overwrite Events option), you must clear the log manually when NT notifies you that the log is full.

To clear a log, make sure the log is active in the Viewer window and choose Clear All Events from the Log menu. A message box will ask you if you want to save the log before clearing it. Answer Yes to save the log as a .EVT, Text, or Comma delimited Text file. Answer NO to discard the contents of the file and clear the log.

Saving and Exporting Event Logs

You must save an event log in the .EVT file format in order to reopen it later in the Event Viewer. For other purposes, such as viewing in a text editor or word processor, the log should be saved in text format or comma-delimited (field delimited) text format. Sort order only has an effect on log files that you export in text formats.

 NOTE: *When you save a log file in the .EVT file format, filtering options in force do not apply, and the entire file is saved. If you export a log file, saving it in a text or comma-delimited text format, it will be saved exactly as displayed.*

To save or export an event log, choose Save As from the Log menu, or during a Clear All Events operation, choose Yes. In the File Name box, enter a filename to save the file under (see Figure 7-8). The default will be to save the file as a native .EVT type file, but you may select a file format in the Save File As Type box. When done, choose the OK button.

You can save or export an event log in one of the following file formats:

- **EVT file format:** Choose this native format if you want to reload the log file in Event Viewer.

- **Text file format:** Use this format to export your log file for use in, say, a word processor.

- **Comma delimited format:** Use this format to export the log file field information to applications that import delimited data such as spreadsheets.

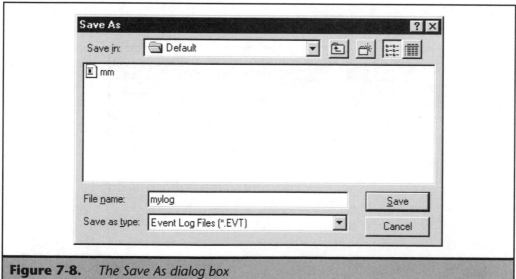

Figure 7-8. *The Save As dialog box*

Displaying EVT Files in Event Viewer

To display a saved .EVT file in Event Viewer, choose Open from the Log menu. Select the file in the File Name list and then choose the OK button. In the Open File Type dialog box (see Figure 7-9), select the kind of log you saved originally—System, Security, or Application—and then choose the OK button.

Using the Performance Monitor

The Performance Monitor helps administrators and users by providing monitoring facilities for performance. Diagnostics for throughput and potential are provided in most of the critical processing areas—such as percentage of CPU usage, storage media read and write speed, network component efficiency, and so on. This section explains how to use the features in Performance Monitor and how to quantify the results of it's operation.

TIP: *Performance Monitor can pinpoint bottlenecked areas within your installation that will help you to understand and change the performance of your local computer and other computers in a network.*

We'll look at the following topics:

- Reasons for using Performance Monitor
- Charting and logging performance statistics
- Setting alerts on performance
- Reports on performance
- Using performance log files

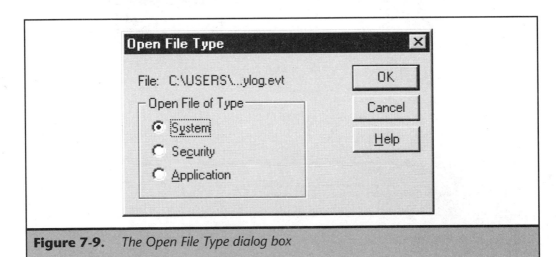

Figure 7-9.   *The Open File Type dialog box*

How It Works

Performance Monitor is a Win32 application used for monitoring the performance of an NT computer locally or on the network. You can measure the load on and performance of NT system objects and various system services—such as number interrupt/sec, Processors (CPU usage), virtual and physical memory, network components, physical and logical disks, threads, and processes.

 NOTE: *Measurements are taken by using an NT object's counters—a set of variables that the operating system updates at periodic intervals for display in Performance Monitor or a similar facility. Each object that Performance Monitor can measure has its own set of counters that may be queried.*

Performance Monitor features also include performance charting, logging, and reporting. When you open Performance Monitor from the Start/Administrative Tools menu, you'll be presented initially with a blank charting window, the main output screen for Performance Monitor (see Figure 7-10).

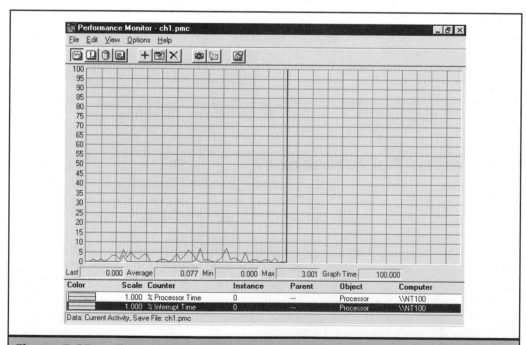

Figure 7-10. *The Performance Monitor main window*

Performance Monitor Prerequisites

There are no special preparations needed for most operations that you will perform with Performance Monitor. A proviso to that statement is the need to be logged on as a member of the Administrators group to use the diskperf command, which turns on and off the counters for physical and logical disk activity on your own or another computer. These counters insert themselves into and intercept the disk driver chain. Because of the way they work, these counters can have a negative effect on disk throughput.

After you run the *diskperf* command to turn the disk activity counters on or off, you must reboot NT to put the counters into effect.

 TIP: *You should only turn these disk performance counters on if you intend to measure physical or logical disk activity. If your Performance Monitor session does not need to work with disk access, leave the counters off, since they can slow disk access, thereby skewing other results such as CPU time.*

Performance Monitor Windows

Performance Monitor has the following data windows—each with their own commands and functionality—which you display by choosing to view them from the View menu:

- Chart
- Alert
- Log
- Report

We will take a look at each of these windows and their functions later in this chapter, but first, let's explore some reasons and uses for Performance Monitor.

Why Monitor Performance?

As a user or administrator of a newly installed or upgraded installation, your first duty will probably be to test and tune the base components or additions that you have just enabled. Without the proper tools, guessing and empirical measurements are going to have to suffice. And that's not always good enough! You are definitely going to want to pin down bottlenecks and problems in a new or changed installation, because there are too many possibilities to just wing it with an estimate of where the problem might lie.

Additionally, you may be asked, as an administrator, to justify network efficiency or system resource usage. How are you going to come up with meaningful and relevant information? If you have a tool such as Performance Monitor, you have a much better chance of quantifying system performance and metrics.

Additionally, as a programmer, you might want to use such a tool to verify and debug program flow or design.

Performance Monitor Capabilities

Most everyone who needs to look at performance will have slightly different reasons and expectations for wanting this data. A network admin may want to monitor network usage and efficiency for quality of service requisites. Failures and load sharing differences may need to be quantified and balanced.

Bottlenecks and system throughput problems can occur when resources are insufficient with regard to demand. This may be a hardware problem, such as a slow network card, an old style I/O card that slows data flow, or lack of enough physical memory. Software also may play a major role in system speed and throughput. Finding out how applications interact with the system and with each other can be of great importance when tuning a system.

Mini-Glossary

COUNTER A variable that holds a "count" to be displayed in the monitor window.

INSTANCES An instance denotes an entire representation of a running application in the computer's memory space. Programs and applications are said to be multi-instanced when more than one copy of the program is running at once.

OBJECT In Windows NT, an object is an abstraction of some logical or physical mechanism, process, or system resource. Objects are created and manipulated by the operating system to represent processes, events, and data.

PROCESS A Windows NT process is created when a program or service is executed. A process may represent an application (such as Microsoft Word or Micrografx Picture Publisher), a service (such as the Network Redirector or Computer Browser), or operating system code and data (such as WOW). In addition to executable code, a process defines a range of virtual memory addresses and at least one executable thread.

THREAD Threads are objects within processes that execute program instructions. They allow concurrent operations within a process. They also enable one process to execute different parts of its program on different threads and, with the right hardware, on different processors simultaneously.

Performance Monitor Counters

Performance Monitor utilizes the concept of *counters* when monitoring the behavior of system objects. Counters are grouped by object type. Counters are provided for the processor, memory, cache, hard disks, threads, processes, and so on.

Objects capable of being monitored can be multi-instanced. If you have more than one hard disk, the PhysicalDisk object will have more than one instance, complete with counters for each instance of that object. Other objects that may have more than one instance include the LogicalDisk, Processor, and Process. There are some object types that never have more than one instance. The Memory object is always single-instanced since there's always only one system-wide virtual memory space.

NOTE: The Process and Thread objects are tied together very closely. Thread object instances exist for each thread running on the system. Thread objects (and their counters) are each associated with the Process object that owns them. Performance Monitor itself (Perfmon, as a Process object instance in the Thread objects list) has four threads associated with it.

Types of Counters

The following list describes a few of the most useful counters and what you would use them for. The complete set of counters for each object may be browsed while adding counters to a chart.

- **Process:Working Set:** Query this counter on a process for which you wish to find how much of the machine's physical memory is allocated. If you use this counter on all application processes, you can derive the minimum working set values for your application mix. This will tell you what your minimum requirements are for physical RAM (with minimal paging).

- **Process:Working Set Peak:** Query this counter on a process for which you wish to find peak usages of the machine's physical memory. If you use this counter on all application processes, you can derive the maximum working set values for your application mix. This will tell you what your maximum requirements are for physical RAM (with minimal paging).

- **Memory:Pages/sec:** Query this counter to ascertain the number of pages per second that are read from or written to the paging file on disk. It's used to ascertain system performance with regard to the system's demand on physical memory. In other words, this counter's value reflects demand on the paging system to meet memory read and write requests. If this value is greater than five pages per second, you should think about increasing physical RAM to minimize paging, a major performance bottleneck.

- **Paging File:% Usage:** Queries the total amount of the paging file in use. If this counter exceeds 90 percent, increase the initial size of your PAGEFILE.SYS through the Start/Settings/Control Panel/System applet.

- **Paging File:% Usage Peak:** Queries the peak amount of the paging file in use. If this counter exceeds 90 percent, increase the initial size of your PAGEFILE.SYS through the Start/Settings/Control Panel/System applet.

- **Processor:% Processor Time:** Query this counter to check the percentage of time that a processor(CPU) is busy executing a thread. Compute bound applications will cause this counter to read high. Instantaneous high readings are not necessarily indicative of a problem, but high Processor usage over time might point to an application or driver that is "hogging" the machine, either because of it's computational overhead, or because it is poorly designed.

- **PhysicalDisk:Avg. Disk sec/Transfer:** Query this counter on a physical disk drive to ascertain total disk throughput. A high value (> 0.3 secs/transfer) may indicate physical drives that are failing on retry or who have slow transfer rates. In either of the above cases, you should probably look further at the physical/electronic disk drive system for problems.

Global Operations

Performance Monitor can provide you with four views of the state reflected by the objects and their counters you choose to query. When working with the different views available, you use the same primary operations, with additional commands appearing in context, in all of the view windows: Chart, Alert, Log, or Report.

To work in any view, first choose the type of view from the View menu. Once you have chosen the type of view, you may setup a new session, with its own settings or choose to open a previously saved view settings file. From the File menu, choose New or Open, respectively. Then, if you want to add objects or counters, from the view's Edit menu, choose the Add to XX command, where XX denotes Chart, Alert, Log, or Report. You use this command to select objects and their counters on one or more computers locally or in your network.

TIP: You can use the Edit menu's commands to make changes to individual items. You can also use the File menu's Save commands to save selections for single views or the Save Workspace command to save selections for all views. Use Save As… to save settings in a new settings file or Save to update the current settings file.

Changing a View's Options

From any view's Options menu, you can change any of the options valid for that view (see Figure 7-11), such as specifying the periodic update, grid setup, labeling, and plotting maxima for data presentation.

Selecting Computers

Performance Monitor allows you to view different counters on different objects residing on different computers. When adding a counter or object to a view, you may specify the computer that this data should come from. To select a computer, from the

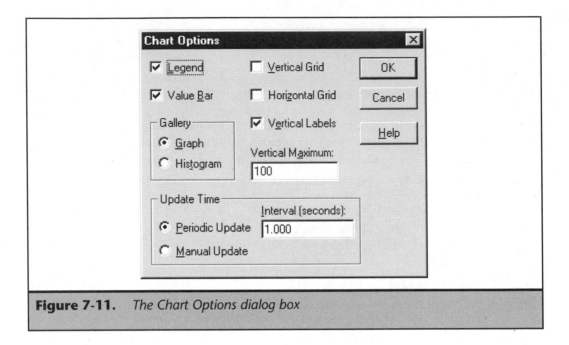

Figure 7-11. *The Chart Options dialog box*

view's Edit menu, choose the Add To command. Then, in the Computer edit field, type the computer's name or click the "..." button to the right of the Computer edit field to display the Select Computer dialog (see Figure 7-12). If you use the Select Computer dialog, double-click the name of a domain controller or workgroup to display the list of servers and workstations available. Choose the name of the server or workstation that you want to monitor and press the OK button.

 TIP: *If you use the view's Edit menu with an object or counter that you have selected while working within a view, that object's owning computer will automatically be used in the Edit operation.*

Clearing and Deleting Displays and Selections

To clear the values displayed in a view, use Clear Display from the view's Edit menu. To delete a selection, select a chart legend, log, or report item and choose Delete from the view's Edit menu or press the DELETE key on your keyboard.

The Data From Command

The Data From command in the Options menu is available for all views. You use this command to specify whether you are going to view current values or whether you want to work with an existing log file. Current values are used as default.

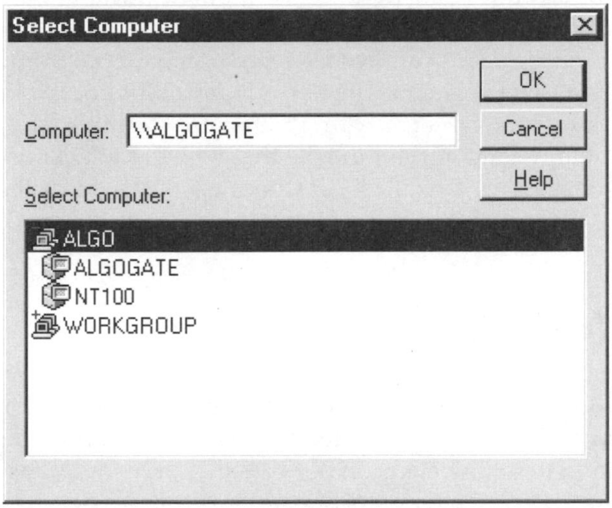

Figure 7-12. *The Select Computer dialog box*

Updating the Display

You may wish to instantaneously update the display of information for an applicable view. Some views have a command under the Options menu and a button on the toolbar for this purpose. This command will only be enabled when relevant. You can use the Edit menu/Update Now command or button to capture data immediately.

If you wish to change the way in which a view is updated, choose periodic or manual updating from the Options menu/Options command dialog box. If you select Periodic Update, type a number in the Interval box to determine the time, in seconds, between updates and then choose the OK button.

CAUTION: Update interval settings can affect the amount of processor time that is used by Performance Monitor. Monitoring can skew your performance data if you update data very frequently or you frequently query large numbers of networked computers.

Exporting Data

Spreadsheets can provide a way to correlate your performance data. They can massage and total numerical values in ways that let you see the data in a different light. A bar chart can often be more informative than a columnar list of numbers. If you need to keep track of performance data over a period of time, or have the requirement to keep records of data trends, you might also want to use performance data in a database.

To export performance data to a spreadsheet or database program, choose the Export command from the File menu. The Performance Monitor Export As dialog box will appear (see Figure 7-13). Select or type a path name (with the appropriate extension for the column delimiter) for the file that you want to export. In the Save as type combobox, choose either Tab (*.TSV) or Comma (*.CSV) delimited, depending upon which type of data your spreadsheet application needs for import. Finally, choose Save.

Charting Performance

Creating and using charts (and to a lesser extent, alerts) may be where you'll find Performance Monitor most informative. Using the chart view, you can often find out why a computer, network, or application is slow or inefficient. You can use the chart view, in addition to setting alerts on performance, to continuously monitor a single computer or a group of computers to find performance degradation and incompatibilities. You can also use charting to quantify load and capacity problems or metrics.

Opening a Chart View

To open a Chart view, choose Chart from the View menu or choose the Chart button on the toolbar. Initially, the Chart view will be blank (see Figure 7-14). The Chart view

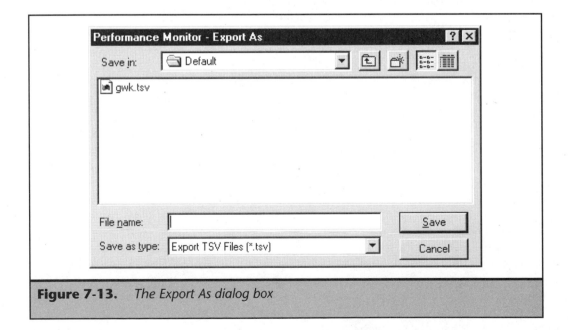

Figure 7-13. *The Export As dialog box*

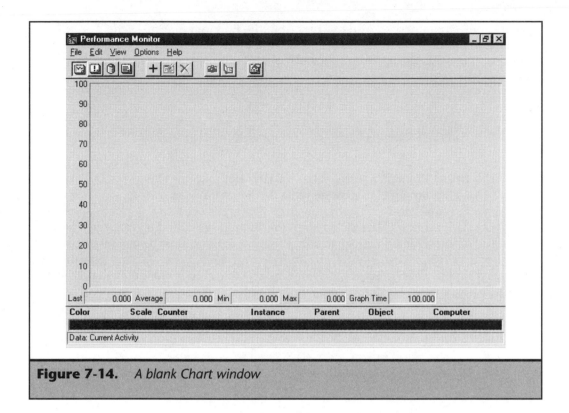

Figure 7-14. *A blank Chart window*

will only contain data if you have already created or opened a chart or have run Performance Monitor from the command prompt with a data file input argument. To create a new blank chart, choose New Chart from the File menu.

NOTE: *To open a previously saved chart settings file, choose Open from the File menu. In the File Open dialog box, select or type the path name for an existing .PMC file and choose the OK button.*

Adding Chart Selections

Looking for bottlenecks and performance problems can involve using Performance Monitor in many different ways. You can create charts with different sets of object instances and relevant counters arranged in an order that you choose. You can then save these chart layouts, using a unique filename, and recall the charts to use whenever you want. Once recalled, these charts can also be edited. In this way, you can build a library of chart settings files to recall and use whenever you suspect a problem in a specific area of performance.

To add selections, choose Add to Chart from the Edit menu or press the Add to Chart button on the toolbar. The Add to Chart dialog (see Figure 7-15) will appear with the default settings, including your NT workstation or server listed in the Computer edit field.

NOTE: *To select a computer whose objects and counters you wish to add to a chart, see the procedure given in the previous section on selecting a computer, and Figure 7-12.*

SELECTING OBJECTS, INSTANCES, AND COUNTERS   In the Object field (Figure 7-15), select an object to monitor from the list of those that are available on the chosen computer. The Counter and Instance fields change to display the selections that are available for that object on the computer that appears in the Computer field.

To actually select an item, in the Counter field, select a counter. In the Instance field, select one or more instances as appropriate, and then choose Add to commit your choices to the chart. Repeat this operation, along with your parameter choices, for all the items you wish to add to your chart.

TIP: *For information that will help you to understand the meaning and scope of a specific counter, press the Explain>> button to display the Counter Definition field. If you have already turned this field on, you will get an explanation automatically as you choose different objects and their counters.*

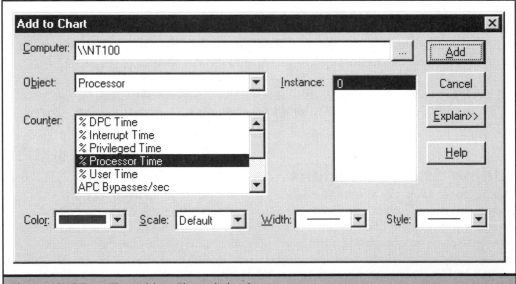

Figure 7-15.   *The Add to Chart dialog box*

CHOOSING PLOTTING COLORS AND SCALE FACTORS   By default, the selection you make will be assigned the next available color for the chart plot, with the default scale, line style, and line width. You may override these defaults by using the Color, Scale, Width, and Style fields in the Add To dialog.

For the Scale field, the word Default will initially appear. Use this scale for most charts since it reflects a choice of scale which will most likely be proper for that counter.

TIP: *To make charts show more detail about a particular counter, you can vary the scale of the item in order to "zoom in" on it. Changing the color, line style, and line width may also help view a specific counter. You can edit and modify these parameters at any time by using the Edit Chart Line command from the Edit menu.*

Customizing Chart Selections

You will sometimes find that without customization a chart will be unreadable or hard to understand. The whole idea of using Performance Monitor is to make performance data more accessible and understandable. If you are charting a counter whose default scale does not allow you to see the level of detail that is required, a way must be found to change the plotting characteristics of the charting process for that item.

Performance Monitor allows you to customize your graphs by changing the scale at which you plot counter information, while leaving the actual data unchanged. You can also change the color, style, and width for each individual item. There is also a mode that allows you to highlight an individual counter's plot. This mode is called Chart Highlighting, and can make data stand out where many counters are being displayed at once, presenting a less confused view of a specific counter. To change the plot characteristics of a selected counter, you can use the Edit command from the Edit menu or in the legend field at the bottom of the screen, select the counter that you want to change.

TIP: *If you are selecting the counter from the legend field, double-click the selected counter or choose Edit Chart Line from the Edit menu. You can also use the Edit Chart Line button on the toolbar.*

When the Edit Chart Line dialog appears, showing selected parameters for the counter that you selected, you can change any of the options in the following list:

Parameter to Change	Uses
Color	Colors differentiate counters and make charts more readable.
Scale	Changing scale can zoom in on events and data that would otherwise go unnoticed or blend into the background "noise" in a chart. Only the chart plot is scaled. Actual data is not.

Parameter to Change	Uses
Width	Highlight counters, making them stand out. Useful for assigning visual levels of data importance.
Style	Differentiate counters, making them unique. Useful for assigning visual levels of data importance or hierarchy.

After you have made your customizations, press the OK button. The plot area and legend field will use and display your new selections.

Editing Global Chart Options

After you have opened a chart view, you may want to change certain global options like how often your chart's values are updated and whether your chart will be a plotted graph of individual items or a histogram. Selecting the Chart command from the Options menu will bring up the Chart Options dialog, enabling you to change these global options.

You can use the Chart Options dialog box (see Figure 7-16) to choose to display or hide the legend field, the value bar fields, grid lines, and labels. You can also control the maximum that the vertical axis should extend to, the type of graph you want, and the update time interval for refreshing the chart from the counter values.

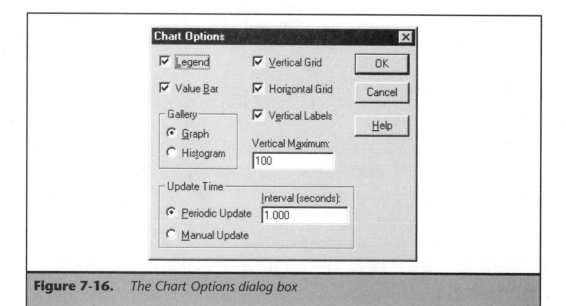

Figure 7-16.   *The Chart Options dialog box*

GRAPH VERSUS HISTOGRAM FORMAT   You can change from graph format to histogram format by using the Options dialog/Gallery field. The histogram may be more useful for charting values of multiple instances of the same object (see Figure 7-17). The graph format is the default, representing data as plotted lines on an XY chart. In the Gallery field, select how you want to display information in the chart and then choose the OK button.

UPDATING CHART INFORMATION MANUALLY   Additionally, the Options menu/Update Time area allows you to control how information gets updated. If you choose to set the Update Manually option, you must explicitly update your chart by using the Update Now command from the Options menu. You can use the Update Now command at any time. This is useful even between automatic updates, when you want to capture instantaneous values.

NOTE: If you choose to set periodic updates in the Chart Options dialog, enter a value in the Update Time field. This value, in seconds, will be used by Performance Monitor to control the frequency of automatic updates to chart elements.

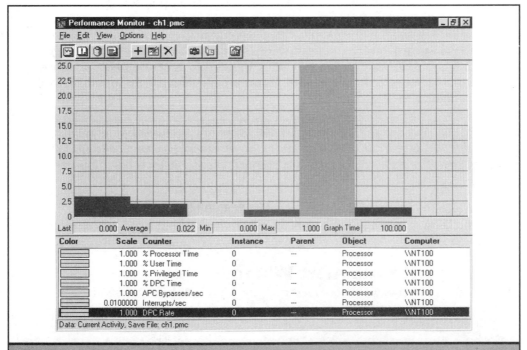

Figure 7-17.   *The Performance Monitor in Histogram mode*

Displaying Your Selections

Once you have added selections to your chart and you have returned to the main chart view, Performance Monitor will immediately start plotting your choices, usually as an average of the last two sampled values. A list of your counter selections will appear in the field at the bottom of the chart window.

Saving Your Chart Selections

To save your chart settings, choose Save Chart Settings As from the File menu. In the Performance Monitor Save As dialog, select or type a filename for the file that you wish to save the present settings in and then choose the OK button. This file can reside on any computer in your network.

Setting and Using Alerts

Alerts are a mechanism that allow you to set alarms based upon parameters that you specify, turning Performance Monitor into a sort of background watchdog that tracks your criteria silently. When your parameters are satisfied, and a counter goes over (or under) the values that you have specified, an event is generated, and you will be notified in a way that you have prearranged.

The way Performance Monitor alerts you is dependent upon settings that you control. An alert may simply bring up Performance Monitor's alert view, or you may create an alert log and log the alarm to that file. You can also direct that the alert be entered in the Event Viewer's application log (see the section on the Event Viewer at the beginning of this chapter). You may setup the alert to generate a network message that is sent to a specific remote computer. These are global settings, applicable to all alerts generated.

 TIP: *You may also direct Performance Monitor to run an application for you when a specific alert is generated. You may specify that the application be run once, on the first alert generated for the criteria you have specified, or every time the criteria are met.*

When a counter meets the alert parameters that you have specified, a date and time stamp, along with the actual event, is entered in the Alert window. No more than one thousand events may be recorded, after which wrapping will occur.

Working with the Alert Window

To bring up the Alert view, choose alert from the View menu or choose the Alert button on the toolbar. Initially, unless already setup and used, the Alert Log view will be blank. The Alert view shows the Alert Interval field where Performance Monitor shows how often, in seconds, the system will be monitored. The view also has a display area for logged alerts and an Alert Legend field where selected alert object counters are displayed.

To open an alert log settings file, choose Open from the File menu, and then select or type the path and name for a .PMA file in the File Name field of the Performance Monitor File Open dialog. To create a new blank alert log file, from the File menu, choose New Alert Settings, and when you have set up your alert parameters, you may save them by using the Save Alert Settings As command from the File menu.

Adding Alert Parameter Selections

To add selections to an alert view, choose Add to Alert from the Edit menu or choose the Add to Alert button on the toolbar. This will cause the display of the Add to Alert dialog (see Figure 7-18). Default settings, and your workstation or server, listed in the Computer field, will appear. You may choose a different computer, as in the Add to Chart dialog in the previous section. In the Object field, select an object to monitor from the list of those given.

ALERT COUNTERS AND INSTANCES   The Counter and Instance fields will reflect items that are available for the object you have chosen. In the Counter field, select the counters you wish to add, and in the Instance field, select the instances you want, if relevant. Choose a color, or let Performance monitor assign the next available color.

ALERT VALUES AND RUNNING PROGRAMS   In order to trigger an alert on parameter excession, you will fill in the Alert If fields. In the Alert If field, you will specify what criteria will trigger an alert. Select either Over or Under and enter the value that corresponds to a limit for the specified counter.

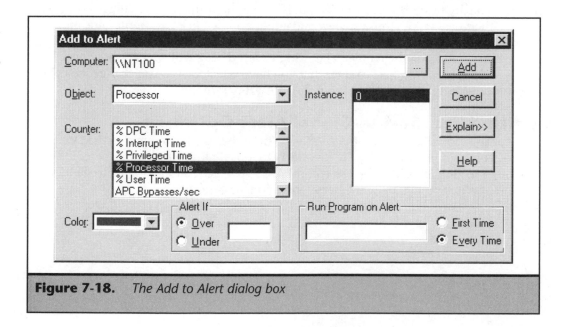

Figure 7-18.   *The Add to Alert dialog box*

If you wish to spawn an application when an alert happens, you will fill in the Run Program On fields. In the Run Program on Alert field, select either First Time or Every Time and type the complete path name for an application or macro that you want the system to run once, or every time, the specified alert occurs. The Alert Log entry will be passed, as the command line argument, to the specified application.

ADDING ADDITIONAL OBJECTS   Choose the Add button and repeat the process for any additional objects or computers you want to watch. When you finish adding object selections, choose the Done button.

Displaying Your Selections

When you are returned to the Alert view, a list of your selections will appear in the Alert Legend field, found at the bottom of the view window. Performance Monitor will then display any alerts generated on the objects you have chosen to monitor in the Alert Log area.

NOTE: Performance Monitor allows you to monitor alert conditions even when working in other views. If an alert occurs while you are in another view, an alert icon will appear in the right side of the status bar showing the number of alerts that have occurred since the last time that the Alert view was displayed. The icon will disappear after you have switched to Alert view and then back to another view.

Editing Alert Parameters

If you wish to change Alert parameters for an object counter, you may do so at any time. If you are in Alert view, you can double-click the counter line in the Alert Legend field. Otherwise, switch to Alert view and either double-click the counter line or choose Edit Alert Entry from the Edit menu. Alternatively, you can choose the Edit Alert Entry button on the toolbar. The Add to Alert dialog will appear, showing parameters set on the object counter that you have selected. You can change the color, Alert If criteria, and/or the Run Program on Alert parameters.

Editing and Saving Global Alert Options

You control global settings for the Alert view from the Alert command in the Options menu. This command will display the Alert Options dialog, which allows you to set options affecting all alerts. You can control Alert view activation, logging to the Event Viewer application log, network alerts, and update methods.

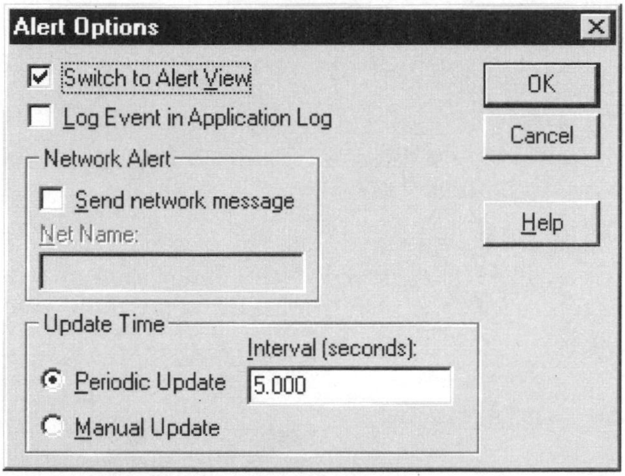

Figure 7-19.   *The Alert Options dialog box*

SETTING GLOBAL ALERT OPTIONS   To display the Alert Options dialog, choose
Alert from the Options menu or choose the Options button on the toolbar. In the Alert
Options dialog (see Figure 7-19), select one or all of the following options:

- **Switch to Alert View:** If you wish Performance Monitor to immediately
  bring up the Alert view when an alert is generated, select the Switch to Alert
  View field.

- **Log Event in Application Log:** If you wish Performance Monitor to log
  alerts to the Event Viewer application log, select the Log Event in Application
  Log field.

- **Send Network Message:** If you wish Performance Monitor to send a network
  message to another computer, select the Send network message field, and then,
  in the Net Name field, type the computer name of the remote computer. The
  NT Messenger service must have been already started and the net name that
  you use must have been previously defined.

■ **Update Time (method) and Interval:** Use these fields to determine the method and interval for alert view updates. Select either Manual or Periodic Update. If you choose Periodic Update, enter a value, in seconds, into the Interval field. This determines the time between updates in alert view.

When you are finished with setting global options, choose the OK button. These new options will take effect immediately.

SAVING ALERT SELECTIONS   To save alert view parameters in a file (.PMA), choose Save Alert Settings As, from the File menu. In the Performance Monitor Save As dialog, select or type a path and name for the file you wish to save these settings in. Finally, choose the OK button.

Logging Information

Performance logging allows you to record events related to the activity of the objects and counters that you have selected. This can be very helpful in gaining an overall view of events and throughput, pointing out general trends, and capturing long term trends in the performance of your system. You can collect data from multiple systems, spanning multiple users and time frames, into a single log file.

Bringing up the Log Window

To display the Log view, choose Log from the View menu or choose the Log button on the toolbar. Initially, the Log view will be blank unless you have previously loaded or created a log file during the present Performance Monitor session.

To create a new log file, choose New Log Settings from the File menu. To open a log settings file that has been previously saved, choose Open from the File menu. In the Performance Monitor File Open dialog, select or enter the path and name for the log settings (.PML) file that you want to use, and then choose the OK button.

Adding Objects to a Log View

When you create and add objects to a log, you are able to collect information that can be examined at any time. You'll have a permanent record of the activity reports on the items you select. You can view objects' behavior from different scenarios or times and do a compare and contrast on the data. You start this process by adding objects to a new log settings collection.

To add objects to the log, choose Add to Log from the Edit menu or choose the Add to Log button on the toolbar. You will be presented with the Add to Log dialog filled in with the default settings plus the name of your workstation or server entered into the Computer field (see Figure 7-20). You may select another computer as in the procedures outlined earlier in this chapter.

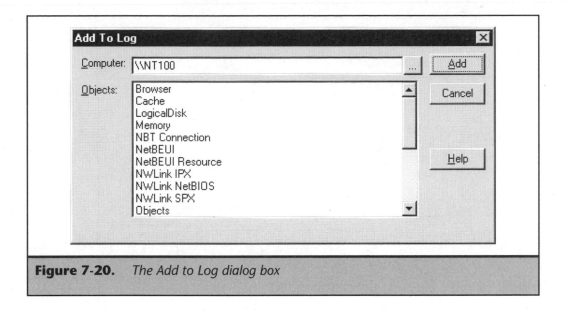

Figure 7-20.   *The Add to Log dialog box*

Select an object or objects to query in the Objects field and then choose the Add button. Repeat this process for any objects and computers that you want to query, and when you have finished, choose the Done button. The log view will then reflect a list of your selections.

Editing Log Options

The Log view has global options you may set anytime. Choosing the Log command from the Options menu enables you to change the data involved in naming the log file, changing the method used for updating log values, and specifying the update interval. The Options dialog (see Figure 7-21) is also capable of being used to start and stop the logging of information.

ENTERING A NAME FOR THE LOG FILE   In the Log File field, type a name for the log file you wish to create, or, if this is the name of an existing file, it will be opened and appended to. To open the file as new, it must have a new name.

CHOOSING MANUAL OR PERIODIC UPDATES   In the Update Time field, you can select either the Manual or Periodic Update options. Also, if you select the Periodic Update option, you must enter a value, in seconds, in the Interval field.

CHOOSING TO START THE LOG   At this point, you can elect to immediately start the log by choosing the Start Log button, which will turn into a Stop Log button when activated. Otherwise, use the Start Log toolbar button when you wish to start logging.

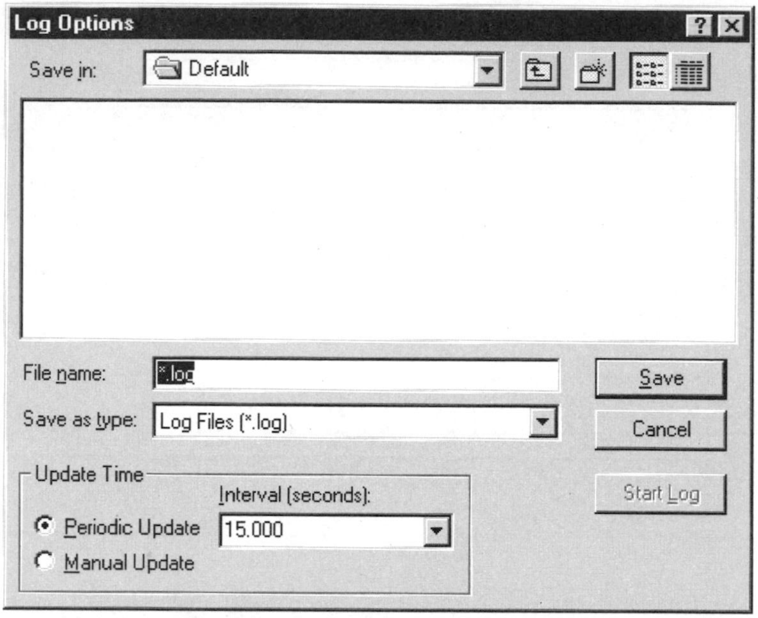

Figure 7-21. *The Log Options dialog box*

Saving Log Parameters

To save log settings to a (.PML) file, choose Save Log Settings As from the File menu. Next, from the Save As dialog, select or type a path and file name you wish to save these settings in, and then choose the OK button.

Insider Info

Just as liner notes help expand understanding and meaning on the cover of a music album, log files can be made more understandable and useful by using a built-in feature called *bookmarks*.

You can add bookmarks at any point while logging. They are textual notes that you can embed within log files at any point. Bookmarks can serve as a way to provide explanation and background for events or scenarios of interest. The Bookmark command is available anytime while you are logging.

To add a bookmark, choose Bookmark from the Options menu or choose the Bookmark button on the toolbar. In the Bookmark Comment field, type your comments and then choose the Add button.

Working with Log Files

Performance log files can help you go into depth to solve a performance problem or metric. Charting provides instantaneous feedback, but at the cost of being unable to put events in perspective. In a log file, your ability to look at the overall performance of a system is enhanced and you are provided with great detail. You use a *timeframe* to specify how much data you want to look at. This timeframe has a start and a stop, both relative to the frame, which slides against the background time limits. In this way, an interval can be setup and moved relative to the actual record, making sort of a movable window on your total data. You can do this from the Log or Chart view. A timeframe has a start and stop time that you control.

Viewing and Using Saved Log Files

The primary purpose of logging data is to be able to quantify results. When you need a graphical view of a log file, you can open an existing one in Chart view to see how the values changed over a defined period of time. You can change the time intervals displayed, choose which objects and counters to view, print the chart, and export the data to a word processor, spreadsheet, or database for special analysis and display.

Selecting Log Files to Manipulate

To view and manage an existing log file, choose the Data From command in the Options menu from the Chart view. This will open a dialog that allows you to select a log file, anywhere on your network, to become the input to your chart view. This action will also activate the Time Window command, grayed out until now, in the Edit menu.

To select the log file, pick Log File in the Data Values Displayed From field. Next, in the Log File edit field, type the log's filename, or choose the gray More ("…") button to the right of the edit field. This will display the Open Input Log File dialog from which you can select a log file anywhere on your network. When you are finished, press the OK button.

 NOTE: *The Data From command is like a toggle switch. It allows you to select where the data, that is charted or viewed, comes from. You can therefore select whether you will gather data live—from the samples Performance Monitor collects on the fly in the present—or from a previously recorded session—where the data is redisplayed by you in a format and analysis mode of your choosing.*

Working with Edit Commands

Once you have selected and loaded a log file, commands on the Edit menu become active. You can manipulate the data in many ways by choosing any of the following commands:

- **Add to Chart:** Use this command to select which objects, and their counters, you wish to chart or manipulate.

■ **Delete from Chart:** Use this command to delete objects, and their counters, which are of no interest or use in the analysis you wish to perform. This helps you weed out extraneous data originally logged alongside the data of interest.

■ **Edit Chart Line:** Use this command to change any of the option settings for an individual chart line, representing an object and it's counter (e.g. color, line style, etc.).

■ **Time Window:** Use this command to manipulate the timeframe on which you will base your analysis. You can change the displayed starting and stopping points and their relation to the overall period represented by the log file.

Manipulating Timeframes

Think of a timeframe as a sliding widow on your data, whose start and stop times, representing the width of that sliding window, are also changeable. You can change the start and stop times for a timeframe in either the Log or Chart view. Essentially, a timeframe allows you to move around in a log file at will. It also allows you to view data events on different logical scales, sort of like working with timebases on an oscilloscope. Selected timeframes apply to all four views.

NOTE: *Working with timeframes is of little value when you are in the Log view, however, since you will want to view the results of your manipulations, and that is only possible in the Chart view.*

After you have edited your chart selections you can invoke the Time Window dialog to directly manipulate start and stop times, and timeframe position, by using a graphical representation of the timeframe. This timeframe graph is superimposed upon the total data width, showing you relative positions and frame width all at once.

TIP: *You can position the Input Log File Timeframe dialog, so that as you move the set points in the dialog, you will see gray-colored, vertical placeholder lines move on the Chart view, which reflect your data width and duration choices.*

Once you have set the proper timeframe limits and setpoints, you will have the opportunity to set alerts on the data. You may also re-log the data, using the new timeframe. This allows you to condense data and create new views of the existing data. Finally, you may wish to create a report, which we will examine in the next section of this chapter.

Operating the Time Window

To setup a timeframe, changing the time window for logged data, you will need to bring up the Time Window dialog. Do this by choosing Time Window from the Edit menu. Now, in the Input Log File Timeframe dialog box (see Figure 7-22), use the following procedures to setup your target timeframe, which will control the revised display of the logged data:

- **Start/Stop points:** Change the start and stop by using the mouse, dragging the ends of the time interval slide bar to new positions. You may also use the ARROW keys to move these setpoints.

- **Window Position:** Change the interval or window position by dragging the entire bar, from the middle, over the slide range. You may also use the SHIFT+ARROW keys to move either end.

- **Bookmarks as Setpoints:** You can set a start or stop point to be equal to a logged bookmark. To do so, select the bookmark and choose either the Set as Start button or the Set as Stop button.

 TIP: *If you manipulate timeframes in Chart view, you can get instant feedback on the data setpoints against the backdrop of your plotted data. As you move the setpoints, the gray vertical setpoint lines, superimposed on the actual data, will move to reflect your choices.*

To finalize your choices, press the OK button. All views will change to reflect the selections you have made for the active timeframe.

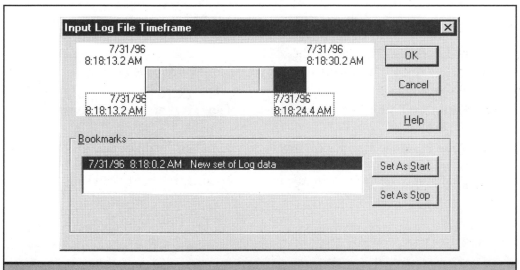

Figure 7-22. *The Input Log File Timeframe dialog box*

Setting and Saving Global Options

To set global options, choose Chart from the Options menu. You may then choose to hide or display items, change the vertical scale, or toggle the plotting format between graph and histogram.

To save your settings, choose one of the following commands from the File menu:

- **Save Chart Settings As:** Use this command to save a new settings file, or to update a settings file, reflecting the changes you have just made.

- **Export Chart:** Use this command to export the chart data in a file format that is compatible with word processors, spreadsheets, and database applications.

Setting Alerts on Input Log Files

Just as you can trigger alerts on data that is collected instantaneously in Performance Monitor, you can also set alerts on the data in an existing log file, pointing out where your logged data went outside the boundary of various alert values. These alerts are added to the Alert log for your inspection.

To set alerts on your input log file, first choose Alert View from the View menu. Choose the Data From command in the Options menu to display the Open Input Log File dialog, which lets you select a log file anywhere on your network. Once you have selected and loaded a log file, commands on the Edit menu become active.

You can manipulate the data in many ways by choosing any of the following commands:

- **Add to Alert:** Use this command to choose the objects and counters you wish to add. All logged objects and their counters will be displayed in the Add to Alert dialog. You can then define your Alert Log by selecting only those objects and counters that you want.

- **Delete Alert:** Use this command to remove any unwanted objects and counters.

- **Edit Alert Entry:** Use this command to change any of the selection settings on an alert.

- **Time Window:** Use this command to manipulate the timeframe on which you will base your analysis. You can change the displayed starting and stopping points, and their relation to the overall period represented by the log file.

Setting, Saving, or Exporting Alert Options

Choose Alert from the Options menu to select the update-time interval. This is the interval on which you wish to sample the logged data, looking for alert criteria excession.

When you have set all of the options and alerts that you wish to look for, and you wish to save those settings or use the data outside of Performance Monitor, choose a command from the File menu. You may use either of the following commands:

- **Save Alert Settings As:** Use this command to create a new alert settings file or to update your present alert settings file to reflect the changes that you have made.

- **Export Alert:** Use this command to export the alert log data for use in a word processor, spreadsheet, or database application.

Relogging Input Log Files

Performance Monitor allows you to use an input log file, with previously recorded data, as if it were instantaneously sampled data. By using this feature, you can reuse and refine collected data many times, either recursively or by constant reapplication of the baseline data. In Performance Monitor, this feature is called relogging.

By manipulating data display and options when relogging, you can create many different views and data sets from the original data points. You can reduce copious data sets to derive only important information, and you can relog with different timeframes and object/counter sets. You can create new output files, or append to existing output files.

To relog an input log file, first switch to Log view from the View menu. Then, choose the Data From command in the Options menu. This will display the Open Input Log File dialog from which you can select a log file anywhere on your network.

Once you have selected and loaded a log file, commands on the Edit menu become active. You can manipulate the data in many ways by choosing any of the following commands:

- **Add to Log:** Use this command to choose the objects and counters you wish to add. All logged objects and their counters will be displayed in the Add to Log dialog. You can then define the subset of these objects and counters for relogging.

■ **Delete from Log:** Use this command to remove unwanted objects and
their counters.

■ **Time Window:** Use this command to manipulate the timeframe on which you
will base your re-log. You can change the displayed starting and stopping
points, and their relation to the overall period represented by the log file.

From the Options menu, you can then choose Log to change the log file name, the
logging interval, and to start relogging. If you select an existing log file for output, the
data will be appended to the log file. If the log filename does not already exist, a new
log file will be created and data will be added from the start of that file.

*NOTE: To enable the Relog File button, you must first provide a valid filename and you
must have selected at least one object/counter to log.*

Saving or Exporting Log Data

When you wish to save the log settings or export the log data for use elsewhere, you
can now, from the File menu, choose either of the following commands:

■ **Save Log Settings As:** Use this command to create a new log settings file or to
update your present log settings file to reflect the changes that you have made.

■ **Export Log:** Use this command to export the log data for use in a word
processor, spreadsheet, or database application.

Creating Log Data Reports

Reports help separate and collate data on a per counter basis (see the next section of
this chapter on the Report view). When you need to create a report using logged data
(rather than from live, instantaneous data), you may do so using the same techniques.
The only difference in your output report will be that it is representative of the logged
data with regards to the timeframe that you have specified, rather than from the live
data you would be deriving from current values.

To create a report based on values derived from an input log file, choose the Data
From command in the Options menu. This will display the Open Input Log File dialog
from which you can select a log file anywhere on your network. Once you have
selected and loaded a log file, commands on the Edit menu become active, and you
can manipulate the data in many ways by choosing any of the following commands:

■ **Add to Report:** Use this command to choose the objects and counters you
wish to have displayed in your report. All logged objects and their counters
will be displayed in the Add to Report dialog. You can then define the subset of
these objects and counters for display.

- **Delete from Report:** Use this command to remove unwanted objects and their counters.
- **Time Window:** Use this command to manipulate the timeframe on which you will base your report. You can change the displayed starting and stopping points, and their relation to the overall period represented by the log file.

Saving or Exporting Reports

When you wish to save the report settings or export the report data for use elsewhere, you can now, from the File menu, choose either of the following commands:

- **Save Report Settings As:** Use this command to create a new report settings file (.PMR), or to update your present report settings file to reflect the changes that you have made.
- **Export Report:** Use this command to export the log data for use in a word processor, spreadsheet, or database application.

Using the Report View

Performance Monitor data may be so copious that cursory inspection yields little or no usable conclusions. A processor counter may change so many times over a short period, that unless you can contrast it against a counter, say, for the current process (the process that affected the CPU load), you may not be able to tell what is really going on.

Using the Report view, you may collate these rapidly changing values in columnar format, listing each individual instance of a particular object. This kind of display tends to point out data trends that graphing alone will not pick up. It gives you a more granular view of the data. The Report view allows you to adjust the intervals that reporting is done on, print reports, and export the report data to other applications for further processing or inclusion in documents.

Opening Report View

To open a Report view, choose Report from the View menu. You can also open a Report view by using the Report button on the toolbar. Initially, the Report view will appear blank unless it has already been opened and setup during the present Performance Monitor session.

You may use settings from an existing report settings file by choosing Open from the File menu. In the Performance Monitor File Open dialog, select or type the filename of an existing report settings file (.PMR) containing the settings you wish to apply to this report. This file may exist anywhere on your network.

Alternatively, you may create a new report file by choosing New Report Settings from the File menu. You will then have the option of saving new settings to a file at any time.

Insider Info

Reports can uncover behavior in objects that would otherwise go unnoticed in a current-value Chart view. They can help you to discover function in individual instances of objects that are obscured when many objects are being sampled or when you need to look closely at an object's activity with regard to another object's actions.

For instance, if you suspect a bottleneck in network communications, finding the exact data that reflects that bottleneck may not be altogether straightforward. You may be suspect of a particular application that uses TCP/IP to communicate, where, in reality, a background utility using the NetBEUI component is causing the problem. Without the capability to collate throughput data on each of these specific objects, looking at their changing values in columnar format in a side by side comparison, you might never find the real problem.

Loading can also be problematical. If you are trying to ascertain load levels on the Processor, reports may be the best way to see these rapidly changing values in context. The Processor object can exhibit wild fluctuations, and without the macro view that a report will give you, load versus application mix will most certainly be obscured by background or system processing events.

Reports can also give you a baseline upon which to judge system performance on an ongoing basis. If you create a report every month, using the same settings file, you may become aware of performance drop-offs. These performance reductions may then be traced to an activity that has changed the system within that last period of time.

For instance, say that within the last month, a performance report indicates that your data throughput to and from an application has dropped drastically. The performance data points to a bottleneck in the paging file (pagefile.sys). You look back in your maintenance logs and discover the addition of a spooler program for printing. You can then rerun the performance report, adding queries to the spooler, to discover that the paging file is being hit heavily by that component, reducing performance in your target application. With this new knowledge, you can easily increase the size of the paging file, or add more paging capability on a different hard disk, to alleviate the problem.

Adding Objects/Counters to a Report

To add object/instance and counter selections to a report, choose Add to Report from the Edit menu or choose the Add to Report button on the toolbar. The Add to Report dialog box will be displayed with default settings, and your workstation or server will be listed in the Computer field (see Figure 7-23).

SELECTING A DIFFERENT COMPUTER   To select a different computer on your network, in the Computer field, type the computer's name or click the "..." button to

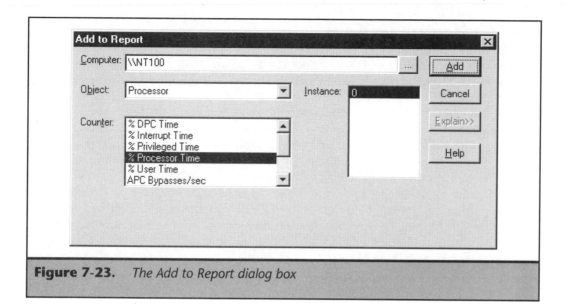

Figure 7-23. *The Add to Report dialog box*

the right of the Computer edit field to display the Select Computer dialog (see Figure 7-12). If you use the Select Computer dialog, double-click the name of a domain controller or workgroup to display the list of servers and workstations available. Choose the name of the server or workstation that you want to monitor and press the OK button.

ADDING AN OBJECT TO THE REPORT   In the Object field (from Figure 7-23), select an object to add to the report from the list of those that are available on the chosen computer. The Counter and Instance fields change to display the selections that are available for that object on the computer that appears in the Computer field. To actually select an item, in the Counter field, select a counter. In the Instance field, select one or more instances as appropriate, and then choose Add to commit your choices to the report. Repeat this operation, along with your parameter choices for all the items you wish to add to your chart.

TIP: *For information that will help you to understand the meaning and scope of a specific counter, press the Explain>> button to display the Counter Definition field. If you have already turned this field on, you will get an explanation automatically as you choose different objects and their counters.*

Displaying Your Selections

Once you have made your object/instance/counter choices, a list of these selections, sorted by computer and object, will appear in the report area. Performance Monitor will then display the counter values in the report.

Editing Report Options

Once you have added objects to the report view, you may want to change how Performance Monitor updates these values for the report. You can also, at any time, get an instant update of the sampled values by using the Options menu/Update Now command.

To set the method that Performance Monitor uses to update the selected counters, use the Report command in the Options menu. You can select either automatic updating, with interval, or manual updating only. To change the report updating method, choose Report from the Options menu or choose the Options button on the toolbar. In the Update Time field, select Periodic Update—entering a value (in seconds) in the Interval field where updating will occur. You may also pick the Interval rate by opening the Interval field to select a value. If you wish to manually control all updating, select Manual Update. To complete the process, choose the OK button.

Saving Report Settings

To save report settings, choose Save Report Settings As from the File menu. This command will result in the display of the Performance Monitor Save As dialog. In the Save As dialog, select or type a filename for the file that will contain the present settings and selections that you have made. When you are done, choose the OK button. This settings file can reside on any computer in your network.

What's Next

In this chapter you have learned how to navigate and configure the Event Viewer and the Performance Monitor applications. These are two of the most important diagnostics that you can use to gain an upper hand over the chaos that can happen simply by adding a service or a piece of hardware to your computer. These tools are also helpful in situations that require bringing untested configurations on line.

In the next chapters (the remainder of Part Two of this book), you'll gain some in-depth information on the user interface, the Console, and some special insights into NT 4's multimedia capabilities.

Chapter Eight

The Command Prompt and Console Applet

This chapter explains how to use the NT 4 command prompt, or console—the character-based, full screen or windowed interface to NT 4 and its subsystems. We'll also cover the command prompt's associated Control Panel/Console applet. The command prompt implements an interface similar to a teletype terminal screen, with a great deal of added functionality. This interface supports most character mode commands and applications designed for NT 3.1–4, Windows 95, Windows 3.x, MS-DOS, OS/2 1.x, and POSIX. The Control Panel/Console applet lets you configure global options to change the default behavior and appearance of all command prompt (console) windows.

NOTE: If you have used MS-DOS or earlier Windows operating systems, you will be instantly familiar with the NT command prompt. The command prompt retains and enhances almost all the commands used in MS-DOS and offers new, NT-specific extensions and commands.

The command prompt supports direct, command line execution of 32-bit executables, 16-bit MS-DOS applications, batch files, interprocess communication and redirection between subsystems and applications. It also supports most of the Windows Clipboard functions, and adds some unique twists, using what NT calls the QuickEdit mode. The command prompt also implements a built-in superset of the MS-DOS Doskey program functionality for command line history and editing.

A Quick Overview

The following sections give you a quick overview of the basic operations and configuration options available with NT 4's command prompt and the Console applet.

Starting and Quitting

Start the command prompt by double-clicking the command prompt icon on the desktop or choosing the Command Prompt command from the Start menu. The command prompt window will display the command prompt, a set of changeable prompt characters, followed by a blinking cursor. The default command prompt characters are the current drive and directory followed by the ">" sign, but you can change this to almost anything you like.

NOTE: *On Intel x86 computers, the command prompt window may be configured to appear in it's own desktop window (the usual default), or it can be shown full screen, taking over the entire display. The desktop and all other applications are still there, only hidden. Use the ALT-TAB combination keys to switch back and forth between the command prompt window and any other windows. This works for full screen or windowed applications, including the command prompt. On most RISC-based computers, a command prompt session is full screen only.*

There are four ways to quit the command prompt:

- Type **exit** at the command prompt
- Choose Close from the System menu
- Double-click the System menu box
- Click the Close box in the upper-right corner of the window

To quit the command prompt when it, or an application started by it, fails to respond, Choose Close from the System menu. The End Task dialog will appear. Choose End Task to terminate the application and the command prompt. (see Figure 8-1).

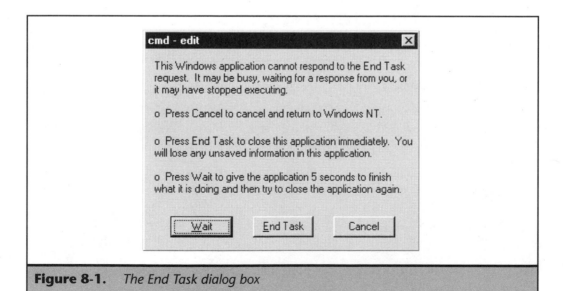

Figure 8-1. *The End Task dialog box*

CAUTION: *Use the End Task dialog method only as a last resort, when everything else fails. You should only quit the command prompt or an application this way in an emergency, because you may lose or corrupt data by using this method. When you quit the command prompt using this method, you will generally not be given the chance to gracefully shut down any applications or utilities that have been started by the command prompt session. If you were running a disk utility, for instance, shutting down the prompt by this method would also shut down the utility, possibly in the middle of an operation on a disk file.*

Changing Window Options

You can configure the options and appearance of an individual command prompt window by using the System menu's Properties dialog or, if you wish to change the defaults for all command prompt windows, by accessing the Settings/Control Panel/Console applet from the Start button. Either way will bring up the same Properties dialog. The only difference being the scope of your changes.

With the System Menu

The icon/box in the upper left corner of any window in NT 4 is that window's System menu. The command prompt window has a System menu with extra commands that refer to operations for command prompt windows only. Although some commands may be grayed (disabled) from time to time, the System menu generally allows you to:

- Move or position the window (if in widowed mode)
- Size the window with the mouse or cursor keys
- Minimize (iconize) or maximize (make window fill screen) a window
- Close the window
- Edit: Mark, Copy, and Paste commands (command prompt specific)
- Open the Properties dialog to change specific options and appearances for this command prompt window (command prompt specific)

To open the System menu, click the System menu box once or press ALT+SPACEBAR. The System menu will open so that you can select from the list of commands.

NOTE: *If you are in full screen mode, the window will minimize and the System menu will appear from the icon.*

With the Console Applet

If you are setting properties for all command prompt windows, you can use the Console applet in Settings/Control Panel from the Start bar. This applet will allow you to configure global settings that will be used as a default for all command prompt windows.

Using the Properties Dialog

The Properties dialog is the key to setting options, whether global or for a specific command prompt window. Parameters can be set using the tabbed properties pages contained within the dialog. The tabbed pages contain settings described in the following sections:

The Options Tab

In the Options tab (see Figure 8-2), the possible selections include:

CURSOR SIZE FIELDS   The displayed cursor can be set to one of the following vertical sizes, with the horizontal size of the cursor dependent upon the size of the font in use:

■ **Small:** Displays the blinking cursor as an underline type character.

■ **Medium:** Displays the blinking cursor as a box—half the vertical size of the vertical font pitch.

■ **Large:** Displays the blinking cursor as a box—the vertical size of the vertical font pitch.

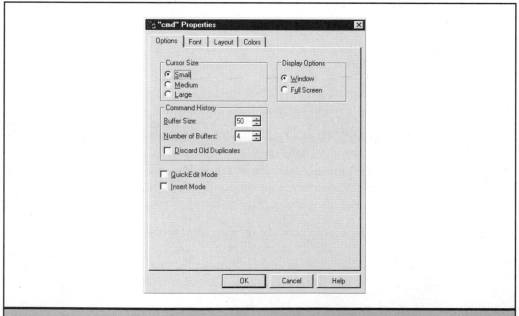

Figure 8-2.   *The Options tab*

COMMAND HISTORY FIELDS   The Command History buffer is used by the built-in command line history and recall facility. The commands executed in a console window are stored in this buffer. If you frequently need to use the same commands, accessing the command history can save you time because you don't have to retype the commands each time you use them.

To access the command history, Press F7 to display a popup box with a list of stored commands. You can then use the arrow keys to scroll through the list until the command you want is selected. Press ENTER to issue the command. You can also type part of a command, and then press F8 as many times as necessary to retrieve the correct command. You can edit the command and press ENTER to issue it.

This feature is very similar to the Doskey program in MS-DOS. The options include:

- **Buffer Size:** The size, in lines, of the History buffer, which when exceeded, will wrap around and discard the earliest entries.

- **Number of Buffers:** The total number of buffers that will be created, system wide, using the Buffer Size parameter. Other programs may need access to a command line history buffer. Use this setting to limit the buffers that are available.

- **Discard Old Duplicates:** Lets the history buffer search for duplicate command lines, discarding them if found. When in a command prompt session, if you have issued the same command more than once, the command history buffer will contain every individual representation of that command. To save buffer space, and keep only one instance of each command that you type, select the Discard Old Duplicates check box.

QUICKEDIT MODE   If checked, the QuickEdit mode permits you to use your mouse to cut and paste, without having to use the Edit menu.

INSERT MODE   This is just like Insert/Overtype on a word processor. If Insert mode is not checked, text typed at the cursor replaces existing text.

DISPLAY OPTIONS FIELDS   These allow you to set the screen mode to either windowed or full screen. To toggle between windowed and full screen mode, press ALT+ENTER, or choose the Properties dialog from the System menu and set the mode in the Options tab. By default, the command prompt opens as a window on your desktop.

   NOTE: Most RISC-based computers do not support windowed mode.

The Font Tab

You can choose different fonts and font sizes for the console window from the Font tab (see Figure 8-3). When you change fonts, the window size changes to accommodate the new font size.

In the Font box, choose a font. These fonts are fixed pitch and may be TrueType or raster fonts. The specific fonts that are available on your computer will appear in this listbox. Next, in the Size box, choose a size. If you want to use bold fonts, select the Bold Fonts check box. When you've completed your selections, choose the OK button.

NOTE: *In the Window Preview box, a display of the resultant size of the window will appear, based on the font and font size you selected.*

The Layout Tab

The Layout tab of the Properties dialog (see Figure 8-4) lets you specify the screen buffer size, the window size, and, optionally, the window position. The window

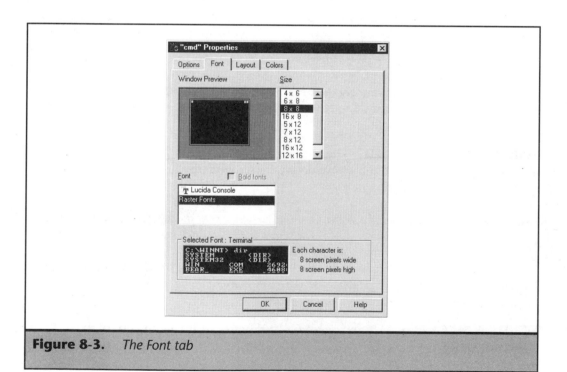

Figure 8-3. *The Font tab*

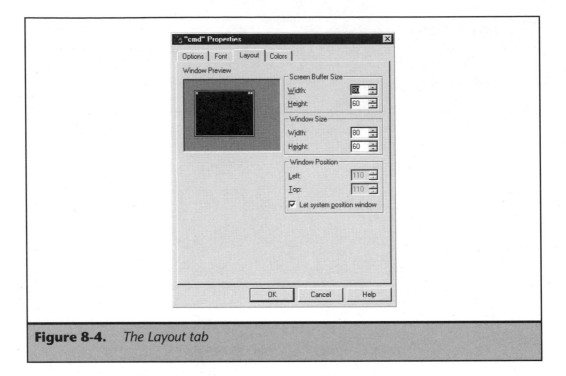

Figure 8-4. *The Layout tab*

position, relative to the top-left corner of the screen, may be entered or left to the system to position automatically.

The Layout options include:

SCREEN BUFFER SIZE FIELD The width setting determines the number of characters per line. The height setting determines how many lines are stored, as a representation of the screen in memory.

NOTE: Scroll bars will be displayed if the current size of the physical window is smaller than the screen buffer size settings. The screen buffer settings set a maximum for the physical size of the window based on font size. No matter what font size you choose, if you have set the width to be 80 and the height to be 25, the maximum physical size of the window will be no larger than would be needed but large enough to fit 80x25 characters in the selected font.

WINDOW SIZE FIELD This box lets you specify the width and height of the window in memory.

WINDOW POSITION FIELD This box lets you specify the left and top position of the window relative to the upper left corner of the screen.

SYSTEM POSITION CHECKBOX Use this check box if you want the system to position the window automatically.

The Colors Tab

The Colors tab of the Properties dialog lets you specify the color of the text (foreground) and background for a console window (see Figure 8-5). You can also specify the color of the text and background of popup windows—small informational windows like the command history window—that originate from console windows.

Choose colors for screen text, screen background, popup text, or popup background by selecting the screen element you want to change and the color you want to assign to that screen element. When you're done, choose the OK button. The selections that you make will appear in the Selected Screen Colors or Selected Popup Colors box.

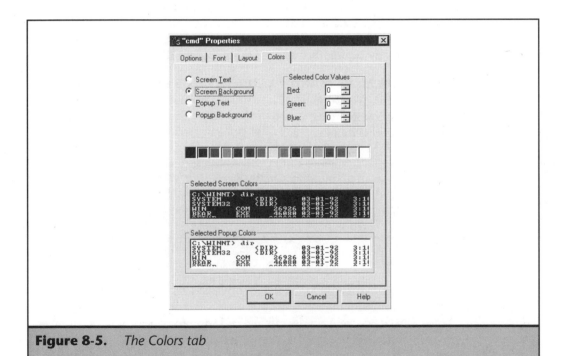

Figure 8-5. *The Colors tab*

Mini-Glossary

ANSI (AMERICAN NATIONAL STANDARDS INSTITUTE)　Refers in this case to the ANSI.SYS file, which defines functions that change display graphics, control cursor movement, and reassign keys. The ANSI.SYS driver file may be loaded so programs that depend upon it can be run.

COMMAND HISTORY BUFFER　A Last-In/First-Out (LIFO) line oriented buffer kept by each console window to store command lines that have been typed during the present session. Once you close the console window, the buffer is discarded. Similar in action to the MS-DOS Doskey facility, the command history buffer stores previously typed commands while you are working in the console window. In this way, you can recall commands that you have typed by using shortcut keys. This saves a great deal of retyping when long command lines must be repeated.

COMMAND PROMPT/CONSOLE WINDOWS　Windows that implement the NT console, sometimes called a command prompt window. The console is the character-based NT interface that looks and acts very similar to MS-DOS. The console also supports OS/2 1.x and POSIX character applications as well as Win32 console and most MS-DOS programs. Most applications can be started from a console window by typing the name of the program file.

OEM (ORIGINAL EQUIPMENT MANUFACTURER) CODE PAGE　A code page is a loadable character set, which can include numbers, punctuation marks, and other symbols. Different languages may be supported by the use of different code pages. For example, ANSI code page 1252 is used for American English and most European languages. OEM code page 932 is used for Japanese Kanji.

SCREEN BUFFER　The screen buffer size is the size reserved in memory for a console window's display. The buffer size is determined by the number of characters wide multiplied by the number of lines high—usually 80x24 or 80x50.

Using the ANSI.SYS File

The ANSI.SYS driver file contains functions that control screen display graphics, cursor movement, and key assignments in a universal way that many programs depend upon. ANSI.SYS supports ANSI terminal emulation to control your system's screen and keyboard. Control is asserted by a program with an ANSI escape sequence. This is a sequence of ASCII characters, the first two of which are the escape character (1Bh) and the left-bracket character (5Bh). The character or characters following the escape and left-bracket characters specify an alphanumeric code that controls a keyboard or display function.

ANSI.SYS can be loaded and used from the command prompt, with the restriction that it can run only in the context of the MS-DOS subsystem. To load ANSI.SYS, add *device=%SystemRoot%\system32\ansi.sys* to the CONFIG.NT file in the NT 4 SYSTEM32 directory. Once ANSI.SYS is loaded, you can use any MS-DOS based program that makes use of this driver.

Insider Info

The command prompt supports Unicode in addition to ANSI/OEM. This allows you to support international character sets and applications and to use characters not included on most computer systems.

The ANSI/OEM/ASCII character set has a maximum length of 255 characters. Unicode display is most important for applications that need to display character sets such as Hebrew, Chinese, or Arabic, where the amount of characters in the language (or the symbols and pictographs available) would not fit into the ANSI/ASCII character set.

Getting Command Prompt Help

Online Help is available for all commands. The following list shows commands that you can type at the command prompt to access different types of help:

- **help** Displays names and short descriptions for all native system commands.
- *command* **/?** Displays description, syntax, parameters, and switches for native commands.
- **help** *command* Displays description, syntax, parameters, and switches for native system commands.
- **net help** Displays names of available command line network commands.
- **net help** *command* Displays description, syntax, parameters, and switches for command line network commands.
- **net** *command* **/help** Displays description, syntax, parameters, and switches for command line network commands.
- **net** *command* **/?** Displays syntax for command line network commands.
- **net helpmsg** *message#* Displays an explanation and action for a numbered network help message.

 TIP: *The Windows NT online Help Reference is available to provide in-depth command syntax, parameters, and details of a command. To use the online Command Reference, click the Help command in the Start menu.*

Exploring NT's Commands and Utilities

Any supported NT 4 command can be run from the command prompt. The NT syntax, symbols, commands, and utilities that we will examine are listed as follows:

- Command syntax
- Command symbols
- NT Console commands: Internal and External

Mini-Glossary

BATCH COMMAND Batch commands are for use in batch programs only. They are commands that direct flow and execution in a batch file.

EXTERNAL COMMAND Commands, such as *chkdsk* and *xcopy,* are external, meaning the command is stored in its own file and loads from disk when you use the command. External commands can be run at the command prompt, from the RUN dialog in the Start menu, from Explorer, or from the Task Manager's Task List/New Task dialog.

INTERNAL COMMAND Commands, such as *dir* and *chdir,* are internal, meaning the command is processed by CMD.EXE and resides in memory at all times. Internal commands can be run only at the command prompt.

NATIVE COMMAND A native command takes advantage of the 32-bit operating system. Most commands familiar to MS-DOS users are now native NT 4 system commands.

Command Syntax

Command Syntax is the exact way in which you must type a command and any arguments or parameters that accompany the command. All commands have at least one part: the command name. Some commands have parameters and switches, or toggles. An example of a syntax for the *xcopy* command is shown here:

```
C:> xcopy a:\*.* c:\newdir\ /s /e /v
```

Command Names

The command name, the only required element in all commands, is usually the name of the function or program that you want to perform or execute. There are a few NT commands that require no other elements, such as *time* or *cls*. Almost all commands, however, have variants that take variable amounts of parameters, arguments, or switches.

Parameters and Switches

When you issue an NT command, you will almost always include some set of parameters and/or switches, which are arguments to that command. The switches are usually one- or two-character toggle-like arguments that change the action of the command subtly. A switch is a forward slash (/) or a hyphen (-) usually followed by words, letters, or numbers. Arguments, if any, are parameters that give the command precise or exact data with which to work. Sometimes, commands will result in an action being taken immediately, and sometimes a command will set the state for overall or global operations. For instance, the *xcopy* command takes a switch in the form of "/v" to verify immediate copy operations, where the *mode* command can take switches and parameters that affect all subsequent operations.

Command Symbols

NT provides a special set of command symbols (shown in the following list) that allow you to manipulate and redirect the input or output of a command. Some of these symbols permit conditional execution of a command, dependent upon the success or failure of the preceding command.

TIP: *The redirection and pipe symbols can be important in working with files and ports. For instance, you can redirect the screen output to a file by typing something like dir > myfile.txt. This would store a directory listing, usually bound for the console screen, in a file named myfile.txt.*

Command Symbol	Use To:
arg > *arg*	Redirect output of left side argument to right side argument.
arg >> *arg*	Redirect output (of left side argument to right side argument) and append to existing data (of right side argument).
arg < *arg*	Redirect input from right side argument to left side argument
arg | *arg*	Pipe output from left side argument to right side argument.
arg | | *arg*	Run the command on the right side of the symbol if the command on the left side of the symbol fails.
arg **&&** *arg*	Run the command on the right side of the symbol if the command on the left side of the symbol is successful.
cmd **&** *cmd*	Separate multiple commands on the command line.
( )	Group commands.
^	Denote the Escape character ($1B) and allow input of command symbols in text.
; or ,	Separate parameters on the command line.

A Listing of NT Commands

The following list describes some of NT 4's most important console commands. Some of these are native (built-in) and some are programs that are run like a command from the command prompt. They are listed here with their principle syntax. Where applicable, see NT Help online for switch (/...) definitions.

TIP: For more information on individual commands, open a command prompt window and type **help***.*

AT   Schedules commands and programs to be run on the specified computer at a specified time and date. The Scheduler service must be running to use the *at* command. The *at* command requires you be a member of the local Administrator group.

```
at [\\computername] [[id] [/delete [/yes]]
```

or

```
at [\\computername] time [/interactive] [/every:date[,...] |
/next:date[,...]] "command"
```

ATTRIB   Displays or changes file attributes. This command displays, sets, or removes the read-only, archive, system, and hidden attributes on files or directories.

```
attrib [+r|-r] [+a|-a] [+s|-s] [+h|-h][[drive:][path] filename] [/s]
```

CACLS   Displays or modifies access control lists (ACLs) of files.

```
cacls filename [/t] [/e] [/c] [/g user:perm] [/r user [...]] [/p user:perm
[...]] [/d user [...]]
```

CHDIR (CD)   Changes the current directory. With no arguments, it displays the current directory.

```
chdir [/d] [drive:][path] [..]
```

or

```
cd [/d] [drive:][path] [..]
```

CHKDSK   Chkdsk lists and/or corrects errors on a disk drive. If *chkdsk* cannot lock the drive for operations, it will offer to run itself automatically the next time the computer reboots. You must be a member of the Administrators group to use *chkdsk*.

```
chkdsk [drive:][[path] filename] [/f] [/v] [/r]
```

CLS   Clears the screen.

```
cls
```

Comp   Compares the contents of two files on a byte by byte basis.

```
comp [data1] [data2] [/d] [/a] [/l] [/n=number] [/c]
```

COMPACT   Displays or alters the compression of files or directories on NTFS volumes.

```
compact [/c] [/u] [/s] [/i] [/f] [/l] filename
```

CONVERT   Converts FAT volumes to NTFS. If *convert* cannot lock down the requested drive, it will offer to convert automatically the next time the computer reboots.

```
convert [drive:] /fs:ntfs [/v] [/nametable:filename]
```

COPY   Copies one or more files from one location to another.

```
copy [/a|/b] source [/a|/b] [+ source [/a|/b] [+ ...]] [destination
[/a|/b]] [/v] [/n] [/z]
```

DATE   Displays and allows you to change the date.

```
date [mm-dd-yy]
```

DEL (ERASE)   Deletes files.

```
del [drive:][path] filename [; ...] [/p] [/f] [/s] [/q] [/a[:attributes]]
```

or

```
erase [drive:][path] filename [; ...] [/p] [/f] [/s] [/q] [/a[:attributes]]
```

DIR   Displays a directory's files and subdirectories. Can display in many ways depending upon switches and arguments.

```
dir [drive:][path][filename] [; ...] [/p] [/w] [/d]
[/a[[:]attributes]][/o[[:]sortorder]] [/t[[:]timefield]] [/s] [/b] [/l]
[/n] [/x]
```

DISKCOMP   Compares the contents of two floppy disks.

```
diskcomp [drive1: [drive2:]]
```

DISKCOPY   Copies the contents of a floppy disk in drive 1 to a floppy disk in drive 2.

```
diskcopy [drive1: [drive2:]] [/v]
```

EXIT   Ends the CMD.EXE program (the console) and returns to the calling program or to the desktop.

```
exit
```

EXPAND   Expands one or more compressed files. Use this command to expand compressed files on distribution disks.

```
expand [-r] source [destination]
```

FC Compares two files and displays the differences between them.

```
fc [/a] [/b] [/c] [/l] [/lbn] [/n] [/t] [/u] [/w] [/nnnn]
[drive1:][path1]filename1 [drive2:][path2]filename2
```

FIND Searches for a specific string of text in a file or files.

```
find [/v] [/c] [/n] [/i] "string" [[drive:][path]filename[...]]
```

FINDSTR Searches for strings in files using literal text or regular expressions.

```
findstr [/b] [/e] [/l] [/c:string] [/r] [/s] [/i] [/x] [/v] [/n] [/m] [/o]
[/g:file] [/f:file] strings files
```

FORMAT Formats the disk in the specified drive with the specified file system. If this is a floppy drive, formats only in the FAT file system. You must be a member of the Administrators group to format a hard disk drive.

```
format drive: [/fs:file-system] [/v[:label]] [/a:unitsize] [/q] [/f:size]
[/t:tracks /n:sectors] [/1] [/4] [/8]
```

LABEL Creates, changes, or deletes the volume label of a disk drive.

```
label [drive:][label]
```

MKDIR (MD) Creates a directory or subdirectory.

```
mkdir [drive:]path
```

or

```
md [drive:]path
```

MODE   Configures system devices and default actions. The *mode* command is a multi-purpose command that can display system status, change system settings, or reconfigure ports or devices. The following is a list of tasks for which you can use the mode command:

- Reconfiguring a printer attached to a parallel port (PRN, LPT1, LPT2, or LPT3) for printing at 80 or 132 characters per line, 6 or 8 lines per inch, or both (if the printer supports these features).

- Configuring the baud rate, parity, and number of data bits and stop bits of a serial communications port (COM1, COM2, COM3, and COM4) for use with a specific printer, modem, or other serial device.

- Displaying the status of all devices or of a single device.

- Redirecting printer output from a parallel port to a serial port so that the serial port becomes the system's default printer port.

- Changing the size of the command prompt window.

- Setting the keyboard's typematic rate.

MORE   Displays one screen of output at a time.

```
command name | more [/e] [/c] [/p] [/s] [/tn] [+n]
```

or

```
more [/e] [/c] [/p] [/s] [/tn] [+n] < [drive:] [path] filename
```

or

```
more [/e] [/c] [/p] [/s] [/tn] [+n] files
```

RENAME (REN)   Changes the name of a file or files.

```
rename [drive:][path] filename1 filename2
```

or

```
ren [drive:][path] filename1 filename2
```

RMDIR (RD)   Deletes a directory.

```
rmdir [drive:]path [/s]
```

or

```
rd [drive:]path [/s]
```

START   Starts an application or command in a separate window. There are many parameters to control how the application starts up.

```
start ["title"] [/dpath] [/i] [/min] [/max] [/separate] [/low] [/normal]
[/high] [/realtime] [/wait] [/b] [filename] [parameters]
```

SUBST   Associates a path with a drive letter. Used to reduce pathnames and simplify commands.

```
subst [drive1: [drive2:]path]
```

or

```
subst drive1: /d
```

TIME   Displays or sets the system time.

```
time [hours:[minutes[:seconds[.hundredths]]][A|P]]
```

XCOPY   Copies files and directories, including subdirectories. There are many switches to control how xcopy performs the operation.

```
xcopy source [destination] [/w] [/p] [/c] [/v] [/q] [/f] [/l]
[/d[:date]] [/u] [/i] [/s [/e]] [/t] [/k] [/r] [/h] [/a|/m] [/n]
[/exclude:filename] [/z]
```

Putting the Command Prompt to Work

The following sections examine the operations you can perform while working in the command prompt window, including:

- Starting applications
- Entering commands repetitively
- Using batch programs
- Cutting, pasting, and editing command line information
- Pausing or canceling command execution

Starting Applications

You may use two methods to start a program from the command prompt. To simply start an application, enter the application's file name (along with a path, if necessary), and then press ENTER. If the application runs as a "console application," the command prompt window will totally contain it. Otherwise, a new window may be started with the application running within it.

> *NOTE:* *In some cases, the command prompt window used to start the program will be unavailable for further use until you exit the application.*

The second method is more flexible and allows you to immediately reuse the command window. To start an application this way, type **start** followed by the application's file name, and then press ENTER. The *start* command has many switches that allow you to control how an application starts up. The command prompt window will also immediately return and accept further commands.

> *TIP:* *You can use the* start *command with the* /separate *switch to run 16-bit Windows applications in their own memory space. This protects other 16-bit Windows programs in case of an application failure. Another set of switches,* /high *and* /realtime, *allow you to control priority boosts when running an application from the command prompt. See the NT online documentation for a complete listing of switches and parameters for the* start *command.*

Using Batch Files

Batch files, or programs, allow you to enter a series of commands into a file so that you can run the file from the command prompt as a single command—really consisting of many embedded commands contained in the batch file.

A batch file has a filename extension of .BAT or .CMD and consists of plain text commands that are entered line by line, as if they were typed at the command prompt.

These commands can consist of any of the commands that you would normally be able to type from the command prompt, plus some special batch commands that allow conditional processing and branching within the context of the batch file playback.

For example, the *goto* batch command directs batch processing to branch to a labeled position, usually dependent upon some prior batch process decision. Conditional batch commands allow you to make choices based upon arguments or results. Other batch commands allow you to input data, output information to the screen, and call other batch files from within a batch file.

Editing Command Prompt Information

Just as the graphical portion of NT has its Clipboard functions to cut and paste data, the command prompt allows you to transfer line oriented data to or from the console window using two methods. The two methods available are the QuickEdit mode and the Edit menu commands.

Using QuickEdit Mode

When turned on from a command prompt window's Properties/Options tabbed dialog, the QuickEdit mode allows you to copy and paste text by using a mouse without having to work with the window's System menu/Edit commands. All data is text oriented, and the QuickEdit mode will work in both full screen and windowed modes.

NOTE: *In full screen mode, you can only paste data. You must be in windowed mode to copy data. You must also use the start command to retain use of the mouse when starting a program from the command prompt when QuickEdit mode is enabled.*

To cut and paste using QuickEdit mode:

1. Use the Command Prompt/System menu/Properties dialog to turn QuickEdit mode on.

2. Position the mouse cursor at the beginning of the text you want to copy, hold the left mouse button down, drag the cursor to the last character of the section you want to copy, and then release the left mouse button. The portion of the screen you want to copy will be highlighted (see Figure 8-6).

3. Press the right mouse button to copy the highlighted area to the Clipboard. This will also dismiss the highlight.

4. When you want to paste the data at the command prompt cursor, press the right mouse button.

Since the data that you copy to the Clipboard is available to all Windows applications, you can also use the Paste command from the Edit menu of any

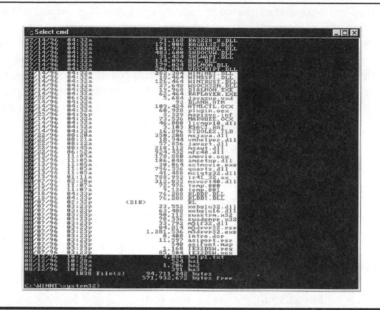

Figure 8-6. *Highlighted data for the copy operation*

Windows application. In this way, you can transfer data to and from graphical applications. You can use a character-based editor, for instance, to pick up text in the command prompt window, and then paste that text into a Windows-based word processor.

Using the Edit Menu

The command prompt Edit menu commands allow you to copy and paste information using the Mark/Copy/Paste methods. The data may be treated as text or graphics, depending upon what graphics mode that the command prompt window is in at the time and how you perform the copy operation.

TIP: These methods also transfer data to and from the Windows Clipboard, so you can also use this method to transfer data between character and graphically based applications.

To copy selected text from a command prompt window, use the following method:

1. Use the mouse, or press ALT+SPACEBAR to open the System menu.

2. From the System menu, choose Edit.

3. From the Edit menu, choose Mark.

4. Select the information you want to copy using a mouse—highlighting data and using the same methods as you would in QuickEdit mode.

5. Press the right mouse button to copy the highlighted data to the Clipboard, or choose Edit and then choose Copy from the System menu.

TIP: *To copy the contents of the entire command prompt window to the Clipboard, as a graphics bitmap, press the PRINT SCREEN key at any time. To copy a specific window as a bitmap, press ALT+PRINT SCREEN.*

6. To paste textual data that is on the Clipboard, use the mouse to place the insertion point where you want it.

7. From the window's System menu, choose Edit (see Figure 8-7).

8. From the Edit menu, choose Paste. Carriage returns will be added to multi-line paste operations.

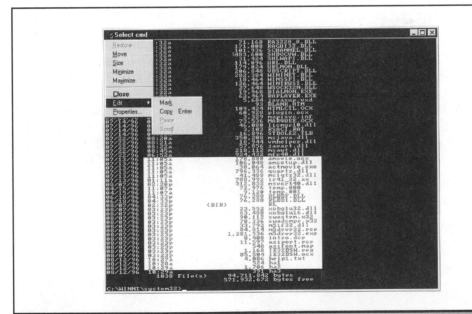

Figure 8-7.   *The Command Prompt Edit menu*

Pausing and Canceling Commands and Applications

While working within the command prompt window, you can pause or cancel the output of a command or stop execution of a program altogether. Many character-oriented commands and applications respond to certain key sequences, either by pausing, or stopping execution and exiting right away.

To pause the output of a command, press CTRL+S or PAUSE. To resume the command's output, press any other key. To cancel a command or application in midstream and stop it from completing, press CTRL+BREAK or CTRL+C. You will be returned to the command prompt. Some commands and applications may also respond by pressing ESC.

> **CAUTION:** *You must be very careful when canceling execution of certain commands and applications. This action does not "undo" what has already been accomplished. If, for example, you are formatting a disk from the command prompt, and you stop the command abruptly, you may render the disk that you were formatting unusable. You will then have to reformat the entire disk. Another example to watch out for would be when your application was writing data to a disk file. If you cancel the application in mid-execution, it may not close the file properly, leaving the entire data file unusable.*

What's Next

Now that we know how to use NT's command prompt utilities—and we can understand NT setup too—it's time to round out our in-depth examination of the basics by taking a closer look at NT's file manipulation utilities: Explorer and File Manager.

In the next chapter, you will learn how to examine, copy, delete, and manipulate files and directories. You'll also learn how to traverse a network, look for files, and perform copy and backup functions. You'll see how easy it is to use another computer's disk drives and share your drives out to another workstation so that your files may be accessed by others.

Chapter Nine

The Explorer and File Management

E very computer user needs a way to work with files and resources. There was a
time when basic operations were all that were needed; dir (ls), copy, move,
delete, and rename were quite enough in the days of CP/M and the first Unix.
Operating systems for microcomputers have become more sophisticated, and their
file-management capabilities have followed suit. Now we have built-in networking
and file systems that exceed the complexity of some of the most sophisticated
machines of ten years ago.

The Way Things Were

As MS-DOS became popular, and was extended in the late 1980s, all of its file
manipulation utilities and built-in commands became very hard to memorize and
work with. And since these commands were all invoked from the old tty-like
command line, remembering and typing in all of the switches and parameters for
more than a few basic commands became almost impossible. The user had the choice
of either sticking with a few well-known commands—back to basics as it were—or
using one of the third-party applications that came to be so well known in the days of
MS-DOS. These utilities unified the tasks of displaying hierarchical directory
structures; navigating through the directory trees; using menu commands for copying,
editing, deleting, and renaming; along with tasks like changing file attributes and time
stamping files.

With the advent of the Windows family of operating systems, a unified file
manager was introduced in the form of a graphical application. No longer dependent
on the character-based interface of MS-DOS, this application showed a graphical
depiction of a hierarchical directory tree, had multiple windows for visual data
organization, and ran within the framework of the main desktop—then called
Program Manager. Its name was equally appropriate: File Manager. As Windows
3.0/3.1 was extended to provide network connectivity, File Manager became capable
of managing network resources as well. Functionality was added to exploit the
networking capability of Windows for Workgroups, and File Manager was extended
so that it not only browsed for, and connected to, network resources but also provided
controlled access to local resources, by sharing local disk drives and directories as
network resources to be used by other peer connections.

When Windows NT 3.1 was introduced, it took on the look of its 16-bit Windows
cousins and inherited the Program Manager/File Manager designs, along with the
same look and feel. There were some extensions to the resource sharing model, along
with support for different file systems, but it was instantly recognizable to anyone
using 16-bit Windows.

NT Today

Then came Windows 95, in which an even newer and more capable design was
employed, and that is essentially the file and resource interface employed in NT today:

Explorer. Explorer takes the designs of Program Manager and File Manager, extending functionality where applicable, and reducing application overhead where possible. Program Manager has been totally replaced by functionality in Explorer, and File Manager is now an old-fashioned subset of what Explorer has become.

Welcome to Explorer

Explorer (see Figure 9-1) is used for file browsing and maintenance, resource sharing and connectivity, application launching, and—as a support tool—it's involved in the operation of other applications. As a file maintenance tool, Explorer unites resources so that files on any media, stored locally or on a remote network share, are accessible in a uniform way.

Files are associated with their viewing or editing applications so that when you open a data file, it launches that file's native viewer or application container and you can execute or edit its data. Added to this application and data launching functionality is the standard set of extended file and directory manipulation tools. You may create, delete, rename, copy, cut, and paste directories and files between connected storage resources. You can also edit files by launching an editor application associated with the file type. A data file can be sent directly to a printer resource, a floppy disk, a mail or fax application (see Figure 9-2), or to the special desktop briefcase replication facility (see Chapter 6).

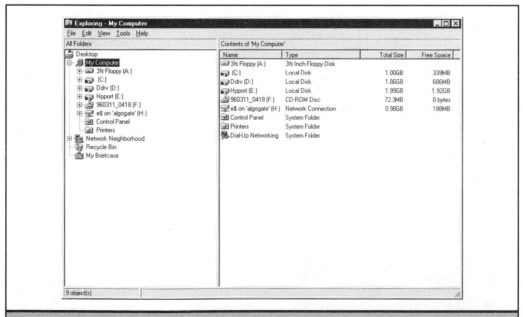

Figure 9-1. *Explorer's main view*

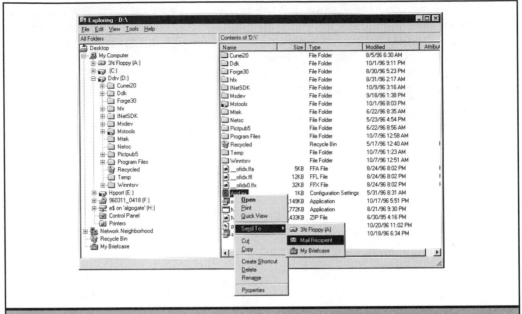

Figure 9-2. *Sending a data file by email in Explorer*

How Explorer Works

Explorer is designed to look like a browsing tool. It presents a connected resource as a hierarchical directory, if applicable, displaying the tree in the left window pane along with the contents of the currently selected directory, or branch of the tree, in the right window pane (see Figure 9-3). To fully exploit Explorer, you should have a mouse attached to your computer, but most commands can also be invoked from the keyboard.

Exploring Your Resources

There will generally always be a standard set of resources available for browsing from the left window pane under the Desktop heading. These resources follow the four standard icons available directly from the desktop (see Chapter 6):

- My Computer
- Network Neighborhood
- Recycle Bin
- My Briefcase

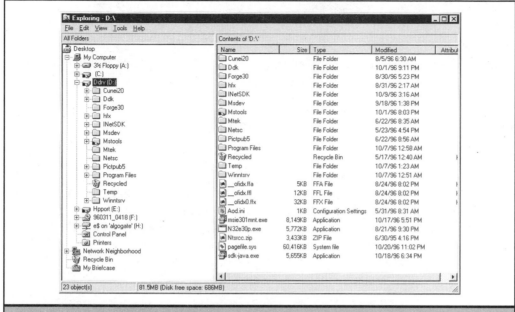

Figure 9-3. *Expanding the branch of a directory tree*

Using the Display

The display in the left window pane consists of icons representing resources, drives, and folders in descending order. A + sign to the left of an item indicates that it can be expanded to display a hierarchy below. When expanded, the + sign next to the item will turn into a − sign. You can toggle the expansion and collapse of a branch of the hierarchical tree by alternately clicking on that item in the left window pane.

As you browse through a resource's tree and expand its branches, the items (other folders or files) contained in the level you have expanded in the left window pane view will be displayed in the right window pane.

NOTE: *If you expanded My Computer/C:/Winnt/help, you would see the contents of the C:\Winnt\help directory listed in the right window pane. Depending on what branch you are in on a particular resource, you might see only individual files or you might see a combination of folders and files.*

Accessing File and Directory Commands

Explorer's file and directory manipulation commands are accessed in the following ways:

■ After selecting a file or folder to work with, you may select a command to apply by choosing one of the commands from the menu at the top of Explorer's window.

■ You may access the most frequently used commands by clicking the right mouse button—after selecting a file or folder or a range of either type of item (see Figure 9-4).

Selecting Ranges of Files or Folders

Selecting ranges of files or folders is accomplished in much the same way as you would select text in a Windows-based text editor. Select the first element of a range by clicking on it once. While holding the SHIFT key down, press the left mouse button, drag the mouse pointer to the last element you wish to select in the range, and then let go of the left mouse button and the SHIFT key. All elements within the range change color to the selected state. To select more than one file or folder individually, hold down the CTRL key, and then select each item you want.

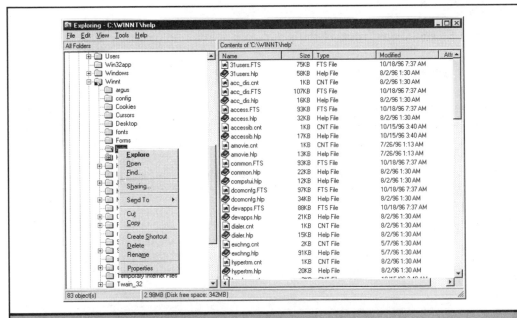

Figure 9-4. *The shortcut menu invoked by clicking the right mouse button*

Working with Explorer Commands

The following sections cover Explorer's commands one at a time, explain their features, and relate them to the advanced tasks and work you can accomplish—such as moving directories and connecting to network resources.

> **REMINDER:** *There are three elements in a typical Explorer window: the left window pane, the right window pane, and the menu area. The Explorer menu can be activated in the usual way by positioning the mouse over a menu item, clicking to drop the menu down, or by using the accelerator key, which is the underlined letter in the menu text in combination with the* ALT *key. For example, to activate the File menu from the keyboard, press* ALT+F.

File Menu

The File menu (see Figure 9-5) is contextually adjustable depending on what kind of element you are operating on. Whether you have selected a disk drive, a directory folder item, or an individual file, the File menu shows only those commands that apply to working with that type of item. The File menu items available for drives, folders, and files are explained in the following sections.

New Folder or Shortcut

To create a new folder, open the folder in which you want to create a new folder. On the File menu, point to New and then select Folder. The new folder appears with a temporary name. Type a name for the new folder, and then press ENTER.

To create a shortcut in a folder, open the folder you want to create the shortcut in. On the File menu, point to New and then select Shortcut. Pick the application or enter

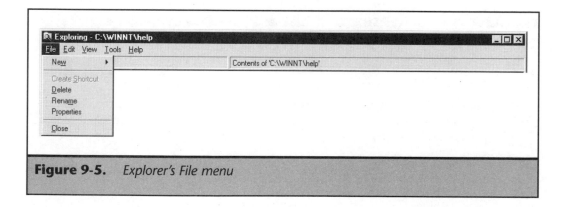

Figure 9-5. *Explorer's File menu*

the command line you wish to execute. You may browse for an application by pressing the Browse button. You can assign an icon and text to the shortcut or accept the default text and icon.

To change any settings for the shortcut—such as what kind of window it starts in or what key combination is used to access it—use your right mouse button to select the shortcut, and then choose Properties. To delete a shortcut, drag it to the Recycle Bin. The original item will still exist on the disk where it is stored.

Delete

To delete a folder or a file, locate the item you want to delete and select it. On the File menu, select Delete. If you want to retrieve a file you have deleted, look in the Recycle Bin. Your deleted items remain in the Recycle Bin until you empty it. You can also drag file or folder icons onto the Recycle Bin icon. If you press SHIFT while dragging, the item is deleted from your computer without being stored in the Recycle Bin.

Rename

To change the name of a folder or file, select the item you want to rename. You do not need to open it. On the File menu, choose Rename. Type the new name, and then press ENTER. A filename can contain up to 255 characters including spaces, but it cannot contain any of the following characters: \ / : * ? " < > |. You can also select the icon in the Explorer list to rename a folder or file. To rename a drive, select it and then choose Properties to change the label.

Properties

To change drive, folder, or file properties, select the item you want to change. On the File menu, choose Properties. You can also right-click an item in the Explorer view and then choose Properties. The Properties sheet that is displayed by selecting this action allows you to inspect and edit the properties relating to the item.

THE DRIVE PROPERTIES SHEET   In the case of drives, the Properties sheet has three tabs: General, Tools, and Sharing.

- **General:** This tab allows you to change the name or label for that drive. Also displayed is the drive's free and used space and its total capacity.

- **Tools:** This tab allows you to perform immediate or scheduled error checking and backup on the drive. You can also perform disk defragmentation if that option is installed.

- **Sharing:** This tab (see Figure 9-6) allows you to share this drive out to remote network users, controlling access and providing a name for the share. Also, if a drive is already shared, you may clone it or stop sharing the drive with this property sheet.

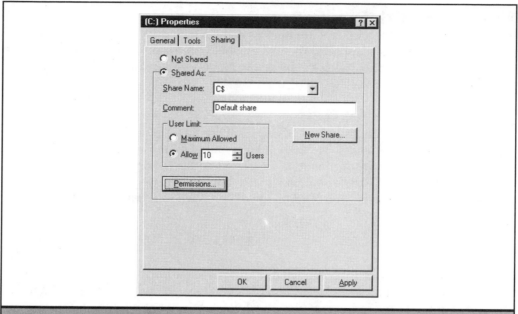

Figure 9-6. *A drive's Properties sheet/Sharing tab*

THE FOLDER PROPERTIES SHEET   In the case of folders, the Properties sheet has two tabs: General and Sharing.

- ■ **General:** This tab allows you to inspect the folder's size and numeric contents in terms of how many folders and files it contains. Also shown is the creation date for the folder, and you can set the attributes for the folder from this sheet.

- ■ **Sharing:** This tab allows you to share this folder out to remote network users, controlling access and providing a name for the share. Also, if a folder is already shared, you may stop sharing it with this property sheet.

THE FILE PROPERTIES SHEET   The File Properties sheet has one tab, General, which allows you to inspect the file's type, location, and size. Also displayed are the file's MS-DOS name, creation date, last modification date, and last access date. You can also set the attributes for the folder from this sheet.

Close
The Close choice on the File menu closes Explorer immediately.

The Open With Dialog Box

If you double-click a file and Explorer doesn't know which program to use to open it, the Open With dialog box appears. You can use this dialog box to specify the appropriate program. This dialog can be invoked directly with this menu command to set file associations for a selected file.

The Send To Menu Item

To quickly send files to another destination, select the file(s) you wish to send and then choose the Send To menu item. You can also use your right mouse button to point to Send To and then select the destination. You can add other destinations to the Send To command. In the Send To folder, which is located in your Winnt folder, you can create shortcuts to the destinations you send files to often—such as a printer, fax, or a particular folder.

Edit Menu

Explorer's Edit menu works very much like the Edit menu in all Windows-based applications. It implements cut, paste, and copy functionality with the Clipboard for directories (folders) and individual files. In addition, this menu provides undo functionality for file moves and the like. The Edit menu items are explained in the following sections.

Undo

To cancel your last action, on the Edit menu, choose Undo. Some actions you perform cannot be undone. If the Undo command is unavailable, you cannot cancel your last action.

Cut

To move a file or folder, select the file or folder you want to move. On the Edit menu, choose Cut. Open the folder where you want to put the file or folder. On the Edit menu, choose Paste.

 TIP: For all cut and copy functions, you can select the first element of a range by clicking on it once. Now, while holding the SHIFT *key down, press the left mouse button, drag the mouse pointer to the last element you wish to select in the range, and then let go of the left mouse button and the* SHIFT *key. All elements within the range change color to the selected state. To select more than one file or folder to move—not within a contiguous range—hold down the* CTRL *key, and then select the items you want.*

Copy

To copy a file or folder, select the file or folder you want to copy. On the Edit menu, choose Copy. Open the folder or disk where you want to put the copy. On the Edit menu, choose Paste.

Paste

Use the Paste command to paste whatever you have previously cut or copied.

Paste Shortcut

Use the Paste Shortcut command to paste whatever shortcut you have previously cut or copied.

Select All

To select all the files and folders in the window, select the Edit menu and then choose Select All. To select a group of files that are next to each other in Explorer, click anywhere in the blank area of the window. A box appears that you can then drag around the files you want to select.

Invert Selection

As its name implies, the Invert Selection command inverts all selections—deselecting those items that were selected, and selecting those items that were not selected.

View Menu

The View menu works very much like the View menu in all NT-based applications. It lets you control showing or hiding of toolbars, the state of status bars, icon sizing, the level of display detail, the arrangement of icons; and it refreshes the display. In addition, this menu provides an Options selection allowing you to control the level of information that Explorer uses to display files and folders. The View menu items are explained in the following sections.

Toolbar

To show or hide the toolbar, on the View menu, select Toolbar. When the command has a check mark next to it, it means that the toolbar is displayed.

Status Bar

To show or hide the status bar, on the View menu, select Status Bar. When the command has a check mark next to it, it means that the status bar is displayed.

Large Icons/Small Icons/List/Details

To change the appearance of items in a folder, select the View menu and then choose one of the following commands: Large Icons, Small Icons, List, or Details.

- **Large Icons:** Makes the right window pane display items in desktop-sized iconic representation.
- **Small Icons:** Displays the right window pane contents in miniature desktop-like iconic representations.

■ **List:** Displays the right window pane items in an abbreviated multicolumn list with miniature icons.

■ **Details:** Displays the right window pane contents as text along with such file details as size, creation date, and attributes.

Arrange Icons by Name, Type, Size, Date

You can sort displayed items by name, size, date, and type, depending on the view. Sorting by type lets you sort on the file's extension, arranging the list so that all files of, say, .doc type are listed contiguously.

Refresh

The Refresh command refreshes the display, updating Explorer views with any changes that have taken place since the display was last refreshed.

Options

The Options sheet (see Figure 9-7) allows you to set parameters for how files will be displayed in Explorer.

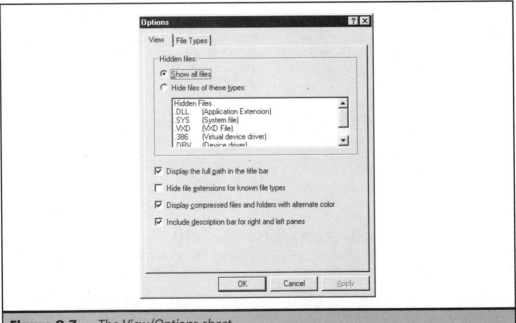

Figure 9-7.   *The View/Options sheet*

The choices are

- **Hidden files:** You can choose to show all files or hide files that match the criteria in the list below this option.

- **Display the full path in the title bar:** Usually, you will want this option checked so you always know where you are in your file hierarchy.

- **Hide file extensions for known file types:** This hides file extensions in the lists of file types that NT knows about.

- **Display compressed files and folders with alternate color:** To make it easy to spot compressed files and folders, check this option to display them in a different color when they are listed in Explorer.

- **Include description bar for right and left panes:** When checked, this option includes a description section for items listed in Explorer.

Tools Menu

The Tools menu includes the option to invoke a file and folder search engine, the mapping or disconnection of network drives and resources, and a way to direct Explorer to jump to a particular drive and directory. The Tools menu items are explained in the following sections.

Find Files, Folders, or a Computer

By choosing the Find menu item and then a subordinate command, you can search for specific files or folders, or you can search for a specific network computer using its computer name. There are three tabs on the Find dialog box. Each tab uses different search criteria to control the search.

- **Name & Location:** You may enter the name of a file that you are searching for. The name may include wildcards if you don't know the full name. For instance, **mydoc*.*** would find all files starting with *mydoc* and ending with any legal filename characters with any extension name. From this tab, you also control where you want to search for these files. Enter the name of the disk volume or drive letter you wish to perform the search on. You may also search on connected network resources. Use the listbox dropdown or Browse button to find a network resource or subdirectory. There is also an option that lets you search subdirectories.

- **Date Modified:** You can control search criteria relating to date and time. You can enter a range of times between file creations, or you can specify files created during a previous period of days or months. The default time criteria is for all files.

- **Advanced:** You may enter criteria pertaining to the type of file you wish to search for. Enter an extension type here, such as **.exe** or **.doc**. You can also search for files that contain a word or phrase by entering the data into the Containing Text field. Finally, you can limit your search to files within a specific size range by entering the size criteria in the Size is fields.

Across the top of the Find dialog box, there are File and Options menus, where you can save the results of a search, open folders that you have found through a search, and control the case sensitivity of a textual search.

Map Network Drive

This command (see Figure 9-8) connects to shared drives and directories on the network. You must have permissions set to actually connect to these displayed resources.

- **Drive:** This displays the first available drive letter for the connection. You can type or select another drive letter.

- **Path:** This specifies the network path for the connection. A network path consists of a computer name followed by the name of a shared directory in the form *computername**foldername*. In the Path dropdown listbox, you can select a previous network path if there are any. Type the name of a computer and shared directory in the Path edit field. In addition to universal naming convention (UNC) names, such as the names of network servers, domain name system (DNS) names can be used in the Path field. DNS names appear with periods as separators, such as *mycompany.vp.com.**accounting*.

- **Connect As:** To connect using a different user account, type the account name in the Connect As field. To connect using an account in a different domain, type the domain name followed by a backslash (\) and the username for the account. By default, you are connected as the username you used to log on.

- **Reconnect at Logon:** Click to clear this check box if you do not want to connect to the shared directory each time you log on.

- **Expand by Default:** By default, the list in the Shared Directories field expands to display all of the computers in your computer's domain or workgroup. To stop automatic expansion of the Shared Directories list, clear Expand by Default. Clear Expand by Default if you are connecting over a slow network or dialup.

- **Shared Directories:** This shows networks, domains and workgroups, computers, and shared directories. Double-click an item to expand the list. Selecting a shared directory places it in the Path field.

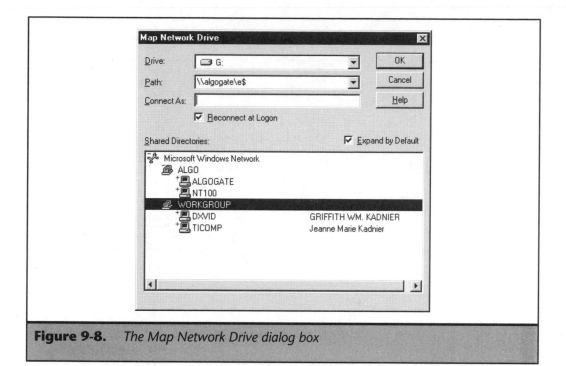

Figure 9-8.   *The Map Network Drive dialog box*

Disconnect Network Drive

The Disconnect Network Drive command disconnects your computer from a network drive. Select the drive or drives you want to disconnect and then choose OK.

Go To

To jump to a directory or drive, select Go To and type in a full path name to a directory or drive root.

Help Menu

The Help menu works very much like the Help menu in all NT-based applications. It invokes help for the application and provides a general NT status dialog. For Explorer, the main Windows NT help file is invoked, and help is available for most Explorer functions in this file.

Using Shortcut Menus

As previously mentioned, most menu items in Explorer can be accessed by clicking the right mouse button when the mouse cursor is positioned over an item. A menu

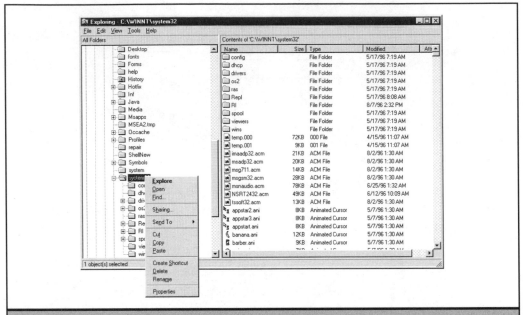

Figure 9-9. *Use the right mouse button to open shortcut menus in Explorer*

appears with the most-used commands for that item, and you may perform many tasks without ever accessing the normal menus.

Use the shortcut menu as you would for items on the desktop (see Chapter 6). Figure 9-9 shows a typical shortcut menu in Explorer.

What's Next

We are now going to examine an aspect of the NT operating system that is not only fun but is making waves in the world of commercials and Hollywood-style special effects, sound, and animation: NT Multimedia. So, let's turn the page and see what's happening in the way of OS support for a very interesting application of the NT platform.

Chapter Ten

NT's Multimedia Capabilities

An exciting trend has developed in modern desktop computing. Whether for business or theatrical presentation, scientific analysis and research, or corporate and entertainment production, multimedia is all the rage, and for very good reason. *Multimedia*—any production or presentation that combines the use of text, graphics, sounds, and still or motion pictures—enables people to look at data in a more natural way. Humans regularly process input from more than one kind of source, synthesizing ideas and solving problems in unified ways (see Figure 10-1).

As a species, we use all of our senses to communicate ideas and data. A speech is always more powerful and effective if given by the speaker to an audience, rather than being distributed on paper. Because we live in a three-dimensional world and use the facilities of sound as well as sight, we understand and grasp ideas better this way. Static, one-dimensional presentations do not excite and engage us.

Presentations of columns of numbers are not nearly as understandable as graphical charts, and in advertising or teaching, a picture is truly worth more than a thousand bytes! (We'll see why this is a double play on words soon.) In business and production settings, NT provides a suite of multimedia tools that will help make your presentations and exhibitions come alive.

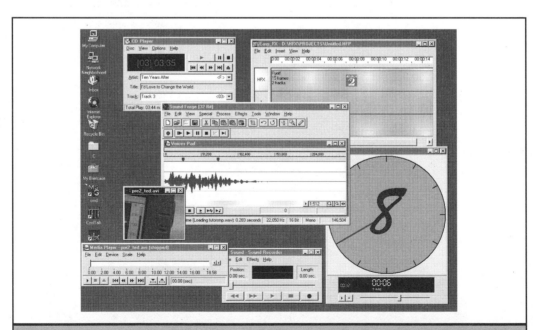

Figure 10-1. *A typical NT multimedia session with multiple applications cooperating*

NOTE: *The new Microsoft DirectX multimedia (discussed later in this chapter) and Internet ActiveX extensions can be used to create real-time animation, games, and multimedia presentation content, and to distribute that content over an intranet or to the Internet. We'll discuss NT and ActiveX in Chapters 25 and 26.*

What Is Multimedia?

In McLuhan's *The Medium Is the Message: An Inventory of Effects* (San Francisco: Hardwired, 1996), electronic multimedia is viewed as a corrupt technology, showcasing and reprocessing industrial-age concepts and legitimizing them as an art form. But multimedia is so much more than the media itself. It has become a basic tool for work, learning, and research. More and more, computers are becoming the transparent, primary delivery and display systems for information. People are sending electronic mail instead of letters. Advertising and marketing concerns are targeting customers directly by using multimedia in mass mailings of demonstration disks and in presentations over the Internet.

Standard television and film production is now permeated with computer-driven multimedia. *Star Wars*-style graphics and digitally composited or synthesized scenes are showing up in almost all facets of distributed entertainment. Children play fully animated games, complete with video, sound, and sensory feedback. As a direct tool, instead of huge printed dictionaries and encyclopedias, you can look up entries that are stored on CD-ROM and illustrated with color graphics, sound, and animation. Even when the focus of an application is to help you produce a printed document or perform calculations, the application can use multimedia elements to clarify and explain the concepts or ideas that you want to express.

Uses for Multimedia

Traditional lines of communication are rapidly breaking down in the new frontiers offered by mixing standard media with computer-based presentation. Printed books will probably never be fully replaced by their electronic cousins, but owners' manuals and bulk catalogs or mailers have already found their way onto CD-ROM and the computer display.

Although Hollywood has embraced multimedia, showcasing it to the public, there are many other commercial uses for multimedia presentation. For example, companies that use catalogs to sell goods or services traditionally use photographs and textual descriptions in print. Printed catalogs can only show limited views and presentations of the items or concepts they are trying to showcase. Models are sometimes used, but with static pictures and presentations, these items cannot be represented as they would be in real life. It's pretty hard to imagine what, for instance, a coat would really look like when viewed as a two-dimensional representation in a still picture, or what a new music CD sounds like, when only the cover is shown.

Also, because old-style catalogs are printed, only limited amounts of information can be presented. If advertising or reference information is distributed on CD-ROM as multimedia applications, it can present many more items, use animated or video sequences to model items from all angles, and provide visual and aural examples of usage and demonstration. Huge amounts of detail can be distributed electronically in an instant or by mailing a CD-ROM, instead of ten pounds of paper, through the mail.

NOTE: *The new Internet "Push" technologies, being developed and integrated now, implement a kind of forced advertising that might end up turning a lot of people off. These technologies send sometimes unsolicited information and advertisements, usually rife with multimedia, to your Internet browser. But never fear, where there's a need, there's a company that can sell you a "Push-blocker" application to filter unwanted content before you even know it's there!*

Creating New Multimedia Applications

Developing a new type of advertisement or bulk mail catalog is only one example of what you can do with multimedia. Many companies and individuals are using multimedia to create business presentations with graphs, sounds, and illustrations; and the creative potential of multimedia for art, music, entertainment, learning, and research is staggering. You can use multimedia to create presentations and applications that capture, edit, and play sounds and images. You can also use multimedia to create applications that control multimedia hardware, such as CD players, videocassette recorders, and MIDI (musical instrument digital interface) devices.

For games and entertainment applications, NT and the Win32 API (application program interface) also support the use of joysticks and custom interface devices for user input, and provide for a high-speed timer mechanism that is more accurate than the standard Win32 timers. This gives NT an advantage when close-coupled live action and user feedback becomes a crucial element in the multimedia experience. This information may contradict what you have heard about NT's real-time response, which we will be covering directly in Chapter 23, but with the advent of DirectX technology (discussed later in this chapter), many of the bottlenecks that have kept NT from performing in this way are gone.

Most multimedia is now delivered by CD-ROM. A standard CD-ROM can handle only about 650 megabytes of data—way too little for, say, a digitized feature-length movie. So you will see new digital video delivery systems coming online rapidly to fill these niches, and as bandwidth over networks increases, direct delivery of multimedia will also become the norm.

NOTE: *More and more applications depend entirely on integrated multimedia sources. Thousands of multimedia applications, such as games, entertainment, and educational programs, and computerized reference works, make extensive use of integrated sound and video. Since multimedia data requires a great deal of storage space, these applications are often distributed on CD-ROM. On an intranet, multimedia can be distributed directly over the network. Multimedia applications typically need network connections of 5 to 10Mbps (megabits per second). This will rapidly change to connection speeds of 100Mbps and greater as rich multimedia content pushes cable modems and high-speed LANs into general use.*

Upgrading Old Applications

Many companies are redesigning older applications and including multimedia elements for an improved look and feel, or to make the applications easier to use and more natural to interact with. For example, attachment of video and sound, including voice annotation, is now possible in most popular word processing applications. The ability to recognize voice input is just coming on the market in usable form. Audio and video clips are used routinely in presentation graphics applications and Internet web sites or advertisements.

Sound and video feedback is being used in applications where formerly only text and dialog output could cue the user for input and instructions. Many computer manufacturers have recently gone to multimedia help files for buyer introduction to features contained in their equipment. Fax and email applications have been designed and upgraded to include voice capabilities and feedback. Multimedia is even showing up in applications that have traditionally been completely text oriented, such as spreadsheets. Data can be presented as animations over time, series of statistical or graphical depictions that show trends, and can bring the data to life in contour plots or the like.

Mini-Glossary

AUDIO COMPRESSION MANAGER (ACM)   When a multimedia application requests that the system open an audio device for input or output, the request specifies an audio format and the target device. The ACM maps and routes these requests to an installed audio device, either physical or logical, and to a compressor or decompressor. The audio device and a supported (de)compressor work in concert, possibly with filtering and wave-shaping elements, to render an audio stream onto storage media, or out into the real world. Synchronization components within the NT multimedia system can be utilized to play or record audio in step with a video stream or clip.

INSTALLABLE COMPRESSION MANAGER (ICM)   Just as the ACM provides services for audio input and output devices, the ICM is the intermediary service layer between an application and the NT multimedia video compression and decompression drivers. When an application needs to display or store compressed video (for all intents and purposes, all digital video is compressed in one way or another), it makes a request to the ICM services that handle compression and decompression of image data, in the specified format. Many competing and complementary formats are used for different purposes, and to support different input and output hardware devices. The ICM acts as a clearinghouse, offering up unified services to any application that needs to work with compressed video, dependent only on which supported (de)compressors are installed.

MEDIA CONTROL INTERFACE (MCI)   The MCI provides an easy-to-use, common API that multimedia-enabled applications can interface with and manipulate to control multimedia hardware, such as VCRs and audio boards. With MCI, an application can pass simple, scripted commands to the operating system without having to know intimate details about the hardware it intends to control. There is also a direct interface providing for the passing of data structures and commands. Many presentation and audio/video editing packages use MCI. MCI is made up of an API available to applications, MCI command parsing and dispatching routines for translating MCI commands, and a variable set of MCI drivers.

MIDI (MUSICAL INSTRUMENT DIGITAL INTERFACE)   A standard software protocol for communication between musical instruments and computers. Used extensively by musicians, MIDI is a message-based protocol that assigns numbers to musical notes and actions. Synthesizers, as well as many other musical instruments, use MIDI to store and generate music on a note-by-note and action-by action basis.

WAVEFORM AUDIO   Audio data that is digitized and stored as a stream of data bits representing the pitch and amplitude of the original data. In concept, waveform audio is like a tape recording in that it is a digitized representation of all sampled frequencies. Some normal sampling rates are 8.0, 11.025, 22.050, and 44.1KHz, in mono or stereo.

WIN32 API   The set of system-defined functions that are exposed and made available by the Win32 subsystem and its adjunct modules and extensions. Win32 is the primary programming interface for applications running on NT 4.

How Multimedia Works

NT supports three distinctly different types of multimedia data: waveform audio, MIDI, and video.

Waveform Audio

Waveform audio is a digitized recording of a sound. Sound is sampled by an audio input device at a chosen rate (frequency) and written to a file, or used directly, as a stream of bits representing the pitch and amplitude of the original sound. The higher the sampling frequency, the better fidelity you will achieve.

Waveform audio can be mono or stereo, and you can edit waveform audio using applications that perform various audio processing operations such as changing pitch and volume, adding special effects and filters—flanging and phasing, for example—and performing insertions and deletions. A waveform sound file can store voice, music, and sound effects, with varying degrees of reproduction quality. In NT, and in Windows generally, waveform audio files typically have a .WAV filename extension, although non-native extensions of .AU and .AIFF are also becoming common.

> **NOTE:** *Editing waveform audio requires sophisticated utilities and can be exacting and difficult. Additionally, the storage requirements for waveform audio are directly related to the sampling rate at which the waveform audio file was recorded. For instance, a stereo file recorded at 44.1KHz/16 bits, the sampling rate used on music CDs, will consume 17K/sec. So you can see how this would lead to very large files within a short time. To reduce storage requirements, applications usually reduce the sampling rate and use a data compressor/decompressor. Beware, however, that most compression schemes also reduce the achievable playback fidelity.*

MIDI Sound

MIDI (musical instrument digital interface) sound is stored as a series of note-based instructions, rather than as a waveform. It is the standard for live digital music presentation, used by most modern musicians and performers today. A MIDI musical instrument (such as a MIDI-enabled piano or guitar), or a synthesizer (usually part of a computer's sound card and driver, but sometimes a dedicated peripheral), recognizes and interprets the instructions to produce musical sound. The sounds are based on the musical note scale but, when using a synthesizer, may be mapped through the hardware to any available instrument sound. For instance, a note can be played with a piano sound, or it can be mapped and changed to sound like an oboe. Different synthesizers support different mapping schemes, and they may interpret MIDI instructions with slight variations. To get optimal fidelity and correct instrument sounds in playback, you use MIDI mapping schemes (set through the Control Panel/Multimedia/MIDI applet) to ensure that the instruction stream is understandable by your output device.

The MIDI sound format can store and reproduce music (in the form of notes) and some sound effects, but since it does not generally digitize input data, and its notation scheme is not suited to that task, it is not capable of storing and reproducing voice, per se. (New MIDI software is coming on the market, actually allowing you to input song notes by humming them!) In NT, and generally in all versions of Windows, MIDI sound files have a filename extension of .MID or .RMI.

 TIP: *MIDI can be easily edited and manipulated by applications that allow you to change the MIDI instruction stream as if it were scored on paper, like sheet music. MIDI applications can also capture music that you play on a keyboard, for instance. The music is captured to a MIDI file and is then available for editing and playback. Since MIDI is note based, very little storage space is required, as contrasted with waveform audio data.*

Video

Video data is recorded frame by frame, sometimes with synchronized waveform audio. Because video data is composed of bits representing each pixel, or picture element, in an image, and each frame is recorded as if it were a whole still image, or field, data requirements are very high. And the amount of data you must store or display depends also on its color information. A so-called TrueColor bitmap will be 24 bits/pixel deep. This is so that 8 bits of resolution for each of the R-G-B values can be stored. Typically, video will be compressed using an encoder in software or hardware, and will then be decompressed on the fly, during playback, by a hardware or software decompressor. In NT, and Windows in general, video files typically have filename extensions of .AVI, .MOV, and .MPG. These extensions denote the type of video file, based on the recording and playback technology utilized.

Since video data requires so much storage space, various video compressor/decompressor schemes have been invented. Some of these are software and/or hardware-assist based, as in the Intel Indeo (Rxx) driver series, and some are hardware based, such as MPEG (Motion Picture Expert Group) adapters (for instance, the ReelMagic series of player boards). The exact mix of hardware and software to achieve capture and playback of any video encoding scheme will depend on your budget; there are hardware accelerators for most of these schemes, but cost goes up as capability and performance increase.

The compression schemes use different algorithms to subtract information from each frame of the picture. Some kinds of compression/decompression are *lossy*—they result in a playback picture that has lost definition. Others are considered *lossless*—rendering video frames that have lost no information through the compression/decompression operation. The available and usable video compressors and decompressors on your machine will depend on which video display adapter and capture equipment is installed. Most capture boards and multimedia-capable video display adapters come with hardware-specific drivers and compressor/decompressor sets.

Insider Info

Applications and drivers can use NT's audio and video multimedia functions to edit, mix, play, and record multimedia elements. Multimedia can be made up of audio and video data using raw or compressible waveform, MIDI, and auxiliary audio, as well as a host of compressible video formats, with or without synchronization. Mixing is accomplished by using the Win32 mixing functions for audio and video, along with the system's capability to route to or from the actual hardware devices, through a driver software layer. The compressors and decompressors for audio and video are functionally exposed to applications, which need these services, through the Audio Compression Manager (ACM) and the Installable Compression Manager (ICM).

An application can also use an audio or video MCI command function set, made available by an MCI driver, to manipulate system software structures, or to pass registered and private driver messages to the multimedia hardware in order to capture video and audio clips and streams, sometimes using the audio functions to capture sound track information simultaneously. The actual capture techniques require video and audio digitization or acquisition hardware, such as a video capture board and VCR, or a sound board with microphone and line input.

Other devices and interfaces can enhance and improve NT 4's multimedia interaction and presentation. Among these are input via joysticks; 360 degree of X/Y freedom linear-input devices that allow the user to interact with a moving element on the screen. NT 4's multimedia Win32 APIs have built-in support and calibration routines for joysticks, and many games use this interface element as their primary input mechanism. The joystick interface (usually part of a multimedia panel or sound card connector on the computer) is actually a miniature X/Y analog-to-digital digitizer. Because of this, unique input devices have also been made available for this input port. Companies sell compatible input devices as esoteric as biofeedback controllers to interact with multimedia displays using this input hardware. For laboratory or production use, many manufacturers supply precision hardware and software that can enhance specialized input and output using NT.

Also available are visual input and output devices such as virtual reality headsets and data gloves, providing tactile input and 360-degree visual field output, through the use of biometric sensors and liquid crystal or video eyepieces. These devices are now rapidly showing up in the engineering station markets, making interactive design and visualization of such things as 3-D chemical molecules and automobile designs finally possible. Of course, they also filter down into the games and home markets as soon as is feasible.

The underlying NT Win32 multimedia APIs, along with custom drivers, make the use of such devices possible now. NT has many system-level support mechanisms that can help a so-enabled application to run efficiently. Along with built-in audio, video, MIDI, joystick, and high-resolution timing features, NT's memory management and synchronization facilities can be used to tailor a multimedia input or output system to exacting performance. As mentioned earlier, the inclusion of DirectX, Microsoft's direct-to-hardware acceleration technology, can make the difference in a real-time response system using video, audio, and custom I/O.

Using NT's Multimedia Services

NT 4, through the Win32 API and its multimedia extensions, provides multimedia services to record, manipulate, and play all of the popular direct input, audio, and video multimedia devices and formats. This includes

- Waveform audio
- Video in a window or full screen
- Input through a joystick, data glove, or other real-world device
- Output to virtual reality and sensory feedback devices
- Control of devices such as audio CD players, audio and video editing decks, VCRs or laser disc players
- MIDI devices and instruments

As mentioned earlier, the primary application interfaces are twofold. First, any multimedia device or program may have as its primary I/O mechanism a custom-registered multimedia driver. This type of interface is usually directly linked to a piece of input or output hardware, using private messages and structures to perform communication and processing. A typical example of this is the driver and application files that support the sound card that will be installed in your NT workstation. These files work in unison to talk with the audio hardware, performing custom I/O steps to accomplish their goals, sometimes directly, and sometimes on behalf of a higher-level program, such as a presentation program that needs to record or play a sound.

Secondly, the programmatic Media Control Interface (MCI) is provided in NT 4 for controlling media devices directly, whether through an abstract scripting facility, such as Adobe Premiere's editing and production application or other program interface, or through direct control of an actual device, such as a Pioneer laser disc player or audio CD changer. The MCI facility allows a device driver or program to register custom commands, using English-like words and phrases, which then become part of the multimedia operating system layer. Any program wishing to use that device may then issue a set of commands similar to the following (shown here for the audio CD player device):

```
>open CDAUDIO alias cdchanger
>play cdchanger track 2
>seek cdchanger from track 2 to track 10
>play cdchanger track 10
>shuffle cdchanger
>close cdchanger
```

These MCI commands are issued directly from an application, or by you, through a custom scripting facility. Notice how, using this interface method, MCI abstracts and hides implementation specifics concerning the make and model of such a device. Only valid macro-like actions need be specified, within context of course. Some hardware devices come ready to install with standard *and* MCI driver support. In most cases, MCI will be easier to work with, but slightly slower to respond, so the trade-off is yours to make.

Other controlling functions and applets allow you to customize your multimedia facilities. The standard taskbar volume control is just a front end for the more feature-laden system sound mixer. Double-click on the taskbar icon to bring up an entire audio mixing panel. And from the Start/Settings/Control Panel/Multimedia/Audio applet, you can choose preferred audio I/O devices and customize the digitization frequencies for waveform input.

For the musician or composer, a MIDI Mapper function, available through the Start/Settings/Control Panel/Multimedia/MIDI applet, supporting standard MIDI patch services, is included. This allows MIDI files to be authored independently of specific MIDI synthesizer setups. Control Panel multimedia options let you install and configure multimedia device drivers, compressors/decompressors (CODECs), and mixer setups, control how devices interact with the system, and configure elements of the multimedia system software.

 NOTE: *The NT multimedia architecture is both extensible and device independent. This architecture accommodates new or improved devices and drivers without change to the underlying operating system. Only new device drivers and support software are needed when a new hardware or software interface is installed. The multimedia architecture is made to be independent of any particular device, so applications can be developed once, using system programming interfaces that are generalized, at that level, allowing the execution of an arbitrary application against another arbitrary set of installed devices and support files.*

Multimedia File Formats

Usually, multimedia files are maintained in one of the formats described in the following list (although *many* other formats are used).

Format	Filename Extension
Digital video	.AVI, .MPG, .MOV
Waveform audio	.WAV, .AU, .AIFF
Musical instrument digital interface (MIDI)	.MID, .MOD, .RMI

The Primary Multimedia Applications

Although many third-party multimedia programs and utilities exist, NT 4 ships with four primary multimedia applications (see Figure 10-2). In this respect, multimedia is defined to be waveform, music CD, MIDI sound, and digital video. With these built-in applications, you can play a wave file, record sounds, play a MIDI file, play an audio

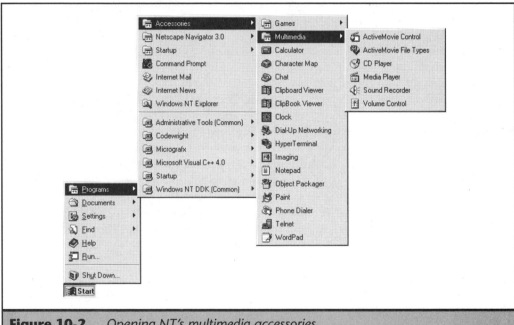

Figure 10-2. *Opening NT's multimedia accessories*

CD, capture and/or play a video file, mix sound and control volume, and use OLE to control multimedia:

■ **Play a wave file:** This kind of multimedia is aural. Waveform (.WAV) files consist of bitstreams of digitized sound, either in mono or stereo. The sampling rate determines storage requirements and playback fidelity. Waveform files can store and reproduce any type of sound that a tape recorder would usually handle—voice, sound effects, or music. You can play .WAV files using the built-in Media Player, shown here:

Mini-Glossary

AUDIO LINES   Physical and logical input and output connections, controlled by the Volume Control/Mixer application or directly, by a multimedia application. These lines may be mono or stereo and are routable by using the mixer controls to mix signals, set volume, and control other parameters.

CODECS (COMPRESSOR/DECOMPRESSORS) AND COMPRESSOR FORMATS The primary data reduction scheme used in NT (Windows) multimedia. Software components compress multimedia data so that storage requirements are reduced. Matching decompressors then allow this data to be played back on the fly. The actual names of these compressors are indicative of the algorithms and standards used in the processes.

■ **Record sounds:** You can use a microphone or auxiliary input from, say, a music CD connected to your computer to record waveform sound, using any valid sampling rate, by using Sound Recorder, shown next.

Insider Info

Before using Sound Recorder, you can use the Start/Settings/Control Panel/Multimedia/Audio/Customize button to bring up the Customize (waveform sampling rate) dialog, or from Sound Recorder, the Edit/Audio Properties/Customize menu choice, tailoring settings for sampling rates and compressor technologies. You use this dialog to control at what sampling rate, and therefore at what fidelity, you wish to digitize the sound. Also, CODEC technology is selectable, controlling the algorithms used to condense and/or unpack the sampled stream of bits on disk. The choice of compressor will depend on how you plan to use the sampled sound, how much fidelity you wish to preserve, and what kind of playback criteria you have.

CODEC algorithms vary depending on

- Specific mathematical/design implementation
- Support for custom features, such as speech decoding
- Convention: International Telephony, Engineering Society, etc.
- Legacy support for older systems

For example, the ADPCM CODEC is used as a default wherever normal adaptive pulse-code-modulation compression can be employed. The DSP Truespeech CODEC is included for specialized voice and telephony use, where that CODEC has been previously used to encode audio data. Use of the GSM 6.10 CODEC insures compatibility with older 16-bit Windows systems. In most cases, audio CODECs allow you to select a sampling rate. However, not all CODECs are suited to all tasks and to all sampling rate values. The sampling rates available for a particular CODEC will be listed in the Customize dialog's Attributes dropdown list.

■ **Play a MIDI file:** This is, again, an audio function, which uses Media Player or a third-party application. MIDI (.MID) files are composed of musical notes and direct instructions to, or from, a synthesizer (instrument, keyboard, or chip) or a MIDI-enabled musical instrument. MIDI files reproduce music exactly as it is scored. Many third-party applications exist that show MIDI files as sheet music, allowing you to directly edit and change the file as if you were working with a musical score. Depending on the output device, MIDI files can sound as good as, if not better than, digitized music recorded in the .WAV format, because musical information is not lost in a digitization and compression/decompression process. The musical notes are re-created and played live, through the output instrument, instead of being recorded and reproduced. This also reduces the size of the data stored on disk by quite a bit. The drawbacks to MIDI include the fact that a MIDI-capable output device must be present, and that MIDI is only truly applicable to musical reproduction. Many newer MIDI-capable sound cards have a feature called WaveTable synthesis. This is a MIDI output technique that uses stored samples of real instrument sound instead of an internal electronic generator. When MIDI is played using WaveTable synthesis, a much truer reproduction of any particular instrument is possible.

Insider Info

MIDI is a serial interface standard that allows for the connection of music synthesizers, musical instruments, and computers. Usually, you will see this interface expressed as a MPU-401-compatible device. The MPU-401 is one of the original MIDI stand-alone serial synthesizer standards, and most sound card manufacturers make their MIDI serial interfaces to this standard. MIDI's standards are based both on hardware and a description of the way music and sounds are encoded. The standard also defines how MIDI devices should communicate with each other.

MIDI is now used in almost all modern musical equipment, and many musicians and studios depend on MIDI to control musical instruments and such things as mixing boards and switchers. Optical fiber communications have made MIDI a standard for on-stage performance gear, and MIDI is used as a development tool by composers, musicians, and producers.

- **Play an audio CD:** The CD Player application (shown in the following illustration) gives you the capability to play red book audio CDs just as if you had a Walkman or CD stereo component installed in your computer. (Of course, you need to have a CD-ROM drive installed, which is a given for any NT 4-capable computer.) Aside from just listening to music, you can use the output from your audio CD as input to the Sound Recorder application. In this way, music can be added to a .WAV file that you record. Third-party recording applications can also use the output from the audio CD player functions to add CD audio to audio and video productions that you might make. You cannot read data from the CD-ROM drive while playing an audio CD unless this is part of the particular CD format, such as Cdi.

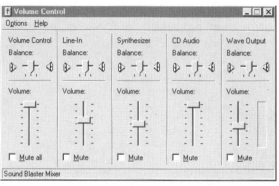

- **Capture and/or play a video file:** This capability (see the illustration on the next page) is probably the most appealing of all. We're visual creatures after all. Windows NT 4 video services provide the resources for capturing video clips, compressing the content, and controlling playback. A host of third-party applications, such as Adobe Premiere and Hollywood FX, allow you to use video capture hardware to import live or prerecorded video into an NT 4 application. You can use this video in many different ways. Depending on how sophisticated your capture hardware is, you can assemble-edit the video, a process akin to what TV stations do when they merge video clips into full productions. You might also apply special effects, such as flying logos, or page peels, to your video production. You can also add to or edit the audio portion of the video clip. After you have produced the finished product, some capture boards allow you to output the video to tape, or, at the very least, you will be able to merge the video into your own multimedia production stored on hard disk or CD-ROM.

Insider Info

The ability to capture, edit, and play video (.AVI, .MPG, .MOV, etc.) files depends on how fast your CPU and video hardware is. Capture and playback is expressed in frames per second (fps), and to be really usable, your hardware must be capable of capturing and reproducing video at rates above 15fps. For normal NTSC (the American broadcast standard), the frame rate is almost exactly 30fps. Most modern computers (especially those capable of running NT) have enough muscle for this task when teamed with capable capture and playback hardware. Although no special hardware is needed for display of small video clips that are to be embedded into multimedia presentations, the newest high-end video capture and playback equipment is based on the PCI bus standard (see Chapter 3 for more information on this standard), which accelerates and improves video throughput. You should make sure that any PC-adapter video hardware you buy is PCI bus based. Also, because of the way disk drives recalibrate themselves when their thermal characteristics change, you should capture video only to an AV-rated hard disk drive.

Nonlinear is the term professionals use when speaking of digital video in this sense. All of the video data is reduced to a stream of bits that is manipulated by multimedia hardware and software, in any sequence desired. Because NT 4 is a true 32-bit operating system, it can move these prodigious amounts of data at higher speeds than that attainable with older versions of Windows. Also, the support for true preemptivity within the operating system helps companies write nonlinear editing and playback software that can run more efficiently. Because of the limited availability of vertical-market capture and editing hardware, the PC/video field has, until recently, been dominated by the (high-end) Apple Macintosh platform. With the advent of Windows-based TrueColor capture hardware and display adapters, and video production software such as SoftImage and TrueSpace, NT 4 has now become the standard for these non-linear-based video systems.

■ **Mix sound and control volume:** PC audio adapter hardware usually implements multiple input and output lines. Inputs such as line level and microphone, as well as speaker and line output, are common. NT 4 includes a Volume Control/Mixer application (shown in the following illustration) so that these audio lines can be manipulated and their various sources and outputs can be mixed and controlled using a graphical application that looks like a studio mixing panel. The NT audio line mixer is also capable of setting advanced options, for those audio boards that support such things as bass and treble control, loudness, or microphone gain boost. Some adapter boards even support a karaoke mode in which lip-sync with other input sources is available.

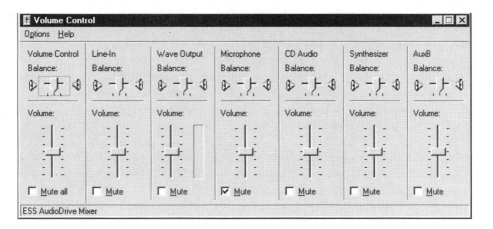

Insider Info

Multimedia audio input and output lines are similar to those you would find in a stereo amplifier component, with MIDI I/O as an addition. In the case of microphone inputs, they are monaural, but most lines are stereo, with right and left channels. Waveform data can be digitized into the system through the line-in or microphone input. Your CD-ROM audio data input is normally brought into the system through its own interface lines on the adapter or motherboard. It may also become an input for digitized waveform data. The MIDI I/O channel is special. In reality, it is the only purely digital input or output from the audio multimedia system. MIDI I/O, through the MIDI connector, is a digital-serial data stream, consisting of instruction bytes coded to the MIDI specification.

The physical audio output lines usually include both amplified speaker output and line-out levels. They are almost always stereo. In addition, there may be audio outputs that map to logical or internal physical devices, such as the synthesizer output. This output comes from the audio adapter's electronic synthesizer, which may be programmed to play arbitrary sounds, or may be the recipient of an internal MIDI data stream. Special software drivers will then interpret this MIDI data, rendering it as played notes through the internal synthesizer output. Depending on your exact hardware, the mixer will display a number of audio lines—some stereo—for playback, recording, and special purposes such as voice commands. These display options, and the mode that the mixer application reflects, are controllable by bringing up the Volume Control application, using the Start/Programs/Accessories/Multimedia menu. You can also double-click the volume control icon on the Start bar. Next, go into the Options menu and choose Properties. You will be presented with a dialog to pick the operational mode for the mixer and to customize which audio lines, with their controls, are displayed, as shown here:

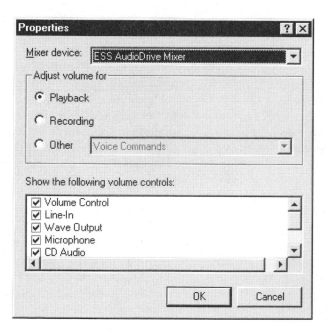

The Media Control Interface

Although the Media Control Interface (MCI) has been lightly covered already, and is largely transparent to the casual user, it is worth a section here to fully explore this operating system service. MCI provides NT applications with device-independent capabilities for controlling multimedia devices such as audio and video hardware, VCRs and videodisc players, and animation recorders and players. This interface works by employing device-specific MCI drivers to run under the direct command of an application, using data structures and function calls, or by parsing and interpreting plain text MCI commands such as Pause, Play, Run, and Stop. MCI has been a part of the Windows family of operating system services since 16-bit Windows 3.0 was introduced.

A fully functional MCI control set can actually consist of up to three components:

- The core MCI interpreter and dispatcher routines in the operating system
- The MCI device-specific driver
- The hardware device, if any

NOTE: *MCI does not necessarily have to control a piece of hardware; applications such as Macromedia Director use MCI to control software presentations and graphic transitions.*

How MCI Works

MCI actually exposes two interface methods: One is a more standard programmatic interface, in which an application or driver must know parameters and data structures, passing these directly, like a function call. The other more interesting interface can be viewed as a sort of extensible command interpreter. Any device or process can expose an MCI command set through its MCI device driver. Once this set of plain English (or pseudo-English) commands are registered with the multimedia system, they are immediately available for use by an application that knows how to converse with the components in the MCI layer. MCI has a set of preregistered core commands that, depending on the device to be controlled, are applicable to a broad range of media devices and applications.

For example, MCI uses the same command (Play), with meanings changed by the specific MCI device driver, to start playback of a MIDI, waveform, or video clip, a VCR or videodisc track, an audio CD, and an animation sequence. Extended or device-specific commands are registered with the operating-system-level MCI layer to provide device-specific capabilities, such as a Route command for a video or audio switcher. The command set is entirely dependent on the MCI device driver's registration routines, so any command set is supportable.

MCI Device Types

A *device type* denotes standard preregistered classes of MCI devices. These device type classes have predefined command sets that, while using the same verbs (such as Play), respond in device-specific ways that are correct for the particular family of hardware or application. The following list shows the currently defined MCI device types:

Device Type	Description
animation	Single-frame animation devices
cdaudio	CD audio player
dat	Digital audio tape recorder/player
digitalvideo	Video in a window (avi)
other	Any device undefined by the base MCI routines
overlay	Video overlay and chromakey device
scanner	Image and text scanners
sequencer	MIDI sequencer/synthesizer
vcr	Videocassette recorder/player
videodisc	Videodisc player
waveaudio	Devices that record and play waveform audio

Selecting an NT Multimedia Computer

Choosing your NT multimedia computer is not a Black Art. The requirements are actually rather straightforward and in many ways are some of the same requirements that make for all-around fine performance. You will find that the base components are probably not going to be any different, whether specifying an NT installation for database, network server, or multimedia work.

First, you should consider the basic box—meaning the motherboard, CPU, and installed RAM. For any NT installation to succeed, a balance of power and resources must be achieved. It would do little good to have a fast CPU, but no memory. Make sure that the machine you plan to use has the right combination of these three components:

■ **CPU power:** The fastest Intel CPUs are now 200MHz or greater. If possible, choose a processor speed above 133MHz for fast processing and response.

■ **Motherboard:** Choose a motherboard that offers PCI and ISA slots, bus-mastering disk I/O for speed, and as little integration of features as possible. (If you buy off the shelf, ask the factory about this before you spend a dime!) A word about integration of features is due here. Many consumer-grade computers have sound and video integrated into the motherboard electronics. This is fine for general-purpose use, but not for custom installation. If, for instance, you want to use a special or new audio card, and your motherboard has audio integrated into it, you might not be able to disable the on-board audio. This would preclude the use of a custom card, keeping you from using new or improved features. Stay away from integrated audio and video!

■ **RAM:** Install as much RAM as is economically feasible. RAM prices are continually fluctuating because they are now a commodity. As prices drop, this will become a non-issue. Start with a base of 48MB, and if you can afford more, go to 64 or 128MB. The larger the amount of RAM, the fewer disk accesses will be needed. This is important for multimedia, especially video capture.

Multimedia performance depends heavily on a range of system components, not just a singly optimized piece of hardware. Your CD-ROM must be capable of greater than MPCII (Multimedia PC II specification) throughput (>300K/sec, quad speed or better), and you should also have a fast disk controller and hard disk drive. The controller should be capable of *bus-mastering*, which is a method by which it can perform transfers without hogging CPU time. It does not matter whether you choose IDE (Integrated Drive Electronics) or SCSI (Small Computer Systems Interface) disk drives. IDE drives of 5 or more gigabytes are showing up on today's market, so you can get any storage capacity you need in either format. Typically, hard drives for multimedia use are rated as AV (audio/visual). This means that they are usually faster at both reading and writing data, and that they do not perform thermal recalibration during a read or write operation. Both of these factors are important for smooth recording and playback performance.

The video display, as well as the video and audio capture, or digitization, subsystems should be capable of handling the sampling and playback rates that you plan to employ. You will be better served by having a fast display subsystem than having the next-higher CPU speed installed in your NT box. So much in a multimedia installation depends on perceived speed. If your CPU is being throttled by inefficient display electronics, the entire machine will appear to be slow.

For best results, the computer should have the following components:

■ **PCI video and disk controller interfaces:** Video and disk drive adapters that use a so-called local bus (a different data path than older adapters have to the CPU) and conform to the PCI 32- or 64-bit bus standard will perform many times better than older style video and storage adapters. PCI has become the standard for high-performance adapters, and you should insist that video and disk adapters conform to this standard. An exponential increase in video and disk performance can be realized, with respect to older style adapters. Without local bus video, your multimedia installation will be severely crippled when it comes to keeping up with the amount of video data that capture and display applications use. Even most of the newer games attempt to display video in a continuous stream, and this requires PCI. Display adapters should also be capable of displaying 24-bit, or TrueColor, graphics. This is required for photographic quality rendition and to get away from palette-based graphics, which use subsets of color. Palette graphics can cause flashing and color distortion on transitional graphics.

- **A 17- to 21-inch color display monitor:** Preferably capable of displaying from 640x480 to 1024x768 or higher 24-bit modes with refresh frequencies above 60Hz for antiflicker and clarity.

- **A quad, eight, or greater speed CD-ROM:** Modern multimedia applications assume greater than double speed data rates, the MPCII standard. They should be capable of quad or better speeds and throughput (600 to 1200K/sec), and should support CD, CD-XA, CD-DA (digital audio), and multisession playback as a minimum.

- **16-bit audio, full-duplex operation, and MIDI support:** Older 8-bit audio cards do not support the throughput, bidirectionality, and data sampling rates needed for modern multimedia applications. All modern sound cards support full-duplex operation, which allows you to record and play back at the same time—a useful feature for real-time mixing. Most multimedia also now makes some use of MIDI, and if you are producing music or controlling instruments, MIDI is a must.

Mini-Glossary

ANALOG-TO-DIGITAL CONVERTER (ADC)   A section of the sound card that electronically converts analog signals (frequencies and amplitudes) to their representation in digital signals and strength (1s and 0s, and a digital value for strength).

DIGITAL-TO-ANALOG CONVERTER (DAC)   A section of the sound card that electronically converts digital data, in the form of digitized frequency and amplitude, into analog signals for playback through speakers or output to tape.

MULTISESSION SUPPORT   In CD-ROM parlance, multisession support denotes CD-ROM/XA type II recording and playback. This effectively means that many small sessions of recording can be linked together and played back as if the entire disk was recorded at one time. Used primarily in multimedia for game, linked video, and Photo CD support.

TRUECOLOR   A buzzword coined by the TrueVision Corporation, this denotes a computer graphics or video display that uses 24 bits of information to describe one pixel (picture element) on the screen. Using 24 bits of color information, a pixel is capable of displaying upwards of 16 million colors, essentially any color imaginable, or TrueColor.

NT Multimedia Video

Use the following pointers when looking for video support in your NT multi-media installation:

- Specify a video card with PCI interface. As mentioned earlier, PCI-based video cards perform much better than older technologies. PCI is also the standard for high-end video capture and editing adapters for nonlinear digital video. The older adapter technologies do not offer a "wide" enough data path for video. This affects throughput and therefore overall performance in both capture and display modes. Some nonlinear editing adapters also offer special professional features such as preview video (live) in a window, time-encoding and decoding, and hardware-based zoom and pan.

- Make sure that the video electronics support 24-bit (TrueColor) graphics. The idea here is to have video rendered in as natural a color format as possible. With 24-bit color, more than 16 million colors can be captured and displayed at once. Some capture systems use 16(15)-bit color, making more than 65,000 colors available, and that is the minimum you should use.

- Obtain a video adapter that supplies NT video drivers for both capture and playback. Driver support is a must! Check with the manufacturer before purchasing any video equipment. Do not accept adapters without guaranteed driver support.

- Check resolution capabilities. The standard for NTSC video capture is 640x480, but you will want more real estate on your display, so look for adapters that are capable of performing all of their functions at resolutions of 88x600 and 1024x768, or higher. This may require adapters with additional video memory or special options.

- Match the display monitor to the adapter capabilities. If, for example, your video adapter is capable of 1024x768 at 75Hz refresh, make sure that the display monitor is also capable of displaying that resolution at the given refresh rate.

NT Multimedia Audio

Use the following pointers when looking for sound support in your NT multi-media installation:

- Look for audio adapters that have 16- or 32-bit internal digitizing circuitry. Audio circuitry works by converting analog sound to a representation that is digital in nature—a number. When playback is desired, the audio circuitry then decodes these digital numbers, turning them back into analog sound that is output to a speaker or recording device. The analog-to-digital converter (ADC) and digital-to-analog converter (DAC) sections of the card do most of the work in the encoding (recording) and decoding (playback) of the analog and digital data, respectively. You want to have the widest data path on an audio card in order to perform sampling at higher rates and accuracy. Make sure there's support for both monaural and stereo recording and playback, with all of the standard sampling rates (digitizing frequencies). Also, as mentioned earlier, make sure that the adapter is capable of full-duplex operation, in which recording and playback are possible simultaneously (this capability is also a must for applications such as "internet phones" and two-way video conferencing).

- Look for 20 or more voice capability. Audio adapters include a synthesizer section that is capable of playing multiple sounds simultaneously. Obviously, the more the merrier! Minimum on good adapters is 20, with 32 voice capability becoming standard.

- Look for WaveTable capability. Some MIDI adapters re-create a musical note using waveform synthesis, a mathematical sound model. This type of reproduction sounds "electronic," and is desirable in some cases. But for most uses, a WaveTable adapter sounds much better, since the reproduced MIDI notes are played with an actual stored sample of a real instrument sound.

- Look for an MPU-401-compatible MIDI port. This type of port is standard on most sound cards. It enables you to plug a MIDI instrument into your computer for recording and playback. Included on most 401-type ports is a dual joystick connector, integral to the design.

Maximizing NT Video Performance

We will now look at some of the issues involved in optimal video performance, since this is the bottleneck where most NT multimedia installations run into trouble. We'll examine several areas in which performance can be improved. As a general note to video performance, a new standard for compressed video (offering higher throughput and greater compression) has finally hit the market and become mainstream. Even the direct broadcast digital satellites use this compression standard now. As mentioned earlier in this chapter, this new standard is called MPEG (Moving (Motion) Picture Experts Group). Until recently, MPEG was seen only as a playback format (because of difficulties in making the encoding process real time), but MPEG adapters are now coming on the market that record and play back in real time. MPEG allows you to play back real-time, full-screen (or windowed) digital video. MPEG is a high-compression technique that reduces the huge data rates of digital video to a fraction of their uncompressed form. MPEG has advanced to become a key technology for Digital Video Disk, CD-ROMs, Cdi, video-on-demand, and multimedia games. MPEG decoders are able to play back MPEG-1 videos up to full screen with 25/30 frames as well as MPEG audio in stereo. Many companies currently use MPEG in multimedia presentations and productions because of its quality and compression ratio. Variants on this theme include MPEG-1 and MPEG-2.

Another related technology for compression is used extensively by video capture adapters and equipment. MJPEG (Motion JPEG) is a video CODEC format supported by many companies selling these adapters. It is fully supported, with the right drivers, by an NT video editing installation.

The disadvantages relative to MPEG are lower compression and higher space requirements, since MJPEG does no interframe compression. On the other hand, MJPEG has distinct advantages over MPEG in a nonlinear editing installation. It allows frame accurate editing, has a more uniform bit rate, so it is more predictable and manageable, and it allows for real-time compression with simple hardware since the compression algorithm is much faster. Of course, MJPEG encoded video can be followed by conversion to MPEG.

Mini-Glossary

AUDIO-VIDEO INTERLEAVE (AVI)   The original (and still very popular) Video for Windows file format. It carries both video and audio information in one file, interleaving the two streams of data.

FRAMES PER SECOND (FPS)   The measure of how many full video frames, at any given resolution, can be displayed per second. An indicator of playback or capture speed; to be realistic looking, it must be more than 15fps. A measure of 30fps is considered real-time playback; 24fps is considered animation speed playback. In the range of 12 to 15fps, the human eye can detect the difference between one frame and the next; this appears as a jerky motion.

KEY FRAMES   In terms of video clips, key frames are full video frames between which recording consists only of the *changes* in the data. In terms of animation, key frames are frames that define the start and end positions of a piece of animation that is tweened; *tweening* being the process of filling in animated action *between* key frames.

MOTION PICTURE EXPERTS GROUP (MPEG)   Both a standards body and the standard itself, MPEG is a popular CODEC for compressing full-screen, VHS-quality digital video into a small data stream so that it can be played across a network connection or from CD-ROM. MPEG allows 640x480x30fps video playback with extremely low data rates.

MPEG-1   MPEG-1 is the international compression standard used in the conversion of analog motion video into digital motion video including both video and audio data. MPEG-1 meets the needs of CD-ROM and video-on-demand applications. Actual compression over uncompressed digital video is about 100:1.

MPEG-2   MPEG-2 is an extension of the MPEG-1 compression standard designed to meet the requirements of television broadcast studios.

JPEG   Joint Photographic Experts Group. This committee was given the task of finding the best way to represent photographic data in digital format. JPEG, the result of their work, is the international compression standard used in the conversion of analog still images to digital still images. The algorithm itself was selected from among competing submissions and is designed to achieve high compression, yet maintain the highest image quality. The algorithm works by eliminating the data to which the human eye is least sensitive. Hence, JPEG is considered to be a lossy algorithm. Actual compression over uncompressed digital images is about 20:1.

MJPEG   Motion JPEG. Sequence of JPEG images when displayed rapidly in a video player, becomes video.

NTSC   An analog video standard format with a resolution size of 640x480.

PALETTE FLASHING AND MATCHING   Multimedia containing video or bitmaps that overlay other background bitmaps often exhibits what is called palette flash. This flash comes from using different color palettes for the background and foreground graphics in palette-using color modes (usually 4- or 8-bit modes). The system code that manages how colors are rendered on a palette-using display will always attempt to accurately render the palette of a foreground window. Background windows have to render themselves after foreground windows, and two things usually occur if the color palettes do not match. First, because the system switches away and reloads a different palette, the colors in the other bitmap will flash. Second, in some cases, the background bitmap, using palette entries from the foreground bitmap, will render itself with the wrong colors. This usually ends up looking psychedelic, or at least very wrong. If you must use palettes, make sure all graphics shown share an "optimized" global palette.

PIXEL   A picture element. The smallest addressable element on a display surface, a pixel is usually made up physically of one or more phosphor triads (red + green + blue) on a color CRT. On a monochrome CRT, a pixel is just a point (dot) on the screen, off or on.

Video Playback Window Sizing and Alignment

If you are planning a multimedia presentation or production, and you have programmatic control over how video will be displayed on screen, you should pay careful attention to window alignment and size. These pointers do not apply to full-screen video, but most multimedia applications depend on video shown in a window.

To achieve optimal video playback, the playback window's active client area (the area where the video gets displayed) should be programmatically aligned, horizontally, on any four-pixel boundary. Without enforcing this kind of alignment, playback may be slowed by up to 50 percent on some video display adapters, because of the way video data gets written into display memory. The CPU is able to move the video data to the display memory more efficiently when the active display area is aligned like this.

You should also enforce optimal window sizing since resizing a video playback window from its original size and shape can also seriously affect playback performance. When designing a multimedia presentation, it's always better to create and show your video in a 1:1 window rather than resizing it up or down, even under program control, afterwards.

 NOTE: Again, some newer, more sophisticated display adapters do not exhibit these problems. These newer adapters do not depend on the main CPU to move video data onto the display surface memory planes. Even so, NT, working in concert with your adapter's display drivers, will almost always try to size and align the video playback window automatically.

Using Optimal Palettes and Avoiding Palette Flash

Because NT uses color palettes in 4-, 8-, and 16(15)-bit graphics modes, files having different palettes that are displayed at the same time will exhibit a phenomenon known as palette flash. Only one window at a time will ever be considered by NT to be in the foreground. The display will flash as the foreground palette (the one belonging to the foreground graphic) is applied, by the system, to the graphic contained in the background window. Add to this the fact that, at the very least, the background graphics will look strange, as if off-color or grainy. If the palettes share few common colors, the background graphics might look solarized or unintelligible.

There are ways to attack this problem. They are listed here in order of usability and effectiveness:

- Use 24- or 32-bit color modes. This obviates the need for palette-based color in the first place and will look correct in all cases. Color modes of 24 bits or greater usually run slower on older display adapters. If you are aiming your final presentations toward a wide audience, you must realize that many people will be using display adapters that are set up for 8-bit palette color (256-color displays). They will not only take a performance hit, but their displays will render your 24-bit color images as 256-color palette-based graphics. Your presentations might look very strange to these users. However, if you are using your system for in-house video capture and editing only, 24- or 32-bit color is the best choice.

■ Dither the graphics to a unified palette. Use the same global palette for all graphic elements, programmatically dithering all graphics to these colors. You will not have flash or color shift in any graphic, but all graphics will look slightly off, especially those rich in one set of colors, or hues. This technique is only possible if you have full programmed control over the application that displays your graphics.

■ Use a normalized palette, containing colors for both graphics elements. Of course, the element count (on screen at any one time) has a direct impact on whether this technique can be used. If you are able to employ this method, you can use a palette normalization utility, such as De-Babbelizer by Equilibrium, to examine, pick, and sort colors in more than one palette. These utilities then allow you to combine palettes by taking the 256 most used colors from the source palettes, producing a normalized hybrid usable by more than one graphic element. This method usually works for two elements, but fails for many simultaneously displayed graphics, or for graphics containing large sets of shaded colors or hues of the same color.

Optimal Audio/Video Compression and Decompression

If you are using lossy compression techniques, the following suggestions will be very important to you. When audio and video data are subjected to lossy compression, they inevitably lose some quality. So applying lossy compression should only be a one-pass, final technique. If the data has been subjected to compression and decompression already, expect some loss of quality, sort of like first- and second-generation videotape.

To achieve the best results in compressing and decompressing audio and video, follow these general suggestions:

■ Use first-generation data only, as input. Do not use compressed or otherwise degraded data as a source for the final cut. Of course, if you are using nonlinear editing, without recompression, *all* data is first generation!

■ Do not compress already compressed data with lossy algorithms. Because lossy-compressed data is already encoded with the loss, further encoding runs two risks: further degradation of data, or worse, loss of encoding information (with certain compressors), resulting in a total loss of data.

■ Use 1:1 interleave, if available and where applicable. This is optimal for most AVI video.

■ Use the most recent and applicable drivers and CODECs for your hardware platform. Always check with the manufacturer for customized drivers. A visit to their Web site might be in order.

Throughput, Data and Frame Rates, and Key Frames

The data rate and frame rate sustainable by your hardware and application depend on many factors, some of which we have already reviewed. Data rates refer to the throughput your hardware can support in providing data to an application. A typical AVI might require a data rate of as little as 300K/sec, or as high as 1.5MB/sec, depending on frame rate (displayed frames/sec) and color depth (i.e., 8-bit 256 color, TrueColor, etc.).

PCI-based video adapters will easily support 15 to 30fps at sizes up to 640x480 pixels, depending on all other factors being optimal. The mitigating factors here are acceleration by specialized playback hardware—such as MPEG adapter cards or on-video-chip acceleration with the S3 V+ or ATI MACH series VGA chipsets.

When capturing video with compression, or when postproducing compressed video, the subject of key frames comes up. Most CODECs compress by taking certain whole frames of information and interpolating information for intervening frames as a delta to the start-key frame, on through to the end-key frame. This process starts over with another key frame pair, and so on.

With most applications, you will simply choose default settings for key frames. If you wish to set the number of key frames, be aware that although fewer key frames can result in a better image capture, data rates will go up since more delta information between keys will have to be stored. This may affect the smoothness of your playback quality. More key frames will result in fewer dropped frames, because the delta data is reduced, and the playback must synchronize to the key frames.

Insider Info

Basic NT hardware performance can be critical in delivering enough throughput to support video and audio capture or playback methods. Multimedia data can be stored on, and read back from, a CD-ROM, a local hard disk drive, a network file server, or another storage medium. The quality of rendition can be limited by the quantity of data that the chosen storage medium and delivery mechanism can continuously supply to the capture and playback transports. For instance, a low-speed modem connection across the Internet is not going to be able to supply enough raw data to the system, in a small enough amount of time, to be able to render video at real-time speeds (more than 15 fps) without buffering and intermediate storage.

When you consider a multimedia setup for recording and playing data that requires high bandwidth throughput, the primary considerations must be

- Match the speed of hardware and software to minimum requirements for data-dependent bandwidth.

- Make sure no bottlenecks occur in system layout and configuration (swapfiles, memory constraints, etc.).

- Network data connections are sufficient for quality of service assurance (no dropouts on continuous data requirements).

- Storage requirements are met (enough local or network storage for minimum recording and playback scenarios).

NT Multimedia and DirectX

Multimedia in NT has, up till now, depended on various and sundry software modules that are really add-ons to the NT operating system proper. While these modules provide basic multimedia services, they are not optimally configured for speed or utility.

DirectX addresses many of the drawbacks and shortcomings in earlier NT multimedia services. DirectX is a suite of low-level routines designed specifically for high performance and utility in 3-D graphics, games, and similar applications. DirectX is OLE based, using COM (the Component Object Model—see Chapter 22). DirectX routines provide the fastest kind of interface—direct access to hardware—and will take advantage of hardware accelerators, if present. DirectX modules include

- **DirectDraw:** Provides new and improved GDI-type (2-D) drawing and graphics services.
- **DirectSound:** Provides new and improved sound playback and mixing services.
- **DirectInput:** Provides new and improved input device services, such as for joysticks.

DirectX Components

While new components are still being designed, and will be added to the DirectX suite as necessary, the base functionality itself is important enough to cover here. Normal GDI (Graphics Device Interface) graphics have been the mainstay of Windows-type graphics programming for years now. Many third-party workarounds have been tried, but none have become a standard. Microsoft is formalizing a built-in interface to bypass most of GDI for high-performance graphics and sound. That interface is DirectX (see Figure 10-3). As an adjunctive technology, DirectX and GDI can (and must) coexist. Graphics can be authored using either technology, and can be rendered to the screen at the same time. In fact, DirectX uses GDI for some of its functions, so what DirectX does not do well, GDI can fill in, and vice versa.

DirectDraw

DirectDraw is an aggregate drawing technology that encompasses services intended to provide for 2-D, 3-D, video, and animation primitives. From the beginning, it was designed to be high performance, and because it's so close to the hardware, you have finer control over what happens and how graphics are rendered. Some of DirectDraw's services include

- High-performance page flipping and blts (block transfers) for quick data movement.
- Hardware overlays, color keying, and bitmap stretching to take advantage of newer graphics hardware technology.
- High-performance color and format conversion, which speed rendering in foreign formats and color-using schemes.

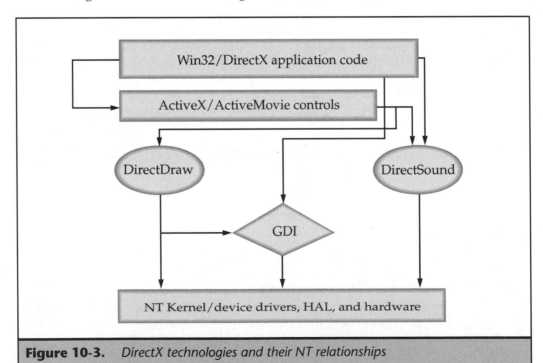

Figure 10-3. *DirectX technologies and their NT relationships*

ActiveMovie

ActiveMovie is a new media streaming design for video and audio, a large step forward when compared with standard AVI/digital video player technology. ActiveMovie uses DirectDraw to accelerate rendering by using graphics adapter accelerators if available. The ActiveMovie control is shown in Figure 10-4. ActiveMovie supports AVI, MPEG, and Apple QuickTime (.MOV) media streams. It is also designed for maximal Internet connectivity and functionality (covered in Chapter 25) using ActiveX technology.

DirectSound

DirectSound is an accelerated low-level interface to your audio hardware, using any available accelerator technology that is present on the audio card. It can provide interfaces for real-time audio mixing, volume, and panning. DirectSound also has the ability to play multiple audio streams simultaneously, effectively mixing waveform audio streams. The ActiveMovie/ActiveX control uses calls to the DirectSound interface.

Figure 10-4.   *The DirectX ActiveMovie control*

DirectInput

DirectInput provides for control of analog and digital joysticks. DirectInput can use any device that can track position in absolute coordinates. For example, DirectInput could use light pens or digitizer pads, head-mounted virtual reality gear, or any game control that outputs absolute position.

DirectInput can query information in six degrees of freedom with 32 input toggle states. This gives designers possibilities not found in the joystick/input services used formerly for Win32 programming. For instance, a virtual reality helmet would need at least four degrees of freedom, or reporting axis, to be usable. DirectInput will enable this type of interface now.

3-D Graphics and OpenGL

Those computer animation sequences seen in films these days take sophisticated graphics applications to produce and, until now, high-end workstations and operating system software. Compared to Silicon Graphics and Sun workstation graphics software, the Windows family has previously been lacking in high-end horsepower and support for this type of application.

History of OpenGL

With its introduction in NT 3.5, and with expanded support and maturity in NT 4, OpenGL now provides application authoring on NT. OpenGL is a powerful, high-end, 3-D graphics support library that enables NT applications to perform the kind of graphics operations that must be used in theatrical and advanced scientific rendering. Silicon Graphics Inc. (SGI) developed OpenGL as a direct result of its effort to port GL—SGI's proprietary 3-D graphics language running on SGI Iris workstations. The principal movers and shakers in this now open architecture are Microsoft, SGI, DEC, IBM, and Intel.

What OpenGL Offers

OpenGL is a library of portable graphics primitives used in rendering 3-D graphics (see Figure 10-5). Over 100 primitives are included for rendering points, lines, polygons, and so on—all in 3-D. OpenGL includes support for lighting, shading, texture mapping, anti-aliasing, and animation. It is a rendering library, so no support exists for graphics file conversion, window creation, or the like.

OpenGL is a portable 3-D rendering library. As such, code written for an SGI Iris workstation will probably run, with very little porting effort, on an NT Pentium-based workstation (although much slower, since the Iris is *very* high performance). OpenGL programs consist of the code to render a 3-D (2-D is also possible) scene to be displayed in an operating system managed window. Animation is possible by flipping scenes in rapid succession, and scenes or scene objects can be rendered photo-realistically with viewing angles, shading, and lighting sources. OpenGL

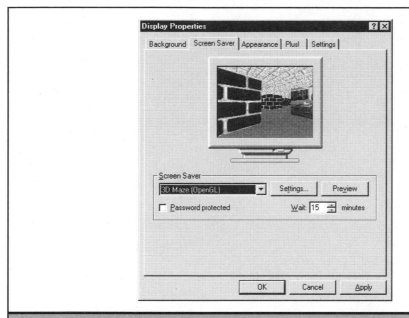

Figure 10-5.   *An NT OpenGL screen saver*

graphics can be bitmapped or polygon based. Most of the portable software for rendering complex, realistic 3-D scenes use polygonal rendering, so OpenGL is capable of handling these tasks.

> **REMINDER:**   *OpenGL is a graphics library, not an end application. As developers discover OpenGL, you'll see more and more applications that employ its services. Three-dimensional programming is mathematically intensive, and any high-end library to offload rendering duties is sure to be a hit. To get a feel for what OpenGL can do, use one of the OpenGL screen savers in the Start/Settings/Control Panel/Display/Screen Saver dialog.*

What's Next

This chapter has only scratched the surface with an overview of some of the capabilities of NT 4 multimedia. There are so many adapter cards, programs, and uses for multimedia, it's not possible to go over them in such a short time. Advertising, game, and simulation producers and manufacturers are driving this industry, so we are likely to see even better hardware and software in the days to come.

Next, we're going more into the area of connectivity—networking, the Internet, and remote access issues. Part 3 of this book is entirely devoted to these subject areas.

PART THREE

Connecting with Windows NT

Chapter Eleven

Networking with TCP/IP

With the rising popularity of internetworks, local area network (LAN) connection protocols have largely been supplanted by the most universally used wide area network standard: the Transmission Control Protocol/ Internet Protocol (TCP/IP). This is a networking protocol that provides communication on any scale that is needed—from small local area networks with a few workstations to large, interconnected networks (especially the Internet).

Because TCP/IP is used whenever you connect to the Internet, and many times is the only network standard in use at university, government, and corporate sites, it is now considered to be the primary protocol for networking and, therefore, for an NT 4 installation. In this chapter, we will go through a description of how to install and configure TCP/IP on a computer running NT 4 Workstation or Server. This chapter also provides background and reference material on the TCP/IP protocol and information about TCP/IP services such as the Peer Web Server and the Simple Network Management Protocol (SNMP) service.

NOTE: The Peer Web Server and SNMP are TCP/IP services that need no special NT Server-side support when used on a client or workstation machine. If you are contemplating an installation of Microsoft's Internet Information Server (IIS) for NT 4 Server, we'll be talking about the special considerations you need to make in support of that configuration, and the services that IIS provides, in Chapters 25 and 26.

Insider Info

Since almost everyone must use the TCP/IP protocol to connect to the Internet, it has become the most accepted, and yet complicated, routable networking protocol available. In addition to Internet connectivity, anyone contemplating deployment within a Unix environment, or any large wide area network (WAN), should seriously consider TCP/IP as the primary networking protocol.

TCP/IP installation, with its multiple settings and configurations, can be daunting. Add to this the matter of valid IP address assignment and the issue of registered domains. Since the TCP/IP protocol presents a set of protocols, or rules, that control the way data is passed between computers on a network, the scope of the network makes a lot of difference in how many of the setup rules you must follow.

If you contemplate a transient or permanent presence on the Internet, or on a network that will ultimately expose your installation to the public, you must absolutely follow all rules for settings that will allow interoperation with the global network. These rules and protocol settings are made so that no matter how large and disparate the interconnections between smaller nets, or single workstations, becomes, an individual node will always be able to communicate with any other single node.

However, TCP/IP can also be used to implement networking *only* within a privately connected LAN or wider area private internetwork. An example of this would be a company with several locations, using dedicated lines, wishing to keep communications entirely "within the family." Here, TCP/IP's rules can be bent somewhat, since for all practical purposes the local network is the world. Settings and rules that govern how a workstation or subnet will expose itself to others running TCP/IP can be totally controlled since you can absolutely guarantee the nature of all other machines that will have, and grant, access.

TCP/IP can be used to communicate with, and between, any version of NT installed on your system. In addition, Windows 95, Windows 3.x, and MS-DOS clients are supported. The TCP/IP protocol for NT 4 also allows you to communicate with Unix systems or any other TCP/IP-enabled installation that you might encounter on a WAN connection, such as the Internet. You can use TCP/IP to interconnect almost any combination of divergent technologies. The thrust in "smart" peripherals is now resulting in printers, closed-circuit cameras, and many other devices that know how to talk TCP/IP and have their own IP addresses. This means that the TCP/IP protocol is becoming a universal network communication standard for all purposes.

You will find a multitude of application support when using TCP/IP. Since TCP/IP has been used so extensively, many software authors have written utilities and applications that fully exploit this protocol. Many standard applications and connectivity utilities are available to access and transfer block data between TCP/IP-connected systems. These include the File Transfer Protocol (FTP) and the Terminal Emulation Protocol (Telnet). These and other utilities are included with NT 4.

NT 4's TCP/IP Package

In brief, the TCP/IP capabilities of NT 4 are as follows:

■ Automatic IP address configuration through the use of the Dynamic Host Configuration Protocol (DHCP) when a DHCP server is available on the network.

■ TCP/IP utilities and system performance counters to make optimization and administrative tasks easier. You can easily track performance of IP protocols, FTP server traffic, and WINS servers. Additionally, IIS servers have full graphical administrative and tracking ability (see Chapter 25.)

■ Name resolution capabilities by using NetBIOS over TCP/IP (NetBT) and the domain name system (DNS), plus, a service that is exclusive to Windows: the Windows Internet name service (WINS). WINS, working in concert with DHCP, provides name resolution services and also includes graphic, centralized management. WINS is a sophisticated computer name-to-IP address resolution and registration service. Both DHCP and WINS are covered in Chapter 12.

■ Simple Network Management Protocol (SNMP) is provided to monitor and administer WINS and DHCP servers (see Chapter 12 for more information).

■ Multiple *homed* TCP/IP configurations are supported. This means an NT system can have more than one network interface card (NIC) assigned with different TCP/IP parameters and addresses. Also available is the option to configure multiple default gateways and IP forwarding, which we will talk about later in this chapter, to ensure reliable and redundant packet routing.

The following sections treat the complete TCP/IP package in greater detail.

The Core TCP/IP Protocols

NT 4 TCP/IP implements and supports all of the basic TCP/IP protocols:

■ The Transmission Control Protocol (TCP), which provides a reliable, connection-oriented delivery service. TCP ensures reliability, flow control, and connection maintenance. To ensure reliability, TCP is able to recover from data reception that is damaged, lost, duplicated, or delivered out of sequence. The receiving host's TCP layer must return an acknowledgment for bytes received within a specified period. If this is not done, the data is retransmitted.

■ The Internet Protocol (IP), which is responsible for addressing and delivering TCP data packets. A connectionless protocol, IP acts to route data from one host to another, working under the assumption that the data may not reach the remote connection.

■ The User Datagram Protocol (UDP), which is used by applications that only need a connectionless, best effort transport service that does not guarantee delivery, much like IP. A datagram is a collection of data that is sent as a single message. Each of these datagrams is sent through the network individually.

■ The Address Resolution Protocol (ARP), which provides IP address resolution to Media Access Control (MAC—the physical 48-bit network adapter address) address resolution.

■ The Internet Control Message Protocol (ICMP), which provides feedback to the sender on problems, as well as settings. ICMP messages such as ECHO REQUEST and ECHO REPLY are typical, and, for instance, *pinging* an address on the net will result in ICMP being used to find the remote host.

Together, these Internet protocols provide the core set of functionality that allows TCP/IP-enabled computers to communicate, and they also dictate how TCP/IP-enabled networks may be interconnected. It is interesting to note that TCP and UDP, as protocols, are commonly used by themselves in making local network connections without regard to the Internet or any other WAN connection. In other words, TCP/IP is a general solution to both local and wide area connectivity, and works well as a primary protocol for almost any network scenario.

There are many single-purpose ancillary Internet protocols. For the most part, these high-level data packet transfer protocols are implemented programmatically by using members of the basic suite. For instance, the Real-Audio streaming protocol is based on data transfer using UDP or TCP. NT 4, through an application, is capable of recognizing and responding to any protocol that is implemented using the TCP/IP framework. Support is also provided for PPP and SLIP, which are protocols used for dial-up access to TCP/IP-enabled networks, and the security challenge/response mechanisms (CHAP, PAP, and clear text) that these communications protocols use (see Chapter 13).

Simple Services

NT 4 can be configured with client support for non-native higher level network protocols, more properly referred to as simple TCP/IP services, that are used extensively in Unix systems, including *Character Generator*, *Daytime*, *Discard*, *Echo*, and *Quote of the Day*. When another system generates a protocol request covered by one of these services, an NT 4 computer can respond to the request as long as it has already been set up by installation of TCP/IP and the "TCP/IP Simple Services," using the Control Panel's Network applet. You do not have to support requests made by any of these services, as they are largely used in making systems appear friendly, and they do not provide critical functionality. However, if you want to be able to respond to these requests, simply install the support; from there on, everything is automatic.

Application Interface Support

For programmers, NT 4 also includes support for TCP/IP application interfaces and direct control. The Windows Sockets 1.1/2.0 application program interface (API) is provided for high-level TCP/IP network programming, and such languages as Visual C++ and Visual Basic can be used to implement applications that use the Sockets standard.

The Windows Sockets specification defines a network programming interface based on the *socket* concept that has been popularized by the Berkeley Software Distribution (BSD) from the University of California at Berkeley. Sockets provide a unified API that developers can use to ensure conformance no matter which network transport is in use. Theoretically, the Windows Sockets API can be used with any network transport, but the existing implementation is geared to TCP/IP.

You may also use calls into the NetBIOS over TCP/IP layer for establishing logical names and sessions on the network, and direct program control of the TCP/IP transport is always available, if somewhat arcane.

Insider Info

NT TCP/IP applications and utilities, along with Services for Macintosh and the Internetwork Packet Exchange/Sequenced Packet Exchange (IPX/SPX) protocol (NWLink) to a lesser extent, utilize many of the Windows Sockets services and APIs. Even 16-bit Windows Sockets applications will run under NT.

Windows Sockets version 2.0 is the successor to version 1.1, which has been the standard since its release in 1993. Version 1.1 was intentionally limited to deal with TCP/IP because the parties involved in its authorship were primarily interested in that standard. However, like its Berkeley Sockets model, Windows Sockets could theoretically support other protocol suites.

Windows Sockets version 2.0 (WinSock 2) does this now, and NT 4 includes support for this version. Protocol suites such as DecNet and IPX/SPX can now coexist with TCP/IP, with full backward compatibility for the existing version 1.1 interface. WinSock 2 implements most of the true Sockets standard, allowing compliant applications to be network protocol independent.

A WinSock 2 application can seamlessly use any protocol it needs to. An application using this new standard can adapt to differences on the fly using the facilities that WinSock 2 provides. Almost all modern applications and utilities are being written to the Windows Sockets standards; most browsers, email clients, and FTP utilities use Sockets.

Command-Line TCP/IP Connectivity Utilities

NT 4 includes Unix-style command-line TCP/IP utilities that look and act exactly like their counterparts on other operating systems. Although many of these utilities are now implemented in graphical Windows form, Unix mavens, administrators who need scripting capabilities, and users who need only basic intercomputer utility can make use of them. These utilities are installed whenever you install the TCP/IP protocol on your NT system.

The utilities that are available include *finger, ftp, lpr, rcp, rexec, rsh, telnet,* and *tftp,* all of which will be instantly recognizable to a user of a Unix system. NT 4 originally shipped with these utilities so that Windows users could converse with other operating systems, either on dedicated lines or across the Internet. In deference to Unix users, they are still shipped with NT 4, although you can find many graphical applications that implement these same utilities in the native Win32 environment, making them much easier to use.

TCP/IP Services and Administrative Tools

Along with the client utilities that NT 4 provides, basic NT TCP/IP provides several workstation services and administrative tools that act as, or allow access to, server-side components. These services do not rely on an NT Server installation being present, and they can be installed at any time, so gradual build out of services is possible.

First, there is the Peer Web Server, which can be installed on any NT workstation. This component allows any NT 4 workstation to act as a fully functional Hypertext Transfer Protocol (HTTP) server, as well as an FTP and GOPHER server. By allowing you to publish Web pages and supply FTP and GOPHER functionality from a workstation, this service supplies Internet/intranet server functionality to any browser-enabled peer on your network. You can use this service instead of NT Server (with IIS) to supply Web pages, FTP sites, and GOPHER publishing services on a lightly loaded, local intranet (for instance, in small, private company LANs where traffic can be controlled and high volume or security is not so much of a concern). You install the Peer Web Server from the Services tab of the Control Panel's Network applet.

Additionally, you can install support for TCP/IP-based printing. This service allows you to access a printer queue on a Unix system or a TCP/IP-based printer that is connected directly to the network and, conversely, if installed along with the LPDSVC service, allows Unix computers to print to printers on an NT system.

Also included is the Simple Network Management Protocol (SNMP) service. This component, or agent, allows an NT computer to report current status and be administered remotely by an SNMP management tool, such as those available from Carnegie Mellon University's CMU-SNMP package or Hewlett Packard's Open View software. SNMP can also be used to monitor and manage DHCP servers and WINS servers, which we'll review in the next chapter.

You will also find command-line TCP/IP trace, setting, and diagnostic tools, including *arp*, *hostname*, *ipconfig*, *lpq*, *nbtstat*, *netstat*, *ping*, *route*, and *tracert*. Using these utilities, you can make manual changes to TCP/IP routing tables, trace routes to remote hosts, and discover what your TCP/IP installation is doing. An example of a TCP/IP setup on NT is shown in Figure 11-1.

> **TIP:** *If you have older operating systems to support, you can still use TCP/IP for your entire network. For Windows for Workgroups and MS-DOS-based computers on a Microsoft network, you can install the new version of NT TCP/IP-32 or the Network Client version 3.0, respectively, from the NT Server version 4 CD-ROM. You'll find this software in the CLIENTS directory. The software includes the DHCP and WINS clients and other elements of TCP/IP software. Windows 95 already includes this support natively. Also, many shareware SNMP service agents are now available for both NT and Windows 95.*

The Hidden Advantages of Installing TCP/IP

As we have seen already, TCP/IP can provide your NT network with a common set of internetworking protocols that are used by, and allow you to connect to, many

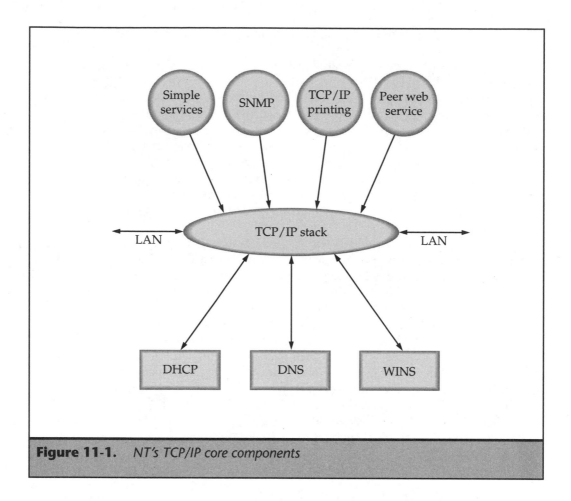

Figure 11-1. *NT's TCP/IP core components*

different types of systems. By using TCP/IP, you instantly gain support for such operations as hypertext document support, email and news, foreign-host file transfer, remote process control and execution, and connectivity to non-NT systems (in a wired LAN or WAN, as well as on the Internet).

You also gain some very important functionality under the hood, as it were. For instance, TCP/IP gives your installation the ability to act as either an end node in a network or as a *router* that will forward network requests to another computer system, or network, through what is called a *gateway*. This routing ability is a central feature of TCP/IP, since some networking protocols do not allow for messages and data across gateways. In fact, this is one of the reasons that TCP/IP works so well on the Internet.

Because routing is a central part of TCP/IP's capabilities, it may also be put to use in securing your network site. The main components used to secure a TCP/IP network from attack and unauthorized access, by screening access, are called *firewalls* and *proxies*. A firewall is able to screen and filter on certain client, service, and other conditions. In principle, three techniques are used:

- IP-level filtering
- Application-level filtering (proxy)
- Connection-level filtering

IP Filtering

The principle of IP-level filtering is that the firewall will pass IP packets between client and server based on information present in the headers of the IP packet. The most important pieces of information are source IP address, destination IP address, destination port, and packet type.

The weakest point of IP-level filtering is that the information on which the connection is to be filtered is rather limited and also not very reliable. For instance, the source address should identify the client; however, it does not identify a real user. This is not very reliable and it is certainly not as reliable as an authentication-based connection, for instance, on username and password or username and some kind of challenge/response mechanism.

Application-Level/Proxy Filtering

The principle of an application-level filter is that it blocks all IP-level traffic between the internal network and the Internet. No IP packet from the internal network will ever reach the Internet and no IP packet from the Internet will ever travel the internal network. This method therefore avoids a lot of the security-related problems of the IP protocol, which was not built with security in mind.

A proxy-based firewall controls how internal clients connect to the firewall, talking to a server on the firewall and not directly to the server on the wider area network. This server on the firewall is called a proxy. The proxy on the firewall understands the client/server protocol and acts as an intermediate; when it decides that the client is allowed to do a certain type of operation, the proxy on the firewall connects to the server on the WAN and will execute that operation on behalf of the client.

Proxies are considered to be the most secure type of intermediary, but they are not transparent for the user and the client program. Every application that uses a proxy must be set up to do so, and the incurred administrative overhead can be prohibitive (see Chapter 25).

Connection-Level Filtering

Connection-level firewalls are somewhere in between IP filtering and proxies. This kind of filtering does not deal with individual incoming and outgoing IP packets.

Rather, this technique deals with the connection that is built between a client and a server. It is able to keep state, or history, and is capable of relating incoming and outgoing IP packets belonging to a single TCP connection between a client and server.

Connection filtering also blocks all IP packet exchange between the internal network and the Internet: A proxy on the firewall mediates the connection, but once the connection is made, it does not screen the type of data being exchanged between client and server.

Installation—Before You Do It!

First, TCP/IP can be installed as part of the NT Setup process, when you are initially specifying network protocols. The following sections pertain equally to this and the second situation, discussed next. Unless you are an expert with TCP/IP, read on.

Second, you can also install TCP/IP after your initial setup. (This is highly recommended! Don't be in too much of a rush to set up this protocol.) Since this is the most common way the protocol will be configured, we'll assume that NT 4 has been successfully installed on your computer and that TCP/IP has not been installed. Remember that you must be logged on as a member of the Administrators group to install and configure all elements of TCP/IP.

The TCP/IP setup dialogs demand specific information from you. The level of this information will vary, depending on the level of server-side support in your network for such things as automatic IP address assignment.

However, no matter what provisions are made on the server side, there are many values that you will have to know about before you can manually configure TCP/IP and SNMP (see "Installing the SNMP Service" later in this chapter). There is also a difference between Workstation and Server setup, and we'll make mention of this where necessary. In many cases, a network administrator will supply these values and settings, so you might not need to figure out some of these parameters on your own. In situations where you *are* the administrator, or have a small LAN that you have set up privately, you will need to determine these settings yourself. In either case, you should know the following information before you attempt TCP/IP setup:

- The IP address and subnet mask (see "IP Addressing, Subnet Masks, and IP Gateways" for reference information on subnet masks) for each network interface card installed in the computer.

- Whether you will use Dynamic Host Configuration Protocol (DHCP) to configure your IP addresses. If a DHCP server is available on your network, and the computer you are setting up will not be a DHCP server, you can choose this option to obtain an address automatically.

- The IP address for any default local gateways, which are IP routers used to access hosts that are beyond your local network, if any.

- Whether you will use PPTP, and whether you want PPTP filtering (see the section "The Advanced Dialog" for more information on PPTP).

■ Whether your computer will use the domain name system (DNS) and, if so, the IP addresses of the DNS servers available on the network.

■ Whether this computer will use the Windows Internet name service for resolution of NetBIOS names to IP addresses. This usually is accomplished through DHCP, if available.

■ If you wish to use WINS and cannot use DHCP for configuration, you need to determine the IP addresses for any WINS servers available on your network.

Additionally, if you are setting up an NT Server you must know

■ Whether this computer will be a DHCP server

■ Whether this computer will be a WINS server

Mini-Glossary

ADDRESS RESOLUTION PROTOCOL (ARP)   A TCP/IP protocol that dynamically maps Internet addresses to physical (hardware) addresses on local area networks. ARP is limited to networks that support hardware broadcast.

DYNAMIC HOST CONFIGURATION PROTOCOL (DHCP)   Established to ease the burden of manual configuration of TCP/IP hosts, DHCP offers a framework for passing configuration information to clients on a TCP/IP network. DHCP is an enhancement to the BootP protocol. It adds the capability to reuse IP addresses and includes a wide variety of options such as subnet mask, default router, and DNS server. Using DHCP for WINS resolution also provides safe, reliable, and simple TCP/IP network configuration.

DOMAIN NAME SYSTEM (DNS)   DNS uses a distributed namespace to maintain and supply name-to-IP address resolution. It is used on the Internet and on large WAN installations to map "friendly" domain names to IP addresses.

FILE TRANSFER PROTOCOL (FTP)   The TCP/IP-Internet standard high-level protocol for transferring files from one computer to another.

INTERNET CONTROL MESSAGE PROTOCOL (ICMP)   ICMP is used for control and error messages, intended for the TCP/IP protocol software itself rather than any particular user program.

NETBIOS   A commonly used transport protocol for PC local area networks first introduced by IBM. Application programs use NetBIOS for client/server or peer-to-peer communications. There are two NetBIOS modes for communicating: the datagram mode and the session mode. The datagram mode is a connectionless protocol that does not guarantee delivery and is usually limited to 512-byte messages. The session mode is a connection-oriented protocol that guarantees delivery of messages up to 64K bytes long.

SERIAL LINE INTERNET PROTOCOL (SLIP)   Commonly used for point-to-point serial connections running TCP/IP. It is not an Internet standard and does not provide for the sophisticated features that the PPP protocol enables.

POINT-TO-POINT PROTOCOL (PPP)   The Point-to-Point Protocol (PPP) provides a method for transmitting datagrams over serial point-to-point links. It was added to the Internet protocol suite to help connect devices where dissimilar transport protocols exist.

TERMINAL EMULATION PROTOCOL (TELNET)   The Internet standard protocol for remote terminal connection service. Telnet allows a user at one site to interact with a remote system at another site as if the user's terminal was connected directly to the remote computer.

USER DATAGRAM PROTOCOL (UDP)   A transport layer protocol for the Internet. It is a datagram protocol that adds a level of reliability and multiplexing to IP datagrams, but does not guarantee delivery.

UNIVERSAL NAMING CONVENTION (UNC)   Used to denote filenames or other resource names, beginning with the string "\\," indicating that they exist on a remote machine or as an abstract resource. This convention allows you to specify resource names on networked computers in your NT domain.

WINDOWS SOCKETS   A Windows-based implementation of the widely used UC Berkeley sockets programming interface. It abstracts the physical networking layer, to provide a universal programming interface.

WINDOWS INTERNET NAME SERVICE (WINS)   A service that maintains a resolution database of computer names and their associated IP addresses in a TCP/IP environment. A WINS client can dynamically update the database.

TCP/IP Installation and Configuration

For TCP/IP to work on your computer, it must be configured with the IP addresses, subnet masks, and (default) gateways for each network adapter card that is installed and used on the computer. TCP/IP can be configured using two different methods:

- If there is a DHCP server on your network, it can automatically configure TCP/IP for your computer using DHCP.
- If there is no DHCP server, or if you are configuring an NT Server computer to be a DHCP server, you must manually configure all TCP/IP settings.

These options are described in the following sections.

With an Available DHCP Server

By using DHCP to configure your local computer with the correct TCP/IP parameters, you insure a smooth and effortless startup. If there is a DHCP server installed on your network, you can take advantage of this technique; however, you cannot use this method if you are using this computer as a DHCP server. If you choose this method, your computer will be configured properly every time you restart it, by automatically using the values supplied by the DHCP server.

Doing It Manually

If you are installing TCP/IP on a DHCP server, or if you choose not to use automatic DHCP configuration, you will have to manually enter valid addressing information at some point during the setup. Before attempting setup, make sure you are logged on as a member of the Administrators group for the local computer.

> *CAUTION: No matter how you are setting up TCP/IP, make sure that the configuration information is correct and does not duplicate settings on another machine. If you are connected to a wider area network, your addressing must be valid. Your network administrator or service provider will supply you with the proper values. If this is not done, your installation may not work at all, or you may find that other computers on the network work improperly.*

Choosing a Network Adapter

When configuring TCP/IP, you will be presented with dialogs that have *adapter* lists. These adapter lists contain the installed network interface cards (NICs) on your computer. You will be entering information for whichever adapter is displayed in this list's primary field, so be careful to choose the correct adapter when working with these dialogs.

IP Addresses and Subnet Masks

When asked to enter values for IP addresses and subnet masks, you will enter four-part values in the IP Address and Subnet Mask fields. These values identify the assigned IP address for your computer (and adapter), and also the network class membership. See the background section, "IP Addressing, Subnet Masks, and IP Gateways," for in-depth information about IP addresses and subnet masks.

> *TIP: If you are going to implement TCP/IP exclusively on a private network, without the chance of connecting directly to a wider network, you can use a specially reserved range of IP addresses that are guaranteed not to be present on any wider area network. Enter IPs in the range of 192.168.0.1 to 192.168.0.254 as the addresses, with a subnet mask of 255.255.0. Use this address range with caution! Never expose machines using these addresses to the Internet or any other WAN.*

The Default Gateway

The value for the default gateway specifies an IP address, or IP router, which is used to forward TCP/IP packets to remote subnets or networks. You will only need to specify a value for this parameter when your computer participates in a wider area, nonlocal network, where IP traffic must be forwarded across a router (software or hardware). If you are connected to a WAN or are on a subnet of a larger network, you will have to provide this parameter to enable communication with the wider network unless a static route is entered into your computer's route table, using the TCP/IP ROUTE command.

NOTE: *If your computer has multiple network adapter cards, additional gateways can be specified using the Advanced TCP/IP IP Address dialog, described later in this chapter.*

To Use the Domain Name System

Because TCP/IP uses IP addresses, you may converse with another computer on a TCP/IP-enabled network by supplying its IP number, as in **net use \ \ 204.182.124 .209\mydir** or **ftp 204.182.124.4**. This is not very convenient, and at any rate can be confusing and unfriendly. To alleviate this problem, DNS is generally used. The domain name system is a name-to-IP address service that has been used extensively on Unix, and hence the Internet, to provide name resolution for IP-enabled computers. Using DNS in the second example just given, one could simply type **ftp algoinc.com** instead of using the four-part numeric IP address, so this will almost always be friendlier and easier to use. Almost all TCP/IP utilities and applications can use DNS, in addition to static HOSTS (or LMHOSTS) files, to enable this mapping ability when trying to find a system on your local or a wider area network.

NT Workstation includes a DNS client that can be used to resolve names on a LAN or WAN. NT Server also provides a DNS server, which can be used in concert with other DNS servers on a wider area LAN to provide name resolution. Additionally, NT is able to dynamically provide name resolution for NetBIOS names via WINS servers and NetBIOS over TCP/IP.

NOTE: *When the TCP/IP protocol is installed, the \systemroot\SYSTEM32\ DRIVERS\ETC directory will contain several files that are needed to support various configuration and service components. These include default HOSTS, NETWORKS, PROTOCOLS, QUOTES, and SERVICES files. Also provided is a template sample of an LMHOSTS file, named LMHOSTS.SAM.*

Installation of TCP/IP from the Control Panel/Network Applet

The Control Panel's Network applet (shown in Figure 11-2), which you reach from the Start I Settings menu, is where you will work with settings and additions to the network layer in NT 4. This includes protocols, services, network interface cards, bindings, and computer workgroup/domain settings (refer to Chapter 6 for a general review of all of the available tabs in this dialog). Here, we will look at several tabs and settings in order to review in-depth information on TCP/IP.

Setting Protocols

The Protocols dialog box displays the currently installed network protocols. The setup dialog boxes for entering or changing parameters for each of the possible protocols are available by selecting a protocol from the list and then choosing the Properties button.

NOTE: *You must be logged on as a member of the Administrators group to install and configure TCP/IP and/or any services.*

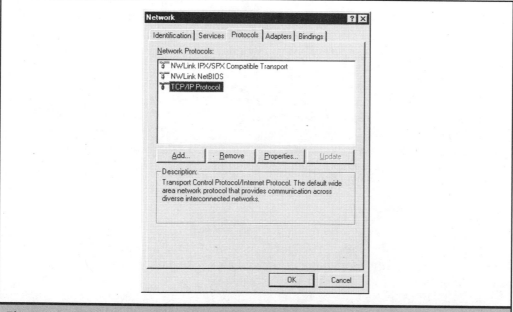

Figure 11-2. *The Network applet*

In our example, we have not yet installed the TCP/IP protocol, so it will not appear in the Network Protocols list. Use the following guidelines to install TCP/IP:

■ In the Protocols dialog, choose the Add button.

■ Another dialog, the Select Network Protocol dialog box, will appear with a complete list of available protocols. Select TCP/IP Protocol from this list, and then choose OK.

■ You will then be asked if there is a DHCP server on the network. If you know there is one, or have been told to choose DHCP, answer Yes; otherwise, answer No to set up your IP addresses later, manually.

■ Setup will now ask for the drive and path where it can find your NT distribution files so it can copy the TCP/IP elements needed to install the protocol. Either use the suggested path or enter a new drive letter and path name for your distribution files. You can specify a drive letter and path name for a hard disk or a CD-ROM drive, or you can enter the path of a shared network directory. You can also choose a universal naming convention (UNC) pathname for a connected network resource, such as \\REMOTE\NT4\i386. Then choose Continue. NT will load and install the files needed for TCP/IP.

■ You will now be returned to the Protocols dialog where TCP/IP will appear in the list of network protocols, as in Figure 11-2. Choose Close to continue your setup.

■ During the Bindings Review, NT will find your newly added TCP/IP protocol, and, if you did not select DHCP server support, you will next be presented with the TCP/IP Properties dialog, where you will enter settings for your particular installation.

NOTE: If you answered Yes to the DHCP server question, earlier, and a DHCP server is indeed available on the network, all settings for the TCP/IP protocol will be automatically entered and you can skip the next section on TCP/IP settings. If you answered No, continue with configuration as outlined in the following sections. If you are entering configuration manually, you will need to successfully complete the following section in order to use the TCP/IP protocol.

Settings for TCP/IP

If you have been presented with the TCP/IP Properties dialog during setup, you have specified that you will not use DHCP for IP assignment and automatic TCP/IP setup. Don't worry; even with automatic setup, you'll almost certainly have to deal with these settings anyway, so we might as well tackle them now.

The TCP/IP Properties dialog contains four, or five, tabbed choices, depending on whether you are installing for Workstation or Server. We'll review each tab dialog and run through the settings that are made in each. You are initially presented with the IP Address tab, as shown in Figure 11-3.

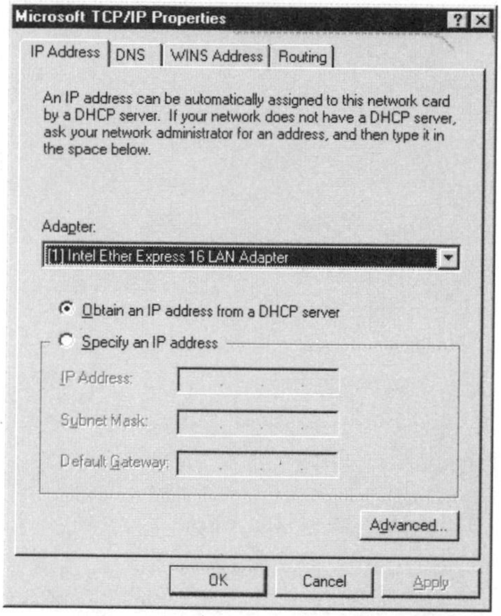

Figure 11-3. *The IP Address tab*

The IP Address dialog allows you to set up IP address assignments for each installed network interface card (NIC) on your machine. The dialog first allows you to pick the adapter that you will be making these settings for. In most cases, you will have only one NIC, so you can leave this alone. Next, you will be asked to pick a DHCP-obtained IP or to specify addresses yourself. Choose "Obtain an IP address from a DHCP server" if there is indeed a Dynamic Host Configuration Protocol server on your network. You should always try to use this method if it is available. If it is not, or you have been given a specific IP address, subnet mask, and default gateway (see "IP Addressing, Subnet Masks, and IP Gateways" later in this chapter), choose "Specify an IP address." You will then have to enter the IP, subnet mask, and default gateway values manually. Normally, these values will be assigned to you by the administrator or your Internet provider contact.

The Advanced Dialog

The IP Address dialog contains an Advanced button. Choosing this button will result in the display of another dialog where you can enter further advanced IP addressing parameters (Figure 11-4). The parameters include

- **Adapter:** Use this dropdown to pick the NIC you want to specify settings for.

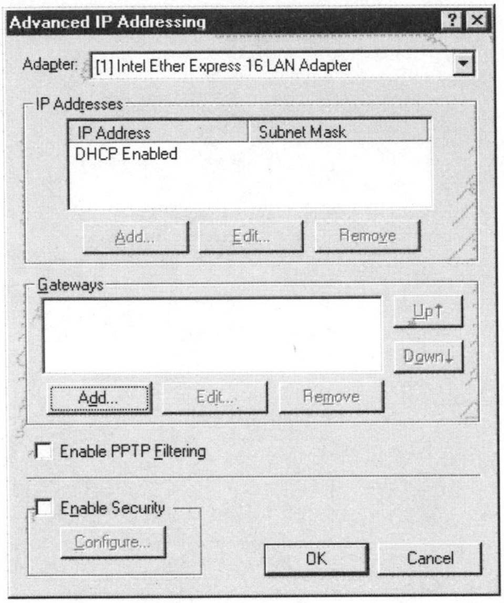

Figure 11-4. *Advanced IP addressing*

■ **IP Addresses:** If your computer is physically attached to a single network with multiple *logical* IP networks, you can specify up to five sets of IP addresses and subnet masks that NT can use to change this NIC's "personality." This feature is used infrequently, and you should only need to specify these values when directed to do so by a system administrator.

■ **Gateways:** This feature allows you to enter up to five additional gateways to use in lieu of the default gateway you specified in the last dialog. Gateways will be used in the order they are listed, and you may adjust their priority with the Up and Down buttons in this section.

■ **PPTP and Security Enable:** PPTP (Point-to-Point Tunneling Protocol) is a secure networking protocol used in concert with TCP/IP to enable secure point-to-point communications over a public network. If you wish to use this connection only for PPTP communication, choose to enable PPTP Filtering. Additionally, enabling Security allows you to configure which TCP and UDP ports you will permit your installation to use, and which IP protocols it can pass. Use these settings when you wish to filter these values for, say, an Internet connection. There are better ways of doing this, as outlined in Chapter 25, so use these settings with caution.

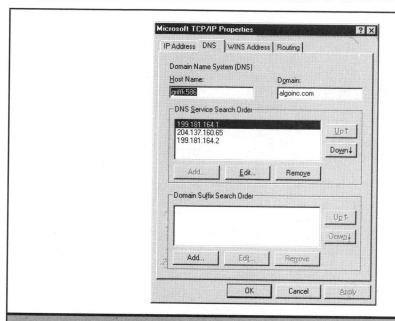

Figure 11-5. *DNS configuration dialog box*

- **DNS:** If you are using the domain name system to resolve name-to-IP addresses, you will know, or have been given, addresses for the DNS servers on your network (see Figure 11-5). Enter your host (computer) name and domain, usually something like "nt100" and "algoinc.com," respectively, in the fields at the top of this dialog. Then, enter the IP addresses of each DNS server that can be reached from your network. Additionally, you may enter suffixes that will get appended to host names when a DNS lookup is done. This helps define a DNS search, but is not necessary for proper operation.

- **WINS Address:** If you are going to utilize WINS, you will set values in this dialog. If you are using DHCP, you can leave this dialog alone since WINS is usually configured automatically through DHCP (see Figure 11-6). Otherwise, and only if you have determined proper settings, enter the IP addresses for a primary and secondary WINS server that can be reached from your network for the chosen NIC. If an address for a WINS server is not specified, this computer will use name query broadcasts (b-node mode for NetBIOS over TCP/IP) plus the local LMHOSTS file to resolve computer names to IP addresses, and name resolution will be limited to the local network. Use this dialog also to enable name resolution through the DNS settings that you made in the DNS dialog. You can enable lookup through, and import, an LMHOSTS

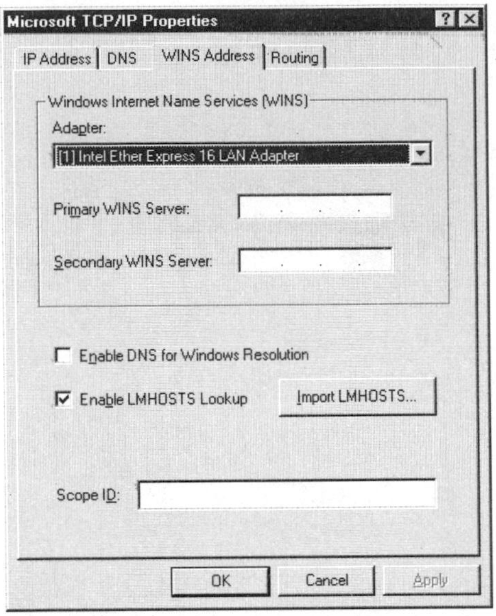

Figure 11-6. *The WINS Address dialog box*

file. An LMHOSTS file carries static computer name-to-IP address mappings for nonlocal computers on the wider area network and is used for NetBIOS name resolution on Windows networks. Finally, you may specify this computer's Scope ID. This value is used to identify "sets" of computers that can communicate with each other using only communication based on NetBIOS over TCP/IP (if no DNS is enabled). Leave this blank unless there is a specific reason to change it.

■ **DHCP Relay:** This feature is found only in NT Server. Use this dialog to specify relay values and target DHCP servers if you want to act as a relay agent for DHCP and BOOTP messages across a router. Enter values here only if you have determined exactly what you want to do. You can enter relay timeout and maximum hop thresholds, and also which DHCP servers, by IP address, that you wish to relay messages for.

■ **Routing:** Use this dialog to enable static IP Forwarding. If you are using more than one NIC in this machine, and you have not installed the Routing Information Protocol service, you should enable IP Forwarding. This option is only useful when your machine is multihomed (has more than one NIC) and you have entered more than one static IP address in the IP Address/Advanced dialogs. It also requires the addition of static routing table entries.

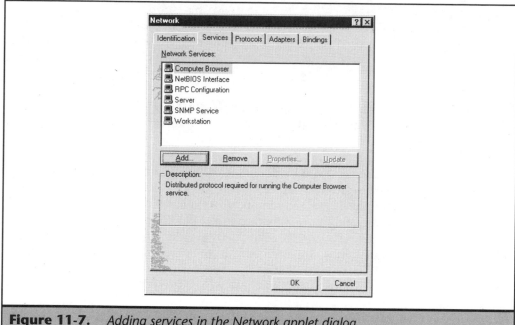

Figure 11-7.   *Adding services in the Network applet dialog*

Network Services Installation

For an NT workstation that is to be used strictly as a nonparticipatory client, one that does not provide ancillary agents or server components to help the domain controller or main network server, setting TCP/IP parameters, as outlined in the preceding sections, is usually all that is required.

However, NT 4 allows you to add TCP/IP network services that will greatly expand and enhance the abilities of your computer and its roles within a Windows domain (see Figure 11-7). Such services, which are modular software components that can be started at machine boot-up time, provide added functionality and ease of use.

The following list describes some of the most important TCP/IP-related service options, plus their installation options and usage.

■ **Simple TCP/IP Services:** This option provides the client software for the Character Generator, Daytime, Discard, Echo, and Quote of the Day services. Select this option to allow this computer to respond to requests from other systems that support these protocols. Upon installation, you will be returned to the TCP/IP Services dialog, as there are no settings or optional components to install.

■ **Peer Web Service:** Select this option to allow this computer to act as a simple Web (HTTP), file transfer (FTP), and GOPHER server (see Figure 11-8). The Peer Web Services are designed to implement a light-load Web server that would be most appropriate for an intranet, where traffic to be handled by the server is limited.

Selecting Peer Web Services Components

All components are selected for installation, except the Internet Service Manager, by default. If the selection box next to a component is checked, NT will install that component.

The only component not checked by default is the Internet Service Manager. To administer the Peer Web Services through a Web browser, select this option. Additionally, selection of the ODBC Drivers and Administration option installs Open Database Connectivity drivers. If you want to provide database access through this service, install the ODBC drivers and then set them up using the ODBC applet in the Control Panel. The Installation dialog also lets you change the directory in which you wish to install the Peer Web Services. You will be asked to specify root directories for each of the services that you choose to install. NT will suggest defaults, which you can use as is.

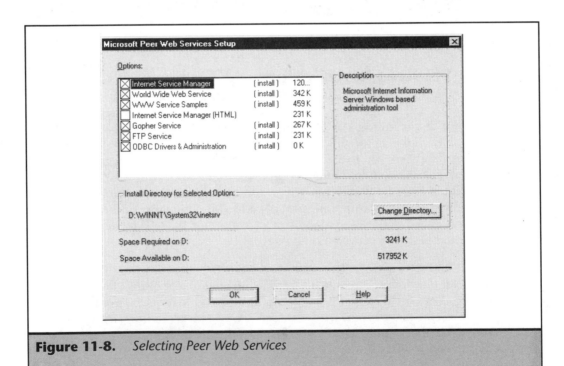

Figure 11-8.   *Selecting Peer Web Services*

After all installation is done, you can make custom settings and changes through the Start | Programs | Microsoft Peer Web Services (Common) menu choice, which will bring up an abbreviated version of the Internet Service Manager in NT Server's Internet Information Server (IIS). The primary operation of the Internet Service Manager is akin to that of IIS, covered in Chapter 25.

- **TCP/IP Network Printing Service:** This component allows the computer to print over the network using TCP/IP. If you want to provide printing services to Unix clients (using the LPDSVC service), or print to Unix print queues or TCP/IP-enabled network printers, install this service. Upon installation, you will be returned to the TCP/IP Services dialog, as there are no settings or optional components to install. You can start the LPDSVC service by using the Control Panel's Services applet.

- **Remote Access Service:** Use the Remote Access Service to configure dialin and dialout capabilities. This component is fully covered in Chapter 13.

- **SNMP Service:** Select this option to allow this computer to be remotely administered by an SNMP manager application. CMU-SNMP Manager, Hewlett Packard's Open View, and many third-party SNMP manager tools can be used with this service. As described in Chapter 7, you can also use

---

Mini-Glossary

COMMUNITIES AND COMMUNITY NAMES   Formally, a pairing of an agent with a set of application entities whose purpose is to identify valid sources for requests and limit the scope of data that can be accessed. A *community* is a group of hosts to which an NT computer running the SNMP service belongs. Used for authentication and identification when the SNMP service receives a request for information.

TRAPS AND TRAP DESTINATIONS   A trap is an operation in which the SNMP agent sends information to a management tool without an explicit request from the manager. Traps alert the manager application to activities that occur on the agent system, such as a reboot. Trap destinations are the names or IP addresses of hosts to which you want the SNMP service to send traps with the selected community name.

ROUTING INFORMATION PROTOCOL (RIP)   Within IP networks, RIP is an interior gateway protocol used to exchange information about reachable networks. Within IPX networks, RIP is a dynamic protocol used to gather and maintain information about the network.

DEFAULT GATEWAY   The gateway (address) that NT will use when attempting to route IP traffic onto a wider area, nonlocal network.

FULLY QUALIFIED DOMAIN NAME (FQDN)   As applied to addressing on a WAN or on the Internet, a name that includes all the enclosing domains up to the top level of the domain system, and so contains all the information needed to locate it uniquely. For example, *ftp.algoinc.com*, rather than just *algoinc*. Some utilities need only a partial pathway because they make certain assumptions about the rest of the address, but most need fully qualified domain names.

IP ADDRESSES   The unique four-part, 32-bit number assigned to each host computer on the Internet or any TCP/IP-enabled network. This number's bits specify the class of network and its number, as well as the subnet that specifies a particular machine or group of machines. The "dotted decimal notation" showing four decimal numbers between 0 and 255 separated by periods is a convenience, for readability.

SUBNET MASK   The IP subnet mask is a configuration parameter used to differentiate between that part of the IP address that represents the network and the part that represents the host.

Performance Monitor to gather statistics for the SNMP services. You must configure SNMP with the correct values and settings so that it will operate properly. The SNMP configuration information includes parameters that identify community names, trap destinations, and IP addresses, or computer names, for SNMP management hosts.

TIP: *If you do not know or care about specific community or trap identification, use the "public" community name when you configure the SNMP service. Remember, this and all community names are case sensitive.*

Installing the SNMP Service

After choosing the SNMP service, NT will display the SNMP Properties dialog. The dialog has three tabs that allow you to set options and values for the various ways the SNMP service can react to SNMP management queries. We will examine each tab here.

THE AGENT TAB   The SNMP Agent dialog, shown in Figure 11-9, allows you to enter textual identifiers and comments about the location of this computer, which will be reported to an SNMP management tool. You can also specify the types of service that you wish your SNMP configuration to report on.

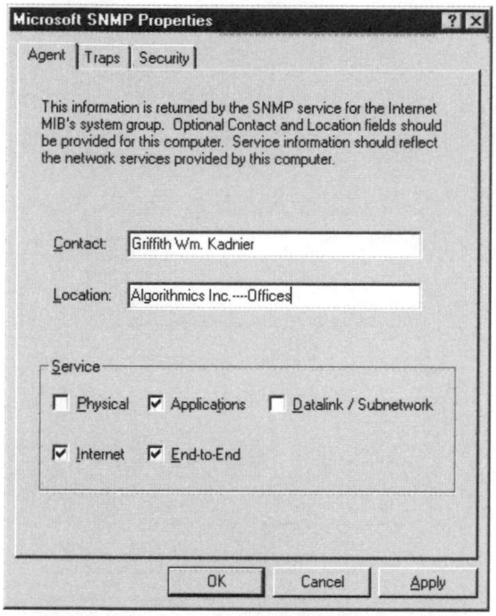

Figure 11-9.   *Entering contact info and choosing agent services*

Type the computer user's name, or a local administrative contact, in the Contact field. Then type a comment or physical location for this computer in the Location field. Now check all services that you wish to report back to a management tool in the Service fields. These choices will depend on the installed network components and capabilities of your NT workstation or server.

THE TRAPS TAB   First, in the Community Names field, enter the name of a community that you wish to send traps to. If you are not sure what to enter here, use the generic "public" community name, and then choose Add (see Figure 11-10). You can enter more than one community name by repeating this procedure. To delete an entry in the list, select it and choose the Remove button.

Next, you can specify hosts by IP or IPX address in the Trap Destination list. These addresses specify hosts for the selected community that you wish to send traps to. After highlighting a community name above this list, choose Add and type the host address into the IP Host or IPX Address dialog that will appear. To edit or remove an entry in the list, select it and choose the appropriate button.

THE SECURITY TAB   SNMP security allows you to specify the communities and hosts a computer will accept requests from, and to specify whether to send an authentication trap when an unauthorized community or host requests information.

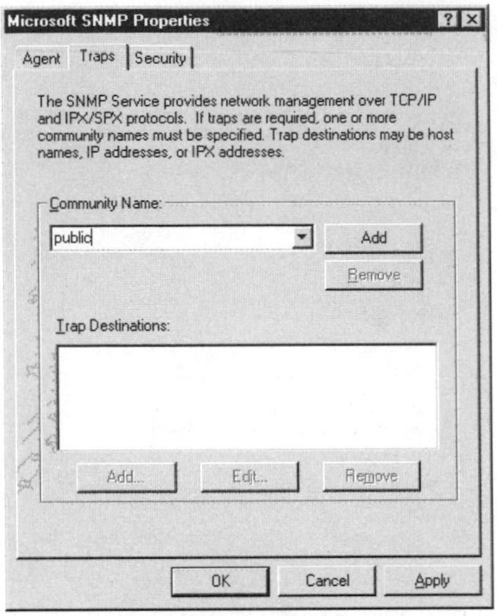

Figure 11-10. Choosing community names and trap destinations

There are three sections in this dialog that you may use to set SNMP security, as shown in Figure 11-11:

- **Send Authentication Trap:** Check this box if you want to send a trap to the hosts that you have previously selected, for failed authentication attempts.

- **Accepted Community Names:** Choose the Add button and enter the community names that you will accept requests from. After typing each and selecting Add from the ancillary input dialog, the name will move to the Accepted Community Names list. Repeat as needed. To edit or remove an entry in the list, select it and choose the appropriate button.

Insider Info

SNMP is a network management protocol that is widely used in TCP/IP networks. It is used to communicate between a management program run by an administrator and the network management agent (SNMP service) running on a client workstation or gateway.

Each type of network management service, responsible for different management protocols and scope, has its own set of management objects. This set of objects, for a service or protocol, is referred to as the object's management information base (MIB).

Using the SNMP service, an NT computer can report its current status, as reflected within its MIB, to an SNMP management tool somewhere on the network. The SNMP agent transmits status when a management system requests such information or when an important event, such as a reboot, occurs. A report from the agent is called a *trap*.

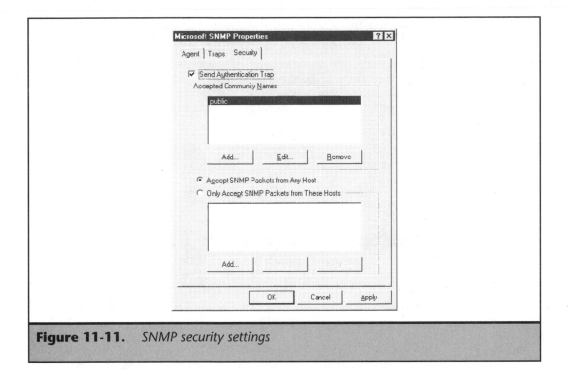

Figure 11-11. *SNMP security settings*

- **Accept SNMP Packets from Any Host:** Specify this action to accept SNMP packets from any host. No SNMP packets will be rejected on the basis of source host address, and the list of hosts under "Only Accept SNMP Packets from These Hosts" will have no effect.

- **Only Accept SNMP Packets from These Hosts:** SNMP packets will be accepted only from the hosts that appear in the list. You may add a host by IP or IPX address. Choose Add and type the host address into the IP Host or IPX Address dialog that will appear. To edit or remove an entry in the list, select it and choose the appropriate button.

Network Services Installation for NT Server

These network services are only available while running NT Server; however, they are installed in the same way as services for NT Workstation. Each of these services appears as an option for installation under the services list in the Control Panel's Network applet.

- **DHCP Server Service:** Installs the server software to support automatic IP address configuration for client computers using TCP/IP on your network. Covered fully in Chapter 12.

- **WINS Server Service:** Installs the server software to support WINS, a dynamic name resolution service for computers on a Windows-based network. Covered fully in Chapter 12.

- **DNS Server Service:** Installs the server software to support the Microsoft NT domain name service and DNS Manager. DNS is a distributed database of host information that resolves computer names to IP addresses.

Mini-Glossary

BERKELEY SOFTWARE DISTRIBUTION (BSD) UNIX   BSD refers to the particular version of the Unix operating system that was developed and distributed by the University of California at Berkeley. A number indicating the particular distribution level of the BSD system, for example, 4.3 BSD, usually precedes the BSD acronym. BSD Unix is very popular, and many commercial implementations are based on or include BSD code.

HOSTS FILE   Contains a list of IP addresses and the host names that they correspond to. In general, the HOSTS file only contains entries for your local machine, and perhaps other important machines, such as your name server or gateway. Your local name server will provide address-to-name mappings for other machines on the network transparently. HOSTS files are largely superseded now by DNS services.

LMHOSTS FILE   The LMHOSTS file maps IP addresses to the NetBIOS names of remote servers with which you want to communicate using TCP/IP. The LMHOSTS file allows NT to communicate across an IP router using NT computer names.

NETWORK INFORMATION CENTER (INTERNIC)   In January 1993 the InterNIC was established by AT&T, General Atomics, and Network Solutions with support from the National Science Foundation. The InterNIC is a service created to provide directory and database services, registration services, and information services for the Internet community. These services are provided by AT&T, Network Solutions, and General Atomics, respectively. In February 1995 the NSF terminated the cooperative agreement with General Atomics, and Network Solutions took over General Atomics' responsibilities.

ROUTING The process of choosing which path or route is optimal is called routing. When speaking of TCP/IP datagrams, or packets, there are two kinds of routing: direct and indirect. A datagram, or packet, is the unit of information that contains source and destination addresses, plus some data. Within a network such as the Internet, a datagram can take many paths to a given address.

You can route a datagram directly when the sending and receiving hosts are in the same network or subnet. A datagram will be routed indirectly when the sending and receiving addresses are in different networks. When routing indirectly, the datagram first goes to a local gateway. The gateway determines where to send the datagram next. The datagram "hops" from one gateway to

INSTALLING A DNS SERVER

- Open the Network applet from Control Panel and select Services.

- Choose Add.

- From the Select Network Service list, choose Microsoft DNS Server, and then choose OK.

- When asked, supply the path to the NT distribution files and choose Continue.

- After files have been copied, you will be returned to the Network/Services dialog. Choose OK to finish installation. There are no other settings or parameters that you must set from within the Network or Network/Services dialogs. Reboot.

- You will now have a new Start | Programs | Administrative Tools (Common) menu entry called DNS Manager, which you will use to customize the DNS service on this computer. Also, if you are moving an existing DNS server to NT 4 Server, you should move your DNS zone, reverse-lookup, and cache files to the %SystemRoot%\System32\DNS subdirectory.

TCP/IP Background and Concepts

This section describes how TCP/IP fits into NT's networking architecture, and then it goes on to review the various components of the Internet Protocol suite and the concepts of IP addressing. It also covers NT's name resolution capabilities, implemented by NetBIOS over TCP/IP and the domain name system (DNS), and will lightly touch on the background for the next chapter's focus, the Dynamic Host Configuration Protocol (DHCP) and Windows Internet name service (WINS).

The TCP/IP Protocol Suite

Transmission Control Protocol (TCP) and Internet Protocol (IP) are only two members of a much larger family. TCP/IP is more correctly a suite of protocols that includes TCP and IP, User Datagram Protocol (UDP), Internet Control Message Protocol (ICMP), plus several others. TCP/IP conforms to only part of the Open Systems Interconnection (OSI) model, and its hierarchy is more exactly expressed in Figure 11-12.

The TCP/IP protocol suite can be implemented on top of a variety of communications schemes and lower level protocols such as T1, X.25, Ethernet, and RS-232, making it very flexible. TCP/IP originated in a research project funded by the United States Defense Advanced Research Projects Agency (DARPA) in 1969.

In 1983, the new protocol suite, TCP/IP, was adopted as a standard, and all hosts on the ARPANET (the precursor to the Internet) were required to use it. By the time ARPANET finally grew into the Internet, the use of TCP/IP had spread to networks beyond the Internet itself. Most notable are local area networks and dial-up networks.

Let's take a look at the protocols that make up this very popular suite.

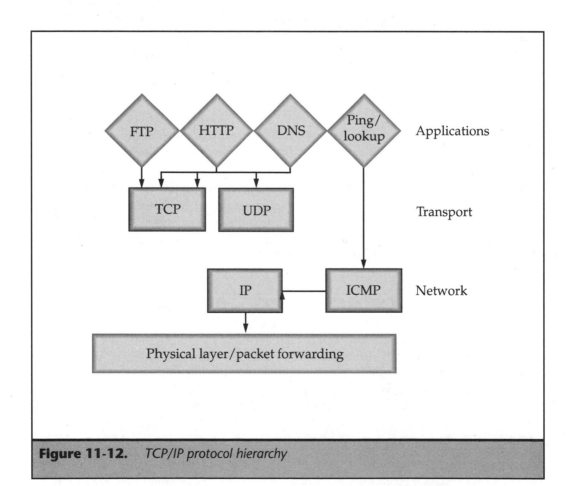

Figure 11-12. *TCP/IP protocol hierarchy*

Transmission Control Protocol (TCP)

The TCP protocol sequentially orders network packets and performs error correction on them. It also implements virtual circuits, or connections, between hosts. The TCP packets contain sequence numbers and acknowledgments of received packets so that any packets received out of order can be reordered, and damaged packets can be retransmitted.

So, TCP is responsible for verifying the correct delivery of data from client to server, and back. Data can be, and is, lost along the way. TCP adds support to detect errors or lost data and to trigger retransmission until the data is correctly and completely received. This level of reliability has a price; TCP requires additional overhead to provide proper sequencing of information, and it implements an additional level of surety with a checksum on both the header and packet data. Such methods generate additional network traffic, affecting the level of data throughput in favor of reliability.

Connection-oriented services, such as FTP and SMTP, require a high degree of reliability and therefore use TCP. Additionally, DNS services use TCP for transmitting and receiving DNS databases.

Internet Protocol (IP)

IP protocol packets are unreliable, connectionless datagrams. The IP protocol does not ensure that IP packets are delivered in sequential order or that they were not damaged by transmission errors. The IP packets contain a source and destination address—the address of the host from which the packet was sent and the address of the host that is to receive the packet, respectively.

The higher level TCP and UDP protocols almost always assume, upon acceptance, that source addressing in a packet is valid. So, an IP address forms the basis of a rudimentary type of authentication for many services. These services infer the validity of the source host by its address value in the packet.

Because of this, IP addressing is easily "spoofable." A clever hacker can appear to be someone else when sending IP packets, since replacement of the source address effectively hides the real source. Source address replacement can also take place when a packet is routed. To some TCP and UDP services, those that rely on valid source addressing in IP packets, a source-routed IP packet appears to have come from the last system in the route as opposed to coming from its true origin. Hackers have long relied on these shortcomings in IP to hide their identities and impersonate other source computers/systems.

The User Datagram Protocol

The UDP protocol interacts with application programs on the same hierarchical basis as TCP. But unlike TCP, there is no error correction or guarantee of delivery and correct sequencing in delivered packets. UDP was not designed to implement connection-based virtual circuits like TCP. It is best suited as a *broadcast* protocol.

UDP data checksums can be used, and they provide a way to use this protocol with better quality of service, without the full overhead of TCP connections. Also, the UDP protocol can be used where a one-to-many service relationship exists, because it can be either broadcast or multicast.

Services that use UDP include Internet applications such as RealAudio, and RPC-based services such as Network Time Protocol (NTP) and DNS.

ARP and ICMP

Two other ancillary TCP/IP protocols have important, if not direct, functions. These protocols are not primary data transports, but perform maintenance and support on behalf of the rest of the framework.

The Address Resolution Protocol (ARP) and the Internet Control Message Protocol (ICMP) are used in the support of a TCP/IP connection, acting in concert with the primary data protocols to provide housekeeping and status or error messages.

ARP   IP packets do not contain all of the data necessary to complete delivery. While source and destination IP addresses are known, the hardware address of the destination system must also be obtained by broadcasting a special information inquiry packet, called an ARP *request packet.*

These ARP request packets contain the IP address of the destination system, which, upon reception of the packet broadcast, replies with its hardware address in an ARP reply packet. If this is not the first time a destination host has been contacted, ARP can use its own local cache to bypass the challenge/response broadcast, because it stores the hardware-to-IP address map after an initially successful round-trip. Other network nodes can use an ARP reply broadcast to update their local caches, so minimization of network requests and replies can be realized.

ICMP   ICMP implements sharable status and error reporting on an IP network. When a high-level application or protocol needs to query status or recover from error conditions, it can use the information retrieved by utilization of the ICMP protocol.

ICMP packets use IP packets as a transport mechanism, but are not considered to be a higher level protocol. When a user or application *pings* a destination host, the mechanism in use is ICMP. In this case, ICMP issues an *echo request packet,* to which the destination host issues an *echo reply packet.* This request-acknowledge conversation determines whether an IP node, or computer system, on a network is functional. Because it is a status and error-reporting protocol, and apart from its normal housekeeping duties, ICMP can also be useful for diagnosing IP network or gateway failures or timeouts.

IP Addressing, Subnet Masks, and IP Gateways

An end node, or host, is any device attached to the network that uses TCP/IP. To transmit and receive data packets between your host (or hosts) and a remote node, you must configure your TCP/IP protocol layer with three pieces of information: your machine's IP address, a subnet mask, and the default gateway that you will be using, if you are connecting to a larger area network.

A network administrator may give these parameters to you, or you may have to deal with them yourself. NT users who have a DHCP server available on the network can take advantage of automatic IP configuration, which makes setup much easier.

If you have a need to manually configure the TCP/IP protocol, or just want to understand the principles involved in deriving each parameter's value, the following sections provide details about IP addresses, subnet masks, and IP gateways.

IP Addresses

Every host interface, or node, on a TCP/IP network is identified by a unique IP address. An IP address looks like this: 204.182.124.68.

The addressing convention used in TCP/IP is a 32-bit binary number, which logically identifies each node on the network as a whole. This means that the Internet, as an example, can have a total of 4,294,967,295 individual nodes. The nodes are referred to as hosts and the 32-bit binary address number as an IP address. This 32-bit IP address is normally represented by breaking the 32 bits into four groups of 8 bits each and representing each 8-bit byte with the decimal value equivalent of the binary number.

This kind of notation is referred to as dotted-decimal notation, or as an *octet string*. For example, assume a network node is assigned the following address:
11001100101101100111110000000001

To represent this address in dotted-decimal notation, the address is first broken up into four bytes, as follows: 11001100 10110110 01111100 00000001

Next, each byte is converted from binary to decimal, as follows:

11001100 = 204, 10110110 = 182, 01111100 = 124, 00000001 = 1

The result is written in dotted-decimal notation as 204.182.124.1.

Although the representation of the address consists of four decimal numbers separated by dots, the octet string as a whole denotes a 32-bit binary number. This is the 32-bit number that is used to identify each communicating device, or node, on the network.

NOTE: Because IP addresses identify unique nodes on a connected network, each host on the network must be assigned a unique IP address, valid for its particular network scope. The network scope is determined by its class and identifier, as outlined next. A specific and unique identifier is issued to each qualified applicant by a standards body, the InterNIC, which serves as a clearinghouse and central database for the entire Internet. Of course, if you will only be using your network within a completely closed organization, where connection to the global network is never allowed, you may derive and use these values as you see fit, without regard to InterNIC registration.

IP Address Derived Network and Host IDs

The IP address has two identification purposes; although an IP address is a single 32-bit value, it actually contains two pieces of information: the network identifier and the host/end-node identifier. These identifiers are used by TCP/IP in determining how TCP/IP data gets routed from node to node and in identifying individual hosts on the network.

The network identifier is used to classify a group of computers and other devices that are all located on the same logical network, which may be separated and/or connected by software or hardware routers. The host identifier is used to distinguish your computer/host, or end node, within the scope of a particular network identity.

Identifiers and IP Address Classes

Network classes, as they pertain to TCP/IP, are used to define and separate networks of varying capacity and size. A network's class can be derived from the first *octet* of its dotted-decimal notation IP address.

Since both source and destination IP addresses are embedded in each IP data packet that is transmitted or received on the network, a node can use the network and host identifiers contained within the IP address to determine which packets are meant for its reception, and which ones it should ignore. The node can also use this information to determine whether it should accept a network broadcast message. Routers use this information to determine how and where an IP packet should be forwarded. The determination involves combining these identifiers with another 32-bit number that is assigned to every node, common to all nodes within a subnet, called a subnet mask, as described in the following section.

Subnet Masks

The IP subnet mask is a parameter used by a TCP/IP end node and by IP routers to differentiate between that part of the IP address that represents a network and the part that represents a host. The original design defined three masks that are used by end nodes and routers. These three masks are referred to as Class A, B, C. When logically ANDED with a specific IP address, the resultant value is the network identifier, which is then used for routing an address. The masks are defined as listed in Table 11-1.

An end node with address 1.2.3.4 would be an example of a Class A address. The default mask for this station would be 255.0.0.0. After ANDING with the subnet mask, the network identifier would be 1.0.0.0.

An end node with address 129.5.10.20 would be an example of a Class B address. The default mask for this station would be 255.255.0.0. After ANDING with the subnet mask, the network identifier would be 129.5.0.0.

An end node with address 210.111.112.213 would be an example of a Class C address. The default mask for this station would be 255.255.255.0. After ANDING with the subnet mask, the network identifier would be 210.111.112.0.

When the network or node portion of an IP address is set to all 1s (255), it indicates that the packet involved is intended for broadcast.

Network Address Class	First Octet in IP Address	Subnet Mask	Networks Allowed	End Nodes Allowed
Class A	1–126	255.0.0.0	256	2^24
Class B	128–191	255.255.0.0	2^16	2^16
Class C	192–223	255.255.255.0	2^24	256

Table 11-1.   *Classes and Subnet Masks*

The class of your network will therefore determine how many end nodes, or workstations/devices, you can have connected. Most networks will be Class B or C, and may even consist of multiple class subnets. Instead of applying for, or making up, more network identifiers, it is better to use subnetting. This makes more effective use of a network ID's range, and if you need a global identifier, it obviates the need to apply for multiple identifiers from InterNIC, which you wouldn't use to the fullest extent at any rate. Within each local subnet, a computer is assigned a unique host identifier, while all local hosts share the same subnet mask.

Note that subnetting may extend further by breaking, for instance, a Class B network into 254 subnets, by manipulating the third octet in the mask, or a Class C network into 16-node subnets by manipulating the fourth octet value, or combinations thereof.

CAUTION: All hosts on your local network (a network, or subnet with the same network identifier) should have the same network identifier and subnet mask. If you do not follow this convention, you risk problems with addressing and routing.

Routing and Gateways

Depending on their level of cooperation and connectivity, TCP/IP networks and subnetworks can be coupled together through the use of routers and/or gateways. A router is a special piece of hardware that knows how to forward an IP packet to a larger internetwork, or subnet. A router can also be a computer that is set up in that role. A gateway is a router that is attached to the wider area network, where remote destinations are found.

The simple way to route IP data is to have each IP host maintain static routes for specific destinations, entering those routes into the route table, or by utilizing a routing file (the HOSTS file), which is then used directly. This only works for destinations that you have entered into the table or file, so a more general solution becomes attractive.

Routing generally works like this: An IP address contains source and destination addresses. TCP/IP checks whether the network identifier of the destination address matches the network identifier of the source address. Three things may happen:

- If both identifiers match, the packet is bound for a local host and is sent directly to the destination computer on the local network.

- If the network identifiers do not match, the static routing table is examined, and if the route is found, the packet is forwarded to the destination.

- Otherwise, the packet is forwarded to the default gateway for onward delivery.

THE DEFAULT GATEWAY   The default gateway is normally a computer that is connected to the local subnet and also to the larger remote network. This computer can, through several methods, determine or discover network identifiers for remote networks, and has the ability to reach them through the wider network. The default gateway can forward an IP packet because it has knowledge of how to reach remote network identifiers on other networks, and will normally pass the IP packet to other intermediary gateways until the packet is eventually delivered to the gateway that serves the destination network, which contains the computer with a destination address that matches. This entire process is known as routing (see Figure 11-13).

If you will be communicating entirely within your own subnet, or if you intend only to have static routes beyond your local net, even if it is connected, a gateway is not required. You can use a HOSTS file or add static routes by using the *route* utility.

If you use a gateway, multiple default gateways can be assigned so that if your first choice of default gateway becomes unavailable, another will be used. When NT TCP/IP is configured to use multiple default gateways, the other gateways will be used, in order of listing, to retry the forwarding operation. Use the Advanced TCP/IP Configuration dialog box to enter multiple default gateways, as outlined in the earlier sections of this chapter on TCP/IP settings and the Advanced dialog.

Name Resolution for NT Networking

When you initially configure NT with TCP/IP, you are required to enter the IP address for your computer and the name of the computer. These are both used in various ways as unique identifiers for the computer on the network. All TCP/IP devices will use your computer's IP address, as described earlier in this chapter, to converse with and recognize your computer on the network. When you entered the host name in the TCP/IP-DNS dialog during setup, that name, plus the name you entered in the Domain field, are used together to identify your computer on a TCP/IP network, such as the Internet. On your local NT installation, this combination can also be used, but

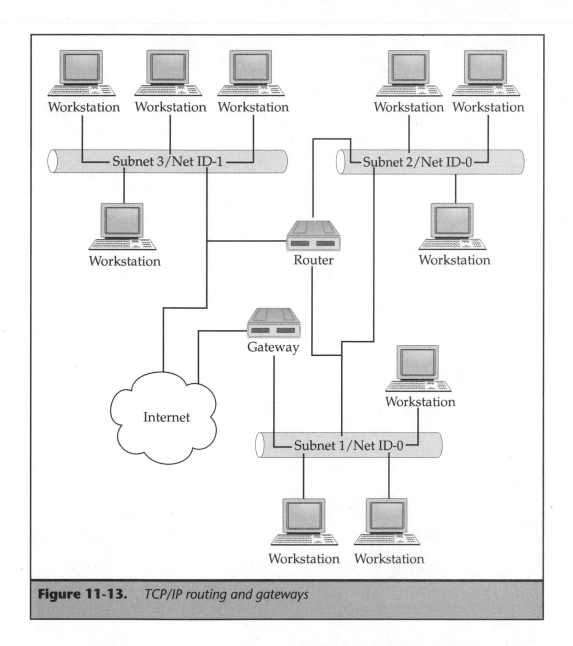

Figure 11-13. *TCP/IP routing and gateways*

more naturally the computer is known on your NT LAN by its NetBIOS name—the name that you gave your computer when you were asked to name it during NT setup.

IP addressing is fine for computer-to-computer communication, but humans work better with names than with numbers, especially 32-bit numbers! So a mechanism is available on TCP/IP networks to resolve names to IP addresses. When an NT computer starts up, it registers its name on the network. The IP-to-name resolution methods that are then available include the following:

- **Windows Internet name service (WINS):** An NT computer can use WINS if a WINS server is available on the network. A WINS server contains a dynamic database that maps computer names to IP addresses. See Chapter 12 for a complete discussion of WINS.

- **Domain name system (DNS):** DNS can provide name-to-address mapping when an NT (or other OS) computer is connected to a remote host, and is set up to query a DNS server. DNS, as it is implemented on the Internet, is a worldwide distributed database, having root servers located at InterNIC, in Herndon, Virginia.

- **LMHOSTS or HOSTS file:** LMHOSTS files specify NetBIOS computer name (local name) and IP address mappings, whereas a HOSTS file specifies a DNS name and IP address. HOSTS files are used by Windows Sockets applications to find TCP/IP host names, and LMHOSTS files are used by NetBIOS over TCP/IP to find Microsoft networking computer names.

- **Broadcast name resolution:** If NetBIOS over TCP/IP is available, an NT computer can use this method to resolve names if each computer on the network registers its name by broadcasting it on the network.

Name Resolution with Host Files

The HOSTS and LMHOSTS files can provide mappings for name-to-IP addresses. This is an older technique, used before DNS and WINS were implemented. Think of a HOSTS file as the equivalent of a limited DNS server. The LMHOSTS file is more like a WINS server equivalent.

You can configure TCP/IP so it uses the HOSTS file to resolve remote host names to IP addresses. Edit the sample HOSTS file that is created when you install TCP/IP to include remote host names and their IP addresses for each computer with which you will communicate.

The LMHOSTS file maps IP addresses to NetBIOS (local) computer names for Windows networks. If WINS and broadcast name resolution fail, the system reads the LMHOSTS file to try to resolve NetBIOS names. Any resolved entries are then stored in a system cache for quicker subsequent access.

Domain Name System Addressing

If you are or want to be on the Internet, or you will be running TCP/IP applications that require you to contact remote or foreign IP addresses and hosts, it's likely that you'll be using the domain name system. DNS was developed to provide a standard mechanism for host name-to-address mapping, and it does this in a distributed rather than in a central authoritative kind of way.

The domain name system presents a hierarchical approach to the problem of organizing the namespace, or *domain of names* in a computer network. DNS is a distributed database providing a hierarchical naming system, and each element of the hierarchy is referred to as a domain. A domain can be used to refer to a host or computer, act as a mail address, or merely be a placeholder for a subdomain. At the top of the hierarchy is the root domain, referred to as simply "." by DNS.

Any number of subdomains can exist in the hierarchy beneath the root domain. Subdomains can also exist within other subdomains. Subdomains found directly beneath the root domain are called top-level domains. Subdomains directly beneath top-level domains are called second-level domains, and so on.

Any domain in the namespace can be referred to by the domain names in its hierarchical path separated by dots. For example, a server connected to the Internet at Algorithmics Inc. has the domain name *algogate.algoinc.com*. The name of the computer is "algogate"; it is part of the "algoinc" domain, which is part of the "com" domain. There is an implied "." representing the root domain at the end. The full name of a domain is also called its fully qualified domain name (FQDN).

Each domain in the DNS has one or more resource records (RRs), which are fields that contain information about that domain. The A field contains the IP address for the machine the domain represents, and the MX field contains the name of the machine that handles mail, among other things.

Machines that store DNS information are called nameservers. The DNS system is composed of two elements: resolvers and servers. A resolver is a client that makes use of the DNS service. The resolver sends queries to a DNS server whenever it wants information from the DNS. NT includes the DNS resolver functionality used by NetBIOS over TCP/IP and by Windows Sockets.

Each nameserver handles a specific part of the DNS. Through delegation, nameservers can allow other nameservers to handle parts of the DNS. For example, a nameserver for *algoinc.com* could delegate responsibility for the *sales.algoinc.com* domain to another nameserver, which contains the information for the domain (computer) *Pent200.sales.algoinc.com*. Through delegation, the task of handling the namespace for large computer networks can be shared among many machines. Each piece of the DNS that is handled by a nameserver is referred to as a zone. A nameserver can handle multiple zones.

Since DNS servers are so important to an interconnected network, a nameserver almost always replicates the information contained in one server to other servers. There is always one and only one computer that contains the master list of DNS information for a particular domain name. This computer is called the primary domain nameserver for the domain. A secondary domain server is a DNS server, which downloads a copy of the primary's domain table periodically. Secondaries do this by querying the primary (usually every 6 to 24 hours) to see if the primary's information has changed. If it has, the secondary simply downloads the entire table again from the primary.

The other primary NT name resolution service, WINS, differs from DNS in two significant ways. First, DNS information for a particular domain is configured by using distributed, but static, configuration databases. The root database files must be updated by hand, or at least by batched computer runs, initiated by a manual request. On the other hand, the WINS information database is built dynamically. When a WINS client boots, it registers its name with the WINS server. If the client's name is valid and unique, the WINS server will allow the client to use that name.

Secondly, WINS and DNS are used to resolve names for different types of services. DNS is used to resolve TCP/IP host names for services such as HTTP Web access, or FTP file transfer and SMTP email transfer. WINS name resolution is used to resolve NetBIOS names such as would be used by an NT computer or a printer shared on an NT server.

There are, however, some important cooperative mechanisms that each service can lend to a mixed DNS/WINS environment. For instance, NT computers can use DNS to resolve names of NetBIOS services and Web browsers can resolve HTTP addresses through WINS using NT TCP/IP.

What's Next

Your future in NT *will* include TCP/IP. Most likely, your installation will include an Internet connection, an intranet, or some interoperability issue. These are the fields for which TCP/IP was designed. If you intend to install NT 4 Server and run an Internet Web service, you must familiarize yourself with TCP/IP.

Next, we'll take a look at DHCP and WINS in depth. Because the TCP/IP protocol is so hard to manually set up and administer, you'll want to know all about these NT services that practically automate the installation and everyday operation of an NT interconnected network.

Chapter Twelve

Configuring DHCP and WINS

N ow that we know a great deal more about TCP/IP, we can finally get our NT network up and running. But as we have already seen, TCP/IP is anything but trivial in its installation and management. And setting up for TCP/IP is only part of the equation as far as full Internet and intranet networking is concerned. A large part of the cost—in time and effort—of implementing TCP/IP on your network is going to stem from the fact that TCP/IP networking is not only difficult to set up, it's also hard to manage properly.

The architects of this protocol's maturation process realized that there were too many configuration parameters and settings needed first to install, and then keep a TCP/IP installation running. So DHCP (Dynamic Host Configuration Protocol) and then WINS (Windows Internet Name Service) were born, each addressing different parts of the TCP/IP management dilemma, and both meant to ease the burden.

Insider Info

Although Microsoft worked with the organization that developed DHCP, it is not strictly a Microsoft invention or product. Only the flavor of DHCP that ships with NT Server is from Microsoft. DHCP is a popular protocol available on many platforms. WINS, on the other hand, is strictly an NT (server-side) platform-specific Microsoft product. It is meant to ease the burden of naming resolution on the Windows platform only and is designed to interoperate with DHCP.

This chapter describes DHCP and WINS, and then goes on to explain how to install and manage servers to support DHCP and how to use WINS and the WINS Manager to administer servers that you have installed this service on.

Mini-Glossary

DHCP SERVER   An NT Server running TCP/IP and DHCP server software. DHCP servers supply DHCP client computers with TCP/IP setup information.

WINS SERVER   An NT Server running TCP/IP and WINS server software. A WINS server maintains a database that maps computer names to IP addresses so users don't have to deal with dotted-decimal notation IP addresses when connecting to and using other computers on a TCP/IP-enabled Windows network. WINS is usually used in concert with DHCP so that the dynamic IP assignments made by DHCP can always be mapped to the correct computer names.

DHCP—What Is It and What Does It Do?

The Dynamic Host Configuration Working Group of the Internet Engineering Task Force (IETF, a volunteer organization that sets standards for the Internet) created DHCP. DHCP's purpose is to enable a networked computer, running TCP/IP, to request configuration information from a DHCP server. A DHCP server's primary currency is IP addresses. It will meter these addresses out to clients when asked to do so. The DHCP server has no specific information about the computer requesting information until that request is made. This is one of the major selling points for DHCP: Its primary purpose is to provide TCP/IP setup parameters to clients who *ask* for them, reducing the administration overhead on TCP/IP networks. And DHCP does so without needing to know who is connecting to the network until they ask for help. Using DHCP on a network provides the following benefits:

- Administration of a TCP/IP network can be managed centrally. Networkwide TCP/IP configuration can be done from a single location. Subnets and reserved addresses, or clients that need fixed IP addresses, can also be defined and managed in a cohesive way.

- DHCP provides statistics and feedback on how a network can be load-leveled and quantified. This helps a network designer to assign resources in ways that improve network efficiency and throughput.

- Individual computers can be moved between locations (networks) and subnets without requiring manual TCP/IP reconfiguration. Every time a client system boots, it is configured automatically with the correct TCP/IP parameters. This can be particularly helpful when a company has a base of mobile employees who need to attach to a network from different locations, perhaps even through the Remote Access Service (see Chapter 13).

- DHCP provides another level of security on TCP/IP networks because IP addresses are *leased* out, to be revoked or renewed at the administrator's discretion.

Insider Info

DHCP is designed around a client/server model on a network containing one or more DHCP servers that maintain TCP/IP configuration information. This data is provided to client computers that make properly formatted requests. The DHCP database supplies configuration parameters and IP addresses for all of the clients, attached to a network, who ask for DHCP's help. IP addresses are provided to clients from a fixed pool, or range of addresses, which are specified by the system or network administrator at server configuration time. These addresses are supplied to a client computer on loan. DHCP calls this an IP *lease*. The duration and control of leases is a primary duty of the DHCP server, and IP lease renewal and revocation parameters are set up ahead of time by the administrator.

You can install DHCP on any NT server on your network. You may have more than one DHCP server installed across your network, and they can act as backup servers for one another. DHCP requests can be routed across subnets, and this creates network traffic; so if you have differing subnets, you'll want to plan for at least one DHCP server per network class, or possibly one per subnet, to save broadcast traffic bandwidth across your routers. A DHCP server can theoretically serve an unlimited number of clients, but 10,000 is probably an extreme upper bound. For most administrators, this means that you don't need more than one DHCP server, unless routing constraints dictate otherwise. Clients will be able to use a DHCP server if they have their TCP/IP configuration set to automatically use DHCP. DHCP can also be used by Remote Access Service clients (see Chapter 13) and by Windows 95 and Windows for Workgroups clients. The latter need to have TCP/IP-32 installed, which is included on your NT Server distribution CD-ROM.

Installing the DHCP Server

When you get ready to install a DHCP server, you will do so by working with the Network applet in Control Panel. We will assume that you have already installed NT Server and that you are logged on as a member of the Administrators group. It is also assumed that you have properly installed the TCP/IP protocol on your server.

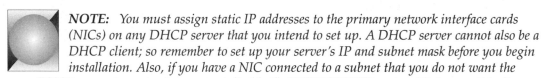

NOTE: You must assign static IP addresses to the primary network interface cards (NICs) on any DHCP server that you intend to set up. A DHCP server cannot also be a DHCP client; so remember to set up your server's IP and subnet mask before you begin installation. Also, if you have a NIC connected to a subnet that you do not want the DHCP server to support, you must disable the DHCP/TCP/IP protocol linkage, or binding, for that NIC or transport wrapper. You can do this by choosing the Control Panel/ Network/Bindings dialog. Select "Show bindings for all services," and then choose Microsoft DHCP Server; expand its TCP/IP dependency list, and highlight the NIC or wrapper that you want to disable. Choose the Disable button, and then choose Close.

Follow these steps to install a DHCP server:

1. Choose the Network applet in Start/Settings/Control Panel, and choose the Services dialog. From this dialog, choose the Add button to display the Select Network Service list.

2. Highlight Microsoft DHCP Server in the Select Network Service list. Then select OK. The DHCP service will be installed from your distribution files. The installer program will ask you to enter the path to these files, and will suggest a default.

3. If the DHCP server service detects that you have not set up a static IP address for your TCP/IP settings, you will be taken to the TCP/IP setup dialog before DHCP is fully installed. At any rate, from the main Network applet dialog, which you will be returned to, choose Close.

4. The DHCP server service will be installed, with changes to your primary TCP/IP settings if necessary, and you will be required to reboot the computer. No settings for DHCP are possible from the Control Panel/Network applet; you will use the Manager application, covered in the next section, to set up and administer DHCP.

5. Finally, reboot the computer and proceed to the DHCP Manager application.

Using DHCP Manager

You can use the DHCP Manager to connect to, and work with, a DHCP server on your local machine, or anywhere else on your network. When DHCP is installed, a menu choice for the DHCP Manager will appear in the Start/Programs/Administrative Tools(Common) menu.

DHCP requires initial setup and then must be maintained whenever the scope or topology of your network changes. The DHCP service needs to know how to hand out parameters to clients and what range of settings it can work with. Additionally, the service must be told about how it will work with other services on your network. You will use the DHCP Manager to perform these tasks and more.

The functionality built into DHCP Manager addresses the ability to create, edit, and delete DHCP *scopes.* A DHCP scope is a cluster of computers that all use a DHCP client service, where these computers also are members of the same logical subnet.

A scope contains values for the range of IP addresses that can be distributed to clients. It also stores a unique subnet mask (see Chapter 11 on TCP/IP subnetting), which determines a particular subnet, given an IP address. IP lease parameters, the address of a DNS or WINS partner that will provide IP-to-name mapping, and custom parameters, are also stored in a scope's database.

When first started, DHCP Manager will display the local machine in its Servers window. Whenever another server is added, or connected to, that entry will subsequently be displayed, upon startup, in this window. The other main window, the Option Configuration pane, displays various options (explained in a later section), set globally, for the scope that is highlighted in the server window or for an individually reserved address. (See Figure 12-1).

Working with Servers and Their Scopes

If this is the first time you are setting up your DHCP service, there won't be any servers listed in the Servers window; it will just show "Local Machine." To add another server, choose Add from the Server menu. In the Add DHCP Server to Server List dialog, enter the name or address of the DHCP server you wish to add and choose OK.

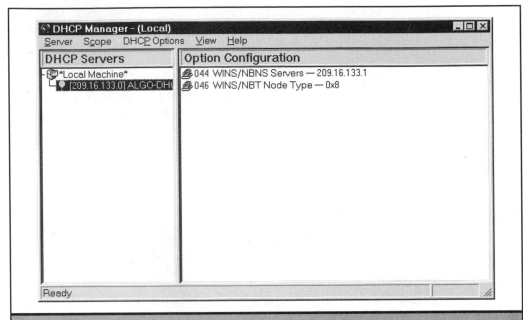

Figure 12-1. *The DHCP Manager*

Mini-Glossary

LOGICAL SUBNET A portion of a network, which may be physically separated, that may share a network address with other portions of the network and is distinguished by a subnet number. The subnet number is the part of an IP address that designates a subnet. This number is used for localized inter-network routing.

SUBNET MASK In a subnetted network, the host portion of an IP address is split into a subnet component and a host component using a subnet mask, which is logically ANDED with the IP address to derive the subnet number.

ADDRESS POOL For DHCP server purposes, the group of IP addresses that the DHCP server can work from when assigning client addresses.

BINDING A logical setup and relationship between layers of support software within a network service. A process that establishes the communication channel between a network protocol or service driver and a network adapter driver.

LEASE The term that DHCP uses to denote the temporary assignment of an IP address to a DHCP client, subject to renewal at intervals that you set up.

TIP: *If you are setting up for the local server, simply highlight the Local Server entry and proceed to creation of a scope. DHCP will calculate the address of the local server for you, adding it to the Servers list under the Local Server heading. You can enter a DHCP server name by using dotted-decimal IP addresses, such as **209.116.229.99,** or you can enter an Internet-type/DNS name, such as **algorithmics.algoinc.com.***

When you initially set up DHCP, your first duty, after connecting to a server, is to create a DHCP scope. One of the primary duties of the DHCP Manager is to create, remove, and activate scopes. We will now review the steps that are required to accomplish these tasks.

Creating and Activating Scopes

To create a scope, first highlight the DHCP server that you wish to work with in the main Servers window. Next, from the Manager's Scope menu, choose Create. The Create Scope dialog will appear (see Figure 12-2).

- Define the range of IP addresses for this scope. Enter the beginning and ending IP addresses in the Start Address and End Address fields. In the Subnet Mask field, enter the subnet mask for this range of IP addresses.

- Define the Exclusion Range for the given IP address pool. If static addresses are to be assigned within the range of IP addresses you have entered, or you wish to reserve an address for broadcast, use these fields to enter the excluded addresses. The Exclusion Range fields take a starting and ending IP address, within the range entered in the Start and End Address fields. If a single address needs to be excluded, enter it in the Start Address field. When you are ready, choose the Add button.

NOTE: *You should exclude all IP addresses that are statically assigned to any other DHCP servers, static clients, or non-DHCP Remote Access Service clients. You can reactivate IP addresses or ranges from those that have been excluded by selecting them in the Excluded Addresses list and then choosing the Remove button.*

- Specify the Lease Duration. If you wish DHCP to hand out IP leases that never need to be renewed, as for permanent servers or workstations, select Unlimited in this area. For IP addresses that will be assigned to clients that may come and go, select Limited To and enter the time limit that you wish to enforce in the fields provided. Finally, assign a name and optional comments to this scope, using the supplied entry fields, and choose the OK button.

- After all scope settings and options (see the following section on DHCP options) have been configured, you must activate the scope so that your DHCP clients can request IP configuration. From the Scope menu, choose

Activate. When the scope has been activated, the menu will change to Deactivate, showing that this scope is now operative. Your NT network is now using DHCP.

TIP: *Do not activate the scope now, even though you will be asked to, unless you will not be setting any options for the scope.*

Removing Scopes

When subnet scopes change or are no longer needed, use DHCP Manager to remove them. If the scope is activated, it is necessary to deactivate it before setting options or removing it. Highlight the server in the main Servers list, and choose Deactivate from the Scope menu. At this time, ensure that the client's active leases are released, or wait for them to release. Now, with the selected scope still highlighted, from the Scope menu, choose Delete.

TIP: *Use **ipconfig /release** from an NT command prompt, or the winipcfg.exe program from Windows 95 to release DHCP leases immediately.*

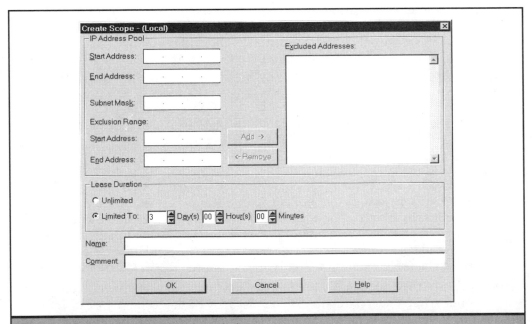

Figure 12-2. *The Create Scope dialog*

DHCP Options

DHCP options are configuration settings and parameters given to clients, along with an IP address. You control which options are supplied to a client, and the values they contain, when you set these options using the DHCP Manager. Many of the standard options have default values, which you won't necessarily want to change or even know about. However, some options have settings that are important to understand and set correctly, especially in concert with WINS use, and we'll learn more about how to configure them now.

DHCP Configuration Options: Addition, Editing, and Deletion

When a client asks for IP addressing configuration, DHCP also supplies other configuration values, which must be defined by you at installation time. Using DHCP Manager, these option settings can be added, edited, or removed globally for all scopes managed by a server or for an individual scope or DHCP client (with a reserved address—see the section on reserved addresses, later in this chapter). You can also set default values that will be used in lieu of those supplied by DHCP.

To add, change, or remove DHCP options:

■ In the DHCP Servers window, select a server and scope that you want to configure. Next, from the DHCP Options menu, choose Scope, Global, or Default to display the Options dialog (shown in the following illustration). This dialog will be used to set option values for any extent that you choose. You can set or remove options that apply to all scopes on the currently selected server, the scope currently selected, or you can edit the default values used by DHCP.

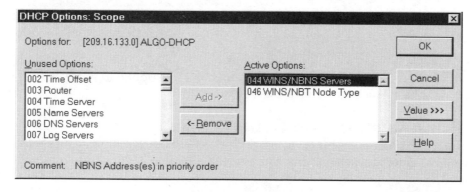

■ From either the Unused Options list or, if options are already assigned, the Active Options list, select the name of the DHCP option that you want to add, change, or remove. If you wish to assign an option, choose the Add button to move the option to the Active Options list. If you want to remove an active option, select its name in the Active Options box, and then choose the Remove button.

■ To enter or edit the value for an option, select its name in the Active Options list, and then either enter a new value in the supplied field or choose the Value | Edit (Array...) buttons, if applicable, to enter new values. You'll be required to enter a value that is valid for the type of option being set or changed; for numbers, enter a numeric value in the number base that is displayed. For IP addresses, enter a dotted-decimal IP number, and so on.

Creating and Deleting Custom DHCP Options

You can add custom options, which will subsequently appear in the list of available options. To add custom options, follow these steps:

1. From the DHCP Options menu, choose Defaults. This will result in the display of the DHCP Options: Default Values dialog as shown in Figure 12-3.

2. The Option Class dropdown list will show "DHCP Standard Options." Choose the New button. This will result in the display of the Add Option Type dialog shown in Figure 12-4.

3. In the Name field of the Add Option Type dialog, enter a name for your custom option. Next, select a data type for the option in the Data Type dropdown list. If the data type is to be held in an array, check the Array box.

4. Enter a unique number between 0 and 255 to be associated with this custom option. Start with values that exceed identifiers already in the list. Currently, the highest built-in default value is 68. Enter a description in the Comment field, and then choose the OK button.

5. You will be returned to the DHCP Options: Default Values dialog, where you should now select your custom option and set the value(s) for it by using the editing procedures described in the next section.

If you need to delete a custom option, highlight the option in the DHCP Options: Default Values dialog and choose the Delete button.

Editing Custom and Default Options

You can edit parameters for both custom and default options. Follow these steps to change a value for a default option or a custom option that you have configured yourself:

1. From the DHCP Options menu, choose Defaults. This will result in the display of the DHCP Options: Default Values dialog (Figure 12-3).

2. Select the option you want to change from the Option Name list, and depending on what kind of value is associated with this option, you will be

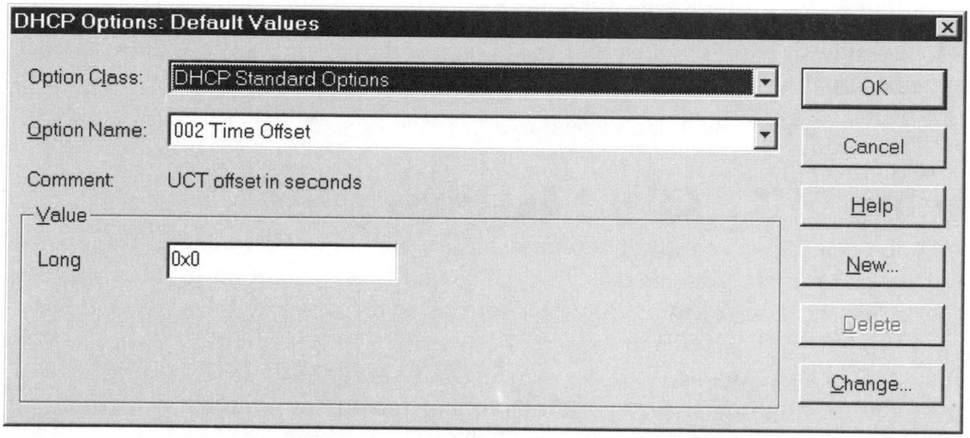

Figure 12-3.   *The DHCP Options: Default Values dialog*

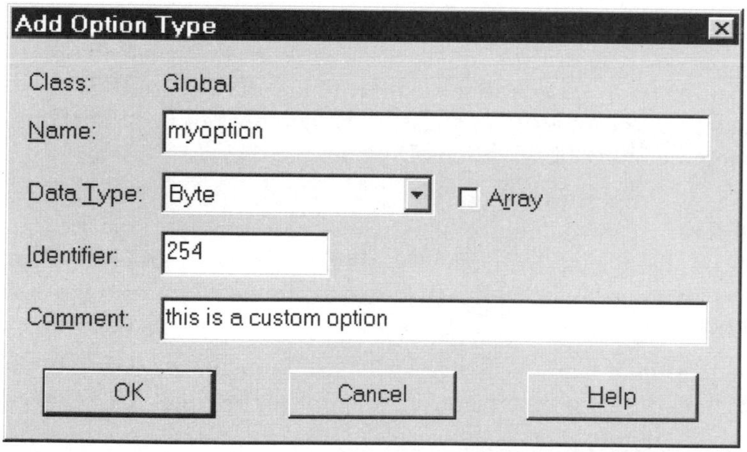

Figure 12-4.   *The Add Option Type dialog*

presented with fields for a numeric value, a string, an array, and so on. If this is an array, choose the Edit Array button to change values in the array.

3. If you wish to edit values for the option's name or comments, choose the Change button, and change the appropriate fields.

4. After you are finished, choose the OK button.

Managing DHCP Client Settings

When you need to have control over how DHCP parcels out client configuration on an individual client basis, you can use DHCP Manager to administer individual leases and client *reservations*. A reservation sets aside a specific IP address for a client. For instance, you might need to make reservations when you have Remote Access Service clients who are incapable of working with a DHCP server and must use a static IP address. Other situations that require reservations include domain name system servers and domain controllers that have defined IP addresses.

Administration of Leases

As mentioned previously, a client lease on an IP address assigned by DHCP can expire, be renewed, or revoked. The DHCP Manager allows you to view lease information for DHCP clients. The procedure for viewing lease information is as follows:

■ In the DHCP Servers window, select a server and scope that you want to configure. Next, from the DHCP Scope menu, choose Active Leases to display the Active Leases dialog (see Figure 12-5). This dialog will be used to display information for active leases and to work with reserved clients (see the next section).

■ Now, from the Client list in the Active Leases dialog, select the client whose lease you want to view. You may control the sort order of the list by using the dialog's sort control area, and you can show only reserved IP clients by checking the Show Reservations Only box.

■ Choose the Properties button. This will result in the display of the Client Properties dialog (see Figure 12-6), where you can view specific information about the client lease, including the Media Access Control (MAC) address for the client computer's NIC, the lease expiration date, and the assigned IP address.

■ To delete a client from the active DHCP configuration, select it in the Client list, and then choose the Delete button. Make sure the client has released the assigned IP before you do this.

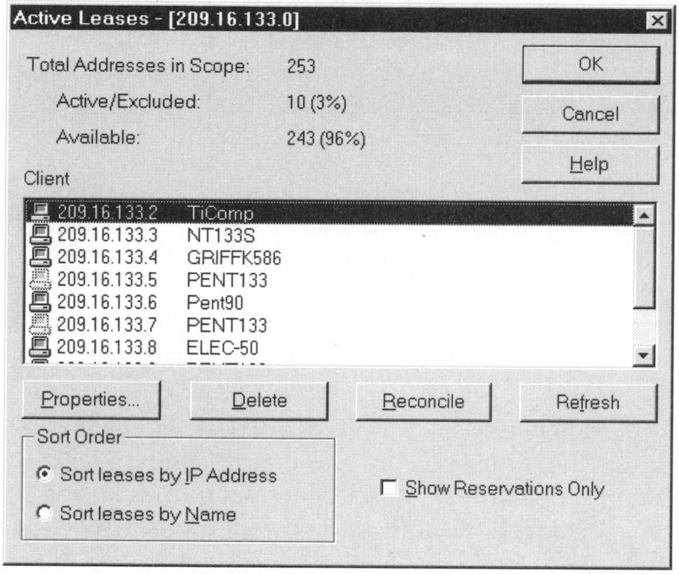

Active Leases - [209.16.133.0]

Total Addresses in Scope: 253
    Active/Excluded: 10 (3%)
    Available: 243 (96%)

OK
Cancel
Help

Client

🖥	209.16.133.2	TiComp
🖥	209.16.133.3	NT133S
🖥	209.16.133.4	GRIFFK586
🖥	209.16.133.5	PENT133
🖥	209.16.133.6	Pent90
🖥	209.16.133.7	PENT133
🖥	209.16.133.8	ELEC-50

Properties...   Delete   Reconcile   Refresh

Sort Order
⦿ Sort leases by IP Address
○ Sort leases by Name

☐ Show Reservations Only

Figure 12-5.   *The Active Leases dialog*

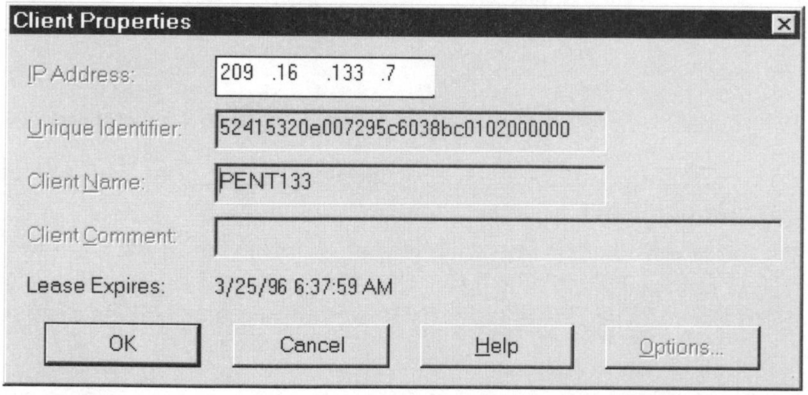

Client Properties

IP Address: 209 .16 .133 .7

Unique Identifier: 52415320e007295c6038bc0102000000

Client Name: PENT133

Client Comment:

Lease Expires: 3/25/96 6:37:59 AM

OK   Cancel   Help   Options...

Figure 12-6.   *The Client Properties dialog*

Administration of Client Reservations

Client reservations can be added, removed, and edited by using the DHCP Manager. Reserved clients can also be viewed using the same procedures for viewing other clients. In addition, options can be set on reserved clients.

Follow these steps to add reserved clients:

1. From DHCP Manager's Scope menu, choose Add Reservations. This will result in the display of the Add Reserved Clients dialog. To add a reserved client, fill in the IP address, of which part is displayed, coming from the scope's IP address pool. Also enter the Unique Identifier, or Media Access Control (MAC) address for the client computer's network adapter. You can display the MAC address by going to the client computer and typing **net config wksta** at any command prompt.

2. Enter the Client Name, if this field is not grayed out, as with MS-DOS clients. This name specifies the computer name that should be displayed for the client, so this does not have to be the actual computer name that you would use on the network. Optionally, you can enter any additional text in the Client Comment field.

3. Choose the Add button to commit this information to DHCP's database. When you have finished adding reservations, choose the Close button.

To change information for a reserved client, follow these steps:

1. From DHCP Manager's Scope menu, choose Active Leases. This will result in the display of the Active Leases dialog.

2. Select the reserved client you wish to change information for from the Client list. Next, choose the Properties button.

3. The Client Properties dialog will now be displayed, where you can change the unique identifier (MAC address), client name, or comment. When you are through, choose the OK button.

Here are the steps for entering or changing DHCP options for reserved clients:

1. From DHCP Manager's Scope menu, choose Active Leases. This will result in the display of the Active Leases dialog.

2. Select the reserved client you wish to change information for, from the Client list. Next (and only available if this client is a reserved client), choose the Options button. The DHCP Options: Reservation dialog will be displayed, as shown here:

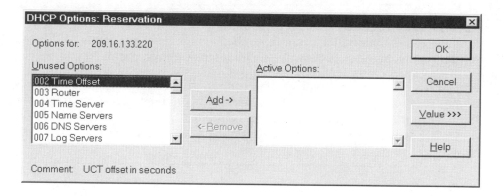

3. Select an option name in the Unused Options list, and follow the instructions for editing global, scope, or individual options, given earlier.

Mini-Glossary

DOMAIN   In relation to NT networking, a collection of computers that share a common database that dictates membership and security policy. Controlled by an NT Server domain controller, which authenticates domain logons. Each domain has a unique name.

IP BROADCAST TRAFFIC   Certain TCP/IP protocols are used, at times, to direct messages to everyone attached to the network, rather than directing datagrams (IP packets) towards a specific destination. Usually, a service or application that doesn't know who's attached to a network, but must inform any node that is active of some event, or must deliver information in this way, will use IP *broadcast*.

HUB   A term used to describe multi-port network repeaters, usually of twisted pair networks such as for 10BaseT or 100BaseT.

HOSTS and LMHOSTS FILES   Files containing lists of known IP addresses mapped to host names or NetBIOS computer names. LMHOSTS is a local text file that maps IP addresses to the NetBIOS computer names of Microsoft networking computers outside the local subnet.

PROXY   A WINS-enabled computer that listens for name queries from non-WINS-enabled computers and helps to resolve them through its proxy cache entries.

PUSH/PULL PARTNER WINS push partners send database update notifications to their pull partners, who then may request an update. WINS pull partners actively seek database updates from their paired partners.

ROUTER A computer, or a dedicated computerized device, that attaches to two or more networks and routes network data traffic from one network to the other. Used sometimes to describe a computer connected to multiple physical TCP/IP networks, capable of routing or delivering IP packets between them.

Preparing for WINS

Unless your TCP/IP network is a very small departmental or private network, you will quickly run up against a wall when trying to resolve IP addresses to your internal Windows-computer names. If you are running DHCP and your clients are coming and going, such as in a mobile sales force, it becomes very hard to manually keep track of which IP maps to which computer. You will quickly tire of having to manually update the mappings kept in HOSTS and LMHOSTS files.

There are two ways you can solve these problems: by using a local domain name system (DNS) service, or by using WINS. The Windows Internet naming service was designed to address this time-consuming task by automatically configuring and dynamically maintaining computer name and IP-address mapping tables. WINS also prevents the registration of duplicate network names and works in concert with DHCP.

WINS is superior to local DNS in a Windows network for one primary reason: It provides a NetBIOS namespace. This makes WINS superior in capability, while running a Windows network, since DNS knows nothing about NetBIOS name resolution, which lets you use local computer names such as \\MYSERVER.

WINS also gives you the ability to centrally manage its database and replication methods. And because WINS allows clients to locate remote systems, replacing LMHOSTS functionality, you can use it across both local and wide area networks for browsing nonlocal domains.

Installing WINS Servers

When you get ready to install a WINS server, you will do so by working with the Network applet in Control Panel. We will assume that you have already installed NT Server and that you are logged on as a member of the Administrators group. It is also assumed that you have properly installed the TCP/IP protocol on your server.

You can plan capacity based on a typical WINS server installation. Without performance degradation, and for a typical Pentium 166 or above, up to approximately 1,000 name registrations and about 800 queries per minute can be serviced per installation. You should plan, as with DHCP, to install a WINS server and backup for every 5,000–10,000 computers on the network.

The procedure for installing the WINS server is as follows:

- Choose the Network applet in Start/Settings/Control Panel, and choose the Services dialog. From this dialog, choose the Add button to display the Select Network Service list.

- Highlight Windows Internet Name Service in the Select Network Service list. Then select OK. The WINS service will be installed from your distribution files. The installer will ask you to enter the path to these files and will suggest a default. The files will be copied to your hard disk drive, and when done, you will be returned to the main Network applet dialog, where you should choose Close.

- After the network bindings review, you will be required to reboot the computer. No settings for WINS are possible from the Control Panel/Network applet; you will use the WINS Manager application, covered in the next section, to set up and administer WINS.

TIP: Remember to set option 44-WINS Servers and option 46-Node Type on your DHCP server if you are going to use DHCP in tandem with WINS. Otherwise, your DHCP clients will not be able to automatically find and use your WINS server.

Using WINS Manager

The WINS Manager is used to set up and administer a WINS server. You can use this application to connect to, and work with, a WINS server on your local machine, or anywhere else on your network. When WINS is installed, a menu choice for the WINS Manager will appear in the Start/Programs/Administrative Tools(Common) menu.

WINS requires initial setup and then must be maintained whenever you need to change the way WINS operates in respect to WINS-enabled clients, replicates database information, and works with other WINS servers. You will use the WINS Manager to perform these tasks and more.

The WINS Servers Window

If a WINS server is running locally when WINS Manager starts, that server will be opened and displayed as active within the WINS Servers window in WINS Manager (see Figure 12-7). If the WINS service is not running locally, the Add WINS Server dialog will be initially displayed. Note that the display of servers is based on how the WINS Manager was initially connected to the WINS server, what IP address was listed for TCP/IP, and what computer name was listed for NetBIOS.

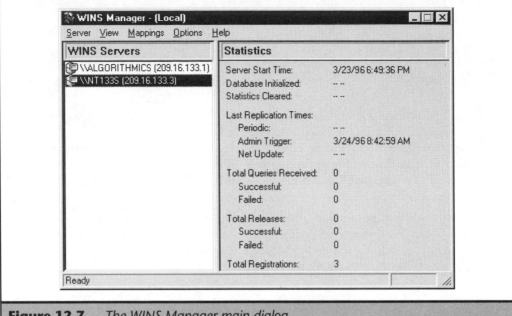

Figure 12-7. *The WINS Manager main dialog*

If the Add WINS Server dialog appears, enter the computer name or IP address of the computer where a WINS server that you wish to administer is located. Then choose OK.

The WINS Manager window will always list all of the WINS servers that you have connected to in prior sessions. You may use the Add WINS Server dialog whenever you wish to work with a WINS server that you have not previously administered. When you are returned to the main Manager window, highlight the server you wish to work with.

The Statistics Window

For any WINS server that is highlighted, the right pane, or window, of the WINS Manager main display will show statistics for this server. These statistics include the following:

■ **Database Initialized:** Time of first database initialization.

■ **Statistics Cleared:** Time when statistics were last cleared.

■ **Last Replication Times:** Times for last WINS database replication by type: Periodic is the last time replicated based on replication intervals; Admin Trigger is the last time replicated by manual administrator intervention using the Replicate Now button; and Net Update is the last time replicated by network push notification.

■ **Total Queries Received:** Total number of name query requests received. Database matches are listed under Successful; failed name resolutions are listed as Failed.

■ **Total Releases:** Total number of notifications of NetBIOS application shut down. Successful releases are listed as Successful; unsuccessful releases are listed as Failed.

■ **Total Registrations:** Total number of client name registrations.

Mini-Glossary

DATABASE CLEANING (SCAVENGING)   A process by which the database is checked for consistency, compacted, and any unused or invalid entries are deleted.

DATABASE REPLICATION   The process of copying the WINS databases to another WINS server, for distributed name services and backup use.

MULTIHOMED RECORDS   Depending on the context, database records that exist on more than one WINS server, or records that map to more than one address (single name->1 IP) on multihomed machines.

REPLICATION PARTNER   The WINS server that acts as a backup/replication recipient for another, primary WINS server.

REPLICATION PERIOD   The time intervals between WINS database replications.

REPLICATION TRIGGER   The event that causes WINS database replication.

Detailed Information

The Server | Detailed Information menu choice lets you inspect information about the currently selected server in more detail. Choose this command to display the Detailed Information dialog (see Figure 12-8), which shows information covering the following items:

■ **WINS Server Address:** Displays computer name, IP address, connection type, and connection statistics.

■ **Last Address Change:** Last time that any WINS database changes were replicated.

■ **Last Scavenging Times:** Last times that the database was scavenged, or cleared of invalid entries, by type: Periodic is the last time database scavenging was triggered by the specified "Renewal interval" times; Admin Trigger is the last time scavenging was triggered by the administrator's choice of the Initiate Scavenging command; Extinction is the last time scavenging was triggered by the "Extinction interval" times; and Verification is the last time scavenging was triggered by the "Verify interval" times.

■ **Unique Registrations:** Number of accepted name registrations. This is broken down into the number of conflicts detected during name registration and the number of renewals of unique names.

■ **Group Registrations:** Number of accepted registration requests for groups. These are broken down into the number of conflicts detected during group name registration and the number of renewals of group names.

Replication Partners

If you are planning for a large network deployment, you can install multiple WINS servers to lessen single-point load and increase name registration throughput. When more than one WINS server is installed, each will be paired with at least one other,

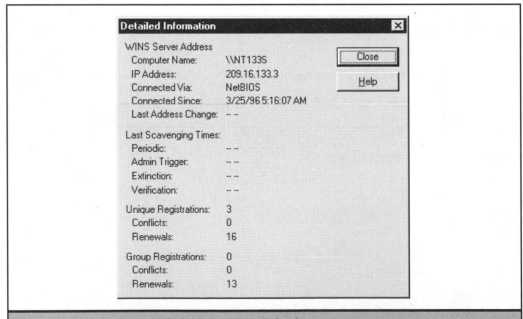

Figure 12-8. *The Detailed Information dialog*

which becomes its replication partner. You control how database entries will be replicated, or copied, between replication partners with WINS Manager.

Two types of replication partners are possible. You can set up a pull partner, whereby the WINS server pulls in database entries from its partner by request. The other type is called a push partner, whereby the WINS server sends, or pushes, database update notifications to its partner. The partner then responds with a replication request, and the push partner sends the database updates.

Push and pull partners may be daisy-chained, or they may have a single relationship with a central, primary WINS server. The specific topology that you choose will depend on your individual network loading.

Proxies

WINS proxies help to resolve name queries for non-WINS computers. Unless otherwise configured, these non-WINS computers use b-node IP broadcasts when requesting name resolution, and WINS proxies respond to these broadcasts.

WINS proxies keep a special cache of IP-to-NetBIOS names. If a WINS proxy receives a name resolution broadcast from a non-WINS computer, it will attempt to resolve the name query through its mappings, contained in its cache. If it cannot resolve the query, it will ask a WINS server for the mapping. WINS proxies can also work in a routed environment. If no local WINS server is available, the proxy will try to query a WINS server on the remote side of a gateway or router. The proxy cache is a temporary storage for these mappings and is updated at regular intervals.

If you have any non-WINS computers using IP broadcast for name resolution, a WINS proxy should be installed on one of the WINS-enabled clients on your network. To make a WINS client act also as a proxy, edit that computer's registry parameter under

HKEY_LOCAL_MACHINE\SYSTEM\CurrentControlSet\Services\Netbt\Parameters

where the parameter to add or edit is EnableProxy, which should be set to 1.

Configuring WINS Servers

The configuration of database replication triggers is the most important set of controls that you will configure using WINS Manager. Specific times, time periods, or numbers of new records are all candidates for triggering replication. As with all other services, you must be logged on with administrator privileges to work with WINS Manager.

To set the triggering controls, from the main dialog, choose the Configuration command on the Server menu. This will result in the display of the WINS Server Configuration dialog. Choose the Advanced button (see Figure 12-9) to show all settings. Now you are ready to work with the interval, pull, push, and advanced options to set up your server's configuration. The options and their meanings are described here.

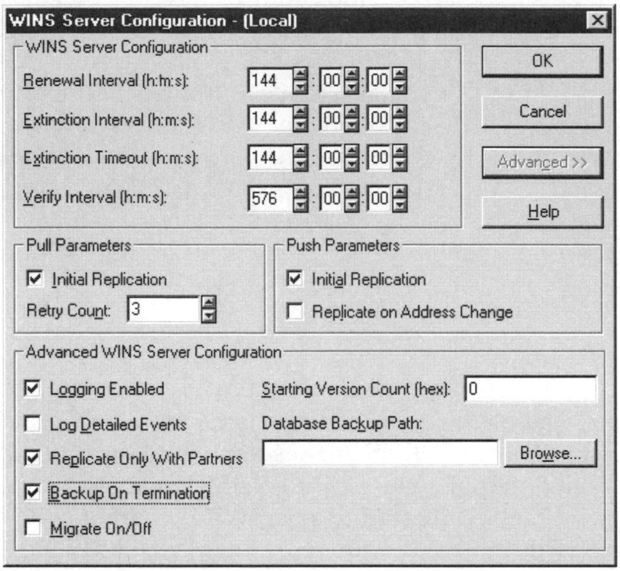

Figure 12-9.   *The WINS Server Configuration dialog*

INTERVALS   This area allows you to enter intervals of time for triggering events and timeouts. Pay particular attention to the renewal interval, as its setting most affects response time. If many regular registrations are expected, reduce the renewal interval to reduce burst traffic.

- **Renewal Interval:** Period after which clients must re-register their names.
- **Extinction Interval:** Interval to wait after an entry is marked released to mark it as extinct.
- **Extinction Timeout:** Interval to wait after an entry is marked extinct to initiate item scavenging from the database.
- **Verify Interval:** Period after which the server must verify that nonowned names are still active.

PULL PARAMETERS   If you are setting up this WINS server so it pulls replicated data from a partner on startup, check Initial Replication. Now, enter a value for Retry Count. The retry count is the number of times a pull partner will attempt connection when pulling database replicas.

PUSH PARAMETERS   If you are setting up this WINS server as a push partner that sends notifications of database updates to other partners on startup, check Initial

Replication. Check Replicate on Address Change to send notification to other partners when the address changes in a database mapping.

ADVANCED WINS SERVER CONFIGURATION   Now, make any settings needed in this area, as required, from the following options:

- **Logging Enabled:** Enables logging of changes to J*.LOG.

- **Log Detailed Events:** Enables verbose log entries. This should only be done for debugging purposes, since the log files will be very large and can affect performance.

- **Replicate Only With Partners:** Enables replications only with push and pull partners.

- **Backup On Termination:** Enables automatic database backup when you exit WINS Manager.

- **Migrate On/Off:** Directs WINS to treat static and multihomed records as dynamic. When a new registration or replication takes place, these records will be overwritten if they are no longer valid.

- **Starting Version Count:** Designates a version number for the database. Used to force re-sync by replication partners to a new database if you need to start clean. If the database is reinitialized after corruption or loss, use this value (set to higher than before) to force synchronization among partners.

- **Database Backup Path:** Points to a directory where WINS database backups can be stored. The directory must be local to the WINS server machine.

After all options are set, choose the OK button to commit your changes.

Adding a Replication Partner

Follow these steps for adding replication partners:

1. Choose the Replication Partners command from the WINS Manager's main menu. This will result in the display of the Replication Partners dialog (see Figure 12-10).

2. In this dialog, choose the Add button. The Add WINS Server dialog will be displayed.

3. Enter the NetBIOS computer name or IP address of the WINS server that you want to add and choose the OK button. The server will be added to the Replication Partners/WINS Server list.

You can control what kind of partner, whether immediate replication will take place, and what the Replication Partners/WINS Server list will display by checking the filter boxes and using the replicate controls. Check either Push Partners, Pull Partners, or both to set up the type of partnership required, and then choose the

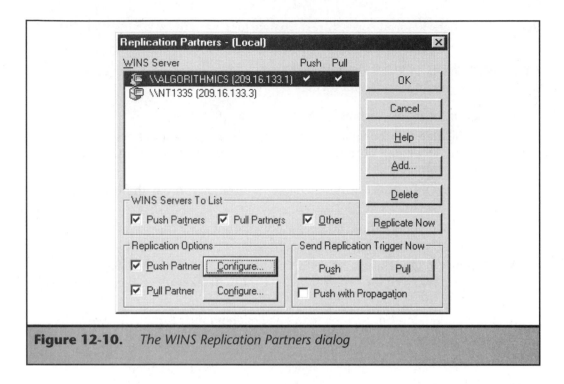

Figure 12-10. *The WINS Replication Partners dialog*

related Configure button. This will result in the display of the appropriate Properties dialog, where you will make settings as listed here:

■ To make pull partner settings, first enter a time in the Start Time field of the Pull Partner Properties dialog, to indicate when replication should begin, as shown here:

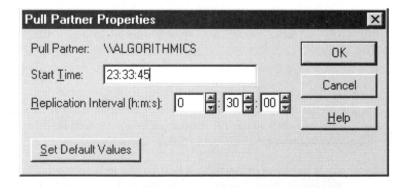

■ In the Replication Interval field of this dialog, enter a time in hours, minutes, and seconds that indicates how often replications will occur.

■ To make push partner settings, enter a number in the Update Count field of the Push Partner Properties dialog, to indicate how many additions and updates can be made to the database before replication will be triggered, as shown here:

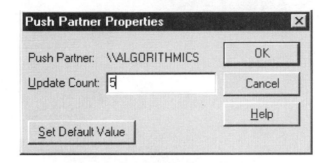

Choose the OK button to commit your changes.

To delete a replication partner, in the Replication Partners dialog, select a server in the Replication Partners/WINS Server list and choose the Delete button.

WINS Static Mappings

Static mappings are permanent computer name-to-IP address mappings that cannot be changed, removed, or challenged, except by the administrator. You use the Static Mappings command to add, edit, import, or delete static mappings for clients that are not WINS enabled (see Figure 12-11). Static mappings should never be assigned to WINS-enabled client computers.

Adding and Removing Static Mappings

You can add static mappings to the WINS database for specific IP addresses by entering them into one of the dialog fields or by using import files that contain these mappings. Working with the Static Mappings dialog, as in Figure 12-11, you may sort and filter what is presented by using the appropriate controls. You can add static mappings to the WINS database manually or by using an import file.

MAKING MANUAL ENTRIES   Follow these steps to add static mappings to the WINS database manually:

1. From the WINS Manager's Mappings menu, choose Static Mappings, which will result in the display of the Static Mappings dialog.

2. Choose the Add Mappings button, which will result in the display of the Add Static Mappings dialog (see Figure 12-12).

3. Enter the target's computer name in the Name field, and its dotted-decimal IP address in the IP Address field. If the type of mapping is designated as Internet Group or Multihomed, this dialog will display additional fields, designed to

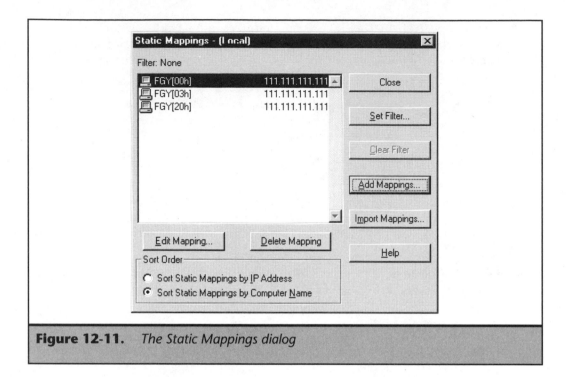

Figure 12-11. *The Static Mappings dialog*

allow you to enter multiple IP addresses. See the following section on this dialog's Type entry area, and the later section on special names, for more information on these types.

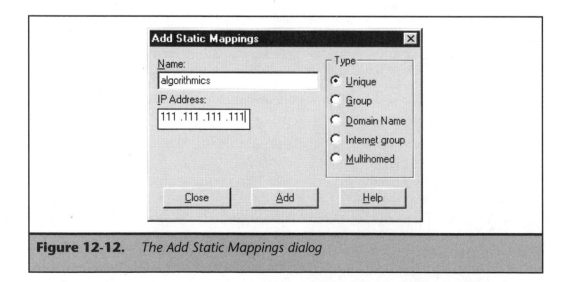

Figure 12-12. *The Add Static Mappings dialog*

4. In the Type area, choose a type to assign to this static mapping. This option flags the entry as a unique name, or as belonging to a group with a special name, as described here:

- **Unique:** Unique name with a single address.

- **(Regular)Group:** A regular group is a designation that does not require the addresses of its members to be stored in the database. Clients use name broadcasts to regular groups.

- **Internet Group:** Internet groups are defined by the user. They have special-character NetBIOS names and can hold up to 25 individual addresses.

- **Multihomed:** A unique name with more than one address. This means that the addresses belong to different NICs or bound services on a single computer (multihomed).

5. After you have entered the appropriate information, choose the Add button. The mapping will be added to the database. When you are finished adding mappings, choose the Close button.

In order to remove existing mappings from the Static Mappings dialog, highlight the mappings you wish to delete from the list, and then choose the Delete Mapping button. When you are completely finished with Static Mappings, choose the Close button.

ENTRIES USING AN IMPORT FILE   Instead of manually entering individual static mappings, you can import these entries using any file that follows the same format as an LMHOSTS file. To import a file containing static mappings, follow these steps:

1. From the Static Mappings dialog, choose the Import Mappings button. This will result in the display of the Select Static Mapping File dialog.

2. Select a filename to use for importing your mappings, and then choose Open. The file import will proceed automatically. A static mapping will be created for each computer name and address listed in the file. An Internet group will be created for each instance of the #DOM keyword, and the address that follows will be added to that Internet group.

Editing Mappings

You can edit the IP addresses for any listed static mapping. From the Static Mappings dialog, edit a static mapping with these steps:

1. Highlight the mapping you wish to edit. Now choose the Edit Mapping button, which will result in the display of the Edit Static Mapping dialog. The

computer name will be displayed, along with the mapping type, and an IP address field will be presented for edit, as shown here:

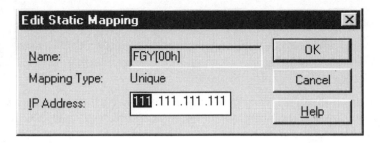

2. Edit the dotted-decimal address in the IP Address field, and then choose the OK button.

Insider Info

Before the development of WINS, the only way to associate Windows machine names with IP numbers was via an LMHOSTS file. An example LMHOSTS (lmhosts.sam) file can be found in the %SystemRoot%\System32\drivers\etc directory. You can view and edit this file for directions and examples of how to properly utilize an LMHOSTS file. The file must be renamed "lmhosts. (no extension)" for actual use.

WINS Special Names

Special group names are used by WINS to signify the special handling and characteristics that WINS will use and recognize when working with these groups. These names and designations are explained in the following sections.

Regular Groups

A regular group is not bound to an address. When a WINS server receives a query for a group name, it returns a broadcast address, which the client can use in a further discovery process. Regular groups can be registered with one or more WINS servers. A regular group name is used to receive broadcasts and to denote a domain name, which is used for browsing purposes.

Internet Groups

An Internet group holds IP addresses for up to 25 primary and backup domain controllers for a given domain. These names are held in a first-in/-first-out list, where the oldest entry is replaced if the limit is reached and new registrations are received.

Replica members—members registered by other WINS servers—are removed and replaced first.

Multihomed Names

Multihomed names contain a unique computer name that maps to multiple IP addresses. A multihomed computer contains multiple network interface cards or bindings, each with its own IP address. As with Internet group names, a multihomed name can contain up to 25 IP addresses.

What's Next

We now have a very good idea of how to use DHCP and WINS to automate the setup and administration of a difficult but very valuable service: TCP/IP. Next, we are going to examine NT's Remote Access Service (RAS) and Dial-Up Networking. If you travel with your portable computer, or you need to gain access to a remote NT machine or Internet service provider, this subject will be of great importance.

We will examine both sides of the NT RAS component. The server side is the part that you use when you wish to make your NT server or network available to the world through a remote access technology. Dial-Up Networking is the other side—the client software that you can use to dial into a RAS server, or into an Internet provider's computers. We'll look at how to install RAS and how to use some of its advanced features. If you ever intend to do remote networking, RAS will be in your future. After you read the next chapter, you won't be caught by surprise!

Chapter Thirteen

The Remote Access Service

W
e are now going to look at RAS (the Remote Access Service), which allows you to connect to your NT computer, with a modem or leased line, and proceed to work as if you were connected directly to the local internal network. You can also connect one NT system (and so its network) to another, using RAS, thereby extending your internal network to transparently include another's. RAS connections are compatible with, and invisible to, any network application running on a RAS-capable client. You can browse a RAS-connected network, and you can use its shared resources as if they existed locally. RAS provides a way for remote clients to securely connect to a private LAN or WAN without having to be wired to a network, or be Internet enabled.

RAS can also be used to couple your NT server and network to a wider area network through a dialup, and we'll cover this kind of connection too. We will look at a new addition for NT 4—Dial-Up Networking. This facility is an outgrowth of its Windows 95 counterpart in name and appearance only. Functionally, NT's Dial-Up Networking is intimately linked to the underlying NT RAS services, and it extends their functionality and usability by presenting RAS dial-out capabilities in an easier-to-use and standardized wrapping. Earlier versions presented the user with an arcane RAS dialing manager, which was not well integrated into NT's user interface.

In addition to the linkage of two NT machines, RAS's server can handle connections that use other types of clients, such as Windows 95, Windows for Workgroups, LAN Manager, and, with TCP/IP, almost any other remote client. Of course, functionality will be lost if the remote client is incapable of using Microsoft networking protocols, which enable full NT network capability. For instance, in cases where generic TCP/IP connections are made, you will lose the ability to browse the server's network using NetBIOS names, and to use its shared resources as you would on a local NT network.

RAS clients can use any of the popular network protocols when connecting to a RAS server, but they must use IPX or NetBEUI for full, transparent NT functionality. If TCP/IP is used solely, you must provide a way to map IP addresses to computer names on the network. Dial-Up Networking supports SLIP (Serial Line Internet Protocol) and PPP (Point-to-Point Protocol), so you can connect to remote SLIP servers, such as Unix systems; and RAS PPP clients using TCP/IP, IPX, or NetBEUI can all connect to a RAS server. In addition, RAS supports a special Microsoft-only protocol, with which you can connect to (or from) NT 3.1 and Windows for Workgroups computers.

Clients and Servers

Because RAS is really two distinct services, providing a way into *and* out of an NT box, it's important to know about both the client and server sides of the setup. As a RAS server operator, it's important to know the mechanics of client dial-in procedures; and even if you are only interested in connecting as a client or, for instance, in using the

Insider Info

RAS client support for Serial Line Internet Protocol (SLIP) is primarily provided to allow connection to non-NT servers, which require this less-than-optimal, older remote access protocol. The Dial-Up Networking client in NT 4 provides support for this kind of connection, typically to a Unix server.

During connection to a remote SLIP server, Dial-Up Networking provides an interactive terminal window, which is then used to enter and display logon and authentication procedures for the remote server. This interactive logon replaces the automatic logon and authentication usually provided by the Dial-Up Networking facility.

You can also specify that interactive terminal windows be provided for any other kind of protocol logon. See the sections on Dial-Up Networking, later in this chapter, for more information.

client side to connect to the Internet, you'll want to understand how RAS accepts your call (see Figure 13-1).

RAS clients can connect to a RAS server or another network provider by using a POTS (plain old telephone service) modem or modem pool, through an ISDN (integrated services digital network) or frame relay connection, or over an X.25 network. If very high speed is required, RAS can be set up to operate with T1, T3,

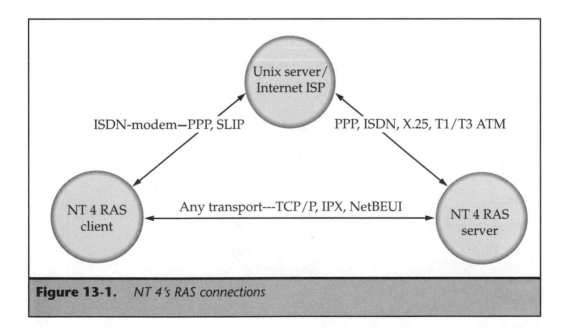

Figure 13-1. *NT 4's RAS connections*

or ATM (asynchronous transfer mode) connections. A local RAS client can also connect to a RAS server by using an RS-232C null modem (a direct serial cable connection).

When accepting a logon from a RAS client, the server provides all NT security and data encryption features that it would normally present to a local workstation. RAS servers also provide a facility for callback: After initial logon, the server must call the remote client back to continue the connection, providing an extra layer of security and authentication.

A RAS server that is implemented on NT Server will permit up to 256 simultaneous client connections, providing access either to the entire network or to the RAS server only. On NT Workstation, RAS will only permit one client connection.

Mini-Glossary

ATM (ASYNCHRONOUS TRANSFER MODE)   A network standard that defines high-load, high-speed (1.544Mbps through 1.2Gbps), fixed-size packet switching along with dynamic bandwidth allocation.

T1-T3 CONNECTIONS   T1 is an AT&T term for a digital network facility used to transmit and receive data at 1.544Mbps. T3 is a term for a digital network facility used to transmit and receive data at 44.746Mbps.

NETBIOS (NETWORK BASIC INPUT/OUTPUT SYSTEM)   The standard interface to networks on systems using DOS, Windows 95, NT, OS/2, and some versions of Unix that provides standard ways for applications to interact with a LAN (e.g., request lower level network services).

NETBEUI (NETBIOS EXTENDED USER INTERFACE)   Pronounced "net-booey," it is an enhanced version of the NetBIOS protocol used by network operating systems such as LAN Manager, LAN Server, Windows for Workgroups, Windows 95, and NT. It formalizes the transport frame that was never standardized in NetBIOS.

MICROSOFT RAS PROTOCOL   The Microsoft RAS protocol is a proprietary protocol supporting the NetBIOS standard. Used in all previous versions of RAS, including NT 3.1, Windows for Workgroups, MS-DOS, and LAN Manager clients. Microsoft RAS requires the NetBEUI protocol, acting as a gateway, to provide access to servers that use the NetBEUI, TCP/IP, or IPX protocols.

ISDN AND FRAME RELAY   RAS may be implemented over an integrated services digital network (ISDN) or frame relay device (FRAD) line. Both technologies provide higher connect speeds than standard POTS modems, and lower connection speeds than T1 or ATM. Telephone companies at both the server and remote site must install an ISDN or FRAD line. ISDN also requires that an ISDN adapter card or modem be installed in both the RAS server and client. Frame Relay devices also require supporting equipment, one type of which is a device called a MONOFRAD, or monolithic frame relay device.

X.25   A network interface for computers and terminals that uses packet switching technology over public data networks.

X.25 PAD (PACKET ASSEMBLER/DISASSEMBLER)   A device, or piece of software, to allow data terminals to communicate over an X.25 network.

Remote Access Clients

Clients may be hosted on NT, Windows 95, Windows for Workgroups, MS-DOS, LAN Manager, or a third-party PPP-capable platform. Many communication options are available to connect clients to servers: POTS, frame relay, ISDN, X.25, T1/T3/ATM, and RS-232C null modem. These various physical connections allow you to choose the right mix of speed, availability, and cost.

Insider Info

Currently, POTS service is capable of carrying data at rates up to 33,600 bits per second (bps). With some proprietary technologies, this will soon increase to 56Kbps, the same rate at which single B-channel ISDN and FRAD devices communicate. Two-B-channel *bonded* ISDN communicates at 128Kbps, three to four times that of the fastest analog modem available today. An ISDN modem can cost $500 to $1,000 dollars, with metered and flat-rate services costing $100 or more per month, but as ISDN becomes more popular, prices are rapidly falling.

An ISDN line consists of two B, or *bearer*, data channels that are rated at 56 or 64Kbps each, and a 16Kbps D channel for signaling and low-speed packet data. You can have two 64Kbps data channels operating as separate pipes simultaneously, or you can *bond* the two B channels to get one 115Kbps or 128Kbps connection. The newest multilink PPP protocols allow you to achieve this B-channel bonding in a nonproprietary way.

RAS also supports connections based on the X.25 standard. You can use an X.25 adapter card, or a modem with dial-up X.25 in place of an X.25 PAD.

If you need to logically link two or more networks that have no physical connection, or if you want to temporarily attach a portable computer with no network adapter to your NT box, you can use a serial RS-232C null modem. A null modem is a crossover serial line that allows direct connection between two PC serial ports. You can use this type of connection the same way modems are used. Both client and server-side RAS software can be set up to communicate over a direct cable connection.

NT 4 and Windows 95 Clients

NT 4 and Windows 95 clients can exploit RAS features fully. They can also be used to connect to any third-party PPP or SLIP server. The Dial-Up Networking facilities provide scripted and nonscripted logons, and can negotiate authentication with the server.

NT 3.1, Windows for Workgroups, MS-DOS, LAN Manager, and Third-Party PPP Clients

Windows NT Server provides RAS services for NT 3.1 RAS clients, a RAS Network Client version 3.0 for MS-DOS, and a Windows for Workgroups RAS client. However, these clients do not support the PPP protocol, and they also require that you install the NetBEUI LAN protocol.

Third-party PPP clients using TCP/IP, IPX, or NetBEUI can access an NT 4 RAS server. The RAS server will automatically negotiate logon and authentication with all PPP clients.

Insider Info

If you use TCP/IP and the PPP protocol on your client connections, the RAS server can be made to provide your clients with an IP address, taken from a static range, assigned initially by the administrator during setup. RAS clients can also specify a fixed IP address if allowed to do so by the administrator.

Name resolution is also required for TCP/IP client connections. This may be accomplished by one of three methods: the Windows Internet Name Service (WINS—see Chapter 12), a domain name system (DNS) server, or by using HOSTS and LMHOSTS files.

If WINS or DNS is used, the RAS client will utilize the services of the WINS or DNS server that the RAS server uses. As an alternative, a RAS client can use a HOSTS or LMHOSTS file for name resolution. This method is faster, but the IP addresses and computer name mappings must be known ahead of time, and must not change.

Remote Access Servers

NT RAS servers are set up and administered through the Control Panel/Network/Services dialog and the Remote Access Admin application, available from the Start/Programs/Administrative Tools (Common) menu.

The Remote Access Admin program, installed along with the RAS service, allows you to choose a RAS server to administer, view connected users and their usage statistics, grant network permissions, and control the amount of data that the Admin program presents.

Insider Info

RAS servers on NT Server permit a maximum of 256 simultaneous dial-in clients. A RAS server on NT Workstation permits only one incoming call. A RAS server can be configured to provide the dial-in client with access to the entire network, or just to the computer on which the RAS server is running. In order for RAS to provide access to an entire network, the RAS server must also have a properly configured network interface card (NIC) that is connected to the rest of your network. If these conditions are met, RAS will allow the remote dial-in client to become a member of the subnet that your local network is part of. This ability is predicated on the assumption that your RAS server supports proxy-ARP (Address Resolution Protocol).

You configure the RAS service during initial setup in the Control Panel/Network/Services dialog. You will be given the chance to make selections for the protocols and network setups that you want a dial-in client to use, access scope, type of modem or remote support, and a logon-authentication method. You can set up multiple RAS ports to provide more than one dial-in/out connection. Each modem or port that you set up to work with RAS can be a dial-out, a receive, or a dial-out and receive connection.

An additional level of authentication can be set up while configuring RAS. Callback allows you to specify that the RAS server will provide an initial logon for a dial-in client, after which it will hang up and call the client back to complete the authentication procedure. You might want to use callback in cases where you absolutely want to ensure both user identity and user location in a logon session.

Novell NetWare Access

If your RAS server will act as a gateway to a Novell NetWare network, you must be running a client NetWare redirector. You install this redirector as a service in the Control Panel/Network/Services dialog. For NT Workstation, install the Client Service for NetWare. For NT Server, install the Gateway Service for NetWare.

By configuring the redirector service, an NT RAS server can provide file access and print services for Novell NetWare; and clients, through the use of the PPP-IPX protocol, can use Windows Sockets applications over IPX.

RAS Security Options

NT security features are fully available when using RAS. Remote clients can be authenticated as users whose accounts exist on any connected domain. Logon and data communications can be encrypted at connect time.

NOTE: In order to use domain authentication, you should have a network domain structure already established. If you are providing access to one machine only, you can use its local domain (its computer name) in place of a networkwide name.

User Accounts and Domain Authentication

One of the ways that RAS enforces security and grants permissions is to enforce user account security. For remote clients, RAS will authenticate against user accounts existing on any connected domain, trusted domain, or connected NT computer. Use the Remote Access Admin utility to select a computer's or domain's user accounts. You then grant RAS permission to the user accounts. You can also set callback behavior per user.

Trusted domains allow one NT Server to be *trusted*, or allowed to use resources on the other NT Server's domain. You use User Manager for Domains on an NT Server to set up trust relationships. If trust relationships exist, RAS servers can find a user's account on a trusted domain after searching for it locally, first.

RAS Data Encryption

NT 4 (and 3.5) RAS can encrypt the actual data stream between client and server, if the Dial-Up Networking client is set up to do so (see the section later in the chapter on installing a Dial-Up client phonebook entry). This feature, which uses bulk data RSA-RC4 data encryption, is a front-line defense against unauthorized interception of the data stream while it is in transit. The RC4 algorithm was developed by RSA Data Security Incorporated and is very secure.

TIP: *You can also use callback to ensure that authorized users connecting only from specific locations will be authenticated for RAS sessions. Configuring callback in Remote Access Admin is covered later in this chapter.*

Installing and Configuring RAS

There are two sides of a RAS conversation: the RAS server and the RAS client. We will examine both setups, but will concentrate our client setup on configuring NT 4's Dial-Up Networking. Other operating systems have clients that need to be set up according to their specific needs and capabilities.

The RAS server is installed by selecting the Start/Settings/Control Panel/ Network/Services dialog from the Start button on the desktop, whereas the RAS client is installed by choosing the Dial-Up Networking icon from the My Computer icon on the desktop. If you are going to provide dial-in RAS server capabilities, install the RAS service. This is not necessary if you intend only to dial out using Dial-Up Networking.

NOTE: *The following setups assume that NT is fully installed and that you are logged on as a member of the Administrators group, or a group that has been given administrator privileges.*

First Things First...RAS Server Protocols and Roles

A RAS server is your client's gateway into the local LAN, so you must decide on and select the protocols that you wish RAS to use in making a connection to the LAN. This is equally important to a Dial-Up Networking client, but how you set up your RAS server will determine which protocols a client can use.

Additionally, when setting up a RAS server, you must decide what role the service will play in the usage and sharing of your communication channels. Since a RAS server can support both dialing in and dialing out (sharing a RAS port for use with Dial-Up Networking), you must tell the RAS server how you want a port to be used. A RAS server's role is mostly determined by how you specify the use of its RAS-enabled ports.

Installing a RAS Server

You begin your RAS server installation by choosing Start/Settings/Control Panel/ Network/Services. This dialog lists all of the services currently installed on your computer. We will assume that the RAS service does not already appear in the list of installed services and that you are logged on with administrator privileges. Also, any LAN protocol that you wish to have RAS support should already be installed as part of your primary network setup.

To add the RAS service, from the desktop:

1. In the Start/Settings/Control Panel/Network/Services dialog, choose the Add button.

2. In the Select Network Service list, select Remote Access Service and choose the OK button.

3. When prompted for the path to the original NT distribution files, type the path (or accept the suggested path) and choose the OK button. The RAS support files will be copied to your NT system directories.

4. After copying has been completed, you will be presented with the Remote Access Setup dialog and its Add RAS Device dialog. In the Add RAS Device/ RAS Capable Devices list, you will see a list of the modems/adapters and ports that RAS can use. Select the device and port you will use for remote access and choose the OK button. You may also invoke the modem installer, or the X.25 PAD installer, to add a specific device at this point (see the following tip).

TIP: *If you have not yet set up a modem or port device, you will first see an information box, as shown here, that asks if you want to invoke the Modem installer to set up a RAS-capable device. See the section on Dial-Up Networking to learn more about the modem installer.*

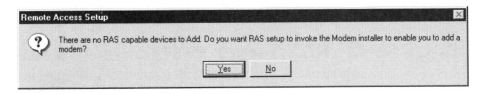

5. In the Remote Access Setup dialog box, the detected or installed modem will be highlighted, as shown next.

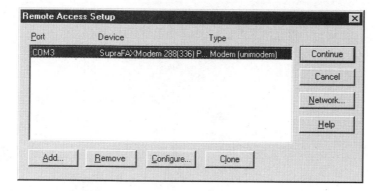

You must now make two configuration choices to set up the device. These choices will determine the device's role and its networking support. Choosing Configure will display the Configure Port Usage dialog where you will specify the role you wish this device to play:

- Choose Dial out only to make this device available to a RAS client only.

- Choose Receive calls only to make this device available to a RAS server only.

- Choose Dial out and Receive calls to make this device available to both client and server. Usage is mutually exclusive; devices can only play one role at a time.

6. Choose the OK button.

7. In the Remote Access Setup dialog box, choose the Network button to configure RAS network settings. You will be presented with the Network Configuration dialog (see Figure 13-2). You will be selecting the network settings for the highlighted device and port in the Remote Access Setup dialog.

8. Select the protocols to use for dialing out in the Dial out Protocols area. These settings determine which protocols will be used when you use Dial-Up Networking as a client, using the selected device.

NOTE: *If you did not configure this port for dialing out in the previous steps, the Dial out Protocols area will be grayed out.*

9. Select the protocols you wish to use for receiving calls in the Server Settings area. These settings determine which network protocols the RAS server will

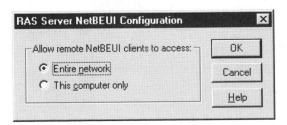

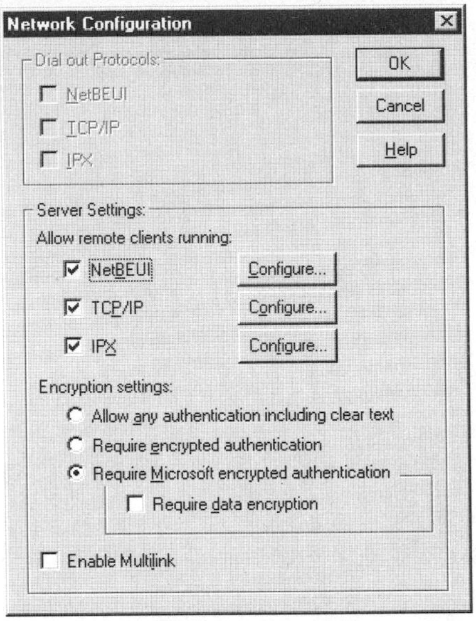

Figure 13-2. *The Network Configuration dialog*

allow when receiving a remote client call. You must also set up each protocol
that you choose to support by selecting the Configure button next to the
checked protocol.

NOTE: *If you did not configure this port to receive calls, the Server Settings area will
be grayed out.*

Configure each selected protocol as follows:

■ **NetBEUI:** When the NetBEUI Configuration dialog is shown, select the access
scope that you wish to grant to incoming calls. Select Entire network or This
computer only to limit the client connection's access (as shown in the following
illustration). Choose OK when done.

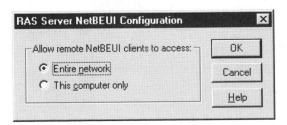

■ **TCP/IP:** When the TCP/IP Configuration dialog is shown, two areas will need setting. First, select the access scope that you wish to grant to incoming calls. Select Entire network, or This computer only to limit the client connection's access (as in Figure 13-3). Next, choose whether to use DHCP (see Chapter 12), or whether to assign the client call an IP from a specified range that you enter into this dialog. If you choose DHCP, you must have a DHCP server running on your network. Otherwise, specify a valid range of IP addresses within your network's subnet and with the same subnet mask. You can exclude single IPs or ranges of IPs if they are to be reserved. Lastly, you can specify that RAS will allow a predefined IP request from the client. Use this setting if your client has a fixed IP address. Choose OK when done.

■ **IPX:** When the IPX Configuration dialog is shown, you have four settings to make. First, select the access scope that you wish to grant to incoming calls. Select Entire network or This computer only to limit the client connection's access (as in Figure 13-4). Now, select how network numbers will be allocated: automatically, or with a fixed range that you assign. If you choose automatic assignment, RAS will determine (by using the NetWare Routing Information Protocol) an IPX network number to assign to the client. Next, select "Assign same network number to all IPX clients" to make RAS assign the same network number to all IPX clients, thereby reducing route overhead and network

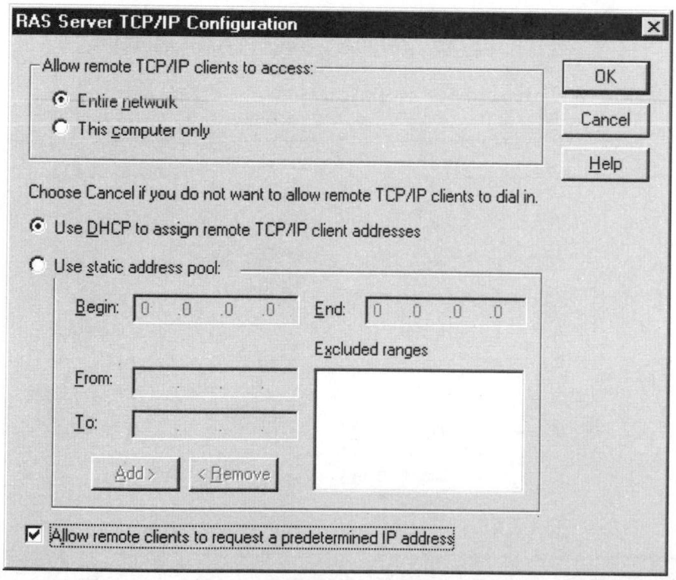

Figure 13-3. *The RAS Server TCP/IP Configuration dialog*

announcement traffic. Last, select "Allow remote clients to request IPX node number" to allow the remote caller to choose its own node number, if requested. Choose OK when done.

10. Now, back in the main Network Configuration dialog (refer to Figure 13-2), select encryption settings as follows:

   ■ **Allow any authentication including clear text:** Select this box if you want to accept connections that use any authentication procedure that is requested by the client (MS-CHAP, MD5-CHAP, PAP, SPAP). This is potentially the least secure authentication scheme.

   ■ **Require encrypted authentication:** Select this box if you want to accept connections that use any authentication requested by the client except PAP (clear text). This requires an encrypted authentication scheme, which is more secure.

   ■ **Require Microsoft encrypted authentication:** Select this box if you want to accept connections that use MS-CHAP authentication. Select the subheading under this choice, Require data encryption, to enforce RSA-RC4 bulk encryption on all data sent or received on the connection. This is the most secure setting and must be used with NT 4 (or 3.5) clients.

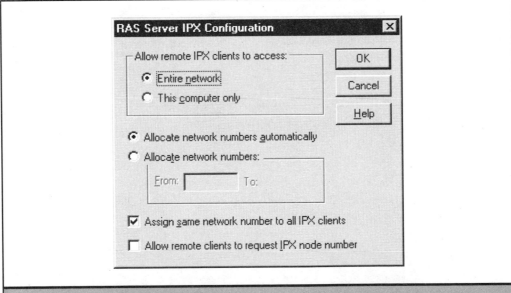

Figure 13-4.   *The RAS Server IPX Configuration dialog*

11. Still in the Network Configuration dialog, choose Enable Multilink to allow NT to combine two or more physical links into a single logical link, as in ISDN B-channel aggregation. This support is similar to MLPP, or Multilink PPP.

12. Finally, choose OK, and return to the Remote Access Setup dialog. Choose the Continue button to commit your changes and exit Remote Access Setup. After NT reviews your settings, you will be taken out to the Network/Services dialog where you should choose Close, after which NT will finalize your RAS settings and ask you to restart your computer. You should answer Yes to reboot, after which the RAS service will be in effect.

Mini-Glossary

CHAP (CHALLENGE HANDSHAKE AUTHENTICATION PROTOCOL)   Using the CHAP protocol, the server sends a randomly generated "challenge" string to the client, along with its hostname. The client uses the hostname to look up the appropriate coded response, combines it with the challenge, and encrypts the string using a one-way hashing function. The result is returned to the server along with the client's hostname. The server now performs the same computation and authenticates the client if its computational result agrees. A major feature of the CHAP protocol is that it sends challenges at regular intervals to make sure that an intruder hasn't replaced the client, for instance, by switching phone lines or networks.

MD5/MS-CHAP (MD5/MICROSOFT-CHALLENGE HANDSHAKE AUTHENTICATION PROTOCOL)   Variants on the CHAP protocol that provide greater security and encryption of the CHAP data passed between the host-server and the client.

PAP (PASSWORD AUTHENTICATION PROTOCOL)   The PAP protocol works in the same way as a clear text login. The client starts authentication by sending the server its username and a password that can be optionally encrypted. The server compares the username and password to one in its database and either authenticates or rejects the client—not a very secure logon protocol.

SPAP (SHIVA PASSWORD AUTHENTICATION PROTOCOL)   A proprietary variant and extension of the PAP authentication protocol developed by the Shiva Corporation, a major remote networking company.

Installing Dial-Up Networking Clients

NT 4 RAS clients are set up by using the Dial-Up Networking icon in the My Computer icon on the desktop. When this icon is selected, the New Phonebook Entry wizard (Figure 13-5) will create a new entry in its phonebook for you to fill out and complete. You may use this wizard, or you may select the "I know all about phonebook entries..." checkbox to take you right into the main setup dialog. Since the wizard assumes so many things, and makes default settings that may not be correct for your installation, we will check this box, which will take us straight to the main setup dialog.

How Dial-Up Works

The following list shows how a remote user accesses resources on the network:

- Through the Remote Access Phone Book, a client dials a Remote Access Server.
- The server sends a challenge to the client.
- The client sends an encrypted response to the server.
- The server checks the response against the user database.
- If the account is valid, the server checks for Remote Access permission.

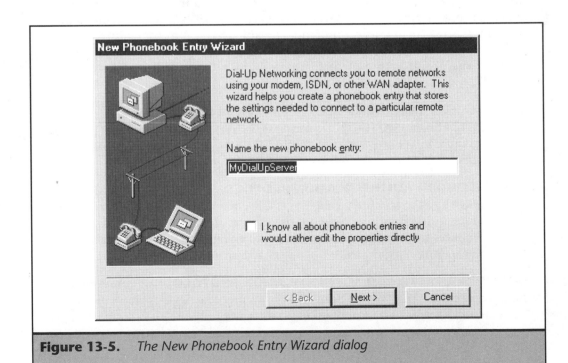

Figure 13-5. *The New Phonebook Entry Wizard dialog*

- If Remote Access permission has been granted, the server connects the client.

- If callback is enabled (see the "User Permissions" section at the end of the chapter), the server calls the client back and repeats the previous steps.

Filling in the Main Phonebook Entry Dialogs

The new Phonebook Entry dialog (Figure 13-6) is where you set up a dial-out connection for a RAS client. The dialog has five tabs, which let you make specific settings for basic information, server settings, script settings, security settings, and X.25 networking. We will examine all of these now.

BASIC This dialog is where you enter basic contact information:

- **Entry name:** A name to identify this phonebook entry.

- **Comment:** Free-form comment field for your own use.

- **Phone number:** The phone number you want your modem to use. The Alternates button allows you to enter a list of alternate phone numbers to use, in case a number is busy or out of service. If you check the Use telephony dialing properties box, telephony settings will be used to choose prefix and suffix dialing codes.

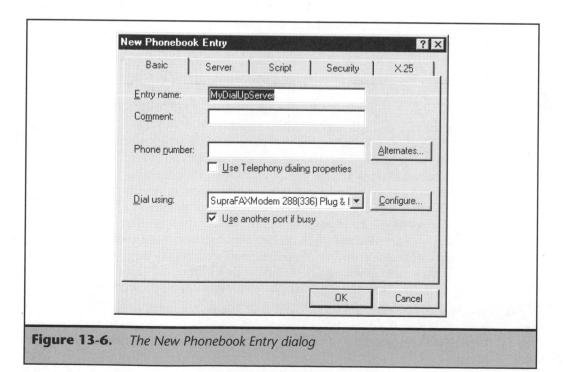

Figure 13-6. *The New Phonebook Entry dialog*

■ **Dial using:** Selects the device to use for this connection. The Configure button displays the Modem Configuration dialog (shown in the following illustration), where settings for initial connection speed, hardware settings, and speaker control may be found. If you check the Use another port if busy box, Dial-Up Networking attempts to try this call on another RAS port, if available.

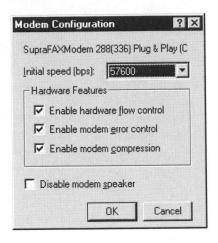

SERVER   Use this dialog to enter information about protocols:

■ **Dial-up server type:** Choose the type of connection you wish to make. Choose PPP, SLIP, or NT 3.1/WfW 3.11. Notice that if you choose NT 3.1, your only choice of network protocol will be NetBEUI.

■ **Network protocols:** Choose the protocols you wish to use when connecting to the server. If you wish to use TCP/IP, also choose TCP/IP Settings to configure the protocol for connection. When selected, the TCP/IP Settings button displays the PPP TCP/IP Settings dialog (see Figure 13-7). The entries here will largely depend on how the server you wish to connect to expects that connection to be made. First, choose whether the server will assign you an IP, or if you have a fixed IP to use. Your administrator will know what is proper. Next, choose whether to enter nameserver addresses, or whether they will be assigned to you at connection time. Again, your administrator should tell you what is proper. If you need to enter values here, IP addresses for DNS and WINS servers may be entered. Finally, two checkboxes are presented. Usually, IP header compression and the use of the default gateway on the remote network are proper settings. Change these only when told to, or if you have determined that these settings need to be changed for a specific reason.

■ **Enable software compression:** Check this box to enable NT to do software compression on the data stream. Usually, this kind of compression will increase throughput and takes the place of hardware compression inside a modem, for instance.

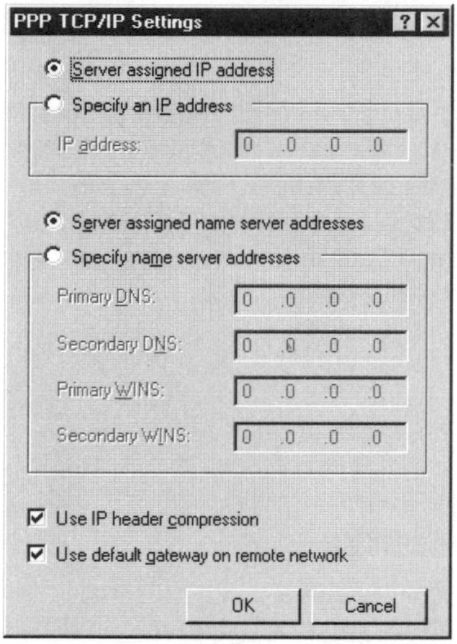

Figure 13-7.   *The PPP TCP/IP Settings dialog*

- **Enable PPP LCP extensions:** To enable newer PPP features. Disable this box only when connecting to older server software, or if you have repeated trouble making a PPP call.

SCRIPT   This dialog allows you to enter a choice of actions to take before and after dialing:

- Choose to do nothing and proceed, to display an interactive terminal window, or to run a script of your choice. The Before Dialing button allows you to choose the same actions before the number is dialed.

SECURITY   This dialog allows you to enter a choice of authentication and encryption policies:

- **Allow any authentication including clear text:** Select this box if you want to accept connections that use any authentication procedure requested by the client (MS-CHAP, MD5-CHAP, PAP, SPAP). This is potentially the least secure authentication scheme.

■ **Require encrypted authentication:** Select this box if you want to accept connections that use any authentication requested by the client except PAP (clear text). This requires an encrypted authentication scheme, which is more secure.

■ **Require Microsoft encrypted authentication:** Select this box if you want to accept connections that use MS-CHAP authentication. This is the most secure and must be used with NT 4 (or 3.5) clients. "Require data encryption" is used to enforce RSA-RC4 bulk encryption on all data sent or received on the connection. "Use current username and password" is used to enforce the use of the same logon name and password that you used at NT logon time.

X.25 This dialog allows you to enter the X.25 provider and address if this kind of connection is to be used. Consult with your network specialist to find out how these parameters affect you and how they should be entered.

Adding a Modem

During RAS setup, working with Dial-Up Networking, or when you are installing any other remote access application, you may be asked to add a modem to NT's database. You can also explicitly add your modem hardware to the data-store that NT keeps. NT uses this information when an application requests data about how it will communicate with the outside world.

The Install New Modem wizard (see Figure 13-8) can be invoked explicitly from the Start/Settings/Control Panel/Modems applet. NT will automatically try to detect the type of modem you have and what communications port it is attached to.

If you check "Don't detect my modem; I will select it from a list," you will immediately be presented with a list of known modems, from which you can pick your model. From here you can also select Have Disk to load a manufacturer's .inf file for your equipment. Otherwise, choose Next, and the wizard will proceed to the detection phase.

Once the modem information has been detected, or has been loaded from the list, NT will finish updating its databases, and the installation will finish. You will then be shown the Modem Properties dialog (see Figure 13-9). This dialog allows you to set properties for the installed modem.

The Modem Properties sheet has several buttons on it:

■ **Add:** Takes you into a new session of the Install New Modem wizard. Use this button to start the wizard if you already have modem devices installed. If there are existing modems in the database, the wizard will not automatically start by choosing the Modems applet, so you must invoke the wizard through the Add button.

■ **Remove:** Removes the highlighted modem from NT's database.

■ **Properties:** Invokes the property sheet for the highlighted modem (see Figure 13-9). Allows you to set speaker volume, maximum connect speed, data format, call preferences, and advanced modem controls.

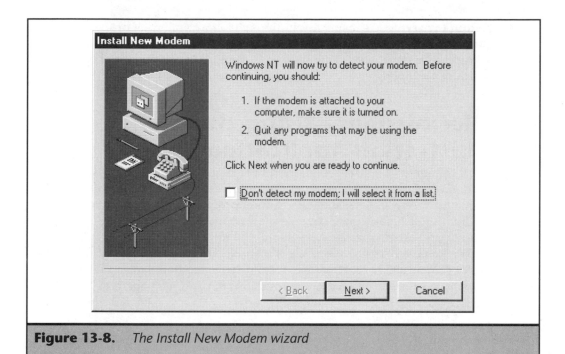

Figure 13-8. *The Install New Modem wizard*

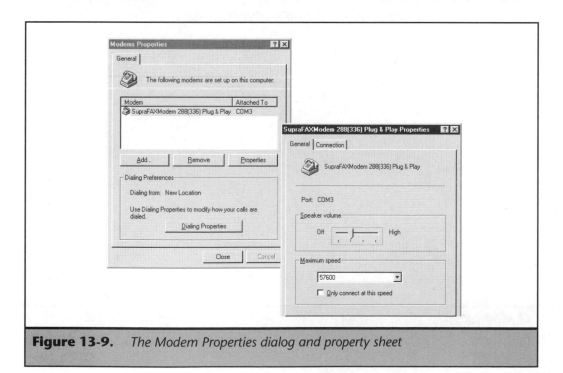

Figure 13-9. *The Modem Properties dialog and property sheet*

■ **Dialing Properties:** Choosing this button will allow you to set properties that affect dialing, such as your originating area code (for long-distance prefixes), calling card and call waiting prefixes, and whether your telephone line uses tone or pulse dialing.

User Permissions—Using the RAS Administration Application

Before users can connect to a RAS server, they must be granted RAS permissions. You can use the Remote Access Admin program to do this and to accomplish other housekeeping tasks. As a status display, the Admin program will also give you up-to-the-minute statistics on how many users are connected, status of RAS ports, and the condition of the system in general (see Figure 13-10).

You use the Remote Access Admin/Users menu to grant permissions. When you first start RAS Admin, a list of RAS servers will be displayed in the main dialog. Highlight the server that you wish to set permissions for, and then open the

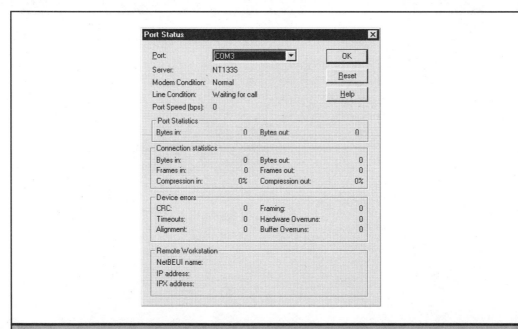

Figure 13-10. *The Port Status dialog*

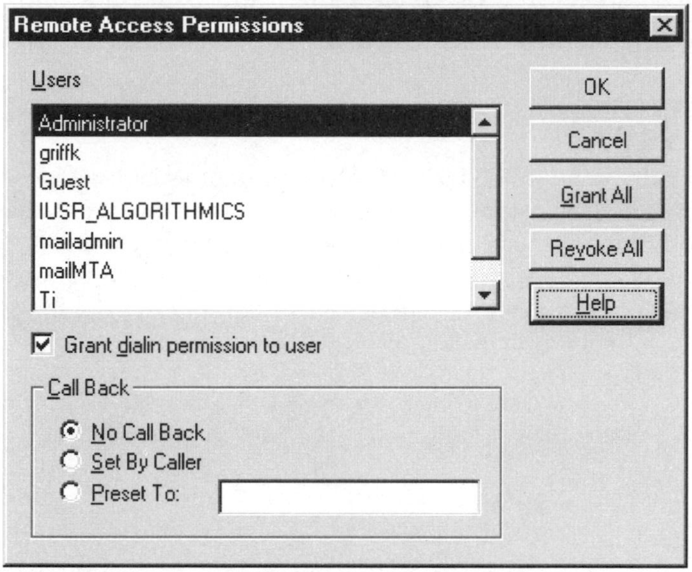

Figure 13-11.   *The Remote Access Permissions dialog*

Users/Permissions dialog by making that menu choice. The Remote Access Permissions dialog will appear (see Figure 13-11). The illustrations and procedures outlined next assume that the user has a valid NT server or domain account.

The Remote Access Permissions dialog has the following fields:

- **Users:** This list shows all users for which RAS permissions on this RAS server may be set. Highlight a user to set his or her permissions.

- **Grant dialin permission to user:** Check this box to grant dial-in permissions to the highlighted user. Then choose OK.

- **Call Back:** Use this area to configure callback security for the highlighted user. Choose No Call Back if you do not wish to use the callback feature. This is the default setting. Choose Set By Caller if you wish to prompt users for callback numbers. Choose Preset To if you wish to require a fixed telephone number for callback. Enter the number in the input field. The server will only use this number on callback. When the user's call reaches the RAS server, the server first determines whether the username and password are correct. Next it responds with a message announcing that the user will be called back, and then it disconnects and calls the user back at the preset number.

- **Grant All button:** Grants everyone in the list RAS dial-in permissions.
- **Revoke All button:** Revokes RAS dial-in permissions for everyone in the list.

What's Next

Remote connectivity is becoming increasingly important as laptops become popular. Many workers are on flextime, or work from home for some part of their day. All of these factors contribute to the need for fast, secure remote access that is easy to set up, and we hope this chapter has given you the information to reach these goals.

Next, in Chapter 14, we take a deeper look inside Windows NT. For starters, we'll be exploring the NT 4 file systems in greater detail.

PART FOUR

Inside Windows NT

Chapter Fourteen

Working with File Systems

One of the most important aspects of any operating system is the way in which it manages files. Even basic computer operations depend heavily on the ability to read and write data in the form of files residing on floppy and hard disk media. This is the primary way that any operating system implements permanent and semi-permanent storage. The actual physical storage medium, however, is of little importance. For instance, IBM is researching holographic-optical storage, but tape is still used extensively for long-term storage. As long as there is sufficient room for system files and user data, physical media can be implemented with any available technology.

Physical File Organization

The way in which files are stored on any physical medium, that is, the logical structure of how files are laid out, is then, the only meaningful and interesting subject to discuss. File systems on PC-type computers have traditionally been based around the most historically popular PC operating system, MS-DOS. Since its conception in the mid '80s, 16-bit Windows has relied on the underlying MS-DOS operating system to implement file handling, with the addition of some Windows-specific 32-bit acceleration modules in Windows 3.1 and Windows for Workgroups.

The most recent versions of Windows—Windows 95 and Windows NT 4—handle their file systems in totally different ways, both with respect to their 16-bit predecessors and in relation to each other. Windows 95 file systems are 32-bit and installable, somewhat like NT, but are implemented, for compatibility, as logical extensions to their MS-DOS/16-bit Windows forebears. There is no built-in support for any file system but FAT (and the CD-ROM file system).

NT, on the other hand, implements installable, totally replaceable file system components that are completely responsible for managing the user's files and drives. There is no dependence on an MS-DOS-type file system, although the FAT file system is fully supported. The most important difference, however, is that NT natively supports multiple file systems simultaneously.

The Basic File Systems

Prior to NT version 4, NT shipped with four different file systems. Although one of these, HPFS (the OS/2 native file system), has been discontinued, all are listed here for completeness. With the exception of HPFS, which is no longer supported, NT 4 has improved and extended these file systems:

File Allocation Table (FAT)

This is the familiar file system currently used by all versions of MS-DOS 16-bit Windows and Windows 95 and is probably the most common NT file system choice. The reasons for choosing this file system include backward compatibility with older workstations and applications. Another reason to use this file system is if you perform dual boot into MS-DOS, 16-bit Windows, Windows 95, or OS/2 on your workstation. The FAT file system is also the only file system that NT supports when floppy disk drives are in use.

New Technology File System (NTFS)

NTFS is the newest file system, created specially for use with NT. It is an advanced file system, having features that both extend and improve on FAT and HPFS and go beyond those designs to support new features and optimizations—such as security and controlled recovery after system failure.

Important features of NTFS include the ability to use very large-capacity media, long filenames, and security attributes on system and user files. NTFS uses Unicode for filenames and directory names. This built-in support for foreign languages and character sets makes NT a truly international standard. NTFS also supports POSIX file system features such as hard links, case-sensitive filenames, and file usage history.

NTFS is an extensible file system, used by an extensible core operating system. Transaction processing, support for fault tolerance, multiple data streams, and support for C2 security are all planned for or already present.

CD-ROM File System (CDFS)

This file system, native to NT, supports long filename Joliet extensions and is used specifically for CD-ROM drives, allowing them to operate as read-only disk drives. More and more software, including NT 4, is shipped only on CD-ROM discs.

High Performance File System (HPFS)

Formerly supported for upgrade reasons, HPFS was originally designed for use with the OS/2 operating system. HPFS was not fault tolerant, and NT now allows HPFS volumes to be converted to NTFS, so all of the reasons for using HPFS in the first place are obviated.

Insider Info

Of primary usefulness is NT's simultaneous support for all of the file systems discussed in this section. You can have one partition on your hard disk formatted for FAT and another formatted for NTFS.

Be aware, however, that these individual file systems contain features that aren't interoperable with other file systems. For example, NTFS saves original creation-time stamps and long filenames. Neither of these features is found in the FAT file system, with the exception of Windows 95's FAT file system (VFAT). You will lose attributes and will have automatically truncated names if you copy files from an NTFS partition to a FAT partition.

> *NOTE:* *In NT 4, Microsoft has dropped support for HPFS, the native file system for OS/2.*

NT File System Support Conventions

NT lays down some ground rules for file systems so its higher-level routines can support them. All file systems must have a hierarchical directory tree, just as the FAT file system does. Directory names and filenames cannot contain the backslash separator character (\ ), ASCII characters below 20 hex (backspace), or other characters explicitly disallowed by any other file systems.

The Win32 subsystem supports mixed case, but searches for directories and files are performed on a case-insensitive basis. Mixed-case creation of directories and filenames that do not differ in any other way will fail. Only the POSIX subsystem fully supports filenames with mixed-case characters.

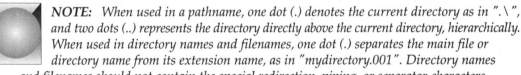

> *NOTE:* *When used in a pathname, one dot (.) denotes the current directory as in ".\ ",*
> *and two dots (..) represents the directory directly above the current directory, hierarchically.*
> *When used in directory names and filenames, one dot (.) separates the main file or*
> *directory name from its extension name, as in "mydirectory.001". Directory names*
> *and filenames should not contain the special redirection, piping, or separator characters*
> *(<, >, | , ;, :, or double quotation marks ("")).*

Physical Disk and File Architecture

A physical disk, such as a floppy or hard disk, is laid out with top and bottom sides that have rings called *tracks*. Within these tracks are sections called *sectors*. A sector is the smallest physical storage unit on a disk, typically 512, 1,024, 2,048, or 4,096 bytes in size. The physical sector size is usually a function of the total size of the disk and the way in which the disk is constructed. The sector size is also a function of the way in which the disk controller works and is usually controllable by formatting commands.

> *NOTE:* *When you issue the Format command, it uses software to direct the disk*
> *controller to organize the disk into tracks and sectors that are appropriate for use by a*
> *particular file system. The sector size is usually determined by the operating system and*
> *the commands issued to the disk controller by the format utility in use, dependent on the*
> *size of the media, controller capabilities, and so on.*

When a file is written to the disk, the file system uses as many sectors as are needed, rounding up to the next integral size, to store the file's data. As an example, a file that is 2,130 bytes long gets written to a disk with three 1,024-byte sectors. Since the 2,130-byte file exceeds the 2,048 bytes that two sectors would take, a third sector is committed. If contiguous physical sectors are available, the file will be written to them.

If a file is written starting in an area of the disk with only one open sector and more are needed, another portion of the disk will be used to write the remainder of the file. In this case, the file is said to be *fragmented*.

Insider Info

File fragmentation becomes a problem, slowing access to a file, when file access is initiated and the file system needs to read or write to many different physical locations. The physical seek/read/write cycle is extended by the motion of the mechanical parts and synchronization needed to orchestrate the entire operation. All of the pieces of the file must be read or written individually, and this takes longer than one continuous operation over consecutive physical locations.

Large sector sizes, when formatted, reduce this delay, since they allow small files a greater chance of ending up in consecutive physical locations, but there is a tradeoff. Large sector sizes commit many partially used sectors to the ends of files. This increases the wasted space on a disk and reduces the amount of files that can be stored on that disk. Programs to defragment an NT disk volume are covered in Appendix A.

The actual way in which data is written and retrieved and the structures that point to that data in the directory depend on the directory and file indexing design used by a particular file system. In the following sections, we'll look at these designs and corresponding storage and retrieval methods for each of NT 4's file systems.

Mini-Glossary

CONTIGUOUS SECTORS   Disk-drive storage that is contained in physically consecutive locations.

DIRECTORIES   A logical construct that organizes files in a hierarchical form, with a root directory and subdirectories underneath the root directory.

FRAGMENTED FILE   A disk file that is stored in noncontiguous sectors.

ROOT DIRECTORY   The primary directory from which all other directories branch.

SECTOR   The smallest logical unit that can be allocated for storage on a physical storage medium.

TRACK   The largest logical unit that can be allocated for storage on a physical storage medium. A track is further broken down into sectors.

VOLUME   A logical partition of a physical disk medium. Volumes are usually identified by drive letters.

The FAT File System

The FAT file system is named for the design it uses to keep track of where a file is located on disk—the File Allocation Table. The FAT is a table of values that stores links to where one allocation unit, consisting of one or more physical disk sectors, is linked to another.

An Expanding Design

The FAT file system is a straightforward design originally targeted at floppy disks with limited directory structures (see Figure 14-1). The design has been extended and improved with time, and the ability to handle much larger media and structure has been added. The original size structures were 12 bits long, making the maximum size of a volume, or *partition,* 32MB. With the advent of larger hard disks, FAT was extended to provide support for larger volumes and extended filenames in NT 4 and Windows 95.

File Allocation Issues

A disk formatted with the FAT file system is allocated in clusters, or *allocation units,* made up of a number of physical disk sectors whose size is determined by the size of the partition. When a file is created, an entry is created in the directory, and the first

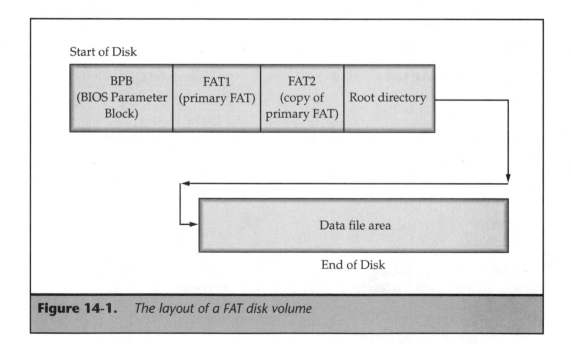

Figure 14-1. *The layout of a FAT disk volume*

cluster number containing data is established. This entry in the FAT either indicates that this is the last cluster of the file or points to the next cluster.

In the FAT file system, the base, or *root*, directory has a predetermined size and location on the disk. Directories are just special files that contain data in the form of entries for each file contained in the directory. The entry for each file includes the filename, attributes, modification time and date, starting allocation unit, and file size. Each file has a pointer to the next allocation unit that holds the next chunk of data, if there is any more data. This pointer scheme is referred to by programmers as a *linked list*.

The directory entry points to the first allocation unit containing the file data. If the file contents extend into another allocation unit, there will be a pointer to the next allocation unit (cluster) in the chain. Figure 14-2 shows how a file is stored in a FAT volume. Because the file spans more than one allocation unit, it has links to the next location. The end of the file chain is marked by the sequence FFF.

NOTE: *The information covered in the preceding paragraphs is common in all FAT file system implementations. However, the base FAT functionality is extended in NT 4. Normal FAT filenames are limited to eight plus three characters. NT adds long filename functionality plus additional time stamps for showing when the file was created or last accessed. Long filenames can support mixed case, 256-character-long names. The time-stamp information is used primarily by POSIX applications.*

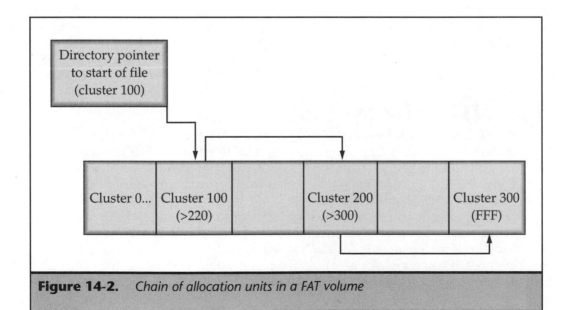

Figure 14-2.   *Chain of allocation units in a FAT volume*

Insider Info

Attribute bytes are usually used in the FAT file system to denote read-only, hidden, or some other status. Some bits are used only by the operating system. There is a bit that indicates that the file is a subdirectory and another that marks the file as a volume label.

NT 4 extends the use of these attribute bits to support long filenames (up to 256 characters) in a way that does not affect normal MS-DOS access to the partition. When a file is created with a long or mixed-case filename, NT creates a conventional directory entry for the file, supplying a normal MS-DOS eight-plus-three name. In addition, one or more secondary directory entries are created for the file. One directory entry is created for each additional 13 characters in the long filename, and NT sets the volume, read-only, system, and hidden file attribute bits of the secondary directory entry to mark it as part of a long filename.

Vanilla MS-DOS does not show directory entries with these attribute bits set, so these entries become invisible to other FAT-based operating systems. Other MS-DOS–based systems, with the exception of Windows 95, only see the eight-plus-three filename.

CAUTION: While most MS-DOS utilities can be used with NT 4, it is dangerous to use old MS-DOS disk utilities that directly manipulate the FAT table. These utilities may regard the long filename entries as errors and try to fix them. This may lead to permanent damage to the logical structure of the FAT volume. Unless a disk utility is certified for use with NT 4, do not use it to perform disk repair or defragmentation. You can use the Windows 95 versions of ScanDisk and Chkdsk to repair a damaged FAT partition, but do not use any other Windows 95 disk utility on an NT 4 FAT partition containing long filenames.

The NTFS File System

The New Technology File System (NTFS) is unique to NT and is NT's native file system. NTFS provides better performance and reliability than the FAT file system. NTFS is optimized to perform read, write, search, and fault-tolerant operations on extremely large media. NTFS files and volumes can be up to 2^{64} bytes (16 exabytes or 18,446,744,073,709,551,616 bytes).

NTFS includes security features such as data access control and ownership permissions that are important for the protection of sensitive and private data. NTFS files and directories can have individually assigned permissions whether they are shared or not. If you want to be able to assign permissions to individual files, you have to use an NTFS volume to store those files.

> **NOTE:**   *NTFS is based on a file-object design. Every piece of information on an NTFS volume is viewed by the operating system as a file, or part of a file. There are no FAT-style system sectors on an NTFS volume. Every sector is viewed as belonging to a file and thus an object.*

The NTFS Master File Table

Each file contained on an NTFS volume has a representative record in a file called the Master File Table (MFT), as shown in Figure 14-3. The first 16 records of this table are reserved for administrative information. The first record of this table holds a description of the MFT itself; the second holds an MFT *mirror record*. If the first MFT record is lost or corrupted, NTFS reads the second record to find the MFT mirror file, whose first record is a copy of the first record of the MFT. The MFT and MFT mirror data is recorded in the boot sector. Another copy of the boot sector is located at the logical center of the disk.

The third record of the MFT is the log file, used for fault tolerance and file recovery. After the first 16, records in the MFT are for each file on the volume. Directories are also viewed as files and are stored as such. The MFT contains a certain amount of space for each file record (see Figure 14-4). The attributes of a file are written to the allocated space in the MFT, and small files or directories can be wholly written to the space left over within the MFT record.

Optimization of Data Access

NTFS optimizes data access. Compared to the FAT file system—which uses a table to store the names and locations, or *indexes*, of each file—NTFS does not need to read a

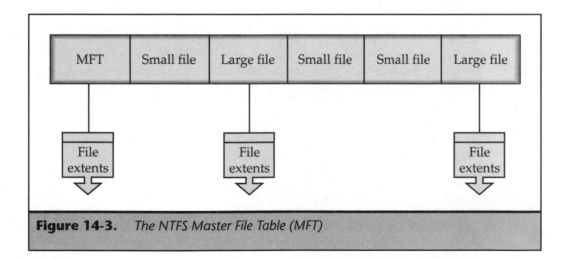

Figure 14-3.   *The NTFS Master File Table (MFT)*

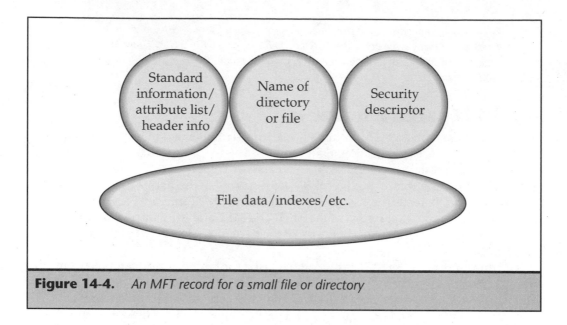

Figure 14-4.   *An MFT record for a small file or directory*

table and then index into the disk. Once you have looked up an NTFS file, the data is in the same place, sometimes within a single record.

Small directory records can reside entirely within the MFT structure. For large directories, a B-trees structure is used with records containing pointers to external clusters, which contain these large directory entries.

NTFS Is Object/Attribute Based

This kind of design treats all files as objects that have user-defined and system-defined attributes. From the file system's perspective, each file or directory is treated as a set of file attributes. File elements such as the filename, security information, and data are treated as file attributes. NTFS file attributes are identified by an attribute type code and, in some cases, by an attribute name.

When attributes can be written within the MFT record, they are called *resident* attributes. When a file is too large to fit all of its attributes in its MFT record, some of its attributes are made *nonresident*, which means they are written in one or more contiguous runs of disk space on the volume.

The following list explains each attribute type:

Attribute Type	Contents
Standard Information	Includes time stamps, link count, etc.
Attribute List	Includes all other attributes; for large files.
Filename	Long filenames are stored as Unicode characters, the standard MS-DOS filename.

Attribute Type	Contents
Security Descriptor	Includes permissions for access, ownership, etc.
Data	Includes actual file data.
Index Root	Used to implement directories.
Index Allocation	Is specific to the type of directory implementation.
Volume Information	Includes data for the volume system file, such as volume name, version, etc.
Bitmap	Records in-use bitmaps for the MFT or directory.
Extended Attribute Information	Related to OS/2 file servers; unused by NT.
Extended Attributes	Related to OS/2 file servers; unused by NT.

Mini-Glossary

BOOT SECTOR　　Read automatically at system startup, the boot sector is the sector of a disk drive that contains the system-defined startup files for the operating system.

FILE ATTRIBUTES　　In respect to NTFS, refers to all aspects of a file or directory, such as the name, data, etc.

LOG FILE　　A special NTFS file that is used to recover data in case of a system crash and holds information on the state of the file system.

MIRROR FILE/RECORD　　A backup copy, kept by the operating system or created by the user, of a file or record.

MASTER FILE TABLE (MFT)　　In NTFS, the primary storage table for all NTFS file objects and attributes.

NONRESIDENT ATTRIBUTES　　Those parts of an NTFS file that cannot be stored in the MFT table.

RESIDENT ATTRIBUTES　　Those parts of an NTFS file that can be stored (will fit) in the MFT table.

SYSTEM FILES　　Special operating system files that are needed for startup or execution of the operating system.

File System Integrity and Recoverability

Before NTFS was designed, two types of file systems were traditionally used to maintain file system integrity: careful write and lazy write systems. With the advent of the NTFS file system, a third type of system is now used in NT: the recoverable system.

Careful-Write Systems

An example of a careful-write system is the FAT file system used in MS-DOS. A *careful-write* system serializes writes to the disk while performing updates and modifications to the volume structure. Most updates are made one at a time, and disk writes for each update are ordered so that if the system fails between any two disk writes, the volume is left in a mostly consistent state, with the possible exception of the last disk operation before the failure. In almost all cases, the volume is usable and repairable.

 NOTE: *On careful-write systems, all disk writes are serialized, which is not optimal, because it slows disk access.*

Lazy-Write Systems

Used by Windows 95's and NT's FAT file systems, as well as almost all Unix file systems, *lazy-write* systems use caching mechanisms to speed up disk access and write back or update to disk their volume information when a machine is idle or when its processing duties are minimal. Usually, lazy-write file systems provide some way to recover data should a failure happen before all data can be committed.

 NOTE: *Recovery from disk failures and crashes with a true lazy-write file system involves scanning entire disk structures and is therefore much slower than with a careful-write file system. Also, more than a single write failure may occur, since caching mechanisms might not flush their buffers until sufficient information, or idle time, is accrued.*

Using lazy write, all data is accessed through a disk cache. While the file system is actively being used, data to be written to disk accumulates in the cache. This way, the user almost never has to wait while physical writes are being performed. Most of the time, those writes can take place during a lull in disk activity, depending on the size of the disk cache.

Also, lazy write shields the user from excessive physical disk activity in which many updates to the same data may take place in a short time period, as in a collection database. The file system accumulates all of the writes in cache memory, committing them to disk only when the cache is flushed. That way, the amount of actual disk activity is reduced, and the overhead involved in physically writing and rewriting similar data is minimized.

Recoverable Systems

Recoverable systems use a combination of lazy-write and transaction-logging technologies. This means that you get the benefits of speed inherent in a lazy-write file system in addition to almost instant fault recovery. NTFS uses transaction-logging and recovery techniques to ensure that a volume is recovered in the shortest time possible at boot time. The transaction logging mechanism has minimal impact on speed, and system overhead is minor when compared to careful-write file systems.

Insider Info

NTFS is designed to recover from system crashes, even though data may still be lost because of I/O errors. To make NTFS even more robust, disk mirroring and parity striping can be used to recover from a failure. Even if the boot record of an NTFS partition is damaged or lost, you can still boot the computer from another partition or another physical drive and have access to the damaged NTFS partition.

NTFS also implements a technique called *hot-fixing*. If a bad sector is encountered during normal operation, NTFS moves the sector's data and marks the offending sector as bad. This operation is transparent and eliminates error messages that are normally generated in such cases—for example, when a FAT file system's "Abort, Retry, or Fail?" message is displayed because of a sector failure.

Transaction and Recovery Mechanisms

NTFS treats every update or write operation on an NTFS volume as a loggable transaction. When an NTFS file, or attribute, is modified, the Log File service stores redo and undo information for that transaction. The *redo* information lets NTFS know how to recover by repeating the transaction, and the *undo* information lets NTFS perform a transaction rollback in case the transaction was not completed or was in error (see Figure 14-5).

When a transaction is successfully completed, the file update is committed to disk. If a transaction is not completed, NTFS rolls back the transaction, using the logged undo information.

NOTE: For boot-time recovery, NTFS performs three passes on a volume: an analysis pass, a redo pass, and an undo pass. NTFS uses the analysis pass to evaluate damage— analyze the extent of what must be updated. Then, the redo pass executes the logged transactions, leading to the undo pass, which rolls back any incomplete transactions.

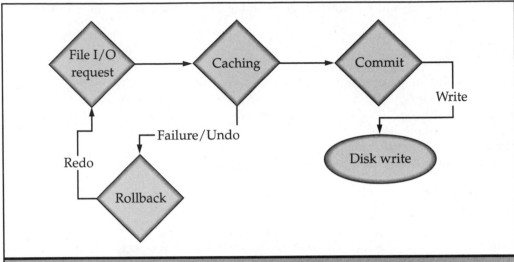

Figure 14-5. *NTFS transactions for recovery and rollback*

NTFS Lazy Commit

Lazy commit is a way of optimizing the NTFS transaction logging mechanism in the same manner as lazy write does for disk file I/O. Transaction completion and commitment information is cached and then logged as a background process. If a failure occurs before this information is logged, NTFS will perform completion checks on the transaction. Since no partial modifications are ever written to an NTFS volume, a transaction that cannot be insured is rolled back.

Periodic Log-File Checkpoints

The transaction log must have waypoints so that transactions can be rolled back to the last commit, in case of a crash. NTFS does this by writing transaction commit status to the log, as a checkpoint on the commit cache, every few seconds.

Mini-Glossary

CAREFUL-WRITE SYSTEM   A file system, such as FAT for MS-DOS, in which all disk writes are performed physically and serially, holding system resources as they occur.

LAZY COMMIT   A method used by NTFS to cache transactional data so that logging of that data is optimally reduced in frequency.

LAZY-WRITE SYSTEM A method used by NTFS and FAT for NT (and Windows 95) that uses a memory cache to optimally reduce physical disk write frequency and duration.

LOG-FILE SERVICE That part of the NTFS file system that implements the logging of transactional data for recoverability.

RECOVERABLE FILE SYSTEM Like NTFS, a file system that utilizes one or more methods, like transactions, in order to implement recoverability after a crash affecting the file system.

POSIX File System Compliance

POSIX file system compliance lets Unix applications be ported to NT. NT 4 is fully compliant with the Institute of Electrical and Electronics Engineers (IEEE) standard 1003.1, which is a standard for file naming and identification. The following POSIX-compliant features are included in NTFS:

- **Case-sensitive naming:** POSIX applications can create case-sensitive filenames where two or more filenames can differ only in case (for example, MyText.Doc and mytext.doc).
- **Hard links:** A POSIX file can be given more than one name. Applications may then use two or more different filenames to access the same data. These filenames can be located in the same or different directories.
- **Additional time stamps:** POSIX files have time stamps that show when the file was last accessed or modified.

NT Services for Macintosh

NT Server includes Services for Macintosh, giving Macintosh users access to files and file sharing on an NT Server. Services for Macintosh stores file sharing folder privileges as NT permissions, so there is only one set of permissions on a folder or file. These permissions are enforced for NT and Macintosh users.

NOTE: Macintosh users cannot see these file permissions because AppleShare only supports folder permissions.

Macintosh clients must access files stored only on NTFS volumes. It is not possible to use FAT volumes when sharing with Macintosh clients. Most Macintosh filenames will remain unchanged, since NTFS supports long filenames. Macintosh resource forks and Finder information on each Macintosh file are stored as NTFS streams.

NOTE: *If you want to automatically create the User Authentication Module volumes for Macintosh clients, an NTFS partition must be available when you enable Services for Macintosh.*

Partitions, Volume Sets, and Stripe Sets

Physical disks must be partitioned before use. The logical partitions that you create may be formatted for use by any of NT's file systems, and you may have more than one partition per physical disk. These formatted partitions, or volumes, are assigned drive letters, depending on their physical position within the system and their type. If there is a primary partition on the first hard drive and it is marked as active, it gets assigned the first drive letter, C:

NOTE: *The floppy disks are always assigned as A: and B: The first hard disk drive letter is always assigned to the first recognized primary partition.*

This process is repeated for all hard drives in the system. Once the letters have been assigned to the first primary partitions on all drives in the system, letters are assigned to the recognized logical disks in the extended partitions using the same scheme. After all of the logical disks in the extended partitions are assigned letters, one last scan is made of the drives, and letters are assigned to any remaining recognized primary partitions. As a default, the CD-ROM drive is always assigned as the last drive letter in the chain, after the hard disk partitions are assigned.

Now, let's review some disk drive formatting terminology:

- **Boot partition:** The part of a physical disk that is formatted to hold the boot system files, which allow the computer to start up. The information contained in the boot sector(s) is only sufficient to start the rest of the operating system load process. This is traditionally called *booting* the computer, since this small piece of software allows the computer to pull itself up by its "bootstraps." On x86 computers, this is always the first hard disk, or disk 0. The boot partition must be a primary partition, and it must be marked as active by the setup software.

- **NT multi-boot:** A special NT boot loader that displays a menu of boot choices. This is especially useful if you have more than one operating system installed on your computer. For instance, if you have NT 4 and Windows 95 installed, the multi-boot menu displays a menu with these choices. The NT multi-boot menu always displays at least two choices: NT and NT in VGA, or default, mode. This second choice is a recovery mode that uses the base display driver to recover from having made system settings that might fault. You can edit the BOOT.INI file to show any number of multi-boot choices or to customize what is seen when the menu is displayed. BOOT.INI is in the root directory on your primary bootable hard disk drive and partition, and it is marked read-only, so to edit it you must first clear that attribute by using Explorer, or edit it with the *attrib* command from the command prompt.

■ **System partition:** The partition that holds the NT system files, usually found under the WINNT subdirectory. In most cases, the boot partition and the system partition are the same.

■ **Primary partition:** Any primary partition can be used as a system partition. This is the part of a physical disk that can be used for operating system files. Each physical disk can have as many as four partitions, all primary, or three primary and one extended partition.

■ **Extended partition:** A partition that can be further subdivided into any number (within system limitations) of logical drives. Since primary partitions cannot be further subdivided, you use an extended partition to divide the disk further, creating logical drives that are then assigned individual drive letters. An extended partition can be used to create volume sets and volumes for fault-tolerance schemes. If the physical drive does not have a boot partition (is not bootable), you can create a single extended partition that spans the entire drive.

■ **Volume set:** When you create primary and extended partitions on hard disk drives, you may by chance, or purposely, end up with leftover free space. This free space is not usable and is uncommitted. If you have many small areas of free space, you may choose to utilize this space by creating a volume set. When you create a volume set, you are choosing to combine multiple areas of free space in order to format these areas and use them as a single logical disk with a single drive letter. You use the Disk Administrator utility to create and manage volume sets. You can include up to 32 areas of free space residing on one or more physical disks. Volume sets can be formatted with the FAT or NTFS file systems, but you can only extend a volume set that has been formatted as an NTFS volume. Other operating systems do not recognize a volume set and do not provide fault-tolerant features. If a volume set is broken because of disk failure, you will lose all data in the entire volume—not just the broken part. Volume sets provide a way to efficiently use leftover free space on hard disk drives.

■ **Disk striping:** A scheme used to increase disk performance by directing the file system to divide the data into blocks, spreading these blocks, in order, across all disks (partitions) in the striping array (see Figure 14-6). The data is transparently broken up or reassembled using the data blocks from these different locations. Because the data blocks simultaneously get written to or read from all partitions in the striped set, striping provides the highest disk performance available in NT. You can create stripe sets using the Disk Administrator utility. This kind of striping is not fault tolerant, and if a stripe is lost, you will lose the entire striped set.

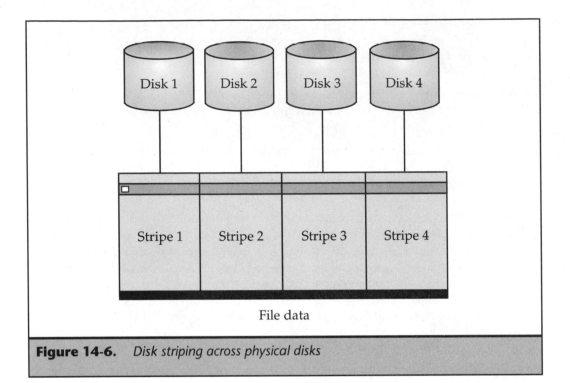

Figure 14-6. *Disk striping across physical disks*

 NOTE: *There are two types of disk striping. NT 4 Advanced Server allows you to create and manage fault-tolerant disk striping with parity (RAID Level 5). This is different from the disk striping just discussed. Striping with parity stores parity information along with the striped data for redundancy. Striping with parity is discussed later in this chapter.*

Setting and Changing a Partition's File System

There are three ways to install a file system on a disk partition. The first way is only available for the boot partition and only during installation. You can tell the NT setup program which file system you want when it asks you where the NT files should be installed. The two other methods are

■ From the command prompt, use the *format* utility with the /FS: parameter to specify which file system you want for an existing partition. The choices are FAT and NTFS.

■ Use the *convert* utility to convert an existing, formatted partition from FAT to NTFS. This is a one-way conversion. Convert will not convert NTFS-formatted partitions back to FAT. Using the convert utility has the advantage of leaving all existing files intact, so you may safely use it without backing up the files already stored on the partition you wish to convert.

TIP: Whether you choose to convert to NTFS or not, ensure that the FAT volume you choose to install Windows NT has at least 80MB (megabytes) of free disk space.

With the Format Utility

By using the format utility, you can format a partition as an NTFS or FAT volume by specifying the /FS:NTFS or /FS:FAT options. You will lose all existing data and be given the chance to rename the formatted volume. You use the format command from the command prompt. This command will not work on the system partition. (It would wipe out the NT system files.)

With the Convert Utility

By using the convert utility, you can convert an existing FAT partition to NTFS while leaving all data files intact. To convert a volume to NTFS, type

convert *volume*: /FS:NTFS

where *volume* is the drive letter of the volume you want to convert.

You cannot choose to convert a volume from NTFS to FAT. Also, if you choose to convert the active boot partition, the convert utility will not run immediately. Rather, an entry will be stored in the Registry, and convert will be started the next time you reboot the computer.

CAUTION: You should not convert the boot partition on most RISC-based computers. RISC firmware is stored on the boot partition of FAT file system–based files on many RISC computers. If you convert such a computer's boot partition, it will then be unusable. You will have to run ARCINST.EXE from the installation CD to fix the partition. If you want to use NTFS in such a computer, create a FAT boot partition large enough to hold the HAL.DLL and OSLOADER.EXE files. You can then use the rest of the disk as NTFS.

NT and File System Fault Tolerance

File system fault tolerance is available in NT Server. We'll look at the methods for implementing a fault-tolerant file system here, including RAID level 5 fault tolerance, in the form of disk striping with parity. Other fault-tolerant mechanisms, covered elsewhere in this book, can be used to enhance file system fault handling. These include tape backup and uninterruptable power supply shutdown and alert methods. Here, we see three primary fault-tolerance mechanisms for use with NT Server:

- Disk mirroring
- Disk duplexing

■ Disk striping with parity

Disk Mirroring

Disk mirroring employs a simple method of duplication to ensure that data is secure in case of hardware failure. This method uses two different partitions residing on different drives but connected to the same physical disk controller. Any file system may be used with disk mirroring. All data on the primary use partition is automatically copied, or *mirrored*, onto the secondary backup partition. In this way, two identical copies of the data are always available in case the physical disk that carries one copy fails. The physical disk drive and created partitions used in disk mirroring do not have to be identical, although for administrative ease, the partition size should be similar. The secondary, backup partition cannot be smaller than the primary-use partition it is mirroring.

Disk Duplexing

Disk duplexing extends the fault tolerance of disk mirroring by utilizing a second disk controller attached to the secondary mirror disk drive. The only difference to the operating system is that by using a second disk controller for the mirror drive, further I/O performance gains can be realized, because simultaneous operations can take place on each disk controller. Otherwise, NT treats mirroring and duplexing exactly alike.

Disk Striping with Parity (RAID Level 5)

Disk striping with parity is similar to normal disk striping in that data is broken into multiple blocks and written to or read from different partitions on different physical drives. Disk striping with parity extends this model, adding fault tolerance by interleaving a parity stripe with the data stripes (see Figure 14-7). The parity stripe is a byte parity stripe of the data stripes.

There must be at least 3 and no more than 32 physical disks in a striped set with parity. Partitions should be approximately the same size on each disk. The disks can use one or more physical disk controllers, and performance is enhanced if multiple controllers are employed.

Insider Info

NT uses a special intercessionary device driver when any of the available fault-tolerant disk schemes are employed. The driver, called FTDISK.SYS, receives commands, processes them, and reacts programmatically with a response based on the fault-tolerant scheme employed. In the case of striping with parity, the file system generates requests to read or write data from a file, and these requests are channeled through FTDISK.SYS.

For a read request, FTDISK calculates the disk stripe the data is in, and by using further information about the number of disks in the set, it calculates the physical disk and location to read from.

Write requests are more complicated, since parity calculations have to be made when breaking up the data into the striped set blocks and since information needs to be dispatched to the different physical disks and disk locations. The parity stripe is updated dynamically, because parity is cumulative, and finally the parity and the new information blocks are written out to the physical disks.

Fault Tolerance with Parity Striping

Scenarios for fault tolerance with parity striping include the broad cases discussed next.

Stripe Unreadable

This scenario can happen when a sector fault affects a particular disk stripe. Inherent in the fault tolerance of the striping with parity scheme is the ability to recreate any one data stripe, so long as all other stripes, along with the parity stripe, are intact. By subtracting, logically XORing the remaining data stripes from the parity stripe, the bad data stripe can be recreated. Writing with a bad stripe is accomplished in the same way. The bad stripe itself is not written, but the parity stripe is updated, and by the same extrapolations as in reading, carries the data stripe information on. The good data stripes are read and subtracted from the parity stripe, leaving the bad data

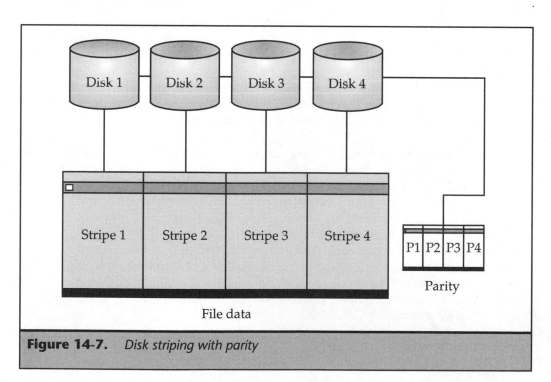

Figure 14-7. *Disk striping with parity*

stripe's information. Then the parity stripe is dynamically updated with that information and written back.

Parity Stripe Unreadable

The only other case for fault-tolerant behavior is when the parity stripe is rendered unreadable. Because the parity stripe is only used during a write operation, reading data is unaffected. Until parity regeneration is accomplished, writes take place as in normal disk striping, without regard to the parity stripe.

Error Recovery and Identification of Broken Sets

When a stripe cannot be written, or a mirrored or duplexed set has a problem, the situation is referred to as a *broken set*. The methods of error detection and error recovery are similar for striping and mirroring schemes.

Insider Info

When errors are detected in these fault-tolerant schemes, NT takes immediate action, because it always tries to keep these fault-tolerant sets from breaking. Most failures are at the sector level, so NT first tries to reassign faulting sectors, recovering data if possible. This sector *remapping* is the first-level response to a file system I/O fault. Remapping is only done for physical disks that support this feature. In general, only disks with Small Computer System Interface (SCSI) interfaces are designed to support sector remapping. If remapping is not possible and the set cannot be prevented from breaking, a high-severity error is written to the event log.

The partition containing a sector failure that cannot be fixed is identified as an *orphan*. An orphan partition is only identified as a result of a write operation. Read failures do not orphan a partition since reads do not affect the physically stored data.

During boot and startup, a severe error is written to the event log if both partitions in mirrored or duplexed sets cannot be located. The remaining partition is then used. If the unlocated partition is part of a parity striped set, a severe error is written to the event log, and the missing partition is marked as an orphan. Then, using the fault-tolerant features of the particular scheme employed, the system continues on in normal fashion.

No matter what kind of fault-tolerant method is employed, partitions are not marked as orphans if all partitions in a set are missing at boot time. This simplifies and speeds the fault-tolerant mechanism since the problem may be as simple as sets contained on drives that have been temporarily disconnected from the disk controller, as in portable SCSI arrays.

Managing the Recovery of Orphan Partitions

Using the fault-tolerant features of the particular scheme in use, NT continues to function normally—with orphan partitions—until the problem that caused a partition to be orphaned is fixed. Usually, a replacement disk or partition has to be supplied, and until it is, the set containing an orphan is not fault tolerant. If another failure occurs in the set, data can be lost. This is a probable scenario because many primary failures are due to a problem with hardware and may cascade. The administrator should employ recovery methods as soon as possible. To perform the recovery process, follow the procedures outlined in the following sections.

With a Mirror of Duplex Sets

If this is a mirror or duplex set, break the set using the Break Mirror option in the Disk Administrator utility. This converts the remaining good partition into a normal partition and assigns the set's drive letter to it. The orphan is assigned the next available drive letter. Next, create a new set using existing free space on another disk, or replace the bad physical drive and reestablish the set relationship using Disk Administrator. Finally, restart the computer, and NT will automatically restore the mirrored data to the newly replaced member of the set.

With Parity of Duplex Sets

If the orphan partition is in a parity-striped set, use Disk Administrator to regenerate the set from the remaining data after disks have been replaced or a new free area has been selected. Once free-space selection has been accomplished, choose the Regenerate command from the Fault Tolerance menu. When the system is rebooted, the stripes will be recalculated and restored to the new space provided.

REMINDER: Choose free space that is the same size as the old area that was orphaned.

Mini-Glossary

BOOT PARTITION The partition where boot files are stored. The boot partition always resides on the first physical disk in x86 machines.

BROKEN SET A fault-tolerant set, one of whose members has been orphaned by an unrecoverable I/O error.

DISK DUPLEXING Disk mirroring using different physical disk controllers for each disk in the mirror set.

DISK MIRRORING   A fault-tolerance scheme in which data from one partition, residing on a physical disk, is automatically mirrored, or copied, to another similar partition residing on another physical disk drive.

DISK STRIPING   A performance-enhancing scheme in which data is written to more than one disk at a time, being first broken up into blocks so it can be *striped* or laid across multiple disk drives. This greatly increases data throughput in file system operations.

DISK STRIPING WITH PARITY   As in normal disk striping, a scheme where data is written and read back in blocks residing physically on different hard disk drives. The addition of a parity channel (stripe) makes this scheme fault tolerant, because the data for any one stripe can be regenerated from the parity stripe if a data stripe is rendered unreadable.

EXTENDED PARTITION   A disk partition that can be further subdivided into sections that can be assigned logical drive letters to appear as if they are distinct, separate physical drives.

FIRMWARE   In RISC-based computers, the software instructions, usually stored on disk, that are loaded at boot time—used as basic instructions or stored for use in extending the capability of the hardware, as opposed to any software that implements application or driver code. Although reference is made here to *RISC firmware*—the actual instruction set extensions for that CPU platform—firmware can exist on any hardware platform and is commonly used in peripherals that have onboard controllers.

ORPHAN   A member of a fault-tolerant set that has exhibited a nonrecoverable I/O error. NT marks this member as an orphan so that administration facilities within NT can exclude it from the set and continue processing normally.

PARITY   The cumulative count, or abstraction by logical operation, of a stream of data. Used generally as a check against which data can be compared for regeneration and integrity assurance.

PRIMARY PARTITION   A disk partition capable of holding system files such as the NT operating system files that are loaded just after initial computer startup.

VOLUME SET   A space-usage scheme that allows the use of otherwise uncommitted free disk space on multiple physical disk drives to be combined into a single logical partition, which is assigned a single drive letter for subsequent use.

EXCLUSIVE OR (XOR)   A logical operation that can be performed on a stream of data. The basic operation is expressed as a truth table. On a bitwise basis, if both elements of an XOR operation are 1, the outcome will be 0. If either element is 0, the outcome will be 1. If both elements are 0, the outcome will be 1. XOR can be used to perform bitwise subtraction.

What's Next

NT 4 offers many file system features. To take advantage of some of the more sophisticated options is overkill for some but the difference that makes a secure, long-lasting installation for others. This chapter has covered the major file system features. Many of these options and methods have control parameter entries in the Registry. The Registry is covered in Chapter 17, so read on.

The next chapter looks ahead to some usage and performance implications in keeping with support for legacy code—Dynamic Data Exchange (DDE). It also discusses Remote Procedure Calls (RPCs), which are found only on high-performance workstation operating systems. These important NT features allow you to take advantage of Interprocess Communication (IPC), data sharing, and a concept called distributed processing.

Chapter Fifteen

RPCs, DDE/NetDDE, and Interprocess Communication

N T 4 contains some powerful mechanisms for interprocess communication (IPC). Interprocess communication allows applications running on the same or different machines to communicate and cooperate at runtime. IPC mechanisms can be as simple as two or more programs having access to a shared disk file, where they leave each other messages and data in a way that serializes access to the file, so the right application gets the right data. This simple example does not really suffice for many real-world situations, and many, more sophisticated examples of IPC exist in modern operating systems. NT 4 contains support for several types of IPC mechanisms, some of which extend into gray areas that demand a redefinition of what IPC schemes can do.

The current IPC facilities in NT 4 include

- Mailslots
- Named pipes
- Component Object Model (COM; covered in Chapter 22)
- Shared memory/shared DLLs/shared file mapping
- The NetBIOS network transport (covered in Chapter 5)
- Windows Sockets (covered in Chapter 11)
- Remote procedure call (RPC)
- Dynamic Data Exchange/Network Dynamic Data Exchange (DDE/NetDDE)

In this chapter we'll take a look at RPCs, DDE, and shared memory techniques.

RPCs: The Distributed Solution

For many years, computer scientists wished that they could tie all of the computers on their networks together. This way they could have one giant distributed computer with the power to process pieces of code on each individual computer in a coordinated way and make an application distribute its workload and processing work across the entire network. These same scientists, wishing for this distributed scheme, also wanted to use the same mechanism to be able to control the amount of front-end processing that their less powerful but still useful user workstations would have to do. After all, if you've got an $8 million computer, capable of servicing many workstations and minicomputers, why not use it to alleviate some of the heavier processing duties of the smaller machines on the network? RPCs do both of these things, simultaneously or individually.

A Real-World Situation

Let's take a look at what an RPC can do in a real-world situation. In our model, illustrated in Figure 15-1, we see that there are three computers on the test network: one workstation running a compute-intensive graphics program and two large multiprocessor "microframes" with state-of-the-art architecture, a lot of RAM, and large disk arrays. Our workstation has been given the task of computing transforms for a large TrueColor animation sequence, spanning many megabytes of data, and having to do calculations involving matrix math, bit transforms, and color quantization (a type of graphics operation that reduces and normalizes color in a graphics picture).

Our workstation has limited processing power, and we have to run the graphics processing application on the workstation, because it outputs its graphics directly to the display on the computer where it is running. In the days before RPC, we would just have to take the performance hit and smile. All of the background processing, disk access, and display functions would have to be handled by the workstation's CPU, as in Figure 15-2. We could store the large graphics file on one of the larger computers, but they cannot help us in processing some of our data and increasing our throughput.

RPC to the Rescue

Now along comes RPC to the rescue. Since we are seriously compute-bound on our workstation, and we want to distribute the processing load, we use RPC. Let's see how RPC works. If we move the code that does our compute-intensive work into a library module (a module of executable code, such as a DLL), which is linked with a special RPC interface stub, and we then recompile our application with other special RPC interface stubs, our application will run much differently.

RPC Glue Routines

When our application, now linked with RPC "glue" routines, needs to perform a matrix calculation, a bit transform, or color quantization, it calls that function through

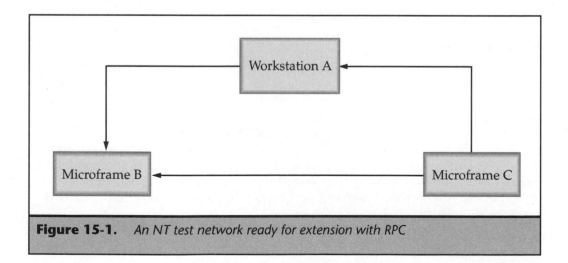

Figure 15-1. *An NT test network ready for extension with RPC*

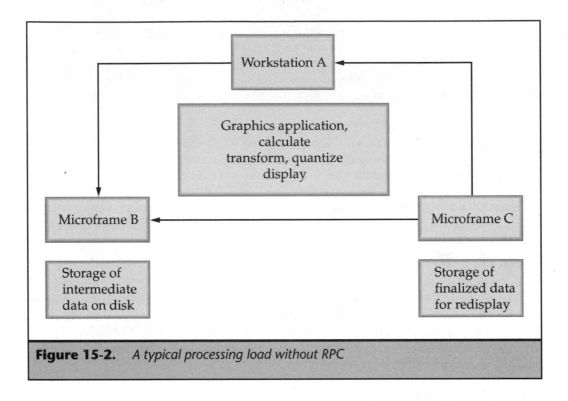

Figure 15-2. *A typical processing load without RPC*

the RPC glue routines. The application does not know the difference. It thinks it is calling its own, linked-in, subroutine. In reality, it invokes special RPC mechanisms in the glue code that connect with the network and search for their counterpart on another computer. This is all done with the agencies of the RPC runtime modules, a part of NT 4, as shown in Figure 15-3.

The Library Code Link

When the right computer is found—the computer with the library code linked with RPC glue routines—the library code is called through that local computer's RPC mechanisms. If data is involved, the RPC runtime modules will format it according to our design time specifications and feed the data to the library too. The library also does not know it's located elsewhere. The routines to be called think that they are running on the local workstation, compiled into the application. This is a round-trip, so the RPC routines in the library code and RPC runtime format the results and return them to the application on our workstation. This round-trip happens for each call that the application makes to RPC and enables library routines sitting on other connected computers.

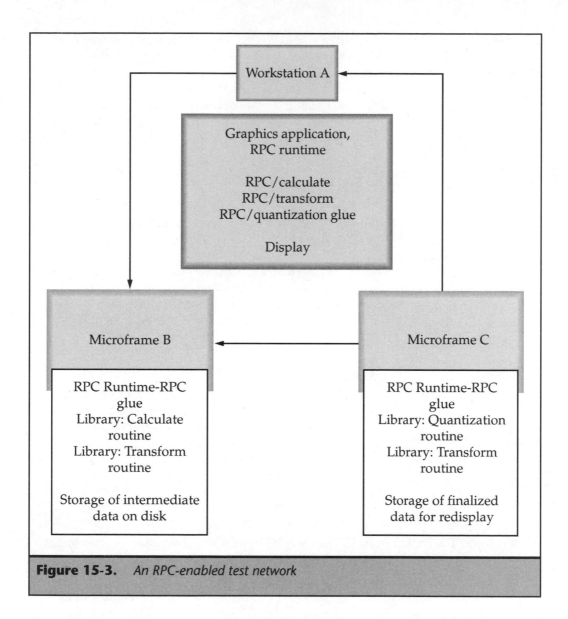

Figure 15-3.   *An RPC-enabled test network*

The End Result

As you can see, this has huge ramifications for systems with compute- or I/O-bound applications. If a program utilizes RPC and is designed right, the compute-intensive operations are performed on a more powerful CPU, and throughput will increase accordingly. This all presupposes that you have studied the situation, and that the increase in network traffic will not have an equally deleterious impact on the application's speed or efficacy.

NOTE: If you have many small remote procedure calls across a heavily loaded network, you run the risk of affecting your total throughput negatively. You should first examine the trade-offs and try to design your applications optimally.

Dynamic Data Exchange

The second IPC mechanism that we will examine is Dynamic Data Exchange (DDE). Although Microsoft's support for DDE has always been problematical (see "Microsoft's Love/Hate Relationship with DDE," later in this chapter), DDE and its cousin NetDDE are still used extensively.

DDE is a conceptually simple IPC mechanism. It has been an integral part of the Windows family of operating systems since the early 16-bit Windows releases. Essentially, DDE uses special messages to pass data and control information between programs that want to be part of the DDE link. With that said, the actual housekeeping mechanisms and DDE link management are a bit more involved.

DDE Servers and Clients

DDE is expressed programmatically in terms of servers and clients. A full DDE link will have a server component (an application that serves up data through a DDE channel) and a client component (an application that asks for data through a DDE link from a DDE server). DDE uses the concept of identifier strings to individualize DDE server "conversations" or links. The DDE link is identified by a hierarchical set of strings that are registered with the system under the following general scheme:

- **Application:** The server's application name. Each server has only one application name, normally the name of the program.

- **Topic:** The topic name. All DDE servers have at least one topic. A topic might be something like "NYSE" or "Automobiles."

- **Item:** The item name. Under each registered topic, a DDE server has at least one and possibly many registered items. This is where the real data will be passed. Typical items for topics might be "DOW" and "FORD," with typical passed data of "6711.30" and "Festiva," respectively.

Types of DDE Conversations

There are three fundamental types of DDE links or conversations: the cold link, the warm link, and the hot link. All three use predefined DDE messages to communicate and oversee their conversations.

The Cold Link

A cold link conversation starts when a client application broadcasts a WM_DDE_INITIATE message containing the application and topic strings for the link it wants to start a conversation on. A DDE server with this application string—supporting the specified topic—answers the client with a WM_DDE_ACK message. The client then requests a specific data item with the WM_DDE_REQUEST message. If the DDE server can, it supplies the requested data by sending a WM_DDE_DATA message to the client application. Otherwise it posts a WM_DDE_ACK with a negative parameter to the client application. The client may or may not send a WM_DDE_ACK message back to the DDE server application (see Figure 15-4). This link is kept up until the conversation is terminated when the client and server post each other WM_DDE_TERMINATE messages.

The Warm Link

The warm link is a combination of a cold link and a hot link (discussed next). The initial conversation is as with cold and hot links. Like the hot link, a client application sends a WM_DDE_ADVISE message to the server application, which acknowledges with a positive or negative WM_DDE_ACK. The difference is that a parameter to the WM_DDE_ADVISE message will tell the server that the client just wants to be kept apprised of changes in data without necessarily receiving new data. Thus, the server sends WM_DDE_DATA messages with NULL data. Once the client has been informed, and wants to get the real data, it sends a WM_DDE_REQUEST message, as it would in a cold link conversation.

The Hot Link

The hot link lets the client know when data has changed without the overhead of the warm link NULL data messages. Everything is as with a warm link except that the server application only sends a WM_DDE_DATA message to the client when data has changed in the server application. This reduces overhead and optimizes the DDE link.

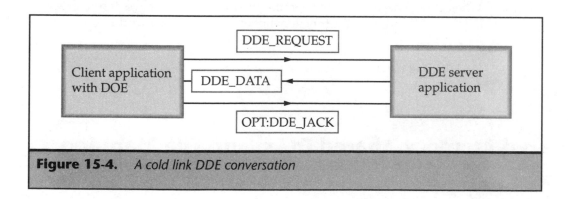

Figure 15-4. *A cold link DDE conversation*

The NetDDE Extension

NetDDE refers to an extension of DDE, whose functionality is limited to links made on the same computer. NetDDE was developed at the behest of programmers who wanted to use DDE conversations as an IPC mechanism over networks between separate computers. The idea of grouping NetDDE with RPC is that, in some ways, they perform similar optimizations.

> *NOTE: Because the NetDDE server application need only reside on one computer in the interconnected network, it acts as a remote server for one or more client applications, reducing processing load for the entire network. In this way, it resembles RPC.*

The only visible difference between DDE and NetDDE is that with the addition of a share name—published by the computer on which the server application resides—NetDDE acts as a network router, sending DDE messages to specified shares and back. The DDE share is published by the server application or, statically, by the computer where the server application is installed. A client wishing to converse with the server need only ask for the application, topic, and item with the share name prepended (share names always end with $).

Microsoft's Love/Hate Relationship with DDE

Microsoft developers have always been ambivalent in offering and supporting DDE and NetDDE. The Windows 95 team has little love for the DDE mechanism in general, hence the scant support and poor performance of DDE and NetDDE in Windows 95. They just didn't make it a priority because of the new technologies coming online for replacement functionality.

The problem is, DDE is extensively used by everything from setup programs (for example, they use DDE to set up program icons) to communications applications that script dial-up utilities using DDE. So where does this leave DDE support in NT 4? In great shape! The NT team has always put compatibility with Windows 3.x at the forefront of their design decisions where similarities existed. They have done a great job in porting the DDE and NetDDE functionality over to the 32-bit world.

> *NOTE: DDE and NetDDE now work better in NT than in Windows 95, the supposed heir to Windows 3.x.*

Shared Memory, Shared DLLs, and File Mapping

Because of the formal IPC mechanisms available in NT 4, some of these sharing techniques have been put on the back burner lately. However, the ability to directly share memory space for storage and manipulation of data between two processes is a time-honored programming design technique.

There are three primary ways in which sharing can be accomplished with NT 4. Before we examine each one, let's talk about why NT treats these memory sharing techniques specially, vis-à-vis earlier Windows offerings and other operating systems too.

Win32, NT, and Security

In older Windows platforms, as well as MS-DOS and other selected operating systems too numerous to list, a programmer could design a simple IPC mechanism that allowed two processes to share data in a globally visible memory arena, accessing that memory space either serially or simultaneously (see Figure 15-5). Besides the obvious synchronization problems, this ability was (and still is!) very handy. In fact, in some cases, it is the only way to perform IPC, since speed and direct programming of, say, a custom adapter card is more important than sticking to the "approved" programming methods.

The Win32 programming interface, the heart of NT's application functionality, makes this kind of memory sharing difficult because all Win32 processes run in their own virtual address space, being protected from all other Win32 processes. That is part of what makes NT so secure and crash proof.

First, because the address space is virtual, a Win32 process that receives the address of a memory arena from another Win32 process will use the address as if it sits within its own address space, pointing to a completely different physical location (see Figure 15-6).

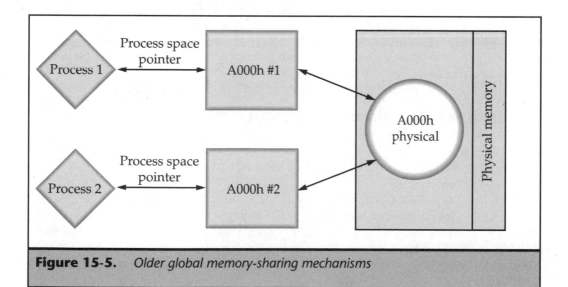

Figure 15-5.   *Older global memory-sharing mechanisms*

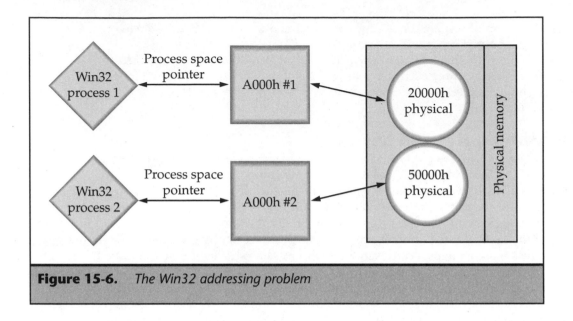

Figure 15-6. *The Win32 addressing problem*

Secondly, NT imposes security attributes on all programmatically created Win32 objects, so without proper security permissions, a calling process might not be able to communicate its data and parameters to another process at any rate.

NT's Memory Sharing/IPC Mechanisms

We will briefly look at each primary shared memory mechanism. These methods can be used to pass large or small quantities of data between processes and do not necessarily have to be implemented between two or more Win32 processes (memory sharing arrangements can be between device drivers—see Chapter 21—and applications, or between different subsystems). Let's review these methods now.

SHARED GLOBAL MEMORY IN A SHARED DLL   This mechanism allows two Win32 (or other) processes to share a specially marked memory area within a DLL that they both link to (see Figure 15-7). DLLs usually have instanced data, so their code may serve more than one application while keeping each application's DLL data separate.

Win32 and NT allow the programmer to declare a variable (which might be the pointer to a DLL-allocated memory space, or just a simple variable or array) as globally shared. In this way, although all other data will be instanced for every application that links with the DLL, the shared DLL variable or memory space will always point to the same instance of the globally shared data area for all Win32 processes that receive a pointer to it.

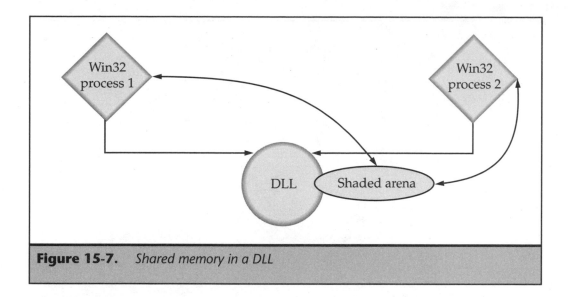

Figure 15-7.   *Shared memory in a DLL*

SHARED GLOBAL MEMORY IMPLEMENTED AT THE DRIVER LEVEL   This
method is much more specialized and requires greater programming overhead and
knowledge. When a Win32 application needs maximum flexibility and speed in using
a global memory arena, either to query and control that memory for custom hardware
or to give other custom Win32 processes speedy access, this method is indicated.

The idea is to have a device driver (at the lowest levels of the operating system)
allocate memory and, through the use of driver calls (IOCTLs or I/O control calls), be
able to map a view of that data into the calling Win32 process's memory space, and
pass a pointer to that memory back up to the Win32 layer (see Figure 15-8).

This method is not available on some RISC platforms, so it is primarily used on
x86 machines where adapter card memory needs to be directly manipulated by a
Win32 application. (See Chapter 23 for more on kernel-shared memory arenas.)

FILE MAPPING   Win32 memory-mapped files are a special memory management
feature that allows NT (and Windows 95) applications to treat files on disk as if the file
space were RAM memory. The method uses pointers to map a view of all or part of a
file on disk, assigning that view to a specific range of addresses within the process's
address space. By using a reference to the pointer (referring to the data that the pointer
is pointing to), you can access the contents of a memory-mapped file as if it were
regular RAM, effectively reading or writing data to or from a file as if you were read
or writing process memory.

Each process that maps a view of a memory-mapped file must have security
permissions equal to the security attributes with which the file was created, and must
be able to identify the file by name (with the exception of child processes, which can
inherit the file-mapping object from their parent processes).

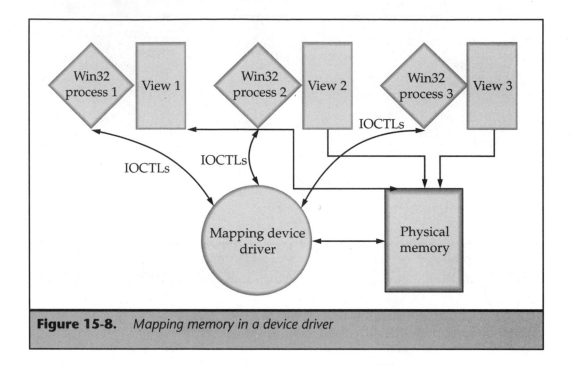

Figure 15-8. *Mapping memory in a device driver*

What's Next

We have looked at several of the major IPC mechanisms in NT 4 and learned a little about their design. We haven't yet visited the Component Object Model (COM), which forms the underpinning for OLE (Object Linking and Embedding) technology, the newest member of the NT IPC function family. We'll be revisiting these concepts in Chapter 22, when we look at COM, which is taking over and extending DDE's functionality for the future.

Next, we will examine NT's security model in depth. This is the chapter to study if you want to run a secure installation or want a better understanding of NT security. Whether you are a programmer, system administrator, or a power user, read on.

Chapter Sixteen

NT 4 Security

Unlike its 16-bit predecessors, and much more capable and complete than Windows 95, security in NT was designed as an integral component of NT, providing extended security methods that are used by all facets of the operating system. NT security was planned from the OS's inception, and its architectural impact is ubiquitous. The NT security model implements control over almost all objects in the system. We speak here of system objects that include everything from file handles (the tokens used to create or work with a file) to device request and basic synchronization and timing elements within the Kernel (see Chapter 19). The security components control the system and user's access to these objects and to processes, which in turn dictate the actions an individual can perform when using a particular object. Additionally, the security subsystem controls and manages which events get audited, when the auditing option is turned on, and how those audits are recorded.

This chapter describes the NT security model and its components. It also explains how NT 4 keeps track of both users and objects—to help you understand why security is so important to other parts of the operating system, and to help you understand what you are looking at when you see system messages and alerts and security information that you might find in the Event Viewer (see Chapter 7). We'll inspect examples of security, showing how NT validates access requests and how it audits and reports on activities performed on protected objects. We'll also take a look at using NT's User Manager application to set security and account information using a graphical administration tool.

The NT Security Model

As shown in Figure 16-1, the NT 4 security model has three major levels of functionality. The subsystem contains the following components:

- **Local and remote logon:** Any logon (initiated at the local workstation or over the network) is performed by using a system-created process that is run in the context of a secure desktop, meaning that it is not owned by any user. This helps to protect the logon from being available to rogue processes that might be used to breach security. Logon processes handle requests and access from both the local machine and from remote users, for instance, as NT Server does for RAS clients (see Chapter 13). The main NT modules involved in this frontline security include the WinLogon and GINA (Graphical Identification and Authentication) components. For local logon processes, these modules control the graphical logon, displaying a dialog box to the user, accepting the user's input, and validating usernames, passwords, and workgroup or domain membership.

- **Local Security Authority (LSA):** This central User mode security component is responsible for ensuring that users have proper system access permissions. The LSA controls and uses the Security Policy Database, and works in tandem with the Security Account Manager (SAM), with its User Accounts Database, to implement the User mode side of the security subsystem. Using the SAM's services to validate a group's and/or a user's account, the LSA generates access permissions (tokens), and is responsible for managing the security policies and audit policies for the local machine.

- **Kernel mode Security Reference Monitor:** This portion of the security subsystem is a Kernel mode component that is responsible for checking to see whether the user has access and execution permission on a protected object. The Security Reference Monitor can carry out validation on object access and cooperative generation of specific audit messages, as defined by the LSA and the Security Policy Database, providing validation services to both Kernel mode and User mode processes. For instance, a kernel process that owns an object to be used by an application, on behalf of a user, will get its permission validation through the Security Reference Monitor.

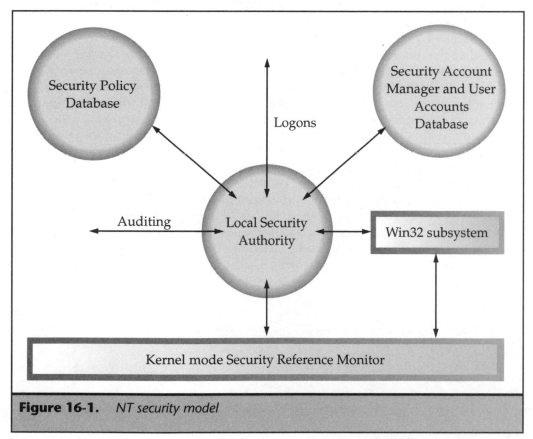

Figure 16-1. *NT security model*

Although we use the term *subsystem* to refer to the security components in NT 4, this is not the same as a protected subsystem, such as Win32 or POSIX. First, the security subsystem comprises both User and Kernel mode components, and second, it is used by almost every other system component in NT. Therefore, unlike a discrete, replaceable, protected subsystem, which has only finite abilities and connection, the security subsystem is part of the base NT operating system. For logical linkage, then, we refer to its components in their entirety as an NT-OS subsystem; really the only homogenous User/Kernel mode entity in NT.

Why NT Implements Object Control and Permissions

Because security is an integral part of NT 4, and because all actions performed and monitored within the OS are based on the abstracted idea of system objects (see Chapters 19 and 20), NT can use its security components to universally control access to these objects. Every object created by the OS, whether on behalf of a user or for the system's internal use, is subject to scrutiny by the security subsystem components. These components keep track of who (which user) tries to create, access, or delete an object and, conversely, the security profiles and permissions on each of the registered users themselves.

Together, these capabilities form a complete system-level security scheme. Instead of trying to layer security on top of a basically insecure operating system, where it could be subject to hacking or circumvention, NT implements security on all of the basic entities that it uses to perform any and (almost) all actions. This model keeps security information for each user, group, and object. Processes that create or use objects, such as User mode applications that open files or use printer resources, or Kernel mode actions that synchronize and carry out actions, are all subject to this vetting process. And by implementing protection at such a low level, network security is automatically included in the scheme, because anyone who accesses any object, local or remote, must first have the proper permissions in place.

NT 4's ability to manage object and user access completely means that it controls which users can access which objects, and how those objects can be accessed. Permissions can be assigned to individual users or groups, which grant or deny access to types of objects. Included are Read, Write, Delete, Execute, No Access, Change of Permission, and Take Object Ownership permissions, usually assigned for, say, file objects. These permissions can be assigned by the "owner" of the object (a user or group who executes an application that uses a file, for instance), or by the administrator, on a systemwide object. This kind of permission assignment is called *discretionary access control*.

TIP: *To keep permission assignment manageable, administrators should assign permissions on groups, not individuals. See the section later in this chapter on the User Manager for information on groups and user accounts. A user can easily have membership in as many groups as are needed. If many different permission profiles are needed, make new user groups and assign the permissions to those groups, subsequently making individual users members of those groups. That way, permission sets can be defined no matter how your users change, making for a streamlined setup. As an example, the administrator of a large corporation, where employees (NT users) change constantly, could easily control access to a server directory for companywide stock quotes by creating and assigning the QUOTES group with read access only, making all employees a member of that group, while controlling read/write access, for employees responsible for the update of that directory, with permission and membership assignments in a more specialized CHANGEQUOTES group. See Chapter 9, on assigning file and directory sharing, for more information.*

Insider Info

NT identifies users in the system by creating and using a construct called a security ID (SID). SIDs are guaranteed to be unique temporally, assuring the fact that there will never be two identical SIDs within the system. Even if the same user is deleted from your NT system and later added back in, NT will create and use a different SID. Even such a scenario as this would not compromise security if, say, that user's permissions were to be changed, and the administrator wanted to be sure the user did not have access to his or her old data or files.

At some time following user registration, a logon will occur. Every time a logon is successfully made, NT 4 creates a *security access token* for the logged-on user. A security access token consists of information that includes the user's SID, membership enumeration and SIDs for the groups in which the user is a member, and account information including any special system privileges and the user's name. NT keeps a list of SID-to-object mappings that allows it to compare permissions on an object with a user's SID, which is passed to any process that is run by the user or on the user's behalf. It is at this time that access is either allowed or denied, on an object-by-object basis.

Logging On

The primary security provided by NT 4 starts with the logon process. This process is created by NT in order to accept logon requests through the interactive facilities of the

WinLogon and Graphical Identification and Authentication (GINA) OS components, as well as remote requests through the network.

Enforcing logon procedures lets NT 4 prevent the user from doing anything on the system before he or she supplies a username and password, with the possible addition of a domain name (see Chapter 4). By supplying this information, users identify themselves to the NT 4 operating system, which uses this information to match with its internal databases for access control and user profile instantiation (see Chapter 17 for information on user profiles in the Registry database).

The typical logon process involves interaction with a username/password dialog, initiated by issuing the NT Secure Attention Sequence (SAS), usually CTRL+ALT+DEL, from the keyboard. An SAS is used so that NT may normally sit idle (in a secure desktop, which we'll talk about later in this chapter) until a user explicitly gains its attention. This prevents the machine from idling in a state in which it would be operational, without a logged-on user, and therefore vulnerable to attack by a local or network-based hacker or username/password-guessing program.

Other SASs may be implemented by custom interface; for instance, by swiping a magnetic card through a reader, or by inserting a smartcard into a card terminal. The U.S. Department of Defense even uses NT with retinal scanners that look at and map the back of a person's eye. Figure 16-2 illustrates a normal interactive logon process.

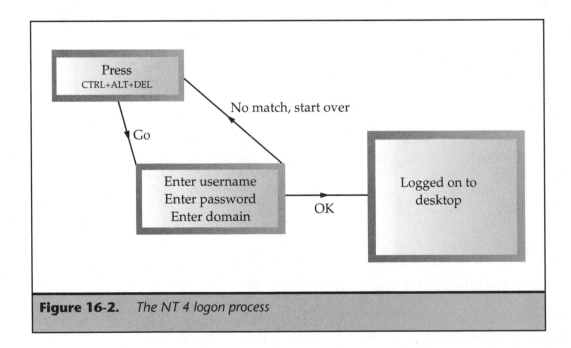

Figure 16-2. *The NT 4 logon process*

Logon Steps

The normal local SAS logon process always follows certain steps. First, the user issues a CTRL+ALT+DEL keyboard sequence—the normal Secure Attention Sequence—to wake NT up. This is handled by the WinLogon and GINA components. The user then enters a username and password, and the logon process calls the Local Security Authority (LSA) through the services of WinLogon.

The LSA then checks the input information against the user accounts database using the local security authentication routines, or package. If the account information is not found, the LSA forwards the logon information to another authentication package, possibly for validation across the network, on another machine. Otherwise, the local logon information is validated at this point.

Once the account information is validated, the Security Account Manager (SAM), the control component that manages the user accounts database, retrieves the user's SID, plus any SIDs referring to groups to which the user belongs.

Next, if the logon is valid, a logon session and the appropriate SIDs are passed back to the LSA. Otherwise, the logon process is terminated and NT goes back to the secure desktop, waiting for another SAS.

Now, the LSA creates a security access token containing the user's SID, the SIDs for groups to which the user belongs, and user rights (described later in this chapter) assigned to the SIDs. Once this information is ready, the access token is returned to the logon session.

The logon session causes an application desktop (see the next section) to be created on behalf of the user, along with the user's attached access token. Together, these elements create an NT *subject*, the combination of a process and the user's security access token. (Subjects are discussed in more detail later in this chapter.)

Window Stations and Desktops

A screen-console, keyboard, and mouse combination is represented in NT 4 as a window station, or workstation. Within a window station there may be several desktops. Desktops represent the entire collection of windows that are visible at any one time.

Normally only one window station is allowed at any one time in NT 4. Future versions of NT promise to allow multiple window stations, with multiple desktops per window station. The default window station is called WinSta0. At SAS-logon time, the NT WinLogon component creates three desktops, one for itself, one for the user's applications, and one for the screen saver.

WinLogon Desktop

The WinLogon desktop is the secure desktop used for interactive identification, authentication, and other logon or logoff and tasking dialogs. This desktop becomes active whenever NT 4 receives a Secure Attention Sequence.

Application Desktop

Each time a user is logged on, an application desktop is created. This desktop is secured within the context of the user's security profile, and only the user, system, and interactive logon session may access it. This is the default desktop where all user applications and interaction will run and take place.

Screen Saver Desktop

This desktop is created for running a screen saver. It will allow access by the logged-on user and by the system. If no user is logged on, this desktop can only be accessed by the system itself, making it secure also.

NOTE: When a user is logged on, and an application desktop is created, NT starts many system-level services and applications for the user. Included in this list are Explorer.exe, Taskmgr.exe, and Systray.exe, as well as several system-level, invisible components. Once proper logon validation has occurred, the user's application desktop security profile and attached access token, with user's rights, will be the security context used for anything the user does, and will be inherited by any process executed on behalf of the user.

Mini-Glossary

DISCRETIONARY ACCESS CONTROL Access that is controlled by the owner of an object, specifying the access that users or groups can have to that object.

SECURITY ACCESS TOKEN When a user logs on, and if the user's password is authenticated, the system produces a security access token and attaches it to the user's process. This access token identifies the user in all subsequent transactions involving securable NT objects. The access token contains the user's SID, group SIDs, user rights (privileges), an owner SID, the SID for the primary user's group, the default discretionary access control list (ACL), the source of the access token, whether the token is a primary or impersonation token, current impersonation levels, and other statistics.

SECURITY ID (SID) A unique value of variable length used to identify a user or group. The SID assigned to a user when he or she logs on becomes part of the access token created for, and attached to, any action attempted by, or process executed for, that user. A SID is always unique, and once it has been used in the identification of a user or group, it cannot be used again to identify any other user or group.

NT Security, Bare to the Bone

Next, we are going to get very technical. When we talk about NT security, there comes a time when we have to discuss the basic elements that make up the model, and how they are used. To understand what NT is doing, and what the OS can tell you about what it's doing, we must bear down and learn about some of the yucky stuff, full of acronyms and interdependent connections!

A Synergistic Relationship: Subjects

How does NT keep track of the level of access a particular user is allowed, at any one time? Under the NT security model, the operating system must ensure that programs run by a user have the same level of access to NT objects (or less) that the user is assigned.

If this were not enforced, any user could, for example, run a program that assigned itself privileged access (beyond the user's normal permissions) that could potentially present a security threat to the entire system. A disgruntled employee with read-only access could run a program with administrator privileges, granting itself rights to delete or change vital system files or confidential data.

NT makes sure that this kind of thing never happens by treating each program executed by the user as a *subject*. This is a term used by the architects of NT to denote an inseparable pairing of a user's access token with a program executed by the user, or acting on the user's behalf. NT treats each application and user access token pair—a single subject—as a unit, and any program executed by a user is then run within the user's security *context*. This context consists of the aggregate of preset user permissions. NT tracks access and manages permissions by looking at a subject, within the user's security context, when any program or service is executed by the user. Then, by using subjects executed within the user's security context, NT prevents a program from granting itself higher privileges on the fly.

NT allows two different types of subjects within its security model: simple subjects and server subjects. A simple subject is a subject that inherits the logged-on user's access privileges. This may be a service or application that is run on behalf of the user, at boot time, or it may be a desktop application, such as a database or spreadsheet program. Simple subjects never have other subjects as clients, such as would happen with a server subject.

A server subject is always implemented as a protected subsystem, such as the Win32 subsystem. As a server process, server subjects necessarily have other subjects as clients—those application-access token pairs that are run as subjects within a user's security context. A server subject almost always inherits the security context of the user who is requesting its services and actions.

The Security Descriptor

Most objects within the NT operating system are secured. The description that they carry along with them, their *security descriptor*, is the primary mechanism used by NT to expose these objects' security attributes to elements of the OS that need this information. The security descriptor for an object consists of four parts: two security IDs (SIDs) and two access control lists (ACLs). These are described in Table 16-1.

SIDs, DACLs, SACLs, and ACEs

As mentioned earlier in this chapter, a security ID (SID) is a unique value of variable length used to identify a user or group. SIDs are assigned by the system to a user or group when an initial logon or group creation is performed. SIDs become part of the user's access token and are always unique.

An access control list (ACL) is made up of zero or more access control entries (ACEs), each of which can specify access or auditing permissions on the object by an

Owner SID	The security ID of the user or group that owns the object. An object's owner can change access permissions on the object.
Group SID	Used only by the POSIX subsystem.
Discretionary ACL (DACL)	This type of ACL lists users and groups that have been granted and denied access on the object. An object's owner controls its DACL.
System ACL (SACL)	This type of ACL lists security auditing permissions (auditing messages that will be generated by the system) and is controlled by the administrator. A SACL is useful when the system administrator wants to log access attempts on a secured object. NT will enter an audit record into the system event log. The Event Viewer can be used to examine entries in the event log, or programs can use the event-logging functions, with the proper permissions, to examine the log.

Table 16-1.   *Parts of an Object's Security Descriptor*

individual user, or group, depending on the context in which the owning ACL is used. ACLs can be discretionary (DACL) or for system use (SACL).

An ACE can be flagged as one of three types:

- **Discretionary ACE: AccessAllowed:** Used in a DACL to grant the specified access rights to the user, group, or logon account.

- **Discretionary ACE: AccessDenied:** Used in a DACL to deny the specified access rights to the user, group, or logon account.

- **System-audit ACE: SystemAudit:** Used in a SACL to generate an audit record when the user, group, or logon account utilizes, or attempts to utilize, the specified access rights, such as who accesses which files.

An ACE is the actual entity used to control or monitor access to an object by a specified user or group. Each ACE contains the following control data:

- A SID identifying the user or group, or logon account. A logon account SID would be used, for instance, by a program such as an NT service component.

- An access mask specifying access rights that are controlled by the ACE.

- An ACE-type flag.

- Inheritance flags to specify whether other objects can inherit the ACE.

The ACE Access Mask

Each ACE has an access mask bit-field whose entries define all possible actions that can be performed on a particular object. Some access control mask bit-field definitions are shown here:

```
#define SPECIFIC_RIGHTS_ALL            0x0000FFFF

#define STANDARD_RIGHTS_REQUIRED       0x000F0000

#define STANDARD_RIGHTS_ALL            0x001F0000
```

ACCESS MASK ENTRY TYPES   Access entry types for the ACE control mask fall into several categories. First, there are *standard* access types, consisting of entries that allow or deny actions on objects of any kind. Next, there are *specific* entry types, applicable only to the actions that can be performed on the object in question. Finally, there are *generic* access entry types, derived from, and mapped to, both standard and specific access entry types.

Specific entry access types are variable and they apply specifically to an object type. For instance, NT file objects may have specific types that include ReadData,

WriteData, AppendData, Execute, ReadAttributes, and WriteAttributes, and the extended attribute ReadEA and WriteEA types. The *specific access mask*, an aggregate of up to 16 possible specific access entry types, is defined when the object is created.

The standard and generic access entry types are listed in Table 16-2. Generic access entry types are mapped from standard and specific types, so they do not appear in audit entries in the security logs, accessible from the Event Viewer (see Chapter 7).

The Object Access Validation Process

Now that we know more about the data types that NT security utilizes in implementing object-level security, let's look at how the operating system actually uses this information when managing access on behalf of a user or process.

NT goes through a rigidly set process whenever a user or process attempts access on an object. When the access attempt is made, NT compares data within the user's (or the logon account's) access token with the data fields contained in the object's security descriptor, as shown in Figure 16-3.

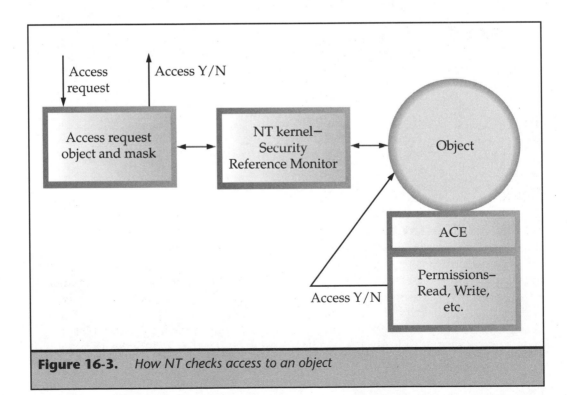

Figure 16-3. *How NT checks access to an object*

Bit Position in Mask	Type	Name	Use
0 through 15	Specific rights	Variable	Contains the access mask specific to the object type associated with the mask.
16	Standard	DELETE	Used to grant or deny delete access.
17	Standard	READ_CONTROL	Used to grant or deny read access to the security descriptor and owner.
18	Standard	WRITE_DAC	Used to grant or deny write access to the discretionary ACL.
19	Standard	WRITE_OWNER	Used to assign write owner.
20	Standard	SYNCHRONIZE	Used to synchronize access and allow a process to wait for an object to enter the signaled state.
21, 22, 23	Reserved	Reserved	
24	Access system security	ACCESS_SYSTEM _SECURITY	Used to indicate access to a system ACL.
25	Maximum allowed	MAXIMUM _ALLOWED	Object will be opened with all rights allowed for the current user or process.
26, 27	Reserved	Reserved	
28	Generic all	GENERIC_ALL	Mapped
29	Generic execute	GENERIC _EXECUTE	Mapped
30	Generic write	GENERIC_WRITE	Mapped
31	Generic read	GENERIC_READ	Mapped

Table 16-2. *ACE Specific, Standard, and Generic Access Mask Entry Types*

How NT Prepares for Object Access Validation

Object access is usually attempted by a process that is being executed on the user's behalf. It may also be attempted by a service running in the user's security context, or by a system logon account. At any rate, the process will typically construct a template access mask based on the specific type of access that is being attempted. The mask is constructed so that it can be compared with one of the target object's security descriptor-DACL-ACEs.

The system compares the process's (user's or logon account's) access token data and constructed access mask with each ACE in the object's DACL, within the object's security descriptor, until access is either granted or denied or until there are no more ACEs to check. It is possible that several ACEs within the object's DACL could apply to an access token. If this occurs, each of the access rights granted by the various ACEs will accumulate.

As an example, if one ACE grants read access to a group in an access token and another ACE grants write access to the user, who is also a member of the group, the user will have both read and write access to the object when the access check is complete.

Steps in Mask Validation with an Object's ACEs

NT first retrieves the target object's DACL from its security descriptor. It then iterates through the DACL's ACEs until a match is found on the ACE's SID vis-à-vis one of the SIDs in the user's access token (subject).

The next step in validation depends on the type of ACE found, denoted by the entry within the ACE's ACE-type flag. If an ACE is flagged as AccessDenied, it will be processed before an ACE that is flagged as AccessAllowed. The process continues, by type, in the following way:

- **AccessDenied:** NT now checks the constructed access mask to see if only a ReadControl and/or a WRITE_DAC bit is set. If true, and the requesting process is also the owner of the object, then access to the object is immediately granted. Otherwise, access bits in the ACE access mask are ANDED (logical AND, 1+1 = 1, else = 0) with the constructed access mask. If there are any matching access bits set within both masks, access is immediately denied (because ACEs flagged as AccessDenied explicitly deny access to a user or group, for preset actions). If this is not the case, processing continues with the next ACE in the DACL's list.

- **AccessAllowed:** For an AccessAllowed ACE, the access bits in the ACE are ANDED (logical AND, 1+1 = 1(TRUE), else = 0(FALSE)) with those in the constructed access mask. If all bits set in the constructed access mask are matched by the bits in the ACE's mask, access is immediately granted. Otherwise, processing continues with the next ACE in the DACL's list, and access is cumulative.

At the end of the list of ACEs within the DACL, if the contents of the desired access mask are still not completely matched, access is implicitly denied.

Implicit Security Access: Empty DACLs and NULL DACLs

The implicit granting or denial of access to an object can be influenced by the type and quantity of DACL within a security descriptor. If a DACL is empty, containing zero ACEs, no access to the object is explicitly allowed, and any access is denied implicitly.

If the security descriptor contains a NULL entry for its DACL, denoting that the object has no DACL at all, any access to the object is implicitly allowed, since there is no protection assigned to the object.

Mini-Glossary

ACCESS MASK   A 32-bit value that specifies the rights that are granted or denied in an access control entry (ACE). An access mask is also used to request access rights when an object is opened.

ACE (ACCESS CONTROL ENTRY)   An entry in an ACL. An access control entry contains a SID and may also contain a set of access rights. ACEs are used to grant or deny access to a user or group and to audit the access attempts of a user or group.

ACL (ACCESS CONTROL LIST)   A list of security protections that apply to an object. An object can be a file, process, event, or anything else having a security descriptor. An entry in an ACL is an ACE. There are two types of ACLs: discretionary (DACLs) and system (SACLs).

SECURITY DESCRIPTOR   A structure that contains the security information associated with an object. An absolute security descriptor contains pointers to the information, and a self-relative security descriptor stores the structure and associated information contiguously in memory.

SUBJECT   The combination of a security token and an associated program that may be a user-level application or a process that uses system services.

A Little Detective Work

One of the most important aspects of security is determining who is actually behind operations of security interest, such as file writes or security policy changes. With the client/server model of NT, user account identification can be rather tricky. Although a thread that requests access to a resource is identified by the user ID, the thread may be impersonating someone else. In this case, it would be misleading to log events by user ID and may not be very useful in finding the perpetrator in the case of a security breach.

To alleviate this problem, two levels of subject identification are used in NT auditing and the security log:

- The user ID (also called the primary ID)
- The impersonation ID (also called the client ID, as applicable)

 NOTE: Impersonation is the ability of a thread to execute in a security context different from that of the process that owns the thread. Typically, a thread in a server application impersonates a client. This allows the server thread to act on behalf of that client to access objects or validate access to its own objects. For example, when a client in a DDE conversation requests information from a DDE server, the server can impersonate the client so the system can verify that the client is allowed access to the information.

The user ID and impersonation ID show security administrators who is performing auditable actions.

 NOTE: In some cases, a security administrator wants to see what is happening with each process. To meet this need, auditing information also includes a subject's process ID where possible.

Process Tracking

When process tracking is enabled (through the Audit Policy dialog box of the User Manager application), audit messages are generated each time a new process is created. This information can be correlated with specific audit messages to see not only which user account is being used to perform auditable actions, but also which program was run.

The Handle ID

Many audit events also include a handle ID, enabling the event to be associated with future events. For example, when a file is opened, the audit information indicates the handle ID assigned. When the handle is closed, another audit event with the same handle ID is generated.

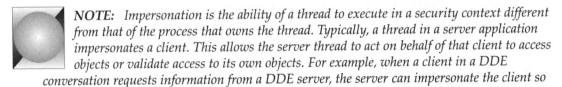 *TIP: With handle ID information, you can determine exactly how long the file remained open. This could be useful, for example, when you want to assess damage following a security breach.*

The Access Token

The following list shows some of the information (also used for auditing) that NT tracks within a process's access token:

- The security ID of the user account used to log on

- The group security IDs and corresponding attributes of groups to which the user is assigned membership

- The names of the privileges assigned to and used by the user, and their corresponding attributes

- Authentication ID, assigned when the user logs on

Audit Determination

NT has an audit determination process similar to its access determination process, described earlier in this chapter. Following access determination, NT evaluates the following information for possible auditing:

- The subject attempting the access (that is, the set of identifiers representing the subject)

- The desired accesses with all generic access types mapped to standard and specific access types

- The final determination of whether access is granted or denied

- The audit ACL associated with the target object

Each ACE in the audit ACL is evaluated as follows:

1. NT checks to see if the type is SystemAudit. If not, the ACE is skipped.

2. NT compares the identifier in the ACE to the set of identifiers representing the subject. If no match is found, the ACE is skipped.

3. The desired accesses are compared to the access mask specified in the ACE.

4. If none of the accesses specified in the ACE's mask were requested, the ACE is skipped. The SUCCESSFUL_ACCESS_ACE_FLAG and FAILED_ACCESS_ACE_FLAG are compared to the final determination of whether access was granted or denied.

5. If access was granted but the SUCCESSFUL_ACCESS_ACE_FLAG flag is not set, or if access was denied but the FAILED_ACCESS_ACE_FLAG flag is not set, the ACE is skipped.

6. If NT performs all of these steps successfully, an audit message is generated.

Mini-Glossary

EVENT ID   The value supplied by a service or application that denotes which event has taken place. It is defined by the module that issued it.

HANDLE ID   In the context of a security event, an ID value that lets another event be associated with the original event. Used mostly for audit tracking.

IMPERSONATION ID   The ID value associated with a user ID, given to a thread that is acting on behalf of another. In programmers' parlance, this introduces one or more levels of ID indirection, letting the base ID be tracked at any time and in any state.

USER ID   The ID value assigned to a specific user when he or she logs on to the system.

The NT Miranda—You Have the Right To...

A word is in order here about the difference between discretionary access—those rights that can be assigned to a user, on a specific system object—and user rights on services and globally available utility applications.

Access Tokens and User Rights

NT controls access to an object by comparing the user and group memberships, in the user's access token, with permissions that have been set for the object itself. This is normally accomplished with discretionary access control, discussed earlier. In cases where specific objects are not linked to an activity, such as shutting down a system from a remote computer, backing up files, setting system time and date, or managing the auditing and security log, an administrator can assign *user rights,* or *privileges,* giving users or groups permission to access or control services that are not covered by normal discretionary access control. A privilege is used to control access to an object or service more stringently than is normally done with discretionary access control. A system administrator can use privileges to control which users are able to manipulate system resources, as stated earlier. An application can also use privileges when it changes a system resource, such as when it changes the system time or shuts down the system.

NT C2-Level Security

The NT security model is designed for C2-level security as defined by the National Computer Security Center (NCSC). C2 is a business level of security criteria that requires a system to have certain secure attributes. Some of the most important requirements of C2-level security are as follows:

- **Discretionary access control:** The owner of a resource (such as a file) must be able to control access to the resource. The system administrator has control over who gets access to what objects, and at what level. The system must protect any one process from gaining access to another's data or resources.

- **Deletion and reuse:** The operating system must protect objects so that they are not randomly reused by other processes. For example, the system protects memory so that its contents cannot be read after it is freed by a process. In addition, when a file is deleted, users must not be able to access the file's data.

- **Identity and authentication:** Each user must identify himself or herself by typing a unique logon name and password before being allowed access to the system. The system must be able to use this unique identification to track the activities of the user. The system must protect itself from external interference or tampering, such as trojan horse logon, unauthorized external system access, or visibility and use of system files.

- **Auditing:** Every system object that is accessed by a user must be auditable. System administrators must be able to audit any and all security-related events. Access to audit data must be limited to authorized administrators.

> *NOTE:* *It is a misconception that the Department of Defense itself rates software such as NT. The NCSC takes submissions, rating them accordingly, against a set of criteria outlined in a set of DoD procedures and regulations. There are also European counterparts to the NCSC that Microsoft has applied to for ratings on the NT operating system. NT's resource kit includes a utility that will let you evaluate your system for C2 compliance. The C2CONFIG.EXE application is used to help you evaluate your system for C2 compliance and make those settings in your installation.*

Controlling Security and Users: The NT User Manager

Several applications listed under the Start/Programs/Administrative Tools (Common) menu are accessible from the desktop, and we have covered some of them already. Of interest here, in a conversation about security, is User Manager. This application is the main route by which security for users and permission groups can be administered (see Figure 16-4). You can use User Manager to perform the following tasks:

- **Create and administer groups:** Assign or delete specific permissions for the groups that exist, or create custom groups, with completely controllable permissions, for assignment to specific users.

- **Create and administer users (their user accounts):** Create new user accounts or change various parameters and settings that affect a user account. These settings include passwords, group membership, user profiles, and dial-in permissions for users who may need RAS services (see Chapter 13).

- **Set and administer account policies:** Set the global policy that your NT computer will use in controlling such things as password expiration and length, and account lockout policy for controlling access after failed logon attempts.

- **Set and administer user rights policies:** Set the global policies that allow you to assign or prevent certain overall rights within the computer's defined permission groups.

- **Set and administer audit policies:** Globally control the events that will be audited, when they happen. These events all pertain to security and access, such as logons and access to files and objects.

The menu choices in User Manager let you completely manage both global and specific security settings for individual users and for all defined permissions groups. But first we have to define some basics, such as what we are given to work with in a just-installed NT 4 system.

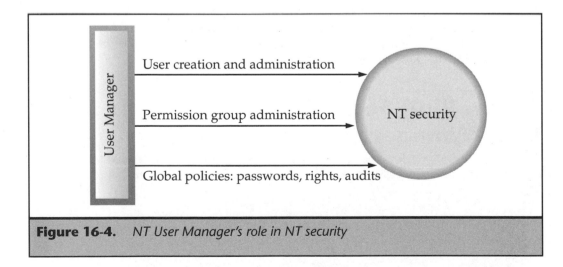

Figure 16-4. *NT User Manager's role in NT security*

Predefined Groups

When you start NT 4 for the first time, certain predefined groups will be available for you immediately. The standard groups are provided to include functionality that covers most of the normal day-to-day operations that you will encounter. They are defined so that their level and scope of functional permission only encompasses those operations that *need* to be accomplished at the implied level of security. The Administrators group has the highest and broadest permissions set. All others are subsets of this group, with exceptions that we shall talk about later in the chapter.

As you can see from Figure 16-5, the standard NT groups you will find on first opening User Manager are as follows:

- **Administrators:** When this group is added to a user's profile, the user can accomplish most normal administrative tasks for the local computer (and domain, if this is a domain controller account). This is a little misleading, as we shall see later on, because even though a user will have normal administrator privileges when this group is part of his or her profile, some operations will still specifically need to be added in special cases where so-called advanced rights must be granted. We'll talk more about this in the "User Rights" section.

- **Backup Operators:** When this group is added to a user's profile, the user is granted access to the file system in order to back up files onto tape or disk. Normally, a user without this group permission (or administrator privileges) could run into file security and locking, preventing the user from performing a backup operation. This is a "permission to read all files, and write them elsewhere" permission.

- **Guests:** When this group is added to a user's profile, the user is granted limited access to the local computer only. This is the lowest, general-level access permission.

- **Power Users:** When this group is added to a user's profile, users have the right to make shared directories and printers available to other users. This gives a specific right to this group that normal users do not have. Grant this privilege, for instance, to users who have local printers that they need to make available to others on a LAN.

- **Replicator:** This is a special permission group set up as standard so that your NT 4 system can act as an import or export server during replication. Replication is the ability of one computer to export files and directories to another computer, in order that identical copies are kept at the remote system.

- **Users:** When this group is added to a user's profile, the user becomes a normal member of the local machine or domain. This permissions group gives a user just about the right mix of rights needed to perform normal application and maintenance functions on local applications and data files.

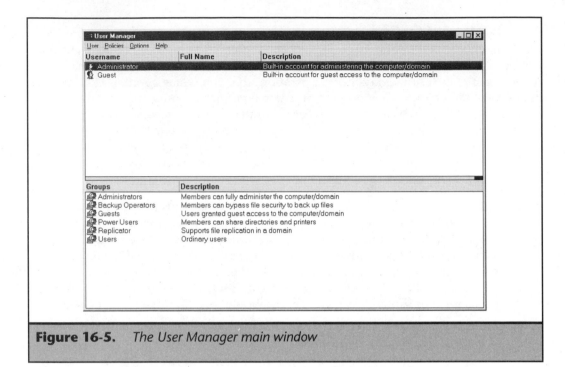

Figure 16-5. *The User Manager main window*

You may add any or all of these groups to any user's group (rights) list, or you may create new groups of your own, adding only those rights that you wish. See the section on "User Rights" for more information.

Usernames (Built-in Users)

Upon first installation, you will normally have two users defined. These are *built-in*, a term Microsoft uses for default accounts that are automatically created at installation time and cannot be deleted. Any users other than the built-in accounts will be defined by you through User Manager.

The User Manager Menus

The menu choices in User Manager allow you to assign new user accounts and groups, edit those assignments, set account policies and global user's rights, and control auditing on a computer, for any auditable security event.

The User Menu

The User menu is where you control creation, editing, and deletion of users and groups. If you are using User Manager for domains on NT Server, you may create users and groups on different computers. Otherwise, this is a local operation. The User menu's options are described next.

NEW USER Use the New User dialog, shown in Figure 16-6, to add a new user account to the user database.

- **Username:** The user's logon name for this new account. A username must be unique on the local computer. Also, it cannot be the same as any group name.

- **Full Name:** The user's full name. Names from this field appear in sorted order in the User Manager window. They are also used in context with certain applications.

- **Description:** Descriptive text for the account; optional.

- **Password and Confirm Password:** Enter the same password for the account in both fields. Passwords can be up to 14 characters.

- **User Must Change Password at Next Logon:** If checked, the user will have to change passwords when next logged on.

- **User Cannot Change Password:** If checked, the user cannot change passwords.

- **Password Never Expires:** If checked, the user will not be forced to change passwords per the Policies/Account Policy dialog.

- **Account Disabled:** Account locked out if checked.

- **Groups:** This button opens the Group Memberships dialog, shown in Figure 16-7, which allows you to assign or remove the user's membership in any registered groups.

- **Profile:** This button opens the User Environment Profile dialog, shown in Figure 16-8, which allows you to assign a user profile and logon script to this user's account. The profile file may be on a remote machine or on the local computer. You can also set the user's home directory. The Connect To field allows you to specify a network connection that must always be made when this user logs on.

- **Dialin:** Grants or revokes dial-in permission to this account (see Figure 16-9). Also controls whether a callback will be used. Using callbacks is a security feature for remote access, covered in Chapter 13.

NEW LOCAL GROUP This menu choice allows you to add a new local group to the list of registered groups. Use this dialog (shown in Figure 16-10) to add custom sets of permissions for user accounts that you will create.

- **Group Name:** Enter a unique name for the custom group here.

- **Description:** Use this field to enter descriptive text for your custom group.

- **Members:** Lists members of this group, which you may add by choosing the Add button in this dialog. Choosing Add will bring up a list of registered users on the local machine, and in the NT domain to which this machine belongs, if any.

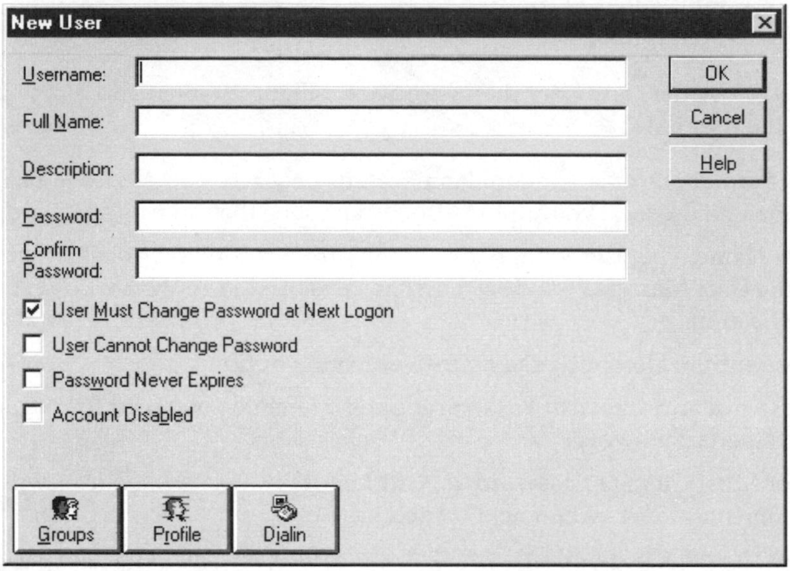

Figure 16-6. *The New User dialog*

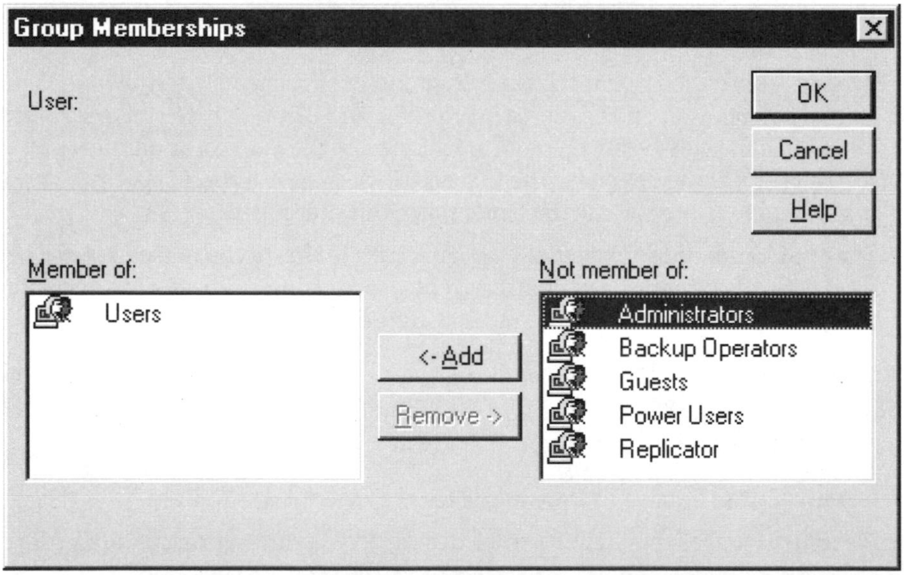

Figure 16-7. *The Group Memberships dialog*

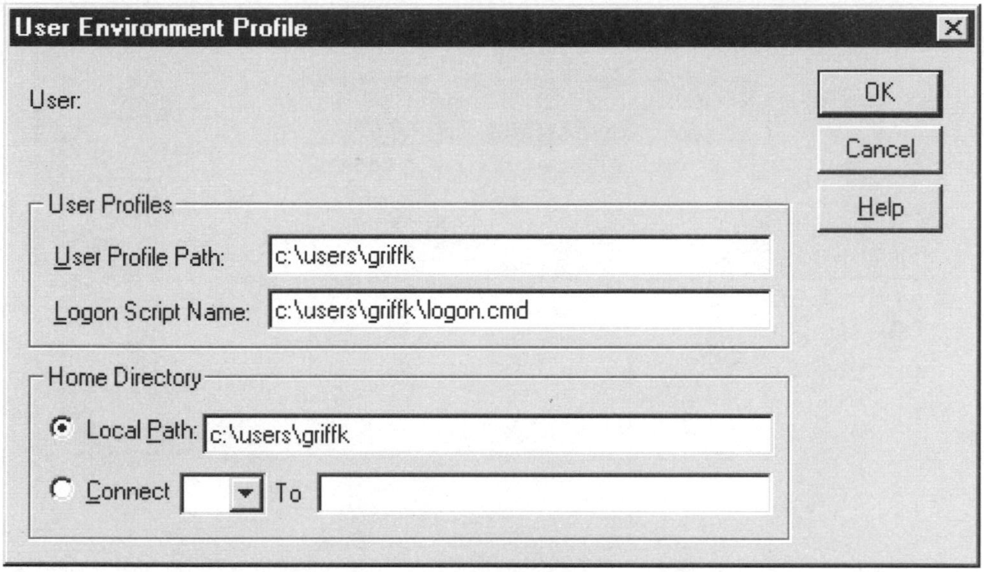

Figure 16-8. *The User Environment Profile dialog*

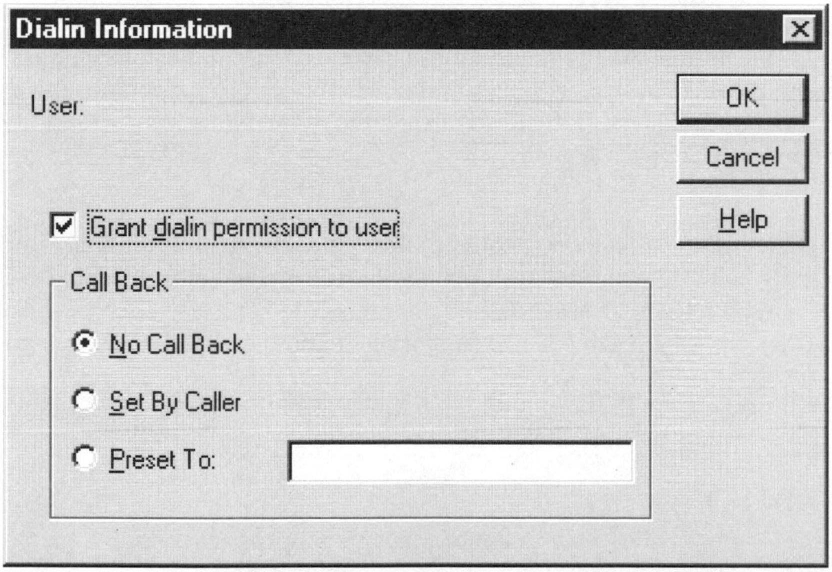

Figure 16-9. *The Dialin Information dialog*

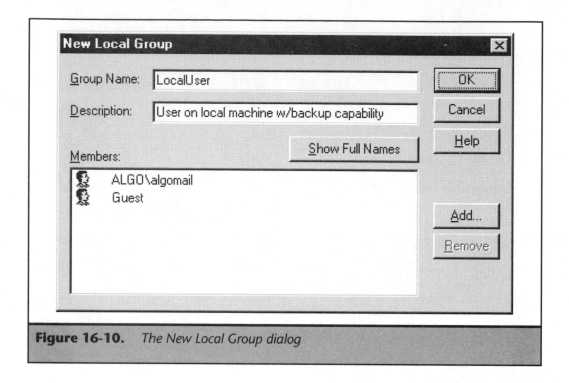

Figure 16-10. *The New Local Group dialog*

COPY, DELETE, RENAME   Use these items on the User menu to act on the currently highlighted selection in the main window. For instance, if you wish to rename a user, highlight the user's name in the main window and choose Rename from the menu. This will show a small dialog where you can enter a new name for the user. Use the Delete menu choice to revoke a user's logon privilege and erase her or him from the user database.

PROPERTIES   Use of this menu choice, or double-clicking a highlighted main window entry, will bring up the appropriate Properties dialog (an example is shown in Figure 16-11). This will be essentially the same as the New User or New Local Group dialog, except you can edit the properties that have already been assigned to the chosen entry.

Use the Local Group Properties dialog (shown in Figure 16-12) to edit membership in a group.

The Policies Menu

The User Manager's Policies menu items affect global properties. Use them to make settings that will be put in force for all users on the local computer.

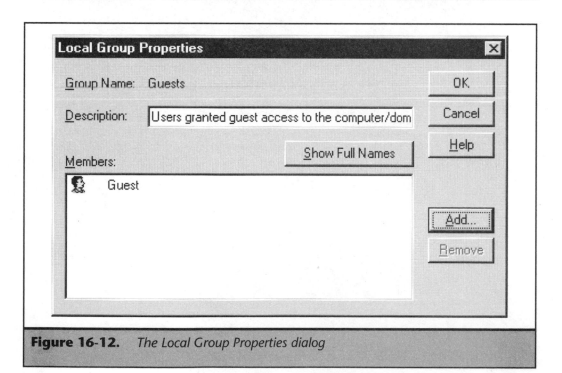

Figure 16-11. *The User Properties dialog*

Figure 16-12. *The Local Group Properties dialog*

ACCOUNT   Use the Account Policy dialog, shown in Figure 16-13, to set global parameters on how accounts will be administered. There are entries to control password aging, length, and uniqueness. Also use this dialog to control your machine's polices on account lockouts, resets, and lockout duration.

USER RIGHTS   Use this dialog to add or remove global permissions for registered groups. These permissions are assigned on an individual basis, using the dropdown list of available permissions (see Figure 16-14).

When you pick a permission, the dialog will list which groups have this permission. To add a group, choose the Add button. To remove a group (to remove its privilege on the highlighted permission), choose the Remove button.

AUDIT   NT lets you use its auditing features to collect information on who is accessing your data, so that you can find out how your system is being used overall. The NT auditing features include facilities that help you monitor access, discover security risks, and quantify any threat or attack on system security.

You use Event Viewer to inspect the security audit messages (see Chapter 7) and User Manager/User Manager for Domains to set the levels and kinds of security audit you wish to generate. Audited events (that you can turn auditing on for) include both system- and application-generated actions. An application may generate its own

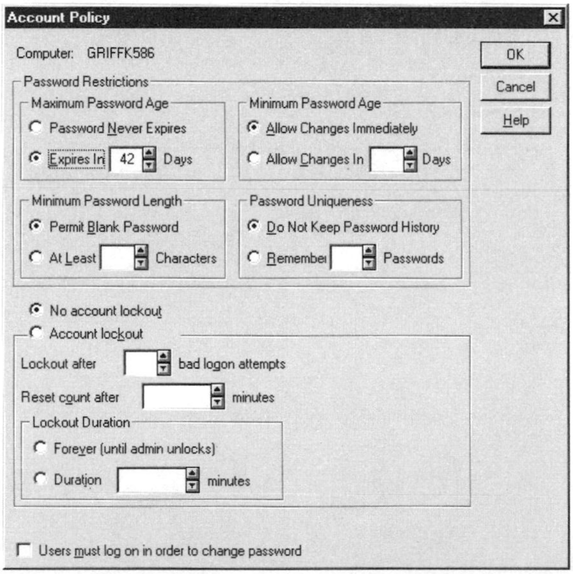

Figure 16-13.   *The Account Policy dialog*

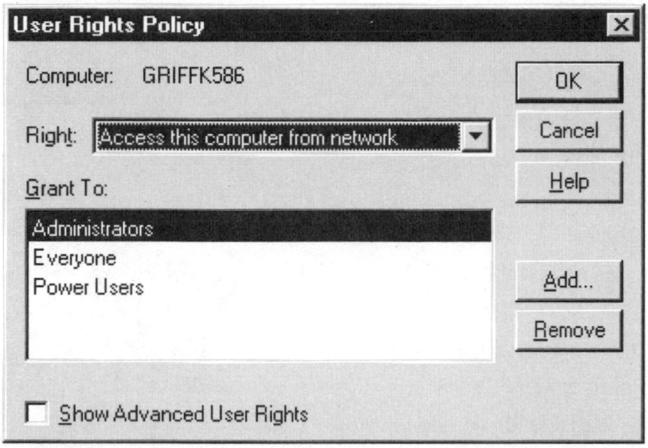

Figure 16-14. *The global User Rights Policy dialog*

audited events by defining them in the Registry (see Chapter 17), where ultimately all auditable events are delimited.

Audit events are entered into the security log by category, event type, and event ID. In cases where an application, rather than the system itself, generates a security audit message, the event type and event ID may be custom defined by the application itself, so you must refer to the application's documentation to determine the origin of these kinds of event messages. The standard security system events and messages will have been generated by events that have entries in the Registry. These events fall into general categories as defined in the User Manager/Policies/Audit Policy dialog, as shown in Figure 16-15. The events shown on this dialog will also be listed in the same general categories within the security log, in Event Viewer.

Table 16-3 lists each of these categories, how they are expressed in both User Manager and Event Viewer, and their meanings.

The Options Menu

Some miscellaneous, fine-tuning options are provided on the User Manager's Options menu.

CONFIRMATION   When certain irrevocable commands are issued, checking this menu item will result in a confirmation dialog being displayed.

SAVE SETTINGS ON EXIT   If checked, all pertinent menu settings will be saved to the Registry. User Manager will restore those settings when next invoked.

FONT   Allows you to choose the font User Manager will use to display its list.

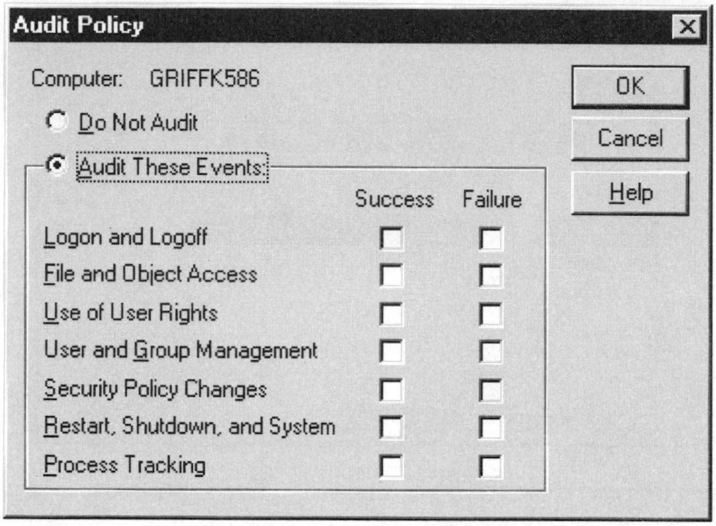

Figure 16-15.   *The User Manager Audit Policy dialog*

Event Viewer Category	User Manager/Policy Dialog Category	Meaning
Logon/Logoff	Logon and Logoff	These events describe a single logon or logoff attempt, whether successful or unsuccessful. Included in each logon description is an indication of what type of logon was requested or performed (that is, interactive, network, or service).
Object Access	File and Object Access	These events describe both successful and unsuccessful accesses to protected objects.

Table 16-3.   *Security Event Categories*

Event Viewer Category	User Manager/Policy Dialog Category	Meaning
Privilege Use	Use of User Rights	These events describe both successful and unsuccessful attempts to use privileges. This category also includes information about when some special privileges are assigned. These special privileges are audited only at assignment time, not at time of use.
Account Management	User and Group Management	These events describe high-level changes to the user accounts database, such as user-created or group membership change. Potentially, a more detailed, object-level audit is also performed (see Object Access events).
Policy Change	Policy Change (Security Policy Changes)	These events describe high-level changes to the security policy database, such as assignment of privileges or logon capabilities. Potentially, a more detailed, object-level audit is also performed (see Object Access events).
System Event	Restart, Shutdown, and System	These events indicate something affecting the security of the entire system or audit log occurred.
Detailed Tracking	Process Tracking	These events provide detailed subject-tracking information. This includes information such as program activation, handle duplication, and indirect object access.

Table 16-3.   *Security Event Categories* (continued)

What's Next

NT security is not trivial. You should, however, brace yourself, and become familiar with its administration and basic structure if your setting requires such knowledge and practice. Many users will be almost totally oblivious to what level of security their actions are validated against. And that is how it should be. Only the system administrator, or programmer, needs to know intimate details, keeping the normal user shielded and unaware.

Another subject the system administrator and programmer should be familiar with is the Registry. Users will definitely *never* touch the Registry directly. This could be disastrous. But there is so much control in the Registry, so many parameters and settings with which to fine-tune and configure your NT 4 installation, that we've devoted an entire chapter to the subject. Next, we're going on a visit to the Registry.

Chapter Seventeen

The System Registry

E ven with its apparent ease of use, NT 4 is a complex operating system. There are hundreds of necessary settings and parameters that control system drivers, boot-up behavior, and installed hardware and software. System administrators, developers, and users are faced with a daunting challenge in managing these settings and options. If all of these parameters and values were stored within their own initialization files (which, in fact, is how Windows operating systems used to work), you would end up with hundreds of tiny files scattered all over your disk drives, or a few very large ones, with hundreds of entries.

In NT, a central database called the Registry helps simplify the storage and retrieval of system and application parameters. The Registry provides a unified and secure data store that holds these setup and configuration values in a hierarchical form that mimics the tree structure found in the file system. The initial addition of Registry values that support any system or application module is usually automatic, but when something has to be changed or tweaked, NT provides two tools, called Registry Editors (REGEDT32.EXE and REGEDIT.EXE), which are used to administer, inspect, and change the Registry. With these tools, power users and system administrators can add to, or customize, Registry entries and values. This can be done locally or from a remote NT machine, and naturally, it is implemented as a point-and-click, graphical application.

How the Registry Works

Under the older 16-bit versions of Windows, booting the system with preconfigured parameters, retrieving user preferences, setting up network and application initialization values, and loading custom startup content involved reading this data from multiple configuration files (usually called .INI files). These files were specific to the operating system component, or application, that used them. They had names like SYSTEM.INI and PUB.INI. Each component or application that needed to store and retrieve startup or operating values had its own .INI file, or stored its values in a global .INI file, under its own heading.

With NT (and partially in Windows 95, which we'll talk about shortly), the operating system and most applications store, retrieve, and use their configuration information by referencing only one file, in one location—the Registry (see Figure 17-1).

The Registry is divided into sections called hives. This curious name comes from the early days of NT 3.1 development, when these parts of the Registry were so named because, purportedly, one of the developers thought of their structure as existing much like the individual cells within a beehive, or honeycomb. Each hive is based at a root key, which is made up of subkeys and value entries, and is physically implemented and housed within a single file in the %SystemRoot%\system32\config directory (usually \Winnt\System32\Config\). We'll look at how hives are implemented and used later in this chapter.

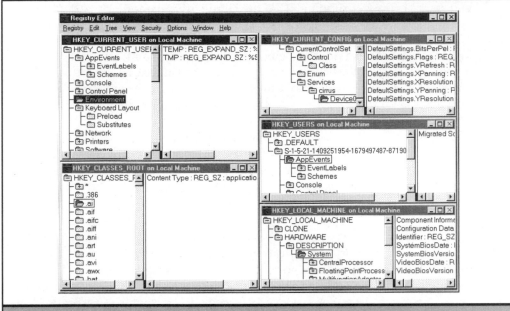

Figure 17-1. *Data in the Windows NT Registry*

NOTE: *If you use Windows 95, which is a 16/32-bit hybrid OS, you'll notice that it employs both Registry and .INI files. This is because legacy software written for 16-bit Windows has to be supported, and that software knows nothing about the Registry. Also, although their use is frowned on officially, programmers may still use .INI files for any Win32 program. Be aware that although the Registry is now the official repository of Win32 and OS configuration information, you may still encounter programs that store private data in an .INI file, even in a brand-new product designed for NT 4!*

In brief, the Registry works as follows:

- **With NT 4 operating system or application setup:** When you initially install NT 4 or upgrade the system by running the NT Setup program, or when you install an application or device that uses a setup program or Control Panel applet for its installation procedure, these setup programs install or upgrade their environment and execution parameters in the Registry. For example, new information about hardware settings and driver files is added when you install a network adapter, a modem, or a new SCSI adapter. For applications, a word processor or spreadsheet program might store its default execution environment variables or its needs for special file type support. Additionally, each time you start a computer running NT 4, the Hardware Recognizer, a part of the operating system boot component, inspects the computer and updates the machine's hardware configuration data in the Registry. This information includes a list of the hardware detected in your system and how that hardware is configured. These are *volatile* Registry entries, updated each time the machine restarts. Most Registry entries are *nonvolatile*, needing to be explicitly updated or changed.

NOTE: On Intel x86-based computers, the Hardware Recognizer is implemented in software by a program found on your boot drive called NTDETECT.COM, working in concert with routines in the NT kernel. On RISC-based computers, the hardware configuration is stored in nonvolatile memory, and NT obtains the information by reading from the ARC firmware (boot) storage areas at restart time.

■ **At system and process, or application, startup:** During system startup, after the Hardware Recognizer has completed its system inspection, the NT kernel components that depend on parametric settings read software configuration data from the Registry. For instance, NT needs to know which OS components and services are to be loaded, such as device drivers for a sound card, SCSI adapter, or other hardware, and system service modules such as Messenger or Network DDE. The Registry also holds data on when and how these components should be loaded and started up, during the boot process. During boot, device drivers need to query from, and store data to, the Registry, in order to properly initialize the hardware or some process that they control. Device drivers and services can reserve and use system resources like blocks of RAM memory, I/O ports, hardware interrupts, and direct memory access (DMA) channels, and they need to know which values and ranges of memory they should use when setting up the actual hardware or process that they provide services for. In some cases, a piece of hardware or process may need to register its usage of a system resource with the OS so that other components can find out about reserved values. This is usually done by publishing these values back to the Registry, where other OS components, drivers, or applications may discover them for installation or execution purposes.

■ **Editing and administration:** When you need to directly inspect or customize the Registry, NT provides three primary tools to do so. First, REGEDT32.EXE and REGEDIT.EXE, the NT Registry editors, provide complete search, replace, and editing services, with which you may change or manipulate any Registry entry or group of entries. You may add, edit, or delete Registry *keys*, the headings under which values are stored, and you may do the same with the actual data and parameters. The Registry Editor does not have a default icon or menu entry, so you must start it from the Start/Run command line, or from a console window session by typing **regedit.exe**. Additionally, the NT diagnostics application, WINMSD.EXE, can be used to inspect Registry information pertaining to the configuration of such information as services, resources, drivers, memory, display, and network components. Although the NT diagnostics program cannot manipulate these settings, it provides a contextual display of various subsystem and component settings in a unified way, so that you may inspect them, determining which values you might want to change with the Registry Editor. We'll discuss REGEDT32.EXE (and its little cousin, REGEDIT.EXE) in depth later in this chapter and WINMSD.EXE in Appendix A.

■ **The Registry versus .INI files:** The Registry implements a unified database-like representation of data that would otherwise be stored in individual .INI files. Both Registry and .INI files store their values under headings, or key fields. These keys provide a way for a program or OS component to query the Registry or an .INI file for parameters and values that are grouped together, supporting a specific setup and instance of a software or hardware component. In the old-style .INI files, key fields, or headings, were denoted by a bracketed text field such as [*myprogram*], and the values stored under those headings were text strings of the form *variable1=some setting*. These .INI headings could not be nested, so if a variable could have more than one value, say for two customized instances of the application associated with the variable, another heading had to be entered into the .INI file with its different settings listed below it, as shown in Figure 17-2. In the Registry, values and parameters can be stored in a completely hierarchical way, supporting different configurations directly. In this way, direct support for different users, with separate preference settings, can be stored and grouped together. As an example, a word processor program could store individual setups for window display and keyboard mapping without having to create a separate .INI file or heading. The keys in the Registry still represent headings like the bracketed strings in an .INI file, but Registry keys can have subkeys, and the subkeys can have subkeys. This helps to keep similar information grouped, and enumeration functions can then easily discover all permutations of a component's settings. Binary values and executable code can also be stored in the Registry, whereas only string values (possibly translated back to some other form by the application or driver) could be stored in an .INI file.

NOTE: *The Registry also contains settings for boot time OS behavior. In 16-bit Windows and Windows 95, direct support for boot time configuration is present in the form of the MS-DOS files AUTOEXEC.BAT and CONFIG.SYS. These files, in their NT form, can still be used to provide compatibility with applications created for MS-DOS or 16-bit Windows.*

Figure 17-2. *Structure of an .INI file (a) versus Registry entries (b)*

Why the Registry Exists

In simpler times, using MS-DOS or even 16-bit Windows 3.1 or Windows for Workgroups, many applications and drivers could be set up and run by supplying the name of the executable, and possibly some command line switches in a form similar to

>   myapp /I /S c:\datafile.dat

And that was it! All of the information needed to execute the application and to work with a data file was contained on the command line.

The Self-Modifying Configuration

The command line parameter-passing scheme is fine for small or simple programs that need very little information to set themselves up and execute. In fact, most NT console-based commands and MS-DOS commands work this way. But what about a more sophisticated program, needing 10 or 20 parameters and filenames (possibly the names of printer driver files, or files for input data) to be executed properly? Well, one of the traditional ways to enter and store this information is to run a specialized option within the executable or its installation application, displaying a setup screen to specify parameters and values that will be stored in a configuration file or within the executable itself for subsequent execution.

Along Came Windows

When Windows became popular, a different type of setup storage method was introduced because of its intrinsic support within the OS, and because Windows enforced so many ancillary dependencies on an application. That method was the .INI file.

As we have learned already, .INI files can be application specific and can have multiple embedded headings and multiple assignment statements under each heading. The primary problems with .INI files stem from the fact that each application or file that needs to have initialization and setup values is forced to create its own .INI file (some use the system .INI files, but that's even more confusing).

Hundreds of .INI files, some with arcane names, can be spread across your computer, creating an unmaintainable mess. Think of the problems involved with remote administration of a client computer's .INI files spanning multiple drives, with .INI files in multiple subdirectories and no set locations for anything. Add to that the fact that each .INI file might point to other files that contain initialization data that is not embeddable in an .INI file. There are even commercial programs available that do nothing more than go out and read, inspect, and unify (à la a pseudo-Registry database) .INI file settings for Windows 3.1x and Windows 95 machines, providing support for installing or uninstalling applications under these operating systems.

This was the state of the technology until the concept of the Registry came along; initially in NT 3.1 and 3.5x, then in Windows 95 (kind of!), and now in NT 4.

The Registry Database Layout

The hierarchical structure of the Registry is designed to keep similar Registry keys and values together; first in an overall scheme that groups functionality and responsibility, and then by individual application, driver, and association. Each key entry in the Registry database can contain discrete data items, called value entries, and can also contain subkeys, with their own value entries and subkeys.

The overall top-down structure is laid out in six subtrees. The headings of these subtrees are keys in and of themselves, sometimes called *root keys*. These subtrees contain keys that consist of per-computer and per-user values, depending on whether the key in question holds global or user-preferred values (see Figure 17-3). Some subtrees contain transient values that the system and application software use for temporary storage.

Global Registry information usually pertains to settings and values that have something to do with hardware settings, for the local machine, or global software settings, such as file associations and user-shared directories and applications. The

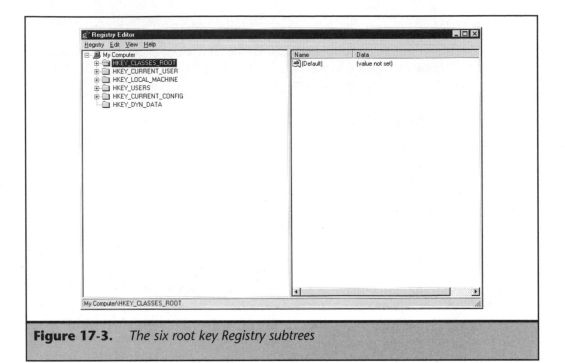

Figure 17-3. *The six root key Registry subtrees*

hardware settings cover the computer itself and all of the drivers and services involved in the global startup and operation of the operating system.

Information that is stored on a per-user basis includes user profiles for things like desktop preferences, individual settings for network connections, applications software, and printer setups.

The expanded Registry subtrees look like the hierarchical structure of a disk drive, with keys, subkeys, and values being similar to directories, subdirectories, and files.

Subtree Functionality and Naming Conventions

All of the main Registry root keys, or subtrees, have names that are prefaced by "HKEY_". This is by convention, designed by NT's developers to denote the Registry headings that have preset "handles" in the system software. A handle is used by programmers to indirectly provide access to the object, in this case a subtree of the Registry, passing that value to system routines that can then reference the object as they would a file or similar item. Each major subtree is prefaced this way, and the Software Developers Kit (SDK) refers to these predefined handles using the same HKEY_ conventions. If a service, driver, or application needs to reference a subkey and value, it will always use the NT Registry programming functions that take one of these HKEY_ handles as a base handle; the root Registry object to reference. Table 17-1 identifies and defines these six root keys (subtrees).

Root Key	Description
HKEY_CLASSES_ROOT	This subtree holds Object Linking and Embedding (OLE) and file, or class, associations. These are used by various system and application components, so that they can automatically bind to or use the right data file types or applications when referenced. This subtree is a mirror of the HKEY_LOCAL_MACHINE \SOFTWARE\CLASSES subtree and is provided for backward compatibility. An example would be the entry for .TXT files; it is normally bound to the NOTEPAD.EXE file, so that when a .TXT file is double-clicked in Explorer, NOTEPAD.EXE is automatically spawned to show the .TXT file.
HKEY_CURRENT_USER	This subtree holds the user settings and profile for the currently logged-on user. The settings and profile include per-user environment variables, personal desktop and display settings, program groups, printers, applications preferences, and network connections.
HKEY_LOCAL_MACHINE	This subtree holds settings and information about the local machine (computer), including hardware data such as installed memory, display, disk drives, and network adapters. Also found under this heading are information and settings pertaining to installed device drivers, system services components, and system boot parameters and control data.
HKEY_USERS	This subtree holds all data for individual user profiles. This information is local to a machine instead of being kept on a server. The HKEY_CURRENT_USER subtree is a mirror of one of the HKEY_USERS profiles, along with any defaults for the local machine.
HKEY_CURRENT_CONFIG	This subtree holds the current configuration settings for software and machine values, such as the current display device setup and control values.
HKEY_DYN_DATA	This subtree holds dynamic data, used internally by the Registry. Not configurable by the user.

Table 17-1.   *The Registry Root Keys*

Registry Hives

Treating some of these root keys, or subkeys beneath them, as associated bodies of values, the static or editable portions of the Registry are composed of what the NT architects call *hives,* as mentioned earlier. A hive may hold data for the security subsystem, or it may be an overall registration base for registered software, and so on. Hives hold most of the subkeys and values for the HKEY_LOCAL_MACHINE, the HKEY_USERS, and the HKEY_CURRENT_USER root keys. Hives are held on disk as data files, with associated log files and possibly alternate files, which will be in the %SystemRoot%\system32\config directory (see Figure 17-4). Profiles for each registered user on an NT workstation or server are also given a hive. The files that implement a user's profile hive are stored, by default, in the %SystemRoot%\profiles*username* directory, but may be put elsewhere or copied to a different machine. A hive can be edited and repaired with the Registry Editor, which we'll talk about later in this chapter.

The .LOG files exist for recoverability. The process of updating a hive has several steps, to ensure Registry data integrity. With the exception of the SYSTEM hive, which we'll discuss next, the process is this: when a hive (part of the Registry) is being updated,

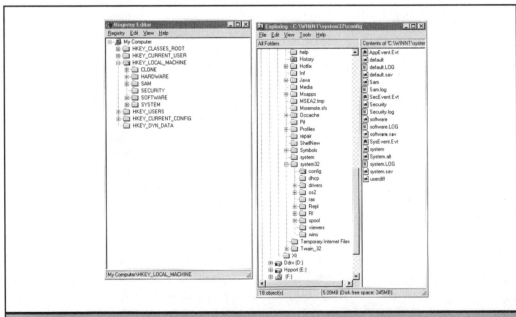

Figure 17-4. *Hives and Registry subkeys*

the first thing that happens is that NT commits the Registry changes to the appropriate .LOG file. Next, the actual hive file is marked as being in the update mode. If a crash happens at this point, the hive is recovered at the next boot by using the changes logged in the .LOG file. Otherwise, the changes are migrated from the .LOG file into the hive itself, after which the hive file is marked as updated.

Because the SYSTEM hive is utilized at a very early stage in the boot process, it cannot be recovered in the same way. During an update of the SYSTEM hive, its file is used directly, followed by an update cycle that is applied to the SYSTEM.ALT hive file. It is thus certain that at least one of these files will contain correct information should a system crash occur during data commit to the SYSTEM hive. At the next boot time, update marks are read from the SYSTEM hive file, and if it does not have the "in-update" mark, it is used. Otherwise, the SYSTEM.ALT file will be used as the basis for re-creating this hive.

Standard Filenames for the Default Hives

The standard default hives and their associated names are as follows:

Hive/Registry Location	Backing Filename(s)
HKEY_CURRENT_USER	%SystemRoot%\Profiles\username\NTUSER.DAT and NTUSER.DAT.LOG
HKEY_USERS\.DEFAULT	DEFAULT and DEFAULT.LOG
HKEY_LOCAL_MACHINE\SAM	SAM and SAM.LOG
HKEY_LOCAL_MACHINE\SECURITY	SECURITY and SECURITY.LOG
HKEY_LOCAL_MACHINE\SOFTWARE	SOFTWARE and SOFTWARE.LOG
HKEY_LOCAL_MACHINE\SYSTEM	SYSTEM and SYSTEM.ALT

The Individual Profile Hives

All user profiles, including the default profile, are implemented as individual hives (files). A hive is created and stored under the %SystemRoot%\Profiles*username* every time a new user is registered on the computer. For instance, if a new user, JohnDoe, is created on the local workstation, a profile hive (file) called NTUSER.DAT (and an NTUSER.DAT.LOG file) will be created under the %SystemRoot%\Profiles\JohnDoe subdirectory. Each user, including the administrator, receives a separate hive file because each profile is a separate entity under NT 4.

Being implemented as discrete files, each profile hive can be viewed, edited, and repaired without affecting other profiles. Also, profile hives may be copied to another computer (usually using the Start/Settings/Control Panel/System/User Profiles dialog). You must have administrator privileges to perform these operations, and, as with any other hive or part of the Registry these actions can be accomplished from a remote computer using the Registry Editor, which we'll examine later in this chapter.

HKEY_CLASSES_ROOT

HKEY_CLASSES_ROOT (see Figure 17-5) contains file association and OLE information used by, for instance, the Explorer associations dialog. This subtree is a mirror of the HKEY_LOCAL_MACHINE\SOFTWARE\CLASSES subtree. HKEY_CLASSES_ROOT provides compatibility with the 16-bit Windows registration database.

NOTE: *As with 16-bit Windows and Windows 95 file manipulation-associations, the NT Explorer application implements file associations for launching support components by file type (extension). NT stores these associations in the Registry under HKEY_CLASSES_ROOT and HKEY_LOCAL_MACHINE\SOFTWARE\CLASSES.*

HKEY_CURRENT_USER

HKEY_CURRENT_USER is the subtree that contains the user profile for the currently logged-on user on the local computer. By providing user profiles that dictate the way

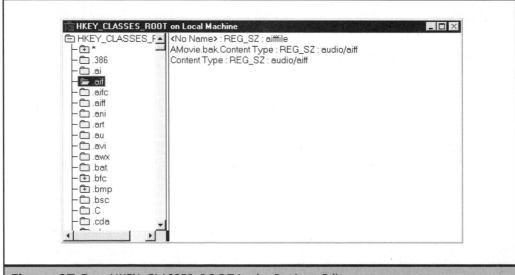

Figure 17-5. *HKEY_CLASSES_ROOT in the Registry Editor*

the desktop looks, the way network connections are made, and how individual preferences for applications and services are presented, NT 4 ensures that no matter where within the local workgroup, or domain that has a user's stored preferences, the user's session settings can be made available, and the interface presented to the user will look and feel the same.

The HKEY_CURRENT_USER subtree contains the complete settings and data necessary to customize the user's environment on an NT workstation or server. Security permissions, network connections, Start menu choices, application settings and preferences, screen size and color, and any other personal settings are stored here.

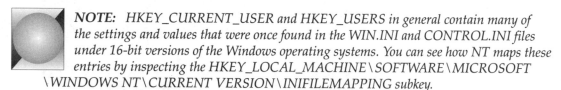 **NOTE:** *HKEY_CURRENT_USER and HKEY_USERS in general contain many of the settings and values that were once found in the WIN.INI and CONTROL.INI files under 16-bit versions of the Windows operating systems. You can see how NT maps these entries by inspecting the HKEY_LOCAL_MACHINE\SOFTWARE\MICROSOFT \WINDOWS NT\CURRENT VERSION\INIFILEMAPPING subkey.*

HKEY_CURRENT_USER may have custom entries but always has the set of default subkeys described in Table 17-2.

How Users Are Loaded

All users are initially entered into, and identified in, the HKEY_USERS subtree by their security ID (SID) string numbers (see Chapter 16 for more information on SIDs). When a new user is initially profiled and registered on an NT workstation or server, a SID string is generated for that user. The settings for that user are then entered into the HKEY_USERS subtree as a new entry and SID subkey. On subsequent boot, the HKEY_CURRENT_USER maps to one of these SIDs (see Figure 17-6). HKEY_CURRENT_USER is a transient subtree that will be assembled at logon time from the information in HKEY_USERS, where the SID matches that of the logged-on user. If no SID matches, the .DEFAULT profile values in HKEY_USERS are used.

HKEY_LOCAL_MACHINE

The HKEY_LOCAL_MACHINE subtree houses all of the parameters and settings data that controls the configuration of the local computer. This information can be entered or queried by many components. The OS uses this information to set up its software components; device drivers read from and write to the various subkeys in this tree for operating modes and parameters to control hardware; and applications and services can get their settings from this tree. This is a global subtree, and all subkeys and values are available for use no matter which user is logged on. HKEY_LOCAL_MACHINE contains six major subkeys, with many subkeys contained under each of the primary headings, listed in Table 17-3.

Primary Subkey	Holds
AppEvents	Subkeys and values that pertain to how registered applications and desktop schemes display themselves.
Console	Subkeys and values for settings pertaining to the options that control the fonts, color settings, edit modes, window size and placement, and other settings for console (DOS Box) windows.
Control Panel	Subkeys and values for various Control Panel applets, such as settings for Accessibility, Desktop, Keyboard, Mouse, and Colors options.
Environment	The values for individual users' environment variable settings. These values are listed in, and set by, the Control Panel/System applet under Environment/User Variables for *user*. Environment variables under MS-DOS and 16-bit Windows are stored in AUTOEXEC.BAT.
Keyboard Layout	Subkeys and values for the individual user's keyboard layout. Set and query these values by using the Control Panel/Keyboard or Regional Settings applet.
Network	Subkeys and values for currently associated, user-defined network connections (shared resources, such as remote drives and directories).
Printers	Subkeys and values specifying printers that are installed and configured for the current user. Set these keys and values through the Start/Settings/Printers or My Computer/Printers, Add Printer or individual printer icons.
Software	Subkeys and values that specify the active user's settings for registered software components whose parameters can be set. Same information types as found in HKEY_LOCAL_MACHINE\SOFTWARE.
Unicode Program Groups	Subkeys and values that specify names and settings for any current program groups; for backward compatibility purposes.
Windows 3.1 Migration Status	Used to store subkeys and values when migrating (upgrading) from 16-bit Windows.

Table 17-2. *Subkeys for HKEY_CURRENT_USER*

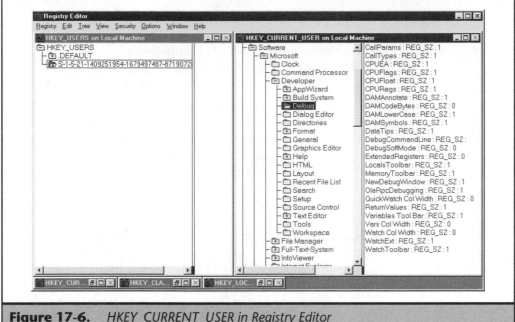

Figure 17-6. *HKEY_CURRENT_USER in Registry Editor*

HKEY_USERS

The HKEY_USERS subtree holds security IDs for all of the registered and loaded users that are known to the local machine. As mentioned earlier, these SIDs hold profiles that are migrated to HKEY_CURRENT_USER when a known user logs on. If no SID exists for the logged-on user, the subkey .DEFAULT is used to fill in values for the HKEY_CURRENT_USER subtree. The HKEY_USERS subtree always contains at least two subkeys. They are

- **DEFAULT:** The subkey that holds an "ideal" generic version of the information that HKEY_CURRENT_USER needs to create its subtree.

- **The SID string for the user who is currently logged on:** The subkey that holds a complete profile for the current user. One of the SID subkeys (or .DEFAULT) in HKEY_USERS will be used to create HKEY_CURRENT_USER.

HKEY_USERS can hold as many SIDs and their profile values and subkeys as there are registered users for the local machine. If this machine were, say, a point-of-sale terminal, HKEY_USERS might hold .DEFAULT and ten or more SID subkeys. This subtree holds subkeys and values as described in the section "HKEY_CURRENT_USER," earlier in this chapter.

Primary Subkey	Holds
CLONE	This subkey and its values are a template for setting up profiles under the \SYSTEM subkey. Correct default values are derived from this subkey, for migration to the \SYSTEM subkey. Read-only.
HARDWARE	This subkey holds a description of the physical hardware in the computer, and the drivers and devices are mapped within the system. These mappings describe which device drivers and kernel and user components are to be used, and which hardware components they map to. The mappings in this subkey are transient, being rebuilt every time the computer boots. In this way, changed components or relationships between components can be registered on the fly. The Description subkey holds values that outline the actual installed hardware. The DeviceMap subkey holds mapping data that is driver or device specific. The OwnerMap subkey holds data specific to which hardware resources own certain driver and service resources. The ResourceMap subkey holds data that registers device driver-to-hardware resource relationships. Read-only.
SAM	This subkey is used by the Security Account Manager (see Chapters 16 and 20). It holds the security database for user, group, and domain accounts. Read-only.
SECURITY	This subkey holds local security policy settings to be used by the security subsystem (see Chapters 16, 19, and 20). Read-only.
SOFTWARE	This subkey holds subkeys and values that pertain to the installed software on the local machine. Configuration data and default operating values for the installed software may be stored here. Read/write.
SYSTEM	The subkeys and values held here control how the machine boots, how (and which) drivers and services are started up, and what actions are taken and settings made at system startup. The current set of drivers, services, and actions are held in the \CurrentControlSet subkey. Read/write.

Table 17-3. *Primary Subkeys for HKEY_LOCAL_MACHINE*

TIP: *User profiles may be copied to a remote machine, so that centralized profiles may be kept, and a user can access his or her profile from anywhere on the local network. You can copy a profile to a remote machine and also delete or change the type of a profile by using the Control Panel/System/User Profiles dialog.*

HKEY_CURRENT_CONFIG

As mentioned earlier, HKEY_CURRENT_CONFIG is built from the current configuration settings for software and machine values, such as the current display device setup and control values. The information in this subtree is the dynamic part of the HKEY_LOCAL_MACHINE\HARDWARE\CurrentControlSet values and any software settings that are configuration dependent. This is a read-only subtree, and it reflects only those parts of the current configuration that can or will change, such as the video adapter mode.

Mini-Glossary

ADVANCED RISC COMPUTING (ARC) FIRMWARE   Refers first to an ARC-based computer (ARC, the RISC-based computer architectural standard, associated with the Advanced Computing Environment (ACE) consortium, a consortium of hardware and software companies formed to promote open computing environments). Second, it refers to the firmware or computing instructions (usually both instructions and data) that are stored in electrically programmable read-only memory (EP-ROM). By storing the basic instructions and configuration data in ROM, a RISC computer can be upgraded or changed easily. Also, because these instructions are stored in ROM, offboard from the CPU chip, they are in a gray area—neither hardware nor software, but "firmware."

DIRECT MEMORY ACCESS (DMA) CHANNELS   DMA is a method of transferring data between a device and the main computer memory without intervention by the CPU. DMA is handled by the device itself (bus-mastering) or by a DMA controller chip in the system, through the use of predefined I/O mechanisms involving channels or I/O pipes.

HANDLE   A unique integer that Windows uses to identify an object created or used by an application, service, or driver. Windows supplies and uses a wide variety of handles, identifying objects such as application instances, windows, menus, controls, allocated memory, output devices, files, and Registry keys.

Normally a programmer has access only to the handle and not to the object it represents. When it is required that the program examine or make changes to an object, it must supply the handle (and possibly a new value or setting for the object), which the OS will then use to process the program's request, setting object data or returning values or representations of object information.

HARDWARE RECOGNIZER   Part of the NT boot loader (usually implemented in NTDETECT.COM, which can be found in your boot directory), which together with the NT kernel, recognizes installed hardware and tells NT about what hardware is installed.

HIVES   A discrete collection of Registry information (keys, subkeys, and value entries), implemented as a file of Registry data. The Registry is divided into *hives*, as in beehive, so named by NT's designers because they thought of each Registry hive as being like a cell in a honeycomb (or, because one of them was an avid beekeeper, and couldn't resist!)

ROOT KEY   A key at the top of the Registry hierarchy. The six root keys in the NT Registry are HKEY_CLASSES_ROOT, HKEY_CURRENT_USER, HKEY_LOCAL_MACHINE, HKEY_USERS, HKEY_CURRENT_CONFIG, and HKEY_DYN_DATA.

SUBKEYS   The keys (or headings) found at any level of a hierarchical relationship within the Registry. These subkeys may have subkeys themselves. They almost always have at least some value entries (see definition of *value entries*).

USER PROFILE   A user profile contains information that defines the appearance and behavior of the individual user's desktop, network connections, and other environment settings.

VALUE ENTRIES   The individual entries within the Registry. These entries are always associated with a key (subkey) and may contain strings, numbers, executable code, or any kind of binary data.

HKEY_DYN_DATA

The HKEY_DYN_DATA subtree holds internally used dynamic data. It is for NT's internal use and is read-only.

Administration: Working with the Registry

The various Control Panel applets and administration tools, as well as NT Setup and most applications, go to great lengths to shield you from having to work with individual Registry keys and values, entering them automatically when needed. Even though most of the interaction that you have with the Registry will be indirect, there will be times when you need to manipulate or inspect the Registry proper. You can do this by using NT's two built-in Registry tools: REGEDIT.EXE and REGEDT32.EXE. Since REGEDT32.EXE is the primary NT Registry Editor, we'll concentrate on reviewing its interface and usage; and since REGEDT32.EXE has an extended superset of the functionality found in REGEDIT.EXE, you'll have no trouble using either.

You can use the Registry Editor to inspect, change, add, delete, and copy Registry entries for the various services, drivers, applications, and components in NT 4. The Registry Editor can be used to perform these functions on the local computer or, with the proper permissions (administrator), on any computer within your network. We are going to review the commands and interface that you will be presented with while using the Registry Editor, as well as some of the advanced operations that can be performed on the Registry and its hives. You'll also want to refer to Appendix A to learn about the NT diagnostics program WINMSD.EXE, in order to take advantage of and fully understand the ramifications of changing or adding values and subkeys to any part of the Registry.

Briefly, we are going to look at using the Registry Editor from the following standpoints:

- Registry Editor's user interface
- Registry Editor's operations and commands
- Registry maintenance
- Working with the Registry from a remote computer

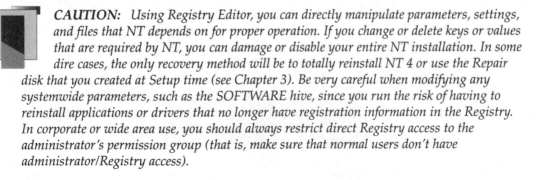

CAUTION: Using Registry Editor, you can directly manipulate parameters, settings, and files that NT depends on for proper operation. If you change or delete keys or values that are required by NT, you can damage or disable your entire NT installation. In some dire cases, the only recovery method will be to totally reinstall NT 4 or use the Repair disk that you created at Setup time (see Chapter 3). Be very careful when modifying any systemwide parameters, such as the SOFTWARE hive, since you run the risk of having to reinstall applications or drivers that no longer have registration information in the Registry. In corporate or wide area use, you should always restrict direct Registry access to the administrator's permission group (that is, make sure that normal users don't have administrator/Registry access).

Using the Registry Editor

Although neither version of the Registry Editor (see Figure 17-7) has a default entry on the Start menu, they are nonetheless automatically installed into the \System32 directory for you during NT Setup. To run the Registry Editor, double-click on \System32\REGEDT32.EXE (or REGEDIT.EXE) using Explorer, or from the Run dialog in the Start menu, type **regedt32**, and press OK. You can also invoke the Registry Editor from a console session by typing **start regedt32**, and then pressing ENTER.

REMINDER: To change values or keys within the Registry, you must have sufficient access permissions. Generally, you can make changes to the Registry if you have the kind of permissions that must be granted to work with Control Panel and Administration applications. You may view Registry keys and values without these permissions, but to effect changes, you must have been granted rights through the Administrators group, or through the use of the Registry Editor's Security/Permissions dialog, covered later in the chapter.

The Registry Editor Menus

The Registry Editor has many commands that allow you to perform almost any operation on the local or a remote Registry. The following overview of the available menu choices gives general usage along with specific instructions for each item.

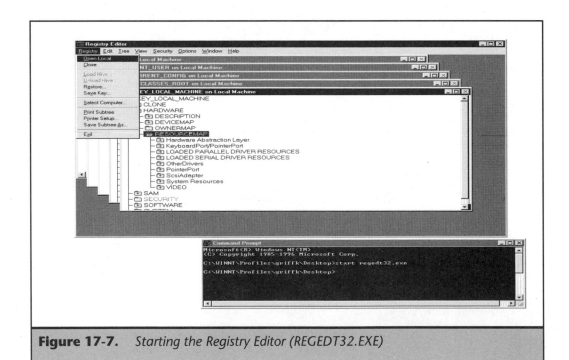

Figure 17-7. *Starting the Registry Editor (REGEDT32.EXE)*

Registry Menu Commands

OPEN LOCAL   This command opens the Registry Editor windows, each of which represents one of the predefined Registry root keys (subtrees):

- **HKEY_CLASSES_ROOT:** Although displayed as a root key and subtree, this is actually a subkey of HKEY_LOCAL_MACHINE\Software. HKEY_CLASSES_ROOT holds information for file associations, such as support for launching the correct container application when a file of a supported type is selected in Explorer, and for associated OLE applications.

- **HKEY_CURRENT_USER:** One of the subkeys of HKEY_USERS, reflecting the currently logged-on user (see the explanation at the beginning of this chapter). This subtree enumerates all of the individually set parameters for the user's personal folders, display settings, and Control Panel settings. In aggregate, this information makes up a user's profile. The hive files for any HKEY_CURRENT_USER are located in the %SystemRoot%\Profiles*username* subdirectory as NTUSER.DAT and NTUSER.DAT.LOG.

- **HKEY_LOCAL_MACHINE:** A globally valid root key and subtree that holds configuration information pertaining to the local computer (machine). This subtree is valid for any logged-on user's profile.

- **HKEY_USERS:** The root key that holds all user profiles on the local computer.

- **HKEY_CURRENT_CONFIG:** A volatile root key or subtree that is built up each time the local computer boots. At startup, this subtree is assembled with current information about the hardware profile used by the local computer.

CLOSE   Closes all open windows.

LOAD HIVE   Loads the HKEY_USERS and HKEY_LOCAL_MACHINE or a specific hive file, such as an NTUSER.DAT profile that is not in use or is on another computer.

You can view or change the contents of hive files on other computers by using the Load Hive command. By utilizing this remote capability, you can repair a hive on a computer that temporarily cannot run NT. You can also view or repair hives for profiles of local or remote users that are not currently logged on.

 NOTE: *The Load Hive and Unload Hive commands are only available for the HKEY_USERS and HKEY_LOCAL_MACHINE root keys, or for an individual user profile hive. You must have Restore and Backup permissions, as normally granted to the Administrators group, to use these commands.*

To load a hive into the Registry Editor, follow these steps:

1. From the Registry menu, choose the Load Hive command.

2. Use the Load Hive dialog box to select the file, local or remote, that contains the hive you want to load, and then choose the OK button.

3. In the Load Hive/Key Name dialog box, type the name you want to appear as a subkey where the hive will be loaded, and then choose the OK button. This action creates a new subkey in the Registry. The new subkey name can be anything you want, but you cannot load to an existing key.

Insider Info

Data from the loaded hive will appear as a new subkey under HKEY_USERS or HKEY_LOCAL_MACHINE, depending on which window was active when you loaded the hive. A new memory space within the local Registry is created by this action and will also involve using the backup .LOG file for the loaded hive. When you are finished inspecting or changing values, you should unload the hive, since the hive will remain in the system until it is unloaded.

UNLOAD HIVE   This command unloads hives that have been loaded into the local Registry from a local or remote computer. You cannot unload a default hive or a hive with an open key.

To unload a hive, select the subkey that represents a previously loaded hive. Now, choose Unload Hive from the Registry menu. The unload action will take place, and the selected key will be removed from the window where it was displayed.

RESTORE   This command allows you to restore a hive from a file you have previously saved, overwriting an existing Registry key. It is a special-purpose command that allows you to overwrite a damaged Registry key, for example, to repair a system. This is a permanent action, and any key overwritten will hold the newly restored information after rebooting the computer.

TIP: You may perform a restore on a local or remote computer, but you cannot restore to an open key or subkey, such as your local SAM, SECURITY, or active profile subtrees, because NT 4 always keeps these Registry keys open and locked.

SAVE KEY   Saves a Registry key, its subkeys, and all values as a hive file. Files created in this way can be reloaded into the Registry with the Load Hive command. Additionally, they may be restored to the Registry with the Restore command.

To successfully use the Save Key command, you must apply the command to a nonvolatile key, and you will need Backup permission, as you would have as a member of the Administrators group.

Insider Info

Volatile keys are those that are destroyed on system shutdown, and then rebuilt on system startup, as in the HKEY_LOCAL_MACHINE\HARDWARE subkey. Any key that is not saved to the Registry because of its volatility cannot be saved to file and loaded or restored. Volatile keys can be saved as text files for information purposes by choosing the Save Subtree As command, as outlined in the explanation of that command given shortly.

As part of a system maintenance plan, you might use Save Key and Restore commands as part of a regular backup routine, so that you always have copies of the Registry on hand. You can do this for all of the computers on your network, storing the backup files in a central backup directory.

SELECT COMPUTER   Use this command to connect to the Registry on a remote computer. Select the name of the computer on your network in the Select Computer dialog. As a default, the names of the computers in your domain are displayed to choose from. You may also type the name of the computer into the edit field in this dialog.

PRINT SUBTREE   This command will allow you to print the currently selected key, including all of its subkeys and value entries. It uses the default Windows NT printer (see next command, Printer Setup).

PRINTER SETUP   This command allows you to specify the printer and paper orientation for printing Registry data.

SAVE SUBTREE AS   This command will allow you to save the currently selected subkey, and every subkey and value entry below it, as a text file.

EXIT   Causes you to exit Registry Editor immediately.

Edit Menu Commands

ADD KEY   This command lets you add a subkey to the currently selected key. You can add new keys to the Registry for support of custom features or additional functionality. If you have installed a new service or device driver, you might want to add a subkey for a feature that has no automatic installation option.

To add a subkey, highlight the key under which you want to add your new subkey, and then choose the Add Key command from the Edit menu, or press the INS key. In the Add Key dialog, enter the new name for your subkey and the class of the key. The class field refers to the type that you wish to assign to this key, most likely REG_SZ, denoting that this key will be a string value. When you are ready, choose OK.

NOTE: *You must have Create permission to add a subkey. This can be assigned, or as administrator, you will have this permission automatically.*

ADD VALUE   This command allows you to assign a value entry to the currently selected key. You can assign a value entry to a newly created key, or you can change the value entry for an existing key. Each value entry is made up of three sections:

- The name of the entry (not the same as the name of the entry's key).

- The type of the value entry. This can be REG_BINARY, REG_DWORD, REG_EXPAND_SZ, REG_MULTI_SZ, or REG_SZ. You could define your own data type, but for the purposes of display and automatic formatting, the Registry Editor only supports these predefined types.

- The data for the value entry. This data can be any size, up to 1MB, in any format except DWORD. It may be binary data or executable code. There is a speed penalty when the Registry grows too large, so if you have copious data in a custom format, it would be better to add a reference to a file where this data could be kept, rather than embedding it in the Registry.

TIP: *Since the Registry deals with Unicode characters (2 bytes per character), and a value name can be 32K long, the actual size of the name cannot exceed 16K. Also, the name can be NULL, or blank, and can contain backslashes ("\"). Case will be preserved but is not evaluated by the normal Registry functions.*

To add a value entry, highlight the subkey for which you want to add (or change) a value entry. Now, from the Edit menu, choose Add Value. The Add Value dialog will be displayed. Into the Value Name edit field, type the name that you wish to assign to the value entry. Next, select the type of the entry in the Data Type dropdown list:

- To enter data as binary values, choose REG_BINARY.

- To enter data as a string, choose REG_SZ.

- To enter the data as an expandable string, choose REG_EXPAND_SZ.

- To enter the data as DWORDs (4 byte values), choose REG_DWORD.

- To represent data as multiple strings, choose REG_MULTI_SZ.

Now choose OK. A second "Editor Box" dialog will appear, the format of which is dependent on what data type you assigned to your new value entry. The Binary and DWORD editors allow you to select the number system base in which you want to enter or edit the data. In the Binary editor, you can choose base 2 or base 16 (binary or hex). Entering or editing DWORDs, you can choose base 2, base 10, or base 16 (binary, decimal, or hex). Data is always displayed in the main windows as hex in these data formats. Finally, enter the data and choose OK. Your value entry will appear in the main Registry Editor pane.

DELETE   Using either this command, from the Edit menu, or the DEL key, you can delete the currently highlighted key or value entry. You cannot delete a root or system-defined key. If a key is deleted, all of its subkeys and entry values are also deleted.

> *CAUTION:*   *Check your selections before deleting a key or value, since you cannot undo this action. If Confirm On Delete, in the Options menu, is checked (this is the default), you will be asked to confirm your actions. If you mistakenly delete a critical subkey or value entry, you can recover it if you immediately reboot the computer, pressing the* SPACEBAR *at the moment when NT starts to load, then choosing the Last Known Good boot option to start up the OS with the last boot's configuration settings. You will lose all changes that you have made in the time since you rebooted the computer the last time.*

BINARY, STRING, DWORD, MULTI STRING (VALUE ENTRY DATA EDITORS)

These commands are only available when a value entry in the Registry Editor's right pane (or value entry pane) is highlighted. They open their respective editors, as if you are entering a new key with its value entry. To edit a value entry in its native type, just double-click on the entry itself, which will open the appropriate editor. You may edit a value entry in any applicable editor. For example, you can edit a DWORD value entry in the Binary editor, which will display a DWORD's worth of binary data.

(See the previous section on the Add Key command for more information on the various formats and editors.)

Tree Menu Commands

EXPAND ONE LEVEL   This command allows you to expand the highlighted key's hierarchical tree, one level down, displaying the subkeys at the first level underneath the highlighted selection. If no subkeys exist, this command will be unavailable.

EXPAND BRANCH   This command allows you to expand the highlighted key's hierarchical tree, completely, displaying all of the subkeys at all levels underneath the highlighted selection. If no subkeys exist, this command will be unavailable.

EXPAND ALL   This command allows you to expand all trees of all of the subkeys in the active window.

COLLAPSE BRANCH   This command allows you to collapse all of the tree levels of the selected key. If the tree is already collapsed, this command will be unavailable.

View Menu Commands

TREE AND DATA   This command allows you to display both window panes of the Registry Editor's main window, showing both the Registry tree, in the left pane, and the value entries of the highlighted key in the right pane. This is the default view.

TREE ONLY   This command allows you to display the Registry tree window (normally the left pane view) only.

DATA ONLY   This command allows you to display the value entry window of the currently selected key (normally the right pane view) only.

SPLIT   This command allows you to select the split view of the active window. If the active window is already split, this command will allow you to control the split view, sizing each side of the window with a central splitter bar. If there is only one window showing either the tree or value entry view, this command will split the window and show both views.

Use the mouse or the arrow keys to move the splitter bar, and then either click the bar or press ENTER. Pressing ESC will cancel the Split command.

DISPLAY BINARY DATA   This command allows you to display the currently highlighted value entry in a binary data view dialog.

REFRESH ALL   This command updates all windows, reflecting any changes. It is not available when Auto Refresh is turned on (see "Options Menu Commands").

REFRESH ACTIVE   This command updates the active window only, reflecting any changes. Not available when Auto Refresh is turned on (see "Options Menu Commands").

FIND KEY   This command allows you to search for a (sub)key name that you enter into its Find What edit field. The search is rooted at the highlighted key or subkey and is performed only on the tree that the highlighted key belongs to.

To start a search for a key, choose the Find Key command. Enter the name of the key you wish to search for in the Find What edit field. You may optionally choose to force a search based on the following options:

- Match Whole Words Only (will not find substrings)
- Match Case (case-sensitive search)
- Search up the tree (from the highlighted selection)
- Search down the tree (from the highlighted selection)

Now choose the Find button. Once you have found a match, you can continue to search for the next selection by choosing the Find Next button.

TIP: *Many keys include underscores, spaces, or other nonalphabetic sequences (such as numbers) within their names. If you know only a portion of the string that makes up a key's name, you can search for just that portion by entering the part that you know to be valid and then performing a search with the Match Whole Words Only and Match Case options unchecked (turned off).*

Security Menu Commands

PERMISSIONS   This command displays the Registry Key Permissions dialog box, allowing you to view a list of users and groups that have permissions set for the highlighted key. It also allows you to add or remove users (or groups), control what type of permission each user or group has for the selected key, and set permissions to be equal for all subkeys under the highlighted key.

To add a user or group, choose the Add button, which will display the Add Users and Groups dialog. Choose a group, optionally choosing an individual user by pressing the Members button, and then press the Add button. Continue this routine until you have added as many groups and users as you want to. You may set their control permissions with the Type of Access dropdown listbox at the bottom of the dialog. Then choose the OK button.

To edit a user's or group's access, from the Permissions dialog, highlight a user or group and choose a permissions level from the Type of Access dropdown listbox. If you choose Special Access, you will be shown the Special Access dialog, where you can finely control access for each user or group on such permissions as Create, Delete, Query, Read, Set Value, and so on.

To set permissions on all subkeys (of the active key), check the Replace Permissions on Existing SubKeys box. You can also delete a user's or group's access to the active key (and all subkeys, if needed) by highlighting and choosing Remove.

AUDITING   Use this command to enable auditing on user- or group-initiated Registry events on the highlighted, active key. Setting up this action will cause specified events, which you choose, to be entered into the event logs, viewable with the Event Viewer (see Chapter 7). You must have specific permissions or be a member of the Administrators group to access this command.

First, you will be presented with the Registry Key Auditing dialog. To enter a user or group on which you wish to enable Registry event auditing, choose the Add button, which will display the Add Users and Groups dialog. Choose a group, optionally choosing an individual user by pressing the Members button, and then press the Add button. Continue this routine until you have added as many groups and users as you want to. Then choose the OK button.

Once you have made your choice for users and groups, you will be returned to the Registry Key Auditing dialog, where you can specify which Registry events you wish audit messages to be generated for. Also, you can check the Audit Permission on Existing Subkeys box to enable audit activity on all subkeys of the actively selected key.

Choose the events that you wish to generate audit messages for by checking the boxes next to each selected event (either to generate an event on a success or failure of the action), and then choose the OK button. Table 17-4 lists the events that can be audited for successful or unsuccessful completion.

OWNER This command displays the Owner dialog box, which identifies the user who owns the selected key and allows you to take ownership of the key, if you have been granted the right to do so by the previous owner. A system administrator can grant this right to a user or can take ownership him- or herself.

Options Menu Commands

FONT Allows you to specify the font and size used for display characters in all windows.

AUTO REFRESH If checked, will automatically update all windows to immediately reflect changes made to the Registry. Mutually exclusive with the Refresh All and Refresh Active commands on the View menu.

Event	Success or Failure of
Query Value	Attempt to read a value entry.
Set Value	Attempt to set value entries.
Create Subkey	Attempted creation of subkeys on a selected key.
Enumerate Subkeys	Attempt to list or identify the subkeys of a selected key.
Notify	Notification events from a key in the Registry.
Create Link	Attempt to create a symbolic link in a selected key.
Delete	Attempt to delete a Registry object.
Write DAC	Attempt, by a user, to gain access to a key for the purpose of writing a discretionary ACL to the key. (A discretionary ACL is a security permission—see Chapter 16.)
Read Control	Attempt, by a user, to access the discretionary ACL on a selected key.

Table 17-4. *Auditing Registry Events and the Actions That Trigger Them*

NOTE: If you are connected to a remote computer's Registry, this command, while appearing to be available, will not work. See the upcoming section, on working with remote computers.

READ ONLY MODE   Checking this menu item will mark the Registry as read-only, preventing any changes from being committed to the Registry database.

CONFIRM ON DELETE   Checking this menu item will cause the Registry Editor to display a confirmation dialog before any data is deleted from the Registry database.

SAVE SETTINGS ON EXIT   Checking this menu item will cause the Registry Editor to save window placement and arrangement, window size, and font size, when exiting the Registry Editor.

Window Menu Commands

CASCADE   This standard application command arranges windows to cascade down the screen, overlapping diagonally from the upper left to the lower right. The system menu and title bars for each window remain visible for easy selection.

TILE   This standard application command arranges windows so that they all are visible, and they all fit within the parent window, much like a tiled floor, so no windows overlap.

ARRANGE ICONS   This standard application command groups any minimized windows, represented by icons, so that they are lined up and arranged along the bottom of the parent window neatly and not overlapping.

Working with Remote Computers

You can provide long-distance support for a workstation or server by working with that computer's Registry remotely. Being able to inspect and make settings from your local workstation, affecting a computer that might be thousands of miles away, is one of the many time-saving administration functions available in NT 4.

This works the same as when you use any of the other remote-enabled administration tools, such as User Manager or Event Viewer (see Chapter 7). The only proviso is that you must have a connection to the remote computer, such as a LAN or modem with RAS and dial-up services enabled (see Chapter 13), and the Server services must be enabled and running on the remote computer.

Mini-Glossary

BINARY DATA   Base 2 data, expressed as 1s and 0s. Usually at least 1 byte in length (8 bits or 8 binary 1s and 0s).

DWORD   A DWORD is a doubleWORD value (a WORD is usually 2 bytes) made up of 4 bytes of data—so, usually a 32-bit quantity.

NONVOLATILE KEY   A Registry key that does not hold transient values and keeps its set value from computer boot to computer boot.

UNICODE   Unicode is a worldwide character encoding standard. It can represent all of the world's characters used in modern computers, including technical symbols and special characters at once, because each Unicode character is 16 bits (2 bytes) wide.

   With 2-byte characters, it is possible to have separate values for up to 65,536 characters, which provides support for such languages as Latin, Greek, Han, Hiragana, Katakana, German, French, English, and Chinese. NT's Registry utilizes the Unicode character set exclusively.

VOLATILE KEY   A Registry key that either holds transient values and does not keep its set value from computer boot to computer boot, or disappears completely.

TIP: If you use one of the newly enhanced voice modems, with the NT RAS and dial-up services, you can share the line for data and voice purposes, enabling you to talk with the user while inspecting the remote Registry over regular telephone lines. As an alternative, NT 4 has good support for ISDN (integrated services digital network) adapters, which can be made to share a 128Kbps line, with 64Kbps high-speed data, and a second voice channel for support and conversation.

Working with a Remote Registry

Preparation is the first order of business. Make sure you have physical connections and access to the remote computer. It must be on a Windows network (using NWLink-SPX/IPX or NetBEUI—see Chapter 5), or it must be available on a modem connection using RAS and dial-up services (see Chapter 13). Also, you must have been given permissions, or be a member of the Administrators group, to effectively work with a remote Registry.

   In the Registry Editor, and from the Registry menu, choose the Select Computer command. This action will result in the display of the Select Computer dialog, shown in Figure 17-8. At this time, from the dialog's Select Computer listbox, select the

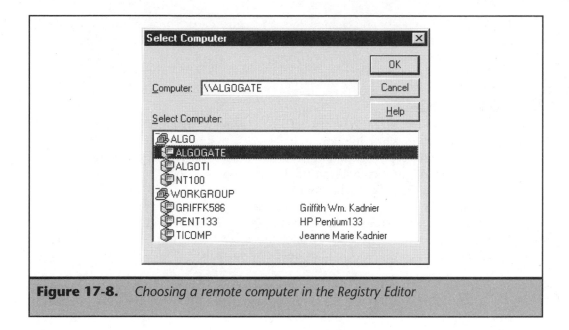

Figure 17-8. *Choosing a remote computer in the Registry Editor*

computer by double-clicking on its name, or type the name of the computer whose Registry you want to access. In the Select Computer listbox, the first name in this list represents a domain name. Double-click the domain name to expand the view if no computers are listed. You may also have one or more workgroups displayed, which you may browse for the name of a computer on the network.

Once you have chosen the remote computer, press the OK button, and you will be returned to the main Registry Editor window, which will now display two additional Registry windows for the key, which you can browse and edit on the remote computer. One window will display the remote root key for HKEY_USERS, and the other window will display the root key for HKEY_LOCAL_MACHINE. You may also explicitly load a remote profile (if not in use on the remote machine) by browsing the remote %SystemRoot%\Profiles subdirectories with the Registry/Load Hive command.

Things to Watch Out for in a Remote Session

Auto Refresh will not work across a remote Registry Editor session. What's more, if Auto Refresh is on while in a remote session, the manual refresh methods will be disabled, and no refresh will be employed until Auto Refresh is turned off. The Registry Editor will try to do this automatically for you. When you open a remote session in the Registry Editor, it will check to see if Auto Refresh is enabled and will then attempt to turn it off. If you override this action, and turn Auto Refresh back on, thinking that it will work over a remote connection (which it appears to do), the other refresh methods that should be used will be unavailable.

Also, you can only view and change keys and entry values on a remote computer if you have been given specific access through the Security/Permissions dialog, or if you are a member of the Administrators group and you are logged on as such.

What's Next

Manipulation of the Registry can be critical when trying to diagnose or recover from an anomalous situation. Knowing how to gain access to and change settings in the Registry, including the types of valid information that resides there, can save you many hours of reconfiguration and multiple installation sessions.

Next, we will briefly look at what makes up the BackOffice suite for NT 4, how to install it, and how to make use of some of its advanced features. BackOffice is becoming the application suite of choice for implementing AS400-NT connectivity, as well as SQL database and Mail services. BackOffice *will* be in your future, and after you read the next chapter, you won't be caught by surprise!

Chapter Eighteen

The NT BackOffice Suite

The NT BackOffice Suite is a loosely woven set of server-based executables that augment and extend the basic "out of the box" NT Server services. BackOffice currently consists of six major add-on modules to NT Server, with more single-purpose modules coming online all the time: SQL Server, SNA Server, Systems Management Server (SMS), Microsoft Proxy Server, Internet Information Server, and Microsoft Exchange Server. Since BackOffice is being extended and enhanced constantly, this chapter also looks at one of the newest NT server add-ons, Index Server, as an example of what you can expect to see offered soon. Since Microsoft has recently concentrated its BackOffice efforts on extending its network-related products, you can count on a blurring of the lines between traditional BackOffice components (those server add-ons that address local data and applications) and the recently introduced Internet-enabled server elements.

Microsoft is already in the process of extending BackOffice into the world of the Internet by adding BackOffice modules that address electronic transactions and commerce on the Internet. The BackOffice Suite will also be a target for extension into such areas as video and multimedia servers for cable companies and entertainment markets, and secure transaction services, such as automated teller machines and terminals.

An Introduction to the Players

Let's quickly run down the list of major BackOffice server modules before covering them in more detail. The list grows longer all the time, targeting more specialized areas (see Figure 18-1). Since BackOffice has traditionally addressed complete functional blocks, we'll review the base set here. Although some of these server products are not *technically* part of the official BackOffice Suite, they nonetheless now belong to the broader BackOffice family. For instance, Microsoft's Internet Information Server (IIS) is not part of the BackOffice product per se; it is currently shipped free, along with NT Server. But it is an add-on BackOffice server product, and it dovetails and interoperates with SQL Server, to name one important relationship. With so many server-side products coming online in the next year, the traditional lines of product demarcation are soon going to fade.

SQL Server—A Database Platform

SQL Server is a client/server relational database platform. Recent releases have improvements to throughput and support for AppleTalk networks using native protocols. Also improved, and added to, are the available Open Database Connectivity (ODBC) drivers. Today, SQL is the most widely used, high-powered, database client/server platform. Support for SQL in the BackOffice Suite enables many large-scale minicomputer tasks to be performed on an NT installation. Small applications can also take advantage of SQL's query and report power, because the impact on performance in these installations, using SQL Server, has been minimized. Working in concert with NT 4, which has specific optimizations for SQL Server, this server component shows drastic increases in speed of execution over prior releases.

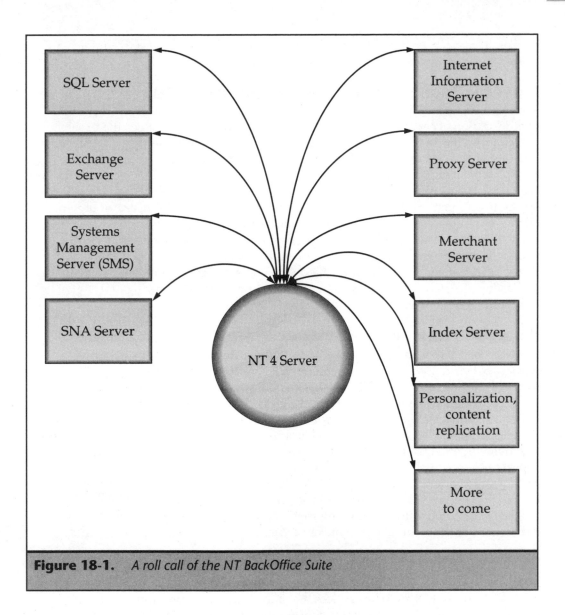

Figure 18-1.   *A roll call of the NT BackOffice Suite*

SNA Server—Connectivity to IBM

SNA Server provides connectivity to IBM mainframes and minicomputers like those of the AS/400 variety. The newest release can handle upwards of 2,000 clients and 10,000 host sessions, making it a powerful gateway server for one or more IBM mini- or mainframe connections. Support for CA/400, IBM's client access software, and native AS/400 client connectivity, is now included with NT 4 and Windows 95, so you don't have to deal with the typical MS-DOS client setup and application set provided by IBM. This has been a problem until now, because PC-based CA/400 required inefficient and buggy MS-DOS driver support.

Systems Management Server—Remote Maintenance

Systems Management Server (SMS) enables you to institute remote inventory and administration of clients on a Microsoft-based network. SMS addresses the problem of software and hardware maintenance overhead inherent in any client/server scenario; software is installed on many clients, each needing to be managed and updated locally, with attention to differences in their specific installations. Traditionally, this has been done by people who have had to visit each client machine site when installing or upgrading a component. SMS relieves the system installer or administrator of many of the duties required when performing traditional on-site installation and management of client hardware and software. SMS can connect to a machine over the network, making it possible to perform a variety of support and diagnostic tasks remotely. These include inventory of installed hardware and software components; software replication, distribution, and installation; and performance monitoring and troubleshooting for networks, client hardware, and software.

IIS and Proxy Server

The Microsoft Proxy Server provides TCP/IP/UDP and Remote Winsock proxy services for virtual WAN and Internet firewall connectivity, working alongside Internet Information Server (IIS), the BackOffice component that provides standard Internet services such as WWW, FTP, and GOPHER (see Chapter 25 for in-depth information on IIS). With the advent of a native proxy server, only available for Unix systems (and the like) until now, NT 4 becomes very attractive in companies that need to provide Internet connectivity along with corporate security. Of course, you should expect to see competitive offerings from Netscape and others, too.

IIS is currently shipped free with NT 4 Server, so you can install this server without having to purchase CALs (client access licenses). It is a capable and complete base-Internet server, and with so many Internet server products charging hundreds of dollars for licensing, this can be a major saving.

Exchange Server—Messaging Services

Microsoft Exchange Server is the email and client/server messaging system component of BackOffice. The services that Exchange Server provides extend to telephony and fax, group messaging functions such as providing standardized company forms and scheduling, and intranet/Internet email. This makes Exchange Server applicable for intranet deployment on a company's private LAN as well as serving that organization's Internet messaging needs. Exchange Server implements all of the most popular Internet-related communication and messaging protocols, such as POP3, SMTP, NNTP, X.400, and MIME. Where possible, Exchange is integrated with other messaging services, such as Internet-based chat and meeting applications, and fax and dial-up networking.

A Glimpse into the Future

As we have learned, Microsoft is expected to extend the BackOffice Suite to include banking and transactional server-side applications and multimedia and network application servers that might be used, say, by telephone, cable, and television companies. You will most likely see such specialized server applications as secure electronic commerce, for handling credit cards and smartcards across the Internet; catalog and purchasing services; and even high-bandwidth imaging, control, and data retrieval servers for vertical markets such as medical records, home automation, and satellite communications.

The BackOffice Components

The following sections discuss the primary BackOffice components currently shipping. Because BackOffice is constantly being extended, this chapter covers the primary components available at the time of this writing, some additional family members being introduced now, and then wraps up with a look to the future.

SQL Server

SQL Server is a high-performance database management system supporting distributed NT client/server computing. The Structured Query Language (SQL) is the industry standard, used in almost all modern, heavy-duty database applications. SQL Server comes with a host of graphically enhanced management tools and allows for full server-side scheduling to enable turnkey operation of multiple servers and automated remote operations.

SQL Server's data replication facilities provide for flexible and reliable distribution of information across an entire network, to and from SQL Server; and they provide linkage to other databases through the use of ODBC (a database interchange specification and implementation, spearheaded by Microsoft). SQL Server also provides for integration with Internet and intranet services and applications. It can provide database access in support of a company's FTP, GOPHER, or WWW site. Using SQL Server's Web Assistant application, you can fill your Web page with data, directly from a SQL database, making the data available to employees only, on an intranet, or to the general Internet public. In addition, the auditing and logging features generated by Internet Information Server (IIS) are directly accessible by SQL Server, so that reports of usage and trend information can be derived explicitly.

SQL Server's Distributed Transaction Coordinator application enables MIS personnel or administrators to create distributed database applications, using automated SQL transaction management spread across multiple servers. This kind of facility saves time and effort when you would otherwise face the task of individually coding, distributing, and customizing separate client applications for use across an entire network.

Exchange Server

Exchange Server is NT's client/server-based, integrated email server (see Figure 18-2). Exchange provides support for, and linkage to, built-in messaging services and functionality that includes Internet mail protocols, fax services, and support for telephony applications (such as automated dialing and voice messaging). With Exchange Server, you get the ability to send and receive secure, encrypted email, to implement group meeting and appointment scheduling (say, through Microsoft's Schedule+ application), to provide and manage companywide forms, send and receive faxes, and to implement applications that let you hold group chats and meetings over the network.

NOTE: In most cases where heavy volumes or large numbers of clients are involved, you will want to run Exchange Server on its own dedicated NT server. Exchange requires a lot of horsepower to run more than just a simple 5- to 10-person messaging facility. Added to this is the fact that Exchange keeps its files (the email and interoffice messaging) for clients, centrally, on the server side, until the clients have deleted those messages, or explicitly moved their messages to private client-side mailboxes. This can require prodigious amounts of hard disk space, so cautious deployment of Exchange is always in order.

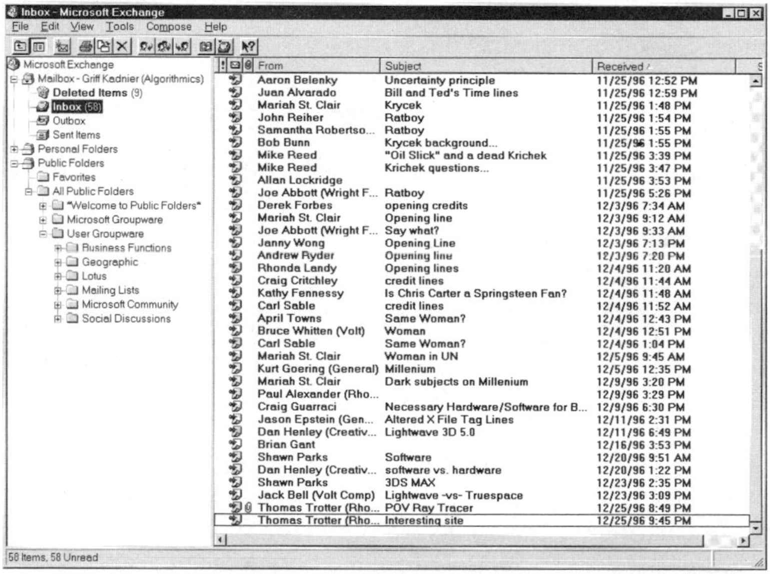

Figure 18-2.   *An Exchange client session*

In this day and age of increased security consciousness, it is important to know that your email and message passing facility is secure from prying eyes. Exchange Server implements digital signatures (for message signing and sealing) and digital encryption for messages and email, both as an intranet and Internet platform. The Exchange Internet Mail Connector provides standard SMTP and POP email services. By using this facility, you can build a wide area private messaging network—for your sales force or remote offices, for instance—by tunneling through the Internet, which Exchange can use as a wide area network to connect private clients and servers to your Exchange Server.

For internal company needs, Exchange Server ships with a complete set of group-related applications. These are the kind of applications that would normally be used by a company for everyday business support, such as special-purpose discussion groups, help desk inquiries and requests, customer logging and tracking, and bulletin board services. Exchange can provide special-interest or targeted group support, with its ability to create customized email aliases. Adding individuals to these group aliases lets you create private mailing lists and distribution lists. For instance, a company's Exchange alias "R&D" might include only those employees and vendors who work directly with a small prototyping group within the organization. By addressing mail to R&D, instead of to the seven or eight individuals within the group, email and discussion can be easily routed to only the members of the alias group.

Exchange Server is expandable. You can start out with an Exchange installation that services a small group initially, and automatically expand services to a wider audience later on. Since Exchange can spread its services by synchronously replicating and distributing shared information across multiple servers, the response time for scaled-up installations generally will not suffer in a correct deployment. Message routing and directory replication can be automatically expanded and configured, so Exchange will provide a path for your messaging services to grow with your needs.

SNA Server

These days, a large group of die-hard IBM users are seriously looking at replacement of their terminal-based data entry and display functions. Although they still require the power of a mini- or mainframe IBM back end, these users are discovering the advantages of client-side environments that allow them to interact with applications written for the Windows platforms. Traditionally, most of the data input and output on the client side of an IBM mini- or mainframe installation has been through the use of, say, a 3270 IBM terminal. These terminals are, for the most part, character- and page-based displays, and have no windowing or simultaneously displayed multitasking capability.

With SNA Server, enabling NT-to-IBM host connectivity, the use of microcomputer front ends is now possible. They can provide reliable and secure access to IBM hosts, including terminal and printer emulation, file transfer, database access, and transaction processing. The SNA Server bridges the NT local area network-to-IBM host communications pathway, providing processing and routing in order to relieve client computers of the responsibility of implementing protocol and interface translation. Your PC clients can use standard protocols, such as TCP/IP or IPX/SPX, to connect to the SNA Server on an NT Server installation. Then, the SNA Server performs the translation and protocol management, which allows it to connect to an IBM mainframe or AS/400 system using the SNA protocol (see Figure 18-3).

Added to this is the inherent facility allowing you to pipe the output from an IBM client session directly into another client-side Windows application, such as a database or spreadsheet. SNA Server includes ODBC and DRDA (Distributed Relational Database Architecture) drivers so that Windows-based clients using Excel, Oracle, or other standard desktop applications can access IBM databases without an additional host database gateway. Support for DB2 for MVS, SQL/DS for VM, and DB2/400 for AS/400 databases is standard.

SNA Server ships with a complete suite of installation and administration tools, allowing you to set up your NT-to-IBM bridge and the client-side sessions. Windows-based tools are included to support host printing and AS/400 shared-folders access. You can implement your SNA gateway with most types of client-side and SNA host

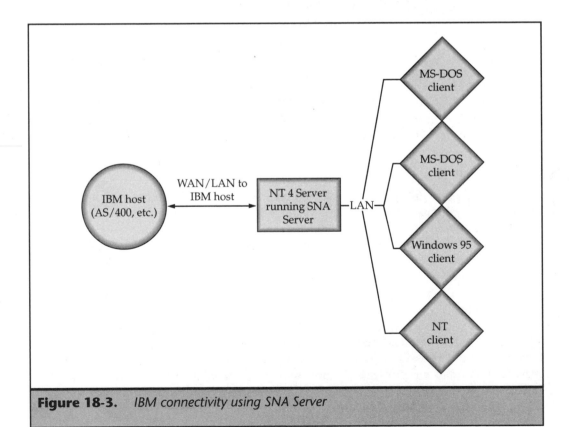

Figure 18-3. *IBM connectivity using SNA Server*

connections, and several scenarios are possible when administering SNA Server. Connections across LAN and WAN routers and bridges, and through remote dial-up transfers, are all possible.

Systems Management Server (SMS)

SMS implements a set of functions and server- or client-side applications that help to centralize administrative tasks and support that would otherwise have to be performed on-site, such as hardware and software inventory, software distribution, installation and setup, software and hardware troubleshooting, and network functions management (see Figure 18-4).

The hardware and software inventory functions track what hardware and software you have and where it is located. You can use SMS to track which clients on your network need updating or maintenance. For instance, SMS will enable you to remotely discover which of your client PCs need updated video or printer drivers and which are running low on disk space or physical memory. This is an important time-saver when you are contemplating a software upgrade on multiple clients. With SMS you

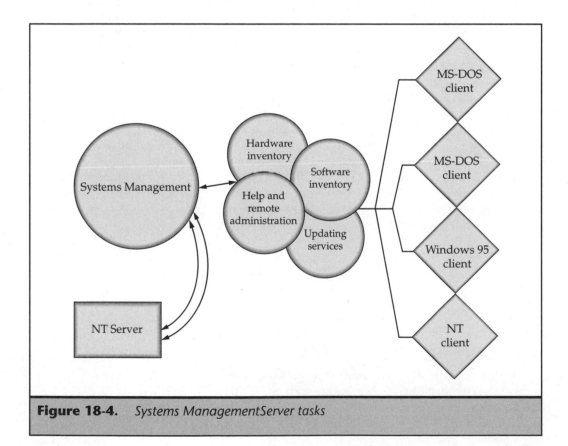

Figure 18-4. *Systems ManagementServer tasks*

can automatically generate inventory and update information for thousands of clients simultaneously; performing these tasks on-site would require many maintenance employees and would take many days or months to do manually.

You can administer PCs remotely with SMS by taking direct control of these client computers if they are running MS-DOS or Windows operating systems. Using this capability, you can perform software installation and troubleshooting, setup and administration of applications and drivers, and you can provide help or update information to the client users. MIS managers will appreciate the possibility of automating software updates and distributing new software and help files from a central location where the manager has control over how and when the software is updated or initially installed.

Internet Information Server

Microsoft Internet Information Server (IIS), which is covered more fully in Chapter 25, is the only Internet and intranet server integrated into and shipped with NT Server. Although servers from Netscape and other competitors will work just fine, IIS is specifically designed to interoperate with NT's other BackOffice components (such as SQL Server), and IIS is a fully capable and complete WWW, FTP, and GOPHER server.

IIS setup is almost automatic, because it asks only a few installation questions, such as where you want to create the default directories that hold the service files and storage space. All of the other setup parameters are given default values, generally designed to get you up and running, for which you can provide custom parameters later (see Chapter 25). You can potentially set up and be operational with an Internet or intranet Web page or FTP service within minutes of installation. IIS provides access to files and content from NT Server or Workstation, Novell NetWare file servers, or IBM hosts (through SNA Server) to the Internet or to your own intranet.

Administration is presented graphically through the IIS management applications in order to monitor and log all activity and grant permissions to users for access to network resources. Since NT provides the capability to remotely administer IIS, these tasks can be done from the local server, or from a remote workstation on the Internet or your intranet.

IIS services and operates with all known client browser applications, such as Internet Explorer, Netscape, and Mosaic. IIS also supports integration with Proxy Server in BackOffice, which we will take a look at next, for increased security and control.

Proxy Server

A *proxy server* is software that runs on a gateway or firewall machine and lets authorized clients make WAN requests such as HTTP and FTP. The BackOffice NT Proxy Server is an integrated proxy server, complete with client software, that enables secure Internet access for every desktop client in an organization. Proxy servers are used in concert with, or as a software extension and replacement for, expensive and difficult-to-maintain hardware routing equipment.

BackOffice Proxy Server supports all popular Internet protocols, including WWW (HTTP), FTP, RealAudio, VDOLive (streaming video), IRC (chat), SMTP, POP, and NNTP mail and news protocols. Proxy Server includes support for the IPX/SPX network protocol, obviating the need to install TCP/IP support over your LAN, making Internet access more secure, and reducing LAN configuration overhead.

Internet and intranet sites can be accessed by client Web browsers running on any operating system, including all Win16 and Win32 Windows Sockets applications. Proxy Server uses active caching technology to speed access to frequently visited sites or documents, automatically updating the cache when needed.

Proxy Server allows you to secure your LAN against unauthorized inbound and outbound traffic. Because you can use IPX/SPX only, no TCP/IP access needs to be available on your LAN through your gateway to the client machine. This secures the inbound route. Administrators can grant or deny outbound access based on user, service, port, or IP domain. Access to specific sites can be blocked and tracked using IIS.

Using a Proxy Server to Implement Secure Links

Typically, small networks have had to resort to insecure scenarios involving an NT Remote Access server (see Chapter 13) acting as a simple TCP/IP packet router between a WAN or the Internet and an internal network. This works very well, by the way. A multihomed NT server—one that has an internal network interface card for the LAN and a modem or WAN connection for the wider area link—is perfectly capable of performing this simple routing duty, but you will encounter two types of problems using this kind of setup.

First, you need a range of static IPs, usually assigned by your Internet service provider or WAN administrator. This is a hassle to administer and set up, even if you use DHCP (discussed in Chapter 12) to assign these IPs on the fly from your IP pool. Also, this obviously requires you to be running TCP/IP on every participating client workstation within your subnet. Second, you have to set a couple of parameters in the NT Server Registry, as well as set up the default gateways and IP addresses or DHCP clients on your Windows client machines. This takes administration time and can be a real pain, unless you have a bunch of TCP/IP experts to go around.

A Remote Access server works so well in this simple router role that you end up with a fully functional two-way connection with the WAN. If this happens to be the Internet, everyone in the world will be able to access every one of your workstations. You can try to seal access by turning off file and print sharing, keeping a tight lid on user permissions and passwords, and so on; but you are still going to end up with a great big security hole.

The traditional means for implementing secure links of this type have been centered around both hardware and software solutions. The hardware solution is to route all WAN traffic through a hardware router. This is an expensive and potentially high-maintenance fix. It works very well, but for small companies it's just too expensive and requires too much hand-holding.

The other solution is to install a proxy server between your WAN and LAN connections. Proxies cache, replicate, and filter on a configurable basis, sort of like a caching router in software. This sounds like a great way to go, since traffic on a proxy can be controlled tightly, and filters can be set on almost any kind of packet traffic. The drawback to this solution is the nature of the proxy server market. Almost all proxy servers that are commercially available have been targeted at Unix or other operating systems. Until now, this has meant that you have to, for example, run a Unix box as your proxy server.

The BackOffice Proxy Server provides CERN-style proxy services (WWW, FTP, and GOPHER) for almost any client and also includes Remote Winsock (RWS) for enhanced services for Windows clients, such as VDO and RealAudio. The really great part of Proxy Server, however, is that it allows you to secure your internal LAN by removing the necessity to run TCP/IP internally. Proxy Server can act as an RWS service that allows client access using only IPX/SPX protocols. You can completely secure your internal network and gain a little speed and memory back by not having TCP/IP installed at all.

When you install Proxy Server, the dialog boxes walk you through the setup of a local address table (LAT) and copy the proxy RWS client setups to your hard disk. The administration of Proxy Server (Proxy and RWS) is done through the IIS administration application, and you can assign Proxy and RWS permissions to individual user groups in your NT domain by using the property sheets for each server (see, for example, Figure 18-5).

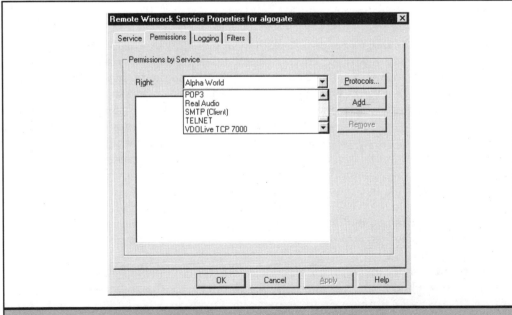

Figure 18-5.   *Setting permissions in Proxy Server*

You install the RWS client on each machine in your LAN, set up browsers and other applications that need to know how to connect through the server proxy to obtain proxied services such as WWW and FTP access, and go! There is a penalty to be paid on the server side, however. Proxy Server uses proactive caching, which chews up a minimum of 50MB of disk space. You can get away with less, but performance of Web browsers almost assuredly will suffer.

You can add new protocols to RWS, in case your favorite service is not listed. You can also set filters on permissions by domain name or IP. You cannot yet filter out certain types of traffic, just whole IPs or domains.

Proxy Server can be administered from an NT client using Internet Service Manager, which is important since remote administration is becoming a must. In its present form, however, Proxy Server has a few limitations:

- It doesn't allow for the use of Web page administration software, such as Netscape.

- It requires that you set up proxy addresses on each client application that needs to be configured.

- Filling out dialog boxes, which are set up on most browsers, to use proxy services (even electronically) will cost some administration time.

A Taste of the Future of BackOffice: Index Server

As an adjunct to NT Server and BackOffice, Microsoft is constantly releasing new, specialized server-side components. As a sample of these technologies, let's take a look at Index Server.

Index Server is a new BackOffice component made to run with NT Server 4. It enables you to query, search, and retrieve all types of stored information in just about any format and across any server using the Microsoft Distributed File System (DFS) and a point-and-click interface. (See Chapter 14 for more information on DFS.)

Index Server enables you to access all types of documents over an Internet or intranet connection in their original format, without the need to convert those documents to HTML or another browser format. Primarily used to create and maintain indexing on all types of documents, Index Server allows you to query the complete text and properties of every document stored on, or accessible to, your Web server. The search engine finds information in file types such as those created by Word, Excel, PowerPoint, and so on.

Index Server queries and searches are customizable. Search parameters can be set on such criteria as author, subject, modification date, or modification time. In addition, Index Server is designed to run in the background, updating its parameters when files change and automatically recovering from power failures or crashes.

Index Server includes built-in administrative tools to help you optimize your query service and give you site and performance information, including number of queries processed and response time. Built-in support for multiple languages is also included.

And More to Come

You will see many more server-side components coming onto the market as NT 4 gains popularity. The inherent ease of porting to, or designing directly for, NT 4 will engender many vertical or task-specific component releases in the near future. In development now are such components as smartcard, encryption, and banking services layers, streaming video and cable TV production servers, and Internet commerce servers featuring secure back channels for credit transactions to and from merchants.

Right now, the BackOffice Suite is growing every month. It seems like an avalanche of specialized server products, but actually each product is fulfilling a need in either a vertical market or in general utility. These products have been asked for, or they are components that implement services on NT which have been available on Unix or other operating systems for a time. This trend only serves to ensure the success of NT as a general OS platform. As NT becomes more capable and encompassing, you can be sure that even fanatic users of other operating systems will take a second look. We leave this section with a brief mention of other new additions to the BackOffice family.

Merchant Server

Following along with IIS, Microsoft has introduced Merchant Server. This server enables corporations to set up commercial Web sites that are designed to be implemented and maintained with little custom support.

Merchant Server integrates a Web site with a merchant's existing order management systems, such as customer databases, inventory management and control, and product ordering applications. It provides dynamic product and ordering content that consumers can browse through to get detailed ordering and specifications. A secure shopping basket, status, ordering, and receipt system is implemented.

Personalization System

Working in concert with IIS, this server component enables an organization to present each customer with personalized interaction and communication.

The Personalization System allows you to create and present custom content based on a customer's identity, online navigation and actions, queried interests, and other preferences. Surveys are also supported, along with customized email to your customers. Included is a scheme that allows the system to identify previous users without necessarily having to resort to re-registration or username/password dialogs.

Conference Server

With the addition of Conference Server to BackOffice, NT now supports online conferencing and real-time communications applications, such as Microsoft's NetMeeting application, as well as IP telephony (i.e., Internet phone). Directory services allow users to look up other users while online.

Conference Server includes two server components: Internet Chat Server (ICS) and Internet Locator Server (ILS). ICS implements real-time communications with support for chat sessions having specific attributes, such as public, secure, by invitation only, and theater/auditorium styles. Standard Internet Relay Chat (IRC) protocols are also supported by Conference Server.

ILS supports search and locate services that allow users to find each other while online. Directory services for ICS's locator are directly supported for Microsoft NetMeeting, the real-time meeting, whiteboard, file transfer, and IP telephony client that ships as part of Internet Explorer, the Microsoft browser.

Content Replication System

The Content Replication system provides facilities to replicate, or move, some or all of a Web site's content across the Internet, between servers. It does so in a secure way, and has the ability to undo replication, in a manner similar to rolling back a SQL transaction. An organization could use the Content Replication system to reliably and securely distribute Web content to many satellite servers, either partially or in total.

Networking, Client Support, and Licensing

BackOffice components run on Windows NT Server. They are variously designed to interoperate with systems running Microsoft LAN Manager, Novell NetWare, TCP/IP-based networks (such as Unix systems), IBM LAN Server, Banyan VINES, DEC Pathworks, AppleTalk and Macintosh systems, IBM SNA for mainframes, and AS/400 miniframes.

Client support is generally available for Windows 95, Windows 3.x, Windows for Workgroups, MS-DOS, OS/2, Unix, NT Workstation, and Apple Macintosh computers.

Microsoft licenses BackOffice server applications on a per-client (per-seat) or per-server basis. You must first acquire a server license for the BackOffice product you wish to use and then buy a client access license (CAL) for each client computer (seat) that will access the server product. CALs allow a client access to the server component, wherever it is situated, on any server on the network.

Since usage patterns among users vary, concurrent use rights are also available for NT Server, SQL Server, and SNA Server. CALs are sold individually or in bulk packs. This kind of licensing model lets you purchase only those licenses that you need for your installation. A BackOffice CAL allows a client to access all the BackOffice applications, whether they are on one computer or distributed throughout the local network.

BackOffice servers are also available in a single, complete package. When you purchase this package, you are granted a BackOffice Server license, which requires you to run all the applications on a single-server machine.

What's Next

Next, we are going to shift gears and take a look at the internals of NT in a more intimate way. This can be important to you, as a user or administrator, when looking to extend or enhance your system with third-party applications, drivers, or custom programming.

Even if you are not planning to customize your NT installation immediately, the information presented in the next chapters can be useful to you in more subtle ways. The more your know about the components that make up the NT operating system, the better you will understand their interaction and purpose. This can make the difference between being lost when presented with a cryptic error or event message and having enough background to know where to look next to solve an error condition or tune a system parameter.

PART FIVE

For Programmers and Power Users

Chapter Nineteen

The HAL, Kernel, and Executive

From a practical standpoint, we can ask ourselves why we should want to know anything about the deep internals of NT. We can safely assume that a programmer will want a firm grounding, but a system administrator or manager may also have to make software and hardware decisions involving many thousands of dollars that also affect all of the users of the system. In these cases, it seems prudent to know as much about the internal workings of the system as possible. This chapter, and the ones that follow, are designed to provide that knowledge.

This chapter covers the basics of NT's architecture, and then focuses on the lowest level of operability—the underpinnings of NT—those modules that allow applications to run and provide the interface to your hardware and storage. As we have already learned, NT 4 is a modular, rather than monolithic, operating system. To review, it is composed of the following collection of more specialized modules (also see Figure 19-1):

- **Hardware:** While not strictly part of the OS, NT supports these hardware platforms: Intel x86, DEC Alpha, MIPS, and PowerPC.

- **Hardware abstraction layer (HAL):** This lowest layer abstracts and hides differences in hardware, providing standard interfaces to any system software above it, and separating hardware dependencies from the rest of the operating system. This is the layer, sometimes written or augmented by the OEM (the computer hardware manufacturer), that allows NT to be logically portable between hardware platforms. All of the common hardware-dependent routines can be found in the HAL, supporting the lowest levels of hardware and memory I/O. This prevents specific computers—those that need to have custom I/O routines for a specific chipset, bus, or hardware feature—from introducing dependencies into the rest of the NT base architecture and codeset. Because most machine dependencies are kept within the HAL, the builders of NT can keep most of the code (almost all in C or C++) that makes up the rest of the OS in one version only, with specialized definitions for each supported platform.

NOTE: The HAL, for example, would be used by a hardware manufacturer to isolate differences in the way each make and model of computer presents a logically standard function block to programs and OS software. If an NEC computer uses a specialized NEC-made chipset to implement memory management, access, or paging for RAM memory, the HAL would do translation and hardware communication, both in and out, so that the rest of NT would (and should) not know about any special features in that NEC computer hardware. As an aside, it's also worthy of note that H-A-L is one off (alphabetically) from I-B-M!

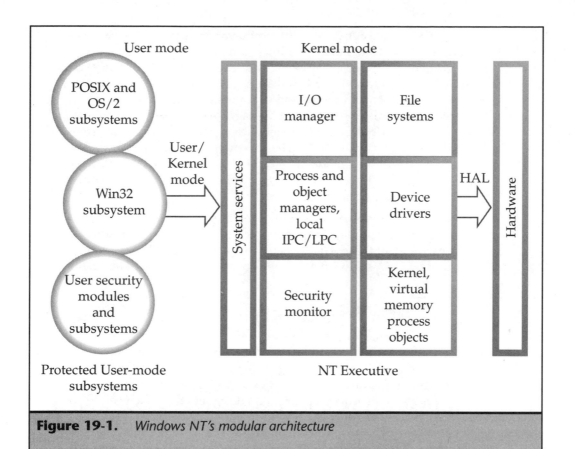

Figure 19-1. *Windows NT's modular architecture*

- **Kernel:** The kernel is at the heart of NT's modular OS design. The kernel manages NT's basic operations such as memory allocation, object synchronization and events, threading, multiprocessor synchronization, and hardware exception handling. The kernel services requests from many "Kernel mode" components and device drivers that utilize its services, which then sometimes results in access to the HAL. A request might be made from another component in which a buffer memory, or a spinlock (a kind of synchronization object), is created for the component's use. The kernel is responsible for fulfilling these requests.

NOTE: When a program at the application (User mode) level requests a buffer, an I/O operation, a thread, system, or synchronization object, or other low-level service, the call will eventually filter down to the kernel, where, in its most basic form, the request will be fulfilled. Security and abstraction through the Kernel/User mode barrier will, of course, hide these operations from the application level.

- **NT Executive:** The Executive is the highest layer of software that represents the entire subset of Kernel mode modules, providing low-level OS services to NT's User mode protected subsystems. (The Executive is the collective name for most of NT's top-level Kernel mode services.) The Executive's modules each manage a particular system service. For instance, object creation and management is handled by the Object Manager. Another component, the Security Reference Monitor, works together with the protected subsystems to provide the security model for NT. The Executive also manages most device driver interaction (although not all, in NT 4) with hardware devices, through the I/O manager and lower level device drivers, on behalf of all User mode processes that require such access.

- **Protected User mode subsystems:** These are User mode protected components that run and support applications native to Win32 and other supported OS-API environments. These subsystems include the Win32 subsystem, the OS/2, and the POSIX subsystem. We will cover these fully in Chapter 20.

The Hardware Abstraction Layer (HAL)

The lowest level and most machine-architecture-dependent part of NT, the HAL, is a small layer of software that obscures and abstracts any hardware differences between hardware platforms, regardless of the processor in use. Through the routines provided by the HAL, all types of hardware look and act exactly alike in respect to the upper layers of the operating system, thus relieving NT's designers from the need to write different versions of any of the other NT system modules, or to design each variant for communication with any specific hardware platform. This does not mean that NT is wholly *binary* compatible. A version of NT is built by Microsoft, using native compilers, for each supported platform.

HAL routines are called from both the base operating system, including the kernel, and from device drivers, through the I/O manager. For kernel routines, the HAL provides a single programmatic model for the OS to use in dealing with hardware devices like the interrupt controller (for x86 machines, this is an 8259 PIC-type device), the memory and processor management chipsets, and the DMA hardware. For device drivers, the HAL provides the ability to support a variety of I/O architectures, rather than NT being restricted to any one model. The HAL also deals with the details of symmetric multiprocessing (where more than one processor is installed, and processing duties are split between these CPUs), and abstracts these details for the rest of the OS.

The Kernel

Tightly bound with the HAL (and just above it logically) is the kernel, at the heart of NT 4. Among the kernel's most important duties is its responsibility to schedule execution time on the CPU for any given process that needs to run. The scheduling of threads is at the core of how NT provides multitasking and preemptivity. Also, for multiprocessor machines, the kernel plays a synchronization role among the various processors, for performance optimization.

Scheduling and the Function of Threads

The functional objects the kernel schedules (which represent an activity to be performed) are called *threads*—the most basic entity in the system that can be scheduled for execution. Threads are defined in the context of a *process*, which we'll look at when we examine the Process Manager, later in this chapter.

 NOTE: *A process represents an address space, a set of objects owned by or visible to the process, and a set of one or more threads that run in the context of the process. The Object Manager manages objects as resources that can be manipulated by the operating system. We'll examine objects more fully when we talk about the Object Manager, also later in this chapter.*

The kernel optimizes scheduling and dispatching of threads in order to maximize utilization of the system's CPU, and the kernel schedules these threads for execution on the basis of their assigned priority, processing the highest priority threads first. There are 32 thread priorities and 2 thread priority classes, which are called real time and variable. This kind of thread-scheduling design helps to make the NT operating system run very efficiently. With the advent of NT 4, a further enhancement has been made to the threading model.

Threads incur overhead. They need to be tracked by the OS, and this requires that information about their state be kept up-to-date at all times. Each thread created needs to have state kept about machine registers, priority, local storage requirements, and so on. When you add all of this up, it means that as the amount of threads created by a process go up, overhead also increases, and in extreme cases, can be debilitating to the system. It is not optimal, or practical, for a process to have large numbers of threads.

With this in mind, NT 4's developers have introduced the idea of a *fiber*. A fiber offers features similar to a thread (and, in fact, is derived from a given thread), but with much less overhead, and some reduced functionality. A fiber is a subunit of a given thread. Because it is created by splitting a thread into one or more fibers, it shares most state and storage with its parent thread, reducing overhead significantly. It has its own execution state and stack, but is scheduled to run on the CPU by its relationship to its parent thread (the parent thread must handle its own scheduling of any of its children-fibers), not as a separate object. Thus, fibers cannot be individually scheduled preemptively, like their parent threads. With that said, fibers can still be a fantastic optimization in a multithreaded process, alleviating the base OS of much of the housekeeping normally incurred in managing large numbers of thread objects.

Insider Info

The kernel is non-pageable, that is, it's always resident in physical RAM. Threads and processes executed entirely within the kernel are not preemptable (there are arcane exceptions) and cannot be switched away from, or context-switched.

Most processes that run outside the kernel are pageable and preemptable and can be context-switched at any time. The kernel can run simultaneously on all processors in a multiprocessor configuration and, by using the HAL's multiprocessor support, can synchronize access and processing when needed.

Kernel Objects

Operating system components at the top of the Executive level, such as the I/O Manager, use the kernel to synchronize their activities. They also call on the kernel to provide synchronization and control entities called *kernel objects*, some of which are made available to user-level application programming interfaces through the Object Manager or indirectly through one of the other Executive services. The kernel creates and manages two different types of objects, which are covered in the following sections.

Dispatcher Objects

Dispatcher objects are said to have a *signal* state (either signaled or nonsignaled) and they are used to control the dispatching and synchronization of system-level operations based on a state, an event, or even a mutually exclusive relationship. Dispatcher objects include the following types:

Object Type	How the Executive Uses It
Events	Used to register an occurrence of an event, possibly signaling some waiting process or thread. Used for synchronization.
Mutants and mutexes	Two very similar objects that the kernel provides for controlling mutually exclusive access to a resource, where the possibility of deadlock must be guaranteed not to occur. Native kernel mutexes are used only in Kernel mode, whereas mutants are used to derive such User mode objects as critical sections and the like.

Object Type	How the Executive Uses It
Semaphores	Used as a gate to control access. May be used to control how many concurrent threads of execution, up to a specified limit, may pass through, using a specified resource. When the gate is in the signaled state, it is open. When nonsignaled, it is in the closed state.
Threads	The entity that executes as program code and is dispatched for execution by the kernel. Each thread is linked to a process object that provides virtual address space and thread control storage. If more than one thread object is associated with a process, execution of multiple threads within the same address space is possible. This is how NT provides multithreading to a process.
Timers	This object is used to signal timer events (as an alarm clock would).

Control Objects

Control objects are used to control the operation of the kernel but do not affect dispatching. Control objects include the following:

Object Type	How the Executive Uses It
Asynchronous procedure call (APC)	Used to interrupt the execution of a thread and cause another procedure to be called out of turn.
Interrupt	Used to set up the logical relationship of an interrupting source to an interrupt service routine by manipulation of entries in an Interrupt Dispatch Table (IDT).
Process	Represents the virtual address space and administrative information needed for the execution of a set of thread objects. Process objects contain a reference to an address map, a list of threads that belong to the process, and so on.
Profile	Profile objects are used to measure processing time within code, both in Kernel and User modes.

Mini-Glossary

I/O (INPUT/OUTPUT)   The way a computer dispatches and fetches information to and from the real world and the hardware it uses to do so. In the x86 world, there are I/O "ports," represented by physical and logical connections to the hardware, that the CPU can use to dispatch or fetch bytes of data to peripheral circuits and devices, such as modems or printers. On other processor architectures, I/O may be accomplished by reading or writing specific memory locations, whose storage is linked to the real world by specialized I/O chips that communicate directly with these memory locations; this kind of I/O is generally referred to as *memory mapped* I/O.

KERNEL OBJECTS   Operating system entities created by the kernel for use in Kernel or User mode execution. These objects allow code to attain and use signaled states and timeouts, gates to control execution, and logical exclusionary schemes.

PROCEDURE CALL   A branching of execution by the CPU to a specified "procedure" or subroutine of executable code.

SYMMETRIC MULTIPROCESSING   The ability to have more than one physical CPU and to utilize those multiple CPUs in a symmetric, or egalitarian way. Each processor might run portions of a routine, in a cooperative way, in order to increase throughput.

THREAD   A thread of execution, or thread, is an entity (of code) scheduled for execution on a processor.

The NT Executive

The NT Executive, which includes the kernel and the HAL, provides a set of services that Kernel mode code (through the System Services layer) and all User mode protected subsystems can utilize. Each group of services is managed by one of the following components of the Executive:

- I/O Manager and device drivers
- Process Manager
- Virtual Memory Manager
- Object Manager
- Local procedure call facility
- Security Reference Monitor (which, along with the logon and security protected subsystems, composes the NT security model)

The top layer of the Executive is an aggregate of "glue" routines and exposed interfaces called the *System Services*. The System Services shown in Figure 19-2 are the places where User mode protected subsystems interface with Kernel mode. Individual Executive components are described further in the following sections.

The I/O Manager and Device Drivers

The I/O Manager is the NT Executive component that supervises input and output operations on behalf of the operating system. A primary role of the I/O Manager is to supervise protocol-bound communications between the operating system and installed device or other drivers. The I/O Manager orchestrates and supervises hardware drivers, file system drivers, network and other device drivers, and presents a uniform interface for these drivers so that they may interact in predictable ways with the OS. The I/O Manager provides a conforming interface to all drivers, so that they

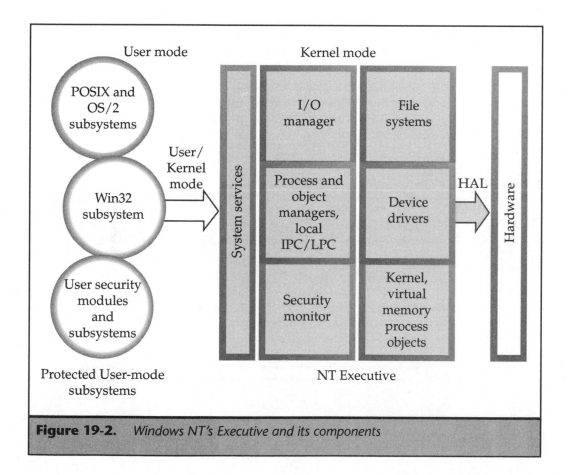

Figure 19-2. *Windows NT's Executive and its components*

can be abstracted in such a way that the rest of NT does not know about or care what real I/O or interface hardware it is communicating with.

A Layered Architecture

NT I/O, within the confines of the I/O Manager, uses an architecture that allows individual drivers to layer themselves on each other, each implementing their respective individual pieces of logical processing. Drivers logically closest to the physical hardware, at the layer where they manipulate the computer's real hardware and devices, are called *device drivers*. They carry on all real-world I/O operations for installed devices, from disk drives to serial ports. There are many combinations of other drivers that may be layered on top of the device drivers, as shown in Figure 19-3. These higher level drivers do not know, and by design should not know, any details about the physical devices. In concert with I/O Manager, higher-level drivers just pass I/O request packets (IRPs) down to the device drivers, which access the physical devices on their behalf.

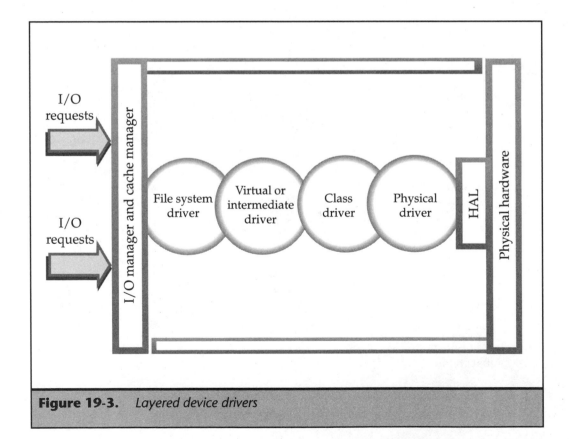

Figure 19-3. *Layered device drivers*

NOTE: *The NT Installable File Systems (IFSs) are examples of high-level drivers that work in this way. They are the highest level drivers in this chain. In the case of IFS drivers, this scheme allows multiple file systems and storage devices to be active at the same time, while being addressed through a single, uniform interface.*

I/O Operations

As mentioned in the previous section, drivers communicate with each other using data structures called I/O request packets (IRPs). The drivers pass I/O request packets to each other via the I/O Manager, which manages the IRPs. Synchronous I/O holds further upper-level execution until completion of the requested I/O operations. When an application performs a synchronous I/O operation, the rest of the application's processing is blocked, hence the name *blocking I/O*. When the I/O operation is completed, the calling process then continues execution. NT allows this kind of I/O but, by providing sophisticated I/O management routines, encourages the use of a better scheme.

Asynchronous I/O

Asynchronous I/O is a better scheme involving built-in architecture that can be used to perform asynchronous I/O. This technique is used to service I/O requests, as they can be fulfilled without stopping upper-level processing, which is used extensively within the NT operating system itself. When processes request I/O, the I/O Manager accepts the request and then returns immediately to the requesting process, signaling that an I/O operation is pending. This allows the process to continue with any other processing duties—waiting only for the completion of the I/O operation. Most I/O devices are very slow in comparison to a computer's processor, so an application can do a lot of work while waiting to be notified that an I/O operation is complete.

After an asynchronous I/O request is made by a process, the I/O Manager will return immediately after putting the request in an internal queue (see Figure 19-4). This is done without waiting for the system and/or the device driver to complete its real I/O operations. While the I/O Manager is accepting requests, and stuffing its queue, it is also running a separate thread that pulls these I/O requests from the queue, in the most efficient order, for dispatch to the drivers and subsequent I/O completion. This is not necessarily done in the order that the requests were received. When each I/O request is finished, the I/O Manager notifies the calling process that the requested I/O operation is done and pending.

NOTE: *Asynchronous I/O permits a process to use the computer's CPU during pending I/O operations. Instead of polling on the I/O Manager for I/O completion, a process may use one of the event or synchronization objects available to it. Some processes or applications will use a separate thread that waits on a synchronization event (in this case, signaled by the completion of the I/O operation), or they will provide a callback function—asynchronous procedure call (APC)—that is called when the asynchronous I/O operation is completed.*

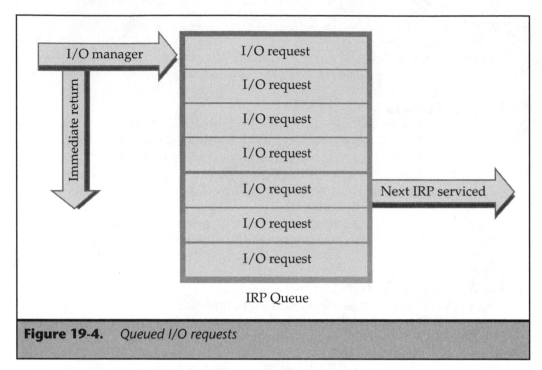

Figure 19-4. *Queued I/O requests*

Cache Management

The NT Executive's I/O architecture includes a Cache Manager that handles caching for the entire I/O system. The Executive's Cache Manager provides caching services to all installed file systems and network components under the control of the I/O Manager. If an I/O request can be fulfilled from the cache, the operation will be much faster than if that request must be physically made from disk or network connection once again. The Cache Manager uses its memory dynamically, adjusting to differing availabilities of physical RAM.

Cache Manager also offers services such as lazy write and lazy commit for the file systems it manages. These schemes, designed to optimize system performance, can increase I/O throughput by intelligently managing real I/O access.

Installable File System (IFS) Drivers

The NT I/O architecture supports multiple file system drivers, which are managed as the highest level drivers by the I/O Manager. This allows NT to provide file systems such as the File Allocation Table (FAT) and the New Technology File System (NTFS), which is designed specifically for use with NT. The FAT file system can be used as a primary file system or for backward compatibility with MS-DOS, Windows 95, Windows 3.x, and OS/2 version 1.x operating systems.

The NT I/O architecture also implements its network redirector and server as file system drivers. Internally, then, the I/O Manager treats access to files stored remotely, accessed through the network, and those stored locally, on a hard disk, in the same way. Because of the way NT treats these network components, and because the I/O manager is capable of managing multiple file systems, it is capable of managing multiple network and redirector modules, too.

Insider Info

When designing a device driver, keep in mind that because NT and the I/O Manager are designed to service many layered drivers, you should not create large, "do-all" driver layers. Create as many drivers as you have logical separations of responsibility. In the end, this will allow your design to be much more flexible, and you will be able to respond to changing designs and installations more easily.

As an example, if you were to write a driver for the Intel 8X930 USB (Universal Serial Bus) controller, you would not want to include specific driver code to service upper-level requests for a smart telephone connected to that controller. If you did, and the telephone control codes were changed, you would have to redo the entire USB driver.

Also, adding functionality becomes problematical as the size and scope of any one driver increase, so keep the minimum amount of functionality in each driver, layering them as needed to implement your design.

Network Redirectors, Servers, and Device Drivers

As previously mentioned, the I/O Manager also has responsibility for handling network file and device drivers. NT includes integrated networking that is supported by a series of network drivers. Network redirectors and servers are implemented as file system drivers and service I/O requests from network layers implemented higher up in the operating system, such as the Windows Sockets layer. Transport protocol drivers, lower in the chain, communicate with redirector and server layers through the Transport Driver Interface (TDI) layer—an intermediate driver. Lower down, toward the actual network interface card (NIC), are the device drivers responsible for actually communicating with the hardware.

 NOTE: NT 4 supports device drivers written to the Network Device Interface Specification (NDIS). NDIS implements standard interfaces for data exchange between transport protocol drivers and NICs. Using NDIS, multihomed network interfaces, where more than one NIC is installed, are possible. This allows the NT installation to provide support for access to multiple types of network servers, with multiple network protocols on each NIC.

Physical Device Drivers

Physical device drivers are the lowest level components of the NT I/O architecture. These drivers are used to access the physical ports and electronics within the computer, which allow hardware to be manipulated by software control. In this respect, I/O can be as simple as output of a byte of information to a printer port, or it can be as complicated as setting up and managing Direct Memory Access (DMA) to a peripheral chipset. Device drivers are written in the C or C++ programming language in concert with the system-development files provided for NT in the Device Driver Development Kit (DDK) by Microsoft. The support routines that are supplied in the DDK make platform-independent driver source code very easy to write.

Since support routines, their names, and operation are the same for all platforms, device drivers written for one NT platform are portable across others. This means that a simple recompilation, using a target processor's native C or C++ compiler, should be sufficient to port almost any device driver to an arbitrary processor platform.

Mini-Glossary

ASYNCHRONOUS I/O   A method of performing I/O operations that uses operating system objects to signal I/O completion, so that the calling piece of code can continue other processing until the I/O operation is complete.

CACHING   Caching is a method used by a memory architecture or file system to improve performance. For example, instead of reading and writing directly to the disk, frequently used files are temporarily stored in a cache in memory, and reads and writes to those files are performed in memory. Reading and writing to memory is much faster than reading and writing to disk.

DEVICE DRIVERS   Those operating system drivers at the lowest level, communicating directly with the computer's hardware.

I/O REQUEST PACKETS   A formal structure used by the I/O Manager and its lower level drivers for interdriver communication and operation.

LAZY COMMIT   Lazy commit is similar to lazy write. Instead of immediately marking a transaction as successfully completed, the committed information is cached and later written to the file system log as a background process.

LAZY WRITE   Lazy write is the ability to record changes in the file structure cache (which is quicker than recording them on disk), and then later, when demand on the computer's central processing unit is low, the Cache Manager writes the changes to the disk.

SYNCHRONOUS I/O   A type of I/O operation in which the requesting code is blocked from further execution until the I/O operation is complete.

NETWORK INTERFACE CARD (NIC)   The actual physical adapter card that implements the hardware network interface.

The Process Manager

The Process Manager is the NT Executive component that manages and supervises two special types of kernel objects—process and thread objects. The process and the thread are central to understanding how NT manages to implement multithreaded, preemptively multitasked operations. The Process Manager manages the creation and deletion of processes. It also provides for the creation and management of threads and processes within the context of User mode protected subsystem code.

In respect to the NT Executive, a *process* can be defined as an address space with a set of objects attached to, and visible to, the process. The process object will have a number of thread objects associated with it, each running a piece of executable code in the context of the process, belonging to an application, subsystem module, kernel routine, and so on.

NT implements the *thread object* as a basic system entity that can be scheduled for execution. The thread object contains a set of registers for saving state, its own stack (in the context of the kernel), a thread environment block (TEB), and process address space user stack.

 NOTE: *The NT process model uses the Security Reference Monitor and the Virtual Memory Manager to provide for interprocess security. Upon creation, or under programmatical control, a process is assigned a primary security access token that is used by the NT access validation routines when threads in the process need to reference protected objects. In this way, access control is enforced on threads that try to communicate with each other, or with system objects, within the model.*

The Virtual Memory Manager

NT 4 uses what is called a *demand paged virtual memory* system. How can a computer with 32MB of physical memory run three programs that each uses up 16MB of RAM? NT does so with virtual memory, which refers to the fact that the operating system can logically reserve and allocate more memory than the computer physically contains, using memory management and disk storage (see Figure 19-5).

Address Paging

Each process is allocated a unique logical address space, which is a set of addresses available for the process's threads to use. This address space is divided into equal chunks, called *pages*. As execution starts, these pages fill with code and data, but there is only so much physical room. When this physical room is nearing a high-water mark, the operating system takes over. It pages code and data in and out of the address space based on how recently some of the code has been used, whether it is discardable, and whether it is referenced in the next instructions to be executed. In this way, a physically limited memory can act as a virtual memory up to NT's limit of 4GB.

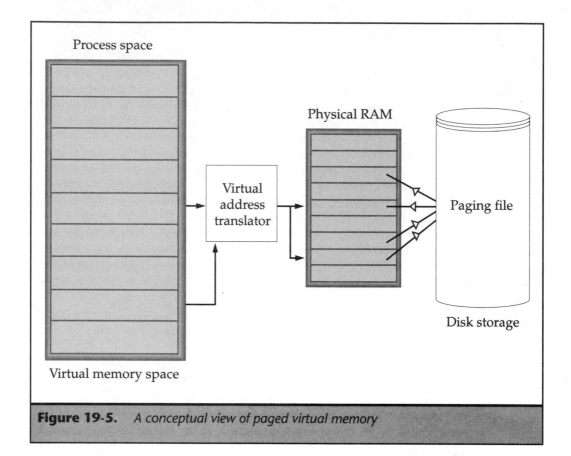

Figure 19-5. *A conceptual view of paged virtual memory*

NOTE: *Very few other operating systems are capable of utilizing this much physical or logical memory, and although nobody expects physical memories of this size to be cost effective in the near future, NT is capable of utilizing as much physical memory as you are willing to throw at it (within the 4GB limit). This ability can greatly increase throughput in memory-intensive applications such as image processing or graphics generation, because as you increase the size of physical memory, the paging mechanism is used less, taking less CPU time away from the application itself.*

Memory Protection

The Virtual Memory Manager transparently manipulates the addressing hardware on the CPU, mapping virtual/logical addresses in a process's address space to actual physical RAM pages in the computer's memory. By doing this, it obscures the physical layout and size of the computer's RAM memory, presenting a 4GB address space to the process's code and data. An important part of this scheme is memory protection. While presenting a different fake address space to each new process, NT also makes sure that each process can only access its own fake address space, keeping code and data from automatically being able to read or write another's process memory. There are cooperative ways around this (for example, memory-mapped files) but only within the bounds of the security model.

 NOTE: *Because each process has a logically separate address space, a thread in one process cannot view or modify the memory of another process without authorization. This memory-protection scheme is one of the principal reasons that NT is said to be "crashproof" and why NT can obtain its C2 security rating.*

The Object Manager

The Object Manager is the NT Executive component that manages instances of NT object types. An NT object consists of a defined object type and its attributes. The Object Manager provides operational rules for instantiation (the creation of an instance), naming, and (along with the Security Reference Monitor) security of objects.

Object Handles

The Object Manager is responsible for creating and providing handles to instantiated NT objects. It is also responsible for tracking the use of these handles. Before a process can use or manipulate an NT object, it must first obtain a handle to the object with access control information. This indirectly gives the process a pointer to the object itself.

The Local Computer Global Namespace

The Object Manager also manages the global namespace for the local NT computer. The global namespace is used to access all named objects that have instances in the local computer environment. For the Win 3.1 programmers reading this book, this is roughly equivalent to an expanded, hierarchical, global atom table. Objects such as Directory, Symbolic link, Semaphore, Event, Process, Thread, and File can have names in this namespace.

Mini-Glossary

DEMAND PAGING   Demand paging refers to a method by which data is moved in pages from physical memory to a temporary paging file on disk. As the data is needed by a process, it is paged back into physical memory.

NAMESPACE   Akin to the global atomic table in Windows 3.x, the Object Manager oversees NT's global namespace. The namespace is a logical construct that defines what names can be given and are given to objects under the control of the local computer. Objects can have arbitrary names that are given and managed within the scope of NT's namespace.

OBJECT HANDLE   An OS-supplied reference to an object. This is usually the value returned when asking for a reference value, which lets a piece of code subsequently refer to a specific object in API calls to the operating system.

PROCESS   A logical entity that represents the virtual address space and administrative information needed to execute a set of threads that belong to the process.

STACK   A part of memory reserved for transient storage, which can enlarge and shrink with need. A stack is always associated with a specific process.

THREAD ENVIRONMENT BLOCK (TEB)   An entity that represents the running state of a thread. The TEB of a thread contains information that determines that thread's stack limit, below which the stack pointer must not be decremented by the thread's executing code. (The stack pointer always has a lower-bounds limit.)

The Local Procedure Call Facility

In NT, the client/server model is followed as faithfully as possible. When an application wishes to communicate with a protected mode subsystem, it passes a message to the protected subsystem by using the services of the local procedure call (LPC) facility. The application does not directly (in most cases) call any underlying code. Rather, the LPC mechanism provides a communication channel between the application code and the protected subsystem. This works very much like the remote procedure call (RPC) facility used in network-distributed processing. The LPC facility is optimized for local execution and messaging between two processes.

Function Stubs

The LPC message-passing process is transparent to client applications. It is implemented, like RPC, by function stubs, which contain nonexecutable call-through placeholders implemented in the system's dynamic link libraries (DLLs), as shown in

Figure 19-6. This client/server stub facility is partly referred to as CSRSS, or the Client-Server Runtime Subsystem. Other system DLLs may also be involved.

Display and Win32/User Mode Optimizations in NT 4

It is worthwhile to note differences in the way NT 4 handles some of its optimizations, for calls from User mode components. New in this version, and beyond the scope of this discussion except for a brief overview, is the addition of new lines of direct communication between selected User mode and kernel components. This new facility is in addition to the client/server I/O model native to all versions of NT.

When an application program interface (API) call from a client (application) is made to a server (protected subsystem), the call stub in the system DLLs or the CSRSS repackages the client parameters and sends them to the server (subsystem) process that has the actual responsibility to implement the call. Almost all application-side requests go through the CSRSS or another LPC facilitator. A performance enhancement, which goes around part of this scheme when it comes to graphics subsystem calls and select subsystem I/O, has been made in NT 4. Part of the GDI and various other formerly User mode component support modules are now down in the kernel, and CSRSS does not go to the subsystem but directly to the

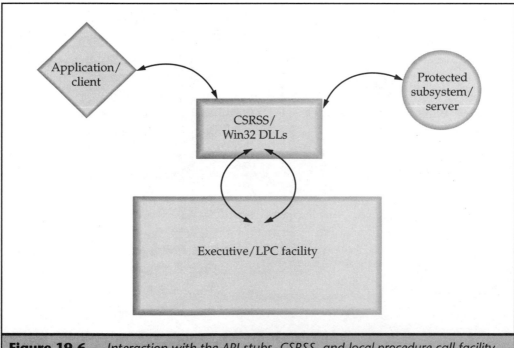

Figure 19-6.   *Interaction with the API stubs, CSRSS, and local procedure call facility*

kernel for certain calls. This is done to optimize display rendering and other direct-to-hardware processes.

The Security Reference Monitor

The Security Reference Monitor is the Executive component that, along with the User mode logon and security subsystem, implements NT's security model. As a Kernel mode component, the Security Reference Monitor has access to security objects that the User mode security components cannot directly query or manipulate. NT implements security (see Figure 19-7) so that applications and processes run on behalf of applications, and users cannot access system resources without secure authorization.

The Security Reference Monitor is responsible for enforcing the access, validation, and audit policies for the security subsystem. The Security Reference Monitor exposes interfaces and services to both Kernel and User mode routines for auditing security, validating access to objects, and enforcing user access privileges.

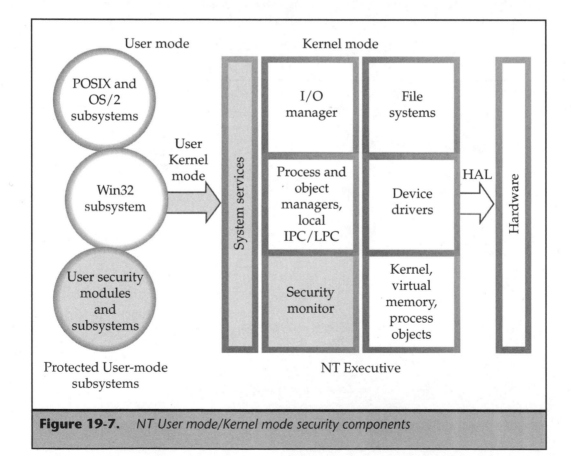

Figure 19-7. *NT User mode/Kernel mode security components*

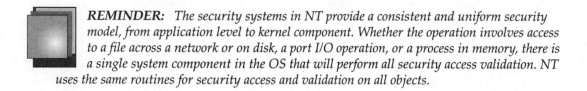

REMINDER: *The security systems in NT provide a consistent and uniform security model, from application level to kernel component. Whether the operation involves access to a file across a network or on disk, a port I/O operation, or a process in memory, there is a single system component in the OS that will perform all security access validation. NT uses the same routines for security access and validation on all objects.*

What's Next

Having gotten a more detailed look at how NT's modular structure works, we are going on now to take a look at protected subsystems in depth. These include Win32, POSIX, and OS/2. The information in the next chapter will help you prepare to author applications or plan for system additions and upgrades.

Chapter Twenty

Protected Subsystems

W hen the architects of NT set out to design a new operating system, one of the major features that they wanted to offer was an extensible and reconfigurable desktop, with support for both legacy operating systems and the new Win32/NT model. The competing operating systems, at the time of NT's original design, were to be emulated, at least in part, for backward compatibility: The Windows 3.x, OS/2, and POSIX applications of the day were to be supported. This intent, along with the introduction of the new base interface, Win32, drove the design decisions that resulted in how NT's protected subsystems were implemented. Although no new (since the OS's inception) protected subsystems have been authored for NT, you can think of protected subsystems as personalities: They have frontline duty to support functionality and application interface, providing native emulation and system services for whatever type of top-level OS, or OS component, they represent. The NT architecture is designed such that protected subsystems are meant to be, if not replaceable, at least augmentable, so that if sufficient time and effort were to be put forth, a team of engineers and programmers *could* come up with a wholly new subsystem, in order to provide native NT support for an even newer OS, or component.

Protected subsystems do not only offer OS emulation functionality. NT's security and printing subsystems are generally considered to be within this realm too. If you can come up with a (mostly) User mode NT interface, representing a whole block of core OS functionality, you will most certainly have the right to call it a protected subsystem.

How NT's Subsystems Work

Protected subsystems refer to code modules implemented as entire support entities—for the OS interface they are designed to emulate—sitting at the middle User mode layers, just above the Kernel/User mode barrier, and below application code. These subsystems implement all of the basic services and application interface that is required for an application of a supported type to run.

NT runs applications written for MS-DOS, POSIX, OS/2 1.x, Windows 3.x, and Windows 95 (both 16-bit and Win32 applications, not dependent on Win95-style device drivers or specialized interface elements), as well as native NT/Win32. These chunks of code make NT what it is. They supply specific functionality for a given user interface and application platform. Graphics, screen output emulation, API (application program interface) support, and individual OS features are all offered and controlled through protected subsystem modules.

NOTE: All protected subsystems are also subject to, and cooperate with, NT's security subsystem, a similar module, with shared functionality, servicing the entire OS. These protected subsystems are also dependent on NT's Executive and kernel, as well as the hardware abstraction layer (HAL) for a specific hardware platform. Although some protected subsystems do not do direct hardware or device access, they are integral and dependent on system and device services offered by these lower level components.

The Kernel and the Executive

Chapter 19 discussed how the kernel and Executive provide services that all protected subsystems call on to obtain operating system functions such as disk file access or basic I/O. Currently, NT protected subsystems, other than the dominant Win32 subsystem, all use translation and transport services derived by code paths that go through the Win32 subsystem. As mentioned briefly in Chapter 19, previous versions of NT also required that all calls from the Win32 protected subsystem (including display I/O) were forced to go through the CSRSS/Executive and I/O manager layers in order to communicate with, and use, kernel and device services. This is no longer universally true, as a new User mode-to-Kernel mode direct code path has been introduced for some Win32/protected subsystem and User mode display elements.

Win32 is all pervasive, and if you wish to build a new protected subsystem, with emulation support for a new OS, you will be using the services of the Win32 and security protected subsystems, along with the Executive and kernel.

Where They Run

As shown in Figure 20-1, protected subsystems run in the same area of NT as applications do, but just under them logically, as User mode processes. Subsystems allow NT to be chameleonlike.

Although NT's primary application support comes from the Win32 subsystem, it might just as well have come from a fictitious subsystem called Win2000, running as a replaceable module. Unlike applications, however, these subsystems are not completely autonomous. All application code is dependent on the Win32 protected subsystem in some way. The Win32 subsystem is the "native" NT subsystem, and it provides some of the functionality, such as cooperative screen output translation, for all of the other OS subsystems.

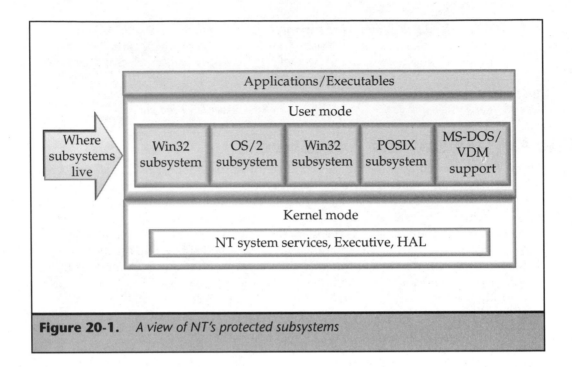

Figure 20-1. *A view of NT's protected subsystems*

 NOTE: *Virtual DOS machines (VDMs) are provided for emulation of MS-DOS and Win16 sessions, and they, too, use the Win32 subsystem for I/O.*

What Comes with NT 4

Currently, the following subsystems and emulation layers are shipped with NT 4:

- Win32 subsystem (NT, Windows 95, and translation services for other emulation)
- Win16 VDM (sometimes called Windows on Windows (WOW))
- MS-DOS VDM (Runs MS-DOS programs in a window, or full screen)
- POSIX subsystem (Unix subset compatibility)
- OS/2 subsystem (runs OS/2 version 1.x applications)

The Win32 Subsystem

NT's primary, and always available, subsystem is Win32. The Win32 subsystem provides functionality and interface to allow native NT and Windows 95 Win32 programs to run as graphical or console (character mode) sessions. The Win32 subsystem also manages I/O for all other subsystems. Mouse and keyboard input, as well as screen output, are all directed by the Win32 subsystem for all applications that run on NT.

How Win32 Differs from Win16

The Win32 subsystem differs from the older Win16 model in several ways. First, Win32 is capable of addressing 4GB of memory. This memory is expressed as an application's process space, and Win32 provides each application process with its own protected view of a 4GB memory space. Obviously, no one has a machine that is capable of handling 4GB of physical memory, so Win32, working in concert with NT's kernel and Executive, provides transparent memory management routines that make it appear that this is the case. The Win16 model could access only 256MB of memory, in aggregate.

Insider Info

All of this might seem academic to you, since computers usually don't come with 4GB of memory. But consider an application that is manipulating an array of bits that represent a 1280x1024 graphical display of, let's say, a NASA flyby animation. In full color (24-bit), that's 4MB of memory, for just one frame!

Obviously, you could run out of physical memory on a 32MB machine real fast. Just one second of this animation could take almost 100MB of memory to hold the bits necessary for calculation and display. In the Win32 model, this could be a flat, memory-mapped file, addressed as if it were a contiguous memory array, making manipulation and calculation much more efficient.

The Tasking and Queuing Model

Win32 also uses a different tasking and queuing model for internal processing and handling of system messages. In Win16, all applications shared a single message queue, and many programs depended on certain messages reaching them in a certain order.

NOTE: If a Win16 application crashed, and was blocking execution when it went down, it could also stop the entire system.

Win32 uses an asynchronous queuing scheme, in which the Win32 application cannot hold up the entire system, and each Win32 process has its own internal message queue, which is threaded to prevent blocking. Also, because of its preemptive multitasking capabilities, a Win32 application that is stuck or not responding for some reason, cannot stop or affect any other process in the system. Figure 20-2 shows how the Win32 subsystem handles input for Win32 and Win16 applications.

Win32 Programming Support

The Win32 subsystem's most important role is to provide program functionality—in the form of a callable application program interface (API)—to application-level code.

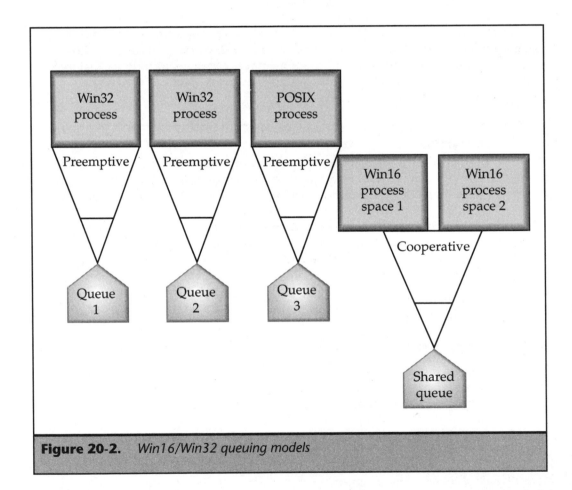

Figure 20-2. *Win16/Win32 queuing models*

An API can be called from code written in many different languages: C/C++, BASIC, Fortran, COBOL, and so on. Win32 libraries and application generators abound, and many popular language packages support Win32.

The Win32 API includes calls to manage memory, create graphics, output characters to the screen or printer; read from and store to files on disk, in memory, or on a network share; and many other specialized functions. Printing, both locally and remotely, is supported programmatically, and access to manipulation of security attributes for NT objects is included.

If you are familiar with the Win16 API, you will instantly recognize Win32. Although some Win16 calls have been made obsolete because of physical addressing, or logical differences between Win16 and Win32, most functions have just been extended and enhanced.

CAUTION: For the seasoned programmer, a word of warning: Parameter packing is different in Win32. Where most Win16 calls took arguments of WORD and LONG size before, they now appear the same, in prototype, but take LONG,LONG, as Win32 is fully 32-bit.

Windows on Windows

Windows 3.x executables (with the exception of Win32-enabled applications) are all 16-bit, using the Win16 software architecture. Because the designers of NT wanted to leverage the vast amount of older Win16 programs, and offer a system that did not require immediate upgrade of, say, every word processor or spreadsheet in an organization, they came up with Windows on Windows (WOW).

NOTE: WOW allows NT to run most older Win16 programs as if they were native NT applications. It does this by extending the emulation layers of NT to include stubs for the Windows 3.1 kernel, user, GDI, and underlying support logic.

Starting Win16 Programs

When a Win16 program is started on an NT 4 box, WOW is automatically loaded into memory behind the application and sits in the background, intercepting the applications calls to (what it thinks is) Windows 3.1 system code. NT loads the application into a special multithreaded virtual DOS machine (VDM), so that the application has no idea that it is running within a 32-bit system architecture.

Insider Info

All Win16 programs share this special VDM because NT must emulate Win16's model in its use and provision of address space and sharable memory arenas. In Window 3.1, there was no security or process space provided to keep one program from sharing another's data or code space. This was one of the shortcomings of Win16, but who can argue with 100,000 applications already sitting on the shelf?

The architects of NT were smart enough to see that if they decided to take the plunge, and offer an OS completely devoid of Win16 application support, NT would be a hard sell to many corporate environments, where millions of dollars had been spent on Win16 software. A company contemplating upgrade to NT/Win32 might not balk at the cost of the OS upgrade, but add in the upgrades of all of their productivity software, and you have some serious change!

Multitasking with the WOW VDM

Win16 applications are cooperatively multitasked with respect to each other, just like in Windows 3.1. But the WOW VDM is preemptively multitasked with respect to all other 32-bit processes executing on the system. This essentially means that Win16 applications will act as poorly toward their 16-bit neighbors as they did under Windows 3.1, but in the context of the entire NT system, they cannot crash the whole computer.

A representation of where WOW fits into the NT model is illustrated in Figure 20-3. With 32-bit NT, all applications have their own message input queue. This is a primary factor in eliminating crashes and lockups due to applications that hold or block the messaging queue, which is the heart of the User mode dispatch mechanism. Under 16-bit Windows, all applications get messages from the same input message queue. This is emulated in WOW.

Thunking 16-Bit to 32-Bit Routines

When a Win16 application calls a Windows 3.1 OS routine, WOW intercepts the call, translating (or *thunking*, as it is called) the call to a similar 32-bit counterpart. The 32-bit routine performs the tasks required and returns through the WOW layer to the Win16 program. This is all transparent to the Win16 application.

 NOTE: *The only true limitation in the WOW system is the support for device drivers, or drivers that directly manipulate hardware (VxDs). These are not supported, due to NT's security model.*

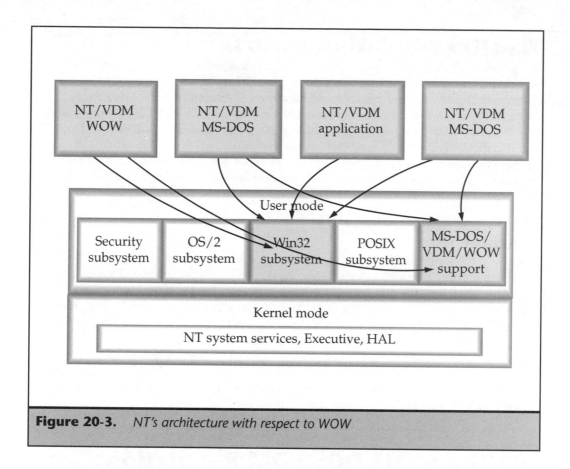

Figure 20-3. *NT's architecture with respect to WOW*

Interprocess Communication (IPC)

A Win16 application running under WOW can use the normal methods of interprocess communication (IPC) when it needs to talk to another Win16 application or to a 32-bit application running natively. These IPC mechanisms include Object Linking and Embedding (OLE), discussed in Chapter 22, and Net Dynamic Data Exchange (NetDDE), discussed in Chapter 15, as well as named pipes.

MS-DOS Emulation Layers

The MS-DOS emulator is similar to WOW but has some distinct differences. MS-DOS programs can individually be given an entire 16MB logical address space. MS-DOS programs typically call built-in software functions by issuing software interrupts. These functions usually reside in the computer's basic I/O system (BIOS), and also in the MS-DOS system software. When running NT, your regular BIOS (the one that's installed on the computer's motherboard) is bypassed. WOW programs also depend on these calls in certain cases, so the MS-DOS emulator must supply a copy of most of these functions. NT can therefore provide an emulated environment for MS-DOS-based programs and support the Win16/MS-DOS calls needed by WOW.

Insider Info

Because NT enforces system integrity through secure methods, it does not allow the use of MS-DOS device drivers that would modify or address hardware directly. Windows 3.1 and some MS-DOS programs also use a memory management scheme called the DOS Protected Mode Interface (DPMI) that must be emulated in NT because it is an integral part of the Win16 architecture and may even be used by 16-bit character mode applications.

DPMI is emulated by a further MS-DOS layer that also includes 32-bit memory management routines for DOS extended (XMS) and expanded (EMS) memory. NT converts an MS-DOS memory request to its native memory allocation or deallocation calls and services the call intrinsically.

WOW and MS-DOS VDM Restrictions

The following list covers some of the major restrictions you may encounter when running NT in WOW or MS-DOS VDM mode:

- **Intel x86 emulation:** On Intel x86 machines, NT is capable of emulating a 486 class computer running MS-DOS or Win16 applications. This is not so in non-Intel boxes, since NT depends on the Intel chip to provide certain higher levels of 16-bit emulation.

 NOTE: *For all other computers, a software x86 emulator is also running underneath all of the Win16 and MS-DOS emulator layers. This soft-pc emulates a 80286 Intel CPU, and therefore, if you are running Win16 applications on a MIPS, Alpha, or PowerPC, it must run in Standard rather than Enhanced mode.*

- **Window or full screen:** On Intel x86 computers, MS-DOS applications can run either in a window or full screen. MS-DOS applications that use video graphics will only run full screen. On RISC (MIPS/Alpha/PowerPC) computers, all applications must be run in a window.

- **Floppy disk drive access:** Floppy disk drive access is supported for the FAT file system only. All MS-DOS functions except task-switching APIs (such as Software Carousel) are supported.

- **WOW subsystem support:** The WOW subsystem on an Intel x86 computer supports Windows 3.1 Enhanced mode, but it does not support VxDs or device drivers that control hardware directly. On RISC computers, support is available in WOW for Standard mode Win16 applications only.

- **Software interrupt support:** In an MS-DOS VDM, limited support for software interrupts is available. There are several MS-DOS interrupt restrictions to be aware of. Interrupts 10, 13, 18, 19, and 2F are most notable because of their systemwide impact. These interrupts will have either partial or full restrictions upon their use, for instance, because interrupt 13 allows direct hard disk manipulation, which is a no-no for any MS-DOS program running under NT.

The Win32 Printing Subsystem

While not strictly a protected subsystem, the Win32 printing routines are a mini-subsystem in their own right. This subsystem is device independent. That is, it abstracts the business of printing to a level where, within the actual engine, the subsystem does not care what printer it is hooked up to (see Chapter 24 for a detailed discussion of NT's printing subsystem).

 NOTE: Win32 controls physical printer options and features through the use of printer drivers, just as all Windows operating systems do. These drivers are sourced by the OEM manufacturer, or by Microsoft, and contain all of the device-specific controls that manage model-dependent printer functions.

Printing Subsystem Features

All of the intrinsic features available within the Win32 printing subsystem—halftoning, rasterizing, plotting, and so on—are not part of any particular printer driver. They reside in the subsystem itself, abstracted and made available in an independent way to any printer driver capable of translating these features to actual print control codes.

The Printing Subsystem's Client/Server Model

As with most other functionality in NT, the Win32 printing subsystem is also built around a client/server model. Within this model, an application and its internal print support are client components, while the physical printing operation—with its attendant device drivers—are on the server side.

The Print Spooler

The drivers communicate with the application through GDI (Graphics Device Interface) and kernel components, and send instructions to the printer through the print spooler. The print spooler is a memory store, router, and database. It does the job of sending the printing job to the specified printer type and, optionally, will route printing jobs across the network to a remote printer. The spooler manages the forms database and also the printer definitions in the Registry.

The Security Subsystem

Although we have covered security in depth in Chapter 16, another mention is due here, since, within the narrow confines of this discussion, the components of security in NT also qualify as a subsystem module. In brief, NT creates tasks, called logon processes, to accept logon requests from users. These include the initial logon, which displays the logon dialog box to the user, and also remote logons, which manage access across a network by remote users. These processes are managed by the NT security subsystem (see Figure 20-4).

The security subsystem comprises the following, functionally separate modules:

- **The Local Security Authority (LSA):** Enforces user permissions for access to the system. The LSA is central to the NT security model. LSA is responsible for generating user access tokens, logon authentication, and local security policies. The LSA also has control over auditing policy, and it manages auditing by logging audit messages sourced by the Security Reference Monitor.

- **The Security Account Manager (SAM):** Maintains a database that stores information on all user and group accounts. The SAM's duty is to provide user validation (from its databases) to the LSA services for logon and internal use.

- **The Security Reference Monitor:** Checks on a user's permission to access an NT object and also performs checks on user actions. The Security Reference Monitor, the only kernel component in the security subsystem, polices access and validation as well as doing the job of generating audits based on the criteria set up by the LSA. It is the final arbiter of whether an NT object can be accessed by a specific user, and it reports back, by audit, on any violation or anomaly. Any process that attempts access to an object must have the necessary permissions. The Security Reference Monitor is the access guard controlling the success or failure of these attempts.

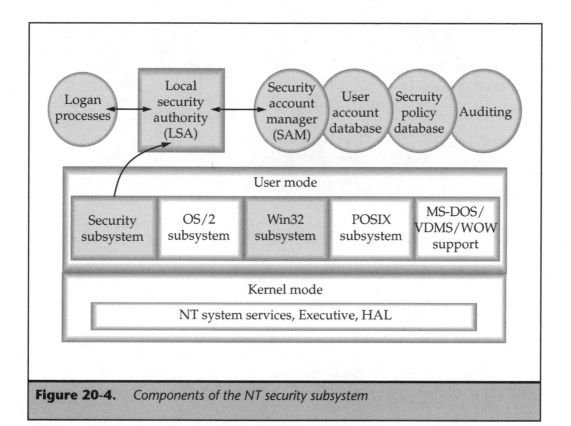

Figure 20-4. *Components of the NT security subsystem*

The POSIX Subsystem

The NT POSIX subsystem executes POSIX code. A POSIX application is very similar to, and in some cases the same as, a Unix program. The NT POSIX subsystem runs in its own protected process space, and NT provides separate process space for each POSIX application. A POSIX application is preemptively multitasked like a Win32 application—with respect to another POSIX program and with respect to all other processes running in the system.

NOTE: *The Institute of Electrical and Electronic Engineers (IEEE) defines POSIX standards, and the NT POSIX subsystem is designed to POSIX 1 standards.*

POSIX applications require specific file system features—like support for case sensitivity in directories and filenames, the ability to distinguish files based on that sensitivity, plus support for files that are hard linked (files that can have more than one name).

NOTE: *The hard linking functionality is only provided by the NTFS file system, and even then, backup facilities may be negatively affected, or may not support hard links completely. If you plan on implementing POSIX applications that access disk files on your NT system, make sure they are executed where an NTFS disk partition is available. If you are running a POSIX application that does not need access to a disk drive, you do not need an NTFS partition.*

POSIX applications do not have direct access to any API or feature found in the Win32 subsystem. They cannot specifically use OLE, COM, DDE (or NetDDE), memory-mapped files or shared memory arenas in DLLs, Win32 networking, GDI graphics, or Win32-specific drivers.

TIP: *The Console applet (see Chapter 8), where POSIX-compliant programs are run, can pipe output from a POSIX application through to a console or Win32 console application.*

The OS/2 Subsystem

The OS/2 subsystem is an orphan starting with NT 4. It supports OS/2 version 1.x character mode applications only on x86-based computers. This subsystem was never supported on MIPS, Alpha, or PowerPC platforms. These other computer architectures can, however, run console-based, real mode (nonbound) OS/2 applications, such as the Brief editor, using the MS-DOS emulator environment.

NOTE: *Support for HPFS (High-Performance File System) has been removed, and though not specifically a subsystem feature (HPFS was one of the installable file systems in earlier releases), lack of this support will render any specific HPFS file system support obsolete.*

The OS/2 subsystem will run OS/2 character mode applications directly. They can be launched from a console window command prompt, from Explorer or File Manager, from the desktop, or from a Win32 or OS/2 application. You cannot run OS/2 version 2.x Presentation Manager (PM) or Advanced Video I/O (AVIO) applications unless you install the NT Add-On Subsystem for Presentation Manager. OS/2 applications will not generally run on RISC-based computers, and OS/2 applications that directly access hardware or memory will not run for system security reasons.

NOTE: *No custom device drivers are allowed, since these would have to be rewritten to the NT device driver specifications, respective of system security and integrity.*

What's Next

NT provides many opportunities to the administrator and programmer alike. When contemplating an update to your system, or an addition of any size, you should take these technical considerations under advisement. Sometimes, a project may seem trivial, only to blow up into a full-fledged logistical nightmare in support or development, just because no one first looked into the technical impact of the work to be performed.

Nothing could be more timely than a look at NT device drivers, their place within the operating system, and their impact and importance. If you are a programmer or technical manager, and need to support a custom device or process within NT, read on with relish.

Chapter Twenty-One

Device Drivers

All hardware is abstracted in NT. When an application opens a file or sends characters to a modem or talks to another application across the network, the program itself should have very little idea of how, or with what resources and methods, the physical devices or transports work. So, at the highest level, a device driver (or any installable driver) is an abstraction mechanism—hiding the actual workings of the hardware and providing applications with a consistent programming interface and calling conventions that are standardized. If the actual computer hardware was being directly controlled by the application, NT's device and platform independence would be seriously compromised. The ideals that drove NT's architects would be shattered, and, as with some other operating systems, you would have to configure your computer in just the right way, with exact hardware and software requirements, in order to run these customized applications.

The Windows Device Scheme

With MS-DOS providing character-based functionality, PCs lacked a truly graphical interface that would sell to the masses. Based on Xerox Parc's work, and in response to the Apple Macintosh graphical interface, Microsoft developed the Windows operating system in the 1980s, which ran on top of and required MS-DOS for its support mechanisms. While Windows solved some of the visual drawbacks of MS-DOS, it did nothing to standardize the device support problem brought up by so many MS-DOS drivers with so many conflicting purposes and hardware usages and requirements. Adding to the confusion, Windows itself could directly support drivers (written to work with the Windows kernel), or it could call through to the underlying MS-DOS driver and use it.

This situation got worse until, at one point, configuring Windows 3.x was (and still is, with Windows 95!) considered a black art. NT's designers were well aware of this when they decided to part company with the schizophrenic way in which 16-bit Windows drivers could be and were implemented (Figure 21-1).

 NOTE: Windows NT is still much cleaner than Windows 95 in its driver implementation. Windows 95 is almost unchanged from 16-bit Windows in its architecture and use of device drivers. In fact, most Windows 3.x device drivers will run fine under Windows 95.

The NT Model

The NT driver model is a complete departure from other Windows operating systems. Instead of a driver structure that allows any or all levels of the operating system to bypass all others and access hardware or logical processes that mimic hardware, the NT model enforces strict adherence to a hierarchical call down, using the kernel and I/O Manager with standardized returns (Figure 21-2). Another important issue for NT drivers is that NT is capable of executing on multiprocessor platforms. A driver will be

Insider Info

In the computing world, the custom configuration situation is actually the norm. For years, large and small companies have made a tidy profit by selling so-called closed systems as turnkey solutions. A company invests many months and many thousands of dollars in providing a computing solution for their customers. At one time, you could only obtain software for a given hardware platform from the hardware's manufacturer. At the same time, they were the only company that could also provide you with a printer, terminal, and network that would operate with the computer that you bought from them.

Times changed, and many software companies sprang up. These companies (such as Microsoft) offered operating systems and applications to a general audience. Many of these companies first concentrated on the minicomputer market, offering corporations software and hardware add-ons as third-party suppliers.

When the IBM PC was introduced in 1982, Microsoft was chosen by IBM to supply the operating system: MS-DOS. Through many iterations, starting with Seattle-DOS, and then going on through many revisions as Microsoft MS-DOS, this operating system was built to run on *any* IBM PC-compatible computer, with minor OEM modifications at times. This was a radical departure from the one computer/one supplier situation that existed in the 1960s and 1970s. As soon as programmers and designers started to embrace the IBM PC as a commercially viable platform, thousands of MS-DOS-based programs appeared on the market, which drove the IBM PC and its clones to their preeminent position today.

But what does this have to do with NT device drivers? Well, the seeds of device-independent operating systems were planted in the 1970s by the Unix crowd. Because of the open and extensible architecture of and available source code for Unix, that segment of the computing world had extensive experience in writing driver layers for various hardware and logical devices that they wanted to support under Unix.

With this in mind, and because of the lessons learned in CP/M (the first ubiquitous microcomputer operating system), whose device support was monolithically built into the OS, the developers of MS-DOS decided to provide and extend support for boot-loadable device drivers. These drivers controlled anything from hard disk drives to optical scanners, and they would load into memory at boot time.

capable of taking this into consideration. Multithreading and interrupts need to be managed in a multiprocessor-safe way.

Drivers for NT will fit into one of three categories: User mode drivers, Kernel mode drivers, and virtual device drivers (VDDs).

Insider Info

As far as a User mode application is aware of I/O, NT views and treats all input and output without making or exposing any distinctions. Any abstracted I/O looks like any other I/O. When an application needs to use stream I/O facilities, the kernel analyzes the request, along with the I/O Manager, and using an internal mechanism known as a symbolic link, decides where dispatches will be sent when a request comes back again, sending the call to the appropriate driver. A User mode handle is returned to the application for use when subsequent I/O requests are made.

Within the bounds of this model, an NT application can, on a handle, indistinguishably use and open a disk file or a printer port or an I/O port for a modem or fax. The application will know what its returned handle refers to and what data it will read from or send to the stream. At lower levels, however, NT does not distinguish the I/O as being unique to a device, until we reach the driver level.

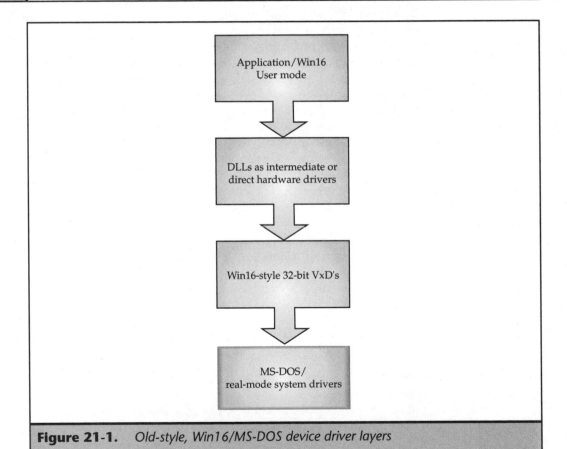

Figure 21-1.   *Old-style, Win16/MS-DOS device driver layers*

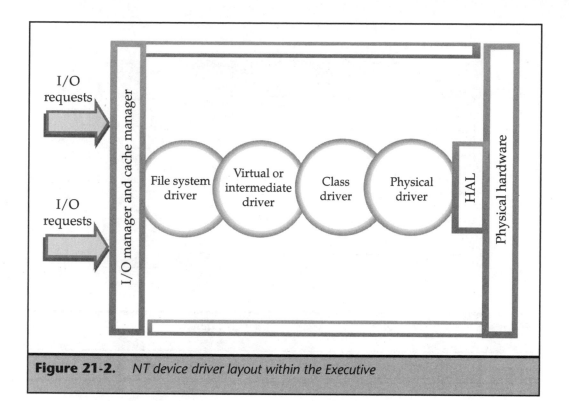

Figure 21-2. *NT device driver layout within the Executive*

 NOTE: *Virtual device drivers (VDDs) is actually a misnomer, since the VxD (virtual device driver) of Windows 3.x and Windows 95 is not the same, and will not run under NT.*

The Service Control Manager

NT provides one mechanism by which drivers can be installed and loaded: the Service Control Manager. The Service Control Manager can control the load sequence and running state of both drivers and system services, which are akin to installable drivers in the Win16 world. The Service Control Manager is active during the entire NT session and assumes a critical role in loading and starting services (Figure 21-3) and devices from Registry entries at boot time. It also provides back-end services to applications that might use this control at runtime, such as the Devices applet (Figure 21-4) in the control panel.

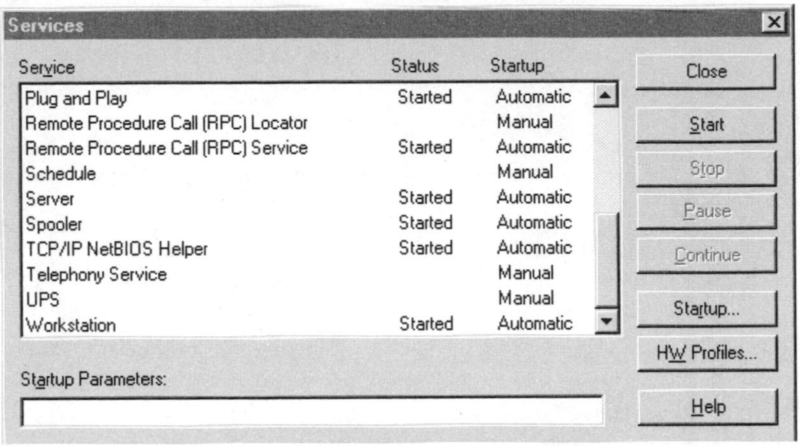

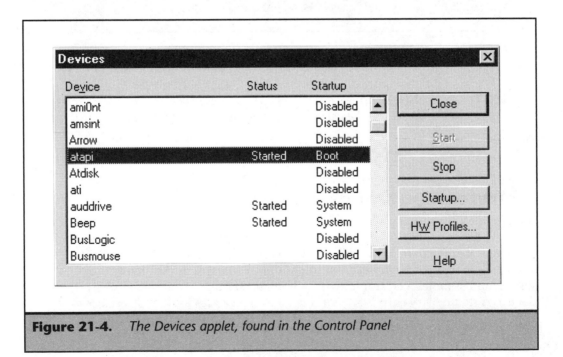

Figure 21-3. *The Service Control Manager's Services dialog*

Figure 21-4. *The Devices applet, found in the Control Panel*

Kernel Mode Drivers

Kernel mode drivers fall roughly into the following categories:

- Lowest level device drivers, such as the mouse, sound card, serial port, or keyboard driver—those drivers that directly control physical hardware.

- Intermediate level drivers, such as a RAM disk, or class drivers (like the SCSI class), that abstract support for underlying lowest level device drivers.

- Highest level file system drivers (FSDs), such as FAT, NTFS, or CDFS drivers.

 NOTE: FSDs are high-level drivers, just under the I/O Manager, whose support is specific to a particular file system architecture. They utilize the services of the lower level intermediate drivers, and ultimately converse with the physical device through a lowest level device driver.

- Specialized highest and intermediate level drivers, such as the network redirector and transport drivers. Also, any custom hardware whose access routines depend on lowest level device drivers and kernel services (such as sound card family drivers).

User Mode Drivers

Win32 User mode drivers are helper drivers for the Win32 protected subsystem. The applicable devices that these drivers handle are primarily concerned with the display subsystem. The graphical environment in Win32 is optimized to use these helper drivers when assembling display output, since this operation involves many calls into Win32, in User mode, and going back and forth across the User/Kernel barrier would degrade performance. Also, as mentioned previously, NT 4 has made changes in the way these drivers, and other User mode processes, can call into the kernel. Direct paths now make display and hardware access much more straightforward. A caveat to this new model is that because the communication is direct, and because faults in the kernel-side portions of this model can be fatal, the robust nature of NT has been somewhat compromised. Devices that use this channel of communication cannot afford to fault or present unhandled failures to the system: Watch out!

Virtual Device Drivers

NT's virtual device drivers are similar in purpose, if not scope, to Windows 3.x/Windows 95 VxDs. They are used to virtualize hardware for use with MS-DOS applications. NT allows concurrent MS-DOS applications. To run properly, and as in 16-bit Windows, they must be run in a fully emulated environment—thinking that they are the only application executing on the PC. This is what virtual DOS machines (VDMs) do for you, as explained in Chapter 20.

What a VDD does is to arbitrate access to system resources—virtualizing the resource—representing it to the MS-DOS session as if no other process has access to it. For instance, if you are running two MS-DOS sessions and each is using the mouse, there must be a way to represent the mouse hardware to each session, so they think that they own the mouse. It's also necessary to pass those mouse requests down to NT, so the proper operating system software can then perform the required functions on behalf of the *correct* MS-DOS session.

Driver Requirements and Operations

All NT drivers have minimum logical requirements that they must fulfill. Drivers can be involved in any or all of the operations covered in the following sections.

Hardware Input/Output Processes

This section applies only to lowest level device drivers. Most communication between software and hardware is accomplished by means of several techniques involving interrupt requests (IRQs), port I/O, and Direct Memory Access (DMA).

Hardware Interrupt Handlers

If a device supports interrupts, the driver will need to include hardware interrupt-handling capability. NT provides macros in the Device Driver Kit (DDK) that intercept and process interrupts. Interrupt handlers are usually optimized to minimize processing time, since disabling them for subsequent service can degrade performance. Also, interrupts can reenter code (overrun), and high-frequency interrupts can bog down the system (see Chapter 23). Interrupt handlers are, therefore, custom implemented in different ways, depending on the device.

Port I/O

Drivers that deal with port I/O service physical ports that are attached to the physical computer system and assigned a number within a range known to the CPU. Reading or writing these ports under the control of a device driver results in the input or output of one or more bytes of information. This information could be data over a modem, through a serial port, or it could be a register belonging to an onboard integrated circuit (controlling an intrinsic device), such as the keyboard controller integrated circuit.

Direct Memory Access

Drivers that use Direct Memory Access (DMA) usually make large data transfers under the control of a DMA controller on an adapter card or device in concert with the DMA controller chips on the computer's motherboard. A shared range of memory is set up, accessible by both controllers, and according to a protocol, these controllers use that memory to communicate without processor intervention.

TIP: *Using DMA, a computer can show big performance gains over schemes that strictly use byte or word I/O with interrupts or polled methods. NT provides DMA services through the HAL, and only lowest level Kernel mode drivers can utilize these services.*

Deferred Procedure Calls and Synchronization Objects

In a driver, software usually waits for or executes asynchronously with hardware. There is usually no way to predict when a hardware flag or signal will come in to set or reset a bit or register in the software layer. The software may not be in a state in which it can service a hardware request immediately, and conversely, the hardware may not be in a state to accept output when the software is ready to perform an operation.

In these cases, a method must exist to allow these I/O operations to be queued. If the I/O request is queued, the driver and hardware can service these queues in a synchronized way without missing requests. Deferred procedure calls, or DPCs (Figure 21-5), are the way in which NT synchronizes these driver processes. NT drivers can also use the full set of kernel synchronization objects, such as semaphores and events, to manage access to data and hardware resources.

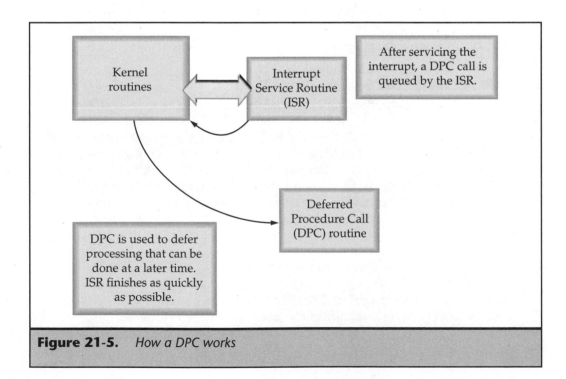

Figure 21-5. *How a DPC works*

Operating System I/O Requests

NT drivers process I/O requests from the operating system by means of the I/O Manager. The I/O Manager assembles packets with I/O request information called I/O request packets (IRPs). These "packets" refer to data structures that are passed from driver level to driver level, each level looking at a different part of the IRP structure. Some drivers modify the IRP structures as they are passed back and forth, but all drivers chain and return the IRPs when they are through with them.

Driver Error Conditions

If error conditions arise during a driver's operation, NT drivers are required to return predefined error codes, outlined in the DDK's NTSTATUS.H include files. These status codes will reflect the state of a driver's query to the hardware, a logical operation success or failure, or some global event. The I/O Manager or kernel will decide on an action, based on the code that the driver returns. If the driver simply returns success, this is packaged by the kernel component and sent back up to the requesting User mode application, if applicable. The kernel also lets drivers log errors or success codes and text to the event log.

Application and Development Tools

Now that you have a basic idea of what it will take to design or plan for an NT driver implementation, let's look at the tools and files you can use to accomplish your goal, as well as to write and debug applications for use with NT.

Tools for Compilers

All drivers and most applications for NT are written in some variant of C/C++ or BASIC (see Figure 21-6), with a few being written in FORTRAN, COBOL, ADA, LISP, and so on. We'll concentrate on C/C++ and BASIC, since these two languages account for upwards of 95 percent of all code development for NT. Compilers and assemblers that generate object modules in the Common Object File Format (COFF) can be used to write NT drivers, although, preferably, a source file debugging format such as CV4 (CodeView) information can also be generated. Structured exception handling must be supported by the compiler, and for drivers, the compiler must support 32-bit execution.

 NOTE: *The executable format for use by 32-bit operating systems built by Microsoft , including NT and Windows 95, is called a portable executable (PE) file. All 32-bit application exe's have this format. The 32-bit DLLs (.DLL), services, and drivers (.SYS) are built as PE files. Your compiler's linker must generate PE executables.*

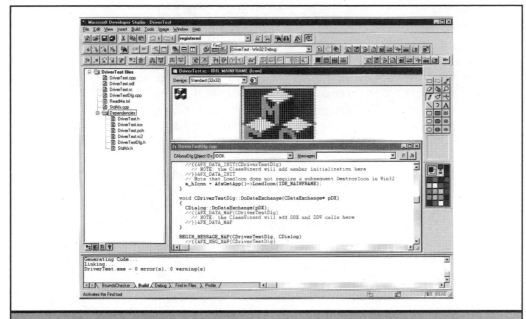

Figure 21-6.   *The Microsoft Visual C/C++ development environment*

Important things to look for in your compiler of choice include

■ **32-bit support:** Support for 32-bit PE executables is critical. Although you can potentially write a 16-bit application that will run in the MS-DOS emulator environment, or the WOW subsystem, native NT applications should all be 32-bit executables.

TIP: *The 32-bit support rule also makes sense from the standpoint of being able to utilize NT's intrinsic functions, since 16-bit support is limited and is really only there for backward compatibility. If you will use your compiler to write drivers, you must write them with a 32-bit compiler.*

■ **Win32 support:** Make sure that the language you choose has support libraries for NT's native subsystem environment, Win32. Unless you are writing POSIX applications, you will want to utilize the many features available to you in Win32.

TIP: *For drivers, Win32 support is not a must, but if you will use your compiler for building applications too, you should target Win32.*

Insider Info

C and C++ are ideal languages for development in NT. The files supplied with Microsoft's NT Device Driver Kit (NTDDK) are almost entirely in C/C++, and if you are going to develop drivers, you generally should write in C or C++. The Microsoft Visual C/C++ language package is the most comprehensive and up-to-date for writing NT drivers and applications. It's capable of generating executables and driver files, proper debugging information, and ships with NT header and libraries for Win32. Other C and C++ compilers may or may not be optimal.

The only BASIC compiler that ships with all the functionality required to author a Win32 program utilizing extended NT functions is Microsoft's Visual Basic. This language is shipped complete with support for OLE, COM, and custom controls, as well as the Data Access Object (DAO) and ODBC libraries.

■ **Good debugger support:** This is essential. You will most certainly have to debug your driver or application, and as the saying goes, The right tool, for the right job.

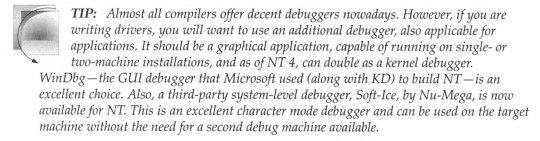

TIP: Almost all compilers offer decent debuggers nowadays. However, if you are writing drivers, you will want to use an additional debugger, also applicable for applications. It should be a graphical application, capable of running on single- or two-machine installations, and as of NT 4, can double as a kernel debugger. WinDbg—the GUI debugger that Microsoft used (along with KD) to build NT—is an excellent choice. Also, a third-party system-level debugger, Soft-Ice, by Nu-Mega, is now available for NT. This is an excellent character mode debugger and can be used on the target machine without the need for a second debug machine available.

■ **Support for additional NT technologies:** For applications, your compiler and its libraries should support OLE, COM, and DAO—three important Microsoft technologies that cover many aspects of NT applications technologies.

Tools for Assemblers

Although assembly is rarely used in NT development, the occasional piece of assembly may be critical in writing a device driver. Two currently capable assemblers include Microsoft's MASM and Borland's TASM.

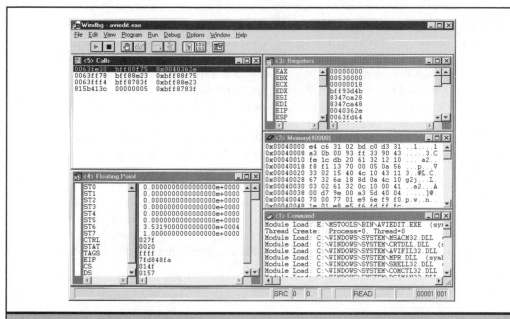

Figure 21-7. *The WinDbg GUI-based debugger*

Tools for Debugging

As it is critical that you use a debugger with teeth, we will concentrate on the best all-around debugger for use with NT today: WinDbg (Figure 21-7). This debugger has been part of every NT release—irrespective of debuggers built into integrated development environments. It was built by the NT development team, and they used it to further debug NT, shaking all of the nasty bugs out of it that way and really customizing it for use with NT.

 NOTE: *Of course, there were other debuggers used by the NT team. KD and NTSD are examples of symbolic debuggers that are available for use. But who wants to use character mode debuggers with no source-level debugging capability when you can have it all with WinDbg?*

Insider Info

With the release of NT 4, WinDbg's capabilities have been extended to debugging any code that an NT developer might want to throw at it. To debug a device or other driver, a special setup must be followed utilizing two machines. If you stop a Kernel mode component (such as a device driver), you stop the kernel. And if you stop the kernel, you can't run a GUI debugger that utilizes Win32 for its own purposes.

The second machine may be an NT machine, or it may be running Windows 95. As long as the right debugging files are available to it, the second host machine's OS is your choice.

As mentioned earlier, Nu-Mega also has a version of its character mode Soft-Ice debugger now available for NT. Using Soft-Ice, you may debug drivers without the two-machine configuration, but you lose the graphical interface and much ease of use. Source-level debugging is also very primitive with Soft-Ice, so WinDbg may still be the best choice, possibly used in concert with Soft-Ice.

What's Next

Although we have gotten a little technical in this overview, the purpose served is twofold. First, if you are a manager or system administrator, you should know a little about what is involved in planning an NT driver upgrade or development project. Although we have not gotten into Win32 development (and indeed, this is not the focus of this book), the same issues apply. If you are a fledgling NT driver developer, you'll have gained enough of a background in how things fit together logically to go on and study more deeply.

We'll now take a look at how those neat embedded objects in word processors and spreadsheets come to life. Among its other capabilities, this is the bailiwick of Object Linking and Embedding (OLE). We will also take a look at the underpinnings of OLE, the Component Object Model (COM) and how it extends the power of NT.

Chapter Twenty-Two

OLE and the Component Object Model

ll Windows operating systems include a technology that enables inter-application and process operability in unique ways. This technology is called Object Linking and Embedding (OLE). The component architecture behind OLE—enabling OLE's features to be generalized and abstracted—is called the Component Object Model (COM). After reading through this chapter, you should be able to gain a firm grasp of the ideas and technologies that make up OLE and COM. We will cover the major features of OLE, give some examples, and go on to look at OLE's underpinnings in COM. An overview of the OLE services available in NT 4 is shown in Figure 22-1.

NOTE: NT 4 has been extended to include some of the features covered by COM that were not to have shown up until the "Cairo" (NT 5 or 6) time frame, so it is valuable to take a look at these features here. (Cairo, now in design, is the release of NT that is to have a fully "object-oriented" file system.

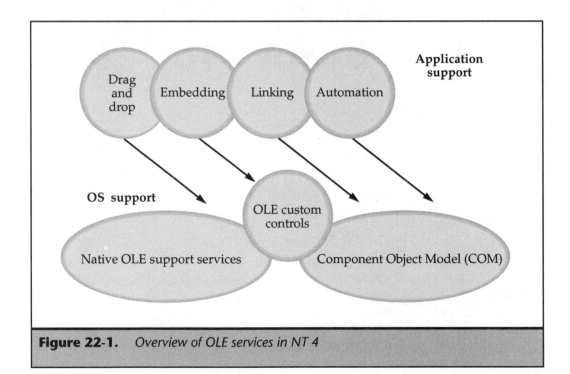

Figure 22-1.   *Overview of OLE services in NT 4*

Together, these architectures define interfaces and methods that allow applications to:

- **Use another's data directly:** Data from OLE-enabled applications can be embedded in other applications' data sets. This is called OLE embedding. The data may be a spreadsheet item that is placed within a word processing document or a .WAV file that is embedded within a presentation slide application's output.

- **Use another's data indirectly:** Pointers to data from applications, stored on disk, may be stored within OLE-enabled documents, which then can cause that data to be loaded and used, sometimes utilizing the services of the originating application. This is called OLE linking.

- **Cause directed changes remotely:** OLE-enabled applications may converse for the purposes of direct control. For instance, an application that displays data may direct a spreadsheet application's operation in calculation or general operation. This is called OLE automation.

- **Provide customized controls:** Applications generally need buttons and controls that allow a user to interact in various ways. OLE custom controls generalize the idea of custom controls. Usually, a custom control will be compiled directly into an application. In the case of OLE custom controls, the major portion of the code for that control is globally stored in one instance by the operating system, making its functionality available to all applications who want to use it. The OLE operating system interfaces are then responsible for passing data back and forth between the control and the application requesting use of the control. These controls are called OLE custom controls.

- **Drag-and-drop:** This feature allows users to select a data object from one application, drag it across the screen to another application's window and drop it in place. For instance, dragging a picture from the Paint application and dropping it into a word processing document at a specified place.

- **Use in-place activation:** While not specifically a separate feature of OLE, in-place activation can be part of both the linking and embedding of data items. Instead of calling up a linked or embedded data item's native application to execute or display the data, in-place activation allows the "container" document, the document in which the data is embedded or linked, to show the active state of the data within its own context. The native application is still called up to act upon the data, but its user interface is hidden, and the data set is run or acted upon within the confines of the application who's document contains the link or data item.

Mini-Glossary

COMPOUND DOCUMENT   An OLE *compound document* is any document that contains any number of linked or embedded objects and/or packages. Two kinds of compound documents can be involved when you create linked or embedded objects and packages; *source* documents and *destination* documents.

DESTINATION DOCUMENT   A destination document is the document or file where the object or package is inserted. This is also called the *container* document.

OBJECT   An OLE *object* is any data set, control (executable and data), document, part of a document, or command that is created or used by an OLE-enabled application.

OLE CONTAINER   An OLE *container*, or client is an application that holds OLE objects within its native document format and may or may not have to invoke an OLE server application for object display or activation. A word processing document that includes an embedded spreadsheet data item (a range of cells for example) would act as an OLE container with server activation if those cells were to be displayed for recalculation, and without server activation if the cells were just to be displayed as they were at the time of embedding.

OLE SERVER   An OLE *server* is an application that can serve up the data in the way it was meant to be displayed or acted upon. If you have a document with a linked object—a .WAV file for instance—the application that will be called upon to play that .WAV file is an OLE server.

PACKAGE   A *package* is an embedded icon that contains an object. A package can be inserted into any document created by an OLE application. You can insert a package into a document—as a directly executable pointer—when you want users to be able to click on it and run a command from within your document, or when you need to display an iconized representation of the information. For example, you might insert a package into an email message pointing to an executable that calculates and shows the stock prices for your company in real time. Your readers can choose the package to open that executable, save it to disk, or ignore it.

SOURCE DOCUMENT   A source document refers to the document where the information in the object or package was created. This is only valid for linked items. An embedded item does not have a source document, since once it is embedded, the OLE container application owns that data. For example, if you want to provide a link to a picture from an art program for use in another document, the file containing the picture would be the source document. You would use this kind of OLE linking when you want to preserve the data in its own file and have updates to that data—no matter what application performed the update—show up in your destination document.

How OLE Works

OLE-enabled programs can accomplish many different tasks, depending upon which core OLE technology is utilized. Simple object linking or embedding uses a different OLE feature set than does in-place activation or automation. Custom controls are an OLE technology unto themselves, but they too can use other OLE features, so the distinctions are almost always unclear. Compound documents only represent one kind of OLE service. Automation, custom controls, drag-and-drop (see Figure 22-2), and the COM services that enable these features are other important technologies that go into making up the OLE mix.

Drag-and-drop is a relatively simple-looking technology that is enabled by OLE. When a user wishes to select an element in a source document and drag that element to a destination document, where it is dropped in place, OLE is involved. This operation is similar to cutting and pasting and using the clipboard, but the operations and their results can be much more sophisticated.

OLE objects can be linked to, or embedded in, other OLE objects in an OLE document. This support of multiple layers of OLE objects can lead to some very

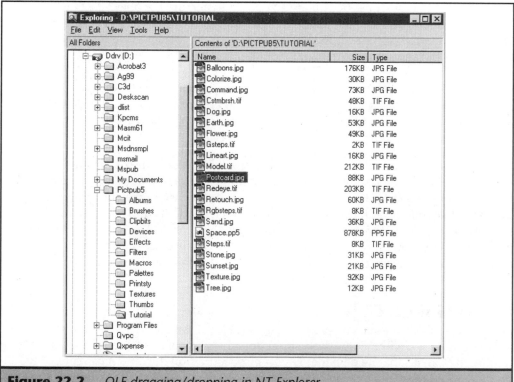

Figure 22-2.   *OLE dragging/dropping in NT Explorer*

sophisticated document design. As an example, you might embed a topological map of a seismically active zone in a document on earthquakes—showing historical features—with an additional link inside of that display pointing to and activating a data display or graph showing earthquakes happening in the last 24 hours in each zone. Changes in the 24-hour charts or displays will affect the overall seismic document—and vice-versa—automatically. Users can access or manipulate the nested objects in this kind of an arrangement, and design time is minimized, since there is no need to have multiple design applications open at the same time to assemble and edit the objects.

Now, let's take a closer look at each OLE technology.

Linking and Embedding

When OLE objects are placed into a document, they normally maintain some sort of association with the original application that they were created by. OLE linking and embedding differs in the ways in which this association is maintained. The type of OLE object is the primary arbiter for how this association will be treated.

Using Embedded Objects

Using embedded OLE objects, you are actually transferring the object *data* into your destination document. The data no longer has direct storage, that is, it is stored as part of your destination document, increasing the size and complexity of the destination document's storage requirements.

TIP: *Normally, you will embed objects when the documents that you create are distributed to other sources, independent of your organization, so that you do not have to provide extra files or links to data that may not be readily accessible to your wider audience.*

Each time you embed an OLE object, whether from a data file or directly out of another application, it becomes part of the destination document that you are creating. Any subsequent change to the original file will not show up in the embedded version. You have to explicitly edit that embedded version (see the section on in-place activation, later in this chapter). Once embedded, these objects are either edited by the original application, brought up in its own window, or in-place—where all maintenance on the object is done within the OLE destination document (see Figure 22-3), using its OLE container services.

Using Linked Objects

Using linked OLE objects, you are using these objects' data indirectly—embedding only enough data within your destination document to be able to access the object by loading it from a separate data file. Thus, your destination document contains only enough additional data to enable it to find the actual object data file on disk, acting upon it as an imported data source.

Figure 22-3. *Embedded/linked OLE objects within container documents*

TIP: *Linking obviously decreases your destination document file size relative to an embedded OLE object. This might be the only way in which you could, say, provide a multi-page excerpt from a law library within a small brochure or brief that you might send out by email.*

OLE linking can provide documents with embedded references to other data items not owned by the document creator. This allows many documents to be created while only keeping a central instance of the object's data, serving many different documents. When a change is made to the linked OLE object, it is automatically reflected in all OLE documents that maintain a link to it (Figure 22-4).

OLE Automation

Linking and embedding allow the user to access the object, whereas OLE automation allows one program, the OLE automation client or controller, to query and control another program, the OLE automation server. In more technical terms, OLE automation defines a capability that allows an application to expose a set of commands and readable and/or writable properties, or variables, making them available to other OLE applications that include programmability features.

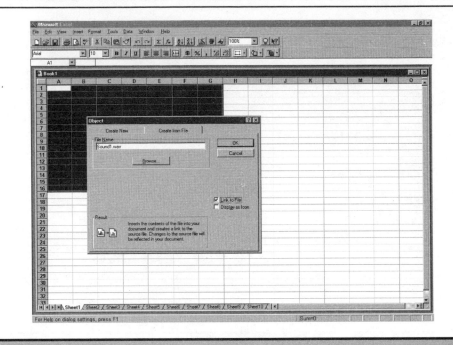

Figure 22-4.   *How a linked item is specified*

Insider Info

OLE services are both language and platform independent. This means that an OLE application written in Visual Basic can interoperate completely, and without change, with one written in C or C++. OLE automation allows OLE components to query other OLE components, directing and using remote services from other OLE-enabled components to accomplish specified tasks. As an example, a stock ticker application, complete with OLE interface, could use an Excel spreadsheet to create and manage trend reports, feeding them back into the ticker application and updating the figures on the fly.

Using OLE Custom Controls, independent developers can create custom, drop-in, components—not complete applications in and of themselves—that can be used like a library of components useful to any other developer wishing to take advantage of these custom controls. Like interchangeable auto parts, these controls can be plugged into any application that is written to the specifications set forth to interface with the control modules. Most modern development tools such as the Microsoft Visual C++ and Visual Basic support the use of OLE custom controls, reducing programming overhead.

The COM architecture, which we will discuss later in this chapter, underlies OLE functionality. Everything in OLE is based on COM, which is a specification for building modules of code and determining how other programs can access and use that code. COM defines independent methods and data structures with which code modules can interoperate. All code capable of using COM to pass data and instructions see the same interfaces and structures. This makes a COM (OLE)–aware application independent of a particular implementation, allowing applications and code fragments written in any language, and with any tool, to interoperate.

NOTE: *Not all applications that support OLE features support OLE automation. Many programs enable you to utilize OLE linking and embedding but not OLE automation.*

Using the OLE automation model, one application can control another through its manipulation of the various properties and commands exposed (see Figure 22-5). This allows a developer or programmer to extend the functionality of, and interact with, an application that exposes its OLE automation interface, but, for commercial or other reasons, would otherwise be closed and only useful through its own user interface.

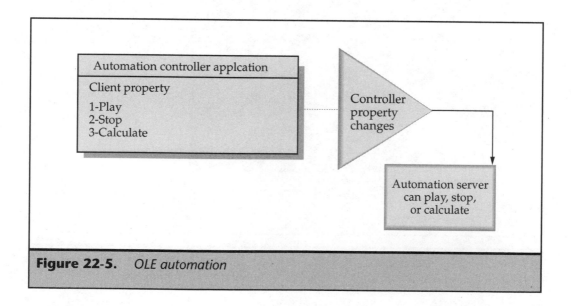

Figure 22-5. *OLE automation*

Custom Controls

Custom controls provide a way in which applications can extend their user interface, provide increased usability and functionality, and generally look better. Instead of the standard Windows interface (a bunch of dialog boxes with check boxes and radio buttons), custom controls can implement unique user interfaces for input and display of data. OLE custom controls are the newest versions of what has been offered up till now (see Figure 22-6).

Additional Functionality

That is not all that custom controls can do. They do not have to be visible. A custom control can implement specific functionality not available from within the standard operating system. An example of this is the MSCOMM.OCX. (OLE custom controls normally, but not always, have the extension .OCX.) This custom control implements specific functionality for, but not limited to, the Microsoft Visual Basic language package. It provides control of the serial ports in an extended way not available through standard operating system calls.

A More Powerful Architecture

OLE custom controls present a more powerful, generalized architecture than older custom controls. Their resources are implicitly used by an application, rather than

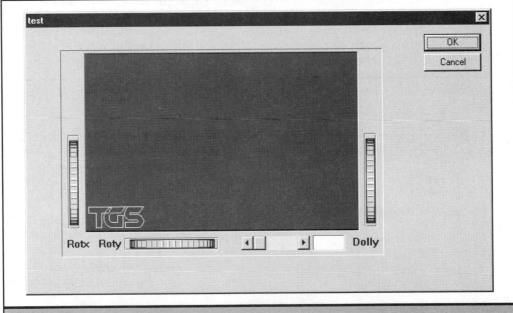

Figure 22-6.   *A typical OLE custom control*

having compile time links into code. The major portion of the custom control's code is stored globally by the operating system, working with OLE. This helps make the control's interfaces and functionality available to all applications who want to use it. The OLE layer of the operating system takes charge of passing data back and forth between the control and the application.

Because OLE is the control manager, multiple instances of the control are managed properly and not left up to the individual applications to sort out. This adds greatly to system stability and decreases overhead in the setup and operation of applications.

TIP: *OLE custom controls can be developed directly in Visual C/C++ using the ControlWizard control generator feature from within the Visual C/C++ Integrated Development Environment (IDE), which automatically generates OLE custom control skeleton code, ready for customization.*

Insider Info

Non-OLE custom controls were first introduced with 16-bit Windows 3.0. A custom control was a dynamically linked library (DLL) that exposed a set of application-usable functions. To the user, the control looks like a part of the application that calls upon its services. In the past, custom controls were usually written by developers for use in their own products. These did not reach the marketplace in great numbers, because at the time, most developers were writing applications for Windows in C, where this was not an issue.

But as development in BASIC stepped up, these new developers wanted to extend the BASIC language, limited as it was, by using custom controls. The problem was that BASIC could not use the original custom control architecture. So Microsoft came up with a set of extensions to custom controls, usable in C and BASIC, called *VBXs*. These extended custom controls took off like a rocket! Whole cottage industries were started to create and sell these controls to BASIC and C programmers, implementing functionality, weirdly shaped input and output dialogs, knobs, LED displays, and so on. VBXs also act as extensions to the BASIC language. VBXs are written in C or C++, so they can perform processing tasks that are too difficult, slow, or just not feasible to implement in BASIC.

With the introduction of NT and later with Windows 95 (both Win32-based operating systems), demand for 32-bit custom controls increased to the point where Microsoft wanted to supply a new, even more powerful control architecture for its development packages. C and C++ users, although capable of using VBXs in a roundabout way, wanted full support for the new 32-bit architecture and APIs, and 32-bit BASIC users wanted access to 32-bit VBX type controls—the older VBX being 16-bit only. Microsoft's answer is the OLE custom control.

Drag-and-Drop

Drag-and-drop allows users to select objects (for instance, spreadsheet cells) from one application, drag them onto another application's data window, and drop them into another document. Up until the inception of drag-and-drop, the most popular Windows method for transferring data between applications was the Clipboard. With the Clipboard, the user can choose to copy a selection in a source application and then paste that selection into the destination. The easier, and more intuitive way to do this is by using OLE drag-and-drop in applications that support this feature.

> **NOTE:** *OLE supports both drag-and-drop, and the older Clipboard method of transferring data and objects from one application to another.*

There are different styles of drag-and-drop. When the user drags and drops between application windows this is called *interwindow* dragging. When the user drags an object that is contained within another object (out of the containing object and into another windows or object), this style is called *interobject* dragging. A final style called *dropping over icons* is commonly used on the desktop and within applications that expose iconized representations of actions, where objects are dragged over the desktop to system icons, such as a printer or to the mail or fax icon, for delivery.

In-Place Activation

When an embedded or linked object needs to be activated in-place (in the case of embedded items, edited too) or from within the container or destination document, two things can be made to happen. First, the object may be activated or edited within the context of its original application. For instance, if you had a spreadsheet object embedded or linked into an OLE destination document, and this object was activated or brought up for editing, the Excel or Lotus 1-2-3 application might be executed, loading your data for editing or displaying.

The other situation that OLE enables is called *in-place activation*, along with an edit function called *visual editing*. This OLE feature, enabled on some OLE compliant applications, allows the object's data to be displayed and/or edited from within the destination or container application. The data's native application is still activated, but its user interface is controlled by the destination application, and usually does not involve separate windows or controls.

> **TIP:** *In-place activation is useful when embedded or linked objects need to be shown as part of a whole—as in a slide presentation where an embedded sound file or a movie clip would need to be shown in the context of the entire slide rather than in its own window housed by its native application's user interface.*

Visual Editing

In *visual editing*, a similar in-place action is initiated. The user double-clicks an object in an OLE document and proceeds to edit and interact with the object in place, rather than switching to a different application window. All of the original application's menus, toolbars, and other controls temporarily replace those of the active document window. The object's creating application temporarily takes over the OLE document window.

NOTE: *Visual editing can include different operations depending on the capabilities of the object. Embedded objects can be played, recorded, displayed, and edited in-place, whereas linked objects can only be activated in place for playback and display.*

When editing objects, instead of switching back and forth between different windows to update objects, users are presented with their contextually appropriate destination document window, which allows them to perform most of their object editing. Visual editing presents data within the context of the enclosing document, allowing focus to be put on the creation and editing of ideas and overall design rather than on the mechanics of manipulating different applications to produce content.

OLE and NT Security

All OLE embedded objects become part of the documents that hold them, so access restrictions that are in force for the document apply equally to the objects within the document. Linked OLE objects are problematical. They carry the access restrictions of their individual data files, or source documents, and the item that you have in your destination is only a moniker, or icon, that represents the link to the actual data.

NOTE: *If you have a linked object whose access is controlled by someone else, and they restrict that access later, you might not have subsequent rights that allow you to use that object.*

When an object has *read* access, you may be able to include it as a linked item, but since you have no *write* access to it, you won't be able to edit it. This can be useful in an organization with intranet capability. You could distribute a document over the intranet—complete with linked objects pointing to documents, data or applications on your local machine—and still restrict access to those pieces of content, keeping others from editing or deleting them. You may also need to examine rights and access when using drag-and-drop or OLE automation across a network and/or with RPC (Remote Procedure Call).

NOTE: *If your access rights are not sufficient to access the remote resources, you will not be able to use them as you had intended. For example, if you are using Explorer on a remote share for which you only have write access, you will not be able to copy a file to your local directory with a drag-and-drop operation between two Explorer views.*

Using Menu Commands

When you open an OLE-enabled application, you will generally use the Edit or Insert menu to work with OLE object insertion, deletion, and editing. Users of Windows applications will be at least somewhat familiar with the commands presented here, since they are in great part extensions to the idea of the Clipboard (see Figure 22-7).

NOTE: *Working with OLE embedding and linking is really an extension of the operations used to edit a single document. The operations on objects in a document, working from an application's menu, are basically similar to those that you would use to perform a Clipboard copy or paste.*

The following list shows typical commands available for inter-application data sharing in a Win32-based program. Although some programs may use different terms, the operations to be performed will generally be similar.

Command	Action
Paste	Normal Clipboard insertion of data into the destination document.
Paste Link	Performs insertion of a linked object using the Clipboard.
Paste Special	Presents a dialog box, allowing you to choose the format for the object before pasting it, and how the paste will be done (e.g. Linked, etc.).
Links	Presents the Links dialog box, allowing you to update, cancel, repair, or edit links.
Insert Object	Presents a dialog box, allowing you to choose the type of object to insert, and then embeds an object in your destination document.
Object (actual names will differ)	Invokes the OLE server application to activate, open, or edit a linked or embedded object. The menu names for this action will depend upon the object, its verbs, or allowable actions.

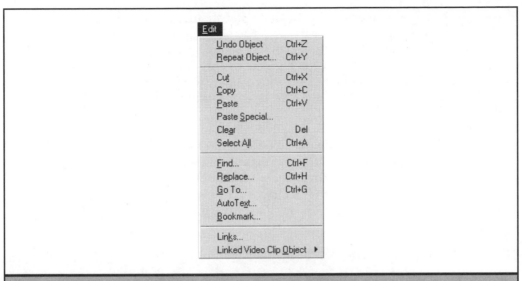

Figure 22-7. *Typical menu commands for linking and embedding OLE objects*

The Component Object Model

The Component Object Model (COM) is a specification for an object-based programming model that is designed to supply interoperability features to applications and software components. OLE uses COM's services extensively as the backbone to most OLE functions. COM supplies the "glue" that allows these components to converse and cooperate with one another—no matter what language they were written in or who wrote them—as long as they adhere to the COM interfaces that they must implement. COM treats these components and applications as abstracted objects.

COM provides the mechanism for different applications and components to connect, and then, when a connection is established, COM disconnects itself, leaving the components connected directly. In other words, COM is an implementation technology, designed to help components open and setup communication, not to act as a runtime library or system component manager.

COM's Component Objects

In COM, an object is a piece of software that contains interfaces and functions that represent what the object is and can do, along with state information for those functions. COM objects are, in the parlance of object technology, *encapsulated*, or made so that they appear to all outside functions as a black box. For instance, an object that represents a file, whose functions include moving the physical data to and from the storage medium, will only "expose" its read and write functions to the outside world.

The external program functions do not know, and should not be concerned with, how the read and write functions in our file object actually work. (See Figure 22-8).

A COM object also presents itself to the operating system as a type of black box, following the rules for exposing certain functions and data that allow the COM architecture, embedded within the operating system, to interoperate with the object, and to introduce this object to other COM objects, linking them together when requested to do so.

COM enables object communication to be programming language independent. Developers and manufacturers do not always use the same languages and interfaces when designing applications and components. To allow developers to use a COM object's capabilities, COM provides a binary standard to which objects conform. Thus, developers do not have to restrict programming to any one language to use the COM object's capabilities. COM objects are designed to be intrinsically interoperable and compatible.

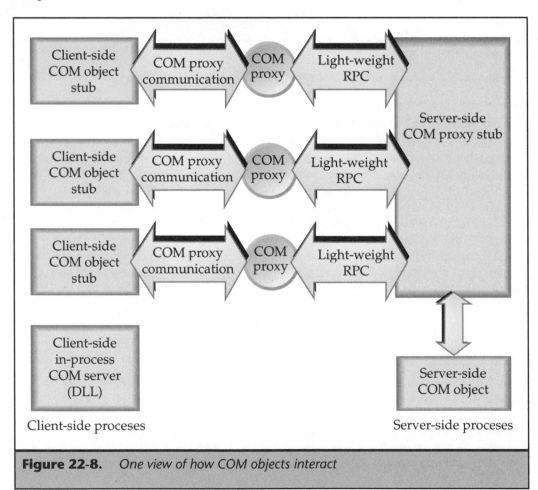

Figure 22-8. *One view of how COM objects interact*

Distributed COM

NT 4 implements Distributed COM. Its COM interfaces can be used across a network; that is, COM allows applications to be split up into a number of component objects, each of which can run on a different computer (Figure 22-9). Since COM implements network-transparent communication, applications that are split in this way do not appear to be located on different machines. This is an extension of the RPC model we talked about in Chapter 15.

Globally Unique Identifiers

COM uses the notion of a numerically and Globally Unique Identifier (GUID) to identify each object. If you have used NT or Windows 95 before, you have probably run across these identifiers in the form of GUID entries in the Registry, and *guid* files within directories. This is an operating system supplied 128-bit number that is almost guaranteed to be temporally unique.

NOTE: *A GUID is the same as a Universally Unique ID (UUID), defined by DCE. These GUID's are used by COM to ensure that COM components do not accidentally connect to the wrong object or COM interface in any case imaginable.*

COM Security

COM uses and complies with the security model inherent in NT. COM objects are subject to the same access rules as any other system object in NT. This includes permissions across a domain or on a local network (where client application access to objects residing on another physical machine will be enforced).

COM's security architecture is based on the DCE RPC (Distributed Computing Environment - Remote Procedure Call) security architecture, the industry standard

Insider Info

Distributed systems carry the potential to address an almost unlimited number of objects and applications. In older systems, the addressing schemes for remote objects or interfaces were generally name based—such as MYDLL, an ASCII identifier meant to uniquely distinguish that component or module within the system.

Unfortunately, as you have probably guessed, these ASCII names, when used as global identifiers, fall short in one important way. They presuppose that all developers in all cases will use different ASCII names. This does not always happen, and even if it did, within a distributed model, two machines with the same ASCII-named component might end up in an object name clash.

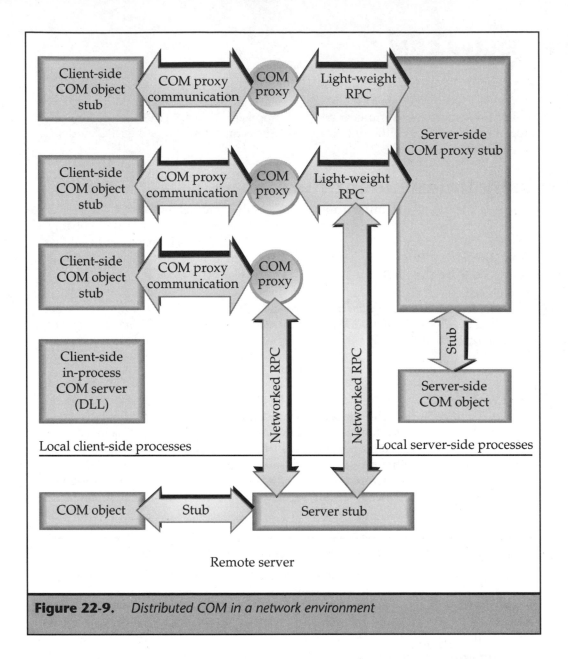

Figure 22-9. *Distributed COM in a network environment*

communications mechanism. COM provides security information about the clients that use its interfaces so that a server can use security on those objects that clients wish to access.

What's Next

OLE and COM encompass so much material that entire books are based upon these standards. We have simply looked at overviews of these components in NT to give you an idea of what underlies the NT 4 operating system, and how you can use some of these features to your advantage.

Next, we'll examine a new frontier in NT computing: Real Time. It has been said that the Windows platforms, and NT in specific, are poor candidates for controlling real time processes—such as an assembly line or a milk bottling plant. Nothing could be farther from the truth, as we'll see. Also, we'll talk about improving the performance and response of NT in all situations. No matter what application you intend to use NT 4 for, these concepts will be applicable.

Chapter Twenty-Three

Real-Time Automation, Control, and Response

Everywhere you look, computers are taking over jobs that once were performed manually. For various reasons, most of which have to do with complexity, hazardous materials, cost control, or quality of service in repetitious tasks, computer control of processes in the real world is increasing. Leaving human work force issues to books on computer ethics, here, we'll study the application of the NT 4 operating system to real-time automation, response, and control.

Real-Time Systems

Almost every tool and appliance you pick up today has some kind of processor built in to control at least one facet of its operation. Even the much satirized allusions to computerized toasters and irons have come true. But even today, information technology cannot claim mastery over all aspects of command and control in the physical world. Computers are very good at taking simple steps and tasks, breaking them down into their most basic elements, and repeating those steps and tasks over and over. The ability to automate a process so that results are obtained in a specified amount of time, usually immediate, is called *real-time control* (see Figure 23-1).

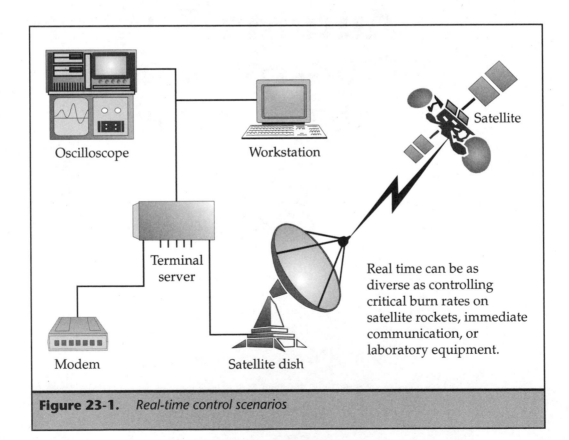

Figure 23-1.   *Real-time control scenarios*

Real-time automation capabilities have traditionally been built into small, single-purpose processors. NT has been considered to be an unspecialized, general-purpose operating system, and the hardware that runs it has been viewed as too generic to be tailored to most automation and control tasks. As we will see, this situation has changed drastically in the last years, and NT 4, in contrast to earlier versions, is specially suited for real-time control.

Categories of Process and Control

Regarding real-time automation, process and control functions tend to fall into two distinct categories: those requiring constant user direction and input, and those requiring initial user direction and input.

Constant User Direction and Input

Computer processes that require constant user supervision and direction, or input, have traditionally been difficult to quantify. What is done today is simple rote repetition. For example, a computer-controlled robot is trained, step by step, to perform the movements and paint metering that allow it to spray paint on a *single* part, over and over again. No regard is given to special cases or differentiation. The computer fails miserably in situations where a human painter would change technique without thought, in midstream, to account for changing conditions. In this case, those conditions might include

- **The item's shape:** The computer is trained to paint one item, invariably, and if that item is changed, the computer will still try to paint with the shapes and moves required for the article that it regularly paints. A human painter would instantly recognize this change of shape, adjusting movement and paint application accordingly.

- **The materials used:** The viscosity of the paint, its flow and drying characteristics, are easily compensated for by a human. Not so with the computer. Its internal model of the paint, both logically and mathematically, is invariable, needing to be reprogrammed for changing media. This does not meet our real-time criteria.

- **The ambient conditions:** Although a computer might have sensors that could sample conditions such as temperature and humidity, these variables directly affect the perceived aesthetic outcome, something that computers are incapable of judging.

NOTE: It can be argued that all of these variable conditions could be compensated for by the addition of sensors and expert routines within the processor control. Indeed, this is what humans do by using their eyes, ears, nose, and sense of touch, along with their knowledge of how different conditions affect the outcome. But almost all of the input that humans process simultaneously, especially that which changes constantly, is difficult to define and process in digital processing terms. Computer vision, touch, and the addition of expert rules systems, make a nightmare out of something as mundane as a general-purpose painting system.

Initial User Direction and Input

The kind of computer-directed automation and control that requires initial user direction is generally well understood and quantifiable. A process that takes well-known initial input parameters and performs unchanging, repetitive tasks on an item or logical system can be easily automated. Examples of this kind of process include

- **Nuclear power/energy plant control:** Critical control processes that depend on fail-safe response to external events. The computer systems controlling these processes must not only respond correctly, but must do so *every* time.

- **Spacecraft guidance, navigation, and weapons systems:** Time-critical monitoring and response to events and external measurements and stimuli. These systems must be capable of fulfilling their duties within a fast, predictable response-time envelope.

- **Medical systems:** Pacemakers, heart monitors that you see in a hospital setting, whose systems alert staff to life-threatening conditions; a computerized insulin pump or pain medication metering device; and the diagnostic machines found in medicine (NMR, CAT, and PET scanners) are examples of this kind of process control.

- **Industrial processes:** Bottling plants, machine milling and drilling, and limiting controls on industrial processes such as chemical manufacturing and smelting fall into this category. The steps to take are well known and easily repeated.

- **Telemetry and communications electronics:** High-speed switching and data delivery mechanisms, such as satellites, routing and storage/retrieval of voice and data, storage and delivery of voice and video media are examples of this kind of process.

- **Control of mechanical systems:** Robotics, automobile engine and braking systems, aircraft computerization, fly-by-wire, and control display, and automation in inventory movement and shipping systems are included here.

- **Household automation:** Media (cable, telephone, data) delivery, security, heating and lighting, control of appliances, and power consumption regulation and management fall into this category.

What Is a Real-Time Process?

Real-time systems can be hosted on any computer topology. The ability to respond to internal or external stimulus within a predictable time frame is what determines the amount of "real-timeness" in any system. Loosely defined, a real-time process is any control or monitoring system that not only performs these functions, but performs them temporally; within a specified and predictable real-world time frame. The time frame is normally defined as immediate, within a specified envelope. The system will respond within a specified time frame, or branching conditions will be met and processing will take an error correction path.

A real-time system must specially respond, in a timely and predictable way, to unpredictable external stimuli or events. In short, a real-time system has to fulfill the following criteria, under any possible load condition:

- **Timeliness:** The system must meet deadlines, and it is required that the application and underlying system support must finish certain tasks within the boundaries of response time that are specified.

- **Simultaneous processing capability:** More than one event may happen simultaneously, and all events must be serviced so that deadlines will be met.

- **Predictability:** A real-time system must service, and react to, all possible events in a predictable way. The system must be capable of following prescribed error condition or correction paths for all possible events.

- **Dependability:** The system must be dependable and reliable, to varying extents.

Hard Real Time

When response time is critical, it's sometimes referred to as *hard* real time. A hard real-time system must respond correctly within a stringently set up time frame. That response time must be repeatable and predictable. An example of a hard real-time system is a fly-by-wire control system of an aircraft: If any system response is not performed within the time specified, the aircraft will not be controllable. The cost of missing a performance deadline, or misexecuting the response, is high, and unacceptable.

Hard real-time requires other processing, if any, to be completely interruptible, and failure paths must be completely recoverable. Latency, or the inherent system overhead and delay that occurs because of electronic and logical response times, must be controllable and foreseeable. Usually, hard real-time systems have dedicated processors and special interrupt handling mechanisms to assure response times (see Figure 23-2).

Soft Real Time

Real-time systems can be set up so that response time is not mission critical and is variably "windowed" or *soft* (see Figure 23-3). As an example, a soft real-time system

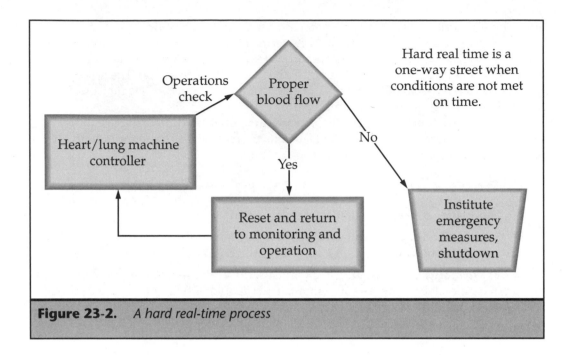

Figure 23-2. *A hard real-time process*

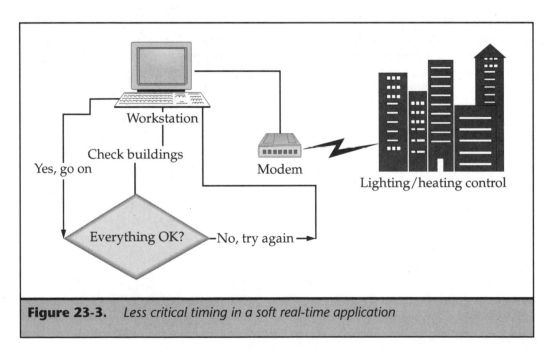

Figure 23-3. *Less critical timing in a soft real-time application*

could be a vending machine: If results are not immediate, there is no critical failure. Rather, less severe penalties are paid:

- Costs rise as results take longer.

- If the performance of the system degrades, fewer customers are willing to use the machine, resulting in decreased revenue.

- Trade-offs are made by weighing cost versus performance versus profit/hour or day. Some lowered performance may be acceptable.

- The system is incapable of handling increased throughput without failure mode being invoked. This may also be acceptable in a soft real-time system.

NT 4 real-time response, without custom drivers and techniques, commonly falls into this category. As a general-purpose operating system that has the capability to provide very fast response times, NT fits the definition of a soft real-time operating system. However, because it was not designed specifically as a real-time OS, its response times to most I/O (which is what we are really talking about) does not necessarily meet the conditions set out in a hard real-time system. Of special note is the fact that NT's scheduling of generic threaded processes is not directly controllable, with exceptions for processing done entirely within Kernel mode drivers, where context switching can be controlled.

 NOTE: A hard real-time system usually requires electronic circuits that meet real-time response characteristics for a given task. This means that if a sensor has to respond to an event within, say, 1 millisecond, it is rated so and is attached to an input circuit on the processor that meets the response time physically and electronically. With special hardware, and the custom device drivers to run with it, an NT system can meet these requirements. Thus, with specialized I/O hardware, an NT system can be made to respond to events in hard real time.

Insider Info

As an example of hard real time, let's consider a circuit board stuffer. This kind of equipment is found in most electronics manufacturing plants. The machine takes, let's say, a capacitor, and places it into holes that are predrilled into a printed circuit board. This takes place at a predetermined time in the manufacturing process, so that the board can make its way down an assembly line and into the solder tank. If the capacitor does not get stuffed into the board at just the right time (in terms of the board's position on the assembly line fixture), the capacitor leads will be bent, the part will not be inserted into the board, and the assembly will be incomplete or defective. So both position and time are a critical part of the manufacturing process. If the conditions are not met, within the specified time and placement, an error occurs and the system goes into failure mode.

As another example, consider a controller on the space shuttle. If it is controlling engine burn, the designers have to make sure that the processing and response will occur within a specified number of milliseconds. The response time is critical and might threaten life and mission if an error occurs.

NT's Real-Time Capabilities

The base NT operating system can be tailored to almost any use, given the constraints of the hardware and application mix that it must run. An NT system that is expected to drive a large database with frequent hits, as well as service asynchronous events coming in from network connections, keyboard, and mouse, cannot be expected to respond in hard real time; but even then, NT 4 is fast enough to service events so that general response time frames should be satisfied. I/O response times, in general, are said to be bus-bound, or dependent on the computer's I/O bus speed, not the speed of the processor or operating system.

NOTE: *To sum up, NT 4 will generally satisfy the requirements of a soft real-time system. In special cases, where custom hardware and drivers are provided, hard real-time systems may be possible.*

Latency and Predictability

With NT real-time systems, latency and its predictability will depend on the following conditions:

- **Number of I/O interrupts per second:** The number of I/O interrupts per second has a direct impact on whether your real-time system is NT compatible. If a hardware/driver combination can only service an interrupt in 10 milliseconds, and the frequency of your input events is less than 100/second, you'll have little problem.

- **I/O interrupt latency:** This is the total amount of time that both your hardware and driver software take to service an I/O event.

- **Processing application mix:** If you are running many applications, or the applications that you are running load the processor greatly, you will have to derive empirical application latency figures to calculate total system latency on I/O.

- **Speed of bus I/O:** This may be critical. Most 8-bit I/O cards, such as serial ports, have an upward limit on bandwidth, which is not directly related to the speed of the computer.

- **Device driver efficiency:** The device drivers that service real-time I/O must be sufficiently fast and capable so as not to allow bottlenecks. They must also handle most I/O errors internally, as calls to other system services would add to latency problems.

- **Thread priority:** The priority assigned to the thread of execution that services the interrupt has a direct effect on system latency. The NT scheduler works on a system of thread priorities (see the section on the scheduler later in this chapter).

- **Number of processors:** You can, with custom device drivers, take advantage of a multiprocessor system to devote more processing power to a specific device or process.

NT 4 Internals

NT 4 contains features that usually are not found in operating systems specifically designed for real-time response. Most real-time operating systems are either single-task, single-thread (that is, they allow only one serialized process and thread at a time), or they allow multitask/threading with exact control on the scheduler.

 NOTE: *Since NT was not specifically designed as a real-time operating system, many features that are considered a must for hard real-time development must be derived from other system services or custom software. Of most interest to anyone wanting real-time response from NT is the interrupt scheme, the scheduler's mechanism for priority boost, I/O completion, and the opportunities to extend the operating system for real-time response through the I/O Manager device driver layer.*

Real Time and NT's Design

NT's general-purpose, modular design means that many decisions were made that directly affect the OS's responsiveness to interrupt events and processing.

The Deferred Procedure Call

In NT, a device driver (the first piece of code to service an interrupt) is supposed to do very little direct processing at interrupt time. The designers of NT provide a mechanism referred to as a deferred procedure call (DPC) that allows drivers to complete their processing after they have returned from the actual interrupt. The kernel-related IRQL, or interrupt request level, is used to prioritize interrupts, and interrupts may be masked out. Generally, kernel code is not preemptable. However, the kernel will respond to an interrupt while executing kernel code if the IRQL is low enough and interrupts are not disabled (see Figure 23-4).

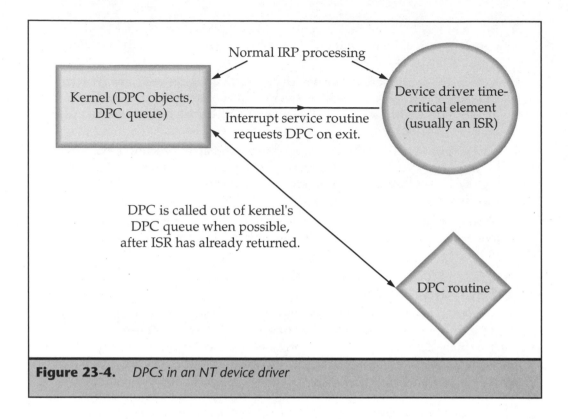

Figure 23-4. *DPCs in an NT device driver*

The Thread Scheduler

Scheduling in NT is performed on a per-thread basis. NT's thread scheduler supports 32 thread priority levels. These priority levels determine when and how often a thread gets scheduled to run on the processor. Sixteen of these priority levels are adjustable by the operating system, depending on other events that may need a temporary priority boost. If a thread is assigned one of these levels, the scheduler will adjust the level as systems requirements change. The other 16 levels are what NT calls real-time priorities. This means that the operating system cannot dynamically adjust the priority level and must service these threads on a highest to lowest priority basis.

TIP: You can set all of the priorities from device or other kernel code. Win32 provides access to setting most priority levels.

Direct Device I/O

With some important exceptions involving the changes in NT 4's internal architecture (see Chapter 20), direct device I/O is not possible from Win32 applications. The services of a device driver must be employed, and if the device is nonstandard, a device driver must be written. In the case of real-time devices, you will probably be dealing with a custom device driver. You may elect to bypass the recommended procedures for interrupt handling and do most of your interrupt processing while actually in the interrupt (see Figure 23-5).

> *CAUTION:* *Be aware that bypassing the recommended procedures for interrupt handling may cause problems in other components of NT.*

In many operating systems, an I/O call is synchronous, blocking until completed. Schemes that block can lead to choppy performance and missed interrupts. NT has full asynchronous I/O support and provides three different asynchronous I/O completion notification mechanisms.

I/O and Interrupt Management

When you design a real-time system around NT, you will invariably deal with the timing and management of I/O. Interrupt and I/O are central to any system that

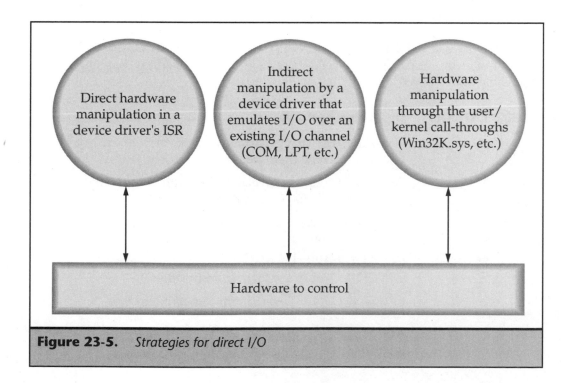

Figure 23-5.   *Strategies for direct I/O*

implements a real-time scheme. If you are familiar with systems software, implementing interrupt service and I/O routines for NT won't be too difficult.

> **TIP:** *The problems faced in getting a general-purpose operating system to behave properly in situations where guaranteed response is crucial mostly stem from following the recommendations set forth by NT's designers for implementing general-purpose applications. You must rise above the crowd and break the mold. The first step in doing this is to further understand what is going on in NT, with thoughts of how to work with the OS, not around it.*

The Critical Nature of Interrupts

Applications and drivers utilize the concept of an interrupt to signal system software that an event should be attended to by the operating system. This scheme offloads the processing power that is usually used in a system where events are polled, or checked for, constantly in round-robin fashion. In any operating system capable of using them, interrupts are important events, needing to be serviced in a timely manner. In real-time systems, the prompt and predictable service of interrupts is critical. NT uses the concept of assigned priority to service interrupts.

The Roles of the Kernel and HAL

The NT components that deal directly with interrupts include the kernel and the Hardware Abstraction Layer (HAL). The HAL maps 24 of the 32 possible interrupt levels into hardware. The remaining 8 interrupts are for the internal use of the kernel and device drivers. The kernel implements a per-processor interrupt dispatch table (IDT) for interrupt dispatch to the rest of the system and can operate at any one of the 32 possible priorities, as described in the following list:

IRQLs/DIRQLs	Definition and Use
31	HIGH_LEVEL: The highest priority interrupt in the system. Used for machine checks and bus errors.
30	POWER_LEVEL: The level used by routines that signal power failures and talk to power failure hardware.
29	IPI_LEVEL: Interprocessor interrupt for multiprocessor system synchronization
28	CLOCK2_LEVEL: Interval clock 2 level. SYNCH_LEVEL: Used for synchronization.
27	PROFILE_LEVEL: Level for timer used in profiling.

IRQLs/DIRQLs	Definition and Use
4–26	Some of these levels are available for use by hardware interrupts, being mapped to physical interrupt levels by the HAL. Some of these levels are also available to interrupt service routines directly as a result of assignation by the kernel and the HAL. Some of these interrupts are sometimes referred to as DIRQLs.
3	WAKE_LEVEL: Used for KD software debugger interrupt only, otherwise part of 3-26.
2	DISPATCH_LEVEL: Kernel reserved, software only, interrupt level for dispatcher prioritization within NT Kernel mode components. DPC execution.
1	APC_LEVEL: Kernel reserved, software only, interrupt level for dispatcher prioritization within NT Kernel mode components. APC execution, page faults.
0	PASSIVE_LEVEL: Kernel reserved, software only, interrupt level for dispatcher prioritization within NT Kernel mode components. Thread execution.

NOTE: *It is the responsibility of any interrupt service routine in a device driver to assure that it returns promptly so that the system does not lose responsiveness or "hang." Changing the interrupt mask only assures that system resources are not held and used by lower priority interrupt service routines until the routines for the higher priority interrupts have been serviced.*

Insider Info

In NT, interrupt dispatch entries are called interrupt request levels (IRQLs). Kernel interrupt service routines or drivers with interrupt service routines are always interruptible and preemptable. The particular IRQL where a piece of Kernel mode code executes determines its hardware priority. When an interrupt with a higher IRQL occurs, that piece of code is run immediately on that processor.

Put another way, when a piece of code runs at a given IRQL, the kernel masks off all interrupt vectors with a lesser or equal IRQL value on that processor. So NT implements a multilevel interrupt mask. Higher priority interrupts can preempt lower priority interrupts and not allow them to occur when the interrupt mask allows them to occur. In terms of a device driver, the IRQL is more properly called a device IRQL or DIRQL.

Asynchronous I/O and Completion

In older operating systems, I/O was implemented as a synchronous process, because that was simpler to design and use. NT offers both blocking (synchronous) and nonblocking (asynchronous) I/O. The ability to perform nonblocking I/O operations gives the NT developer an ideal tool for implementing real-time applications. In cases where I/O can be performed without immediate completion notification, or where the design allows separate threads of execution to be devoted to asynchronous completion routines, the application or device driver can queue I/O and continue processing. The ability to wait or not (on event notification for I/O completion) gives the application direct control over the strategy it will use. Synchronization objects are used, and either method can be implemented efficiently in a threaded application (see Figure 23-6).

The I/O system uses efficient synchronization and scheduling routines to distribute I/O completion processing. This asynchronous I/O and completion is an almost zero overhead optimization that you can design in, making your application I/O extremely efficient, which is especially notable on multiprocessor systems.

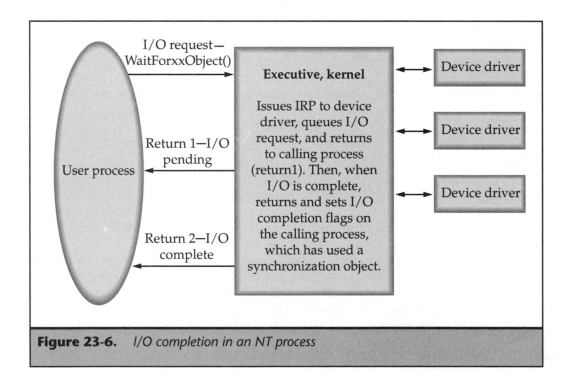

Figure 23-6. *I/O completion in an NT process*

Thread Priorities and the Scheduler

Because NT is a multithreaded, preemptively multitasking operating system, and allows little direct control over actual time slice granularity and allotment, it is important for the designer to know exactly how threads get scheduled for execution. NT uses the concept of time slicing as the unit of scheduling for threads, which are the most basic objects that can be scheduled. The time slice is also referred to as a *quantum*.

The NT Scheduler

The NT scheduler works on a system of priorities. It uses 32 numbered thread priorities, ranging from the lowest (1) to the highest (31), with zero reserved for system use. The base priority of a thread is the assigned level. The current priority of a thread is called its dynamic priority. Threads with assigned priorities of 1 through 15 can be varied by the scheduler, which will adjust the thread's priority based on thread behavior. If threads with a base level in this range yield before their time slice expires (or they are returning from an I/O operation or User mode call), they usually get a temporary increase in current priority; whereas threads that do not yield will usually get their current priority decreased so that other threads can run. This adjustment can be up or down, but never below the base level.

NOTE: *Thread priorities 16 through 31 are labeled real time, and the scheduler will not adjust their current priority. By using the real-time priorities, you can design the real-time parts of a system to be more predictable, since the scheduler does not make any algorithmic priority changes to these threads' priorities.*

The Dispatch Queue

The scheduler works from a dispatch queue of threads and processes that are ready to run. The queued entries are in priority order, and an interval timer and driver will periodically interrupt to call the thread scheduler. The thread scheduler determines the thread in the queue with the highest priority and dispatches it for execution. The scheduling algorithm merely selects the highest priority ready-to-run thread and allows it to run uninterrupted until the next clock tick. The scheduler then takes control and reevaluates which thread is the highest priority and ready to run.

NOTE: *If the previously running thread, however, is still highest priority and still ready to run (has not blocked on I/O or otherwise changed states), it will be run again.*

The Priority Parameter

From the Win32 application level, processes can set priority on threads relative to the priority of the parent process. The priority parameter can have one of the following values: Idle, Lowest, Below Normal, Normal, Above Normal, Highest, and Time Critical. The starting priority set for the thread will be based on that parameter and the current priority of the process starting the thread.

TIP: *From the desktop, you can make global changes to how the scheduler boosts thread priorities by using the Start/Settings/Control Panel/System/Performance tab to adjust the degree of foreground priority boost that applications will receive. Setting this slider to maximum results in a priority boost of two levels.*

The System Process

Of primary interest to developers of real-time systems is the system process. Direct access to the kernel and the HAL is possible from a process run in the context of the system process, such as a device driver. The system process may have multiple system threads, and it runs the kernel, I/O manager, the rest of the Executive, and all device drivers. These components share a single address space, making the developer's job easier in terms of memory and process management. The kernel (an Executive component or device driver) can create and use a system thread at any time, and many kernel components use this mechanism to multithread their system processes. Keep in mind that on entry to a Kernel mode driver, you cannot assume that you are in context to any particular thread.

Real Time and NT Memory

A virtual memory system, such as the one found in NT, is a drawback to most real-time development. Virtual memory is implemented using disk paging, which can cause a switch away from a process that needs to manage a real-time process. Disk paging also takes a great deal of time with respect to other processes running on the system. It requires access to a physical medium that runs several orders of magnitude slower than random access, physical memory.

Virtual Memory Paging

NT 4 has several memory-related features that can be of use to developers of real-time systems. NT makes the impact of demand paging controllable with thread priorities. You may avoid background paging while your code is executing by declaring your process to be of real-time priority. Since background virtual memory paging is done at a lower priority level than a process that is declared with any of the real-time priority levels, NT's "housekeeping" type of memory paging is guaranteed not to take place at an inopportune time.

Physical Memory Shared I/O

NT allows the application designer to utilize Kernel mode device drivers to implement a shared memory arena, allocated from and directly controllable by an application that calls down into the driver to obtain the memory space. Any other application may also call down to receive a pointer to this shared area.

This is a lot like shared memory in the older Windows operating systems, and this technique can be dangerous from a security standpoint, but very powerful. In many cases, there will be no more direct access to shared arenas than this scheme allows. Be very careful *not* to use this kind of design if your NT system must keep its C2 security rating, since this breaks the model for process protection.

File to Physical Memory Without Win32

NT has a set of Kernel mode routines to directly create, read, and write files from a Kernel mode component, such as a device driver. Using the "Zw" set of kernel routines, you can directly manipulate file I/O, direct to Ring 0 device driver memory.

This allows the application designer to perform file I/O much more efficiently than would be possible with the User mode routines. The technique carries with it responsibilities to ensure proper usage and fault tolerance, since a fault in the kernel may be fatal to the entire system. Use these routines with care!

Physical Memory Locking

Like all Windows operating systems, NT also allows an application or driver to lock its memory space into physical memory. This assures that paging within the context of the real-time process does not take place at all. Any amount of physical memory may be locked down (within the physical and logical limits of the operating system), so large buffers for quick manipulation and direct storage (such as for large DMA operations) are possible.

Real Time and NT Synchronization Objects

Real-time systems are often singly threaded, with no multitasking or completion mechanisms. This greatly reduces the burden on the developer or designer because threading, multitasking, and completion are variables that, when introduced into a design, complicate the deterministic flow of code. The real-time system designer must have complete control over the completion paths and synchronization of threads and tasks within a real-time process. A processing task, dependent on externally collected data, cannot be allowed to complete a process before the I/O task that gathers the data returns.

As a further illustration of how important synchronization is, take the case in which data must be output to, say, a logger. To avoid overruns, the real-time application has to be able to determine whether the logger is ready to accept this data. If the process tries to output data before it is signaled to go ahead, the output will be partially or wholly lost.

NT provides synchronization and completion services that help the real-time developer make sure that errors, resulting from mistimed task execution and improper code return flow, are not introduced into program design.

The Role of the Kernel

The kernel is the primary component providing synchronization for dispatching and execution in NT. It provides an extensive set of synchronization and dispatch objects. Synchronization objects serve to insure that the processes that use them have serialized, managed access to shared resources or processes. Not only are these objects used to derive Win32 or other User mode synchronization mechanisms, but they can serve to synchronize execution within NT Kernel mode and device driver components too. Any time that a shared resource is to be managed, you will probably call on one of these objects to help you do so. Mechanisms for mutually exclusive access, locking of code or data access, flag-type access control, and timed events are supplied by the following classes of kernel objects:

- Events
- Mutexes
- Spinlocks
- Semaphores
- Timers

Events

Events are signaling objects that are normally used as gatekeepers or traffic cops. They have two states: nonsignaled and signaled. For instance, when a secondary worker thread, which has been spawned by a primary worker thread and initially sets an event to the nonsignaled state, performs some kind of work, it may signal the primary worker thread to continue by setting the event to the signaled state. The primary worker thread waits in suspended state until the event becomes signaled, consequently to wake up and continue on. In this way, an event can control the execution of mainline code while some initialization, I/O, or other synchronous task is run to completion. A real-time process could use worker threads and events to wait on multiple I/O operations without having to suspend mainline execution.

Mutexes

A mutex is used as a synchronization object whose state is set to signaled when it is not owned by any thread and nonsignaled when it is owned. Deriving its name from its use as a coordinating mechanism for mutually exclusive access to a shared resource, only one thread at a time can own a mutex object.

As an example for real-time drivers, a mutex could be used to coordinate access for two threads to a pool of shared memory or an I/O port. By using a mutex, the designer assures that the two threads cannot access the memory or port at the same time. Only the thread that has ownership of the mutex object will have clear access to the memory pool, or port addresses, giving the other thread access by releasing ownership of the mutex.

Spinlocks

A method of implementing synchronization to data in real-time drivers and applications is the spinlock. A spinlock protects access to global data structures. The spinlock mechanism provides a way to lock access to a global structure so that only one thread can get access at any one time. When a thread takes a spinlock, no other thread is allowed access to the data structure that the spinlock is protecting. When the thread is done, it releases the spinlock, and other threads may then take the spinlock to gain access. NT device drivers and real-time code can use spinlocks to guarantee that only one interrupt or driver task has access to structures carrying data that must be accessed serially.

Semaphores

Working as a gate, a semaphore is a synchronization object that maintains a count between zero and some specified maximum. The count is decremented each time a thread completes a wait for the semaphore object and incremented each time a thread releases the semaphore. The state is set to signaled when a semaphore's count is greater than zero and nonsignaled when its count is zero. The semaphore object is used in controlling access to a shared resource, where the instantaneous number of threads accessing the resource must be limited to some fixed number. When the count reaches zero, no more threads can wait for the semaphore state to become signaled, and so no more threads can be allowed to access the resource.

A real-time driver or application might enforce limits on the number of I/O operations it will try when servicing interrupts or user requests. It could use a semaphore with a maximum count equal to the I/O operation limit, decrementing the count whenever an I/O operation is completed and incrementing it whenever an I/O operation is requested. Using waits on the semaphore, the code could effectively limit operations to some maximum for purposes of preventing overrun or other error conditions.

Timers

NT provides timer services that are sufficiently granular to be used in real-time systems. Within a polled environment, by using simple loops, a real-time system might lose data or exhibit timing errors. This can happen with an operating system like NT, whose virtual memory and caching operations (along with thread scheduling) might make empirically derived timing loops fault.

NT offers kernel services that can be used to obtain precise periodic timer interrupts for firing off and supervising events in real-time environments. A timer might typically be combined with one of the other synchronization objects to provide a frequency-controlled polling mechanism to check a mutex or semaphore for availability.

Real-Time Reaction and Response

A system that cannot respond to an event in the specified time frame will not qualify for use in a real-time design. It is critical to quantify and understand how quickly the operating system can respond to an external event. Regardless of how fast your hardware can react to an incoming signal, the onus will be on system software to service that request in a repeatable and reliable manner.

In vetting the operating system components, there will always be a fixed list of criteria that your system must meet to pass muster as a reliable real-time platform. Further performance factors may be added to this list for individual situations, but the factors covered in the following sections always form the basis for your design.

Hardware Elements

The hardware elements of a real-time system are generally well defined and quantifiable. What makes this a variable in your design equation is individual component interaction within the aggregate hardware installation. The hardware we are thinking about here runs the gamut—from the speed and quantity of processors installed in the NT system, to the specialized I/O hardware that you may have custom built for front-end data capture or output.

It is not enough to throw the fastest individual components together in an NT multiprocessor frame, hoping to get maximum speed and reliability. While the discrete pieces of hardware that you initially choose might have excellent speed and compatibility ratings, they might form a very different and unwanted assemblage when used together.

For instance, a video card with an 8-bit BIOS, rather than 16- or 32-bit, will typically slow down the speed of graphical output to the screen by as much as 75 percent. As another instance of this kind of performance problem, a 256K L2 cache on an x86 machine, versus 512K or 1MB, might slow down overall processing by as much as 50 percent or more. If the L2 cache is invalidated by running instruction mixes that force the smaller cache to be flushed frequently, it's almost like running with no cache at all!

TIP: *Real-time designers should be very sensitive to the hardware platforms that they intend as targets. An installation that has not had its hardware mix tuned will run worse than a well-tuned mix that is rated much slower overall.*

Interrupt Latency

Interrupt latency refers to the aggregate time that an interrupt takes to trigger, complete, and return. There are two components to interrupt latency: hardware latency and software latency. Hardware latency is composed of the time involved in generating an interrupt to the processor, being triggered to do so by some kind of signal change, usually a strobe's rising or falling edge. If this trigger happens on the falling edge of a logically high event, or on the rising edge of a logically low event, the width of the event should also be taken into consideration.

Once the processor has received an interrupt signal, the rest of the hardware time is represented in the actions taken by the CPU and interrupt controller. The CPU must first finish processing the current instruction, possibly flushing the instruction queue. Then the CPU must read the interrupt vector and branch to a trap handler. The trap handler saves state and vectors through the processor's IDT (interrupt dispatch table) to transfer control to an interrupt service routine (ISR) or to an internal kernel routine. The ISR is provided by a device driver for the particular device that caused the interrupt.

At this point, the interrupt service routine starts the transfer of data between the device and the processor. When the transfer is complete, the device again interrupts the CPU for service. From the time that the processor vectors to an ISR, the latency period consists primarily of software overhead, the second component of interrupt latency.

 NOTE: *In real-time systems, latency usually refers to the total of both hardware and software time—the time that it takes for all of these steps to be initiated and executed.*

Driver and Application Processing

Once the service routine has finished its job, the driver will most likely do some more work and pass the rest of the processing up to a User mode application. The application will do the actual job of presenting the data to the screen or printer, if needed. The application will also be involved in initiating the collection or dissemination of data using the driver's services.

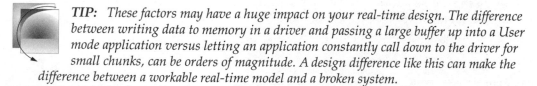 **TIP:** *These factors may have a huge impact on your real-time design. The difference between writing data to memory in a driver and passing a large buffer up into a User mode application versus letting an application constantly call down to the driver for small chunks, can be orders of magnitude. A design difference like this can make the difference between a workable real-time model and a broken system.*

Application Load

The most obvious but overlooked bottleneck for real-time design is deciding what application mix will be allowed to run on the machine. You will have a very hard time determining real-time response in a system that is also running a multiuser SQL database. Response times in systems that do a lot of background processing can be degraded to the point where real-time processes are not consistently predictable.

> **TIP:**   *The idea of running a background accounting system on a computer that is supposed to be controlling the pumps in a gas station might seem silly. Stranger things have been tried, so watch out for the obvious.*

Applications and High-Priority Assignments

It is possible to assign a very high priority (High—a priority of 13—or RealTime—a priority of 24) to application code. At first, this sounds like the ideal solution to real-time systems programming. Just assign one of these priorities, and you're done! But a unique situation will take place when you run an application in these priority classes: You run the risk of starving all other threads in the system, because a program that is running in the High or RealTime priority class can take so much of the available CPU resources that none will be available for other processes or threads. For RealTime, this includes both the mouse and keyboard. In other words, the user I/O may become inoperative, or other programs will not be allowed to run at all.

> **NOTE:**   *Win32 applications are the only User mode processes that can be assigned High and RealTime priorities. WOW, MS-DOS, POSIX, and OS/2 applications may only run at Normal priority.*

What's Next

Real-time applications are just starting to be authored for NT systems. This is the Wild West, and just like in the 1840s, a lot of gold is yet to be discovered. We leave NT internals now, and in the next chapter, touch on a very real world concern: printing. The subject of printing in NT is much deeper than loading a local printer with paper and pressing the online button. As we shall see, the NT printing facilities are varied and cover use with networks and local devices. We are going to look at both scenarios in depth, including the applets that control printing in total.

Chapter Twenty-Four

The Printing Subsystem

The NT printing subsystem (not a true subsystem in comparison to Win32 or POSIX, but usually referred to as one because of its scope) is sufficiently complex and complete to be covered in its own right. NT's printing facilities are much more advanced than its Windows OS predecessors. The printing subsystem includes facilities to accommodate many different printer models and technologies—from thermal printers to plotters. A user may print to a printer anywhere on the network through the remote printing capabilities of the subsystem. NT implements genuine remote printing facilities. Remote printing gives you the ability to use a printer not directly attached to your own workstation or even to your local network. Once installed, NT remote printing operations are transparent to the user and to an application on the local workstation. It is as if the printer was directly attached.

NOTE: NT supports almost all commercially available printers as well as network interface print devices, such as HP JetDirect laser printers and network-compatible printer devices connected by AppleTalk and TCP/IP remote protocols. Novell NetWare connected devices are also supported.

The NT Printing Model

NT implements its printing system in the same way that it implements most everything—as a modular subsystem. First we'll take a look at the layout of the NT printing model, as illustrated in Figure 24-1. We'll look at how jobs are handled when NT acts as a print client and as a print server. Physical print devices (printers, plotters, or a file, for example) do not map directly to the concept of printers, at the application level, in NT. Rather, a *printer* in NT is implemented as a logical software interface whose function is to control various aspects of the print job before it reaches the physical printer.

The NT Spooler

The printing subsystem is implemented as a collection of system files (dynamic link libraries or DLLs) that are responsible for processing the print job and routing it to the print media. These DLLs are what NT calls the *spooler*. Older operating systems also use this term, but in a different way. A traditional spooler is largely responsible for buffering output and managing data flow to a physical device or storage medium. NT's print spooler does much more. When it receives a print request, it examines aspects of the job and acts to route the print request through a series of system components that, depending on the desired output, act on the data in different ways. The NT Print Processor components are key to this universal functionality.

The spooler consists of system components that act to route the print job and process an application's print output (using GDI—the Graphics Device Interface—to do graphics, halftoning, and other rendering) into a data format that may be output to any supported printer. The spooler is also involved in sending these print jobs to the

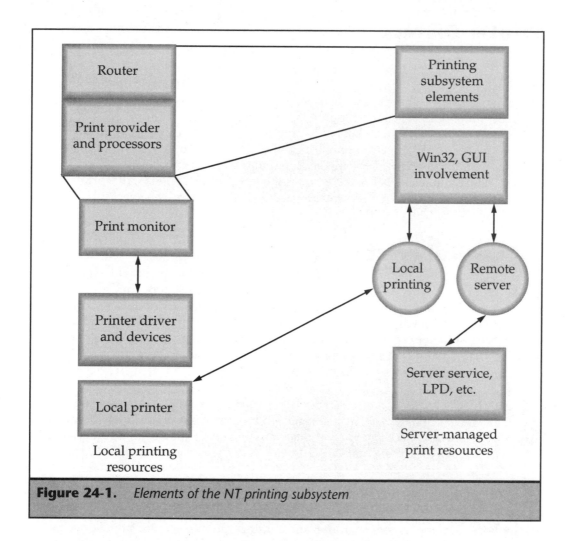

Figure 24-1. *Elements of the NT printing subsystem*

correct physical target. If the printer is physically attached to your local workstation, the spooler sends it to the local processing components. If it is on a remote print share, the spooler has responsibility to see that it gets there too.

NOTE: *The NT printing model takes different actions to render a print job depending on factors such as whether the print job is bound for a local or remote printer, whether it is a graphic or text, and which printer driver is involved.*

NT Printer Drivers

An NT *printer driver* is a module that takes the application's printer output, rendered by the NT spooler, and translates the uniform graphics and text data into a printer-specific control language, such as PostScript or HPGL (Hewlett-Packard Graphics Language). There are so many standards for printer control languages it would be impossible to include support code for every model within an application itself. Added to that is the fact that NT is supposed to abstract this interface, making it unnecessary for applications to know which physical printer they are outputting to. NT ships with printer drivers for almost all popular makes and models of printers and plotters. When you install NT and create a printer or printers, you install a printer driver and, optionally, make the printer available on the network by sharing the printer.

An NT Logical Printer

An NT logical printer, then, holds the definition of where a document will go, when it will go, and how it will be rendered. When users connect to printers, they are connecting to logical printer names that represent one or more print devices on local workstations or somewhere on the network. Using NT, you may establish a multiple point relationship between logical printers and physical printers. You may assign multiple logical printers to a single physical printer or a single logical printer to multiple physical printers of the same kind.

 NOTE: *The ability to assign more than one printer to a print device gives users flexibility in printing documents. For example, two printers associated with a single print device may offer different print properties—one may print separator pages and the other may not. One printer could hold documents and print them at night, while the other processes documents 24 hours a day.*

Remote Operation and Administration

NT supports genuine remote operation and administration. An application, or client, can browse the network for available Windows network printers and use them as if they were directly attached to the local workstation. Additionally, no manual setup is required when NT and Windows 95 (partial support) operating system workstations try an initial connection to a properly installed NT print server. If an NT or Windows 95 client makes an initial connection to such a server and does not have a printer driver installed locally for the target printer model, the printer driver is either automatically downloaded from the server and installed on the local client or a request is made of the administrator to provide the local files needed.

NOTE: *If driver software is updated on the NT print server, those revisions will be automatically downloaded and installed on NT clients when they next connect and try to use the printer.*

Connecting to a Printer

When you are installing or using the print capabilities in NT, the first thing you will want to do on a workstation, or client, is to connect to a printer. NT printers are given global names that identify them to an application or utility. This name can refer to a printer setup that represents a make and model of printer anywhere on your network (including your local workstation) or non-Windows network printers connected to your Windows network through gateway services such as Macintosh printers.

Foreign Printing Clients

Foreign printing clients such as those running MS-DOS and Windows 3.x have full access to NT printers. They cannot use abstracted names as NT and Windows 95 clients (full Microsoft network client support) can, but they easily connect by using redirection to a sharename such as *\\printserver\myprinter*. The built-in fonts and NT forms available from an NT print server are not accessible from foreign OS clients. Also, in cases where the printer is used by or installed on one of these foreign networks, the automatic driver setup functionality will not be available, and you will have to manually install the target printer drivers on your local workstation when first setting up.

NOTE: *In terms of permissions, you must be logged on as an administrator or you must be given permissions in the Power Users group to be able to make a printer connection to a printer server running on a foreign operating system.*

The Printer Browsing Function

Finding a printer on an NT 4 network is greatly simplified. In older versions of NT, this meant setting up a local printer or knowing the sharename (e.g., *\\printserver \myprinter*) and typing that into a connection dialog. NT 4 simplifies this process by providing a graphical printer browsing function. This works exactly like browsing for a computer on your network. The browsing function (see Figure 24-2) can be accessed through the desktop Network Neighborhood icon or while installing through the Add Printer wizard. You may also browse for printers from the Print Setup dialog, in an application, from NT and Windows 95 workstations. Print shares on Windows 3.x/Windows for Workgroups machines may also be used but with reduced setup and configuration functionality.

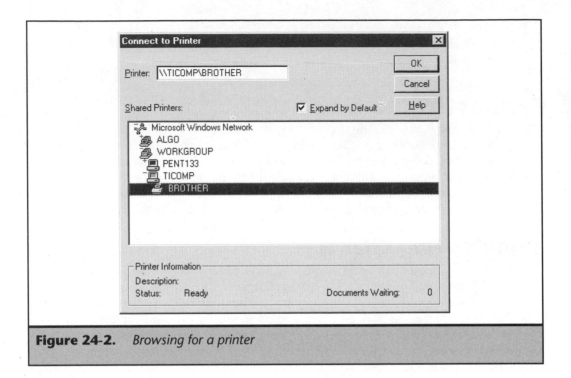

Figure 24-2. *Browsing for a printer*

 NOTE: *If the target printer is attached to a LAN Manager 2.x print server or it resides on a Novell or Macintosh system that you have connected through a gateway, you may browse for these print shares also.*

Installation and Administration

As an administrator, you can remotely connect to NT print servers and printers, controlling installation and configuration of shares, settings, and printer drivers. Printer drivers for NT and Windows 95 clients can be centralized to one location, cutting administration and distribution overhead. Let's look at the basic steps in setting up your printer, printer driver, and print shares.

A Dedicated Print Server Is Not Always Necessary

Dedicating an NT machine totally to the print server role is only necessary when high-volume and high-density jobs are anticipated. You may use an NT installation that is already set up for file sharing, since print sharing typically uses very little resources, unless great numbers of print jobs are expected to be queued or the composition of each print job requires large amounts of temporary local disk storage, as in high-density graphics print jobs.

> **NOTE:** *NT computers set up for file sharing will not be affected by adding moderate use print servers, since the file sharing activity will always have priority.*

Property Sheets

You access a logical printer's settings by using its property sheet. The property sheet (see Figure 24-3) is a tabbed dialog that allows you to set parameters for both server and individual logical printers. You access these property sheets through Start/Settings/Printers, the My Computer/Printers icon on the desktop, the File/Server Properties command, or an individual printer's Properties command.

The installation and configuration of logical printers and connections to physical ports (printer devices) is accomplished by using these property sheets. As we go through the stages of setup, we'll refer heavily to the use of the property sheet applicable for the specific operation.

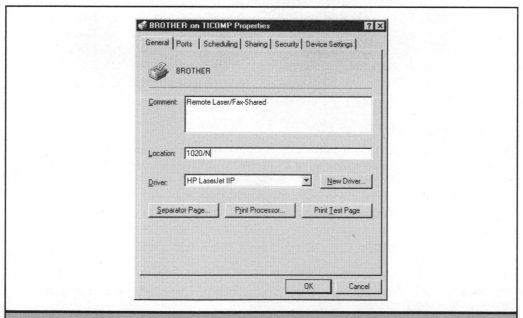

Figure 24-3. *A printer property sheet, General tab showing*

Installing and Configuring Physical Printers

Once you have decided how your physical print resources will be utilized, you'll be ready to make the actual hookup. Physical printers can be attached to a parallel, serial, or network port on the print server or workstation. If the device is network compatible, such as in an HP JetDirect interface, it can be hooked up directly to the network. The guidelines covered in the following sections should be used to plan for your physical installations.

 NOTE: The figures given for throughput on any printer are ideal and do not reflect reality. Many factors figure into the speed of printing that you can expect out of any particular installation. Printer buffering of incoming data, printer engine throughput limits, and printer job mix are major elements that can affect the actual throughput. The general installation guidelines to follow are dictated by the electrical characteristics of the interface of your printer. If speed and distance from computer to printer are factors in your choice of printer, you can expect the following general guidelines to hold.

Parallel Printers/Ports

Printers with parallel interfaces are usually easiest to install. Parallel printers are capable of medium throughput speeds—more than serial, but less than direct network interfaces. Most printers are available with a parallel interface port as standard. The interface requires a cable with 36 wires, so cables for parallel ports are usually more bulky than serially or network interfaced printers. Because of the chance of crosstalk and also the low voltages involved, parallel cables must be less than ten feet long unless you have special repeater equipment that can extend that length. Normal IBM PC-compatible computers are capable of supporting two or three parallel printers, although with special interface cards (and drivers compatible with NT 4), this may be boosted to eight or more ports. Ideal throughput is usually between 8,000 and 24,000cps (ideal parallel output can reach 300Kbps).

Serial Printers/Ports

Serially interfaced printers are a bit more flexible than their parallel counterparts. Interfacing is usually done with a 9- or 25-pin cable, and cables can be 50 to 100 feet long without repeaters. Serial printer interfaces are slower, exhibiting ideal throughput of usually no more than 1,600cps (ideal serial output for most printers is 19.2Kbps or ~2,100cps). Standard IBM PC-compatible computers can interface with up to four serial devices, but serial port cards exist (compatible with NT 4) that will allow up to 64 serial attachments.

NOTE: As with the parallel interface cards, device drivers must be available for NT 4 in order to extend the number of ports available.

Serial Handshaking

When you set out to configure printers and ports, you have to deal with how the printer tells the computer that it's OK to send more data, or vice versa. This is called flow control, or *handshaking*. The actual settings for a particular computer/printer combination will probably involve setting both printer jumpers or switches, and setting parameters in NT through the Start/Settings/Ports dialogs (see Chapter 6).

No NT settings are usually involved when you install parallel or network-compatible printers, so for the most part, these guidelines involve serial printers. Serial devices usually require flow control. Using the NT Control Panel/Ports dialog, you can configure your serial port for speed, data length, and no flow control (XON/XOFF, which involves software flow control), or hardware flow control, which is usually the best choice.

NOTE: *Serial printer speed and data length will normally be 9600 or 19,200 baud, with no parity, 8 data bits, and 1 stop bit.*

Network Interfaced Printers

Printers that can connect directly to a network—those that have a network interface card (NIC) or external network interface—have many unique features that make them ideal for medium to large corporate or businesswide settings. First, they can be placed almost anywhere and do not have to be physically attached to a computer at all. The only requirement is that a network tap, or connection, must be available for them to plug into. A network-compatible printer has its own NIC or adapter built in, so it appears on your network as just another node, like a workstation or server. Physical location has no effect on printing throughput and performance, and because the printer appears on the network as a node, an NT 4 print server can control any number of this type of printer—only dependent on your network topology, server processing capacity, and logical layout. If network connected printers have internal RAM buffering, ideal throughput to the printer I/O port can reach network speeds of between 5 and 100Mbps.

Installing a Network Protocol

Depending on which network protocol your printer uses, you will need to install either the TCP/IP printing service, the Data Link Control (DLC) protocol, or the AppleTalk protocol. If you will be printing over TCP/IP, you will first need to determine the printer's IP address so that you can specify its network location in the next step. If you will be using an AppleTalk printer, you'll need to know the AppleTalk zone for the printer.

Using the Add Printer Wizard

You need to tell NT about your print hardware after connecting the physical printer. NT calls this *creating a printer*. The process involves using the Add Printer wizard (see Figure 24-4), which you will find in the My Computer/Printers folder or from the Settings/Control Panel/Printers icon. You will use this wizard application to set up the physical to logical relationships and to set other parameters for the logical printer.

> **NOTE:** *Permission to create a printer is only granted to administrators and server operators. If you don't have the correct permissions, you will only be able to connect to an existing printer when using the wizard.*

The process of using the wizard to create a printer involves the following steps:

1. First, you specify the basic parameters—the choice of physical port to use and the make and model of printer.

2. Then you choose a name for the logical printer. This name can be anything you like, although descriptive names usually work best, since other people will be connecting to the printer and its name gives clues to its capabilities.

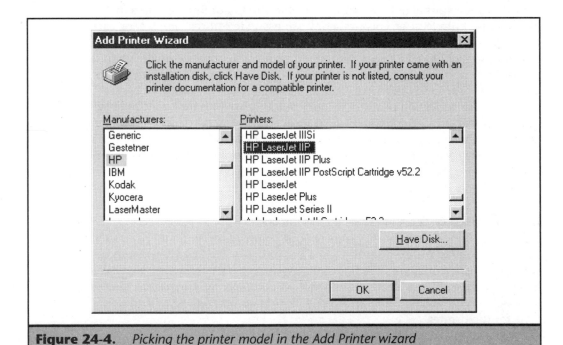

Figure 24-4.   *Picking the printer model in the Add Printer wizard*

3. Also, at this point, you will be asked if this printer should be the default printer (on the local machine) for applications to use.

4. Now, set the printer sharename if it is to be available to network users. NT will suggest a name, but be aware that you should use names with eight characters or less if Windows 3.x and MS-DOS clients are to easily connect to this printer.

5. In this part of the wizard dialog, you will also be asked to specify which operating systems (and revisions) and hardware platforms this printer should support (NT for Intel x86, Alpha, MIPS, PowerPC, and Windows 95). NT asks you to specify these parameters so that the drivers for those specific OS revisions can be installed to support the automatic use and download feature when a remote printing operation is requested from a supported client.

6. Next, you'll be asked to print a test page.

7. NT will try to install the drivers and their various revisions from CD-ROM or a network share, if necessary. If you have chosen versions of NT other than 4, or Windows 95, the wizard will ask you to insert disks that contain printer .INF and driver files for those platforms. Be aware that the requested driver files must be reachable or you will not be able to install the drivers for those configurations. You also have to provide the driver files for Windows 95 in the extracted form, since NT 4 does not extract files from Windows 95 .CAB archives. See your Windows 95 documentation on using the EXTRACT utility. You can add support for these other platforms later from the Sharing tab of the printer's properties sheet.

8. Once you have followed all the previous steps, and optionally loaded drivers, you will be shown the properties dialog for the specific printer model that you have chosen. You will be allowed to assign physical, printer-specific parameters such as security, separator pages, sharing properties, color and fonts (if applicable), printer memory settings, and so on. If you do not choose to set specific properties at this time, NT will use its default settings for that physical printer type.

NOTE: Once you have stepped through the wizard and the printer's property dialog (see the following section), you will be ready to use the printer. If you have shared it, the printer will now appear in the network printer browse list when an application tries to find it. Only NT 4 and Windows 95 clients will be able to choose this printer by name or from their Add Printer wizards. By using a sharename, such as \\printshare\myprinter, any compatible application will be able to utilize this printer.

Using the Printer's Properties Sheet

After the Add Printer wizard has helped you create a logical printer, you will be shown that printer's properties sheet, or dialog. This tabbed dialog allows you to set the parameters discussed in the following sections.

The General Properties Tab

The selections on the General tab (see Figures 24-3 and 24-5) of the properties dialog box let you make choices about the location of your printer, the drivers, and some other special elements.

COMMENTS In this area you may enter a comment to be displayed when NT clients are browsing for a printer. This is helpful in announcing to others what the printer can do, who it belongs to, and so on.

LOCATION In this area you may enter text describing the location of the physical printer to be displayed to clients who are browsing for a printer.

DRIVER The chosen printer driver is displayed here. You can choose a new driver, using the New Driver button, if you wish to update or change driver types for this printer.

SEPARATOR PAGE When you choose this button, a small dialog will appear asking for the name of the separator page. If you want to set up a printer so that separator pages are generated at the beginning of each document, enter the name of the separator page file here.

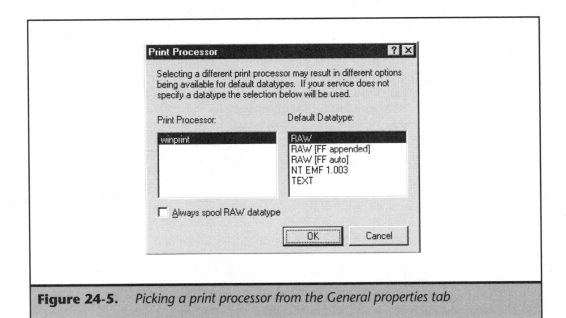

Figure 24-5. *Picking a print processor from the General properties tab*

NOTE: Separator pages are sometimes used where shared printers generate jobs from many users. They can have anything you like printed on them, but typically state the owner of the document and show the time printed.

You may use one of the three separator page files included in NT or a custom file that you create. To create a custom page, you can use one of the included files, renaming and editing it. The included separator pages can be found in the systemroot\system32 directory. They are

- **SYSPRNT.SEP:** A generic separator page
- **PCL.SEP:** A separator page compatible with Hewlett-Packard PCL printers
- **PSCRIPT.SEP:** A separator page compatible with PostScript printers

PRINT PROCESSOR   By using the dialog that is shown when you choose this button, you can change or install new print processors. The print processor controls how the document will be rendered and routed. NT will usually make the best choice here, and only system administrators should ever change this setting.

The Ports Properties Tab

You can use the Ports tab (see Figure 24-6) on a printer's properties sheet to check and change which port a printer is connected to. You can choose buttons to add a port, delete a port, or configure a port. The type of port will determine what processes you must go through to work with it. If you add a network port, you might have to add support files and drivers for that configuration. The available ports will be listed in the dialog, and you may direct output to more than one port. NT will send your print job to the first available port that is checked in this dialog. Usually, only one port will be used, but you can direct NT to use any number of ports by checking them in this dialog. Of course, those ports must have compatible physical printers attached.

If the physical printer has a direct network connection, use the Add Port button and choose the port type based on the following criteria for the particular type of printing job:

- **Print to a local parallel or serial, or UNC (universal naming convention)-shared device:** This is the most straightforward type of connection. Simply choose the port from the dialog.
- **Print to a LPR (line printer remote) device:** You will first need to install the NT TCP/IP Printing Service from the Control Panel/Network applet, and then use the NT LPD/LPR services.

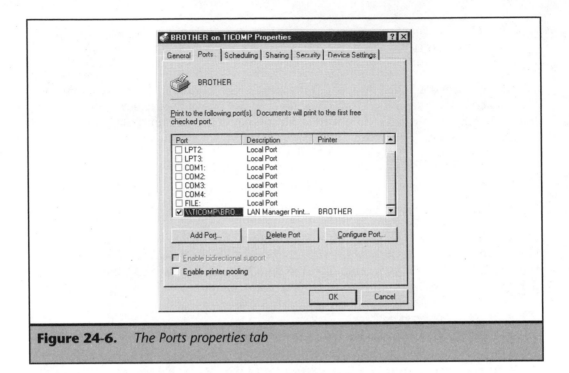

Figure 24-6. *The Ports properties tab*

- **Print to an HP JetDirect-type device:** The DLC protocol must first be installed from the Control Panel/Network applet.

- **Print to a DEC-type device:** The TCP/IP or DECNet protocols must first be installed from the Control Panel/Network applet.

- **Print to an AppleTalk device:** The AppleTalk protocol must first be installed from the Control Panel/Network applet.

The Scheduling Properties Tab

You can set scheduling and spooling options for the logical printer in the tab shown in Figure 24-7. The option sections are described next.

TIMES OF PRINTER AVAILABILITY   The first section of the Scheduling tab allows you to set availability times for this printer. This is useful in order to limit usage at peak hours or to schedule maintenance.

PRINT JOB PRIORITY   Print priority is based on a scale of 1 to 99. The relative priority can be set for each logical printer on the network, thereby allowing a staggered relationship to be set up. The default is priority 1. If two logical printers are connected to a single print device, print jobs with the highest priority (according to the setting in their associated logical printer) will print first.

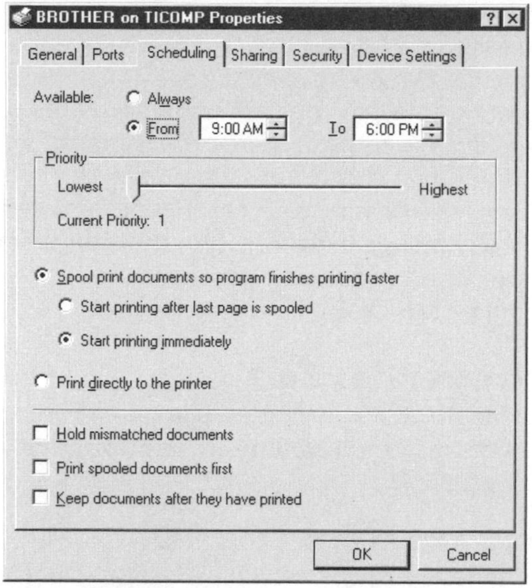

Figure 24-7. *The Scheduling properties tab*

SPOOL PRINT JOBS   Use the spooling settings to enable the printing spooler. This allows applications to spool their printing jobs to memory and return faster. You can choose to wait until the last page of the job has been spooled or start printing immediately.

PRINT DIRECTLY TO THE PRINTER   Use this setting to bypass NT's memory spooling mechanism. If you have a large amount of physical printer memory, and the device is on a high-speed connection, you may want to choose this setting. Also, some printing devices may require full control of a physical port, necessitating this option's usage. Usually, this setting will slow down application printing.

HOLD MISMATCHED DOCUMENTS   Use this setting to direct the memory spooler to hold off printing jobs if they do not match the loaded form. Other documents will print while the new form is loading.

PRINT SPOOLED DOCUMENTS FIRST   Use this setting to direct the memory spooler to print in FIFO (first-in/first-out) order. This option will cause the printing to start immediately.

KEEP DOCUMENTS AFTER THEY HAVE PRINTED   Use this setting to direct that printing jobs should be saved in memory after they have printed once. This allows faster print resubmission for copies.

The Sharing Properties Tab

Use the Sharing tab (see Figure 24-8) to provide a sharename so that other computers on your network can use the printer by referring to it in the form of \ *printshare* *myprinter*. NT clients can connect to your printer by using the printer name or the sharename. Other operating systems can connect by using the sharename. If you provide a name with 31 or fewer characters, with no spaces or special characters, you will be able to provide this sharename to clients on your network other than NT and Windows 95. To use the sharename with MS-DOS clients, limit it to eight characters, optionally followed by a period and three extension characters (such as .doc). This is the so-called eight-dot-three MS-DOS naming convention.

The Security Properties Tab

Use the Security tab of the printer's properties dialog (see Figure 24-9) to set the following NT security features for controlling access to printers, auditing access, and to take ownership of printers.

PRINTER PERMISSIONS AND ACCESS CONTROL   Choose the Permissions button to show the Printer Permissions dialog, which will allow you to set permissions on

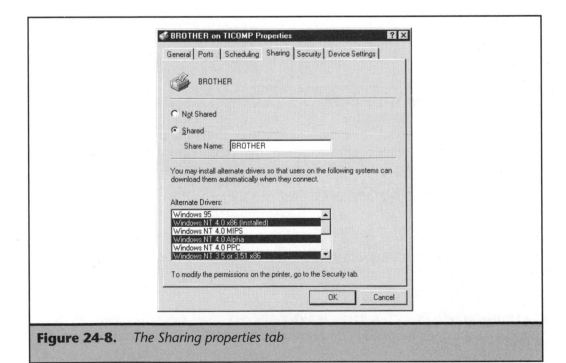

Figure 24-8.   *The Sharing properties tab*

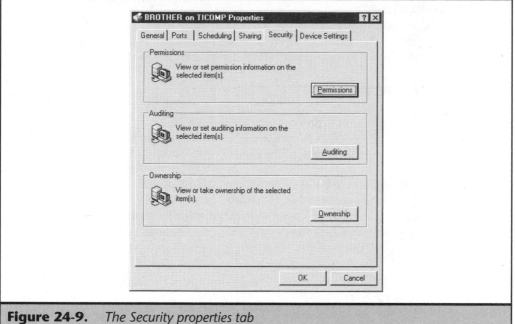

Figure 24-9. *The Security properties tab*

user groups and individuals by printer. Shared printers are available to all network users unless permissions are explicitly set otherwise. You can restrict usage by altering permissions on the group or individual that you choose here. In order to change printer permissions, you must own the printer or have Administrator/Full Control permission on the printer. You can set permissions to No Access, Print, Manage Documents, and Full Control.

NOTE: *Unless explicitly set otherwise, administrators, print operators, and server operators have Full Control permission if the machine is a print server. If the machine is a workstation, administrators and power users have Full Control permission. Any user has permission to manage her or his own documents.*

PRINTER AUDITING To track the usage of a printer, by group or user, you can set the actions to be audited. You do so by choosing the Auditing button, which will bring up the Printer Auditing dialog. You then add groups or individuals to your audit list, setting the actions you want to audit. The events you choose may be audited for success or failure. You may audit Print, Full Control, Delete, Permission Change, and Ownership events. You can use Event Viewer to view the audit information, but you must make sure that the audit policy is set to audit file and object access, using User Manager first.

PRINTER OWNERSHIP   If you want to set permissions on a printer, you must have ownership of that printer. You use the Ownership button to display the Ownership dialog and take ownership of the printer. You can take ownership if you are logged on as an administrator or have Full Control permission granted on the printer.

The Device Settings Properties Tab

You can use the Device Settings tab (see Figure 24-10) to discover and set options and configuration for the physical target device that is described by your logical printer. Depending on what kind of physical printer is targeted, you can view and set options for paper trays, font cartridges, installed memory, and so on.

FORMS   NT printing is form based. The print administrator configures the printer by defining the form loaded in each paper source, or tray. Size, margins, and form name are configurable. When users need to print on an NT client, they can choose a form instead of a physical tray on the printer, relieving the user of knowing specifics about the physical configuration.

NOTE: *These properties can also be viewed and set from the printer's Document Properties sheet by opening the Printers folder, selecting a printer, and choosing Document Defaults from the File menu.*

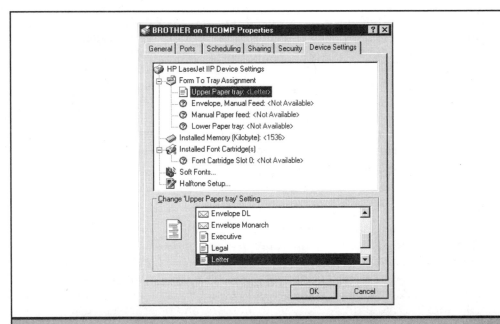

Figure 24-10.   *The Device Settings properties tab*

FONTS   As a WYSIWYG (what you see is what you get) graphics system, NT uses three types of screen fonts for reproduction on printers. These include TrueType, raster, and vector fonts. NT will also use soft fonts, stored in disk files, that are specific to particular printers. For any given print job, NT will upload the required screen and soft fonts into printer memory.

- TrueType fonts, rendered from stored shape files, are device independent and can be used by all types of physical print devices.

- Raster fonts are device-specific bitmaps that are tailored for an individual display device. They may or may not be directly renderable on a specific physical printer. Unlike TrueType fonts, they are not scalable.

- Vector fonts are used by physical devices such as plotters. They are line oriented and can be scaled or rotated in any way.

PRINTER MEMORY   Laser, LED, and other types of page printers work by taking a complete page of information from the computer at one time. They must store this information in their internal memory, so it's important that NT knows exactly how much memory is installed on your physical page-type printer. If NT thinks that there is more memory in your printer than is actually installed, serious print problems and faults could occur because of buffer overruns. If NT thinks that there is less than there actually is, print performance will suffer.

> **TIP:** *The Device Settings property tab will display what it thinks is correct for your printer's memory settings. Set the memory amount to match your specific page printer's internal memory. You can usually find the correct amount by running self-diagnostics on the printer. It will print out a page of its settings, including installed memory.*

Setting Up and Using a Printing Pool

NT will allow the use of what is referred to as a *printing pool*. When high-volume printing is to be managed on an NT server or system, a printing pool can even out loads and expand throughput and capability. The pool is made up of multiple, identical, physical print devices connected through one logical printer. Because the physical devices are identical, NT can be set up to output a print job, destined for a single logical printer, to any connected port with an identical physical device. Thereafter, the next physical print device that goes idle will receive the next print job.

Setting It Up

You set up a printing pool by creating a printer using the Add Printer wizard, or by opening a logical printer's Ports property sheet. You then assign as many output ports as you wish to this printer, each port having identical physical print devices attached. The physical printer ports can be of the same type or a mixture of parallel, serial, and network.

Creating Flexible Configurations

Flexible configurations are possible with NT printing. A printer may be part of a printing pool and, by creating another logical printer, can be at the same time separate from the pool. By associating another logical printer with the same physical printer, the physical printer may be referred to in two different ways. So, logical printers may be associated with more than one physical printer, and physical printers may be associated with more than one logical printer.

Remote Printer Management

If you have Administrator/Full Control permission on a printer, you can administer and manage it from any NT client on the network. You can select a printer from the Network Neighborhood folder, set printer properties, and create new printers. However, you must administer a printer locally to add, delete, or configure ports. Any user on the network can check the status of a remote printer. If you want to manage documents other than your own, you must have Administrator/Full Control, or Manage Documents permission for the particular printer.

NOTE: Some management functions will be unavailable on printers attached through stations running older versions of NT or other operating systems.

AppleTalk Networks and the Macintosh

NT Workstation and NT Server installations can print to AppleTalk devices and AppleShare print servers. However, only NT Server, which includes Services for Macintosh, can enable Macintosh clients to print to Windows NT print servers.

Macintosh networking only provides support for file security. Print devices are not covered. Macintosh clients always have permission to access print devices or print servers. There is no password or username mechanism in the AppleTalk protocol, and Macintosh print clients cannot identify themselves on the network. Because of this, NT print servers cannot enforce user-level security on these Macintosh clients.

NOTE: By default, the NT Server MacPrint service logs on as the System account. To enforce a set of custom permissions on all Macintosh users, create a different user account, set permissions for that account, and then set the MacPrint service to log on using this account.

Using Novell NetWare Networks

You must install the NT Client Services for NetWare (CSNW) on each client in order to enable NT clients to print directly to NetWare printers. To set up a print server with which Microsoft network clients can print to a print device shared by Novell NetWare, install Windows NT Gateway Services for NetWare (GSNW) on the print server. To allow NetWare clients to print to NT network printers, and Microsoft Network clients to print to NetWare PServers, use File and Print Services for NetWare (FPNW). FPNW is an optional product, not shipped with NT.

What's Next

Printing is very flexible in NT 4. Whole books could be written on the many ways both servers and clients interact in the printing subsystem. We have only scratched the surface, and if printing is a favorite subject of yours, or you need to be proficient in administering large print farms, there is plenty of room for study.

Part 6 of this book looks toward the future of NT client/server technology (a future that is rapidly coming upon us), the Internet (and intranets), and how you can use NT 4 to make your place in this future better. We'll examine the modules and applications that can have you up and publishing your own Web pages and advertisements to millions, within hours. So read on, and soon you'll be cruising the NT wires through cyberspace!

PART SIX

Internet and Intranet Functionality

Chapter Twenty-Five

The Internet and NT's Internet Information Server

With the heightened interest in the Internet these days, almost all connected organizations want some sort of Web presence. This may be only for information dissemination within an organization—for use by an organization's employees exclusively (what is now generally called an *intranet*)—or it may encompass plans to publish advertising and support material to the connected public at large, on the *Internet*. Targeted customer sales and support is a very important aspect of having a connected public presence, and many companies are moving away from printed newsletters and handouts for their employees, using local area networks and private Web pages instead.

Internet and Intranet Basics

Connectivity that exposes a network to the public WAN (wide area network)—known as the Internet—is just part of the equation. The Internet is a global network of computers that communicate using a common language and protocol. Its composition is understandable and explainable once you have heard its strange birth story, starting 30 years ago, with the RAND Corporation, America's premier Cold War think tank.

What Is the Internet, and Where Did It Come From?

Back in the "Dark Ages" (1960s), the RAND Corporation was given a contract to find a solution to a serious strategic problem: How could U.S. leadership successfully communicate after a nuclear war? After a nuclear attack, America would need a command-and-control network, but after an attack, the network's computer nodes, cabling, and switching stations would be in shambles, with only a very few connections and nodes still operational. The thought that a central control and command authority could survive an enemy attack was ludicrous.

The RAND proposal, under the direction of Paul Baran, was released in 1964. The network would have no central authority. It would be designed, from the outset, to operate after a nuclear strike, in shambles. It would be assumed that the network would always be unreliable, and its design would overcome this drawback. All network nodes would be equal in status to all other nodes, each node with its own authority to originate, pass, and receive messages. The messages themselves would be divided into packets, each packet separately addressed. Each packet would begin at some specified source node and end at some other specified destination node. Each packet would find its way through the network on its own, with the specific route being unimportant. Although inefficient, this scheme would ensure that packets could get from here to there after half of the network had been destroyed.

In 1968 and 1969, the Pentagon's Advanced Research Projects Agency (ARPA) decided to fund and install a project based on the RAND study, with help from UCLA and MIT. The first node was installed in UCLA, and by 1970 there were four nodes on the infant network, which was named ARPANET. The four supercomputers so connected transferred data on dedicated transmission lines. In 1971, 15 nodes made up ARPANET; by 1972, it had 37 nodes. Throughout the 1970s, ARPA's network expanded because of its decentralized structure and the need for computing resources. As long as individual machines could speak the packet-switching communication protocol, their architecture and operating system software were not important.

ARPA's original communications standard was the Network Control Protocol (NCP), quickly evolving into the more advanced TCP/IP protocols. TCP (Transmission Control Protocol) converts communications data into streams of packets, reassembling them at the destination. IP (Internet Protocol) handles addressing, seeing to it that packets are routed across multiple nodes and even across multiple networks with multiple standards.

In 1983, the government branched off of this increasingly academically inclined network to become the MILNET (Military Network), leaving a bunch of contractors and academic institutions interconnected through the primary network, now becoming known as the "Internet." At the time, most connected institutions used this network to exchange ideas and rudimentary email. Anyone with connectivity could barge in and become a node on this, now civilian, free-for-all, network.

The individual nodes were assigned extensions to their basic addressing names: six basic Internet domains, named .gov, .mil, .edu, .com, .org, and .net. For instance, .com stands for "company" or "commercial" entities, .org for nonprofit organizations, and .net for the gateway computers between networks and "backbones," mostly privately owned commercial high-speed "trunks." Just like the international telephone and telegraph systems, each country has control and ownership, either nationally, or privately, of their network backbone infrastructures, but they provide interconnects so that, as a whole, it works like a homogeneous worldwide network. As a user on this network, you may be allowed to access any other computer that is connected, as long as the remote computer's security safeguards are set up to allow you to do so. Web services are just one facet of what is available to an Internet-connected user; you can also transfer binary files directly (FTP), use global email, do specialized information searches, and more.

The Intranet Spin-Off

Internet-type services, without the public network exposure, are becoming very popular. These services have distinct advantages over printed material when a document or notice must be distributed companywide. More and more organizations want to utilize Internet-like capabilities *within* a company or group, excluding public access. This kind of private data connection has been popularly dubbed an intranet. We'll use the term intranet here to refer to any TCP/IP, or IPX/SPX with remote Winsock, local/wide area network, not connected to the Internet, but using Internet protocols and applications to provide access to information.

As an example, a company might set up Web servers, accessible only by employees, to publish company newsletters, sales figures, and other corporate documents. This data can be accessed by using Internet-capable Web browsers and file transfer applications within the company's local area network.

> *NOTE: Internet protocol servers are just that: they provide the services and protocols that are needed to provide remotely connected users with Web, file transfer, email, and search capabilities. These servers can just as easily be configured to provide an intranet with the same features and services, without having to be connected to the global network at all. Of course, both intra- and Inter-net connections may be provided for at the same time, giving a company the best of both worlds.*

Mini-Glossary

GOPHER   Developed at the University of Minnesota, this is a standard Internet protocol supported by a menu-driven application that allows you to skip around the world searching for information. It has largely been replaced by search engines in Web browsers as an access tool, but many servers still offer GOPHER.

Similar to Web browsers, GOPHER lets you "burrow" into a server's subdirectories until you find the information that you are looking for. Since it is text only, and is more difficult to navigate than the World Wide Web, its popularity is waning. The aggregate of GOPHER clients and servers is called "gopherspace."

FILE TRANSFER PROTOCOL (FTP)   An Internet protocol supported by an application that allows users to access remote computers and retrieve files from these computers. Almost any Web browser is also capable of accessing an FTP server, and this is often the preferred method.

Usually, FTP is used to download (transfer from a remote computer to your computer) files from FTP servers all around the world, called anonymous FTP sites. An FTP site is just another computer connected to the Internet that is running FTP server software and has available data files stored on it. The "anonymous" part of this definition means that anyone can log in from around the world and you don't need to have an account at the FTP site. Some FTP sites, however, will require a username and password to access their directories and files. FTP sites can have any type and quantity of data or executable files, and are usually kept for the convenience of users who need to transfer large files or great quantities of files.

HYPERTEXT TRANSFER PROTOCOL (HTTP)   A generic, object-oriented Internet protocol that is usually used to transfer HTML (Hypertext Markup Language-Web browser files), but can be used for many other tasks. HTTP has been used for document transfer and display on the World Wide Web since 1990.

HYPERTEXT Information on electronic "pages" that has embedded links to allow users to skip around and read the information in any order they wish. These links also provide direct pointers to documents and data contained on other hypertext pages, connected server directories, and remote files. Hypertext provides information in a way that is more flexible than text in books and magazines. It allows documents to contain adjunct material such as multimedia, pictures, and references to files and executables.

INTRANET A collection of Web, FTP, or other Internet-type services that have been installed on an internal (private) LAN or WAN. Intranets provide exactly the same display, data, and functionality as computers connected to the Internet, but the data that is accessible is only made available to a private group, say, within a corporation or institution. Any intranet may also be connected to the Internet, at large, and can access all of the public data, protecting any private data from being accessed by the public.

INTERNET A worldwide interconnection of computer networks and gateways that are linked, in most cases, with the TCP/IP suite of protocols. Originally used by government entities, defense contractors, and connected research universities as the ARPANET (Advanced Research Projects Agency Network), the Internet now allows a broad spectrum of businesses, academic institutions, government agencies, and private users to exchange documents, email, files, and other information.

INTERNET SERVICE PROVIDER (ISP) A business concern that provides individuals and businesses with connections to the Internet backbone. When you get on the Internet, your connection is passed through to the Internet backbone (the main, high-speed, network interconnections that allow individual computers and servers to communicate using the Internet), by an ISP. This makes connection to the Internet cost effective for individuals and businesses. Otherwise, you would need one of these high-speed links, and you would have to provide services, such as DNS and newsgroup servers, yourself. If you were directly connected to the Internet backbone, you would pay thousands of dollars per month in connection charges, and you would need a minimum of $10,000 to $20,000 dollars worth of server and routing equipment.

INTERNET INFORMATION SERVER (IIS) The Microsoft suite of Internet-related servers and services that allow you to publish and provide World Wide Web, FTP, GOPHER, and other services for an Internet site using NT 4. Part of the Microsoft BackOffice Server Suite (see Chapter 18).

OPEN DATABASE CONNECTIVITY (ODBC) The database portion of the Windows Open Services Architecture (WOSA), an interface that allows Windows-based applications to connect to multiple, and different, computing environments without rewriting the application for each platform. ODBC allows users to access data in more than one data storage location, on multiple servers, in more than one type of DBMS (such as DB2, Oracle, SQL Server, or dBASE) from a single application.

WORLD WIDE WEB (WWW)   That part of the services provided on the Internet, or through the use of a privately published intranet, that allows the reading and publishing of documents and data using the Hypertext Markup Language (HTML).

NT's Internet Information Server (IIS)

NT Server version 4 ships with a Web, FTP, and GOPHER server called Internet Information Server (IIS) When you install NT Server, you will be given the choice to automatically install IIS. Although technically a BackOffice product, IIS and the license to use it are included in the base NT Server product. This means that it is essentially free, shipping as an out-of-the-box component. This is in contrast to Netscape's Web server (or other Web server products), some costing many hundreds of dollars extra.

IIS also has the advantage of being written specifically for NT, by NT's authors. Other Web server products on the market target many OS platforms, making them less capable of taking advantage of NT's unique capabilities and interface. IIS provides enhanced performance and management features, and is fully integrated into the NT operating system. This integration allows IIS to take full advantage of NT's security and performance features.

NCSA, CERN, and PPTP Support

IIS also supports both NCSA- and CERN-style image map files, facilitating Unix porting efforts. It provides Web-based administration from any Web browser, or through the Internet Information Server Manager application, with which you can manage all your Web servers, anywhere on your network. With this management tool, administrators can configure ports, directories, permissions, and virtual connections. IIS also supports the Point to Point Tunneling Protocol (PPTP). It can use PPTP, which is built into NT Server, to create secure, private intranets, tunneling through public networks with a secure transmission protocol. Used in conjunction with Index Server (see Chapter 18), IIS enables content indexing and search capabilities for HTML and other types of files in multiple languages (see Figure 25-1).

An Array of Servers

Shipped with IIS as standard are three different servers. Microsoft Internet Information Server is a Web server that enables you to publish information on an

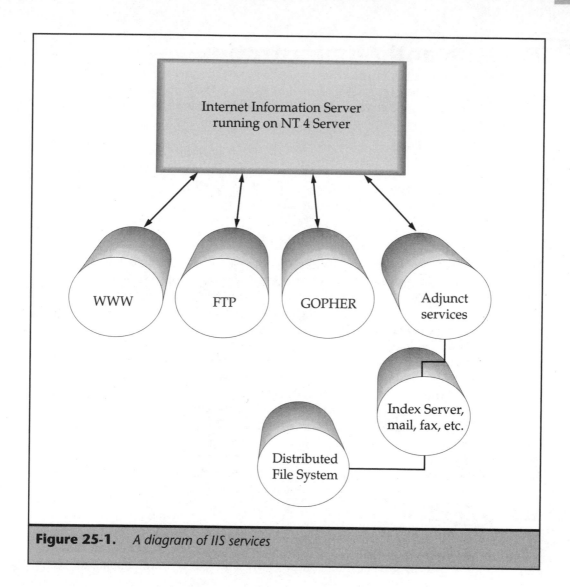

Figure 25-1.   *A diagram of IIS services*

intranet or on the Internet. Internet Information Server transmits World Wide Web (WWW) information by using the Hypertext Transfer Protocol (HTTP). Internet Information Server can also be configured to provide File Transfer Protocol (FTP) and GOPHER services. The FTP service enables users to transfer files to and from your Web server site. The GOPHER service—while largely superseded by HTTP—uses a menu-driven protocol for locating documents.

IIS Setup and Administration

You can install Internet Information Server at the same time you install NT Server. When prompted to install Internet Information Server, make sure that the IIS installation checkbox is selected and click OK. IIS will automatically be installed along with the base OS.

TIP: *If you already have the necessary Internet or intranet connection, you can accept all of the default settings during setup and then add your Hypertext Markup Language (HTML) content files to the WWW root folder. The default setup configurations are suitable for almost all WWW publishing scenarios without any further modifications.*

Installing IIS after NT Server Setup

First, insert the NT Server CD into the CD-ROM drive. Double-click the Install Internet Information Server icon on the Windows NT Server desktop. Follow the instructions on the screen. Alternatively, you can install IIS by using the Start / Settings / Control Panel applet. In Control Panel, double-click the Network icon. Next, on the Network property sheet, click the Services tab, and then click the Add button. From the Network Services list, select Internet Information Server and then click the OK button. In the Installed from box, type the letter of the drive where your compact disc is located and click the OK button. Follow the instructions on the screen.

There is a third way to install IIS directly from the NT Server CD (see Figure 25-2) by using the NT Explorer or by issuing commands at the command prompt. First, change to the drive containing the server CD and start IIS setup. To start IIS setup from Explorer, double-click the file named Inetstp.exe in the Inetsrv folder of the compact disc. To start setup from the command prompt, change to the Inetsrv folder of the compact disc and then type **inetstp**. Follow the instructions on the screen.

IIS Setup Options

All of the IIS setup options—except HTML administration—are selected during setup by default. Click the OK button to install them all. If you do not want to install a particular item, clear the box next to it and then click the OK button to install the rest.

Web Service Management

Internet Service Manager installs the administration program for managing the Web services. The World Wide Web Service creates a WWW publishing server. The FTP Service creates an FTP publishing server, and the Gopher Service creates a GOPHER publishing server. When prompted to create the service folders (Wwwroot, Gophroot, and Ftproot by default), click Yes.

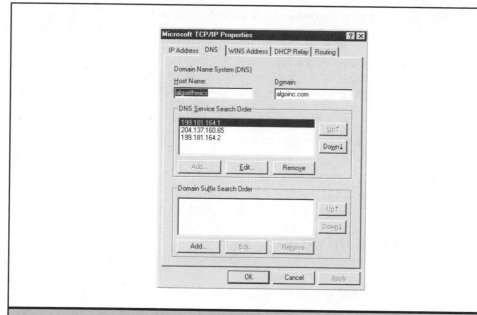

Figure 25-2.   *Installing IIS from the NT Server CD*

Open Database Connectivity Drivers

ODBC Drivers and Administration installs Open Database Connectivity drivers. These
are required for logging to ODBC files and for enabling ODBC access through the
Internet Database Connector (IDC) from the WWW service.

TIP: *You can use the Setup program later to add or remove any or all IIS components.*

Installation Requirements

Internet Information Server requires a computer with at least the minimum
configuration to support NT Server. Once IIS is installed, you can administer it
from a remote computer running NT Workstation. Install the Peer Web Services
Internet Service Manager on that computer, and then connect to the server you
want to administer.

TCP/IP network support is needed in most cases to implement an IIS server. Use the Network application in the Start/Settings/Control Panel to install and configure the TCP/IP protocol and related components. If you are also using Proxy Server for intranet or Internet applications, you may need to install the IPX/SPX protocols for use by your internally connected workstations (see Chapter 5). Additionally, in order to enforce NT object security on file access to your Web site, you should consider using the NT File System (NTFS) on all IIS connected server drives.

To Publish on an Intranet

As a minimum, you need a network adapter card and local area network (LAN) connection to publish on an intranet. You may optionally install the Windows Internet name service (WINS) server or the domain name system (DNS) server. These components will resolve IP addresses to "friendly" names, easing the burden on users.

To Publish on the Internet

Again, as a minimum, you need an Internet connection and an Internet Protocol (IP) address from your Internet Service Provider (ISP), in place of or in addition to a network adapter card and local area network (LAN) connection, to publish on the Internet.

TIP: *You should seriously consider getting an official DNS registration for your ISP-assigned IP address. InterNIC—the company responsible for issuing domain names in the United States—can help you obtain a domain name, such as mycompany.com. Other countries have issuing authorities also; check with your ISP, since they will most likely handle the domain registration for you. As with using WINS or DNS locally, this step allows remote users to use "friendly" names instead of IP addresses when connecting to your WWW server.*

Configuring IIS for the Internet

You must configure your NT Server networking component so that your Web server can operate on the Internet. Security configuration is also an important step to prevent remote users from tampering with your computer or network. In the sections that follow, we'll take a look at a minimum configuration session when preparing to use IIS.

NOTE: *In order to install the services for IIS, you must be logged on to the server with administrator privileges. You also need administrator privileges to configure the services remotely through Internet Service Manager. To publish on the Internet, you must have a connection to the Internet from an ISP. There are ISPs in almost all medium-to-large cities around the world and ISPs that also do business nationally.*

Server Network Configuration

After installing NT Server and Internet Information Server, you will need to configure the TCP/IP protocol layers. Open the Network applet in the Start/Settings/Control Panel menu, and install the NT TCP/IP protocol and connectivity utilities. If you have any Internet services installed, such as another FTP service, remove them now.

NOTE: *Your ISP will have provided you with your server's exposed IP address, IP subnet mask, and the ISP's default gateway IP address. The default gateway is the ISP's server computer through which your computer will route all of its Internet traffic.*

CONFIGURING THE DOMAIN NAME   Through the TCP/IP Properties dialog box of the Network applet in the Control Panel (see Figure 25-3), you must now configure your site's domain name—sometimes called the hostname—and the DNS servers that you will use for domain name resolution. On the Internet, your IP address (for example, 111.111.111.1) can be used to contact your Web server. However, if you obtain a registered domain name, your server can then be contacted by using its domain name instead, for example, www.mycompany.com.

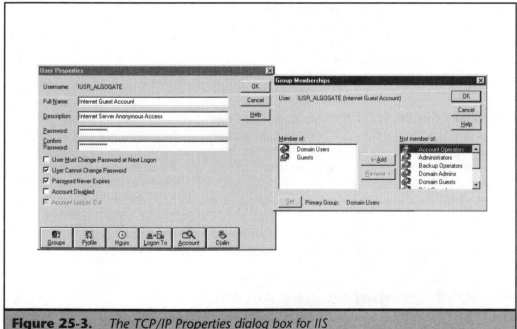

Figure 25-3.   *The TCP/IP Properties dialog box for IIS*

CONFIGURING DNS OR WINS   On an intranet, you can use either local DNS or WINS. Your network must have DNS or WINS servers to match IP addresses to hostnames, and client computers must know the IP address of the DNS or WINS server to contact. A limited alternative to DNS is to use a HOSTS file. A limited alternative to WINS servers is to use an LMHOSTS file.

ENTERING IP ADDRESSES   On the Internet, you will most likely be given the IP addresses of the DNS servers that your ISP maintains. Enter these IPs in the DNS listbox. As an alternative, you may run your own DNS server in concert with your ISP. Check with your ISP for details on this subject.

ADVANCED CONFIGURATION SETTINGS   Use the Network application in Control Panel to make the appropriate Advanced TCP/IP Configuration setting for this server's name resolution. For more information on installing and configuring WINS or DNS, see Chapters 11 and 12.

> **TIP:**   *If you obtain multiple registered domain names, you can host these on the same computer running IIS. Use the Advanced TCP/IP Configuration settings to assign multiple IP addresses to the network adapter card connected to the Internet.*

Server Security Configuration

Steps should be taken to enhance the security of your NT Server intranet or Internet installation. These steps include password and permission settings, as well as setting security access on file system elements. Once you have installed IIS, review the IUSR_computername account rights (see Figure 25-4).

> **TIP:**   *Choose difficult passwords, set strict account policies, and limit the membership of the Administrators group using the User Manager or User Manager for Domains application.*

DISABLING GUEST ACCOUNT ACCESS   During the setup process, a screen will appear asking you whether you want to disable access by the Guest account to your FTP server. In most cases, select Yes to protect the contents of your system. If you choose the No option and enable guest access to your server, all existing files and any new files are available to the Guest account through FTP. You will need to disable access to each file or folder individually to prevent unauthorized access.

> **NOTE:**   *Disabling FTP access for the Guest account will not affect the IUSR_computername account that is created during setup.*

The IUSR_computername Account

IIS setup will create an anonymous user account called IUSR_computername. On domain controllers, this account is added to the domain database. After setup

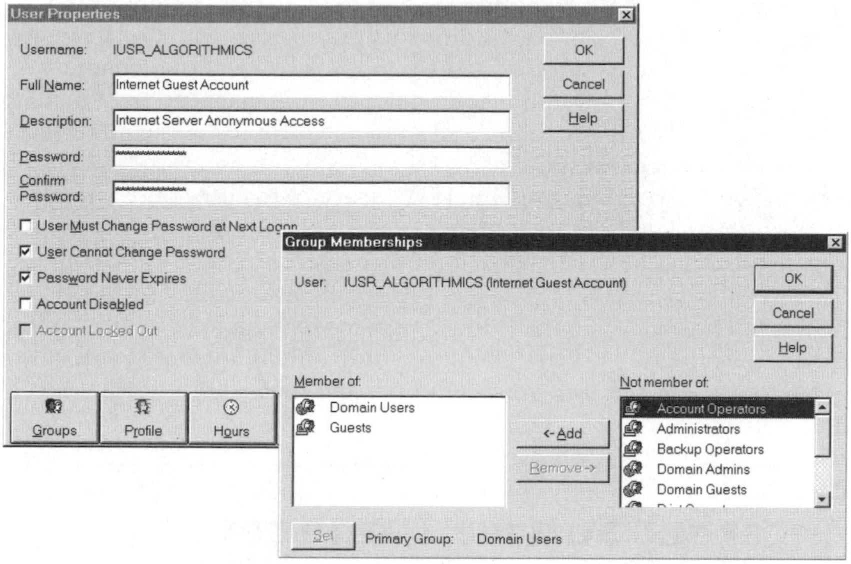

Figure 25-4.   *Setting IUSR_computername account rights*

completes, you may change the username and password for this account using the
Service property sheet in Internet Service Manager, making sure that the new
username and password are entered into the accounts database using NT User
Manager or User Manager for Domains.

> **NOTE:**   *The WWW, FTP, and GOPHER services use the IUSR_computername account
> by default for anonymous access. You can set the rights for IUSR_computername with
> User Manager and file permissions on NTFS drives with NT Explorer.*

Insider Info

When you allow remote users to run applications on your computer, you run the
risk of amateur or professional hackers attempting to break into your system. IIS's
default configuration is meant to reduce the risk of malicious intrusion by
applications in two important ways.

First, the virtual directory Scripts contains your applications. Only an
administrator can add programs to a directory marked as an execute-only
directory. Thus, unauthorized users cannot copy a malicious application and then
run it on your computer without first gaining administrator access.

It is recommended that you grant read and execute permission for the IUSR_computername account on the directory associated with the virtual folder, and grant full control only to the administrator. Perl scripts (.pl filename extension) and IDC files (.idc and .htx filename extensions) need both read and execute permission. However, to prevent someone from installing an unsafe file on your server, do not grant write permission.

Second, if you have configured the WWW service to allow only anonymous logons, all requests from remote users will use the IUSR_computername account. By default, the IUSR_computername account is unable to delete or change files by using the NT File System (NTFS) unless specifically granted access by an administrator. Thus, even if a malicious program were copied to your computer, it would be unable to cause much damage to your content because it will only have IUSR_computername access to your computer and files.

The Internet Service Manager

You can use IIS's Internet Service Manager application—available through the Start/Programs/Microsoft Internet Server(Common) menu—to configure settings and performance on your IIS/NT Server (see Figure 25-5). There are three views supplied in Internet Service Manager: Reports, Servers, and Services.

- **Report view:** The Report view is the default view. Report view alphabetically lists selected computers, with each installed service shown on a separate line. Click the column headings to sort the entire list alphabetically.

- **Servers view:** Servers view displays services running on servers listed by computer name. Click the plus symbol next to a server name to expand the list of services that the selected server is running. Double-click a particular service name to see its property sheets.

- **Services view:** Services view lists services—grouped by service name—on selected computers. Click the plus symbol next to a service name to expand the list of servers running that service. Double-click the computer name under a service to see the property sheets for the service running on that computer.

The Service Properties Sheet

The Service properties sheet (see Figure 25-6) controls who can use your server and specifies the account used for anonymous client requests to log on to the computer. If you allow anonymous logons, then all user permissions for the user—such as

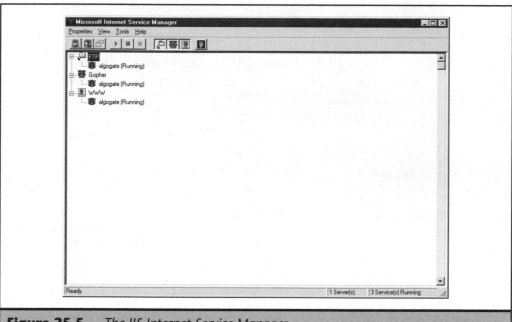

Figure 25-5.   *The IIS Internet Service Manager*

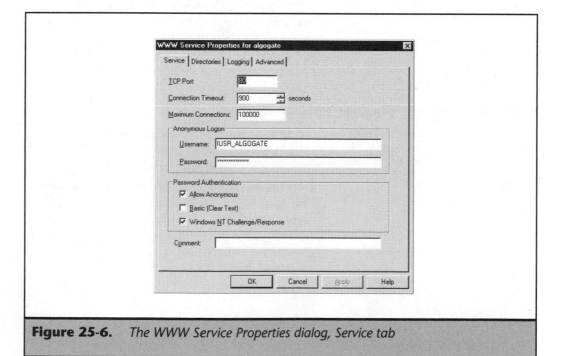

Figure 25-6.   *The WWW Service Properties dialog, Service tab*

permission to access information—use the IUSR_computername account. The following list describes the available options:

TCP Port	Determines the port on which the WWW service is running. The default is port 80. You can change the port to any unique TCP port number. You must restart your computer if you change this port.
Connection Timeout	Sets the length of time before the server disconnects an inactive user.
Maximum Connections	Sets the maximum number of simultaneous connections to the server.
Anonymous Logon	Sets the NT user account to use for permissions of all anonymous connections. IIS creates, and by default uses, the account IUSR_computername. Even though the password for this account is only used internally, this account must have a password, matching both here and in User Manager.
Password Authentication	Specifies the authentication protocol that will be used if anonymous access is not allowed or if a request for authentication is made by the remote client. The Basic authentication protocol is encrypted and is often used in conjunction with Secure Sockets Layer (SSL). Most browsers support Basic authentication. The NT Challenge/Response mechanism encrypts usernames and passwords.

The Directories Properties Sheet

The Directories properties sheet sets directories and directory behavior for the WWW service (see Figure 25-7). The following list describes the options:

Directory listbox	Lists the directories used by the WWW service. The Alias column is the path used for virtual server directories. The Address column lists the IP address for the virtual server using that directory. The Error column indicates system errors, such as difficulty reading a directory.

Add, Remove, and Edit buttons	To administer directories, press the Add button, or select a directory in the Directories listbox and press the Edit button. The Remove button removes the directories that you select.
Enable Default Document and Directory Browsing Allowed	These settings are used to set up default displays that will appear if a remote user does not specify a particular file. When a remote user does not specify a particular file, the default document in that directory is displayed. A hypertext directory listing is sent to the user if directory browsing is enabled and no default document is in the specified directory.

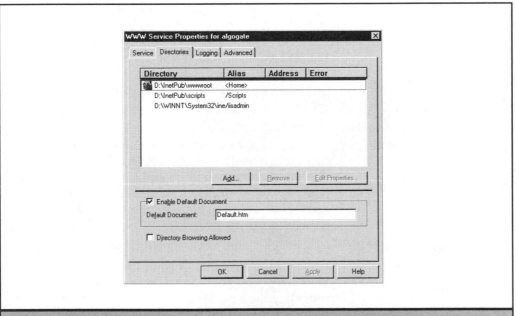

Figure 25-7. *The Directories properties sheet*

Configuring WWW Service Directories

To configure the WWW service directories, press the Add button on the Directories property sheet to set up new directories. The following list explains the options:

Directory	Sets the path to the directory to use for the WWW service.
Browse button	Selects the directory to use for the WWW service.
Home Directory	Choose this to specify the root directory for the WWW service. Internet Information Server provides a default home directory, \Wwwroot, for the WWW service. The files that you place in the WWW home directory and its subdirectories are available to remote browsers. You can change the location of the default home directory.
Virtual Directory	Choose this to specify a subdirectory for the WWW service. Enter the directory name or alias that service users will use to gain access. You can specify the physical location of a virtual directory and the virtual name (alias), which is the directory name used by remote browsers. Virtual directories will not appear in WWW (or FTP) directory listings. Virtual directories on network drives must be on computers that are members of the same NT domain as the IIS server machine.
Account Information	Active only if the directory specified is a universal naming convention (UNC) server and sharename. Enter the username and password that has permission to use the network directory. Virtual directories on network drives must be on computers in the same NT domain as the IIS server.
Virtual Servers for WWW	Select the Virtual Server checkbox and enter an IP address to create a directory for the virtual server. The IP address must be bound to the network card providing the service. Use the Network applet in Control Panel to bind additional IP addresses to your network card. The default directories created during setup do not specify an IP address. You may need to specify IP addresses for the default directories when you add virtual servers.

Access checkboxes

The Access checkboxes control the attributes of the directory. If files are on an NTFS drive, settings for the directory must match these settings. Read must be selected for information directories. Do not select if directories contain programs. Execute allows clients to run any programs in this directory. Put scripts and executable files into this directory. Select the Require secure SSL channel box if using Secure Sockets Layer (SSL) encryption.

The Logging Properties Sheet

The Logging properties sheet (see Figure 25-8) sets logging for the selected information service. You can send log data to files or to an ODBC database. If you log to a file, you can specify how often to create new logs and which directory to put the log files in. If you log to an ODBC data source, you must specify the ODBC Data Source Name (DSN), table, valid username, and password to the database. The following list explains the options:

Enable Logging   Selected to start or stop logging.

Log to File   Option to log to a text file.

Log Format   Choose Standard format or National Center for Supercomputing Applications (NCSA) format.

Automatically open new log   Generates new logs at the specified interval instead of using one log file always.

Log file directory   Path to the directory containing log files.

Log file filename   Name for the log file.

Log to SQL/ODBC Database   Logs to an ODBC data source. Input datasource name, table name, username, and password. Use the ODBC Control Panel applet to create a system data source.

The Advanced Properties Sheet

The Advanced properties sheet (see Figure 25-9) allows you to set accesses by specific IP address. This can be used to block individuals or groups from gaining access to

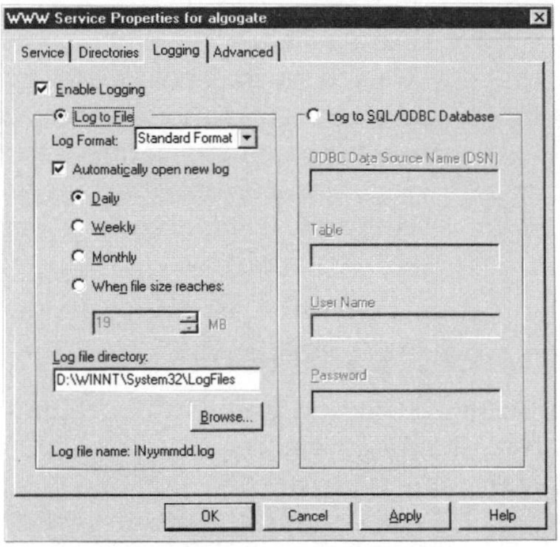

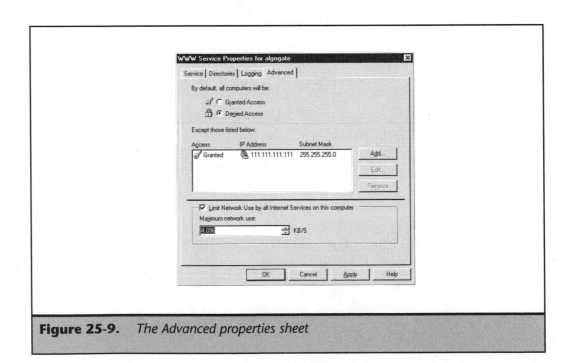

Figure 25-8. *The Logging properties sheet*

Figure 25-9. *The Advanced properties sheet*

your server. You can also set the network bandwidth to control the maximum amount of traffic on your server. The following list explains the options:

IP Access Control	You can control access to each Internet service by specifying the IP address of the computers to be granted or denied access. If you choose to grant access to all users by default, you can then specify the computers to be denied access. For example, if you have a form on your WWW server, and a particular user on the Internet is entering multiple forms with fictitious information, you can prevent the computer at that IP address from connecting to your site. Conversely, if you choose to deny access to all users by default, you can then specify which computers are allowed access.
(By Default, all computers will be) Granted Access (except those listed below)	If you choose this radio button, you may then press the Add button to specify and list (in the listbox) computers that will be denied access. The list, and the Add operation, specify individual computers that will be denied access.
(By Default, all computers will be) Denied Access (except those listed below)	If you choose this radio button, you may then press the Add button to specify and list (in the listbox) computers that will be granted access. The list, and the Add operation, specify individual computers that will be granted access.
Add	To add computers to which you want to deny access, select the Granted Access button and click Add. The computers you list will be granted access. Conversely, to add computers to which you want to grant access, select the Denied Access button and click Add. The computers you list will be denied access. Add computers by their IP addresses and subnet masks (e.g., 111.111.111.111). You may use DNS to look up a computer by its name by pressing the ellipsis button and then entering the name of a computer, such as *nt100.algoinc.com*.
Limit Network Use by all Internet Services on this computer	You can control your Internet services by limiting the network bandwidth allowed for all of the Internet services on the server. Set the maximum kilobytes of outbound traffic permitted on this computer.

WWW Grant or Deny Access	Choose Single Computer and provide the IP address to exclude a single computer. Choose Group of Computers and provide an IP address and subnet mask to exclude a group of computers. Press the button next to the IP address to use a DNS name instead of an IP address. Your server must have a DNS server specified in its TCP/IP settings. You are specifying, by IP address or domain name, which computer or group of computers will be granted or denied access. If you choose to—by default—grant access to all users, specify the computers to be denied access. If you choose to, by default, deny access to all users, specify the specific computers to be allowed access. You should fully understand TCP/IP networking, IP addressing, and the use of subnet masks to use this option.

Authentication Options

In addition to the anonymous username and password options, the Service properties sheet of Internet Service Manager contains the following authentication options:

Allow Anonymous	When selected, anonymous connections are allowed. When unchecked, all anonymous connections are rejected, and Basic or NT Challenge/Response authentication protocol is required for access.
Basic	When selected, the WWW service will process requests using Basic authentication.
NT Challenge/Response	When selected, the system accepts requests by clients to send user account information using the NT Challenge/Response authentication protocol.

The FTP Service Properties Sheet

Use the FTP Service properties sheet (see Figure 25-10) to control FTP access to your server. If you allow anonymous logons, then all user permissions for the user—such as permission to access information—use the IUSR_computername account. The following list describes the options:

TCP Port	Port on which the FTP service is running. Defaults to port 21. If you change the port, you must restart your computer.

Connection Timeout	Length of time in seconds before the server disconnects an inactive user.
Maximum Connections	Maximum number of simultaneous connections to the server.
Allow Anonymous Connections	By default, the account IUSR_computername is used for all anonymous logons.
Allow only anonymous connections	When selected, allows only anonymous connections. Users cannot log on with usernames and passwords. Used to prevent access to the server by an account with administrator privileges.
Comment	Used to enter the comment displayed in Internet Service Manager's Report view.
Current Sessions	Displays current FTP users.

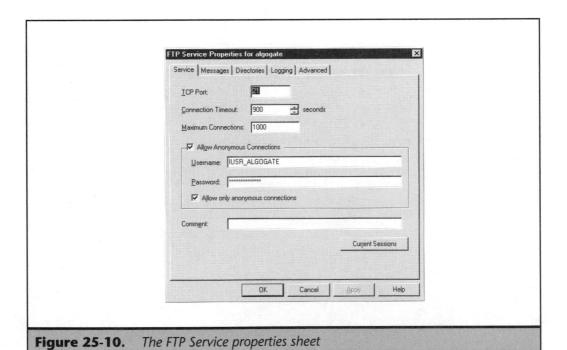

Figure 25-10. *The FTP Service properties sheet*

The Gopher Service Properties Sheet

The following options are used to set properties for the Gopher Service (see Figure 25-11).

TCP Port	Sets the port to use for the Gopher Service. The default is port 70. For this option to take effect, you must restart your computer.
Connection Timeout	Length of time before the server disconnects an inactive user.
Maximum Connections	Limits the maximum number of simultaneous connections.
Service Administrator	Sets the values reported to GOPHER service users.
Anonymous Logon	By default, the user account IUSR_computername.
Comment	Used to specify the comment displayed in the Internet Service Manager Report view.

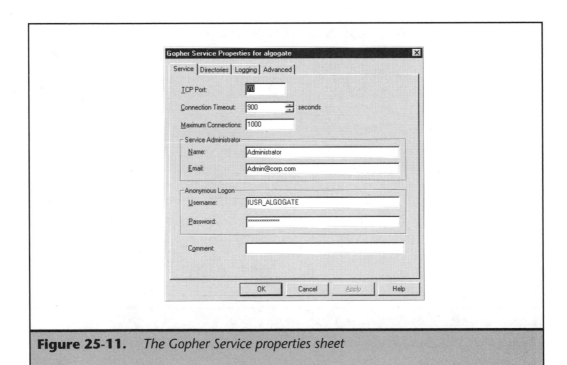

Figure 25-11. *The Gopher Service properties sheet*

What's Next

Now that we've covered IIS basics, we are going to look at authoring for Internet and intranet usage with the Internet Information Server's APIs and NT's support of the Common Gateway Interface (CGI). In the next chapter we'll take a look at the technologies that are just now coming up on the horizon for using distributed COM and ActiveX content with WWW browsers and related applications. We'll also run down the list of enhancements NT adds to the world of the Net and speculate on advances now being brought out of the laboratory to extend the power of NT networking.

Chapter Twenty-Six

Authoring for the Intra/Internet

The Internet's most important service component today may be the World Wide Web (WWW). The Web gives you a graphical and navigable interface for looking at documents, playing movies, listening to sounds, and linking information in any form. This service is equally important and available on an intranet or on the Internet, so named because the files and documents, as well as the links that join them together and provide references between them, constitute a spider's "web" of networked information.

World Wide Web Basics

Files and documents on the World Wide Web are, ideally, completely interconnected. You connect to Web pages by typing in a Uniform Resource Locator (URL), usually in the form of http://www.xxx.xxx or by clicking on special text or graphic hyperlinks. Web pages can contain text, images, movies, sounds, and links to other pages or files. If you are connected through the Internet, these pages can be located on computers anywhere in the world.

Hyperlink Connections

Hyperlinks are words or graphics on a Web page that have Web addresses embedded in them. By clicking a hyperlink, you jump to a particular page on a particular Web site. You can usually identify hyperlinks by their color or by the fact that in a browser, the cursor will usually change shape when it is positioned over the hyperlink.

You can create links to almost any kind of file that is either natively supported by the popular browsers or is supported with add-on applications. You will have to make sure that remote users have the correct viewing application to view non-HTML files or embedded applications. As an example, if you know that all remote users will have Microsoft Word, you can include links to Word .doc files. The user can click the link and the document appears in Word on the user's computer.

Web Pages

Each Web page, including a Web site's home page, has a unique address called a URL, for example, http://www.algoinc.com/default.htm. The URL specifies the name of the computer on which the page is stored and the exact path to the page. URLs may also take the form of ftp:// for direct browser connection to File Transfer Protocol (FTP) server sites, where you can transfer files directly.

Web Browsers

NetScape Navigator and Microsoft Internet Explorer are two popular Web browsers. These applications are tools that you use to navigate through and access ("browse") information on the Web. Browsers usually provide a range of detailed functions and commands for setting options and navigation. There is almost always an address bar

below a toolbar or menu that displays the address, or URL, of the currently displayed
Web page or FTP directory, as shown here:

You can use this address bar to go to a new Web page by typing the page's URL
directly into the edit space and pressing the ENTER key to initiate the process. You can
also go to a new page by clicking a hyperlink on a displayed Web page.

NT's Internet Explorer

NT 4 includes Microsoft's Internet Explorer for NT. Internet Explorer is also available
for NT 3.51, Windows for Workgroups, Windows version 3.1, Windows 95, and
Macintosh. Using NT Server and IIS, you can publish both information and
applications. This means that your Web site can contain anything from static pages of
information to interactive applications. You can also find and extract information from
and insert information into databases.

The Hypertext Markup Language

Most Web pages are formatted in Hypertext Markup Language (HTML). HTML
files are simple ASCII text files with codes embedded to indicate formatting and
hypertext links. HTML specifications are changing constantly, and it's still a wild
and woolly environment.

 NOTE: *You should probably refer to the most current HTML specifications,
usually available somewhere on the Internet, in order to fully plan the design of your
HTML pages.*

Authoring on the Web

You can use any text editor—for instance WordPad or Notepad—to create and edit
your HTML files, but you will probably find an HTML editor—such as Corel
WebDesigner (see Figure 26-1), Microsoft FrontPage, NetScape Navigator Gold, or
Internet Assistant for Microsoft Word—easier to use. You use the HTML editor or
other application to create HTML files, which can include hyperlinks to other files on
your system. If you want to include images or sounds, you will also need appropriate
software to create and edit those files.

 NOTE: *Once you have created your information in HTML or other formats, you can
either copy the information to the default directory InetPub\Wwwroot in IIS, or you can
change the default home directory to the directory containing your information.*

Figure 26-1. *Example of an HTML editor*

Mini-Glossary

ACTIVEX   The newest incarnation of OLE/COM custom controls (see Chapter 22). This type of custom control can be imbedded in a standalone application *or* a Web page, akin to how a Java applet is embedded and used for Web page development. ActiveX controls can incorporate any functionality that an application can, on it's own. This makes ActiveX much more flexible and sophisticated than Java, or plug-ins, since the latter always have to run in the context of their environments, usually protected from the machine and underlying software. This makes Java and various plug-ins portable, but because they are more abstract, they cannot do as much.

AMERICAN STANDARD CODE FOR INFORMATION INTERCHANGE (ASCII)

The dominant standard for coding character-oriented information on computers and computerized equipment. The normal ASCII code scheme assigns the numeric values 0 through 255 (one byte) to letters, numbers, punctuation marks, and specially designated characters and non-printing actions, such as Form-Feed, in order to facilitate the exchange of information between computers, and between computers and peripherals, such as printers.

COMMON GATEWAY INTERFACE (CGI)   CGI is an interface for executing external programs or challenge/response filtering applications on an information server. HTTP information servers are the only platform that CGI interfaces run on at the present.

CGI is a common way of implementing server-side response mechanisms for Web page information input and output. As time goes on, CGI is being supplanted by newer technologies.

DATA SOURCE NAME (DSN)   The globally visible name of a data source that applications can use to request a connection to that data source. For Open Database Connectivity (ODBC), a data source name can be registered through the ODBC Administrator program.

MICROSOFT FOUNDATION CLASSES (MFC)   MFC is an "application framework" for writing applications in Microsoft C++, targeting Windows or any other platform that supports the Win(16)32 API. MFC is implemented as a group of C++ classes, representing abstractions of objects that are Windows specific and non-Windows specific, such as document containers, windows, dialog boxes, toolbars, and so on.

MULTIPURPOSE INTERNET MAIL EXTENSION (MIME)   A standard Internet protocol developed to allow the exchange of electronic mail messages with varied content, such as embedded files and non-text content, to be exchanged across unlike networks, machines, or email applications and environments. MIME enabled applications do not have to be email oriented, and many purposes have been found for MIME document encoding. When you see a MIME document embedded in a word processor or email edit window, it usually looks like a collection of gibberish characters, but in actuality, these characters represent the original document or file, encoded into the MIME protocol.

INTERNET DATABASE CONNECTOR (IDC)   The IDC uses ASCII files saved with an .IDC extension to get information on how to connect to an ODBC data source and how to execute an SQL statement.

INTERNET SERVER APPLICATION PROGRAMMING INTERFACE (ISAPI)
ISAPI is a high-performance alternative to CGI executable files. Unlike CGI executable files, ISAPI functionality is implemented by ISAPI dynamic link libraries (DLLs) that are loaded into the same address space as the HTTP server application.

By this means, all of the resources that are available to and from the HTTP server process are also available to the ISAPI DLLs. This allows the ISAPI application to run with minimal code and execution overhead, incurring no penalty for individual requests and responses, as CGI does.

STRUCTURED QUERY LANGUAGE (SQL) SQL is a high-end, high performance, client-server relational database management system (RDBMS). SQL is designed to support high frequency and volumes of transaction processing, lending itself to large management applications and projects, as well as smaller tasks that require SQL's in-depth support for complicated and specialized database queries.

UNIFORM RESOURCE LOCATOR (URL) Using the Hypertext Transport Protocol (HTTP), a URL is the globally unique address of a single HTML page or file on the Web. The address includes a domain name such as mycompany.com, which is actually a unique Internet server address, and a hierarchical pointer to the directory in which a file is located on the server.

Publishing Dynamic HTML Pages

One of the most useful features you get when you use IIS as a Web server is the ability to develop applications or scripts that remote users start by clicking HTML links or by filling in and sending an HTML form. Using programming languages such as C, C++, Visual Basic, or Perl, you can create applications or scripts that communicate with the user in dynamic HTML pages.

Creating Interactive Scripts

Interactive applications or scripts can be written in almost any 32-bit programming language, such as Visual Basic, C++, Perl, or as NT batch files (which have the .bat or .cmd file-name extension). When you write your applications or script, you can use one of two supported interfaces: ISAPI or CGI. CGI is the basis of most previous interactive Web applications.

Insider Info

Developers use languages such as Visual Basic, Perl, or Visual C++ to develop CGI applications. Interaction with other Windows applications is easier using a specialized CGI implementation called Windows CGI. Windows CGI is supported in IIS by using the IS2WCGI.DLL part of the IIS SDK (Software Development Kit). By supporting CGI, IIS provides instant functionality while technologies such as ISAPI are still being developed and finalized. CGI tutorials and sample code is available freely on the Internet and allows developers to get started quickly.

Developers familiar with DLL development will be able to quickly develop ISAPI DLLs that extend the functionality of IIS. Using tools such as Visual C++, developers can create high performance DLLs that work in conjunction with IIS.

Web applications developed using CGI or ISAPI follow the same basic set of steps. They first interpret information entered by the user via a Web browser. Based on this input, the CGI program or ISAPI DLL performs the appropriate functions. Then they send the output back to the user's Web browser in HTML format. ISAPI also provides the ability to create filters that are called every time a user accesses the Web server, allowing the addition of custom logging, auditing, and security capabilities to IIS.

The Internet Server API (ISAPI)

ISAPI for NT can be used to write applications that Web users can activate by filling out an HTML form or clicking a link in an HTML page on your Web site. The remote application can then take the user-supplied information and do almost anything with it that can be programmed, and then return the results in an HTML page or post the information in a database.

DYNAMIC LINKED LIBRARY APPLICATIONS   ISAPI can be used to create applications that run as DLLs on your Web server. If you have used CGI scripts before, you will find that the ISAPI applications have much better performance because your applications are loaded into memory at server run-time. They require less overhead because each request does not start a separate process.

PRE- AND POST-REQUEST PROCESSING   Another feature of ISAPI allows pre-processing of requests and post-processing of responses, permitting site-specific handling of HTTP requests and responses. ISAPI filters can be used for applications such as customized authentication, access, or logging. You can create very complex sites by using both ISAPI filters and applications. ISAPI extensions can also be combined with the Internet Database Connector to create highly interactive sites.

EXECUTE PERMISSION FOR ISAPI APPLICATIONS   IIS executes ISAPI applications in the security context of the calling user. An access check is performed against that calling user. To restrict execution to selected users, New Technology File System (NTFS) permissions can be used with ISAPI applications such as the Internet Database Connector (IDC). Access will be allowed only if execute permission has been granted for a user.

NOTE: Once an ISAPI application has been loaded, it remains loaded until the WWW service is stopped. IIS does not track security descriptor changes after the ISAPI application has been loaded, so if you change permissions for an ISAPI application after it has been loaded, you must stop and restart the WWW service before the change will take effect.

The Common Gateway Interface

The Common Gateway Interface (CGI) is a set of specifications for passing information between a client Web browser, a Web server, and a CGI application. A client Web browser can start a CGI application by filling out an HTML form or clicking a link in an HTML page on your Web server. As with ISAPI, the CGI application can take the information the client Web browser supplies and do almost anything that can be programmed, then return the results of the application in an HTML page or post the information to a database. IIS can use most 32-bit applications that run on NT and conform to the CGI specifications.

NOTE: *Because some simple CGI applications are often written using scripting languages such as Perl, CGI applications are sometimes referred to as scripts. IIS can use most 32-bit applications that run on NT and conform to the CGI specifications.*

THE CLIENT/SERVER RELATIONSHIP CGI works by using the client-server relationship inherent in an Internet or intranet connection (see Figure 26-2). The CGI application runs on the server, waiting for information to be passed to it, and then

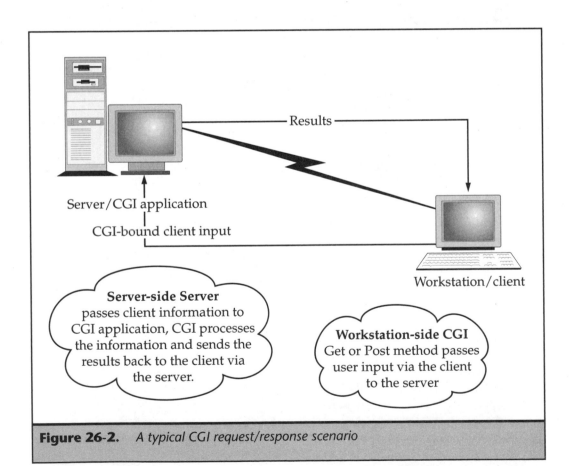

Figure 26-2. *A typical CGI request/response scenario*

executes it in response to a client-side request. The client-side browser or application can request server-side services by passing CGI parameters in one of two ways: using the Get or Post methods, which allow you to pass information via the HTTP protocol back to the server. Once the server has received a client side request, parameters are passed to the CGI application on the server. The CGI application does its thing, and passes response parameters back to the server, who passes these responses back to the client. This round trip is finished when the client passes the responses back to the browser or application on the client side.

CGI LIMITATIONS   The IIS WWW service supports the standard CGI specification. However, as of this writing, only 32-bit CGI applications work with the WWW service. Also, the REMOTE_USER environment variable is not present when the user is logged in as the anonymous user, accessing the Web server anonymously. Additionally, you should be aware that all of the variables defined for ISAPI applications are passed to the CGI application as environment variables.

NOTE: *CGI applications are typically stand-alone executables. This is in contrast to ISAPI applications, which are typically loaded as DLLs and are therefore server extensions. Because of this, ISAPI applications offer enhanced performance when compared to CGI applications and scripts.*

SECURITY CONSIDERATIONS FOR CGI EXECUTABLES   CGI executables must be used with caution because of their potential security risk to the server. Give only Execute permission to virtual directories that contain CGI or Internet Server API (ISAPI) applications.

CAUTION: *World Wide Web content directories should be assigned Read permission only. Any executable files intended for downloading from NT File System (NTFS) drives should have only Read access enabled.*

Using Visual Basic Script

A subset of Visual Basic—called Visual Basic Script—is used by Microsoft's browser to create active HTML applications. This implementation of the Visual Basic language is available to other browser vendors who license Microsoft's browser technology. Visual Basic supports the creation of OLE components that can be used on the Internet. VBScript enables developers to write Visual Basic code that is embedded in the HTML document.

VBScript Support

When the browser parses a VBScript <Script> tag, it calls VBScript to compile and execute the code. To use this feature, the browser needs to have VBScript support and must be able to integrate scripting with controls or applets embedded in the HTML data stream. Microsoft's Internet Explorer, as well as browsers from Oracle, Spyglass, and NetManage are doing this now.

OLE Automation

OLE Automation can be used with VBScript to manipulate both the browser and other applications on the desktop. It can be used to set properties and methods on OLE Controls and Java applets (see the following section on Java).

Using ActiveX Controls

ActiveX controls—formerly known as OLE controls or OCX controls—are components (or objects) you can insert into a Web page or other application to reuse preprogrammed functionality. The ActiveX controls that are included with Microsoft's Internet Explorer allow you to enhance your Web pages with high-level text features, sound, and animation (see Figure 26-3).

With Other Programming Languages

ActiveX controls, in contrast to Java applets and Netscape plug-ins, can also be used in applications written in C, C++, Visual Basic, and many other programming languages. There are many hundreds of ActiveX controls available today, and developers are

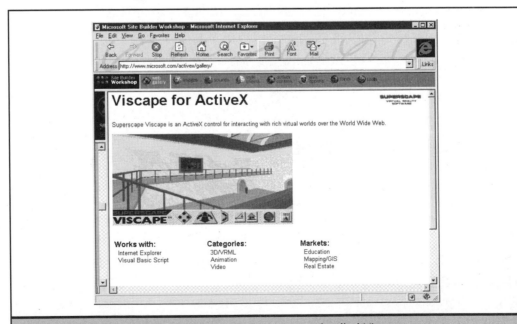

Figure 26-3. *A Web page using an ActiveX control called Viscape*

continually authoring more. You add ActiveX controls to your Web page by using standard HTML tags. You can set parameters for a control that changes the appearance and behavior of the control.

With Internet Explorer

The ActiveX controls provided with Internet Explorer get installed automatically when the user installs Internet Explorer. Once installed, ActiveX controls run when a Web page containing them is displayed, or they are activated by an application's code. Unlike some applet technologies, users do not need to download any additional files.

Writing ActiveX Controls

The following are the basic ways to write ActiveX controls:

- The easiest method is to use the OLE control development environment in Visual C++ and the Microsoft Foundation Classes (MFC), which include classes for OLE *and* Internet development. This has overhead for control clients, since they must have, or download, the MFC DLLs.

- Another way to write ActiveX controls involves programming the control interface directly, using an expert knowledge of OLE COM and the ActiveX control architecture. This kind of programming is generally left to an expert, so it's not very useful as an authoring tool.

- The third method, which is much easier than programming the control interface, described just above, allows easy creation of very fast and small C++ controls using the ActiveX Template Library (ATL) contained in Visual C++. The templates require very little code overhead, so they move across networks easily.

Using Java

Java was developed by Sun Microsystems and licenses have been snapped up by many of the main Internet companies, including Netscape. Formerly known as oak, it is an object-oriented programming language that shares many superficial similarities with C, and C++. It is not based, however, on any of those languages nor have efforts been made to make it compatible with them.

The Author Applets Context

Java is used in this context to author applets. An applet is a program that runs in the context of an applet viewer or Web browser, with access strictly limited to the host system (see Figure 26-4). There are already browsers with built-in Java capability for all major computer platforms—PCs, Unix, and the Macintosh. Before Java, most of the compute-intensive work was carried out at the Web server end. The results were then transmitted back over the intranet or Internet to the browser. The browser was responsible only for the static display, and thus, much of its computing capacity was

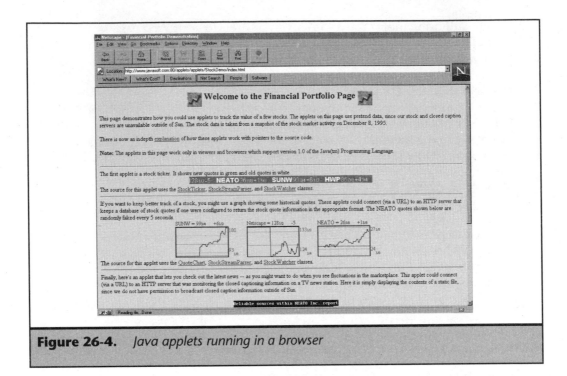

Figure 26-4. *Java applets running in a browser*

underutilized. As with other control and applet technologies, a Java program can balance the computing load by spreading it from a single server to many browsers. Sometimes it is even possible to split the load by minimizing the size of the communications between the server and the browser.

For example, a Web site that uses a lot of graphics might make the browser responsible for calculating complex sequences, while the server keeps track of user interaction. User interface changes might be abstractly transmitted over the network in relatively compact codes. This kind of use for a Java applet can alleviate a high-demand communications load on the server. Compared with a scenario where the server calculates all graphical images for all users—continually having to transmit changed images—Java can make a real difference in these situations.

Form Design Capabilities

Java can also be used to design forms (for HTML submittal) that encompass a higher level of security and data integrity. Java can be used in this way to enforce range checking and automatic forms population, relieving the server-side application from duties involving parameter checking and forms rejection.

Using Visual J++

Visual J++ is Microsoft's visual Java development environment. Using the same integrated development environment found in Visual C++, Visual J++ includes a visual debugger, shown in Figure 26-5, wizards to build applets and ActiveX controls, an advanced editor with syntax highlighting, and a compiler which translates at very high rates. Visual J++ is

- Certified as Java compatible and allows users to build cross-platform applications, with specific optimization for the Windows 95 and Windows NT platforms.

- A tool to enhance and speed Java development . It fully supports Java language standards and extends Java by integration with ActiveX control technology.

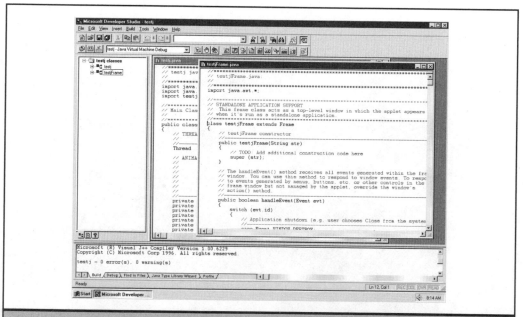

Figure 26-5. *The Visual C++/J++ integrated development environment*

NOTE: *Microsoft has an agreement with Sun Microsystems (the creators of Java) to author a reference implementation of Java for Windows. Applications built with Visual J++ will work with any major browser, including Internet Explorer and Netscape Navigator.*

Using Microsoft FrontPage

Since building Web pages has a lot to do with graphic layout—rather than being all hard programming—tools have started to appear that make the task easier for nonprogrammers. Corel, Asymmetrix, and Microsoft all have no or few Web programming/authoring tools available. We'll take a look at one of these here: Microsoft's FrontPage—a wizard-based application that walks you through the steps of building Web pages without having to have any programming knowledge (see Figure 26-6).

TIP: *If you already have textual content, you may also want to consider one of the many assistant-type plug-ins for the most popular word processors and spreadsheets. They can convert your documents into standard HTML for inclusion on a Web page.*

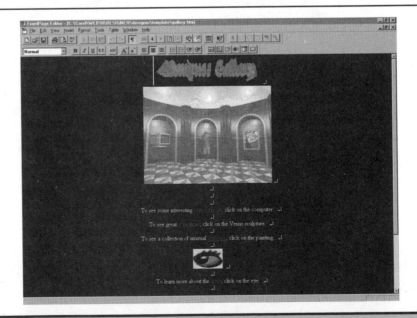

Figure 26-6. *The FrontPage editor environment*

A Tool for Nonprogrammers

FrontPage is designed for nonprogrammers, but its features may be of interest to almost all Web site developers. FrontPage gives you a word processor-like WYSIWYG editor for page layout, page templates, wizards to step you through the creation of your Web site content, and integration with other Microsoft applications for content import and export. Added to this base functionality are pseudo-controls that Microsoft calls WebBots. These are components that you can use to create interactive functionality on a Web page with little knowledge of what they really do.

The Features of FrontPage

The FrontPage Editor helps you create and edit Web pages without having to know HTML. Very much like a word processor on the front end, the FrontPage Editor automatically generates the HTML code representing your layout. Other features that make authoring faster and easier include:

- Automatic conversion of images to GIF or JPEG format
- Creation of hot spots by tracing an area and converting it to an image map with the hotspot editor
- A drag-and-drop interface to create hyperlinks within a page, to other pages, or to other Web sites
- A forms editor to create forms with text fields, check boxes, radio buttons, drop-down lists, and push buttons
- Creation of WYSIWYG HTML tables
- Frame support using the Frames wizard
- WebBot components to automate CGI programming

FrontPage comes with a suite of Server extensions to allow it to work with Web servers from NetScape, Microsoft, Spry, and more. Hosting is on NT 4, Windows 95, and Unix, and it comes with a local Web server to allow you to be self-hosted—not having to be connected to a remote server while developing your Web content.

 NOTE: You are going to see offerings like FrontPage from most of the major players within the coming months. Web content and authoring tools are rapidly becoming more suitable for graphic artists and content providers, rather than requiring programmers to implement HTML and CGI code and features directly.

Installing Server-Side CGI or ISAPI

After you have written a CGI or ISAPI application or script, place it in the Scripts directory—a default virtual directory meant for executing applications. This directory has Execute access, and you must make sure that any process started by your application is also running in the context of an account with adequate permissions.

NOTE: *By default, applications run using the IUSR_computername account, which must have administrator and execute permissions for these application files.*

Running Your Application

If the application does not require input data, it will likely be the target of a simple hyperlink within an HTML document. If it needs input from the user, you can use an HTML form or send a URL with data parameters to invoke a program.

TIP: *If you wish to create an application that requires input from the user, you can use wizard programs like FrontPage to create the client- and server-side components, or you can program directly in HTML—using forms—and implement server-side components in ISAPI or CGI.*

Publishing with Database Access

Using IIS's WWW service and the ODBC drivers provided with NT 4 (see Figure 26-7), you can easily integrate data access methods into your content and applications. With

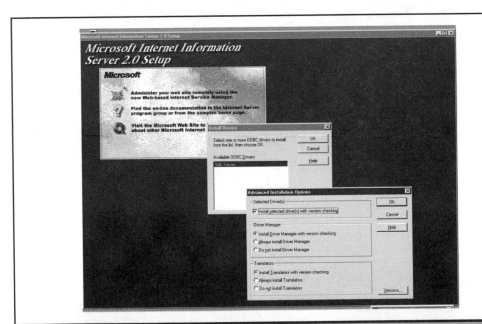

Figure 26-7. *Setting up IIS*

these tools you can create Web pages with information contained in a database, update and use information in a database based on user input from a Web page and, more technically, you can directly execute various SQL database commands.

The Internet Database Connector

Web access to databases on an IIS-enabled NT 4 server can be accomplished using a component called the Internet Database Connector (IDC). The IDC is an ISAPI DLL that uses ODBC to enable database access. Output is typically in the form of a HTML document for return to client-side services.

The IDC uses special files (.IDC and .HTX) to control how the database is accessed and how the output HTML page is constructed. The IDC files contain the necessary information to connect to the appropriate ODBC data source and execute a database SQL statement. The IDC formats database returns for subsequent return to the calling application.

Installing ODBC

If you want to provide ODBC functionality to your Web site, you must install ODBC when setting up IIS. You must use ODBC version 2.5, as that version supports System Data Source Names (DSNs). System DSNs allow NT services to use ODBC. The ODBC drivers are installed during IIS setup. If you did not install these drivers, and their administration application, use the following steps:

1. Click the IIS Setup icon in the Microsoft Internet Server menu on the start bar. You will also need the NT 4 Server CD or a connection to a shared network directory containing the CD image.

2. Once you have restarted IIS Setup, select the ODBC Drivers and Administration option.

3. When the Install Drivers dialog box appears, select the SQL Server driver from the Available ODBC Drivers list box, and click the OK button. Setup will copy and install the SQL driver files.

4. To create the system data sources, open the Control Panel from the Start/Settings menu and choose the ODBC control panel applet.

5. When the ODBC Data Sources dialog appears, click the System DSN button. The System Data Sources dialog box appears. (Be sure to click the System DSN button. The Internet Database Connector will work only with System DSNs.)

6. Choose the Add button, and when the Add Data Source dialog appears, select an ODBC driver from the list (usually SQL) and click OK. A dialog specific to the chosen driver appears.

7. Enter the name of the data source. The data source name is a logical name used by ODBC to refer to the driver and any other information required to access the data, such as the actual server name or location of the database. The data source name is used by the IDC files to instruct the Internet Information Server where to access data. (For Microsoft SQL Server, the server name, network address, and network library displayed by Setup are specific to your installation. If you do not have a reason to change the displayed parameters, just accept the defaults.)

8. Click the OK button, and then dismiss the System Data Sources dialog by clicking the Close button, which will bring you back to the main Data Sources dialog. Click close to dismiss it, and then OK to complete the ODBC and DSN setup.

NOTE: *The Internet Database Connector requires the 32-bit ODBC drivers shipped with Microsoft Office 95 and Microsoft Access 95. The ODBC driver for Microsoft Access 2.0 will not work with Internet Information Server.*

The MIME Mapping Configuration

If your Web site includes files that are in multiple formats, your computer must have a Multipurpose Internet Mail Extension (MIME) mapping for each file type. If MIME mapping on the server is not set up for a specific file type, browsers may not be able to retrieve the file. To configure additional MIME mappings:

1. Start the Registry Editor (regedit.exe) and open HKEY_LOCAL_MACHINE\ SYSTEM\CurrentControlSet\Services\InetInfo\Parameters\MimeMap.

2. Add a REG_SZ value for the MIME mapping required for your computer with the syntax: *<mime type>,<filename extension>,<unused parameter>,<gopher type>* The string associated with the value (that is, the value content) should be blank. The default entry with the file-name extension specified as an asterisk (*) is the default MIME type used when a MIME mapping does not exist. This will cause most browsers to save such a mapped file to disk.

What's Next

Now that you've completed this final chapter in the book, you can look forward to many enjoyable experiences as a well-informed NT user. You certainly know by now that NT 4 is a powerful and multi-featured program. As you further explore and refine your application, you may be surprised to find that this book also functions as an excellent reference resource. Should you encounter any problems on your journey, be sure to consult Appendix A.

Many years of smooth operation and happy computing!

Appendix A

Diagnosis and Troubleshooting

If your NT installation goes smoothly, and you are up and running right away, congratulations! For the rest of us, especially those with more sophisticated and complicated hardware and software setups, this appendix describes steps for troubleshooting the various problems that can arise while installing, starting, and running NT. We will also cover some of the more esoteric NT features that can be used to tailor performance and execution to suit particular needs.

We'll begin by reviewing NT's diagnostic capabilities and discussing problems with hardware configuration and compatibility, and then move on to startup difficulties and problems with networking. Finally, we'll cover what to do when performance is poor, reviewing diagnosis and techniques that you can use to improve and tune NT 4's operation. We'll end with a quick discussion of why NT must always be set up from distribution files.

NT 4's Diagnostic Tools

There are many ways to examine and diagnose a faulty NT system. Two tools that you can use to inspect different facets of operation are of primary importance: WINMSD, the NT diagnostics application, and for NT Server, the Network Monitor (a *very* sophisticated software-based network diagnostic tool and sniffer—formerly code named "Bloodhound"). These tools address different facets of diagnosing NT installation and operation problems, throughput/bottlenecks, and integration. We'll discuss the elements of WINMSD first, since this is of more general use in diagnosing and resolving system conflicts. Then we'll lightly touch on the Network Monitor and how to install support for it across your NT network.

 NOTE: Though it may seem obvious, it should be noted that these tools can only be used if the basic system is in a functioning state. If your PC is not running at all, or won't boot up, see the sections later in this appendix on getting a non-booting NT system up and running.

WINMSD (Windows NT Diagnostics)

NT 4 includes a primary diagnostic tool for the base hardware and environment called WINMSD.EXE (see Figure A-1). This tool allows you to inspect and determine hardware and system installation settings for any NT computer that can be reached from your network. You must, of course, have the proper permissions when using this tool remotely.

You can invoke WINMSD from the command line or from the Start/Programs/ Administrative Tools (Common) menu. WINMSD (or Windows NT Diagnostics, as it is called on the Start menu) can be used to view almost all crucial configuration information for a local or remote computer. To reach a remote computer on the network, you must invoke WINMSD with a command line argument equal to the Windows network computer name of the target you are trying to connect to, as in

WINMSD \\nt133s

where the computer name is preceded by "\\". You may also use the IP address of the remote computer, just as long as there is some way to resolve the address, as in:

WINMSD \\209.16.133.11

While diagnosing problems with hardware settings, or services that have trouble with startup or initialization, WINMSD will soon become an old friend. Using WINMSD's tabbed dialogs, you can inspect values and parameters in the following areas of interest:

- **Version:** Operating system version and service-pack revision. Also lists registration information.
- **System:** Identifies the type of computer and the HAL version in use (see Chapter 19 for an explanation of the HAL software layer). Also identifies the computer's BIOS version and the number and types of CPUs installed on the machine.

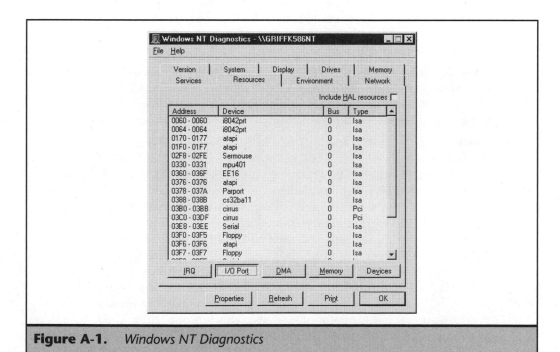

Figure A-1. *Windows NT Diagnostics*

- **Display:** Identifies the type of video adapter that is installed. Also lists its BIOS identifier string, the current settings for display resolution, adapter chipset type, and installed video driver information.

- **Drives:** Provides a hierarchical list of installed and network-reachable disk drives for the computer being inspected. You can list drives by type or by drive letter using the buttons at the bottom of this dialog.

- **Memory:** Provides statistics on both physical and logical memory amounts and usage. Lists available and total physical/file cache/kernel (paged and nonpaged)/commit memory. Also displays statistics on total open handles, threads, and processes, as well as both paging file space and usage.

- **Services:** Lists all services or devices, using the selection buttons at the bottom of the dialog, as well as their state (running, stopped, etc.).

- **Resources:** Lists combined resources for the computer in question. This is probably the most helpful dialog when trying to identify conflicts in hardware or driver settings. The selection buttons at the bottom of the display allow you to change the list to show various information. Click the IRQ button to list IRQs in use and to determine which hardware device has claimed which IRQ. The I/O Port button shows you the ports in use and which hardware device has claimed which I/O port or port range. In the same way, the DMA button and Memory button show you the DMA channels and memory addresses in use, and which hardware devices have claimed them. The Devices button allows you to show device classes that claim some number of system resources. You can inspect total resource commitment for any listed device class by double-clicking on any member of the list.

- **Environment:** Lists the environment strings, parameters, and settings for both the system and individually logged-on local user. Use the Start/Settings/Control Panel/System applet, Environment dialog to edit these values or add environment variables to those listed (see Chapter 6).

- **Network:** Lists general and specific statistics covering this computer's network settings and connection to the network. Using the selection buttons at the bottom of the dialog, you may view various types of information. The General button lists overall parameters and values for the computer's network layer. The current user's access level, workgroup or domain, version information, and logon parameters are listed here. The Transports button lists installed network transports and their address bindings for the primary NIC. This generally covers only NetBIOS (NetBT/NWLink—see Chapter 5) transports. The Setting button lists network-related settings such as buffer sizes, read ahead throughput, encryption, and transfer size. The Statistics button lists statistics for data transmission over the network transports. Read and write totals, failed operations, connects and reconnects, and use counts are but some of the values listed in this dialog.

The NT Network Monitor

Network sniffers can be simple, generally informative applications, or they can be sophisticated and all-encompassing system tools. Network Monitor for NT falls into the latter category. An entire book could be written about this application alone. Although we cannot hope to pay enough attention to this tool here, we will briefly review some of the salient features and then describe how to support the application across your entire network.

The Network Monitor application is installed on an NT Server. It can be invoked from the Start/Programs/Administrative Tools (Common) menu. It is a tool that allows you to quantify and qualify network data and performance across your entire installation (see Figure A-2). Any NT computer connected to the network whose installed network services include the Network Agent (a helper service that enables a workstation to respond to Network Monitor's control messages), can be queried for throughput statistics, and its network data and control packets can be inspected and catalogued.

The Network Monitor and its agent are installed like all other network services, through the Start/Settings/Control Panel/Network applet, under the Services dialog. To add monitoring support to any NT workstation, use this dialog to install the

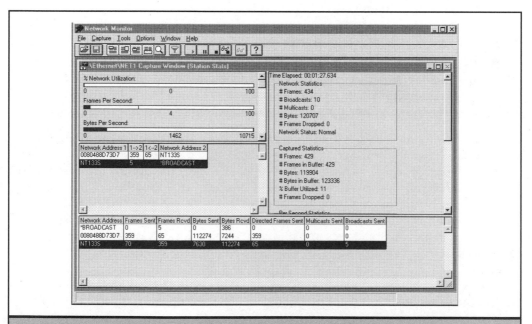

Figure A-2.   *Network Monitor in action*

Network Agent (see Chapters 6 and 11 on working with the Control Panel/Network applet). All installed network protocols can be monitored.

The principal areas that Network Monitor addresses are

- **Per second statistics:** The % Network Utilization field gives you instantaneous statistics on the percentage of network bandwidth utilized. The Frames Per Second field gives you the number of frames being transmitted over the network. The Bytes Per Second field gives you the number of bytes being transmitted over the network. The Broadcasts Per Second field gives you the number of broadcast frames on the network. The Multicasts Per Second field gives you the number of multicast frames on the network.

- **Network card (MAC) statistics:** Total number of frames, bytes, broadcasts, and multicasts on the network, sourced by the NIC since capture began.

- **Network card (MAC) error statistics:** Total number of errors seen by the NIC. Errors include CRC errors, frames dropped because no buffer space was available, and frames dropped because of hardware limitations.

- **Capture:** Network Monitor allows you to capture packet data that is inbound to a particular network address or outbound from any address. Captured data is fully viewable in several different formats.

- **Query:** Network Monitor can query a network for all monitor users and router locations. It can also resolve names from addresses and invoke the Performance Monitor (see Chapter 7). To perform some of these noncritical tasks, you must have the version of the Monitor that ships with Systems Management Server (see Chapter 18).

- **View:** Network Monitor's main windows show throughput and utilization statistics for the target network address. These windows also list total and capture statistics for such parameters as network and MAC (NIC) frames, broadcasts, multicasts, number of bytes transferred, and errors.

Network Monitor includes a sophisticated filter and trigger setup for capturing only the data you are interested in. Many parameters and settings affecting what data is captured for display, and what qualifiers are set for the data capture, are available for use. Full help on working with the Monitor is available within the program and is covered in the NT Resource Kit documentation.

One use of this application is the determination of the source of a broadcast storm. By sorting statistics on broadcasts and multicasts, you can easily determine the source of a broadcast storm by looking at the machine sending the greatest number of broadcasts.

This is not an application for casual use, and it is recommended that you get a good night's sleep before you are first introduced to the intricacies of working with this program!

NT Hardware and Software Installation Problems

Finding and configuring the proper mix of hardware to run NT is probably one of the most frustrating and exacting processes you can be challenged with. If you are simply setting up a standard workstation or server, with no special devices, multimedia support, or compatibility and integration issues, you can be fairly sure that all will go well using the standard setup. All bets are off, though, when your requirements include additional hardware components or adapters that are not considered to be part of a base NT configuration. Microsoft generally considers the base configuration to be as follows:

- **Processor and motherboard:** Any standard brand name listed in the NT hardware compatibility list (HCL), which can be found on the NT CD-ROM and on Microsoft's Internet site. These HCL configurations include at least 16MB of RAM and such peripherals as the keyboard, floppy drive, and standard parallel and serial ports. Many no-name brands based on similar chipsets and designs will work just as well, but they are untested.

- **VGA/SuperVGA display adapter (with compatible display monitor):** Most of the modern VGA and SuperVGA display adapters are supported directly. Many manufacturers also ship display drivers for their newer offerings.

- **(E)ISA and/or PCI-based IDE or SCSI controller(s) and hard disk drive(s):** Again, compatible controller types will be listed in the HCL. Almost all IDE and SCSI drives that are compatible with these controllers will work under NT.

To add to the mix, most specialized configurations require software drivers that may or may not be sourced or supported by Microsoft. Driver interaction and setup can be just as confusing, yet critical, as making the initial hardware settings. NT does not need special adapters, multimedia cards, or a video capture device to run, and Microsoft has designed the driver model so that the third-party company that makes a new hardware product is responsible for providing the necessary driver support. This works well in singular cases. If you are running a base NT configuration, and a single audio adapter is added, you will probably encounter very few hitches. The most likely scenario where problems will be encountered is when multiple adapters and drivers must cooperate. Most adapters and devices need to communicate with the computer bus using one or more of the following methods:

- **Input/output (I/O) ports:** The physical data gateway between an adapter (or chipset) and the main computer bus (specially on Intel x86 architectures). I/O port values will usually be expressed in hexadecimal (base 16) notation, and can be singular or specified within a range.

- **Interrupt request (IRQ) lines:** The physical signaling lines used by an adapter or computer chip to request immediate service by the CPU. Hardware interrupt requests—those we are interested in here for the x86 PC architecture—are usually in the range of 0 through 15, with 0, 1, 6, 8, and 13 always reserved for internal use. IRQ 2 is usually mapped to IRQ 9 because of the way PC hardware is designed.

- **Physical memory buffers:** Many adapters require RAM buffers to transmit large blocks of data between the adapter and the CPU. These buffers are sometimes used directly by the adapter and CPU, and can also be used by the adapter for Direct Memory Access (DMA). The addresses of these buffers will usually be expressed as a 32-bit number in hexadecimal (base 16).

- **Adapter read-only memory (ROM) addresses:** Some adapters have their own startup and utility I/O routines. They keep these software procedures in ROM, which then is assigned to a memory address within the computer's addressing range. The addresses where the adapter's ROM can be located will usually be expressed as a 32-bit number in hexadecimal (base 16).

The PNPISA Driver

Although NT is still catching up to the consumer market demands for seamless hardware installation and integration, it does indeed have limited plug-and-play capability when teamed with an ancillary driver called PNPISA.SYS. This driver can be found on the distribution CD-ROM under the \DRVLIB\PNPISA\<*computertype*>\ directory.

To install this driver, open Explorer, go to the correct subdirectory on the CD-ROM, and right-click the mouse over the PNPISA.INF file. Select Install from the quick menu and the driver will be copied to your NT installation. Then reboot the machine. Any plug-and-play devices present will be automatically recognized and an install will be attempted.

The "Blue Screen of Death" (B.S.O.D.)

Let's hope you never encounter the B.S.O.D. during your interaction with NT 4. What we are talking about is the unrecoverable fault display that is shown when NT encounters a fatal error that stops the system with a diagnostic display (see Figure A-3). This is technically called a STOP error by NT and actually has a blue background with white lettering; hence the nickname.

This diagnostic display contains clues as to where the unrecoverable fault happened, as well as a general diagnostic module and stack listing. Although explanation of each module and section of the display is beyond the scope of this appendix, you can use this information to diagnose what happened to cause a STOP error. If you call Microsoft technical support with a STOP error problem, they too will want to query you about values and information displayed on the B.S.O.D.

You can also automatically perform a *core dump*, or memory image dump, upon encountering a STOP error. Just check the "Write debugging information to" box in the Start/Settings/Control Panel/System applet, under the Recovery section in the

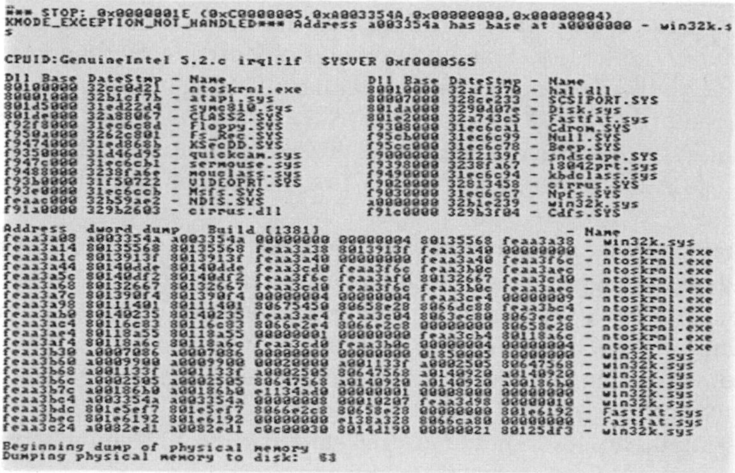

Figure A-3. *The B.S.O.D. —NT's blue screen of death*

Startup/Shutdown dialog. On subsequent STOP errors, the system will write the complete memory image of NT to disk with a default name of MEMORY.DMP. This file can later be used with WinDbg, the NT graphical debugger, to diagnose where and why the fault took place.

Using the Recovery section of the Startup/Shutdown dialog, you can also select the "Write an event to the system log" checkbox if you want to have NT write an event containing information about the error to the system log when a STOP error occurs.

You can also select the "Send an administrative alert" checkbox if you want to have NT send an alert to the members of the Administrators group when a STOP error occurs.

NOTE: *To use the Write an Event, Send an Administrative Alert, or Automatically Reboot options, the computer must have at least a 2MB paging file on the system drive (the drive defined by the SYSTEMROOT environment variable). To use Write Debugging Info, the paging file on the system drive must be large enough to hold all of the physical RAM plus 1MB.*

When you encounter a B.S.O.D., you will inevitably have to reboot the machine by means of hardware reset or power cycling unless you have also checked the "Automatically reboot" box in the Recovery section of the dialog mentioned previously.

Where to Look for Problems

The most common difficulties will be found in hardware settings for devices that cannot share interrupt request (IRQ) settings, memory buffer addresses, or ROM (read-only memory) addresses. A common set of problems you might encounter in an NT computer involves supported devices with conflicting interrupts and/or I/O ports and/or memory ranges. Where possible, NT will try to identify conflicts and suggest alternatives. However, many adapters and peripherals do not present enough information about themselves to let NT resolve a problem, when queried programmatically.

If an adapter or device does not function after installation, you should first make a checklist based on the suggestions in the following sections. The most obvious conflicts can be found by checking all other adapters installed on the machine for duplicate settings in these areas. Some of the settings for newer adapters are totally software based, within the driver setups, while older devices may have rows of hardware switches and jumpers.

The discussion that follows should get you started on troubleshooting your installation.

Free/Used Interrupts

As a guide to choosing interrupts for adapter cards, the standard IRQ assignments for x86-based computers are listed here:

IRQ	Assigned To
0	Timer
1	Keyboard
2	Interrupt controller #1 cascade to IRQ 9 (Free)
3	COM2 and/or COM4 or Free
4	COM1 and/or COM3 or Free
5	LPT2 or Free
6	Floppy disk controller
7	LPT1: or Free
8	Internal PC clock tick
9	(IRQ 2) Free
10	Free
11	Free
12	Bus mouse or Free
13	Math coprocessor

IRQ	Assigned To
14	IDE primary hard disk controller or Free
15	IDE secondary hard disk controller or Free

IRQs cannot generally be shared; although you can, for instance, share LPT1 with a sound card on IRQ 7 (especially if the printer port does not use its IRQ), as long as you don't *ever* want to print while you are playing a sound file. PCI and MCA bus adapters generally are capable of sharing interrupts, but this depends heavily on support for this feature in the device driver for the adapter.

Although the first four COM ports share two IRQs (by convention—which, by the way, severely limits their usefulness), a device or adapter's IRQ should never be shared on an IRQ line that is used by one of the active COM ports. A common problem with serial devices such as mice and modems stems from trying to use them on a shared COM IRQ simultaneously with another serial device attached and active on the other port that shares the IRQ. If a mouse is, for example, assigned to COM2 (IRQ 3), COM4 (IRQ 3) will be unavailable for any use, since the mouse is always active. Therefore, COM4 is unusable. An alternative would be to assign COM4 to another free IRQ, but this is only possible with some serial adapters or motherboards.

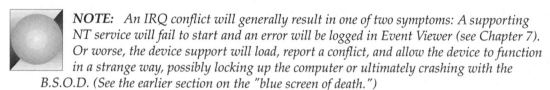

NOTE: *An IRQ conflict will generally result in one of two symptoms: A supporting NT service will fail to start and an error will be logged in Event Viewer (see Chapter 7). Or worse, the device support will load, report a conflict, and allow the device to function in a strange way, possibly locking up the computer or ultimately crashing with the B.S.O.D. (See the earlier section on the "blue screen of death.")*

TIP: *Before you assign IRQs, use the NT Diagnostics/Resources/IRQ dialog to find out which IRQs are currently in use.*

I/O Port Addresses

Most adapters have one or more selectable I/O port addresses. Usually, these will not conflict, and some adapters can even respond themselves to a conflict (see the earlier section on the PNPISA.SYS plug-and-play driver). The following I/O addresses are usually taken in an x86 computer, and therefore should not be assigned to an adapter card:

I/O Port Address	Assigned To
0000-00FF	Internal PC use
0278	LPT2
02F8	COM2

I/O Port Address	Assigned To
0378	LPT1
03BC	Primary-alternate LPT1
03F0-03F7	Floppy disk controller
03F8	COM1:

TIP: *Before you assign port addresses, use the NT Diagnostics/Resources/I/O Port dialog to find out which ports are currently in use.*

Memory Addresses

Make sure that memory needed by a particular adapter does not conflict with the memory address assigned to another adapter. These addresses are variable, so no clear rule can be made on addresses that are reserved, other than the general range between 000A0000-000BFFFF, which is devoted to display memory in almost all modern PCs.

TIP: *Before you assign memory addresses, use the NT Diagnostics/Resources/Memory dialog to find out which memory ranges are currently in use.*

Application/Driver Problems

Many device drivers, and some rare applications, need to know which IRQs, I/O ports, and memory addresses to use, along with any adapter-specific settings, when conversing with installed hardware. Many times, device drivers will automatically be set up, upon installation, with system registry values that do not match the jumpers and switches you have set on the adapter itself. In this case, you will have to bring up the driver's configuration dialog to change these software settings to the correct values. In extreme cases, you may have to edit these values directly, using the Registry Editor (see Chapter 17).

PCMCIA/Cardbus Problems

PCMCIA or Cardbus support is problematical in NT 4. Very few controller chipsets are supported right now, although Cardbus support is planned for a future release. If you do not have a standard Intel-compatible PCMCIA controller, there is a good chance that you will have trouble installing or running card services under NT 4.

Look to companies such as Award, Phoenix, and SystemSoft to provide third-party socket services for the bulk of the PCMCIA/Cardbus controllers. These companies either already market or have announced full support for NT 4.

Unsupported Hardware and Software

Many OEM manufacturers have specifically updated drivers and system software that will support a nonstandard adapter or device. Look at the manufacturer's Internet site of updated drivers and software. Also check with Microsoft, or look on the distribution disk under the \Drvlib directory, where manufacturers have provided updated drivers and registry files for their nonconforming hardware and adapters.

(E)IDE and SCSI Problems

There are two kinds of problems you might encounter with either (E)IDE or SCSI devices. First, the controller-adapter might be the source of your problem. Check IRQs, I/O port assignments, and memory addresses. If all appears well, proceed to the device itself. In any case, check the connections between the controller and device first. Make sure cables are free from bends and kinks and that connectors are securely seated.

PROBLEMS WITH AN (E)IDE DEVICE If the problem cannot be solved on the controller side, examine the device for settings, usually in the form of jumpers or switches, that tell the controller what kind of device this is and what its role in the device chain will be.

Look for the Slave/Master/One Device Only settings to make sure they are correct. If you have more than one device (drive), one will have to be jumpered as the master (this will be your primary boot drive) and one as the slave. Also, check the power connections to the device.

Make sure that your BIOS supports the device in question. Some PC BIOS revisions do not support drives of over about 540MB. And still others do not support drives over about 2GB. It's very dependent on the age of the BIOS and computer, since most PCs made in the last year or so now support (E)IDE drives of any size.

PROBLEMS WITH A SCSI DEVICE If there is trouble with a SCSI device, first make sure that the device is properly addressed. Most SCSI devices need to be jumpered or switched to address them in the SCSI device chain. The device numbers can be set to values ranging from 0 to 7 for SCSI1 and SCSI2, and 0 to 15 for SCSI3.

Also make sure the SCSI bus is properly terminated with SCSI termination resistors. Each physical end of a SCSI bus must have termination installed. For instance, if devices are attached only to the internal or external SCSI bus, make sure termination is installed on the SCSI adapter (one end) and the last physical SCSI device on the connecting cable (the other end).

If both internal and external SCSI devices are connected, the adapter becomes the middle component, and termination should only be installed on each device that is physically at the end of its cable, internally or externally.

Also, check to see which device is configured to provide power for the termination resistors. Usually, this will be the SCSI adapter in the computer, but it can be one or more of the SCSI devices.

CAUTION: *If a SCSI device that is terminated is removed, be sure to install termination in the device that then becomes the physical end-device on the chain.*

Video Display Adapters and Drivers

Potential troubles may be exhibited when installing a new adapter or driver for the video display in your NT machine. The three areas that make up 95 percent of the problems encountered with video adapters are resolution and refresh rates, color depth settings, and driver settings.

- **Resolution and refresh rates:** If you are changing resolution, or increasing the vertical refresh rate at which your display adapter produces a signal, there can be potentially damaging problems. Make sure the adapter card you use is capable of producing the resolution *and* the refresh rate that you choose. Some adapters need extra memory to achieve high resolution at a color depth that is satisfying to you. Refresh rate can usually be set to anything the adapter is capable of. However, if your monitor is incapable of handling a particular refresh rate, the best-case failure scenario will result in an unreadable display (see the section "Reboot, Recovery, and Configuration" a bit later in the chapter). The worst case is that when you change the refresh rate to a value too high for your monitor, the signal can do permanent damage to the CRT. This rarely happens but is possible.

CAUTION: *Check your monitor's documentation before attempting any refresh rate increase!*

- **Color depth settings:** When setting color depth, make sure the mode you choose (256, 32K, 64K, or 24/32-bit TrueColor modes) is actually supported by your adapter/display memory configuration. NT will automatically try to enforce valid modes, but it is ultimately up to the display driver, some of which do not check the hardware before attempting a mode change. If you pick a color depth that is not supported, the display may become unreadable. Reboot in VGA-safe mode (see the upcoming section "Reboot, Recovery, and Configuration").

- **Driver problems:** Display drivers come in two flavors: those that are provided with NT and those that are provided by a third-party OEM or manufacturer. Some display chipset makers provide generic drivers for their products that may or may not work. Check with your video adapter's manufacturer to make sure the newest drivers they supply for NT 4 support your model. Many drivers assume IRQ, I/O port, and memory addresses that may conflict with other adapters in your machine. If this is the case, NT will usually boot up in 640x480, 16-color mode, and then warn you that the adapter settings are in error. In extreme cases, NT may crash on boot-up, displaying the B.S.O.D. In this case, reboot in VGA-safe mode and change the driver or its setup.

Audio and Video Playback and Capture Cards, Other Adapters

Configuration and execution problems that arise from the use of audio or video playback and capture cards, or by, for instance, network adapters, commonly are found to be caused by software driver setup, or by the basics: IRQ, I/O ports, or memory addressing.

Video capture cards present a further problem—noise. Because most computers are built only to the least common denominator with respect to electromagnetic frequency emanations, and because most video capture equipment is not immune to this leaking electronic noise, a capture card may seem to malfunction in this environment. In reality, the video capture adapter is just picking up electronic noise, which may easily be shielded by the addition of special metal barriers, such as Mu metal.

A common fault in network adapter installation that will actually keep NT from starting, is the failure to terminate a thinnet (coax) ethernet adapter. Without the 50ohm termination, the network cabling is in a floating, indeterminate state that can keep the hardware from functioning altogether. This fault does not exhibit itself when using a twisted-pair 10/100BaseT topology.

NT Startup Problems

When NT is set up and installed on your computer, it rewrites the system partition boot record. Thereafter, upon boot, a file called NTLDR, existing in the root directory of the boot drive, is loaded and run before any other file.

When NTLDR is executed, it reads a file, also existing in the root directory of the boot drive, called BOOT.INI. This is a plain text file that contains instructions for NTLDR, so that a menu of available operating systems can be displayed for you on the multiboot startup screen (see Figure A-4).

Once NTLDR has read BOOT.INI, and you have made your OS choice, it executes another root directory file, NTDETECT.COM. This program inspects your computer's hardware and builds a list of the system's components, which will be used later to update the Registry (see Chapter 17).

Booting continues with the loading of the HAL, kernel, and other low-level NT system components, the initialization of device and system drivers, and the startup of NT services. Boot-up then proceeds with the loading of protected subsystems, security, and initial applications, including WinLogon, which allows you to interact with the mechanism that finally logs you on as an active user.

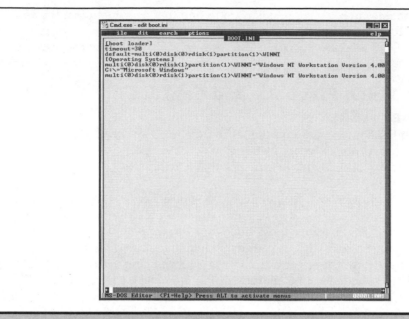

Figure A-4. *A BOOT.INI file's contents*

> **TIP:** *Usually, BOOT.INI contains values that allow the multiboot menu to be displayed with a default OS choice highlighted. It also contains a timer that starts according to a value contained in the file. You are allowed to select any displayed OS from the multiboot menu, and if you do nothing, the timer will count down to zero and start the OS selection that is highlighted. You can control the period in which the timer will count down by entering a value directly into the BOOT.INI file, or by entering a value in the Start/Settings/Control Panel/System applet, under Startup/Shutdown—"Show list for xx seconds" entry field. If you don't want the multiboot menu to show up at all, enter zero for this value. You can also control the default OS highlight using the same dialog, or by directly editing BOOT.INI (see "NT Won't Boot—Examining BOOT.INI," coming up).*

Reboot, Recovery, and Configuration

When you encounter a nonfatal error or you have set up, for instance, video hardware that makes the screen unreadable (because of bad refresh rates or drivers), you can recover from these errors easily. What you need to do is to reboot the machine with minimal configuration, similar to "safe mode" in Windows 95. To accomplish this, select the operating system you wish to start from the multiboot OS loader menu, and make sure your selection is labeled as follows:

Windows NT (Workstation/Server) Version 4.xx [VGA Mode]

This will select the minimal driver set needed to enter NT without video customization and the like. You may then proceed to change the settings that caused problems before.

Likewise, if you have encountered problems with settings or Registry corruption, you may reboot and choose a special recovery mode that loads backup versions of the important Registry databases in order to recover from bad settings or loss of Registry data. To revert to a good backup, upon boot, select

Press spacebar NOW to invoke Hardware Profile/Last Known Good menu

which will take you into the Hardware Profile/Configuration Recovery Menu (See Figure A-5). From this menu, you can choose a configuration to boot with. Usually there will be an Original Configuration menu choice, along with any custom profiles you have set up using the Start/Settings/Control Panel/System/Hardware Profiles dialog.

You will use this same technique with a portable computer that has different hardware configurations when, say, docked or undocked. You can have differing configurations for custom hardware support on a desktop machine also. You might use hardware configurations to support sets of installed adapters and peripherals, for instance, when special video production setups or multimedia devices are only in use transiently.

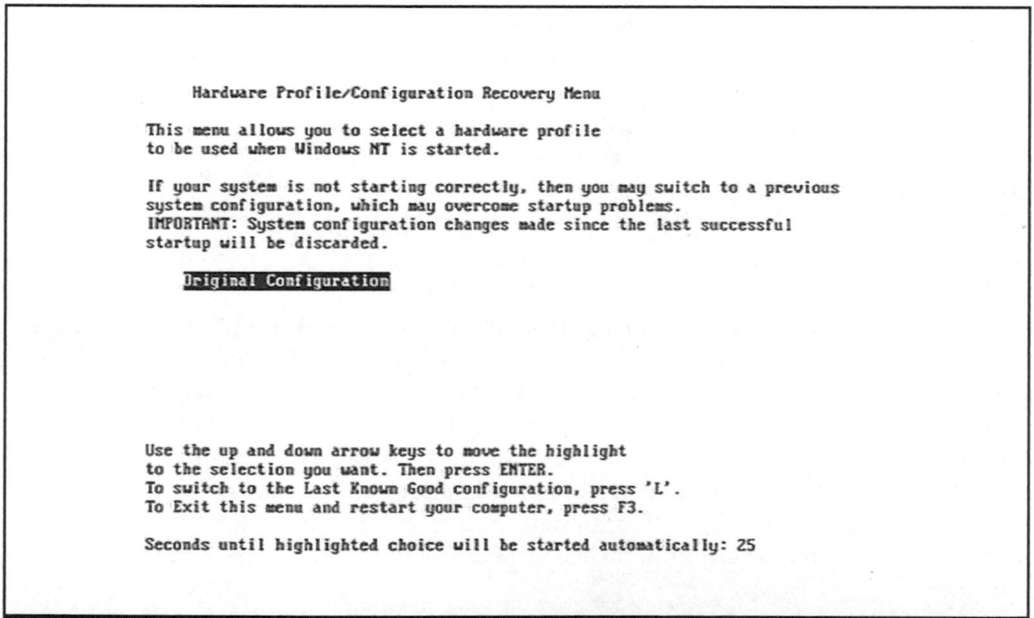

```
        Hardware Profile/Configuration Recovery Menu

    This menu allows you to select a hardware profile
    to be used when Windows NT is started.

    If your system is not starting correctly, then you may switch to a previous
    system configuration, which may overcome startup problems.
    IMPORTANT: System configuration changes made since the last successful
    startup will be discarded.

      Original Configuration




    Use the up and down arrow keys to move the highlight
    to the selection you want. Then press ENTER.
    To switch to the Last Known Good configuration, press 'L'.
    To Exit this menu and restart your computer, press F3.

    Seconds until highlighted choice will be started automatically: 25
```

Figure A-5. *The Hardware Profile/Configuration Recovery menu*

Maintaining the Startup Configuration

Once NT 4 starts successfully, back up your configuration directory (*systemroot*\
SYSTEM32\CONFIG), and maintain current backups as you change your
configuration and accounts. If you have to use the Repair option in NT Setup to
restore the system, you can restore the configuration from your backup.

NT Won't Boot—Examining BOOT.INI

If NT completely fails to start, check hardware and power first, as in the suggestions
outlined in the previous sections of this appendix. Then, check for errors in the
statements contained in the BOOT.INI file:

- The first section specifies which OS will be the default system that is
  highlighted. The timer countdown value is also specified here.

- The second section lists and specifies all of the operating systems and variants
  that can be started by using the multiboot menu.

If you need to edit BOOT.INI, use the Attrib command from a command prompt,
or from Explorer, open BOOT.INI's properties, setting all attribute bits off. Proceed to
edit the file and then set its read-only, system, and hidden bits back on.

 *CAUTION: If certain system files on the boot partition are deleted, NT will not start.
Do not delete the root directory files: NTLDR, BOOT.INI, BOOTSECT.DOS, or
NTDETECT.COM. Your emergency repair disk, created when you set up NT (see
Chapter 3) will allow you to recover these files if accidental deletion or damage does
happen. System repair is discussed next.*

System Repair

What can you do if your NT operating system needs to be repaired? If it has a corrupt
or incomplete Registry database? Or what if some of the boot files have inadvertently
been deleted?

Depending on what has happened, there are repair methods for almost all cases of
loss and corruption. Up front, we are going to discuss the ramifications of using these
methods so you don't set your hopes too high. Any method of repair that is applied to
the Registry will mean data loss of some kind. Unless Registry values become corrupt
right after you have backed up the Registry, any restoration, especially from an
out-of-date repair disk, is going to result in a rollback of values and settings to some
earlier date. You may end up with a running system, but one in which some
applications that you have recently installed will just up and disappear from your
Start menu.

The Registry is the repository of most of the configuration information that is
needed to properly use NT. There are two ways to insure that no matter what

happens, you will end up with a more or less intact Registry. First, you can use RegEdt32.exe and perform regular Save Key operations on each hive. These can later be restored using the Load Hive or Restore commands. Second, and more convenient and complete, is to use the NT Repair Disk utility, RDISK.EXE, which lets you update your system backup information and create a revised repair disk from the updated files.

There are also methods for restoring corrupt and/or missing boot sectors, and boot or system files. You can use the Repair option in NT 4's Setup program to accomplish these tasks. The methods using Setup's Repair option may or may not need your emergency repair disk—the disk you created when you originally set up NT 4 or have created or upgraded through the RDISK.EXE utility (RDISK is discussed shortly).

NT Setup's Repair Options

Depending on what portion of your NT system is in need of repair, you will use different methods to solve your problem. If system files or the boot sectors have been corrupted or lost beyond recovery using the Last Known Good Configuration boot method (covered earlier in this appendix), you can use Setup's Repair operation to recover from the error condition. How current your resultant recovery will be depends on the last time you updated the repair files on your emergency disk, or in your *systemroot*\Repair directory. Setup will need access to these files in order to repair your NT installation. If you do not have copies of these files available, you will have to completely reinstall NT 4.

Making Sure Repair Information Is Current—RDISK.EXE

The principal way to insure that your NT repair information is current, and so reflects the current state of your software and hardware setup, is to use the RDISK.EXE utility, shown here:

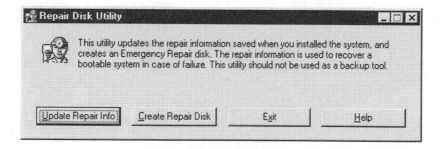

This utility allows you to accomplish two separate, but connected, operations.

First, RDISK lets you update the backup Registry and boot files in your *systemroot*\Repair directory. These files reflect the state of the important Registry hives (see Chapter 17 for more information on the Registry). This directory also contains backup files for your startup parameters when using the MS-DOS program's command line interface.

Second, RDISK lets you create an emergency repair disk, just as if you had created this disk at setup time. A by-product of using RDISK to create your emergency repair disk is that the files used to create the disk are taken from the *systemroot*\Repair directory. If you first choose to update the repair information in this directory, and then to create a repair disk, you will have performed a snapshot of the most current repair information that you can obtain.

To use RDISK, start the application from the Start/Run dialog on the desktop. Type **rdisk** into the Run dialog's entry field, and choose OK. You will be presented with the Repair Disk Utility display, where you can either perform a system configuration update (Update Repair Info) or create an emergency repair disk. Choose the operation that you wish to perform. You will need a 1.44MB disk for a new repair disk. It will be formatted and written to by RDISK automatically.

Using Setup|Repair

In order to repair an NT installation, you must boot up into the Setup program. This means you will need access to the original distribution files, either on CD-ROM, with your Setup boot disk in your primary floppy drive (A), or from an MS-DOS/network-enabled connection, where the distribution files are reachable before NT comes up.

Follow these steps to effect a repair of your NT installation using the Setup | Repair method:

1. Start Setup by inserting the Setup boot disk into the primary boot floppy drive, and then restart the computer. Alternatively, if you are booted into MS-DOS, access the distribution files and start Setup by entering the command line

   \\<*distribution location*>\i386\WINNT.EXE /b

   where <*distribution location*> is a network resource or your CD-ROM drive letter.

2. Once Setup has started, you will be presented with the first screen, where NT asks if you want to install NT or repair files. Enter **r** to continue the repair process.

CAUTION: *You can have more than one NT installation on your computer. Be sure to choose the installation that you actually intend to repair!*

3. Setup will now ask you for an emergency repair disk. Insert the disk into the floppy drive; or if you do not have a repair disk, Setup will search for NT installations, presenting a list that lets you select which NT installation you wish to repair.

4. Repair will proceed to completion under your direction, as outlined in the following sections, and you will finally be prompted to reboot the computer when the process is finished. Press CTRL+ALT+DEL or press your hardware-reset button to restart your computer.

Types of Repair

Setup allows you to choose the type of repair you wish to make on your NT system. The following sections list repair types, what files are affected, and the ramifications of each type of repair.

REGISTRY FILES   Setup will check all of the Registry files for errors and let you specify which files should be repaired and restored. The restoration will take place using the Registry files created when you first set up NT. You will lose all changes you have made unless you have backed up the Registry files in the *systemroot*\ SYSTEM32\CONFIG directory or you have used RDISK, as outlined earlier, to update your system configuration files.

STARTUP ENVIRONMENT   This option allows you to configure the BOOT.INI file to reflect the current state of your installed NT systems. Setup will rewrite the BOOT.INI file to include choices that allow you to pick from among all of the currently installed NT systems on your computer.

SYSTEM FILES   Use this option to verify and restore any corrupt or missing NT system files. Files are restored from the distribution source. Using this option, Setup will also check and restore NT boot files on the system partition. You can use this option to remove security on files that have been inadvertently marked with permissions that do not allow access on an NTFS partition.

BOOT SECTOR   Use this option to recover from the situation in which you cannot boot any OS from your system partition. Setup will write a new boot sector and restore the original boot configuration so that NT will be able to start.

Problems with Logon, Accounts, and Passwords

Once you have successfully booted NT, there are still potential problems that may crop up within the logon process. Some of these difficulties can be traced to the lack of orientation for novice users, and other problems may be due to limits and improper or unintentional settings made within the security and account setups.

The principal way of determining why a user is having difficulty with the logon process is to use the security audit logs in Event Viewer (see Chapter 16 for security auditing details and Chapter 7 for more information on the Event Viewer). Audit policies must be set in User Manager/Policies/Audit or User Manager for

Domains/Policies/Audit to include logon and logoff events in order to view those events later (see "Controlling Security and Users: The NT User Manager" in Chapter 16 for more information on how to set the audit trail).

Logon failures may be due to network transport or hardware problems, especially within a domain where remote users are depending on transient network or dial-up connections. Along with password and account difficulties, the problems encountered most often are listed here:

- Make sure the user's password is correct and is entered in the correct case, since passwords can be mixed case and are case sensitive. The administrator can check and/or reset the user's password if it has been forgotten. If the user is required to change his or her password, it might have been entered without regard to password length or reuse restrictions.

- Make sure the user's account or password has not expired or been locked out. Using User Manager, the administrator can reactivate an expired account or password, or unlock an account that has been locked for system-perceived security breaches. Also make sure that the account's logon hours in User Manager are valid for the times that the user is trying to log on, and that the Logon To dialog in User Manager includes all workstations, or at least the workstation that the user is trying to use.

- Check to make sure that another user has not previously locked the workstation. If this is the case, the previous user, or an administrator, must first unlock the machine.

- Check to see if the NT system on the workstation has been reinstalled or the machine name has been changed without resetting the domain machine account. The administrator for the domain must reset the machine account, or create a new one, to re-enable domain logon. Also check to make sure that the user is trying to log on to the correct domain or to a local machine (domain) that he or she has a local account on.

- Check for general network operation. The electrical or logical operation of the network may be at fault. If one exists on the network, check the domain controller's network connection and routing tables. Check all cables, routers, hubs, and physical connections. See the next section for more pointers on network diagnosis.

Network Hardware and Software Problems

Network problems are common partly because of the difficulty in setting up topologies and routing strategies that work in all cases. Also, problems with hardware setup and operation, or transports and protocols that are incompatible, can cause many difficulties.

The character of the physical network, whether there are electronic protocol translators, such as hubs that route thinnet onto 10BaseT, and the characteristics of the physical cabling can all have an impact on how your network performs. We'll discuss the most common problems that you will encounter when trying to diagnose and repair a network or network connection.

Cabling, Hubs, and Routers

Check all cabling for kinks, breaks, and fraying. If you are using twisted-pair cable, it should be CAT 5 or better. Check all thinnet/coax connections for proper termination with resistors.

If you have concentrators or hubs, check them with their internal diagnostics, if available, for proper operation. Also, try to qualify your network topology. Determine whether in some cases routing fails due to the way the network is physically connected, or whether, for instance, you may have a loopback condition in some cases.

For dedicated routers within the network, check their diagnostics and setup parameters for errors. Make sure that the installed software revision supports your chosen network protocol suite. If the router is connected to a WAN, check that it has been assigned with a valid address or IP address.

Domain Names, Computer Names, and Addresses

Each domain and each computer on a network must have a unique name and/or address. If two entities with the same name or address exist on an interconnected network, NT networking will not run properly, or in the worst case, will not start at all.

Also, computer names cannot be the same as domain or workgroup names. Make sure that when using TCP/IP, the IP address assigned to the workstation's NIC is unique, at least across your internal network. Also check the subnet mask and default gateway for routing data packets off the local network.

NIC Setup

Network interface cards come in many different configurations. Make sure that the basics—IRQs, I/O ports, and memory addresses—are correct upon installation. Also make sure that if the NIC is capable of using more than one kind of connection standard, coax or twisted pair, for instance, that the card and its driver software are set up to support the chosen technology.

Services Startup

Check the Event Viewer for network service startup failure. In many cases, a service is dependent on some other hardware or software component that may be at fault. By inspecting the events that have been logged due to the service startup failure, a pointer to the problem may be discerned. Also check the Services and Devices applet lists in the Control Panel to view the current status of any dependent components; whether NT has started the service or device driver and what its running state is when queried.

Tools for Problems with TCP/IP

The primary problems you will encounter while configuring and using the TCP/IP protocol are mostly related to IP address, subnet mask, and routing problems. The next sections outline two tools you can use to diagnose TCP/IP difficulties. These tools are primarily derived from the Unix world, and they work exactly the same on both platforms, so if you are already familiar with ping and tracert, you will immediately recognize these utilities on the NT platform. These tools require that you issue their commands from an NT command prompt. You must also have TCP/IP installed to use them.

Ping

Ping is a utility used to test the connection between your TCP/IP workstation and another TCP/IP-enabled host (see Figure A-6). To diagnose a connection between two computers using TCP/IP, use ping as follows:

1. Determine the IP addresses of each computer. Use ipconfig on the local machine to view the assigned IP address. If you have a static IP address, you can also open the Network applet in Control Panel to view TCP/IP parameters, where the IP address will be listed. Find the IP of the remote host, either by using a DNS lookup utility directly, or by asking the administrator of that machine for the IP.

2. Check your local loopback address by entering **ping 127.0.0.1** from a command line. You should immediately see a set of four responses, with time statistics listed. If you do not, check your TCP/IP configuration in the Network applet, and also check the Event logs for any TCP/IP service-related startup or operation failures.

3. Now use ping to check the connection to the remote host. Enter **ping** *xxx.xxx.xxx.xxx*, where this number is the IP of the remote host. If ping does not return a sequence of statistics that indicate a connection with the remote host, use the following checklist:

   ■ Your computer is TCP/IP enabled and is properly configured.

   ■ Ping your default gateway with the command line ping *xxx.xxx.xxx.xxx*, where this number is the IP address of your gateway. If ping does not return a series of statistics indicating successful connection, check your local network connections and the default gateway addressing.

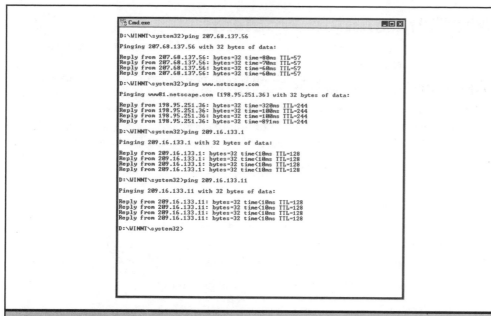

Figure A-6. *Output from the ping utility*

- If you can ping your default gateway but not the remote host, check to see that the Enable IP Forwarding checkbox is selected in the TCP/IP—Routing dialog for the default gateway, if it is an NT computer. Also check any hardware routers for proper forwarding operation.

- If the default gateway is routing IP traffic to the WAN, check the IP address of the remote host, and also check to see if the remote host is online. Use the IP of a well-known remote host to recheck your connection. If your DNS services are enabled, you can quickly check your TCP/IP connection by entering **ping www.microsoft.com**, for instance.

There are command line switches that you can use to change the behavior of the ping command. Enter **ping** alone on a command line to list these options.

Tracert

Tracert is similar to ping in that it tests a connection. In the case of tracert, all of the interim connections—the routes—are also tested and return the turnaround times and statistics to you. Tracert is useful when you need to know where a route to a remote host is failing, or where the most time in connecting to a remote host is spent.

Again, there are command line switches that you can use to change the behavior of the tracert command. Enter **tracert** alone on a command line to list these options.

DNS/Name Resolution Problems

When using ping, if an IP address responds, but you get the response "Bad IP Address <*name*>"; or using tracert, you get "Unable to resolve target system name <*name*>," you have a DNS or some kind of name resolution problem. Problems with HOSTS and LMHOSTS configuration files can cause difficulties and errors with name resolution. DNS server address problems are another area of concern, as well as the physical connection to the DNS server itself. When failing to connect to or resolve a specific host, check the following list of difficulties and suggestions to resolve these name resolution problems.

For HOSTS file errors:

- No entries for a particular hostname.
- The hostname entry is misspelled or is the wrong case. Names are case sensitive.
- Invalid IP address is associated with a hostname.
- There are multiple line entries for the same hostname.

For LMHOSTS file errors:

- No entries for a particular remote host.
- The hostname entry is misspelled. Names are not case sensitive.
- Invalid IP address is associated with a hostname.

Check the Control Panel/Network/Protocols/TCP/IP/DNS and WINS Address dialogs for proper values for the DNS setup and LMHOSTS files.

You can also use the utility netstat to diagnose remote connection problems. Enter **netstat -a** to view the status of all TCP and UDP ports on the local computer. Netstat will list the states of all connections. If data is blocked on a connection, you have a problem with the local TCP/IP transport.

Performance Problems and Cures

Performance is sometimes, but not always, subjective. A machine that is perceived as unresponsive by a local user may be just as fast at internal number crunching or disk caching as any other computer; it has a slow video adapter, so the speed at which it redraws its display makes it *seem* slow. On the other hand, with NT and Performance Monitor (see Chapter 7), we can quantify many of the performance issues that otherwise would be unknown. There are also performance-enhancing rules of thumb that apply not only to NT, but to any OS.

We'll next look at some of the methods and procedures you can use to get rid of performance bottlenecks:

■ Check to see that the CPU's internal and external cache memory is enabled. This is usually done through the chipset portion of the BIOS setup.

■ Check to see that your computer's speed is not de-rated by a turbo function switch being set in the slow mode.

■ Install as much RAM as is feasible. With more RAM, NT will page to virtual memory with less frequency, speeding up all operations on the computer.

■ Use the minimum display color depth that is acceptable for the job. High color depths, such as 24- and 32-bit color, are fine for paint and design applications. But if you need response time rather than color, reducing the color depth will allow the display adapter to respond much quicker.

■ Check the size and amount of NT paging file that you have set up. A good rule of thumb is to have twice as much paging file as you have physical RAM installed. Also, one paging file per physical disk is a good rule of thumb. Place the paging file on the first partition on each physical disk drive (set these parameters in the Control Panel/System applet).

■ Match NICs to the system bus size for maximal throughput. Never use an 8-bit adapter! If you have only a 16-bit bus, use a 16-bit network adapter; otherwise, use a PCI adapter that is capable of 32- or 64-bit transfers.

■ Keep minimal network connections open. The time it takes to browse, query, and connect to remote network resources can severely degrade overall perceived performance. If you are using your NT system for real-time control or response, close all network connections—even consider removing all unnecessary network adapters and protocols.

■ Keep your disk drive defragmented. Fragmentation of files on hard disk drives causes a general slowdown in both reading and writing the drive. The drive mechanism must seek to many different physical locations on the disk when attempting to transfer physically fragmented data. Use one of the commercial defragmenter applications, such as Norton Utilities for NT 4 or DiskKeeper, to defragment files on both FAT and NTFS partitions.

■ Increase general performance by turning off CD-ROM autorun. The autorun feature found in NT 4, for support of automatic insertion and program execution from CD-ROM, degrades machine performance. The CD-ROM is polled every so often, which results in a switch away from normal processing to make this check. Setting the Registry parameter

    \HKEY_LOCAL_MACHINE\SYSTEM\CurrentControlSet\Services\Cdrom
    \Autorun

to 0 will keep NT from performing this check. This setting is critical, for instance, if you are planning on creating CD-ROMs with a CDR writer.

■ Keep 16-bit applications closed when not needed. WOW and MS-DOS VDMs are certainly capable of running many of the popular 16-bit Windows and

MS-DOS programs. But you pay a price in general performance on the Win32 side when an active 16-bit application is left open. Close all 16-bit applications when not in use.

■ Control the foreground (active) application response in relation to background response. Use the Control Panel/System/Performance dialog to set the mix that gives you the best response for your application set.

■ If you are using NT Server, open the Control Panel/Network/Services dialog and double-click on the Server service. This will bring up a dialog where you can set the NT Server optimization mix and resource allocation characteristics. This service establishes sessions with remote workstations and servers and receives Server Message Block (SMB) I/O requests from those remote workstations and servers. You can configure for Minimize Memory Used, designed to support up to 10 remote users simultaneously. You can also choose Balance, which is the option you should pick for support of up to 64 remote users. The Maximize Throughput for File Sharing option is meant to support 64 or more remote users and gives priority to file cache access to memory. The Maximize Throughput for Network Applications option is for 64 or more remote users and gives priority to application access to memory.

■ Look for sources of broadcast/multicast traffic (use the Network Monitor). A faulty NIC, or its driver software, generating more than 100 broadcasts or multicasts per second, is suspect. This can cause serious performance degradation over the entire network, as well as in the local machine.

■ Look to collision rate on your ethernet backbone as an indicator of network load. Keep the number of collisions down to a total of 10 percent to 15 percent of your total output. Network Monitor will not help you quantify collisions, but there are third-party software and hardware solutions that can do the job. It is a good rule of thumb to keep ethernet utilization to under 75 percent to avoid excessive collisions, and conversely, the number of collisions is a direct indicator of network load. Rethink the network topology and judiciously use routers and subnets if necessary.

Performance and Resource Kit Utilities

The NT 4 Resource Kit, a separate product that comes with copious documentation and utility programs, contains two applications that are directly applicable to performance tuning and monitoring. QSLICE.EXE and PVIEWER.EXE have different uses, but complement each other in that their diagnostic capabilities can be used in concert.

QSLICE (see Figure A-7) gives you graphical information about the percentage of total CPU usage for each process in the system. This utility can easily point you in the direction of a CPU hog, giving you quick detail on the process in question and displaying statistics about its CPU usage. For all active processes, QSLICE displays the following information:

- The process ID number in hexadecimal format
- The executable filename or associated process
- The percentage of total CPU usage for a process

The main QSLICE (Quick Slice) window shows a graphical representation of the CPU usage. A red bar indicates time spent executing kernel code, and a blue bar represents time spent executing user code. The length of the graphical bar represents two different ratios. In the main window, it shows

(usage for this process / usage for all running processes) x 100

In a child, or secondary window, it shows the ratio

(CPU usage for one individual thread / CPU usage for all the threads in this process) x 100

Use this utility to get a bird's-eye view of which processes are taking a great deal of CPU time. Then, hone in on a particular process and find out which thread is hogging the processor.

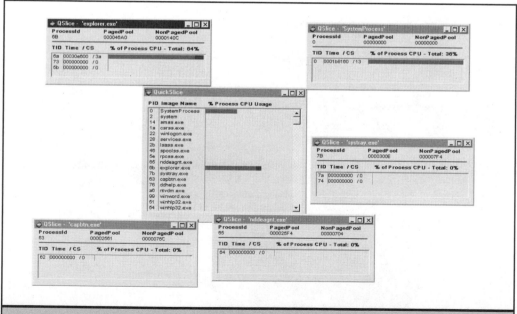

Figure A-7. *The Quick Slice process viewer*

Now open PVIEWER.EXE (see Figure A-8). PVIEWER (Process Viewer) is a more sophisticated tool that lets you inspect a process and its threads further to determine causal relationships and either change the priority of a thread on the fly or kill a running process. It can be used on a remote computer as well.

The PVIEWER window shows which computer it is currently diagnosing. Also in the display is a list of currently running processes for the computer under scrutiny. Under that window, a list of threads for the highlighted process is displayed. Thread information is given, and the main window also contains radio buttons that allow you to set the base priority of a thread. By selecting the Kill Process button, you may also kill the highlighted process, no matter what state it is in.

CAUTION: *With the Kill Process button, you can kill internal NT OS processes that will crash your computer. Be careful!*

It is important to understand the time quantities displayed in PVIEWER. Processor Time denotes the percentage of elapsed time that a processor is busy executing a non-idle thread. Privileged Time denotes the percentage of processor time spent in Privileged mode on non-idle threads. The NT Executive, kernel, device drivers, and most of the GDI and service layer are all included in this number. User Time denotes

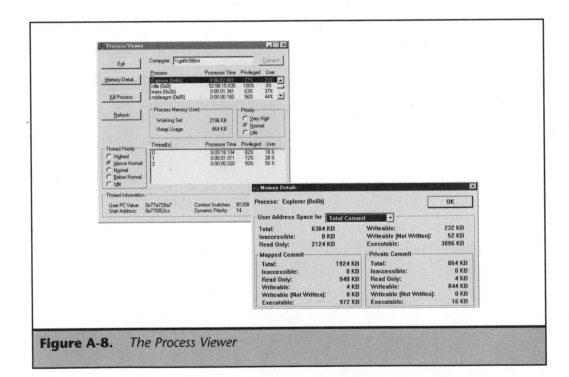

Figure A-8. *The Process Viewer*

the percentage of processor time spent in User mode on non-idle threads. All application code and protected subsystem code, the top layer of GDI, the window manager, and printer drivers are included in this number.

The Memory Details window displays the working set of memory for this process. Here, you can determine whether a process is leaking memory or hogging the virtual memory system, and what percentage of total memory resources it is taking up.

With Quick Slice and Process Viewer, you can find out a lot about the processes and applications running in your computer. Use this information to tune your application mix and to identify inefficient drivers and programs.

Performance and the Distributed File System (DFS)

The Distributed File System (DFS) is a performance-enhancing utility that enables an administrator to set up a single, hierarchical representation of all the file servers and file server resources on a network. DFS allows NT to present a single directory to an application or browsing user whose subdirectories consist of all the servers and shares arranged in terms of their logical position within the hierarchy.

DFS subdirectories can be assigned separate descriptive names, and searches for files and data can be made with the normal NT (and Windows 95) search tools. By using DFS, a client workstation that would normally have five or ten open network connections, can now have one. This reduction in persistent network connections increases local performance because the overhead of keeping network connections active, along with the setup time for browsing those connections, can seriously degrade NT's performance.

File backup performance and virus detection performance are both increased as well. NT Backup can act on a DFS directory tree as if it were a single share, so multiple connects and reconnects are not needed. The operations for virus scanning, or any other process that needs to span multiple servers and shares, are also performance enhanced by only having to deal with one logical network connection.

Why NT Can't Be "Cloned"

There comes a time in the experience of all NT users and administrators when the idea of copying an already setup NT "image" to a network hard disk becomes very attractive. If only you could set up NT once and then copy it to a network drive, all other installations could take place just by copying the image off the network. In effect, you could clone NT onto many different machines, rather than wading through a tedious 30-minute setup.

There are many technical reasons why this is not feasible. Least of all are the issues having to do with NT's storage of machine hardware parameters and system driver files in the Registry. Unless everything about each "clone's" hardware and machine setup is exactly the same, the clone will fail with an inconsistency in the Registry's view of hardware reality versus the real world.

That is the least of the problems. Because each valid user is registered with the system using the NT security model, internal user IDs and security IDs have different numerical values for different machines. Add to that the fact that each NIC/MAC address, the address of the physical hardware adapter, plays a part in the local and domain security model. And this model extends to the workstation/domain controller arena, where, if a machine's name is changed, or the operating system is upgraded, its machine account on the domain controller must be reset, and the machine must rejoin the domain, as if it had never been a member.

Index